Aviation
Fundamentals

Second Edition 1989
Third Edition 1991
Fourth Edition 1992

JS314755D (Hard Cover)
JS314766D (Soft Cover)

PREFACE _____

The Jeppesen Sanderson *Aviation Fundamentals Textbook* is designed for people who are interested in learning more about aviation. It also can be used as the first step toward learning to fly. Whatever your personal goals may be, the textbook is based on the "study/review" concept of learning. This means that detailed material is presented in an uncomplicated way, then important points are summarized through use of bold type and color. The text incorporates many design features that will help you get the most out of your study and review efforts. These include:

- **Margin Notes** — The margin notes, which are printed in color, summarize key points from the text. They emphasize material contained in the FAA written exam, as well as other important data.

- **Illustrations** — Illustrations are carefully planned to complement and expand upon concepts introduced in the text. Color in the illustrations and the accompanying captions flag them as items that warrant your attention during both initial study and review.

- **Bold Type** — Important terms in the text are printed in bold type.

- **Checklist** — A checklist appears at the end of each section to help you verify your understanding of principal concepts.

- **Glossary** — The glossary defines commonly used aeronautical terms.

- **Abbreviations** — Abbreviations explains the most frequently used aviation acronyms and abbreviations.

The textbook is the key element in the Jeppesen Sanderson training materials. Although it can be studied alone, there are several other components which we recommend to make your flight training as complete as possible. One of these is a book of *Federal Aviation Regulations*, which includes exercises to test your understanding of pertinent regulations. You should study this book and complete the exercises if you plan to become a private pilot. Other materials include the *Chapter Test Book, Aviation Fundamentals Exercise Book,* and *FAA Private Pilot Question Book.* You may also note that the table of contents for your manual contains cross-references to video presentations. These video programs are available for your use at participating schools and are designed to enhance and complement your study.

When taken together, these elements represent an exciting new concept in aviation training. They combine the most modern teaching techniques with presentation of all of the information you need to be knowledgeable about aviation, to pass the FAA written exam, or to become a safe pilot if you elect to do so. Outstanding educators from across the country have made significant contributions to this new *Aviation Fundamentals* program.

TABLE OF CONTENTS

ACKNOWLEDGEMENTS ━━━━━━━━━━━━━━━

We wish to thank the following people for their contributions to the development of the *Aviation Fundamentals Textbook:*

Dr. Peggy Baty — Embry-Riddle Aeronautical University
Dr. Thomas J. Connolly — Embry-Riddle Aeronautical University
Dr. Donald Doran — Embry-Riddle Aeronautical University
Mr. William D. Geibel — University of Illinois
Mr. Bruce Hoover — Palo Alto College
Dr. Henry R. Lehrer — Embry-Riddle Aeronautical University
Mr. Kent W. Lovelace — University of North Dakota
Dr. Wallace R. Maples — Middle Tennessee State University
Dr. Lamon I. Marcum — Middle Tennessee State University
Dr. Elaine McCoy — Ohio State University

We wish to thank the following agencies and corporations for providing us with photographs:

AMI AirLife
Department of Defense
General Dynamics
Lyndon B. Johnson Space Center
Martin Marietta
National Aeronautics and Space Administration
National Center for Atmospheric Research
United States Army
United States Navy

PRINCIPLES OF FLIGHT

INTRODUCTION

This chapter is the foundation for your entire course of training. You will encounter many new concepts in principles of flight that may be unfamiliar to you at first. Recognizing this, we begin with a brief overview of airplanes and their components. In the next section, we introduce basic aerodynamic principles related to the four forces of flight. Then we present the four forces in action during maneuvering flight and conclude the chapter with a discussion of the design features that give airplanes their basic stability.

SECTION A

AIRPLANES

One of the first things you are likely to notice during a visit to your local airport is the wide variety of airplane styles and designs. Although, at first glance, you may think that airplanes look quite different from one another, you will find that their major components are quite similar. [Figure 1-1]

THE FUSELAGE

The fuselage serves several functions. Besides being a common attachment point for the other major components, it houses the cabin, or cockpit, which contains seats for the occupants and the controls for the airplane. The fuselage usually has a small baggage compartment and may include additional seats for passengers.

THE WING

When air flows around the wings of an airplane, it generates a force called "lift" that helps the airplane fly. Wings are contoured to take maximum advantage of this force, as you will see in Section B. Wings may be

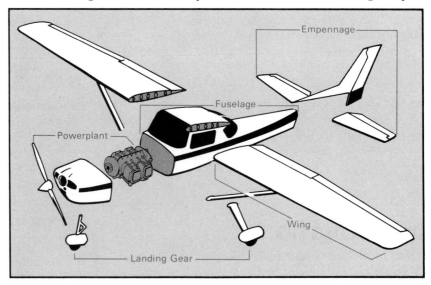

Figure 1-1. Typically, an airplane is made up of five major parts. The fuselage is considered to be the central component, since the powerplant, wings, empennage (tail section), and landing gear are attached to it.

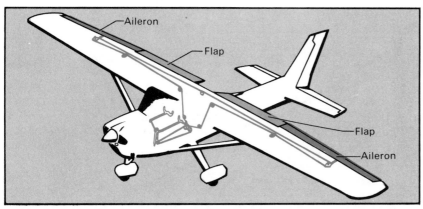

Figure 1-2. You can move the ailerons by turning the control wheel in the cockpit. When you turn the wheel to the left, the left aileron moves up and the right moves down. During flight, this is how you start a turn to the left. Turning the wheel to the right has the opposite effect. You can operate the flaps using a switch or handle located in the cockpit. They are used primarily for takeoffs and landings.

attached at the top, middle, or lower portion of the fuselage. These designs are referred to as high-, mid-, and low-wing, respectively. The number of wings can also vary. Airplanes with a single set of wings are referred to as **monoplanes**, while those with two sets are called **biplanes**.

To help you fly the airplane, the wings have two types of control surfaces attached to the rear, or trailing, edges. They are referred to as ailerons and flaps. **Ailerons** extend from about the midpoint of each wing outward to the tip. They move in opposite directions — when one aileron goes up, the other goes down. **Flaps** extend outward from the fuselage to the midpoint of each wing. They always move in the same direction. If one flap is down, the other is down. [Figure 1-2]

> The wings have two types of control surfaces called the ailerons and flaps.

THE EMPENNAGE

The empennage consists of the **vertical stabilizer**, or fin, and the **horizontal stabilizer**. These two surfaces are stationary and act like the feathers on an arrow to steady the airplane and help you maintain a straight path through the air. [Figure 1-3]

> The horizontal and vertical stabilizers help you maintain a straight path through the air.

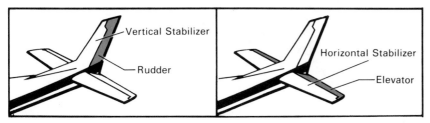

Figure 1-3. Besides the two fixed components, the empennage has two important movable surfaces called the rudder and the elevator.

Figure 1-4. You operate the rudder with your feet, using pedals located in the cockpit. When you press the left rudder pedal, the nose moves left, while the right pedal moves the nose right.

The **rudder** is attached to the back of the vertical stabilizer. You use it to move the airplane's nose left and right. Actually, you use the rudder and ailerons in combination during flight to initiate a turn. You will learn the details about this later. [Figure 1-4]

The **elevator** is attached to the back of the horizontal stabilizer. During flight, you use it to move the nose up and down so you can direct the airplane to the desired altitude, or height. [Figure 1-5]

Figure 1-5. The elevator is moved by using the control wheel. When you pull back on the wheel, the nose moves up; when you push forward, the nose moves down.

Most airplanes have a small, hinged section at the back of the elevator called a **trim tab**. Its purpose is to relieve the pressure you must hold on the control wheel to keep the nose in the desired position. In most small airplanes, you control the trim tab with a wheel or crank in the cockpit. Your flight instructor will direct you in the proper use of the trim control for the airplane you are flying.

STABILATOR

Some empennage designs vary from the type of horizontal stabilizer just discussed. They have a one-piece horizontal stabilizer that pivots up and down from a central hinge point. This type of design, called a **stabilator**, requires no elevator. You move the stabilator using the control wheel, just as you would the elevator. When you pull back, the nose moves up; when you push forward, the nose moves down. An antiservo tab is mounted at the back of the stabilator, to provide you with a control "feel" similar to what you experience with an elevator. Without the **antiservo** tab, control forces from the stabilator would be so light that you might "over control" the airplane or move the control wheel too far to obtain the desired result. The antiservo tab also functions as a trim tab. [Figure 1-6]

> The stabilator is a variation of the standard horizontal stabilizer. It does not require an elevator.

LANDING GEAR

The landing gear absorbs landing loads and supports the airplane on the ground. It typically is made up of three wheels. The two **main wheels** are located on either side of the fuselage. The third may be positioned either at the nose or at the tail. If it is located at the tail, it is called a **tailwheel**. In this case, the airplane is said to have **conventional landing gear**.

> Landing gear usually consists of two main wheels and a third wheel mounted on either the nose or the tail.

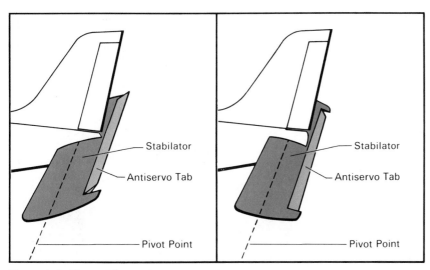

Figure 1-6. The stabilator pivots up and down as you move the control wheel. The antiservo tab moves in the same direction as the trailing edge of the stabilator.

Conventional gear is common on older airplanes, as well as on some newer ones. It is desirable for operations on unimproved fields, because of the added clearance between the propeller and the ground. However, airplanes with this type of gear are more difficult to handle during ground operations.

When the third wheel is located on the nose, it is called a **nosewheel**. This design is referred to as **tricycle gear**. An airplane with this type of gear has a steerable nosewheel, which you control through use of the rudder pedals.

Landing gear can also be classified as either fixed or retractable. **Fixed gear** always remains extended, while **retractable gear** can be stowed for flight to reduce air resistance and increase airplane performance.

SHOCK STRUTS

Just as you need shock absorbers on your car, you need some shock-absorbing device on the landing gear. **Shock struts** are designed for this purpose. They absorb bumps and jolts, as well as the downward force of landing. [Figure 1-7]

BRAKES

Airplane brakes usually are located only on the main wheels and may be operated independently from one another.

Airplane brakes operate on the same principles as automobile brakes, but they do have a few significant differences. For example, airplane brakes usually are located only on the main wheels, and are applied by separate

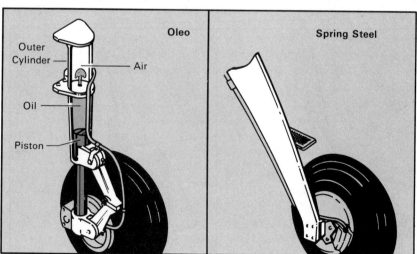

Figure 1-7. There are two primary shock-absorbing systems in use. The oleo strut consists of an enclosed cylinder which houses a piston, oil, and air. It absorbs pressure rapidly and then slowly releases it. The spring steel strut, as its name implies, is made of steel that is designed to "give" as pressure is applied.

pedals. Because of this, you can operate the brake on the left independently of the brake on the right, or vice versa. This capability is referred to as **differential braking**. It is important during ground operations when you need to supplement nosewheel steering by applying the brakes on the side toward the direction of turn. In fact, differential braking is extremely important on conventional gear airplanes, since some do not have a steerable wheel.

THE POWERPLANT

In small airplanes, the powerplant includes both the engine and the propeller. The primary function of the engine is to provide the power to turn the propeller. It also generates electrical power, provides a vacuum source for some flight instruments, and, in most single-engine airplanes, provides a source of heat for the pilot and passengers. A **firewall** is located between the engine compartment and the cockpit to protect the occupants. The firewall also serves as a mounting point for the engine. [Figure 1-8]

The engine drives the propeller which, in turn, produces thrust. It also provides electrical power, a vacuum source, and heat for the cabin.

AIRCRAFT CLASSIFICATION

So far, we have only talked about airplanes. Actually, there is a much broader grouping called "aircraft" which contains not only airplanes, but such things as helicopters, gliders, and balloons. These various aircraft, with their wide range of size, complexity, and capability, must all share the same skies.

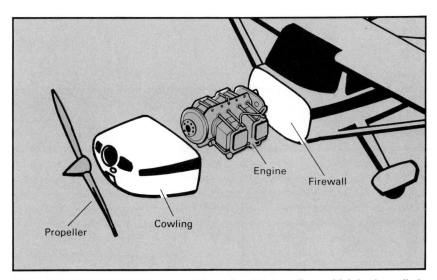

Engine

Firewall

Propeller

Cowling

Figure 1-8. The engine compartment is enclosed by cowling, which is also called a nacelle. Besides streamlining the nose of the airplane, the cowling helps cool the engine by ducting air around the cylinders. The propeller, mounted on the front of the engine, translates the rotating force of the engine into a forward-acting force called "thrust" that helps the airplane fly.

The FAA uses category, class, and type for both aircraft and pilot certification.

To help divide these aircraft into similar groupings, the Federal Aviation Administration (FAA) has established two systems of category, class, and type. One applies when aircraft designs are approved, or certified, for flight. The other is used to describe certification of pilots.

For aircraft certification, **category** relates to the intended use of an aircraft and sets strict limits on its operation. The **normal** and **utility** categories are common to most small airplanes. You will find that many airplanes used in flight training are certified for both of these categories, depending on how they are loaded. When loaded for the utility category, the airplane can withstand heavier stresses than it can in the normal category. **Acrobatic** aircraft have the fewest operating limitations because their design requirements demand more strength than those of the normal or utility category. **Commuter** aircraft are designed to carry passengers, but they are limited to 19 seats and 19,000 pounds or less. **Transport** usually refers to airliners and other large aircraft that exceed certain weight limits or passenger-carrying capacity. [Figure 1-9]

The **restricted** category is for special-purpose aircraft such as agricultural spray planes or slurry bombers used to fight forest fires. **Limited** refers to military aircraft that are now allowed to be used only for limited purposes in civil aviation. The **provisional** category is really an interim measure for newly designed aircraft which have not met all requirements for initial certification, but still can be operated for certain purposes. **Experimental** refers to a wide range of aircraft such as amateur-homebuilt and racing planes, as well as research and development aircraft used to test new design concepts.

For pilot certification, aircraft are again broken down into category, class, and type. In this case, though, category and class have different meanings than when used for aircraft certification. [Figure 1-10]

AIRCRAFT CERTIFICATION			
Category		**Class**	**Type**
Normal	Restricted	Airplane	Specifies make and model such as: PA-28-161 Hughes 500 Boeing 747
Utility	Limited	Rotorcraft	
Acrobatic		Glider	
Commuter	Provisional		
Transport	Experimental	Lighter-Than-Air	

Figure 1-9. For aircraft certification purposes, the FAA establishes broad categories first. These are further broken down into one of four classes, then into types, which are essentially the make and model.

PILOT CERTIFICATION		
Category	**Class**	**Type**
Airplane	Single-Engine Land Multi-Engine Land Single-Engine Sea Multi-Engine Sea	Specifies make and model such as: PA-28-161 Hughes 500 Boeing 747
Rotorcraft	Helicopter Gyroplane	
Glider	- - - - - - - - - - - -	
Lighter-Than-Air	Airship Balloon	

Figure 1-10. For purposes of pilot certification, category is the broadest grouping and contains only four entries. With the exception of gliders, each category is further broken down into classes. Finally, the type designates the make and model. When you complete your training, your pilot certificate will probably specify "airplane single-engine land." The type normally is not listed for small airplanes.

CHECKLIST _____

After studying this section, you should have a basic understanding of:

✓ **Major airplane components** — What they are and what functions they serve.

✓ **Control surfaces** — Where the major control surfaces are attached, how they work, and what they do.

✓ **Landing gear** — What the difference is between conventional and tricycle gear.

✓ **Brakes** — How airplane brakes differ from those found on an automobile.

✓ **Powerplant** — What the powerplant does and what functions the cowling and the firewall serve.

✓ **Aircraft classification** — How aircraft are classified and how the system differs between aircraft certification and pilot certification.

FOUR FORCES OF FLIGHT

The four aerodynamic forces are lift, weight, thrust, and drag. They are in equilibrium during straight-and-level, unaccelerated flight; lift equals weight and thrust equals drag.

During flight, the four forces acting on the airplane are lift, weight, thrust, and drag. **Lift** is the upward force created by the effect of airflow as it passes over and under the wings. It supports the airplane in flight. **Weight** opposes lift. It is caused by the downward pull of gravity. **Thrust** is the forward force which propels the airplane through the air. It varies with the amount of engine power being used. Opposing thrust is **drag**, which is a backward, or retarding, force that limits the speed of the airplane. (Figure 1-11)

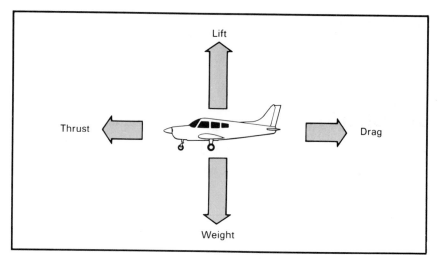

Figure 1-11. In straight-and-level, unaccelerated flight, the four forces are in equilibrium. Weight is equal to and directly opposite lift; thrust is equal to and directly opposite drag. Notice that the arrows which represent the opposing forces are equal in length, but all four arrows are not the same length. For example, the lift arrow is longer than the drag arrow.

The arrows which show the forces acting on an airplane are often called **vectors.** The magnitude of a vector is indicated by the arrow's length, while the direction is shown by the arrow's orientation. When two or more forces act on an object at the same time, they combine to create a resultant. (Figure 1-12)

These basic examples of vector diagrams will be helpful during the following discussion. Now let's consider the four forces in greater depth, starting with lift.

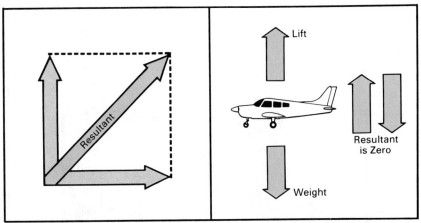

Figure 1-12. When vertical and horizontal forces are applied, as shown on the left, the resultant acts in a diagonal direction. When two opposing vertical forces are applied, as shown on the right, they tend to counteract one another. If the forces are equal in magnitude, the resultant is zero.

LIFT

Lift is the key aerodynamic force. It is the force that opposes weight. In straight-and-level, unaccelerated flight, when weight and lift are equal, an airplane is in a state of equilibrium. If the other aerodynamic factors remain constant, the airplane neither gains nor loses altitude.

When an airplane is stationary on the ramp, it is also in equilibrium, but the aerodynamic forces are not a factor. In calm wind conditions, the atmosphere exerts equal pressure on the upper and lower surfaces of the wing. Movement of air about the airplane, particularly the wing, is necessary before the aerodynamic force of lift becomes effective.

During flight, however, pressures on the upper and lower surfaces of the wing are not the same. Although several factors contribute to this difference, the shape of the wing is the principal one. The wing is designed to divide the airflow into areas of high pressure below the wing and areas of comparatively lower pressure above the wing. This pressure differential, which is created by movement of air about the wing, is the primary source of lift. Later, you will see that several other factors influence total lift.

BERNOULLI'S PRINCIPLE

The basic principle of pressure differential of subsonic airflow was discovered by Daniel Bernoulli, a Swiss physicist. **Bernoulli's Principle**, simply stated, says, "as the velocity of a fluid (air) increases, its internal pressure decreases."

Bernoulli's Principle explains how air pressure decreases as velocity increases.

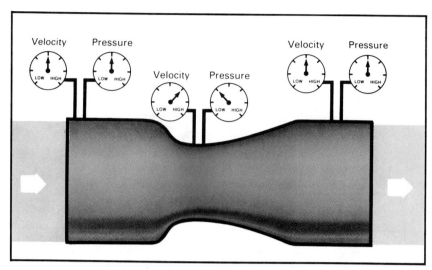

Figure 1-13. As the air enters the tube, it is traveling at a known velocity and pressure. When the airflow enters the narrow portion, the velocity increases and the pressure decreases. Then, as the airflow continues through the tube to the wider portion, both the velocity and pressure return to their original values.

One way you can visualize this principle is to imagine air flowing through a tube that is narrower in the middle than at the ends. This type of device is usually called a **venturi**. (Figure 1-13)

It is not necessary for air to pass through an enclosed tube for Bernoulli's Principle to apply. Any surface that alters airflow causes a venturi effect. (Figure 1-14)

When air flows over the curved upper surface of a wing, it increases in velocity. This increase reduces the pressure above the wing and produces the upward force of lift.

The wing of the airplane is shaped to take advantage of this principle. The greater curvature on the upper portion causes air to accelerate as it passes over the wing. The resulting pressure differential between the upper and lower surfaces of the wing creates an upward force. This difference in pressure is the main source of lift. (Figure 1-15)

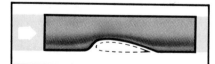

Figure 1-14. Even after the upper portion of the tube is removed, the venturi effect applies to air flowing along the lower section of the tube. Velocity above the curvature is increased and pressure is decreased. You can begin to see how the venturi effect works on a wing, or airfoil, if you picture an airfoil inset in the curved part of the tube.

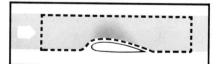

Figure 1-15. Air flowing over the top of an airfoil reaches the trailing edge in the same amount of time as air flowing along the relatively flat bottom. Since both the upper and lower surfaces pass through a block of air at the same speed, the air flowing over the curved upper surface travels farther. This means it must go faster, resulting in lower pressure above the airfoil than below.

NEWTON'S THIRD LAW OF MOTION About 25% of Lift

The remaining lift is provided by the wing's lower surface as air striking the underside is deflected downward. According to Newton's Third Law of Motion, "for every action there is an equal and opposite reaction." The air that is deflected downward also produces an upward (lifting) reaction.

Since air is much like water, the explanation for this source of lift may be compared to the planing effect of skis on water. The lift which supports the water skis (and the skier) is the force caused by the impact pressure and the deflection of water from the lower surfaces of the skis.

Under most flying conditions, the impact pressure and the deflection of air from the lower surface of the wing provide a comparatively small percentage of the total lift. The majority of lift is the result of the decreased pressure above the wing rather than the increased pressure below it.

There are many other factors that determine the lifting capacity of a wing. Before we look into these, let's first discuss some basic terminology.

AIRFOILS

An airfoil is any surface, such as a wing, which provides aerodynamic force when it interacts with a moving stream of air. Remember, an airplane's wing generates a lifting force only when air is in motion about it. Some of the terms used to describe the wing, and the interaction of the airflow about it, are listed here. [Figure 1-16]

Leading edge — This part of the airfoil meets the airflow first.

Trailing edge — This is the portion of the airfoil where the airflow over the upper surface rejoins the lower surface airflow.

Chord line — The chord line is an imaginary straight line drawn through an airfoil from the leading edge to the trailing edge.

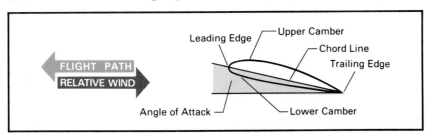

Figure 1-16. This figure shows a cross-section of a wing in straight-and-level flight. Chord and camber are terms which help to define the wing's shape, while flight path and relative wind help define the movement of the wing with respect to the surrounding air. Angle of attack is determined by the wing's chord line and the relative wind.

Camber — The camber of an airfoil is the characteristic curve of its upper and lower surfaces. The upper camber is more pronounced, while the lower camber is comparatively flat. This causes the velocity of the airflow immediately above the wing to be much higher than that below the wing.

The flight path and relative wind are always parallel to and opposite each other.

Relative wind — This is the direction of the airflow with respect to the wing. If a wing moves forward horizontally, the relative wind moves backward horizontally. Relative wind is parallel to and opposite the flight path of the airplane.

You shouldn't confuse the actual flight path with the flight attitude of the airplane. For example, the airplane's fuselage may be parallel to the horizon while the aircraft is descending. (Figure 1-17)

The angle formed by the wing chord line and relative wind is called the angle of attack.

Angle of attack — This is the angle between the chord line of the airfoil and the direction of the relative wind. It is important in the production of lift. (Figure 1-18)

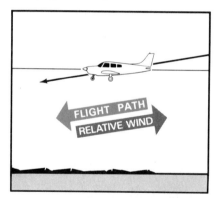

Figure 1-17. This airplane is in a level flight attitude, while the actual flight path is forward and down. Notice that the relative wind is upward and back, parallel to and opposite the flight path.

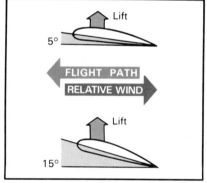

Figure 1-18. As the angle of attack increases, lift also increases. Notice that lift acts perpendicular to the relative wind, regardless of angle of attack.

AIRFOIL DESIGN FACTORS

Wing design is based on the anticipated use of the airplane, cost, and other factors. The main design considerations are wing planform, camber, aspect ratio, and total wing area.

Planform refers to the shape of the airplane's wing when viewed from above or below. Each planform design has advantages and disadvantages. (Figure 1-19)

Camber, as noted earlier, affects the difference in the velocity of the airflow between the upper and lower surfaces of the wing. If the upper

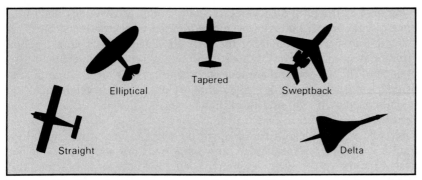

Figure 1-19. The straight wing has excellent slow-flight characteristics, and it is economical to build. However, it is inefficient from a structural, weight, and drag standpoint. The elliptical wing is more efficient in terms of weight and drag, but it has less desirable slow-flight characteristics and is more expensive. The tapered wing is relatively efficient with reasonable weight, drag, and construction costs, as well as good slow-flight capability. The sweptback and delta wings used on higher performance aircraft are efficient at high speeds, but not at low speeds.

camber increases and the lower camber remains the same, the velocity differential increases.

There is, of course, a limit to the amount of camber that can be used. After a certain point, air will no longer flow smoothly over the airfoil. Once this happens, the lifting capacity diminishes. The ideal camber varies with the airplane's performance specifications, especially the speed range and the load-carrying requirements.

Aspect ratio is the relationship between the length and width of a wing. It is one of the primary factors in determining lift/drag characteristics. At a given angle of attack, a higher aspect ratio produces less drag for the same amount of lift. (Figure 1-20)

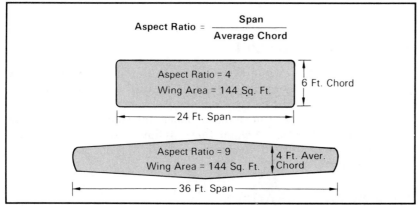

Figure 1-20. Aspect ratio is the span of the wing, wingtip to wingtip, divided by its average chord. In general, the higher the aspect ratio, the higher the lifting efficiency of the wing. For example, gliders may have an aspect ratio of 20 to 30, while typical training aircraft have an aspect ratio of about seven to nine.

Wing area is the total surface area of the wings. Most wings don't produce a great amount of lift per square foot, so wing area must be sufficient to support the weight of the airplane. For example, in a training aircraft at normal operating speed, the wings produce only about 10.5 pounds of lift for each square foot of wing area. This means a wing area of 200 square feet is required to support an airplane weight of 2,100 pounds during straight-and-level flight.

You can see that design has a lot to do with a wing's lift capability. Planform, camber, aspect ratio, and wing area are some of the major design factors. When we discuss drag, you'll see how design factors also affect drag.

Angle of incidence is the angle between the chord line and a line parallel to the longitudinal axis of an airplane. You cannot control this angle.

Once the design of the wing is determined, the wing must be mounted on the airplane. Usually it is attached to the fuselage with the chord line inclined upward at a slight angle, which is called the **angle of incidence**. (Figure 1-21)

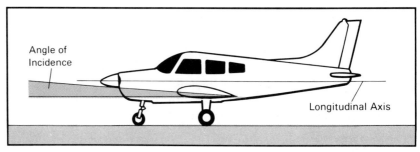

Figure 1-21.   Angle of incidence refers to the angle between the wing chord line and a line parallel to the longitudinal axis of the airplane. A slight positive angle of incidence provides a positive angle of attack while the airplane is in level flight at normal cruising speed. It also improves over-the-nose visibility when the airplane is in a level flight attitude.

PILOT CONTROL OF LIFT

Changing angle of attack or airspeed are the two primary ways to control lift.

Thus far in our discussion of lift, we have looked at only those factors which are controlled by aircraft design. Now, we'll examine the actions you can take to control lift. For example, you can change the angle of attack and the airspeed. You can also change the shape of the wing by lowering the flaps. Keep in mind that anytime you do something to change lift, drag is affected. If you increase lift, drag increases. Drag is always a by-product of lift.

CHANGING ANGLE OF ATTACK

You have direct control over angle of attack. During flight at normal operating speeds, if you increase the angle of attack, you increase lift. Anytime you move the control column fore or aft during flight, you

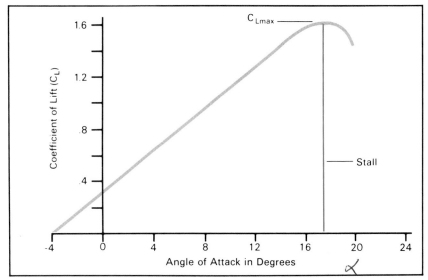

Figure 1-22. As angle of attack increases, C_L also increases. This continues to a point where C_L peaks. This point of maximum lift is called C_{Lmax}. In this example, C_{Lmax} occurs at about 17°. If the maximum lift angle is exceeded, lift decreases rapidly and the wing stalls.

change the angle of attack. At the same time, you are changing the coefficient of lift. The **coefficient of lift** (C_L) is a way to measure lift as it relates to angle of attack. C_L is determined by wind tunnel tests and is based on airfoil design and angle of attack. Every airplane has an angle of attack where maximum lift occurs. (Figure 1-22)

A **stall** is caused by the separation of airflow from the wing's upper surface. This results in a rapid decrease in lift. For a given airplane, a stall always occurs at the same angle, regardless of airspeed, flight attitude, or weight. Since training airplanes normally do not have an angle of attack indicator, the important point to remember is that you can stall an airplane at any airspeed, in any flight attitude, or at any weight. (Figure 1-23)

An airplane can be stalled at any airspeed and in any flight attitude.

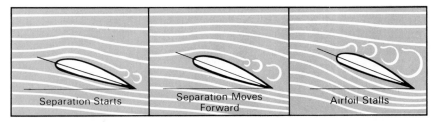

Figure 1-23. Increasing the angle of attack beyond C_{Lmax} causes progressive disruption of airflow from the upper surface of the wing. At first, the airflow begins to separate at the trailing edge. As angle of attack is further increased, the airflow separation progresses forward until the wing is fully stalled.

Stall characteristics vary with different airplanes. In most training airplanes, the onset of a stall from a level flight attitude is gradual. The first indications may be provided by a stall warning device or a slight buffeting of the airplane.

To recover from a stall, you must decrease the angle of attack.

All you have to do to recover from a stall is to restore the smooth airflow. The only way to do this is to decrease the angle of attack to a point below the critical angle.

An airplane always stalls when the critical angle of attack is exceeded, regardless of weight or airspeed. The indicated airspeed of a stall, however, varies with weight and configuration. Maneuvering can also affect stall speed.

Although the stalling or critical angle of attack does not vary with weight, the stalling speed does. It increases slightly as the weight of the airplane increases and decreases as weight decreases. This means you need slightly more airspeed to stay above the stalling speed in a heavily loaded airplane. If you want to fly an airplane at a given weight, there are many combinations of airspeed and angle of attack which will produce the required amount of lift.

CHANGING AIRSPEED

Lift is proportional to the square of the airplane's velocity. If an airplane's speed is doubled, lift increases fourfold.

The faster the wing moves through the air, the greater the lift. Actually, lift is proportional to the square of the airplane's speed. For example, at 200 knots, an airplane has four times the lift of the same airplane traveling at 100 knots if the angle of attack and other factors are constant. On the other hand, if the speed is reduced by one-half, lift is decreased to one-quarter of the previous value.

Although airspeed is an important factor in the production of lift, it is only one of several factors. The airspeed required to sustain an aircraft in straight-and-level flight depends on the flap position, the angle of attack, and the weight.

ANGLE OF ATTACK AND AIRSPEED

The relationship between angle of attack and airspeed in the production of lift is not as complex as it may seem. Angle of attack establishes the coefficient of lift for the airfoil. At the same time, lift is proportional to the square of the airplane's speed. Since you can control both angle of attack and airspeed, you can control lift.

Total lift depends on the combined effects of airspeed and angle of attack. When speed decreases, you must increase the angle of attack to maintain the same amount of lift. Conversely, if you want to maintain the same amount of lift at a higher speed, you must decrease the angle of attack.

USING FLAPS

When properly used, flaps increase the lifting efficiency of the wing and decrease stall speed. This allows you to fly at a reduced speed while maintaining sufficient control and lift for sustained flight. Remember, though, that when you retract the flaps, the stall speed increases.

The ability to fly slowly is particularly important during the approach and landing phases. For example, an approach with full flaps permits you to fly slowly and at a fairly steep descent angle without gaining airspeed. This allows you to touch down at a slower speed. In addition, you can land near the approach end of the runway, even when there are obstacles along the approach path.

Flaps allow you to steepen the angle of descent on an approach without increasing airspeed.

In training airplanes, **configuration** normally refers to the position of the landing gear and flaps. When the gear and flaps are up, an airplane is in a clean configuration. If the gear is fixed rather than retractable, the airplane is considered to be in a clean configuration when the flaps are in the up position. During flight, you can change configuration by raising or lowering the gear, or by moving the flaps. Flap position affects the chord line and angle of attack for that section of the wing where the flaps are attached. This causes an increase in camber for that section of the wing and greater production of lift and drag. In contrast, landing gear position normally has little or no effect on chord line or angle of attack. (Figure 1-24)

There are several common types of flaps. The **plain flap** is attached to the wing by a hinge. When deflected downward, it increases the effective camber and changes the wing's chord line. Both of these factors increase the lifting capacity of the wing. The **split flap** is hinged only to the lower portion of the wing. This type of flap also increases lift, but it produces greater drag than the plain flap because of the turbulence it causes. The **slotted flap** is similar to the plain flap. In addition to changing the wing's camber and chord line, it also allows a portion of the higher pressure air

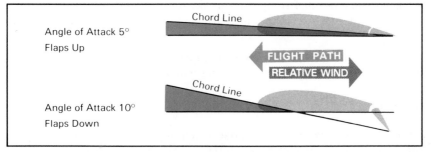

Figure 1-24. Flaps increase lift (and drag) by increasing the wing's effective camber and changing the chord line, which increases the angle of attack. In some cases, flaps also increase the area of the wing. Most flaps, when fully extended, form an angle of 35° to 40° relative to the wing.

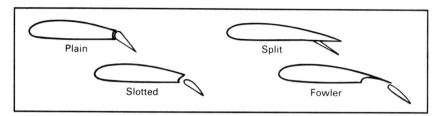

Figure 1-25. Flap types include plain, split, slotted, and Fowler. Although some flaps increase the wing's surface area, most change only the effective camber and the chord line.

beneath the wing to travel through a slot. This increases the velocity of the airflow over the flap and provides additional lift. Another type of flap is the **Fowler flap**. It is attached to the wing by a track and roller system. When extended, it moves rearward as well as down. This rearward motion increases the total wing area, as well as the camber and chord line. The Fowler flap is the most efficient of these systems. As you might expect, it also is the most expensive. (Figure 1-25)

Although the amount of lift and drag created by a specific flap system varies, we can make a few general observations. As the flaps are extended, at first they will produce a relatively large amount of lift for a small increase in drag. However, once the flap extension reaches approximately the midpoint, this relationship reverses. Now, a significant increase in drag will occur for a relatively small increase in lift. Because of the large increase in drag beyond the half-flap position, most manufacturers limit the takeoff setting to half flaps or less.

WEIGHT

Weight varies with aircraft equipment, cargo, fuel, expendable loads, and flight maneuvers. It acts downward toward the center of the earth.

The weight of the airplane is not a constant. It varies with the equipment installed, passengers, cargo, and fuel load. During the course of a flight, the total weight of the airplane decreases as fuel is consumed. Additional weight reduction may also occur during some specialized flight activities, such as crop dusting, fire fighting, or sky diving flights. You will see later in this chapter that weight is also affected by airplane maneuvering.

In contrast, the direction in which the force of weight acts is constant. It always acts straight down toward the center of the earth.

THRUST

The airfoil shape and angle of attack of the spinning propeller create a pressure differential which is similar to that created by the wing.

Thrust is the forward-acting force which opposes drag and propels the airplane. In most airplanes, this force is provided when the engine turns the propeller. Each propeller blade is cambered like the airfoil shape of a wing. This shape, plus the angle of attack of the blades, produces reduced pressure in front of the propeller and increased pressure behind it. By accelerating a relatively large mass of air through a relatively small velocity change, the propeller produces thrust, the force which moves the airplane forward.

During straight-and-level, unaccelerated flight, the forces of thrust and drag are equal. Later you will see that thrust and drag also are equal in stabilized turns, climbs, and descents.

You increase thrust by using the throttle to increase power. When you increase power, thrust exceeds drag, causing the airplane to accelerate. This acceleration, however, is accompanied by a corresponding increase in drag. The airplane continues to accelerate only while the force of thrust exceeds the force of drag. When drag again equals thrust, the airplane ceases to accelerate and maintains a constant airspeed. However, the new airspeed is higher than the previous one.

When you reduce thrust, the force of drag causes the airplane to decelerate. But as the airplane slows, drag diminishes. When drag has decreased enough to equal thrust, the airplane no longer decelerates. Once again, it maintains a constant airspeed. Now, however, it is slower than the one previously flown.

DRAG

As you have seen, drag is associated with lift. It is caused by any aircraft surface that deflects or interferes with the smooth airflow around the airplane. A highly cambered, large surface area wing creates more drag (and lift) than a small, moderately cambered wing. If you increase airspeed, or angle of attack, you increase drag (and lift). Drag acts in opposition to the direction of flight, opposes the forward-acting force of thrust, and limits the forward speed of the airplane. Drag is broadly classified as either parasite or induced.

PARASITE DRAG

Parasite drag includes all drag created by the airplane, except that drag directly associated with the production of lift. It is created by the disruption of the flow of air around the airplane's surfaces. Parasite drag normally is divided into three types: form drag, skin friction drag, and interference drag.

Parasite drag increases with an increase in airspeed. It consists of all drag not associated with the production of lift.

Form drag is created by any structure which protrudes into the relative wind. The amount of drag created is related to both the size and shape of the structure. For example, a square strut will create substantially more drag than a smooth or rounded strut. Streamlining reduces form drag.

Skin friction drag is caused by the roughness of the airplane's surfaces. Even though these surfaces may appear smooth, under a microscope, they may be quite rough. A thin layer of air clings to these rough surfaces and creates small eddies which contribute to drag.

Interference drag occurs when varied currents of air over an airplane meet and interact. This interaction creates additional drag. One example of this type of drag is the mixing of the air where the wing and airframe join.

Each type of parasite drag varies with the speed of the airplane. The combined effect generally is proportional to the square of the airplane's speed. (Figure 1-26)

INDUCED DRAG

Induced drag is associated with the production of lift. It is directly related to angle of attack and increases as angle of attack increases. Normally, induced drag decreases as airspeed increases.

Induced drag is the main by-product of the production of lift. It is directly related to the angle of attack of the wing. The greater the angle, the greater the induced drag. Since the wing usually is at a low angle of attack at high speed, and a high angle of attack at low speed, the relationship of induced drag to speed also can be plotted. (Figure 1-27)

TOTAL DRAG

Total drag for an airplane is the sum of parasite and induced drag. The total drag curve represents these combined forces and is plotted against airspeed. (Figure 1-28)

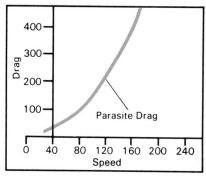

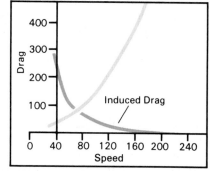

Figure 1-26. If airspeed is doubled, parasite drag increases fourfold. This is the same formula that applies to lift. Because of its rapid increase with increasing airspeed, parasite drag is predominant at high speeds. At low speeds, near a stall, parasite drag is at its low point.

Figure 1-27. Induced drag is inversely proportional to the square of the speed. If speed is decreased by half, induced drag increases fourfold. It is the major cause of drag at reduced speeds near the stall; but, as speed increases, induced drag decreases.

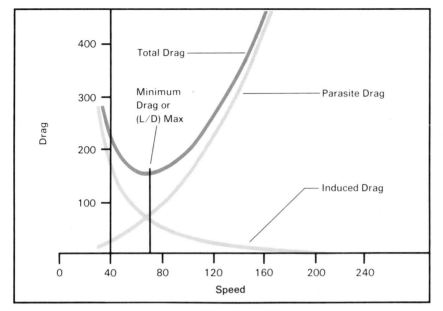

MAXIMUM
LIFT per
unit of drag,
Best speed at
which airplane
will glide.

Figure 1-28.   The low point on the total drag curve shows the airspeed at which drag is minimized. This is the point where the lift-to-drag ratio is greatest. It is referred to as L/D_{max}. At this speed, the total lift capacity of the airplane, when compared to the total drag of the airplane, is most favorable. This is important in airplane performance.

CHECKLIST

After studying this section, you should have a basic understanding of:

✓ **The four forces** — What they are, how they act, and their relationships during straight-and-level, unaccelerated flight.

✓ **Lift** — The key aerodynamic force, how it is created (including Bernoulli's Principle and Newton's Third Law of Motion), and how it acts.

✓ **Airfoil terminology** — The meanings of camber, chord, flight path, relative wind, angle of attack, angle of incidence, and other basic aerodynamic terms.

✓ **Airfoil design** — How lift is affected by basic design considerations, including aspect ratio, camber, planform, and wing area.

✓ **Pilot control of lift** — How you control lift during flight by changing the airspeed, angle of attack, or the airplane's configuration (including the use of flaps).

✓   **Stalls** — How an airplane stalls, exceeding the maximum lift angle of attack, the stalling or critical angle of attack, stall recovery.

✓   **Angle of attack and airspeed** — How angle of attack establishes the coefficient of lift for the airfoil, and how angle of attack and airspeed combine to produce lift.

✓   **Weight** — How it changes during flight, and the direction in which it acts.

✓   **Thrust** — How it is produced, how it acts, and the relationship between thrust and drag.

✓   **Drag** — How it acts, what causes it, the main classifications, and the relationships between drag, angle of attack, and airspeed.

AERODYNAMICS OF
MANEUVERING FLIGHT

This section takes you beyond straight-and-level flight to the aerodynamics of maneuvering flight. You will find that specific aerodynamic principles apply to climbs, descents, and turning maneuvers. These concepts will help you understand the performance limitations of your airplane. At the same time, you will learn important safety-of-flight considerations related to these performance limitations.

THREE AXES OF FLIGHT

All maneuvering flight takes place around one or more of three axes of rotation. They are called the **longitudinal**, **lateral**, and **vertical axes** of flight. The common reference point for the three axes is the airplane's **center of gravity** (CG), which is the theoretical point where the entire weight of the airplane is considered to be concentrated. Since all three axes pass through this point, you can say that the airplane always moves about its CG, regardless of which axis is involved. The ailerons, elevator, and rudder create aerodynamic forces which cause the airplane to rotate about the three axes. [Figure 1-29]

The three axes of flight pass through the airplane's center of gravity.

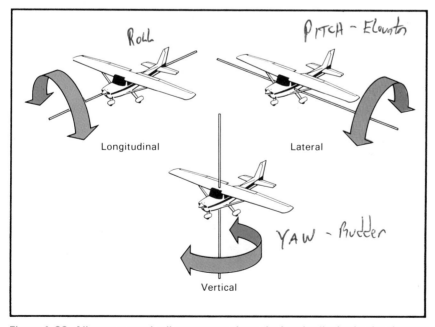

Roll

PITCH - Elevator

Longitudinal

Lateral

YAW - Rudder

Vertical

Figure 1-29. Ailerons control roll movement about the longitudinal axis; the elevator controls pitch movement about the lateral axis; and the rudder controls yaw movement about the vertical axis.

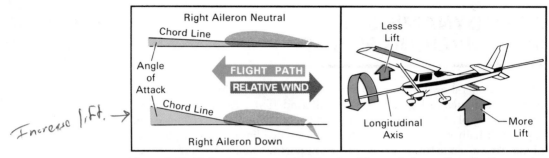

Increase lift. →

Figure 1-30. Deflected ailerons alter the chord line and change the effective camber of the outboard section of each wing. In this example, the angle of attack increases for the right wing, causing a corresponding increase in lift. At the same time, you can see that the left wing will lose some of its lift because of a decrease in its angle of attack. The airplane will roll to the left, because the right wing is producing more lift than the left wing.

LONGITUDINAL AXIS

Roll movement about the longitudinal axis is produced by the ailerons.

Now consider what happens when you apply control pressure to begin a turn. When you deflect the ailerons, they create an immediate rolling movement about the longitudinal axis. Since the ailerons always move in opposite directions, the aerodynamic shape of each wing and its production of lift is affected differently. [Figure 1-30]

One of the first things you will learn during flight is that the rolling movement about the longitudinal axis will continue as long as the ailerons are deflected. To stop the roll, you must relax control pressure and return the ailerons to their original, or neutral, position. This is called neutralizing the controls.

LATERAL AXIS

Pitch movement about the lateral axis is produced by the elevator (or stabilator).

Since the horizontal stabilizer is an airfoil, the action of the elevator (or stabilator) is quite similar to that of an aileron. Essentially, the chord line and effective camber of the stabilizer are changed by deflection of the elevator. [Figure 1-31]

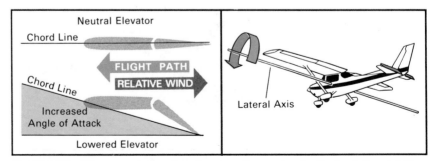

Figure 1-31. When you lower the elevator, the angle of attack of the stabilizer increases, and it produces more lift. The lifting force created by the stabilizer causes the airplane to pivot forward about its lateral axis. The net result is a decrease in the angle of attack of the wings, and an overall decrease in the pitch attitude.

Movement of the control wheel fore or aft causes motion about the lateral axis. Typically, this is referred to as an adjustment to pitch, or a change in pitch attitude. For example, when you move the control wheel forward, it causes movement about the lateral axis that decreases the airplane's pitch attitude. A decrease in pitch attitude decreases the angle of attack. Conversely, an increase in pitch attitude increases the angle of attack.

VERTICAL AXIS

When you apply pressure on the rudder pedals, the rudder deflects into the airstream. This produces an aerodynamic force that rotates the airplane about its vertical axis. This is referred to as yawing the airplane. The rudder may be displaced either to the left or right of center, depending on which rudder pedal you depress. [Figure 1-32]

Yaw movement about the vertical axis is produced by rudder.

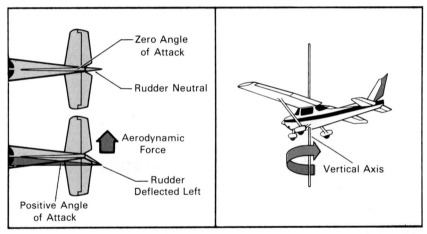

Figure 1-32. Since the vertical stabilizer also is an airfoil, deflection of the rudder alters the stabilizer's effective camber and chord line. In this case, left rudder pressure causes the rudder to move to the left. With a change in the chord line, the angle of attack is altered, generating an aerodynamic force toward the right side of the vertical fin. This causes the tail section to move to the right, and the nose of the airplane to yaw to the left.

FORCES ACTING ON A CLIMBING AIRPLANE

When you transition from level flight into a climb, you must combine the change in pitch attitude with an increase in power. If you attempt to climb just by pulling back on the control wheel to raise the nose of the airplane, momentum will cause a brief increase in altitude, but airspeed will soon decrease.

An airplane climbs because of excess thrust, not excess lift.

The amount of thrust generated by the propeller for cruising flight at a given airspeed is not enough to maintain the same airspeed in a climb. Excess thrust, not excess lift, is necessary for a sustained climb. In fact,

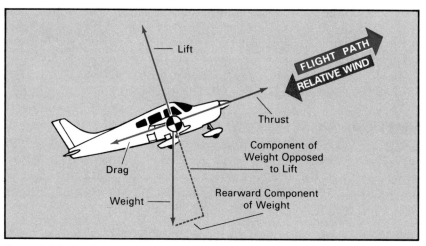

Figure 1-33. The forces of weight, lift, thrust, and drag are in equilibrium during a stabilized climb, just as they are during straight-and-level flight. When an airplane is climbing, though, the force of weight consists of two components. The first opposes lift and is perpendicular to the flight path. The second is called the rearward component of weight and acts in the same direction as drag, opposite to the relative wind.

during a true vertical climb, the wings supply no lift, and thrust is the only force opposing weight. [Figure 1-33]

FORCES ACTING ON A DESCENDING AIRPLANE

In a descent, a component of weight acts forward along the flight path.

Let's continue our discussion by considering the forces of weight, lift, thrust, and drag as they affect a descending airplane. If you are using power during a stabilized descent, the four forces are in equilibrium. During the descent, a component of weight acts forward along the flight path. As speed increases, this force is balanced by an increase in parasite drag.

During a power-off glide, the throttle is placed in an idle position so the engine and propeller produce no thrust. In this situation, the source of the airplane's thrust is provided only by the component of weight acting forward along the flight path. In a steady, power-off glide, the forward component of weight is equal to and opposite drag.

CONSTANT AIRSPEED DESCENT

Once you have established a state of equilibrium for a constant airspeed descent, the efficiency of the glide will be affected if you increase drag. For example, if you lower the landing gear, both parasite and total drag increase. To maintain the airspeed you held before the landing gear was extended, you have to lower the nose of the airplane.

You also can increase drag by descending at a speed that creates more drag than necessary. Any speed, other than the recommended glide speed, creates more drag. If you descend with the speed too high, parasite drag increases; and if you descend with speed too slow, induced drag increases. [Figure 1-34]

GLIDE ANGLE AND GLIDE SPEED

During a descent, the angle between the actual glide path of your airplane and the horizon usually is called the **glide angle**. Your glide angle increases as drag increases, and decreases as drag decreases. Since a decreased glide angle, or a shallower glide, provides the greatest gliding distance, minimum drag normally produces the maximum glide distance.

The way to minimize drag is to fly at an airspeed that results in the most favorable lift-to-drag ratio. This important performance speed is called the **best glide speed**. In most cases, it is the only speed that will give you the maximum gliding distance. However, with a very strong headwind, you may need a slightly higher glide speed, while a slower speed may be recommended to take advantage of a strong tailwind.

LIFT-TO-DRAG RATIO

The lift-to-drag ratio (L/D) can be used to measure the gliding efficiency of your airplane. The airspeed resulting in the least drag on your airplane will give the maximum L/D ratio (L/D_{max}), the best glide angle, and the maximum gliding distance.

The higher the value of L/D_{max}, the better the glide ratio.

GLIDE RATIO

The glide ratio represents the distance an airplane will travel forward, without power, in relation to altitude loss. For example, a glide ratio of

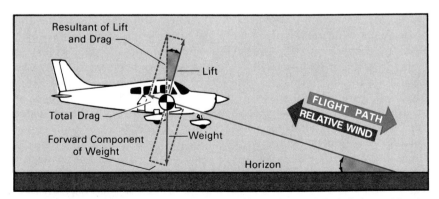

Figure 1-34. In a constant-airspeed, power-off descent, weight is balanced by the resultant of lift and drag. Notice that the angle between the lift vector and the resultant is the same as the angle between the flight path and the horizon. This is the glide angle of the airplane. If drag increases, the angle between the lift vector and the resultant vector increases and, consequently, the glide angle steepens.

10:1 means that an airplane will descend one foot for every 10 feet of horizontal distance it travels. Since the throttle is closed in a power-off glide, the pitch attitude must be adjusted to maintain the best glide speed.

If a power failure occurs after takeoff, immediately establish the proper gliding attitude and airspeed.

In the event of an engine failure, maintaining the best glide speed becomes even more important. This is especially true for a power failure after becoming airborne. Promptly establishing the correct gliding attitude and airspeed is critical. For a loss of power during flight, using the right speed could make the difference between successfully gliding to a suitable area or landing short of it.

EFFECT OF WEIGHT ON THE GLIDE

An airplane's maximum gliding distance is unaffected by weight, but the best glide airspeed increases with weight.

Variations in weight do not affect the glide angle, provided you use the correct airspeed for each weight. Normally, optimum, or best, glide speeds are given in the pilot's operating handbook (POH) for typical weight ranges. A fully loaded airplane requires a higher airspeed than the same airplane with a light load. Although the heavier airplane sinks faster and will reach the ground sooner, it will travel the same distance as a lighter airplane as long as you maintain the correct higher glide speed for the increased weight.

FORCES ACTING ON A TURNING AIRPLANE

From our discussion about the three axes of rotation, you learned that ailerons control roll movement about the longitudinal axis, and the rudder controls yaw movement about the vertical axis. Coordinated turns require you to use both of these flight controls. You use the ailerons to roll into or out of a bank and, at the same time, you use the rudder to control yaw.

The horizontal component of lift causes an airplane to turn.

Before your airplane turns, however, it must overcome inertia, or its tendency to continue in a straight line. You create the necessary turning force by banking the airplane so that the direction of lift is inclined. Now, one component of lift still acts vertically to oppose weight, just as it did in straight-and-level flight, while another acts horizontally. To maintain altitude, you will need to increase lift by increasing back pressure and, therefore, the angle of attack until the vertical component of lift equals weight. The horizontal component of lift, called **centripetal force**, is directed inward, toward the center of rotation. It is this center-seeking force which causes the airplane to turn. Centripetal force is opposed by **centrifugal force**, which acts outward from the center of rotation. When the opposing forces are balanced, the airplane maintains a constant rate of turn, without gaining or losing altitude. [Figure 1-35]

ADVERSE YAW

When you roll into a turn, the aileron on the inside of the turn is raised, and the aileron on the outside of the turn is lowered. The lowered aileron

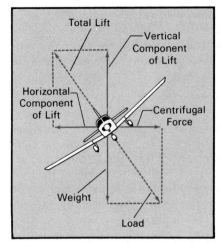

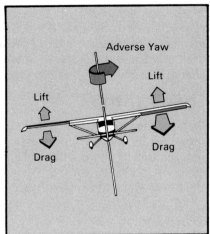

Figure 1-35. The resultant of the horizontal component (centripetal force) and the vertical component of lift is the total lift provided by the wings. The resultant of centrifugal force and weight is the total load the wings must support.

Figure 1-36. If you roll into a turn without using rudder to help establish the turn, the airplane will yaw about its vertical axis opposite to the direction of the turn. Adverse yaw is caused by higher induced drag on the outside wing, which is producing more lift.

on the outside increases the angle of attack and produces more lift for that wing. Since induced drag is a by-product of lift, you can see that the outside wing also produces more drag than the inside wing. This causes a yawing tendency toward the outside of the turn, which is called **adverse yaw.** [Figure 1-36]

The coordinated use of aileron and rudder corrects for adverse yaw when you roll into or out of a turn. For a turn to the left, you depress the left rudder pedal slightly as you roll into the left turn. Once you are established in the turn, you relax both aileron and rudder pressures and neutralize the controls. Then, when you want to roll out of the turn, you apply coordinated right aileron and rudder pressure to return to a wings-level attitude.

The basic purpose of the rudder on an airplane is to control yawing.

OVERBANKING TENDENCY

During your initial flight training, you will learn how to maneuver the airplane through coordinated use of the controls. As you enter a turn and increase the angle of bank, you may notice the tendency of the airplane to continue rolling into an even steeper bank, even though you neutralize the ailerons. This **overbanking tendency** is caused by the additional lift on the outside, or raised, wing. The outside wing is traveling faster than the inside wing. This adds to the lift, and the combined effects tend to roll the airplane beyond the desired bank angle.

The overbanking tendency is most pronounced at high angles of bank. To correct for this tendency, you will have to develop a technique of holding just enough opposite aileron, away from the turn, to maintain your desired angle of bank. Overbanking tendency exists, to some degree, in almost all airplanes.

LOAD FACTOR

So far in this discussion, you have looked at the combination of opposing forces acting on a turning airplane. Now it's time to examine load factors induced during turning flight. To better understand these forces, picture yourself on a roller coaster. As you enter a banked turn during the ride, the forces you will experience are very similar to the forces which act on a turning airplane. On a roller coaster, the resultant force created by the combination of weight and centrifugal force presses you down into your seat. This pressure is an increased load factor that causes you to feel heavier in the turn than when you are on a flat portion of the track.

The increased weight you feel during a turn in a roller coaster is also experienced in an airplane. In a turning airplane, however, you must compensate for the increase in weight and loss of vertical lift, or you will lose altitude. You can do this by increasing the angle of attack with back pressure on the control wheel. The increase in the angle of attack increases the total lift of the airplane. Keep in mind that when you increase lift, drag also increases. This means you must also increase thrust if you want to maintain your original airspeed and altitude. An airplane in a coordinated, level turn is in a state of equilibrium, where opposing forces are in balance. This is similar to the state of equilibrium that exists during unaccelerated, straight-and-level flight.

The load factor imposed on an airplane will increase as the angle of bank is increased.

During turning maneuvers, weight and centrifugal force combine into a resultant which is greater than weight alone. Additional loads are imposed on the airplane, and the wings must support the additional load factor. In other words, when you are flying in a curved flight path, the wings must support not only the weight of the airplane and its contents, but they also must support the load imposed by centrifugal force.

Load factor is the ratio of the load supported by the airplane's wings to the actual weight of the aircraft and its contents. If the wings are supporting twice as much weight as the weight of the airplane and its contents, the load factor is two. You are probably more familiar with the term "G-forces" as a way to describe flight loads caused by aircraft maneuvering. "Pulling G's" is common terminology for higher performance airplanes. For example, an acrobatic category airplane may pull three or four G's during a maneuver. An airplane in cruising flight, while not accelerating in any direction, has a load factor of one. This one-G condition means the wings are supporting only the actual weight of the airplane and its contents. [Figure 1-37]

A positive load occurs when centrifugal force acts in the same direction as weight. Whenever centrifugal force acts in a direction opposite weight, a negative load is imposed. For example, if you abruptly push the control wheel forward while flying, you would experience a sensation as if your weight suddenly decreased. This is caused by centrifugal force acting upward, which tends to overcome your actual body weight. If the centrifugal force equaled your actual body weight, you would experience a "weightless" sensation of zero G's. A negative G-loading occurs when the centrifugal force exceeds your body weight. In rare instances, you may experience a rapid change in G-forces. For example, in extremely turbulent air, you might be subjected to positive G's, then negative G's, and sometimes sideward G-forces. Sideward G's are called transverse G-forces.

LOAD FACTOR AND STALL SPEED

Earlier you learned that you can stall an airplane at any airspeed and in any flight attitude. You can easily stall an airplane in a turn at a higher-than-normal airspeed. As the angle of bank increases in level turns, you must increase the angle of attack to maintain altitude. As you increase the angle of bank, the stall speed also increases. [Figure 1-38]

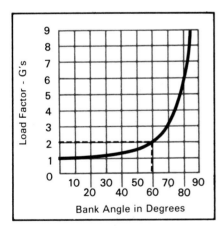

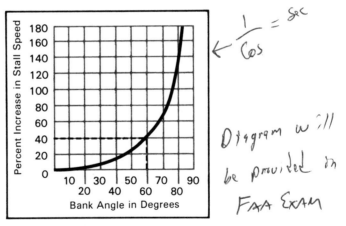

handwritten: $\frac{1}{Cos}$ = Sec

handwritten: Diagram will be provided on FAA EXAM

Figure 1-37. During constant altitude turns, the relationship between load factor, or G's, and bank angle is the same for all airplanes. For example, with a 60° bank, two G's are required to maintain level flight. This means the airplane's wings must support twice the weight of the airplane and its contents, although the actual weight of the airplane does not increase.

Figure 1-38. If you attempt to maintain altitude during a turn by increasing the angle of attack, the stall speed increases as the angle of bank increases. The percent of increase in stall speed is fairly moderate with shallow bank angles — less than 45°. However, once you increase the bank angle beyond 45°, the percent of increase in the stall speed rises rapidly. For example, in a 60°, constant-altitude bank, the stall speed increases by 40%; a 75° bank increases stall speed by 100%.

Increasing the load factor will cause an airplane to stall at a higher speed.

Actually, stall speed increases in proportion to the square root of the load factor. If you are flying an airplane with a one-G stalling speed of 55 knots, you can stall it at twice that speed (110 knots) with a load factor of four G's. Stalls that occur with G-forces on an airplane are called **accelerated stalls**. An accelerated stall occurs at a speed higher than the normal one-G stall speed. These stalls demonstrate that the critical angle of attack, rather than speed, is the reason for a stall. Stalls also can occur at unusually high speeds in severe turbulence, or in low-level wind shear.

LIMIT LOAD FACTOR

When the Federal Aviation Administration certifies an airplane, one of the criteria they look at is how much stress the airplane can withstand. The **limit load factor** is the number of G's an airplane can sustain, on a continuing basis, without causing permanent deformation or structural damage. In other words, the limit load factor is the amount of positive or negative G's an airframe is capable of supporting.

Most small general aviation airplanes with a gross weight of 12,500 pounds or less, and nine passenger seats or less, are certified in either the normal, utility, or acrobatic categories. A normal category airplane is certified for nonacrobatic maneuvers. Training maneuvers and turns not exceeding 60° of bank are permitted in this category. The maximum limit load factor in the normal category is 3.8 positive G's, and 1.52 negative G's. In other words, the airplane's wings are designed to withstand 3.8 times the actual weight of the airplane and its contents during maneuvering flight. By following proper loading techniques and flying within the limits listed in the pilot's operating handbook, you will avoid excessive loads on the airplane, and possible structural damage.

In addition to those maneuvers permitted in the normal category, an airplane certified in the utility category may be used for several maneuvers requiring additional stress on the airframe. A limit of 4.4 positive G's or 1.76 negative G's is permitted in the utility category. Some, but not all, utility category airplanes are also approved for spins. An acrobatic category airplane may be flown in any flight attitude as long as its limit load factor does not exceed six positive G's or three negative G's.

A key point for you to remember is that it is possible to exceed design limits for load factor during maneuvers. For example, if you roll into a steep, level turn of 75°, you will put approximately four G's on the airplane. This is above the maximum limit of 3.8 G's for an airplane in the normal category. You also should be aware of the conditions specified for the maximum load limit. If flaps are extended, for instance, the maximum load limit normally is less. The POH for the airplane you are flying is your best source of load limit information.

MANEUVERING SPEED

An important airspeed related to load factors and stall speed is the **design maneuvering speed** (V_A). This limiting speed normally is not marked on the airspeed indicator, since it may vary with total weight. The POH and/or a placard in the airplane are the best sources for determining V_A. Although some handbooks may designate only one maneuvering speed, others may show several. When more than one is specified, you will notice that V_A decreases as weight decreases. An aircraft operating at lighter weights is subject to more rapid acceleration from gusts and turbulence than a more heavily loaded one.

Any airspeed in excess of V_A can overstress the airframe during abrupt maneuvers or turbulence. The higher the airspeed, the greater the amount of excess load that can be imposed before a stall occurs. V_A represents the maximum speed at which you can use full, abrupt control movement without overstressing the airframe. If you are flying at or below this speed, any combination of pilot-induced control movement, or gust loads resulting from turbulence, should not cause an excessive load on the airplane. This is why you should always fly at or below V_A during turbulent conditions.

The amount of excess load that can be imposed on an airframe depends on the aircraft's speed.

The design maneuvering speed also is the maximum speed at which you can safely stall an airplane. If you stall the airplane above this speed, you will generate excessive G-loads. At or below this speed, the airplane will stall before excessive G-forces build up. By staying at or below V_A, you avoid the possibility of overstressing or even damaging the airplane.

STALLS

All pilots should be knowledgeable about the causes and effects of stalling. This knowledge is a training requirement and it is especially important during flight at slow airspeeds where the margin above the stall speed is small. Keep in mind, slow airspeeds are necessary for every takeoff and landing.

CAUSES OF STALLS

As indicated earlier in this chapter, a stall occurs when the maximum lift angle of attack (C_{Lmax}) is exceeded. If you do not recover promptly by reducing the angle of attack, a secondary stall and/or a spin may result.

A forward CG causes a higher stalling speed than a more rearward CG. Besides CG position, load factor, flap setting (configuration), and weight, other factors can affect the actual stalling speed. Turbulence, lack of coordination, and snow, ice, or frost on the wings are examples. As you might expect, these factors can increase the stalling speed.

STALL RECOGNITION AND RECOVERY

There are any number of ways to recognize that a stall is imminent. Ideally, you should be able to detect the first signs of an impending stall and make appropriate corrections before it actually occurs. If you have a good understanding of the types of stalls, recognition is much easier. Recovery at the first indication of a stall is quite simple; but, if you allow the stalled condition to progress, recovery becomes more difficult.

Knowing the flight characteristics of the airplane you are flying and being aware of the specific phases of flight where stalls are most likely to occur are additional factors in stall recognition. For example, power-on, turning stalls often occur during a departure or climb after takeoff, and power-off, turning stalls are common during the turn to the final approach for a landing.

A typical indication of a stall is a mushy feeling in the flight controls and less control affect as the aircraft's speed decreases. The reduction in control effectiveness is primarily due to reduced airflow over the flight control surfaces. In fixed-pitch propeller airplanes, a loss of revolutions per minute (r.p.m.) may be noticeable as you approach a stall in power-on conditions. Also, a reduction in the sound of air flowing along the fuselage is usually evident. Just before the stall occurs, buffeting, uncontrollable pitching, or vibrations may begin. Finally, your kinesthetic sense (ability to recognize changes in direction or speed) may also provide a warning of decreased speed or the beginning of a sinking feeling. These preliminary indications serve as a warning for you to decrease the angle of attack and add power to increase the airspeed.

LEFT-TURNING TENDENCIES

Propeller-driven airplanes are subject to several left-turning tendencies caused by a combination of physical and aerodynamic forces — torque, gyroscopic precession, asymmetrical thrust, and spiraling slipstream. You will need to compensate for these forces, especially when you are flying in high-power, low-airspeed flight conditions following takeoff or during the initial climb. If you know what is happening to the airplane, you will have a better idea of how to correct for these tendencies.

TORQUE

Torque effect is greatest in a single-engine airplane during a low-airspeed, high-power flight condition.

In airplanes with a single engine, the propeller rotates clockwise when viewed from the pilot's seat. **Torque** can be understood most easily by remembering Newton's third law of motion. The clockwise action of a spinning propeller causes a torque reaction which tends to rotate the airplane counterclockwise about its longitudinal axis. [Figure 1-39]

Generally, aircraft have design adjustments which compensate for torque while in cruising flight, but you will have to take corrective action

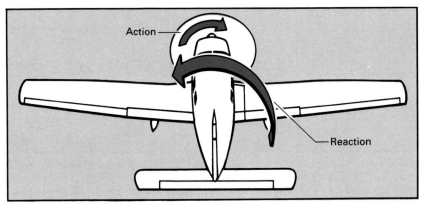

Figure 1-39. In a single-engine airplane, you will experience the greatest effect of torque during takeoff or climb when you are in a low-airspeed, high-power, high angle of attack flight condition.

during other phases of flight. Some airplanes have aileron trim tabs which you can use to correct for the effects of torque at various power settings.

GYROSCOPIC PRECESSION

The turning propeller of an airplane also exhibits characteristics of a gyroscope — rigidity in space and precession. The characteristic that produces a left-turning tendency is precession. **Gyroscopic precession** is the resultant reaction of an object when force is applied. The reaction to a force applied to a gyro acts in the direction of rotation and approximately 90° ahead of the point where force is applied. [Figure 1-40]

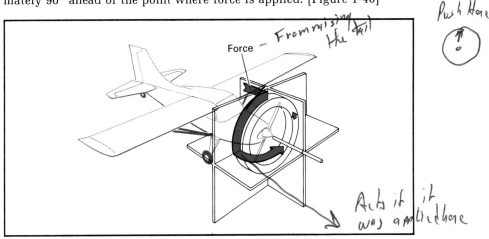

Figure 1-40. If the pitch attitude of an airplane is changed from a nose-high to a nose-level position, a force will be exerted near the top of the propeller's plane of rotation. A resultant force will then be exerted 90° ahead in the direction of rotation, which will cause the nose of the airplane to yaw to the left. This typically happens when the tail of a conventional-gear airplane is raised on the takeoff roll.

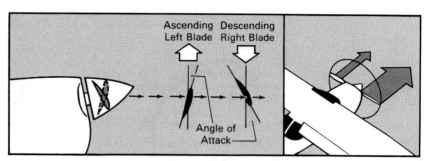

Figure 1-41. Asymmetrical thrust occurs when an airplane is flown at a high angle of attack. This causes uneven angles of attack between the ascending and descending propeller blades. Consequently, less thrust is produced from the ascending blade on the left than from the descending blade on the right. This produces a tendency for the airplane to yaw to the left.

ASYMMETRICAL THRUST

P-factor results from the descending propeller blade on the right producing more thrust than the ascending blade on the left.

When you are flying a single-engine airplane at a high angle of attack, the descending blade of the propeller takes a greater "bite" of air than the ascending blade on the other side. The greater bite is caused by a higher angle of attack for the descending blade, compared to the ascending blade. This creates the uneven, or **asymmetrical thrust**, which is known as P-factor. **P-factor** makes an airplane yaw about its vertical axis to the left. [Figure 1-41]

You should remember that P-factor is most pronounced when the engine is operating at a high-power setting, and when the airplane is flown at a high angle of attack. In level cruising flight, P-factor is not apparent, since both ascending and descending propeller blades are at nearly the same angle of attack, and are creating approximately the same amount of thrust.

P-factor causes an airplane to yaw to the left when it is at high angles of attack.

A good way to learn more about asymmetrical thrust is to take a look at a tailwheel-type airplane the next time you're on an airport ramp. Its high angle of attack is quite apparent, and you can easily see the difference between the ascending and descending blade angles.

SPIRALING SLIPSTREAM

As the propeller rotates, it produces a backward flow of air, or slipstream, which wraps around the airplane. This **spiraling slipstream** causes a change in the airflow around the vertical stabilizer. Due to the direction of the propeller rotation, the resultant slipstream strikes the left side of the vertical fin. [Figure 1-42]

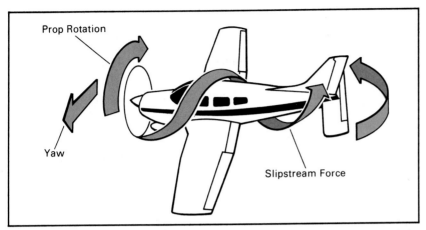

Figure 1-42. As the slipstream produced by the propeller rotation wraps around the fuselage, it strikes the left side of the vertical fin. A left-turning tendency is created as the air "pushes" the tail of the airplane to the right and yaws the nose left.

GROUND EFFECT

Another significant aerodynamic consideration is the phenomenon of **ground effect**. During takeoffs or landings, when you are flying very close to the ground, the earth's surface interferes with the airflow and actually alters the three-dimensional airflow pattern around the airplane. This causes a reduction in wingtip vortices and a decrease in upwash and downwash.

An airplane is usually in ground effect when it is less than the height of the airplane's wingspan above the surface.

Wingtip vortices are caused by the air beneath the wing rolling up and around the wingtip. This causes a spiral or vortex that trails behind each wingtip whenever lift is being produced. Wingtip vortices are another factor contributing to induced drag. Upwash and downwash refer to the effect an airfoil exerts on the free airstream. **Upwash** is the deflection of the oncoming airstream upward and over the wing. **Downwash** is the downward deflection of the airstream as it passes over the wing and past the trailing edge.

If you remember how angle of attack influences induced drag, it will help you understand ground effect. During flight, the downwash of the airstream causes the relative wind to be inclined downward in the vicinity of the wing. This is referred to as the **average relative wind**. The angle between the free airstream relative wind and the average relative wind is the **induced angle of attack**. In effect, the greater the downward deflection of the airstream, the higher the induced angle of attack and the higher the induced drag. Since ground effect restricts the downward

Ground effect reduces induced angle of attack and induced drag.

deflection of the airstream, both the induced angle of attack and induced drag decrease. When the wing is at a height equal to its span, the decline in induced drag is only about 1.4%; when the wing is at a height equal to one-tenth its span, the loss of induced drag is about 48%. [Figure 1-43]

Ground effect allows an airplane to become airborne before it reaches its recommended takeoff speed.

With the reduction of induced angle of attack and induced drag in ground effect, the amount of thrust required to produce lift is reduced. What this means is that your airplane is capable of lifting off at lower-than-normal speed. Although you might initially think that this is desirable, consider what happens as you climb out of ground effect. The power (thrust) required to sustain flight increases significantly as the normal airflow around the wing returns and induced drag is suddenly increased. If you attempt to climb out of ground effect before reaching the speed for normal climb, you might sink back to the surface.

In ground effect, induced drag decreases, and excess speed in the flare may cause floating.

Ground effect is noticeable in the landing phase of flight, too, just before touchdown. Within one wingspan above the ground, the decrease in induced drag makes your airplane seem to float on the cushion of air beneath it. Because of this, power reduction usually is required during the flare to help the airplane land. Although all airplanes may experience ground effect, it is more noticeable in low-wing airplanes, simply because the wings are closer to the ground.

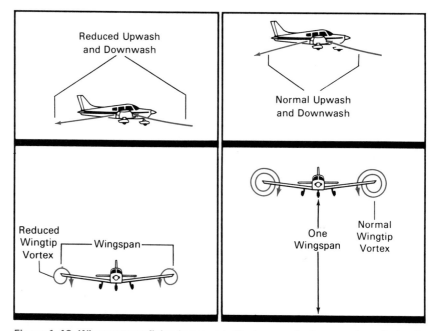

Figure 1-43. When you are flying in ground effect, upwash, downwash, and wingtip vortices decrease. This results in a reduction of induced drag. Ground effect is most noticeable near the surface, and it decreases rapidly until it becomes negligible at a height approximately equal to the wingspan of the aircraft.

CHECKLIST _____

After studying this section, you should have a basic understanding of:

✓ **Three axes of flight** — What they are and how control surface deflection creates movement about them.

✓ **Center of gravity** — Where an airplane's entire weight is considered to be concentrated and where the three axes of flight intersect.

✓ **Forces acting on a climbing airplane** — Why a sustained climb requires excess thrust, and how the four forces are in equilibrium during a stabilized climb.

✓ **Forces acting on a descending airplane** — The significance of glide angle, glide speed, glide ratio, and the effect of weight on a glide.

✓ **Forces acting on a turning airplane** — What causes an airplane to turn, how forces are balanced in a stabilized turn, and how to compensate for adverse yaw.

✓ **Load factor** — What it is, and how it relates to angle of bank, stall speed, and maneuvering speed.

✓ **Stalls** — Their causes, how to recognize them, and recovery techniques.

✓ **Left-turning tendencies** — How the forces of torque, gyroscopic precession, asymmetrical thrust, and spiraling slipstream affect propeller-driven airplanes.

✓ **Ground effect** — How an airplane is affected when it is less than the height of its wingspan above the surface.

SECTION

D

STABILITY

In this section, you will learn about the various aspects of stability that are designed into an airplane. Although no airplane is completely stable, all airplanes must have desirable stability and handling characteristics. An inherently stable airplane is easy to fly, and it reduces pilot fatigue. This quality is essential throughout a wide range of flight conditions — during climbs, descents, turns, and at both high and low airspeeds. You will see that handling characteristics are directly related to stability. In fact, stability, maneuverability, and controllability are all interrelated design characteristics.

Stability is a characteristic of an airplane in flight that causes it to return to a condition of equilibrium, or steady flight, after it is disturbed. For example, if you are flying a stable airplane that is disrupted while in straight-and-level flight, it has a tendency to return to the same attitude. **Maneuverability** is the characteristic of an airplane that permits you to maneuver it easily and allows it to withstand the stress resulting from the maneuvers. An airplane's size, weight, flight control system, structural strength, and thrust determine its maneuverability. **Controllability** is the capability of an airplane to respond to your control inputs, especially with regard to attitude and flight path.

Large transport aircraft are normally designed to be very stable, since passenger comfort is a primary consideration. On the other hand, light training aircraft are designed to be more maneuverable, and somewhat less stable. The two major categories of stability are static and dynamic. Within each of these, there are subcategories called positive, neutral, and negative stability. In addition, since stability applies to all three axes of rotation, it may be classified as longitudinal, lateral, or directional.

STATIC STABILITY

Static stability is the initial tendency that an object displays after its equilibrium is disrupted. When you fly an airplane with **positive static stability**, it tends to return to its original attitude after displacement. A tendency to move farther away from the original attitude following a disturbance is **negative static stability**. If an airplane tends to remain in its displaced attitude, it has **neutral static stability**. [Figure 1-44]

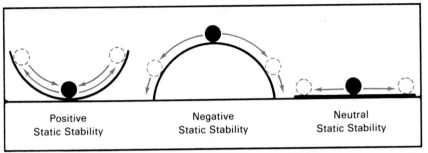

Figure 1-44. Positive static stability is the most desirable characteristic, because the airplane attempts to return to its original trimmed attitude. Almost any airplane you fly exhibits this characteristic. Both negative and neutral static stability are undesirable characteristics.

DYNAMIC STABILITY

Dynamic stability describes the time required for an airplane to respond to its static stability following a displacement from a condition of equilibrium. It is determined by its tendency to oscillate and damp out successive oscillations after the initial displacement. Although an airplane may be designed with positive static stability, it could have positive, negative, or neutral dynamic stability.

Assume the airplane you're flying is displaced from an established attitude. If its tendency is to return to the original attitude directly, or through a series of decreasing oscillations, it exhibits **positive dynamic stability**. If you find the oscillations increasing in magnitude as time progresses, **negative dynamic stability** is exhibited. **Neutral dynamic stability** is indicated if the airplane attempts to return to its original state of equilibrium, but the oscillations neither increase nor decrease in magnitude as time passes. [Figure 1-45]

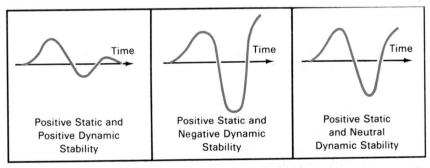

Figure 1-45. The most desirable condition is a combination of positive static stability with positive dynamic stability. In this situation, you need less effort to return the airplane to its original attitude because it "wants" to return there.

LONGITUDINAL STABILITY

When you consider the overall stability of an airplane, remember that the airplane moves about three axes of rotation. **Longitudinal stability** involves the pitching motion or tendency of the airplane about its lateral axis. An airplane which is longitudinally stable will tend to return to its trimmed angle of attack after displacement. This is good, because an airplane with this characteristic tends to resist either excessively nose-high or nose-low pitch attitudes. If an airplane is longitudinally unstable, it has the tendency to climb or dive until a stall or a steep dive develops. As a result, a longitudinally unstable airplane is dangerous to fly.

BALANCE

To achieve longitudinal stability, most airplanes are designed so they're slightly nose heavy. This is accomplished during the engineering and development phase by placing the center of gravity slightly forward of the center of pressure.

The location of the center of gravity with respect to the center of lift determines the longitudinal stability of an airplane.

The **center of pressure** is a point along the wing chord line where lift is considered to be concentrated. For this reason, the center of pressure is often referred to as the **center of lift**. During flight, this point along the chord line changes position with different flight attitudes. It moves forward as angle of attack increases and aft as angle of attack decreases. As a result, pitching tendencies created by the position of the center of lift in relation to the CG vary. For example, with a high angle of attack and the center of lift in a forward position (closer to the CG) the nose-down pitching tendency is decreased. The position of the center of gravity in relation to the center of lift is a critical factor in longitudinal stability. If the CG is too far forward, the airplane is very nose heavy; if the CG is too far aft, the airplane may become tail heavy.

The horizontal stabilizer is set at a negative angle of attack. This offsets the nose-down pitching tendency caused by the CG being located forward of the center of lift.

When the airplane is properly loaded, the CG remains forward of the center of lift and the airplane is slightly nose heavy. The nose-heavy tendency is offset by the position of the horizontal stabilizer, which is set at a negative angle of attack. This produces a downward force, or negative lift on the tail, to counteract the nose heaviness. The downward force is called the **tail-down force**. It is the balancing force in most flight conditions. [Figure 1-46]

With the exception of T-tail airplanes, additional downward forces are exerted on horizontal tail surfaces by downwash from the propeller and the wings. The strength of the downward force is primarily related to the speed of the airplane, but the position of the stabilizer in relation to the wings and the propeller also affects it. T-tail designs are not subject to the same downwash effect, simply because the horizontal tail surface is above most, or all, of the downwash. [Figure 1-47]

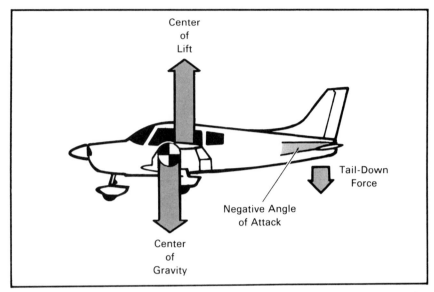

Figure 1-46. To sustain level flight, the lift produced by the wings must support the weight of the airplane plus the tail-down force that results from the negative angle of attack on the stabilizer.

Power changes also affect longitudinal stability. If you reduce power during flight, a definite nose-down pitching tendency occurs due to the reduction of downwash from the wings and the propeller. This decreases the associated downward force on the tail, and reduces elevator effectiveness. Although this is a destabilizing factor, it is a desirable characteristic, because it tends to result in a nose-down attitude during power reductions. The nose-down attitude helps you maintain, or regain, airspeed.

On airplanes other than T-tails, a power reduction decreases the downwash on the horizontal stabilizer from the wings and propeller slipstream. This is what causes the nose to pitch down after a power reduction.

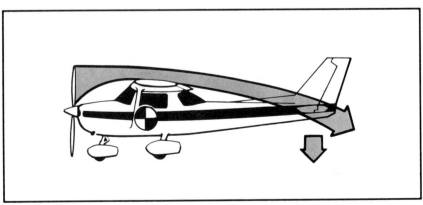

Figure 1-47. As the downwash from the propeller and the wings passes over the horizontal stabilizer, it "pushes" the tail section down. This tail-down force helps to balance the airplane about its lateral axis, and it influences the longitudinal stability of the airplane.

Increasing power has the opposite effect. It causes increased downwash on horizontal tail surfaces and tends to force the nose of the airplane to rise. The influence of power on longitudinal stability also depends on the overall design of the airplane. Since power provides thrust, the alignment of thrust in relation to the longitudinal axis, the CG, the wings, and the stabilizer are all factors. The **thrustline** is determined by where the propeller is mounted and by the general direction in which thrust acts.

In most light general aviation airplanes, the thrustline is parallel to the longitudinal axis and above the CG. This creates a slight pitching moment around the CG. If thrust is decreased, the pitching moment is reduced and the nose heaviness tends to decrease. An increase in thrust increases the pitching moment and increases nose heaviness. Notice that these pitching tendencies are exactly the reverse of the pitching tendencies resulting from an increase or decrease in downwash. This thrustline design arrangement minimizes the destabilizing effects of power changes and improves longitudinal stability. [Figure 1-48]

Although the tail-down force is excellent for longitudinal stability and balance, it is aerodynamically inefficient. The wings must support the negative lift created by the tail, and the negative angle of attack on the stabilizer increases drag. If an airplane design permitted two lifting surfaces, both the wings and the horizontal stabilizer, aerodynamic efficiency would be much greater.

CANARD

The canard design utilizes the concept of two lifting surfaces. A **canard** is a stabilizer that is located in front of the main wings. Canards are something like miniature forward wings. They were used in the pioneering

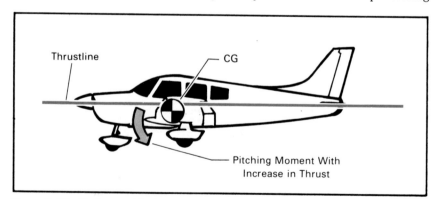

Figure 1-48. Airplanes with the thrustline parallel to the longitudinal axis and above the CG produce a pitching moment about the CG which partially counteracts downwash effects on the stabilizer. An increase in power, or thrust, increases downwash on the stabilizer and produces a nose-up pitching tendency. At the same time, the increased thrust also creates a nose-down pitching tendency because the thrustline is above the CG.

days of aviation, most notably on the Wright Flyer, and are now reappearing on several original designs. [Figure 1-49]

Since both the main wings and the canard produce positive lift, the design is aerodynamically efficient. A properly designed canard is stall/spin resistant. The canard stalls at a lower angle of attack than the main wings. In doing so, the canard's angle of attack immediately decreases after it stalls. This breaks the stall and effectively returns the canard to a normal lift-producing angle of attack before the main wings have a chance to stall. Ailerons remain effective throughout the stall because they are attached to the main wings. In spite of its advantages, the canard design has limitations in total lift capability. Critical design conditions also must be met to maintain adequate longitudinal stability throughout the flight envelope.

CENTER OF GRAVITY POSITION

The position of the center of gravity (CG) is another key factor in longitudinal stability. Distribution of weight in an airplane determines the position of the center of gravity. This weight includes the basic weight of the airplane itself, as well as the weight of fuel, passengers, and baggage. Since the weight of the airplane and the distribution of that weight normally are fixed, the CG location is largely determined by what you put into the airplane, and where you put it. For example, if you load heavy baggage into an aft baggage compartment, it might cause the CG to shift to an unfavorable position. This could be critical, so let's look briefly at what happens when the position of the CG shifts beyond acceptable limits.

As you might expect, for an airplane to be controllable during flight, the CG must be located within a reasonable distance forward or aft of an optimum position. All airplanes have forward and aft limits for the position of the CG. The distance between these limits is the **CG range**. [Figure 1-50]

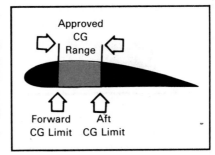

Figure 1-49. With its location in front of the wings, the canard is actually a small, forward wing, as well as a stabilizer. It provides longitudinal stability about the lateral axis by lifting the nose of the airplane.

Figure 1-50. An airplane must be loaded so the effect of weight distribution does not adversely affect longitudinal balance. The CG will remain within the approved CG range if the distribution of weight is acceptable.

When the CG is within the approved CG range, the airplane not only is controllable, but its longitudinal stability also is satisfactory. If the CG is located near the forward or aft limit of the approved CG range, a slight loss of longitudinal stability may be noticeable. However, stabilator (elevator) effectiveness is still adequate to control the airplane during all approved maneuvers.

CG TOO FAR FORWARD

If you load your airplane so the CG is forward of the forward CG limit, it will be too nose heavy. The condition gets progressively worse as the CG moves to an extreme forward position. This actually makes the airplane too stable. Eventually, stabilator (elevator) effectiveness will be insufficient to lift the nose. [Figure 1-51]

CG TOO FAR AFT

An airplane loaded to its aft CG limit will be less stable at all speeds.

A CG located aft of the approved CG range is even more dangerous than a CG that is too far forward. With an aft CG, the airplane becomes tail heavy and very unstable in pitch, regardless of speed. [Figure 1-52]

An airplane becomes progressively more difficult to control as the CG moves aft. If the CG is beyond the aft limit, you will be unable to lower the nose to recover from a stall or a spin.

CG limits are established during initial testing and airworthiness certification. One of the criteria for determining the CG range in light airplanes is a spin recovery capability. If the CG is within limits, a normal category airplane must demonstrate that it can be recovered from a one-turn spin; and a utility category airplane that is approved for spins must be recoverable from a fully developed spin. The aft CG limit is the most critical factor. As the CG moves aft, stabilator effectiveness decreases. When the CG is at the aft limit, stabilator effectiveness is adequate; but, when the CG is beyond the aft limit, the stabilator may be ineffective for stall or spin recovery.

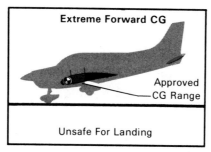

Figure 1-51. If the CG is well forward of the approved CG range, stabilator effectiveness will be insufficient to exert the required tail-down force needed for a nose-high landing attitude. This will cause the nosewheel to strike the runway before the main gear.

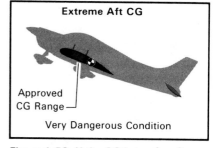

Figure 1-52. If the CG is too far aft, you will not have enough stabilator effectiveness to raise the tail and lower the nose of the airplane. As a result, you will be unable to recover from a stalled condition and a spin may develop.

As a pilot, there are certain actions you can take to prevent an aft CG position. You can make sure the heaviest passengers and baggage, or cargo, are loaded as far forward as practical. Lighter passengers and baggage normally should be loaded in aft seats or compartments. The main thing you must do is follow the airplane manufacturer's loading recommendations in the POH. If you do this, your airplane will be loaded so the CG is within the approved range where longitudinal stability is adequate and, at the same time, where you can control the airplane during all approved maneuvers. Two important points to remember are that a CG beyond acceptable limits adversely affects longitudinal stability, and the most hazardous condition is an extreme aft CG position. You will learn more about the effects of adverse loading in the section on weight and balance in Chapter 3.

LATERAL STABILITY

Stability about an airplane's longitudinal axis, which extends nose to tail, is called **lateral stability**. If one wing is lower than the opposite wing, lateral stability helps return the wings to a wings-level attitude. This tendency to resist lateral, or roll, movement is aided by specific design characteristics of an airplane. Four of the most common design features that influence lateral stability are dihedral, keel effect, sweepback, and weight distribution. Two of these, keel effect and sweepback, also help provide directional stability about the vertical axis.

DIHEDRAL

The most common design for lateral stability is known as wing dihedral. **Dihedral** is the upward angle of the airplane's wings with respect to the horizontal. When you look at an airplane, dihedral makes the wings appear to form a spread-out V. Dihedral usually is just a few degrees.

If an airplane with dihedral enters an uncoordinated roll during gusty wind conditions, one wing will be elevated and the opposite wing will drop. This causes an immediate side slip downward toward the low wing. The side slip makes the low wing approach the air at a higher angle of attack than the high wing. The increased angle of attack on the low wing produces more lift for that wing and tends to lift it back to a level flight attitude. [Figure 1-53]

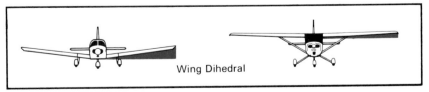

Wing Dihedral

Figure 1-53. Wing dihedral contributes to lateral stability. Low-wing airplanes commonly have more dihedral than high-wing airplanes. The center of gravity is well below the wing in a high-wing airplane. Because this CG position has a stabilizing effect, very little dihedral is necessary.

KEEL EFFECT

Lateral stability is also provided by keel effect. During flight, the vertical fin and side area of the fuselage react to the airflow very much like the keel of a ship. This **keel effect** is the steadying influence exerted by the side area of the fuselage and vertical stabilizer. When the airplane rolls to one side, a combination of the pressure of the airflow against the keel surface, along with the airplane's weight, tends to roll the airplane back to a wings-level attitude. [Figure 1-54]

SWEEPBACK

In many airplanes, the leading edges of the wings do not form right angles with the longitudinal axis. Instead, the wings taper backward from the root of the wing to the wingtips. This is called **sweepback**. In higher performance airplanes with pronounced sweepback, the design helps maintain the center of lift aft of the CG. In light training airplanes, sweepback helps improve lateral stability. [Figure 1-55]

Sweepback also may aid slightly in directional stability. If an airplane rotates about its vertical axis or yaws to the left, the right wing has less sweep and a slight increase in drag. The left wing has more sweep and less drag. This tends to force the airplane back into alignment with the relative wind.

WEIGHT DISTRIBUTION

You have no control of the design features that help maintain lateral stability, but you can control the distribution of weight and improve lateral stability. For example, most training airplanes have two fuel tanks, one inside each wing. Before you take off on a long flight, you normally fill both tanks. If you use fuel from only one tank, you will soon notice that

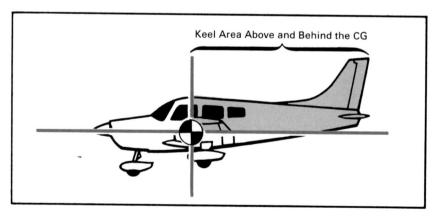

Keel Area Above and Behind the CG

Figure 1-54. Laterally stable airplanes are designed so that a larger portion of the keel area is above and behind the center of gravity. Since more of the keel area is aft of the CG, the keel area also acts as a weather vane about the vertical axis. This helps maintain vertical (directional) stability.

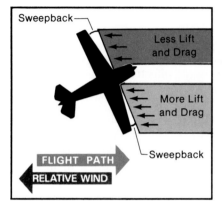

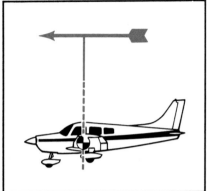

Figure 1-55. If an airplane with sweepback inadvertently rolls about its longitudinal axis and a side slip occurs, the leading edge of the lower wing meets the relative wind more nearly perpendicular than the higher wing. This increases lift and drag on the lower wing and decreases them on the higher wing, which tends to restore the wings to a level position.

Figure 1-56. An airplane must have more surface area behind the CG than it has in front of it. The same is true for a weather vane; more surface aft of the pivot point is a basic design feature. This arrangement helps keep the airplane aligned with the relative wind, just as the weather vane points into the wind.

the airplane wants to roll toward the wing with the full tank. The distribution of weight is uneven and lateral stability is affected. In this case, you can easily correct the imbalance in weight by using an equal amount of fuel from the full tank.

DIRECTIONAL STABILITY

Stability about the vertical axis is called **directional stability**. Essentially, an airplane in flight is much like a weather vane. You can compare the pivot point on the weather vane to the center of gravity pivot point of the airplane. The nose of the airplane corresponds to the weather vane's arrowhead, and the vertical fin on the airplane acts like the tail of the weather vane. [Figure 1-56]

EFFECTS OF LATERAL AND DIRECTIONAL STABILITY

Although airplanes are designed with stabilizing characteristics which lighten your workload while you are flying, there are normally some undesirable side effects. Two of the most common ones are Dutch roll and spiral instability.

Dutch roll is a combination of rolling/yawing oscillations caused either by your control input or by wind gusts. In a typical case, when equilibrium is disturbed, the rolling reaction precedes the yaw, and the roll motion is more noticeable than the yaw motion.

When the airplane rolls back toward level flight in response to the dihedral effect, it continues to roll too far and side slips the other way. Each oscillation overshoots the wings-level position because of the strong dihedral effect. Dutch roll actually is the back-and-forth, rolling/yawing motion. If the Dutch roll tendency is not effectively dampened, it is considered objectionable.

The alternative to an airplane that exhibits Dutch roll tendencies is a design that has better directional stability than lateral stability. If directional stability is increased and lateral stability is decreased, the Dutch roll motion is adequately suppressed. However, this design arrangement tends to cause spiral instability.

Spiral instability is associated with airplanes that have strong directional stability in comparison with lateral stability. When an airplane with spiral instability is disturbed from a condition of equilibrium, a side slip is introduced. In this case, the strong directional stability tends to yaw the airplane back into alignment with the relative wind. At the same time, the comparatively weak dihedral effect lags in restoring lateral stability. Due to the yaw back into the relative wind, the outside wing travels faster than the inside wing and, as a result, more lift is generated by the outside wing. The yaw forces the nose of the airplane down as it swings into alignment with the relative wind. The net result is an overbanking and nose-down tendency which generally is considered less objectionable than Dutch roll.

As you can see, even a well-designed airplane may have some undesirable characteristics. Generally, designers attempt to minimize the Dutch roll tendency, since it is less tolerable than spiral instability. Because of this, many airplanes have some degree of spiral instability which generally is considered acceptable.

The overall stability characteristics of an airplane are closely related to its tendency to enter a spin after stalling. A stable airplane tends to resist spin entry, while an unstable airplane is less spin resistant.

STALL AND SPIN AWARENESS

No discussion of the aerodynamics of flight would be complete without considering spins. Your awareness of what causes spins, and how you can avoid them, is very important. You also need to know how to recover from a spin, if necessary. Since private pilot applicants are not required to demonstrate flight proficiency in intentional spins, this discussion is primarily concerned with fundamental concepts and relationships associated with unintentional spins.

For many years, stall and spin related accidents have accounted for approximately one-quarter of all fatal general aviation accidents. National Transportation Safety Board (NTSB) statistics indicate that most stall/spin accidents result from incidents where a pilot is momentarily distracted from the primary task of flying the aircraft. Because of these factors, regulations stress stall and spin awareness training which is intended to emphasize recognition of situations that could lead to an unintentional stall and/or spin. This is accomplished by use of instructional exercises that include realistic distractions during flight at slow airspeeds. The practice of intentional stalls and recovery techniques is also included in this training. However, only flight instructor candidates are required to demonstrate proficiency in actual spin entry, spins, and spin recovery techniques as a requirement for certification.

Stall and spin awareness is emphasized during flight training. The use of realistic distractions during flight at slow airspeeds is part of this required training.

SPINS

The spin is the most complex of all flight maneuvers. There are actually hundreds of factors that contribute to the spinning of an airplane. In a light, training airplane a **spin** may be defined as an aggravated stall which results in autorotation. During the spin, the airplane descends in a helical, or corkscrew, path while the angle of attack is greater than the critical angle of attack.

PRIMARY CAUSES

A stall must occur before a spin can develop. However, a stall is essentially a coordinated maneuver where both wings are equally or almost equally stalled. In contrast, a spin is an uncoordinated maneuver with the wings unequally stalled. In this case, the wing that is more completely stalled will often drop before the other, and the nose of the aircraft will yaw in the direction of the low wing.

To enter a spin, an airplane must first be stalled. In a spin, both wings are in a stalled condition.

Typically, the cause of an inadvertent spin is exceeding the critical angle of attack while performing an uncoordinated maneuver. The lack of coordination is normally caused by either too much or not enough rudder control for the amount of aileron being used. The result is a cross-controlled condition. If you do not initiate the stall recovery promptly, the airplane is more likely to enter a full stall that may develop into a spin. The spin that occurs from cross controlling usually results in rotation in the direction of the rudder being applied, regardless of which wing is raised. In a skidding turn, where both aileron and rudder are applied in the same direction, rotation will be in that direction. However, in a slipping turn, where opposite aileron is held against the rudder, the resultant spin will usually occur in the direction opposite the aileron that is being applied.

When an airplane is in a stalled or nearly stalled condition, uncoordinated use of the flight controls (aileron and rudder) can easily cause a spin. In most cases, the spin rotation will be in the direction of rudder deflection.

Coordinated use of the flight controls is important, especially during flight at slow airspeeds. Although most pilots are able to maintain coordination of the flight controls during routine maneuvers, this ability often deteriorates when distractions occur and their attention is divided between important tasks. Distractions that have caused problems include preoccupation with situations inside or outside the cockpit, maneuvering to avoid other aircraft, and maneuvering to clear obstacles during takeoffs, climbs, approaches, or landings. These kinds of distractions are another causal factor in stall/spin accidents. Because of this, you will be required to learn how to recognize and cope with these distractions by practicing "flight at slow airspeeds with realistic distractions" during flight lessons under the guidance of your instructor.

PHASES OF A SPIN

Many different terms may be used to describe a spin. The **incipient spin** is that portion of a spin from the time the airplane stalls and rotation starts until the spin is fully developed. A **fully developed** spin means the angular rotation rates, airspeed, and vertical speed are stabilized from turn to turn and the flight path is close to vertical. In light, training airplanes, a complete spin maneuver consists of three phases — incipient, developed, and recovery. [Figure 1-57]

Normally, the recovery from an incipient spin requires less time (and altitude) than the recovery from a fully developed spin. Higher altitudes tend to prolong a recovery. The less dense air is not as responsive to anti-spin controls as the heavier air at lower altitudes.

While some characteristics of a spin are predictable, every airplane spins differently. In addition, the same airplane's spin behavior changes with variations in configuration, loading, and several other factors.

WEIGHT AND BALANCE

Airplanes with an aft CG tend to be less stall/spin resistant than airplanes with a forward CG.

Even minor weight and balance changes can affect an aircraft's spin characteristics. Heavier weights generally result in slow spin rates initially; but, as the spin progresses, heavier weights tend to cause an increasing spin rate and longer recovery time. Distribution of weight is even more significant. Forward center of gravity positions usually inhibit the high angles of attack necessary for a stall. Thus, an airplane with a forward CG tends to be more stall and spin resistant than an aircraft with an aft CG. In addition, spins with aft CG positions are flatter than ordinary spins. A **flat spin** is characterized by a near level pitch and roll attitude with the spin axis near the CG of the airplane. Recovery from a flat spin may be extremely difficult or even impossible.

In a training airplane, the addition of a back seat passenger or a single suitcase to an aft baggage compartment can affect the CG enough to change the characteristics of a spin. Instead of an ordinary spin, a flat spin could easily occur. You also should be aware of other unfavorable loading possibilities. A concentration of weight, or unbalanced weight distribution, a long way from the CG is undesirable. This type of loading may occur with tip tanks or outboard wing tanks. If the fuel in these tanks becomes unbalanced, an asymmetrical condition exists. The worst asymmetric condition is full fuel in the wing on the outside of the spin and no fuel in

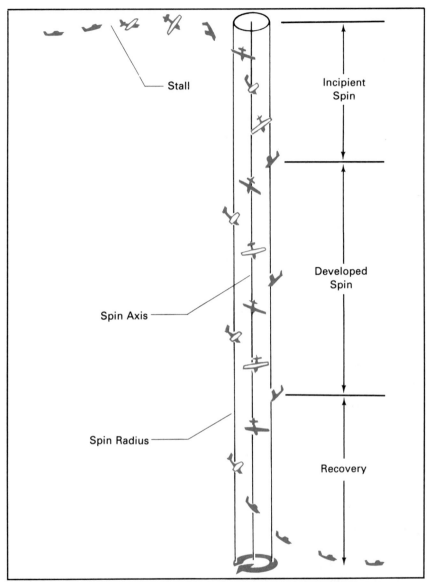

Figure 1-57. The incipient spin usually occurs rapidly in light airplanes (about 4 to
6 seconds) and consists of approximately the first two turns. At about the half-turn
point, the airplane is pointed almost straight down but the angle of attack is usually
above that of the stall because of the inclined flight path. As the one-turn point
approaches, the nose may come back up and the angle of attack continues to
increase. As the airplane continues to rotate into the second turn, the flight path
becomes more nearly vertical, and the pitching, rolling, and yawing motions become
more repeatable. This is the beginning of the fully developed spin. The last phase,
recovery, occurs when anti-spin forces overcome pro-spin forces. During recovery,
the angle of attack on both wings decreases below the critical angle and the
rotation rate slows. This phase can range from one quarter of a turn to several
turns.

the tanks on the inside of the turn. Once the spin is developed, the momentum (inertial force) makes recovery unlikely under these conditions.

From this discussion, it is apparent that observing weight and balance limitations is essential. In fact, all operating limitations are imposed for safety purposes. This is particularly important for limits concerned with spins.

There is no guarantee that a normal category airplane will recover from a fully developed spin.

Single-engine, normal category airplanes are prohibited from intentional spins. This is indicated by a placard with words such as "No acrobatic maneuvers, including spins, approved." However, during aircraft certification tests, normal category airplanes must demonstrate recovery from a one-turn spin or a three-second spin, whichever takes longer. The recovery must take place within one additional turn with normal control inputs. Since airplanes in the normal category have not been tested for more than one-turn/three second spins, their performance characteristics beyond these limits are unknown. The one-turn margin of safety only provides a check of the airplane's controllability in a delayed or aggravated stall which is early in the incipient phase of a spin. This does not provide any assurance that recovery is possible from a fully developed spin.

Acrobatic category airplanes must fully recover from fully developed spins within one and one-half additional turns. Certification in this category also requires six turns or three seconds, whichever takes longer, before the recovery controls are applied.

Utility category airplanes may be tested under the one-turn (normal) criteria or they may satisfy the six-turn (acrobatic) spin requirements. However, spins in utility category airplanes may be approved only with specific loading, such as at a reduced weight and with a forward CG position. It is extremely important for you to understand all of the operating limitations for your airplane. Applicable limitations are placarded and/or included in the POH.

SPIN RECOVERY

It should be clear that you, as an applicant for a private pilot certificate, are not required to demonstrate flight proficiency in spin entries or spin recovery techniques. Even though your flight instructor may demonstrate a spin at some point during your training, you should never intentionally enter a spin. As already mentioned, the emphasis in stall/spin awareness training for private pilots is awareness of conditions that could lead to an unintentional stall or spin. You also need to have a basic understanding of how to recover from a spin.

Spin recovery techniques vary for different aircraft; therefore, you must follow the recovery procedures outlined in the POH for your airplane. The following is a general recovery procedure, but it should not be applied arbitrarily without regard for the manufacturer's recommendations.

Since an airplane must be in a stalled condition before it will spin, the first thing you should do is try to recover from the stall before the spin develops. If your reaction is too slow and a spin develops, move the throttle to idle, neutralize the ailerons, and raise the flaps. Next, apply full rudder deflection opposite to the direction of the turn. When the rotation rate slows, briskly position the elevator forward to approximately the neutral position to decrease the angle of attack. As the rotation stops, neutralize the rudder and smoothly apply back pressure to recover from the steep nose-down pitch attitude. During recovery from the dive, make sure you avoid excessive airspeed and high G-forces. This could cause an accelerated stall, or even result in structural failure.

CHECKLIST ───────────────────────────

After studying this section, you should have a basic understanding of:

✓   **Stability** — What it is and how it causes the airplane to return to a condition of equilibrium after it is disturbed.

✓   **Static stability** — What it is, and the difference between positive, negative, and neutral static stability.

✓   **Dynamic stability** — What it is, and the difference between positive, negative, and neutral dynamic stability.

✓   **Longitudinal stability** — How a longitudinally stable airplane tends to return to its trimmed angle of attack after displacement.

✓   **Balance** — How the location of the center of gravity with respect to the center of lift affects longitudinal stability.

✓   **Tail loads** — How tail-down forces caused by the angle of attack of the horizontal stabilizer, downwash, and the location of the thrust-line affect longitudinal stability.

✓   **Center of gravity position** — How a CG location beyond approved limits can alter an airplane's controllability and adversely affect its longitudinal stability.

✓   **Lateral stability** — How dihedral, keel effect, sweepback, and weight distribution affect an airplane's lateral stability about its longitudinal axis.

✓   **Directional stability** — How Dutch roll and spiral instability affect the aircraft.

✓   **Stall and Spin Awareness** — Why training is required, what a spin is, what causes a spin, what the phases of a spin are, and how to recover from a spin.

CHAPTER 2

THE FLIGHT ENVIRONMENT

INTRODUCTION

The flight environment includes a broad range of information that you will need for any flight operation you may conduct. Acquiring the knowledge to safely operate an airplane in today's complex flight environment is essential to becoming a proficient pilot. We begin by discussing scanning and other collision avoidance factors that relate directly to safety of flight. The next section details the different types of airports you will encounter, and includes information about taxiway and runway marking and lighting. Following that, you learn about the structure of the entire airspace system. This section also describes the operating rules and equipment requirements that apply in each airspace segment. In the next section, you will learn about radio communications and how to talk over the radio using appropriate words and phrases. Finally, you will become familiar with the capabilities of radar and transponders and see how you can benefit from various air traffic control services.

SECTION A

SAFETY OF FLIGHT

In this section, we will discuss various aspects of the flight environment that you will encounter each time you fly. These include scanning, collision avoidance, blind spots in aircraft design, right-of-way rules, altitude rules, and special safety considerations. You will also be introduced to some of the Federal Aviation Regulations, and you will receive an overall view of important factors related to the safety of flight.

VISUAL SCANNING

The most effective way to scan during daylight is through a series of short, regularly spaced eye movements in 10° sectors.

One of the primary factors involved with safety of flight is your ability to see and avoid other aircraft. When you are flying, you should spend at least 70% of your time **scanning**, or looking outside your airplane. For scanning to be effective, though, you must develop a pattern that is compatible with how your eyes function. For example, your eyes require time to refocus when switching from the instrument panel to distant objects outside the airplane. Another characteristic of your eyes is that only a very small area in the back of the eye can send clear, sharply focused images to the brain. Since the eyes require time to focus on this narrow viewing area, scanning is most effective when you use a series of short, regularly spaced eye movements. This will help to bring successive areas of the sky into the central visual field. The FAA recommends that your eye movements not exceed 10°, and that you focus for at least one second on each segment. Be sure that the scan pattern you develop covers all of the sky you can see from the cockpit, both horizontally and vertically.

Effective scanning habits help you compensate for a phenomenon called **empty field myopia**. This condition usually occurs when you are looking at a featureless sky that is devoid of objects, contrasting colors, or patterns. Flying in haze or reduced visibility is an example. In this situation, your eyes tend to focus at only 10 to 30 feet. At this distance, spots on the windshield may look like airplanes and aircraft further away may go undetected. With empty field myopia, an aircraft must be two or three times larger (closer) before you are able to see it. If you feel that you are experiencing empty field myopia, you should consciously increase your scan rate and focus your eyes alternately far and near.

Focusing on the different sectors as you scan can be difficult when flying into the sun, just as driving a car into the sun is a problem. You may want to consider a different route or departure time that will minimize the sun's effects. Also, you know from experience that a clean windshield and sunglasses improve your ability to see objects more clearly in bright sunlight. Keep in mind that when two aircraft are flying on a head-on collision course and both are traveling at 150 knots, they will travel one quarter of a mile toward each other in the three seconds that it usually requires for the pilots to take action. This makes early detection of other aircraft very important.

Your peripheral vision also plays an important role in spotting other aircraft because it is especially effective in detecting relative movement. This movement becomes apparent only during the moments when your scan is stopped. Relative movement usually is your first perception of a collision threat as you stop to focus on successive sectors of the sky. Remember, however, that you should be especially alert for an aircraft which shows no movement in relation to your airplane. It is likely to collide with you unless you take evasive action. When you are considering evasive action, you will need to estimate the other airplane's relative altitude. [Figure 2-1]

If there is no apparent relative motion between another aircraft and yours, you are probably on a collision course.

Remember that the other pilot may be occupied with tasks other than scanning and may not react in the manner that you anticipate. As you take evasive action, watch the other aircraft to see if it makes any unusual maneuvers and, if so, plan your reaction accordingly. You should also be aware that there may be more than one potential collision hazard in an area at the same time. The more time you spend on developing your scan in the early part of flight training, the more natural it will become later. The scanning techniques described here will help you to see potential conflicts earlier and allow you to take the proper action to avoid a collision. Also, being aware of the blind spots in your aircraft's design will improve your awareness of potential hazards.

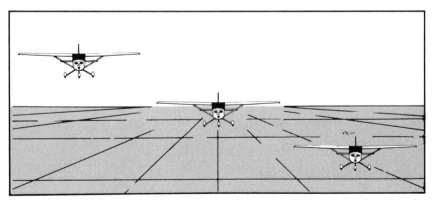

Figure 2-1. To determine if you are at about the same altitude as another aircraft, use the horizon as a reference. If the aircraft appears to be above the horizon, the aircraft is probably at a higher altitude than you are. If the aircraft appears to be below the horizon, the aircraft is probably at a lower altitude than you. If the aircraft is on the horizon, it may be at your altitude. You must decide quickly if it poses a threat and, if so, take the appropriate evasive action.

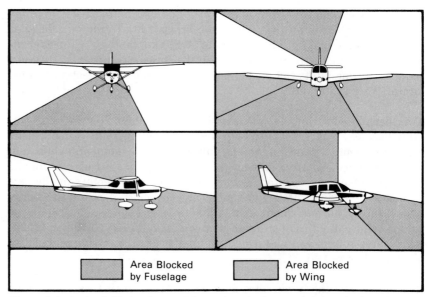

Figure 2-2. In both high-wing and low-wing designs, portions of your view are blocked by the fuselage and wings. This can make it difficult to see conflicting traffic.

BLIND SPOTS AND AIRCRAFT DESIGN

Airplanes, like automobiles, have problems associated with **blind spots**. Due to the nature of airplane design, blind spots are of special concern. High-wing airplanes make it difficult to see above the airplane, but it is very easy to see below the airplane. On the other hand, it is very easy to see above a low-wing aircraft and difficult to see below it. This is important to remember while climbing or descending, particularly when operating in the area around an airport. [Figure 2-2]

Turns require special consideration, too. Before you initiate a turn, always look in the direction of your turn. In a low-wing airplane, this presents no difficulty. In a high-wing airplane, your view is blocked as soon as you lower the wing to start a turn. By gently lifting that wing and looking before you start the turn, you can "clear" the area of other aircraft.

AIRPORT OPERATIONS

Any operation in the vicinity of an airport warrants extra caution. Even airports with control towers may be hazardous because of the large amount of air traffic. A controlled environment does not relieve you of the responsibility to see and avoid other traffic. In some cases, you may need to be even more vigilant. At airports without control towers, which are referred to as uncontrolled airports, you have other concerns. At these airports, you may see a combination of experimental aircraft, ultra-light aircraft, gliders, and aircraft both with and without radios. This variety of aircraft increases the chance that conflicting traffic can be blocked by blind spots in aircraft design. This can develop into a serious problem, particularly during the approach and landing phases of flight. [Figure 2-3]

If you are flying a high-wing aircraft that is climbing out on departure, the blind spot created by the wing will not allow you to see above the airplane. At the same time, it is possible that a low-wing aircraft may be descending for a landing and the pilot cannot see below the wing.

A good way to reduce the possibility of a collision during extended climbs or descents is to make shallow S-turns and avoid climbing or descending at steep angles. Climbing at a faster airspeed permits a shallower angle. This, in turn, enables you to see better over the engine cowling. Making shallow S-turns as you are climbing increases your

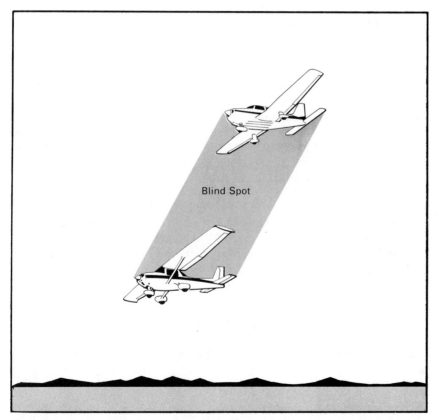

Figure 2-3. When a high-wing airplane is below a low-wing airplane on approach to landing, both airplanes can easily remain out of sight of each other. Similar problems can occur during departures.

range of vision, too. If you are flying a low-wing airplane, plan your descent so that it won't have to be steep, and make S-turns as you descend.

MANEUVERS IN THE TRAINING AREA

Prior to starting any maneuvers, make clearing turns and carefully scan the area for other aircraft.

As you continue your flight training, your instructor will teach you to make **clearing turns** when you are in the practice area, which is the area used to practice flight maneuvers. It is important not only to clear the area for traffic, but to maintain your scan while practicing the maneuvers. Your instructor will demonstrate the various types of clearing turns for you. They usually consist of at least a 180° change in direction. These turns allow you to see the areas blocked by the blind spots of your aircraft, and they make it easier to maintain visual contact with other aircraft in the practice area. Remember to make clearing turns and carefully scan the entire area for other traffic before you begin each maneuver.

In cases where traffic conflicts arise, it is necessary for you to know what action to take. This usually is based on who has the right-of-way.

RIGHT-OF-WAY RULES

Throughout your training, you will become more and more familiar with **Federal Aviation Regulations**, or FARs. FARs are the rules that the FAA asks you to follow when you are in the flight environment. They are very specific about right-of-way rules. First, the regulations state very clearly that the pilot in command is responsible for seeing and avoiding all traffic in visual flight conditions. This is a big responsibility, and one that you and every pilot must fulfill in the interest of safety.

An aircraft in distress has the right-of-way over all other aircraft.

The regulations also specify that an aircraft in distress has the right-of-way over all other air traffic. You can think of an aircraft in distress as one that may not be able to maneuver as well as it could in normal conditions.

Additional rules apply when similar aircraft are approaching each other. For instance, if your airplane and another airplane are on a collision course, both pilots should take the proper action to avoid each other. Primarily, there are three situations where these rules apply: aircraft approaching from the side, or converging; approaching each other head-on; and overtaking, or passing, another aircraft. [Figure 2-4]

If two aircraft are approaching each other head-on or nearly so, both aircraft will give way to the right. In other converging situations, airplanes and helicopters need to give the right-of-way to airships, gliders, and balloons. [Figure 2-5]

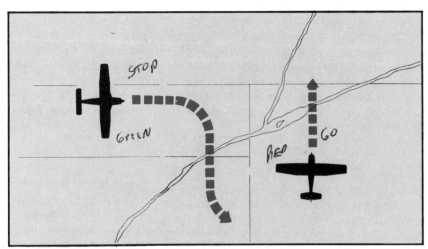

Figure 2-4. When aircraft are approaching from the side, or converging, the aircraft to the other's right has the right-of way. The aircraft to the left must give way to the one on the right. If you are flying the aircraft on the left and need to give way, make a turn away from the other aircraft in a manner that will not interfere with its flight path.

In a situation where you are going fast enough to overtake a slower air-craft, pass the other aircraft to the right and stay well clear. Watch the other airplane carefully until you are safely beyond it. [Figure 2-6]

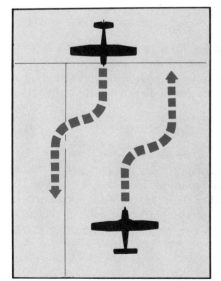

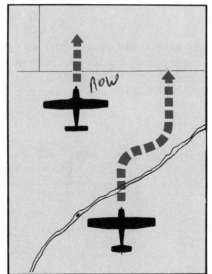

Figure 2-5. In the event that you see an aircraft coming straight at you, or head-on, both of you are required to alter course to the right. If there is safe altitude separation, this action is not necessary.

Figure 2-6. There will be situations where you will be overtaking another aircraft traveling in the same direction. The aircraft being overtaken has the right-of-way, so you must pass well clear on the right.

In general, the least maneuverable aircraft normally has the right-of-way.

The FARs also state that when aircraft are converging (except head-on or nearly so), a balloon has the right-of-way over all other aircraft. A glider has the right-of-way over any airship, airplane, or rotorcraft; and an airship has the right-of-way over any airplane or rotorcraft. Finally, an aircraft that is towing or refueling another aircraft has the right-of-way over all other engine-driven aircraft. The general rule concerning right-of-way is that the least maneuverable aircraft usually has the right-of-way over all other air traffic.

If two or more aircraft are approaching an airport for landing, the aircraft at the lower altitude has the right-of-way, but the pilot should not take advantage of this to cut in front of another aircraft.

The last right-of-way rule concerns your actions at an airport when you intend to land. An aircraft on final approach or an aircraft that is landing has the right-of-way over other traffic in the pattern and those on the ground. If you are entering the traffic pattern at the same time as other aircraft that are also preparing to land, the aircraft at the lowest altitude has the right-of-way. However, this is not intended to allow you to enter the pattern below the specified traffic pattern altitude and disrupt or cut in front of those already established in the pattern.

MINIMUM SAFE ALTITUDES

For safety reasons, there are minimum altitudes that you must maintain during flight. These rules apply at all times except during takeoffs and landings.

The minimum safe altitude anywhere must allow an emergency landing, following an engine failure, without undue hazard to persons or property on the surface.

The lowest altitude at which you can fly anywhere is one which allows an emergency landing without undue hazard to persons or property on the surface. The FAA wants you to have enough altitude so that you have more options for emergency landing sites in the event your engine fails.

Over a congested area, such as a city or metropolitan area, you are required to fly 1,000 feet above any obstacle within a horizontal radius of 2,000 feet of the aircraft. If you keep in mind that 1,000 feet is a minimum altitude and fly at altitudes higher than that over congested areas, you will have more time to troubleshoot any problems and can choose a better landing site if you have to make an emergency landing.

When flying over an uncongested area, you must fly at least 500 feet above the surface. The minimum safe altitude is slightly different for sparsely populated or open water areas. There, you cannot fly within 500 feet of any person, vessel, vehicle, or structure. Remember to observe these rules and to stay at an altitude high enough so that you can make a safe landing if your engine fails. [Figure 2-7]

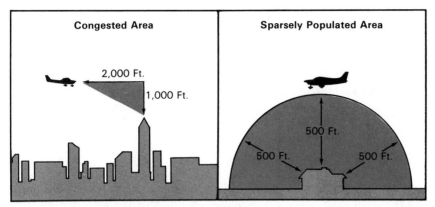

Figure 2-7. Minimum safe altitudes over congested areas are based on obstruction clearance. A congested area may be a city, town, settlement, or an open air assembly of people. Notice that obstacle clearance over sparsely populated areas is reduced significantly.

VFR CRUISING ALTITUDES

Along with minimum safe altitudes, the FAA also has regulations to keep aircraft separated. These are called **VFR cruising altitudes**.

VFR is a term you will see and hear often during your training. It means **visual flight rules**, which are frequently referenced in FARs. These rules apply to contact, or visual, flying where you navigate by maintaining visual contact with objects on the surface. Cruising altitudes are one example of these rules.

To apply the rules for cruising altitudes, you need to know your altitude above mean sea level (MSL), as well as your altitude above ground level (AGL). This can be done accurately only with a current altimeter setting. If you fly out of an airport that has weather reporting capabilities, you can get the current pressure setting and dial it into your altimeter before you take off or before you enter the traffic pattern to land. If the airport has no weather reporting equipment or your aircraft has no radio, you can set your altimeter to the field elevation before you take off.

When you are enroute, you must set your altimeter to the current reported setting of a weather station within 100 n.m. of the aircraft. This is necessary because the barometric pressure can change significantly over a 100 n.m. distance, which will have an effect on both your indicated and true altitudes. If no station is within 100 n.m., you can use the setting from an appropriate available station. If you are not equipped with a radio, you can use the elevation of the departure airport or an appropriate altimeter setting obtained before departure. This last situation is rarely used, since most airplanes today are radio equipped. The important thing is to keep resetting your altimeter as new reports become available. The main reason for this is so all aircraft in the area will be using the same setting for altitude reference.

Anytime you fly in level cruising flight above 3,000 feet AGL, you must follow the VFR cruising altitudes, which are also referred to as east/west cruising altitudes. Aircraft flying on instruments and aircraft flying under visual flight rules have different cruising altitudes, which are assigned to separate aircraft.

For a magnetic course of 0° — 179°, fly odd thousands plus 500 feet; for a magnetic course of 180° — 359°, fly even thousands plus 500 feet.

If you are flying a magnetic course of 0° through 179°, you must fly an odd thousand-foot altitude plus 500 feet. This will give you cruising altitudes of 3,500 feet MSL, 5,500 feet MSL, 7,500 feet MSL, or higher. If you are flying a magnetic course of 180° through 359°, you will need to fly even thousand-foot altitudes plus 500 feet: 4,500 feet MSL, 6,500 feet MSL, 8,500 feet MSL, or higher. As a safety precaution, it is customary to fly at a VFR cruising altitude, when practical, even if you aren't above 3,000 feet AGL. [Figure 2-8]

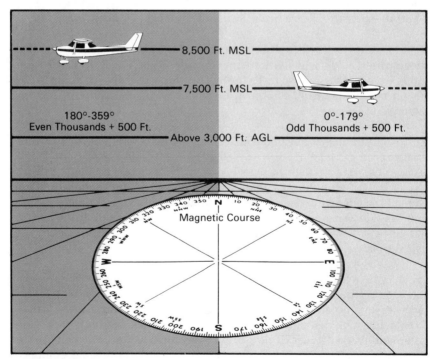

Figure 2-8. Cruising altitude rules are designed to provide a minimum of 1,000 feet vertical separation between VFR aircraft. An eastbound aircraft might be at 7,500 feet while a westbound aircraft could be at 8,500 feet. The rules officially apply above 3,000 feet AGL and below 18,000 feet MSL, and the altitudes are based on magnetic course.

SPECIAL SAFETY CONSIDERATIONS

So far, we have discussed many aspects of scanning, collision avoidance, right-of-way, FARs, obstruction clearance, and cruising altitudes. This final discussion covers some aspects of the flight environment which require special safety considerations and development of good personal flying techniques.

We've already discussed the need for extra care in the vicinity of airports. You also face the potential for heavy traffic on airways and around navigational aids. Airways are similar to highways for cars. They represent routes from one place to another, and they tend to attract air traffic. Therefore, it is important to maintain your scan, use the correct VFR cruising altitude, and make shallow S-turns if you need to climb or descend while on an airway. Airways intersect above navigational aids, or navaids. With the increase in air traffic around navaids, you must be especially alert for other aircraft.

If you need to climb or descend while on an airway, make shallow turns to look for traffic.

If you find yourself spending more time than necessary looking for charts or at your instruments, you should consider organizing the cockpit a little better before your flight. Take some time to plan your flight and be sure you have everything you need. This should include a check of the windshield to be sure it is clean. Remember, if the outside visibility is good, you have a better chance of spotting a hazard than if you are flying in haze or other low visibility conditions. Haze tends to make traffic and terrain features appear farther away than their actual distance. Think about the blind spots that exist in the airplane and plan to compensate for them. Mentally review the safety information you learned in this section.

Objects typically are closer than they appear when you view them through haze.

Finally, there are two suggestions to help make your flight a safer one. **Operation Lights On** is a voluntary program that encourages you to use your landing lights during departures and approaches, both day and night. This practice is recommended especially when operating within 10 miles of an airport, or in conditions of reduced visibility. It is recommended that you check the pilot's operating handbook for your aircraft for any limitations on the use of the lights.

You are also encouraged to turn on anticollision lights whenever the engines are running, day or night. However, anticollision lights need not be turned on when they might interfere with safety. For example, strobe lights should be turned off when their brightness might be detrimental to the vision of others.

CHECKLIST ─────────────────────────────

After studying this section, you should have a basic understanding of:

✓   **Scanning** — The best method for scanning, and how much time you should spend looking outside.

✓   **Empty field myopia** — When it may occur, and how you can recognize and correct for it.

✓   **Blind spots** — What areas of vision are blocked by blind spots and what you can do to increase your visibility during climbs and descents.

✓   **Clearing turns** — Why and when they are done, and how many degrees you should turn.

✓   **Right-of-way** — Which aircraft have the right of way when converging, approaching head-on, and overtaking.

✓   **Minimum safe altitudes** — What your minimum safe altitude is over congested areas, over uncongested areas, and over sparsely populated areas.

✓   **VFR cruising altitudes** — When they must be used and what the east/west cruising rules are.

✓   **Operation Lights On** — What the concept is and when you use it.

AIRPORTS

You have learned that developing an awareness of safety factors is an important step in understanding the flight environment. In this section, you will become familiar with several new terms and concepts related to operations in the airport environment. Knowing how to determine the correct runway to use and understanding the markings on taxiways and runways will be essential every time you fly. The various types of lighting used at airports is another important area for study, which will have direct application when you begin flying at night.

CONTROLLED AND UNCONTROLLED AIRPORTS

Air traffic controllers direct operations at controlled airports from the tower. At uncontrolled airports, you are responsible for determining the active runway and following local procedures. There are two types of airport environments that you will operate in — controlled and uncontrolled. A **controlled airport** has an operating control tower. All aircraft in the vicinity, as well as those on the ground, are subject to instructions issued by air traffic controllers. In order for you to operate in the controlled airport environment, a two-way radio is required for contact with the controllers. At an **uncontrolled airport**, control of VFR traffic is not exercised. Although you are not required to have a two-way radio, most pilots use radios to transmit their intentions to other pilots. You are also responsible for determining the active runway and how to enter and exit the traffic pattern.

Self Announce

RUNWAY LAYOUT

Because airplanes are directly affected by wind during takeoffs and landings, **runways** are not arbitrarily placed by builders. If there is only one runway at an airport, it is placed so that you can take off and land in the direction of the prevailing wind. If there is more than one runway, the main runway is aligned with the prevailing wind and the remaining runway or runways are placed so that they are aligned with other common wind directions.

The numbers that you see on runways are not arbitrary, either. First of all, you normally fly magnetic courses and headings, as opposed to true courses and headings. Secondly, since the wind direction at airports is also given to you in degrees relative to magnetic north, the number on the runway correlates to a magnetic north reference. The runway's magnetic

Runway numbers are derived from the runway's direction in degrees relative to magnetic north.

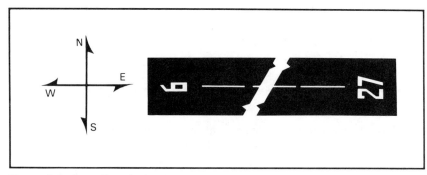

Figure 2-9. Even though there are numbers on both ends of a runway, they are different because the runway designators are 180° apart. A runway labeled "9" on one end is labeled "27" on the opposite end. The runway may be referred to as either 9 or 27, depending on the direction you are using for takeoff or landing. You will use runway 9 if you are taking off or landing to the east and runway 27 if you are taking off or landing to the west.

direction is rounded off to the nearest 10°, with the last zero omitted. So, a runway with a magnetic heading of 268° is rounded off to 270° and, with the zero dropped, becomes runway 27. A runway with a magnetic heading of 088° becomes runway 09. To further simplify runway numbers, any runway that is between the headings of 010° and 090° is designated with a single-digit runway number, so runway 09 is marked as runway 9. [Figure 2-9]

At some airports, there may be two or three parallel runways with the same runway number. If there are two parallel runways, one is labeled the left runway and the other is the right; for example, "36L" and "36R." If there is a third parallel runway, the one in the middle is the center runway and the respective runways are marked "36L," "36C," and "36R." [Figure 2-10]

AIRPORT ELEVATION

In the previous section of this chapter, we mentioned setting your altimeter to the airport elevation prior to takeoff if an altimeter setting isn't available. The official **airport elevation** is the highest part of usable runway surface, measured in feet above mean sea level. The airport elevation is available from several sources, including aeronautical charts.

TAXIWAYS

Your link between the airport parking areas and the runways are the **taxiways.** They are easily identified by a continuous yellow centerline stripe. Sometimes, the edges of the taxiway, as well as the centerline, will be marked by double yellow stripes. Many times, taxiways are labeled "Taxiway A," "Taxiway B," and so on, to help you identify routes to and from runways.

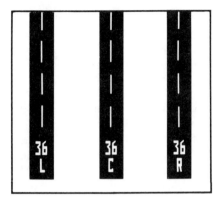

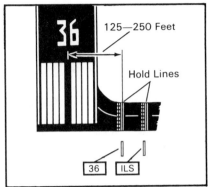

Figure 2-10. At large airports with heavy air traffic, it is common to have parallel runways. When assigning runways for takeoffs and landings, air traffic controllers will refer to these runways as "three-six-left," "three-six-center," or "three-six-right."

Figure 2-11. Holding position markings consist of hold lines painted across the taxiway and a sign identifying the runway. They may be painted wherever taxiways and runways intersect. ILS hold lines are placed farther away from the runway.

INSTRUMENT LANDING SYSTEM CAN GET IN WAY OF SIGNAL

As you transition from the taxiway to the runway, you will see hold lines. **Hold lines**, which are generally 125 feet to 250 feet from the touchdown area, keep you clear of the runway in use. Usually, there will be a small sign nearby which identifies the associated runway. At an uncontrolled airport, you should stop and check for traffic and cross the hold lines only after ensuring that no one is on an approach to land. At a controlled airport, the controller may ask you to hold short of the runway for landing traffic. In this case, you should stop before the lines and proceed only after you are cleared to do so by the controller, and you have checked for traffic. [Figure 2-11]

For your safety at an uncontrolled airport, stop and check for traffic before crossing the hold lines.

At airports equipped with an instrument landing system (ILS), it is possible for aircraft near the runway to interfere with the ILS signal. If this is the case, you will find the hold lines placed farther from the runway to prevent any interference. This means you may find two hold lines for some runways. The closest one is the normal hold line, while the one farthest away is the ILS hold line. At other locations only an ILS hold line may be used. When ILS approaches are in progress, you may be asked by the controller to ". . . hold short of the ILS critical area."

RUNWAY AND TAXIWAY MARKINGS

Runway markings vary between runways used solely for VFR operations and those used in conjunction with IFR operations. **Instrument flight rules** (IFR) apply to flights conducted by reference to the aircraft instruments when visibility is reduced. This often requires the pilot to conduct an instrument approach at the destination. You must have an instrument rating to fly in IFR conditions.

Instrument approaches are classified according to whether or not they use an electronic glide slope for guidance to the landing runway. If they do, they are called precision approaches, such as an "ILS." If they don't, they are called nonprecision approaches, and the corresponding runway markings vary accordingly.

Runway markings differ, depending on whether the runway is used only by VFR traffic or by both VFR and IFR traffic.

A basic VFR runway will have the runway number and a dashed white centerline. When a basic VFR runway is used in conjunction with a nonprecision instrument approach, threshold markings are added. Touchdown zone markers, fixed distance markings, and side stripes are added when the runway is used in conjunction with a precision approach. Occasionally, you may see fixed distance markings and side stripes on a nonprecision runway.

A **STOL runway**, or short takeoff or landing runway, is built for specially designed aircraft that require shorter distances for takeoff and landing. It is not advisable to use this type of runway unless you are flying an aircraft that has these short-field capabilities. [Figure 2-12]

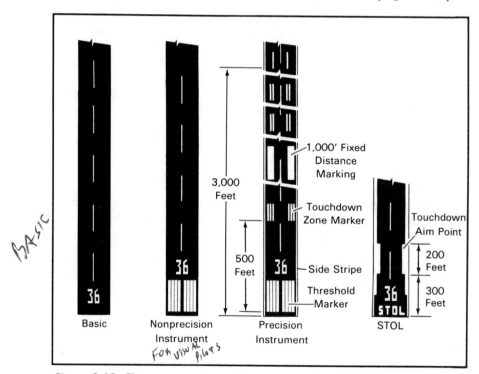

Figure 2-12. The common types of runway markings for VFR, precision, nonprecision, and STOL runways are shown here. As a VFR pilot, you are not restricted from using the precision and nonprecision instrument runways. The threshold marker, touchdown zone marker, fixed distance marking, and side stripes on the precision instrument approach runways are there to aid pilots who are making instrument approaches. STOL runways are clearly marked to avoid any confusion.

It is not uncommon to fly into an airport that has a runway with another type of marking called a **displaced threshold**. Usually, if the threshold is displaced, it is because of an obstruction off the end of the runway. This might prohibit you from making a normal descent and landing on the beginning portion of the pavement. Trees, powerlines, and buildings are typical examples of such obstructions. The beginning of the landing portion of the runway, or threshold, is marked by a solid white line with yellow arrows leading up to it. Even though the first few hundred feet of pavement may not be used for landing, it may be available for taxiing, the landing rollout, and takeoffs.

At airports with a displaced threshold, the beginning portion of the landing zone is marked with a solid white line with yellow arrows leading up to it.

A **blast pad/stopway area** is different from the area preceding a displaced threshold because it cannot be used for either takeoffs or landings. The blast pad is an area where propeller or jet blast can dissipate without creating a hazard to others. The stopway area is paved so that, in the event of an aborted takeoff, an aircraft can use it to decelerate and come to a stop. The pavement strength may be able to support the weight of an airplane, but not be strong enough for continuous operations. Because of its reduced weight-bearing capabilities, no one is allowed to use a blast pad/stopway area for landing or departing. The beginning of the landing portion of the runway is marked with a solid white line, just as it is with the displaced threshold. [Figure 2-13]

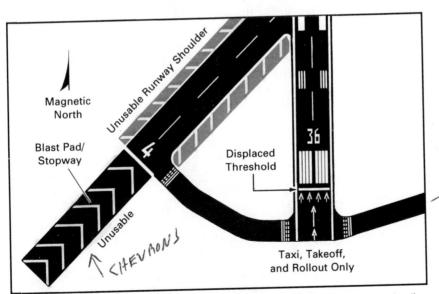

Figure 2-13. You will recognize a displaced threshold by the yellow arrows leading up to a solid white line. The line is the displaced threshold and indicates the beginning of the landing zone. The blast pad/stopway area is painted with yellow chevrons, which indicate the structure of the pavement is unusable for normal operations. Because of this, taxiways will not extend into the area. There also may be areas with yellow diagonal stripes on each side of the runway where the pavement strength is reduced. Operations are not permitted on these areas, either.

Large "Xs" painted on runways or taxiways indicate that they are closed.

Another airport marking you will need to become familiar with is the one associated with a closed runway or taxiway. For one reason or another, a runway or taxiway may not be usable, so there will be a large "X" painted on both ends. Although the surface may appear to be usable, this runway or taxiway cannot be used safely.

WIND DIRECTION INDICATORS

During takeoffs and landings, you need to know which runway to use. At a controlled airport, there are various methods of obtaining the current airport information, including the "active runway," or runway in use. At an uncontrolled airport, you may be the one to determine which runway to use, depending on the type of services available. In many cases, your decision will be based on what you see when looking at a wind direction indicator.

There are two types of wind direction indicators usually located near the runway. The most common is the **wind sock**, which is used at both controlled and uncontrolled airports. Although a wind sock may not be your initial source of wind information at a controlled airport, there will still be a wind sock positioned near the runway. It will tell you the wind conditions near the touchdown zone of the runway. In gusty conditions, the wind sock moves back and forth. Also, the stronger the wind, the straighter the extension of the wind sock. [Figure 2-14]

The other type of wind direction indicator is a **wind tee**. The tail of the tee aligns itself like a weather vane into the wind. However, it does not indicate wind intensity or gusty conditions. In some cases, a wind sock and tee may be at the same location. If so, the tee may be manually aligned to show which runway is active. [Figure 2-15]

Figure 2-14. A wind sock may be your key to choosing the correct runway at an uncontrolled field. The sock aligns itself into the wind because the wind blows into the large end and out the small end. The small end of the wind sock points downwind. When possible, you should select the runway that is the closest to paralleling the sock, and take off or land into the wind.

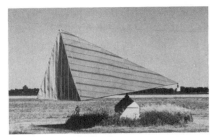

Figure 2-15. The wind tee is not as common as the wind sock. However, it is still effective in helping you to determine the wind direction and favored runway. Because the wind tee is similar to an airplane, it will weathervane into the wind. You need to take off or land into the wind on the runway that most closely parallels the direction of the tee.

Figure 2-16. A tetrahedron is typically used as a landing direction indicator. The tetrahedron may swing around with the small end pointing into the wind, or it may be manually positioned to show landing direction. In either case, you are cautioned not to use it solely as a wind direction indicator, but to use it in conjunction with a wind sock.

A **tetrahedron** is a landing direction indicator, usually located near a wind direction indicator. It may swing freely, as the wind sock does, or it may be manually positioned to show the direction of landing. [Figure 2-16]

SEGMENTED CIRCLE

When installed at uncontrolled airports, the wind sock and wind tee are usually placed in the middle of a **segmented circle** at a central location on the airport. The segmented circle has a two-fold purpose. First, it helps to identify the location of the wind direction indicator. Second, there will be extensions on the segmented circle if the traffic pattern is other than left-hand traffic as the FARs require. [Figure 2-17]

At uncontrolled airports, unless otherwise specified, all turns in the traffic pattern should be made to the left.

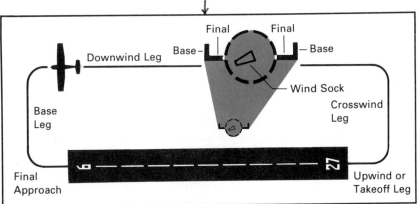

Figure 2-17. At this airport, the segmented circle with the wind sock is located on the north side of runway 9/27. The wind sock shows that the wind is coming from the northeast and that runway 9 should be the active runway. A check of the "L" extensions on the segmented circle shows that runway 9 has a left-hand turn from base leg to final, so you will fly a standard pattern. However, runway 27 has a nonstandard traffic pattern, since a right-hand turn is required from base to final.

A traffic pattern with right-hand turns, called a nonstandard pattern, may be necessary due to noise abatement procedures, terrain, or obstructions. The "L-shaped" extensions are placed so they indicate the direction you should turn in the traffic pattern for a given runway. You can think of the "L" as your base and final legs to the runway. If it is a right turn from "base" to "final" on the "L," then you need to make a right-hand pattern on your approach. If right-hand turns are required for the approach, they normally will be used for departure as well.

When approaching an uncontrolled airport that you are not familiar with, it is recommended that you overfly the airport at 500 to 1,000 feet above the traffic pattern altitude to observe the flow of traffic and to locate the segmented circle. If no traffic is observed, follow the directions indicated by the "L" extensions and land on the runway indicated by the wind direction indicator. If there are no extensions for the runways, they all have standard left-hand traffic patterns. At night, the segmented circle is normally illuminated by overhead lights that allow you to see both the wind direction indicator and the segmented circle.

Some uncontrolled airports also have radio operators who are able to tell you the wind direction and speed, and advise you of the runway in use. Usually, airports have a designated calm-wind runway. This runway is used whenever the wind is five knots or less. However, you must still watch carefully for other traffic that may be using other runways. Also, remember that even though there may be someone at an uncontrolled airport to advise you of the current winds and active runway, you must make the final decision as to which runway to use.

TAXIING IN WIND

Takeoffs and landings are not the only times you are concerned about wind. Taxi operations can become critical in high winds or gusty conditions, too. Strong winds passing over and around the wings and horizontal stabilizer during taxi can actually lift the airplane. In the most adverse conditions, it is possible for the airplane to flip or roll over.

When taxiing into a quartering headwind, hold the aileron up on the side from which the wind is blowing and maintain neutral elevator.

Proper use of the aileron and elevator controls normally will counteract the wind and help you maintain control of the airplane. For example, if the wind is blowing from the left front quarter, you should hold the left aileron up to counteract the lifting tendency of the wind. The elevator should be in a neutral position to prevent the wind from exerting any lifting force on the tail. [Figure 2-18]

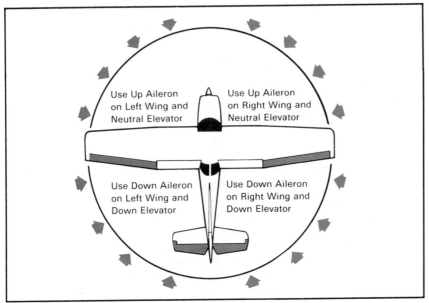

Figure 2-18. Your knowledge of proper control use during windy conditions will help you control the airplane while taxiing. With a quartering headwind, you position the control wheel as if you want to turn into the wind and maintain level flight. With a quartering tailwind, you position the control wheel as if you want to turn away from the wind and descend.

The most critical situation is when you are taxiing a tricycle-gear airplane with a high wing in a strong quartering tailwind. The high wing is susceptible to being lifted by the wind. In extreme conditions, a quartering tailwind can cause the airplane to nose over and flip on its back. [Figure 2-19]

A quartering tailwind is the most critical wind condition when taxiing a tricycle-gear, high-wing airplane.

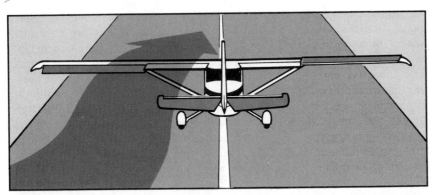

Figure 2-19. Taxiing with strong quartering tailwinds is the most critical situation. In the most severe conditions, the flow of air beneath the horizontal stabilizer and wing can lift the airplane and tip it over. With a tailwind from the left side, position the control wheel full forward and to the right. The correct flight control positions are: left aileron down, right aileron up, and elevator (or stabilator) down.

You will find a difference between taxiing tricycle versus conventional, or tailwheel, airplanes. Weathervaning, or turning into the wind in direct crosswinds, is a tendency of tailwheel airplanes. Weathervaning also is possible in tricycle airplanes, but it normally is not a problem. This is due to the ground friction caused by the nosewheel and the more aft position of the main gear. When you turn while taxiing, the flow of air around the airplane changes direction, and you will have to compensate by altering the position of the control surfaces.

RAMP AREA

The area where airplanes are parked and tied down is called the **ramp area,** or parking area. The airport terminal and maintenance facilities are often located near the ramp area. Aircraft refueling is also done there, so you should be alert for fuel trucks driving on the ramp and trucks in the process of refueling. When you are taxiing through the ramp area, you should be especially alert for people who are walking to or from their aircraft. The prop blast generated by your airplane can blow dust and gravel at them. This is a good reason to avoid starting your aircraft when someone is walking behind it. You should also use low idling r.p.m.'s just after starting your engine. As you proceed to the taxiway, your taxi speed should be only as fast as a brisk walk. At this speed, you can stop the aircraft in time to avoid conflicts with people or vehicles on the ramp.

Also, remember to tie the airplane down whenever you leave it for any length of time. This will prevent the aircraft from rolling into other aircraft on the ramp or being turned over by wind in the event of gusty conditions.

NOISE ABATEMENT PROCEDURES

The FAA, in conjunction with airport proprietors and community leaders, is now using **noise abatement** procedures to reduce the level of noise generated by aircraft departing over neighborhoods that are near airports. The airport authority may simply request that you use a designated runway, wind permitting. You also may be asked to restrict some of your operations, such as practicing landings, during certain time periods. There are three ways to determine the noise abatement procedure at an airport. First, if there is a control tower on the field, they will assign the preferred noise abatement runway to you. Second, you can check the *Airport/Facility Directory,* which will be discussed in Chapter 6, for information on local procedures. Third, there may be information for you to read in the pilot's lounge, or even signs posted next to the runway that will tell you what to do.

AIRPORT LIGHTING

Your flying experiences will soon take you from flying only in the daytime to flying at night, as well. You will notice that airport lighting is similar from one airport to the next. Airports that are lighted for night-time operations use FAA-approved colors, so there is continuity from airport to airport.

AIRPORT BEACON

At night, **airport beacons** are used to guide pilots to lighted airports. Airport beacons may be of the older rotating type, or the newer flashing variety which produces the same effect. If you have enough altitude, beacons can be seen at great distances in good visibility conditions. The combination of light colors from an airport beacon indicates the type of airport. As a routine measure, you are not permitted to operate at military airports. [Figure 2-20]

For seaplane pilots, a water airport is marked with a beacon that has flashing white and yellow lights. Heliport beacons alternate between green, yellow, and white lights.

Generally, you will find that an airport's beacon is on from dusk until dawn. The beacon usually isn't on during the day unless the ceiling is less than 1,000 feet or the flight visibility is less than three statute miles, the normal VFR minimums. Remember, though, the airport beacon may not always be turned on when the weather is below VFR minimums.

If an airport beacon is on during the day, the weather is probably below VFR minimums.

APPROACH LIGHTING SYSTEMS

Some airports have complex lighting systems to help instrument pilots transition to visual references at the end of an instrument approach. These **approach lighting systems** can begin as far away as 3,000 feet

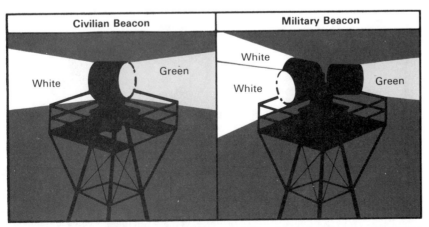

Figure 2-20. Airport beacons that indicate civilian land airports use alternating white and green lights. Beacons at military airports have two flashes of white that alternate with a single green light.

along the extended runway centerline, and can aid VFR pilots operating at night. The most complex systems are for precision instrument runways. Usually, these systems have sequenced flashing lights that look like a ball of light traveling toward the runway at high speed. Closer to the runway, more lights guide you to the touchdown zone. For nonprecision instrument runways, the approach lighting is simpler and, for VFR runways, the system may consist only of visual glideslope indicators.

VISUAL GLIDESLOPE INDICATORS

These are light systems that indicate your position in relation to the desired glideslope to the runway. The indicator lights are located on the side of a basic or instrument runway and they can be used for day or night approaches. One of the most frequently used installations is the **visual approach slope indicator** (VASI).

You should remain on or above the glide path when approaching a runway served by VASI.

VASI configurations vary and may have either two or three bars. Two-bar systems have near and far bars and may include 2, 4, or 12 light units. The VASI glide path provides safe obstruction clearance within 10° of the extended runway centerline out to four n.m. from the threshold. You should not begin a descent using VASI until your aircraft is aligned with the runway. When landing at a controlled airport that has a VASI, regulations require you to remain on or above the glide path until a lower altitude is necessary for a safe landing. [Figure 2-21]

At larger airports, there may be a three-bar VASI system that incorporates two different glide paths. The lower glide path is normally set at 3°, while the higher one is usually one-fourth of a degree above it. The higher glide path is specifically for certain transport category aircraft with high cockpits. This ensures they will have sufficient altitude when

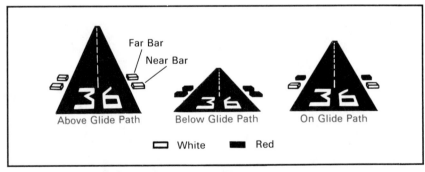

Figure 2-21. The two-bar VASI shows whether or not you are on a glide path that will take you safely to the touchdown zone of the runway. The lights are either white or red, depending on the angle of your glide path, and may be visible from 20 miles at night. If both light bars are white, you are too high; if you see red over red, you are below the glide path. If the far bar is red and the near bar is white, you are on the glide path. The memory aid, "red over white, you're all right," is helpful in recalling the correct sequence of lights.

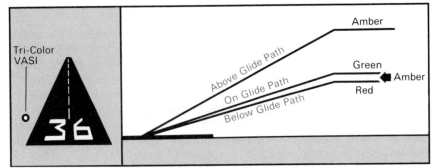

Figure 2-22. The tri-color system also gives you information as to whether or not you are on a safe glide path. If you see amber, you are too high; and if you see red, you are too low. If the light is green, you are on the glide path. As you descend below the glide path, you may see dark amber during the transition from green light to red, so you should not be deceived into thinking that you are too high.

crossing the threshold. If you encounter a three-bar VASI system, use the two lower bars as if it were a standard two-bar VASI.

A **tri-color system** uses a single light unit to project a three-color visual path. It has some similarity to the two-bar VASI because you will see a red light if you are too low. [Figure 2-22]

Some airports may have a **pulsating system** which projects a two-color visual approach path into the final approach area. A pulsating red light normally indicates below glide path; above glide path is normally pulsating white; and the on-glide path indication is a steady white light. The useful range is about four miles during the day and up to 10 miles at night.

With a pulsating system, the below-glide-path indication is normally a pulsating red light.

Another system is the **precision approach path indicator** (PAPI). It has two or four lights installed in a single row instead of far and near bars. The PAPI is normally located on the left side of the runway and can be seen up to five miles during the day and 20 miles at night. [Figure 2-23]

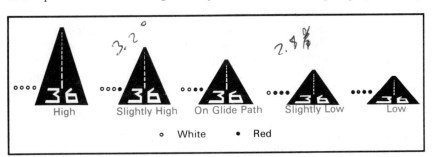

Figure 2-23. If all of the PAPI system lights are white, you are too high. If only the light unit on the far right is red and the other three are white, you are slightly high. When you are on the glide path, the two lights on the left will be white and the two lights on the right will be red. If you are slightly low, only the light on the far left will be white. If you are below the glide path, all four of the lights will be red.

THRESHOLD LIGHTS

If your destination airport has a VASI system, it will lead you down to the touchdown zone on the runway. At night, there are three ways to tell where the runway begins. If the runway has a displaced threshold, there will be a set of green lights on each side of the white threshold line to indicate the beginning of the landing portion of the runway. If the threshold is not displaced, the beginning of the runway pavement will have a row of green lights across it. These lights are two-sided. If you were taking off or landing on the opposite end, they would appear red to mark the end of the usable portion of the runway. Because they are different colors when viewed from opposite directions, you will see green lights designating the approach end of the runway and red lights for the departure end.

Sometimes high intensity white strobe lights are placed on each side of the runway to mark the threshold. These are called **runway end identifier lights** (REILs) and can be used in conjunction with the green threshold lights.

RUNWAY EDGE LIGHTS

You may already be familiar with runway edge lights. They consist of a single row of white lights bordering each side of the runway. Runway edge lights can be classified according to three intensity levels. **High intensity runway lights** (HIRLs) are the brightest runway lights available. **Medium intensity runway lights** (MIRLs) and **low intensity runway lights** (LIRLs) are, as their names indicate, dimmer in intensity. At some airports, you will be able to adjust the intensity of the runway lights from your cockpit by using your radio transmitter. At others, the lights are preset or are adjusted by air traffic controllers.

Some runway edge lights incorporate **runway-remaining lights** on the last half of the runway (or last 2,000 feet of runway, whichever distance is less). They have yellow edge lights to inform you of the amount of runway left. The lights are two-sided, so they appear white when viewed from the opposite end of the runway.

Some airports may have flush-mounted centerline lighting. This system helps instrument pilots determine the amount of runway remaining in very low visibility situations. These lights are placed on the last 3,000 feet of the runway. From the 3,000-foot point to the 1,000-foot point, alternating red and white lights appear, with the last 1,000 feet of lights changing to red only.

TAXIWAY LIGHTING

As you taxi off the active runway, blue taxiway lights guide you from the runway to the ramp area. Because they can be seen from any direction, they are said to be omnidirectional lights. The lights line both edges of the taxiway. At some airports, green taxiway centerline lights may also be installed. These lights are located along the taxiway centerline in both straight and curved portions of the taxiway. They also may be located along designated taxiing paths in portions of runways, ramps, and apron areas. [Figure 2-24]

Taxiway edges are identified at night by blue lights that can be seen from all directions.

PILOT CONTROL OF AIRPORT LIGHTING

For practical and economic reasons, the approach, runway, and taxiway lights at some unattended airports may be on a timer that will turn off the lights 15 minutes after they have been activated. If this is the case, you need to be able to turn them on again as you prepare to depart or approach to land. **Pilot-controlled lighting** is the term used to describe

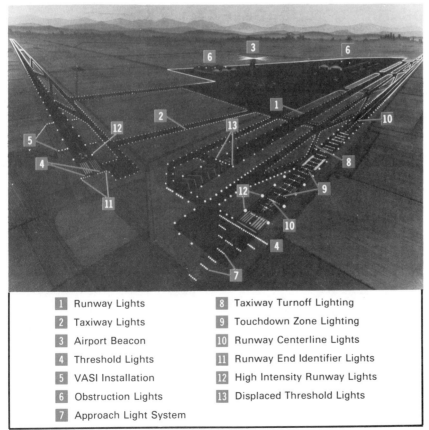

1	Runway Lights	8	Taxiway Turnoff Lighting
2	Taxiway Lights	9	Touchdown Zone Lighting
3	Airport Beacon	10	Runway Centerline Lights
4	Threshold Lights	11	Runway End Identifier Lights
5	VASI Installation	12	High Intensity Runway Lights
6	Obstruction Lights	13	Displaced Threshold Lights
7	Approach Light System		

Figure 2-24. This pictorial summary shows the various types of airport marking and lighting typically found at large, controlled airports.

systems that you can activate by keying the aircraft's microphone on a specified radio frequency. Keep in mind that other types of airport lighting may be pilot controlled, not just approach and runway lighting. For example, VASI and REIL lights may be pilot controlled at some locations.

After three-step runway lights are initially turned on, you can select medium intensity by keying your microphone five times.

The following example shows the general procedures you would use at an airport with three-step pilot-controlled runway lights. Initially, you should key your microphone seven times on the specified frequency to turn all the lights on at maximum intensity. If conditions dictate a lower intensity, key your microphone five times for medium-intensity lighting and three times for the lowest intensity. For each adjustment, you must key the microphone the required number of times within a period of five seconds. Remember though, using the lower intensity lighting on some installations may turn the REILs completely off. The *Airport/Facility Directory* contains a description of the type of pilot-controlled lighting available at individual airports.

OBSTRUCTION LIGHTING

You will see obstruction lighting both on and off the airport, during the day and at night. The purpose of this type of lighting is to give you advanced warning of obstructions. For example, obstruction lights are installed on prominent structures such as towers, buildings and, sometimes, even powerlines. Bright red and high intensity white lights are typically used and may flash on and off. Remember that there may be guy-wires extending from the top of the tower to the ground, so be sure that you are well clear of the object.

CHECKLIST

After studying this section, you should have a basic understanding of:

✓ **Runways and Taxiways** — How they are marked, and what the different markings indicate.

✓ **Wind direction indicators** — The types of indicators and what information they provide.

✓ **Tetrahedron** — What it is primarily used for.

✓ **Taxiing in wind** — What wind situations are most critical and how to position your controls.

✓ **Airport lighting** — What the various types are, how they are used, and which can be pilot-controlled.

AIRSPACE

In this section, you will learn about the various airspace classifications
that are designated throughout the country. Of equal importance are the
operational requirements that might affect you within the different airspace segments. You also need to know which flight restrictions or aircraft equipment requirements apply in certain situations and what areas
you should avoid altogether.

Another reason for being familiar with the airspace structure is that visual flight rules require you to maintain certain minimum flight visibilities and safe distances from clouds. Since these rules vary from one type
of airspace to another, you need to know which rules to apply in each
situation. In general, there are two broad classifications of airspace —
controlled and uncontrolled. Additional classifications of airspace include special use airspace and other airspace areas.

CONTROLLED AIRSPACE

You will soon realize that the major portion of airspace that covers the
conterminous U.S. is controlled. Actually, **controlled airspace** includes
the following subdivisions which are designated by regulation — positive control area, continental control area, control areas (which include
airways), transition areas, airport radar service areas, terminal control
areas, and control zones. Each of these classifications will be covered in
the following discussion.

To provide you with an overview of the kinds of airspace you may
encounter, the next two pages present a comprehensive diagram of the
airspace system. This diagram includes the operational requirements, as
well as the cloud clearance and visibility minimums, appropriate to the
various airspace classifications.

As you read through the entire section, you may find it helpful to refer
back to this diagram to see how the various segments interrelate. In
practice, the airspace structure is not as limiting to flight operations as
it may seem. After you become familiar with the system, you will see
that it is possible to fly under visual flight rules, or VFR, with comparatively few restrictions. [Figure 2-25]

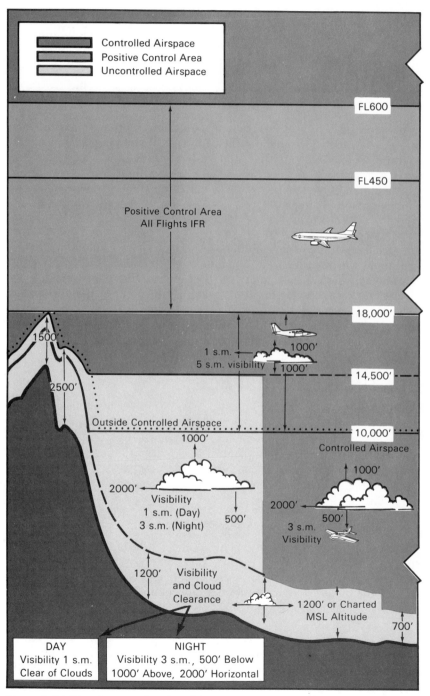

Figure 2-25. To enhance safety for all aircraft, the airspace that covers the U.S. is divided into controlled and uncontrolled airspace. Operational requirements depend on the type of airspace you are flying in, as well as your altitude. Along with these

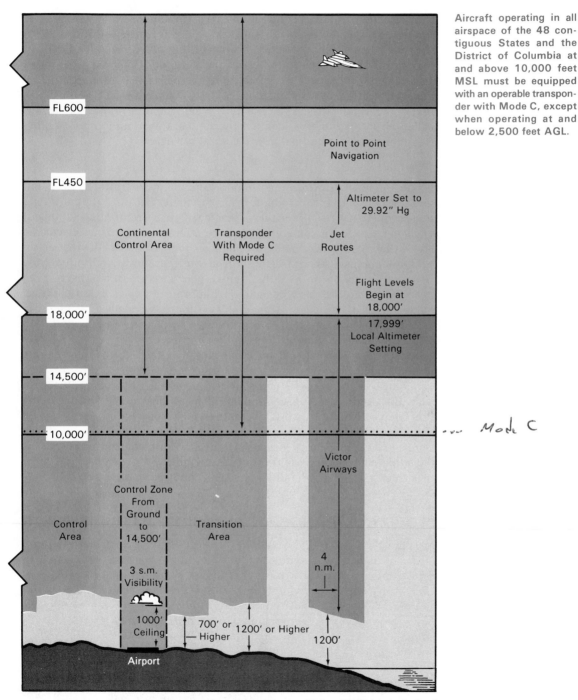

Aircraft operating in all airspace of the 48 contiguous States and the District of Columbia at and above 10,000 feet MSL must be equipped with an operable transponder with Mode C, except when operating at and below 2,500 feet AGL.

FL600

Point to Point Navigation

FL450

Altimeter Set to 29.92" Hg

Continental Control Area

Transponder With Mode C Required

Jet Routes

Flight Levels Begin at 18,000'

18,000'

17,999' Local Altimeter Setting

14,500'

10,000'   ~~~ Mode C

Victor Airways

Control Zone From Ground to 14,500'

Control Area

Transition Area

4 n.m.

3 s.m. Visibility

1000' Ceiling

700' or Higher

1200' or Higher

1200'

Airport

requirements, you also must be aware of the minimum flight visibilities and cloud clearance requirements that apply at various altitudes in controlled and uncontrolled airspace.

The important thing to know about operating in controlled airspace is that you may be subject to air traffic control. **Air traffic control** (ATC) is a service provided by the FAA to promote the safe, orderly, and expeditious flow of air traffic. As a routine measure, IFR flights are controlled from takeoff to touchdown, since they are permitted to operate in all kinds of weather. As a VFR pilot, your contact with ATC typically is limited to terminal areas. For example, when you take off or land at controlled airports, you must contact the control tower, and you will often use radar approach and departure control services.

Separation of air traffic is the primary function of air traffic control, and radar is one of the controller's principal tools. Because of this, FARs require you to use the aircraft transponder (if your aircraft is so equipped) whenever you fly in controlled airspace. A **transponder** is an electronic device aboard the airplane that enhances your aircraft's identity on an ATC radar screen. An air traffic controller may assign an individual code to your transponder to help distinguish your aircraft from others in the area. Transponders carry designations appropriate to their capabilities. For example, those used in general aviation have Mode A capability. Usually they can be set to any of 4,096 codes, and many are able to indicate, or encode, your altitude on the controller's radar screen. A Mode A transponder with altitude encoding equipment is referred to as having Mode C capability. Another type of transponder which uses advanced technology is the Mode S transponder, which also is compatible with Mode C altitude reporting equipment. FARs require that, if you are flying at or above 10,000 feet MSL, excluding the airspace at and below 2,500 feet AGL, your transponder must have altitude encoding capability. This requirement applies in all airspace (controlled or uncontrolled) within the 48 mainland states and the District of Columbia. Transponders and radar are discussed in more detail later in this chapter.

CLOUD CLEARANCE AND VISIBILITY REQUIREMENTS

As clouds lower and flight visibility is reduced, it soon becomes impractical and unsafe to fly under VFR. VFR cloud clearance and visibility requirements are specified in regulations. These regulations also prohibit you from flying when conditions are below basic VFR weather minimums. When this occurs, all aircraft in controlled airspace must be flown by instrument rated pilots in accordance with IFR clearances issued by ATC.

VFR cloud clearance and visibility requirements are designed to help you avoid flying into clouds, as well as to maintain adequate forward visibility in flight. They are also designed to meet other practical requirements, such as seeing and avoiding other air traffic and navigating to

VFR IN CONTROLLED AIRSPACE		
Altitude	**Flight Visibility**	**Distance From Clouds**
1,200 ft. or less above the surface (regardless of MSL altitude)	3 s.m.	500 ft. below 1,000 ft. above 2,000 ft. horizontal
More than 1,200 ft. above the surface, but less than 10,000 ft. MSL	3 s.m.	500 ft. below 1,000 ft. above 2,000 ft. horizontal
More than 1,200 ft. above the surface and at or above 10,000 ft. MSL	5 s.m.	1,000 ft. below 1,000 ft. above 1 s.m. horizontal

Figure 2-26. In controlled airspace, you will notice that the cloud clearance and visibility requirements are greater for flights at and above 10,000 feet MSL than they are for flights below 10,000 feet. One of the reasons for this is that pilots of high-performance aircraft typically fly at higher altitudes and airspeeds; they need better visibility and more cloud clearance to see and avoid other aircraft.

your destination. The altitude at which you fly in controlled airspace usually is the determining factor for the specific cloud clearance and visibility that you must maintain. [Figure 2-26]

Keep in mind that these values are legal minimums. You may need to establish higher personal minimums until you have acquired more practical experience. Your instructor can advise you in this area.

POSITIVE CONTROL AREA

The airspace extending from 18,000 feet MSL up to 60,000 feet MSL is defined as the **positive control area** (PCA). It covers the majority of the conterminous U.S. and extends 12 nautical miles out from the U.S. coast. Within the positive control area, all pilots must be instrument rated. In addition, all aircraft must be transponder equipped, operated under IFR, and controlled directly by ATC. Because of the overall increase in speed of aircraft operating in the PCA and the corresponding increase of the closure rates between these aircraft, VFR flight is not allowed.

Also, because aircraft in the PCA operate at such high speeds, it would be impractical for the pilots to reset their altimeters every 100 n.m. So, within the positive control area, pilots are required to set their altimeters to the standard setting of 29.92 in. Hg. This means that all pilots will be maintaining their assigned altitudes using the same altimeter reference.

At and above 18,000 feet MSL, all pilots set their altimeters to 29.92 in. Hg.

Altitudes within the positive control area are expressed differently. At 18,000 feet MSL and above, altitudes are prefaced by the letters "FL," meaning flight level, with the last two zeros omitted. As an example, 35,000 feet is referenced as FL 350.

CONTINENTAL CONTROL AREA

Another type of airspace that covers the majority of the conterminous U.S. is called the **continental control area**. It extends out to 12 nautical miles from the U.S. coast and upward from 14,500 feet MSL, except for airspace less than 1,500 feet above the surface. The continental control area has no defined upper limit. Within this airspace, you have no additional operating requirements beyond those mentioned previously. For example, you must operate the Mode C feature of your transponder and apply the appropriate cloud clearance and visibility requirements. Remember that you cannot fly VFR above FL 180 because of the positive control area. [Figure 2-27]

CONTROL AREAS

Airspace designated as colored Federal airways (in Alaska), VOR Federal airways, additional control areas, and control area extensions are classified as **control areas**. The continental control area is not included in the definition of control areas. Of the various types of control areas, your chief concern is VOR Federal airways.

FEDERAL AIRWAYS

Federal airways normally begin at 1,200 feet above the surface, extend upward to 18,000 feet MSL, and include the airspace within four nautical miles each side of the airway centerline.

When you begin flying cross-country, you will notice that aeronautical charts depict a network of routes connecting one navaid to another. These air routes are used by VFR, as well as IFR aircraft, and are called

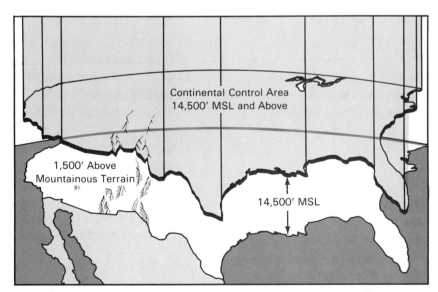

Figure 2-27. You will find a few areas of the country that are not included in the continental control area. For example, prohibited areas and most restricted areas, as well as airspace less than 1,500 feet above the earth's surface, are excluded.

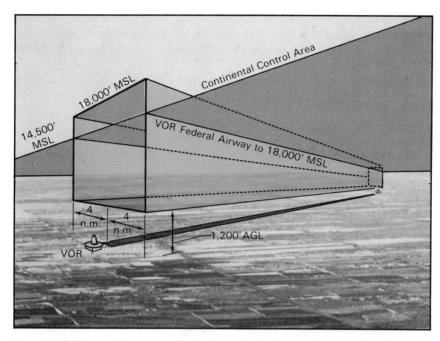

Figure 2-28. Federal airways are part of the airway route system that you can use to navigate across the country. They are commonly called Victor airways.

Colored Federal airways or **VOR Federal airways**. They are usually eight nautical miles wide, begin at 1,200 feet AGL, and extend up to but not including 18,000 feet MSL. VFR cloud clearance and visibility requirements on an airway depend on your cruising altitude. [Figure 2-28]

TRANSITION AREAS

The links between airports and the airway route system are called **transition areas**. They extend controlled airspace closer to the ground. This allows IFR traffic to remain in controlled airspace while transitioning between the enroute and airport environments. Transition areas usually begin at 1,200 feet AGL if they are associated with an airway. When associated with an airport environment, they begin at 700 feet AGL. They terminate at the base of the overlying controlled airspace. Transition areas are shown on aeronautical charts.

AIRPORT RADAR SERVICE AREAS

Factors considered in designating controlled airspace include safety, users' needs, and the volume of air traffic. Because of these considerations, many busy airports are surrounded by the controlled airspace of an **airport radar service area** (ARSA). ARSAs are established by regulation. Within an ARSA, ATC services are provided for all IFR and VFR aircraft.

Participation in this ARSA service is mandatory. You will find that ARSAs usually have very similar physical dimensions from one location to another, although some may be modified to fit unique aspects of a particular airport's location. [Figure 2-29]

The minimum radio equipment required to take off or land at the primary airport within an ARSA is a VHF transmitter and receiver.

Within an ARSA, all aircraft are subject to FAA operating rules. One of these rules applies to arrivals and overflights. Prior to entering the area, you must establish two-way communications with the ATC facility having jurisdiction and maintain it while you are operating within the ARSA. When you are departing the primary airport, you must maintain radio contact with ATC until you are clear of the area.

Normally, the radius of the outer area of an ARSA is 20 n.m. from the primary airport.

The "outer area" associated with an ARSA extends 10 n.m. beyond the outer circle. VFR pilots are not required to contact ATC prior to entering the outer area, but it is helpful to do so. For approach, departure, or overflights, ATC normally provides the same ARSA services for you in the outer area as it does within the ARSA.

If you are departing a satellite airport within an ARSA, you must establish two-way communications with ATC as soon as practicable after departure.

There may be times when you fly into a satellite airport located within an ARSA. If so, you must be in contact with ATC while you are in the ARSA airspace. The ARSA service provided to you will be discontinued early enough for you to change to the appropriate tower or airport advisory frequency at your destination. When departing a satellite airport, you should contact ATC as soon as practicable after takeoff. Keep in mind that ATC facilities may not operate full time at some ARSA locations, so ARSA service may not be available at all times. If the ATC facility is closed, the operating rules for the ARSA are not in effect either. Hours of

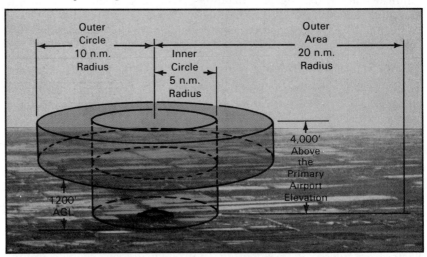

Figure 2-29. An ARSA consists of two circles of airspace extending upward from the primary airport. The first circle begins at the surface and has a five nautical mile radius from the center of the airport. The second begins at 1,200 feet AGL and has a 10 n.m. radius. Both circles have an upper limit of 4,000 feet above the elevation of the primary airport. An ARSA may have one or more satellite airports.

operation for ATC facilities are listed in the *Airport/Facility Directory.* Most of the airports where ARSAs have been designated were once called **terminal radar service areas**, or TRSAs. Operating procedures for TRSAs are covered later in this chapter.

In addition to the two-way radio requirement, all aircraft operating in an ARSA and in all airspace above an ARSA, beginning at its ceiling and extending upward to 10,000 feet MSL within the lateral confines of that ARSA, must be equipped with an operable transponder with Mode C. Aircraft operating in the airspace beneath an ARSA are not required to have a transponder with Mode C.

TERMINAL CONTROL AREAS

Another type of controlled airport environment that helps aircraft into and out of the country's major airports is called a **terminal control area** (TCA). TCAs are more restrictive than ARSAs in terms of operating rules and equipment requirements and typically serve several airports in the area. A TCA has different levels of airspace that are portrayed as a series of interconnected circular patterns around the airport. You may notice that a TCA looks something like an upside-down wedding cake. [Figure 2-30]

Although TCAs and ARSAs have some similarities, TCAs have more than one basic design. Each TCA is individually designed to serve the needs of the particular airport that it surrounds. Terrain, the amount and flow of air

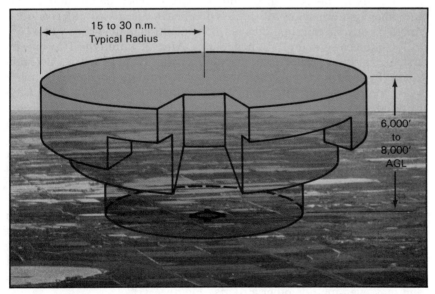

Figure 2-30. Each TCA layer is designated by an upper and lower altitude, commonly referred to as the ceiling and floor for that segment of the TCA. Each layer is a building block for controlling the airspace in the area and for funneling air traffic into the terminal area.

traffic, and the location of other airports all influence each design. Generally, you will find that TCAs surround the busiest airports in the country.

A private pilot certificate is required for operations at the primary airports of the nation's busiest TCAs.

To operate within a TCA, your aircraft must have two-way radio communications capability and a transponder with Mode C. With certain exceptions, the transponder is required within 30 nautical miles of the TCA's primary airport from the surface to 10,000 feet MSL. A VOR or TACAN is only required for IFR operations. In order to fly within TCA airspace, or to take off or land at an airport within a TCA, each pilot-in-command of a civil aircraft must possess at least a private pilot certificate. However, student pilots may be permitted to conduct flight operations within certain TCAs by obtaining specified training and a logbook endorsement from a certified flight instructor. In addition, student pilot operations are prohibited at the primary airports within a number of the nation's busiest TCAs. You should refer to FAR Part 91 for specific rules pertaining to student pilot operations within a TCA.

Authorization from ATC is required before you may operate an aircraft within a TCA.

Before entering any part of a TCA you are required to contact ATC on the appropriate frequency. Before departing an airport in a TCA, you must advise ATC of your intended altitude and route of flight. ATC permission is required before you can fly through the TCA, even after a departure from an airport that is other than the primary airport. You will find that some TCAs have VFR corridors which have been designated to permit you to fly through the area without contacting ATC. Within a VFR corridor, you are not actually in the TCA, so you do not have to meet the operational and equipment requirements. Most TCAs don't have designated VFR corridors. Another concern you should have when operating in the vicinity of a TCA is flying too close to the TCA boundaries. Aircraft within the TCA may be assigned altitudes at or near the floor of the TCA. If you do not give yourself an extra margin of clearance when you are circumnavigating a TCA, you are actually increasing the potential for a collision. Also, keep in mind that regulations specify a speed limit of 200 knots indicated airspeed when flying in the airspace underlying a TCA. Remember, the FAA encourages non-TCA aircraft to avoid the TCA whenever practical. The boundaries of TCAs are clearly shown on sectional and terminal area charts, which are covered in Chapter 6.

CONTROL ZONES

Within the conterminous U.S., control zones extend from the surface up to the base of the continental control area.

Control zones surround selected airports and extend controlled airspace to the surface. A **control zone** is usually a circular area with a radius of five statute miles from the center of an airport that has an instrument approach. It may also have extensions to accommodate instrument arrivals and departures. Therefore, control zones may be of varying sizes and shapes, and may even include other airports. [Figure 2-31]

In order to have a control zone, an airport requires both ATC communications capabilities and an FAA-qualified weather observer on the field.

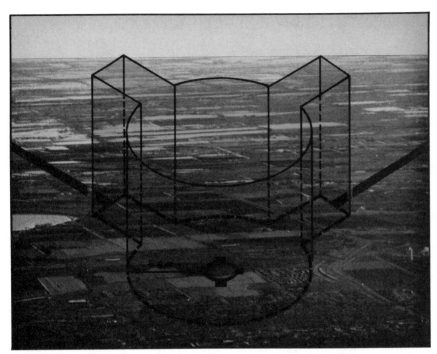

Figure 2-31. A control zone extends from the surface up to the base of the continental control area at 14,500 feet MSL. If a particular control zone is not under the continental control area, it has no upper limit.

Control zones are located at uncontrolled airports, as well as controlled airports. Since there are many uncontrolled airports that have instrument approaches, control zones permit an instrument pilot to communicate with ATC during an approach. If a qualified weather observer is not available at all times, the control zone is in effect on a part-time basis. Control zone boundaries are shown on sectional charts, and part-time control zones are also indicated.

For VFR operations in a control zone beneath a ceiling, the ceiling must be at least 1,000 feet and the flight visibility must be at least three statute miles. To take off, land, or enter the traffic pattern, you still need at least a 1,000-foot ceiling and ground visibility of at least three statute miles. If ground visibility is not reported, you can use flight visibility. The exception to these rules is special VFR minimums. If there is no conflicting IFR traffic in the control zone, a **special VFR clearance** may be available. This allows certificated private pilots to take off or land if they maintain one statute mile visibility and remain clear of clouds. Because of the difficulty in seeing clouds at night, special VFR clearances are not issued at night unless the aircraft is IFR equipped and the pilot has a current instrument rating. In addition, you will find that special VFR clearances are not issued to fixed-wing aircraft (day or night) at the nation's busier airports.

If the visibility is less than three statute miles, student pilots are not authorized to request a special VFR clearance.

UNCONTROLLED AIRSPACE

The *Airman's Information Manual* defines uncontrolled airspace as those areas that have not been designated as continental control area, control area, control zone, terminal control area, or transition areas. As a result, ATC has neither the authorization nor the responsibility to exercise control of air traffic in uncontrolled airspace. The amount of uncontrolled airspace has gradually diminished, so that remaining large areas are located mostly in the western U.S. and Alaska. In a few places, uncontrolled airspace may extend to the base of the continental control area, which begins at 14,500 feet MSL. An exception to this rule occurs when 14,500 feet MSL is lower than 1,500 feet AGL. In this event, uncontrolled airspace continues up to 1,500 feet above the surface. Day cloud clearance and visibility requirements are somewhat less stringent than they are in controlled airspace. However, night visibility and cloud clearance rules are the same as they are in controlled airspace. [Figure 2-32]

SPECIAL USE AIRSPACE

Large segments of controlled and uncontrolled airspace have been designated as **special use airspace**. Operations within special use airspace are considered hazardous to civil aircraft operating in the area. Consequently, civil aircraft operations may be limited or even prohibited, depending on the area. To help you determine the type of operations and the rules for the various areas, special use airspace is divided into prohibited, restricted, warning, military operations, and alert areas.

PROHIBITED AREAS

Areas where, for reasons of national security, the flight of aircraft is not permitted are designated as **prohibited areas**. Prohibited areas are depicted on aeronautical charts.

VFR IN UNCONTROLLED AIRSPACE		
Altitude	**Flight Visibility**	**Distance From Clouds**
1,200 ft. or less above the surface (regardless of MSL altitude)	Day: 1 s.m.	Clear of clouds
	Night: 3 s.m.	500 ft. below 1,000 ft. above 2,000 ft. horizontal
More than 1,200 ft. above the surface, but less than 10,000 ft. MSL	Day: 1 s.m. Night: 3 s.m.	500 ft. below 1,000 ft. above 2,000 ft. horizontal
More than 1,200 ft. above the surface and at or above 10,000 ft. MSL	Day and night: 5 s.m.	1,000 ft. below 1,000 ft. above 1 s.m. horizontal

Figure 2-32. For day flights in uncontrolled airspace within 1,200 feet of the surface, you are required to remain clear of any clouds and maintain one statute mile visibility. Above 1,200 feet AGL during the day, cloud clearance increases significantly. At and above 10,000 feet MSL, the requirements are the same as they are in controlled airspace.

RESTRICTED AREAS

In certain areas, the flight of aircraft, while not wholly prohibited, is subject to restrictions. These designated **restricted areas** often have invisible hazards to aircraft, such as artillery firing, aerial gunnery, or guided missiles. Permission to fly through restricted areas may be granted by the controlling agency. In many cases, the dimensions of these areas may be such that you can avoid them altogether. In any case, extra caution is appropriate, even when you are flying near a restricted area.

You may fly through a restricted area only if permission is granted by the controlling agency.

WARNING AREAS

A type of airspace that may contain hazards to nonparticipating aircraft over international or coastal waters is a **warning area**. It may contain many of the same operations that are found in restricted areas, except that they are conducted outside U.S. coastal borders. Some warning areas are established between 3 and 12 n.m. from the coast and are subject to U.S. regulations. Flight into an active warning area, whether within 12 miles of the coast or over international waters, can be hazardous and should be avoided.

Unusual, often invisible, hazards such as aerial gunnery and guided missiles may be encountered in a warning area.

MILITARY OPERATIONS AREAS

Another area that warrants extra caution is a **military operations area** (MOA). MOAs are blocks of airspace in which military training and other military maneuvers are conducted. MOAs usually have specified floors and ceilings for containing military activities. VFR aircraft are not prevented from flying through MOAs while they are in operation, but it is wise to avoid them when possible. [Figure 2-33]

If you must fly through an MOA when it is in operation, use extreme caution.

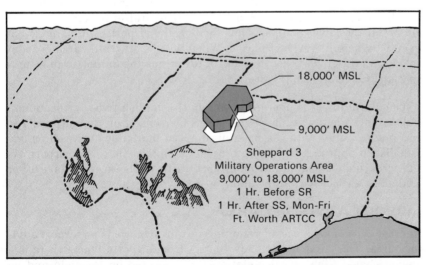

18,000' MSL

9,000' MSL

Sheppard 3
Military Operations Area
9,000' to 18,000' MSL
1 Hr. Before SR
1 Hr. After SS, Mon-Fri
Ft. Worth ARTCC

Figure 2-33. FSSs within 100 n.m. of an MOA are provided with information regarding the hours of operation. When MOAs are not in operation, there should be no problem in flying through them. If you need to fly through an MOA, contact the controlling agency for traffic advisories.

ALERT AREAS

All pilots flying in alert areas are responsible for collision avoidance, without exception.

Areas shown on aeronautical charts to inform you of unusual types of aerial activities or high concentrations of student pilot training are **alert areas**. You should be especially cautious when flying through them. Pilots of participating aircraft and pilots transiting the area are equally responsible for collision avoidance.

CONTROLLED FIRING AREAS

The distinguishing feature of a **controlled firing area,** compared to other special use airspace, is that its activities are discontinued immediately when a spotter aircraft, radar, or ground lookout personnel determine an aircraft might be approaching the area. Since nonparticipating aircraft are not required to change their flight path, controlled firing areas are not depicted on aeronautical charts.

OTHER AIRSPACE AREAS

As indicated in the *Airman's Information Manual*, **other airspace areas** mainly consist of airport traffic areas, airport advisory areas, and military training routes. Other segments of airspace in this category may be designated by temporary flight restrictions or flight limitations/prohibitions. Parachute jump areas are also classified as other airspace areas.

AIRPORT TRAFFIC AREA

The purpose of an airport traffic area is to provide a smooth flow of aircraft landing and taking off from an airport with an operating control tower.

Airspace that begins at the surface in the airport environment and that is served by an operating control tower is called an **airport traffic area**. Air traffic control is exercised within this area to help provide better separation between aircraft and an orderly flow of traffic in and out of the airport. If the tower is a part-time facility, the airport traffic area is not in effect when the tower is closed. When the airport traffic area is collocated with a control zone, the control tower has the authority to issue a special VFR clearance. [Figure 2-34]

If the control tower is operating, you must establish two-way communications with the tower for all operations to, from, or on that airport. You also must comply with the prescribed speed limitations, as well as any established approach/departure procedures applicable to the airport. As a general rule, you should avoid airport traffic areas except to take off or land at an airport within the area.

AIRPORT ADVISORY AREA

An airport advisory area includes the airspace within 10 s.m. of an airport with an FSS but without an operating control tower.

Another type of airspace surrounding certain airports is an **airport advisory area**. This airspace extends 10 s.m. from airports where there is a nonautomated **flight service station** (FSS) located on the field and no operating control tower. The service includes advisories on wind direction and velocity, favored runway, altimeter setting, and reported traffic within the area.

Figure 2-34. An airport traffic area consists of the airspace within a five statute mile radius from the geographical center of an airport with an operating control tower. It extends up to, but not including, 3,000 feet above the airport elevation. Because of their standard dimensions, airport traffic area boundaries are not shown on aeronautical charts.

Airport advisory areas and the associated services are gradually being phased out as automated flight service stations replace existing nonautomated facilities. Currently, pilots who fly into an airport with an automated FSS will not be able to receive airport advisory service on the advisory frequency, 123.6 MegaHertz. The airspace and the service will be completely eliminated by 1995, when the last nonautomated FSS is scheduled to close.

MILITARY TRAINING ROUTES

Low-level, high-speed military training flights are conducted on **military training routes** (MTRs). Generally, MTRs are established below 10,000 feet MSL for operations at speeds in excess of 250 knots. Routes at and below 1,500 feet AGL are generally designed to be flown under VFR; routes above 1,500 AGL are developed primarily to be flown under instrument flight rules (IFR). MTRs are classified as "VR" where VFR operations apply and "IR" where IFR operations apply. Operations on IRs are conducted under IFR regardless of the weather conditions.

Regardless of weather conditions, military training flights on MTRs may be conducted at speeds in excess of 250 knots.

Even though you are not restricted from flying through MTRs, you need to check with an FSS within 100 n.m. to obtain the current information regarding MTR activity in your area. MTRs are marked on sectional charts.

TEMPORARY FLIGHT RESTRICTIONS

Temporary flight restrictions apply to a specific hazard or condition. When necessary, these restrictions are imposed by the FAA to protect persons or property on the surface or in the air. The objectives are to provide a safe environment for rescue/relief operations and to prevent unsafe congestion of sightseeing or other aircraft above an incident or event which may generate high public interest. The FAA will issue a Notice to Airmen (NOTAM) designating the area in which a temporary restriction applies. Situations which warrant these restrictions include toxic spills, volcano eruptions, nuclear incidents, aircraft hijackings, forest fires, and so forth.

For rescue/relief aircraft operations, the restricted airspace is normally limited to 2,000 feet above the surface within a two nautical mile radius. Incidents within an airport traffic area or a TCA are handled through existing procedures, and usually they do not require issuance of a NOTAM. In other cases, the FSS nearest the incident site is normally the coordination facility.

When a NOTAM is required, the format will include the facility establishing the temporary restriction, location, effective times, the area defined in statute miles, and the affected altitudes. The NOTAM also will contain the FAA coordination facility, the reason for the restriction, the agency directing any relief activities, commercial telephone numbers, and other information considered appropriate by the issuing authority.

FLIGHT LIMITATIONS/PROHIBITIONS

Limitations in proximity to space flight operations are designated by NOTAM. These limitations provide protection for space flight crews and prevent costly delays. A NOTAM also may be issued to create flight restrictions in the proximity of the President, Vice President, foreign heads of state, and other persons who may attract large numbers of people. When such NOTAMs are issued, they are considered to be regulatory.

PARACHUTE JUMP AREAS

Parachute jumping sites are tabulated in the *Airport/Facility Directory*. The busiest periods of activity are normally on weekends and holidays. Sites that have been used on a frequent basis and that have been in use for at least one year are depicted on sectional charts. Times of operation are local, and MSL altitudes are listed unless otherwise specified.

EMERGENCY AIR TRAFFIC RULES

Other situations may arise when the FAA needs to issue emergency air traffic rules. These rules are issued immediately after determining that, without such action, the air traffic control system cannot operate at the required level of safety and efficiency. If this happens, a NOTAM is issued to communicate information about the emergency rules governing flight operations and the use of navigation facilities. It designates the airspace in which these rules apply. When a NOTAM is issued with this information, no one may operate an aircraft in conflict with it.

ADIZ/DEWIZ

All aircraft entering domestic U.S. airspace from outside must provide identification prior to entry. **Air Defense Identification Zones** (ADIZs) are established to facilitate this identification in the vicinity of U.S. international airspace boundaries. Generally, you must file an IFR or defense VFR (DVFR) flight plan for all operations that enter or exit an ADIZ. In addition, you normally are required to have a two-way radio and make periodic position reports. A transponder, with Mode C (or Mode S) capability is required, and the transponder must be transmitting pressure altitude information. Failure to follow these rules may result in your aircraft being intercepted by U.S. security.

The **distant early warning identification zone** (DEWIZ) is the same as an ADIZ, except that it lies along the coastal waters of Alaska. The DEWIZ and the ADIZ have somewhat different operating rules. If you are thinking of flying into either of these areas, you should refer to the *Airman's Information Manual* for detailed procedural information.

During a defense emergency or during air defense emergency conditions, special security instructions may be issued in accordance with the Security Control of Air Traffic and Air Navigation Aids (SCATANA) plan. Under the provisions of this plan, the military will direct the necessary actions to land, ground, divert, or disperse aircraft and take over control of navaids in the defense of the U.S. If SCATANA goes into effect, ATC facilities will broadcast instructions over available frequencies.

CHECKLIST

After studying this section, you should have a basic understanding of:

✓ **Controlled airspace** — What the major divisions are, the operating requirements for each type, and what purposes they serve.

✓ **Uncontrolled airspace** — What the definition is.

✓ **VFR cloud clearance and visibility requirements** — What they are, where they apply, and how they change with altitude.

✓ **Special use airspace** — What the types are and what restrictions apply to each type.

✓ **Other airspace areas** — What these areas include, and what rules and procedures apply within each type.

✓ **Emergency air traffic rules** — When these rules may be put into effect and what flight operations may be restricted.

✓ **ADIZ/DEWIZ** — Why these zones are established, and general rules for operations within them.

SECTION D

RADIO COMMUNICATIONS

In previous sections, you became aware of a number of situations that require you to be in two-way radio contact with controllers, flight service stations, and other facilities. In fact, nearly any service you obtain during flight requires radio communications. In this section, you will learn about radio communications equipment and how you should talk on the radio. You will need to become familiar with a number of unique words and phrases which are commonly used in aviation. Depending on your background, talking on the radio may be a new way of communicating, but it will soon become as natural to you as flying the airplane.

VHF COMMUNICATIONS EQUIPMENT

Communications radios in general aviation aircraft use a portion of the **very high frequency** (VHF) range, which includes the frequencies between 118.0 MegaHertz (MHz) and 135.975 MHz. Communications radios are classified according to the number of channels they were designed to accommodate. Most radios of current manufacture have either 360- or 720-channel capability. A 360-channel radio uses 50 kHz (.05 MHz) spacing between channels, such as 118.05, 118.10, 118.15, 118.20. A 720-channel radio doubles the frequencies available by using 25 kHz (.025 MHz) spacing, such as 118.025, 118.050, 118.075, 118.100.

Most VHF radios you will encounter have both communications and VOR navigation receiver capability in one unit. Use of the VOR receiver for navigation is discussed in Chapter 7. [Figure 2-35]

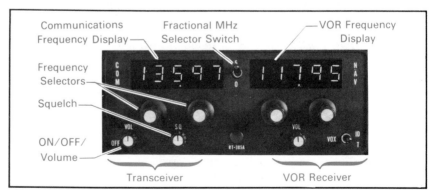

Figure 2-35. Radios normally have frequency selectors and a frequency display, along with the on/off/volume and squelch controls. The switch in the center permits selection of .05 or .025 MHz fractions for communications frequencies. Because communications radios usually include a combination transmitter and receiver, they are called transceivers.

You will find that 720-channel transceivers are a necessity if you want to receive full ATC services, particularly in busy terminal areas. If you have only 360-channel capability, you can still operate in most areas, but delays can be expected and some services may not be available. Occasionally, you may encounter transceivers with only 90-, 100-, or 180-channel communications capability. When you do, be sure your frequency capability will be adequate for the type of facilities you plan to contact.

When you need to change from one frequency to another, use the frequency selectors and check the display to verify that the correct frequency has been set in the transceiver. Because of varying noise levels inside the cockpit, you can adjust the volume of the receiver with the on/off/volume control. If you want to adjust the volume when no one is talking on the frequency, turn the squelch control until you hear background noise. Then, adjust the volume and turn the squelch down until you can't hear the background noise. Most of the time, you will keep the squelch turned down, although turning it up actually increases reception range. This can be important in situations where you want to hear a station that is almost out of range.

The range of VHF transmissions is limited to **line of sight**, meaning that obstructions such as buildings, terrain, or the curvature of the earth block the airwaves that carry radio signals. In areas where the terrain is not mountainous, reception is still limited to line of sight because the curvature of the earth eventually blocks the radio waves. [Figure 2-36]

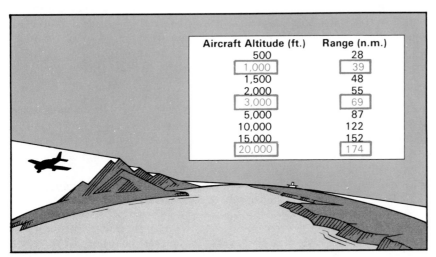

Aircraft Altitude (ft.)	Range (n.m.)
500	28
1,000	39
1,500	48
2,000	55
3,000	69
5,000	87
10,000	122
15,000	152
20,000	174

Figure 2-36. Because VHF radio signals are limited to line of sight, aircraft flying at higher altitudes are able to transmit and receive at greater distances. For example, an aircraft at 1,000 feet AGL over flat terrain may receive transmissions from 39 miles. At 3,000 feet AGL, the distance may be 69 miles; an aircraft at 20,000 feet AGL may transmit and receive from as far away as 174 miles.

Figure 2-37. Normally, a VHF antenna is installed for each transceiver in the airplane. An airplane equipped with two transceivers usually has a microphone selector switch for the respective radios, so a second microphone is not required.

Your transceiver requires a VHF antenna for proper operation. You will notice several different antennas mounted on airplanes, but VHF antennas usually are the bent whip rods or plastic-encapsulated blade types that are mounted on top of the cabin. [Figure 2-37]

FEDERAL COMMUNICATIONS COMMISSION

Within the U.S., one of the functions of the **Federal Communications Commission** (FCC) is to regulate types of aircraft radios. When a radio is used for transmitting, it becomes a radio station. As a result, the FCC requires a **radio station license** for communications radios used for aviation purposes. Although this is not an FAA requirement, the FCC does require that this license be carried on board the aircraft.

The FCC also requires U.S. pilots who fly internationally to have a **restricted radiotelephone operator permit**. The only time that this permit is required within the U.S. is when long-range, high frequency (HF) radios are used. This permit can be obtained by completing an application form obtained from an FCC field office and returning it to the FCC. If you fly within the 48 mainland states, you typically use only VHF communications radios, so the permit normally is not required.

INTERNATIONAL CIVIL AVIATION ORGANIZATION

As you know, the FAA is the regulatory agency for U.S.-based aircraft flying within the country. Throughout the world, an agency of the United Nations, known as the **International Civil Aviation Organization** (ICAO), coordinates international flight activities.

Due to the nature of international travel, it would be difficult for pilots to speak all of the languages that could be involved. Therefore, the English language is recommended by ICAO for international air/ground communications. In countries where English is not the official language, ICAO member states have agreed to make English available upon request. ICAO also adopted a phonetic alphabet to be used in radio transmissions. [Figure 2-38]

You will learn to use the phonetic alphabet as a routine measure when you identify your aircraft during initial contact with ATC or other facilities. The phonetic equivalents for single letters should also be used to spell out difficult words or groups of letters when conditions are adverse to good communications.

USING NUMBERS ON THE RADIO

Sometimes, there may be confusion when you transmit or receive numbers over the radio. Use of proper procedures will eliminate most of these problems. Each number is spoken the same way you are used to saying it, with the exception of the number nine. It is spoken as *"niner"* to distinguish it from the German word *"nein,"* which means "no."

When talking to ATC, you can expect to receive numerous headings, altitudes, and frequencies, all of which contain numbers. To reduce confusion between the sets of numbers included in these instructions, they

Numbers above 9,900 are spoken by separating the digits preceding the word "thousand." For example, the number 10,000 is spoken as *"one zero thousand."*

ICAO Phonetic Alphabet							
A	Alfa	(*Al*-fah)	•—	N	November	(No-*vem*-ber)	—•
B	Bravo	(*Brah*-voh)	—•••	O	Oscar	(*Oss*-cah)	———
C	Charlie	(*Char*-lee)	—•—•	P	Papa	(Pah-*pah*)	•——•
D	Delta	(*Dell*-tah)	—••	Q	Quebec	(Keh-*beck*)	——•—
E	Echo	(*Eck*-oh)	•	R	Romeo	(*Row*-me-oh)	•—•
F	Foxtrot	(*Foks*-trot)	••—•	S	Sierra	(See-*air*-rah)	•••
G	Golf	(Golf)	——•	T	Tango	(*Tang*-go)	—
H	Hotel	(Hoh-*tell*)	••••	U	Uniform	(*You*-nee-form)	••—
I	India	(*In*-dee-ah)	••	V	Victor	(*Vik*-tah)	•••—
J	Juliett	(*Jew*-lee-*ett*)	•———	W	Whiskey	(*Wiss*-key)	•——
K	Kilo	(*Key*-loh)	—•—	X	X-ray	(*Ecks*-ray)	—••—
L	Lima	(*Lee*-mah)	•—••	Y	Yankee	(*Yang*-key)	—•——
M	Mike	(Mike)	——	Z	Zulu	(*Zoo*-loo)	——••

Figure 2-38. Because letters such as ''B,'' ''C,'' ''D,'' and ''E'' all sound alike, they can easily be mistaken for one another, especially during radio transmissions. The phonetic alphabet was developed to avoid misunderstandings of this type. The associated Morse code is also helpful when tuning and identifying navigation facilities, which typically use three-letter identifiers.

Numbers in Radio Communications	
Headings:	
087°	"Zero eight seven"
259°	"Two five niner"
Altitudes:	
8,500	"Eight thousand five hundred"
12,500	"One two thousand five hundred"
FL 330	"Flight level three three zero"
Frequencies:	
121.5	"One two one point five"
135.9	"One three five point niner"
Airways:	
V11	"Victor eleven"
J521	"J five twenty-one"
Altimeter Settings:	
29.92	"Two niner niner two"
30.14	"Three zero one four"

Figure 2-39. If you study these examples, you will become more familiar with correct pronunciation of numbers. Although you normally pronounce groups of numbers by their individual digits, notice that airways are an exception.

usually are referred to as individual numbers. When you state radio frequencies, the decimal is pronounced as *"point,"* but the decimal is dropped when you state an altimeter setting. [Figure 2-39]

COORDINATED UNIVERSAL TIME

Because a flight may cross several time zones, it would be very confusing to estimate your arrival time at the destination using only the local time at the departure airport. To overcome this problem, aviation uses the 24-hour clock system, along with an international standard called Coordinated Universal Time (UTC). The 24-hour clock eliminates the need for a.m. and p.m. designations, since the 24 hours of the day are numbered consecutively. For instance, 9 a.m. becomes 0900 hours; 1 p.m. becomes 1300 hours, and so on.

In the U.S., add hours when converting local time to Zulu; subtract hours when converting Zulu time to local.

Coordinated Universal Time, which is referred to as Zulu time in aviation, actually places the entire world on one time standard. When a given time is expressed in UTC or Zulu, it really is the time at the 0° line of longitude which passes through Greenwich, England. All of the 24 time zones around the world are based on this reference, so you will need to

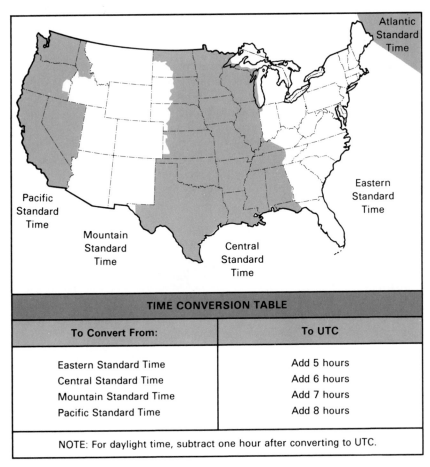

TIME CONVERSION TABLE	
To Convert From:	**To UTC**
Eastern Standard Time	Add 5 hours
Central Standard Time	Add 6 hours
Mountain Standard Time	Add 7 hours
Pacific Standard Time	Add 8 hours
NOTE: For daylight time, subtract one hour after converting to UTC.	

Figure 2-40. ATC operates on UTC or Zulu time regardless of which time zone the facility is located in. When you need to refer to a specific time, first convert it from your local time to the 24-hour clock and then to UTC.

convert local time to Zulu time and vice versa. In the United States, when you convert local time to Zulu time you add hours; when you convert Zulu time to local time you subtract hours. [Figure 2-40]

USING THE RADIO

Talking on the radio should be done in a professional manner, because slang, CB jargon, and incorrect radio procedures can compromise your safety and the safety of others. One of the most important items in radio communication is for you to speak in a manner that will ensure that others understand what you have said. Before you depress the microphone button to talk (key the mike), first think of what you will say. Radio transmissions usually can be quite brief. You should state who you are, where you are, and what type of service you are requesting.

Any other information may be excessive, especially in busy terminal areas. Next, listen for a few moments before speaking to make sure that someone else is not already talking or waiting for a response.

When you are ready to talk, hold the microphone very close to your lips. Then, key the microphone and speak into it in a normal, conversational tone. It may take a few moments for the facility you have called to respond. If you do not get a response, try again. If there is a lack of sounds from your speaker, check your radio to see if it is working properly. Make sure the microphone is not stuck in the transmitting position. This can block other transmissions on the frequency in use and disrupt communications for an extended period of time.

RADIO PROCEDURES

On initial contact, state the name of the facility you are contacting and then state your aircraft type and full call sign.

Generally, you will be the one to initiate radio contact with ATC or other facilities. Therefore, it is important to make your initial contact correctly, so the important information will be received and understood the first time. On initial callups, you should state the name of the facility you are calling and then give your aircraft type, model, or manufacturer and registration number. If you state the manufacturer's name or model, you may drop the "N" prefix of the registration.

In the U.S., each aircraft is identified by a registration number which is painted on the outside of the airplane. Registration numbers are usually a combination of five letters and numbers. They are sometimes referred to as the "tail number," or "N-number," because all U.S.-registered aircraft have an "N" preceding the number.

An example of an initial callup is, *"Great Falls Tower, Cherokee 8458R."* If your message is lengthy, it is better to wait until ATC asks you for it, because this means they are prepared to receive your information. If your request is short, you may also include the request and your position and altitude with the callup. An example of a short request to a control tower might be something like, *"Great Falls Tower, Cherokee 8458R, 5 south, 5,500, landing, Information Charlie."* If there is not another aircraft nearby with a similar number, the controller may shorten your call sign to the last three numbers or letters. In this case, the controller may respond with, *"Cherokee 58R, Great Falls Tower, report entering left downwind runway 21."* Shortening the call sign reduces the amount of air time needed for further transmissions. If there are other aircraft in the area with a similar number, the controller probably will not shorten the number. You are not allowed to shorten your call sign until the controller does so first.

An **air traffic control clearance** is defined as an authorization by ATC for an aircraft to proceed under specified traffic conditions within controlled airspace. Its purpose is to prevent collisions between known aircraft. If you receive an ATC clearance and do not hear all of it or do not understand it, ask the controller to "*say again*" and the controller will repeat the last message. If you are having a difficult time because the controller is talking too fast, ask the controller to "*speak slower*" and the controller will repeat the previous transmission more slowly. Sometimes either you or the controller may repeat what was said to verify that it was heard correctly. The response in these situations usually is, "*that is correct.*" The use of the word "*over*" indicates that your transmission is complete and that you expect a response. On subsequent contacts, the ground station name and the word "*over*" may be omitted if the message requires an obvious reply and there is no danger of misunderstanding. An example of an abbreviated request to Great Falls Tower is, "*Cherokee 58R, entering left downwind runway 21.*"

When you are talking to controllers, they may answer you right away, or they may ask you to "*stand by,*" which means that they know you called and will get back to you as soon as they can. They may be talking to someone else on a different frequency.

If a controller contacts you with a request, you should acknowledge it and quickly restate any instructions given to you in order to reduce the possibility of a misunderstanding. For example, if asked to turn right to a heading of 210°, you should respond with, "*Cherokee 58R, roger, turn right heading 210.*"

There are occasions when controllers issue time-critical instructions such as, "*Cherokee 58R, expedite your turnoff at the next available taxiway.*" You may acknowledge these with "*roger,*" "*wilco,*" "*affirmative,*" or "*negative,*" as appropriate, preceded by your call sign. You should respond immediately to time-critical requests. If, at any time, you are given an instruction that is beyond the capabilities of your airplane, is not safe to follow, or would cause you to violate an FAR, you must inform the controller that you are "*unable*" to comply with the directions. The controller should then give you an amended clearance with instructions that you can follow without compromise.

Time-critical instructions require that you respond immediately to the controller's request, which may include the word *"expedite."*

If you are asked to contact the same controller on a different frequency, the controller will state your aircraft call sign and say, "*. . .change to my frequency, 123.4.*" This means the controller wants you to change frequencies, not contact another controller. In these situations, you can abbreviate your callup by saying, "*Cherokee 58R on 123.4.*"

At times, such as when you are flying into an ARSA or TCA, you may talk to a succession of controllers on different frequencies. Each controller will tell you when to change to the next frequency and what frequency to use. This is called a "handoff" from one controller to another. Before you change frequencies, you should ensure that you heard the new frequency correctly. You can do this with a readback such as, "*Cessna 145, roger, contact tower 118.3.*" This informs the original controller that you received the instruction correctly. Since the two controllers have already coordinated the handoff, the tower will be expecting your call. Usually, the tower controller will acknowledge your call quickly and provide additional landing instructions.

As a student pilot, you can request additional assistance from ATC simply by identifying yourself as a student pilot. For example, assume you were approaching a controlled field with heavy traffic and you were unfamiliar with the airport. In this situation, you should make your initial callup as follows: "*Centennial Tower, this is Cessna 5289T, student pilot.*" This procedure is not mandatory, but it does alert controllers so they can give you extra assistance and consideration, if needed. Identifying yourself as a student may be advantageous in other situations, too. For example, you may want to do so when you self-announce your position over the CTAF at uncontrolled fields.

COMMON TRAFFIC ADVISORY FREQUENCY

Communications procedures at uncontrolled airports are significantly different from those at airports with an operating control tower. Without ATC, it is your responsibility as pilot-in-command to determine which runway to use and how to enter the pattern. You also must see and avoid other air traffic and maintain proper spacing in the pattern. In these situations, the **common traffic advisory frequency** (CTAF) is used by pilots in the area to receive advisories and to broadcast their intentions. When available, advisories usually include wind direction and speed, favored runway, and known traffic. To achieve the greatest degree of safety possible, it is essential that all aircraft equipped with radios use the same frequency. The designated CTAF varies with the type of airport and its facilities. [Figure 2-41]

Transmitting in the blind is a way for you to communicate your position to other pilots at uncontrolled fields.

At some airports, the control tower does not operate 24 hours a day. In this case, you should announce your intentions "in the blind" using the CTAF, which usually is the tower frequency. Transmitting in the blind is part of the **self-announce concept**, in which you broadcast your position and intentions to other traffic in the area.

If you use the self-announce concept when inbound, you should make your initial call when you are 10 miles from the airport. You should also report when entering your downwind, base, and final legs, and when leaving the runway. An example of a radio call for entering the pattern might be as follows: "*Alameda traffic, Piper 5280Q, entering downwind for runway 17, Alameda.*" Because there may be other uncontrolled airports within reception range using the same frequency, it is helpful to repeat the name of the airport at the end of your transmission.

Communications/Broadcast Procedures	Facility at Airport	Frequency To Use
Inbound 10 miles out; entering downwind, base, and final; leaving the runway	Tower or FSS Not in Operation	Self-announce on CTAF.
	FSS Closed (No Tower)	Self-announce on CTAF.
	No Tower in Operation, FSS Open	Communicate with FSS on CTAF frequency.
Outbound Before taxiing and before taxiing on the runway for departure	No Tower, FSS, or UNICOM	Self-announce on MULTICOM frequency 122.9.
	UNICOM (No tower or FSS)	Communicate with UNICOM station on published CTAF frequency 122.7, 122.725, 122.8, 122.975, or 123.0.

Figure 2-41. The principal concept of a common traffic advisory frequency (CTAF) is to provide a method for pilots to communicate with each other at uncontrolled airports. By broadcasting their positions at specified locations, it is much easier for pilots to establish and maintain visual contact.

When departing an airport with a CTAF, you should announce your intentions before taxiing from the parking ramp and before taxiing onto the runway for departure. Here is a typical radio call that you might hear in this situation: *"Mid Valley traffic, Cessna 9668H, departing runway 35 to the northeast, climbing to 8,500, Mid Valley."* By announcing what you intend to do, you alert inbound aircraft to your departure.

While use of the CTAF is highly recommended, you will find certain situations when you can benefit from using other air/ground communications facilities at an uncontrolled airport, in addition to the CTAF. For example, if a part-time FSS or Tower is closed, airport advisory service is not available on the CTAF. However, you can often receive similar information about the airport from an aeronautical advisory station or **UNICOM**. In this case, the UNICOM frequency is not the CTAF and you must return to the designated CTAF to listen for other aircraft and self-announce your position and intentions.

At other airports, the UNICOM may be the designated CTAF and you do not have to change frequencies to get advisory information. Since UNICOMs are privately operated, you can also request other information or services through these facilities. A request for refueling service is an example. Announcing your position and intentions is also standard procedure at airports where the designated CTAF is the UNICOM frequency. There are a limited number of UNICOM frequencies available. If an airport has pilot-controlled lighting, the frequency required to

UNICOM stations handle a variety of information and service requests, including refueling, at many airports.

operate the lighting is usually the same as the CTAF. This eliminates the need for changing frequencies to activate the lighting and allows for continuous monitoring for other traffic.

At nontower airports without an FSS or UNICOM, MULTICOM is used by pilots to self-announce their position and intentions to other pilots.

If your flight takes you to an airport that does not have a tower, an FSS, or a UNICOM, the CTAF will be the **MULTICOM** frequency, 122.9 MHz. The purpose of MULTICOM is to provide a frequency for aircraft in the area to use for air-to-air communications. At airports where MULTICOM is the CTAF, pilots are responsible for determining the favored runway and self-announcing their position and intentions. For example, consider the following announcement: *"Coronado traffic, Mooney 7806L, departing runway 17, remaining in the pattern, Coronado."* If you were departing or arriving, you would know that at least one other aircraft was in the traffic pattern. Common traffic advisory frequencies are listed in the *Airport/Facility Directory* and indicated on sectional and VFR terminal area charts. CTAFs also may be obtained from the nearest FSS.

FLIGHT SERVICE STATIONS

Aside from providing airport advisory service and issuing NOTAMs, flight service stations provide many other services, including search and rescue operations. FSSs are responsible for processing flight plans. When you file a **flight plan** with an FSS, a record is made which includes your destination, route of flight, arrival time, and number of people on board. Once airborne, you "open" your flight plan so the FSS can keep track of your airplane's estimated arrival time. If, 30 minutes after the estimated arrival time, you have not closed or cancelled the flight plan, the FSS initiates search and rescue procedures to find your aircraft. The FAA does not require pilots of VFR aircraft to file flight plans. However, if you file and open a VFR flight plan, you must close it after arriving at your destination. If you decide not to go to your original destination, or if you will be at least 15 minutes later than you had planned, inform the nearest FSS accordingly.

After you open your flight plan, you should give occasional position reports to FSSs along the way. In the event that an aircraft does not arrive at its destination, the FSS has an idea of the aircraft's last known position. Usually, the Civil Air Patrol (CAP), a civilian extension of the U.S. Air Force, assists in search and rescue operations.

If you get disoriented while on a cross-country trip, an FSS specialist may be able to locate you with a **VHF direction finder** (VHF/DF). Direction finding equipment requires two-way radio communications with the FSS. The FSS specialist will ask you to key your microphone while the direction finding equipment "homes" in on your radio signal. The specialist can determine your location from the FSS and then give you headings to guide you to an airport or provide other assistance. Unlike radar, DF determines only your direction from the FSS. It does not reveal how far away you are. Many air traffic control towers also have direction finding equipment. Towers and FSSs with DF service are listed in the *Airport/Facility Directory.*

At times, you will talk to an FSS on one frequency while listening for a response over the frequency used for a navigation aid in the area. Most often, this is done using a VOR station, which is a common type of navigation aid that we will discuss in detail later in Chapter 7. Whenever you initiate contact with an FSS, give the name of the facility followed by "radio," such as "Prescott Radio." If you are listening for a response over a VOR frequency, tell the FSS which VOR you are listening to. Consider this example: *"Albuquerque Radio, Piper 8852P, listening Corona VOR."* If contact is initiated in this manner, the FSS specialist, who can respond over several VOR frequencies, knows which frequency to use in answering your call.

CHECKLIST ━━━━━━━━━━━━━━━━━━━

After studying this section, you should have a basic understanding of:

✓ **Very high frequency** — What the characteristics of VHF radio waves are and what advantages they have for communications purposes.

✓ **Line of sight** — What it means with respect to radio communications and how range increases with altitude.

✓ **Coordinated universal time** — How to apply the 24-hour clock and how to convert local time to Zulu time.

✓ **Common traffic advisory frequency** — The purpose of CTAF and what types of airports use it.

✓ **UNICOM** — What the function of an aeronautical advisory station is, which airports have it, and which frequencies are used for this purpose.

✓ **MULTICOM** — How to communicate with other aircraft, what frequency to use, and why transmitting in the blind enhances safety.

✓ **Flight plan** — Where to file it, what information it contains, and when search and rescue is initiated.

✓ **Direction finding equipment** — What to do when you are lost, who to contact, and what is required to get the service.

SECTION E

RADAR AND ATC SERVICES

So far, we have discussed important safety-of-flight issues, described airports and airspace, and explained how to use the radio. In this section, we will discuss a variety of air traffic control services that are available when you operate under VFR. To use these services effectively, you must become proficient in radio communications and also acquire an understanding of the capabilities of radar and transponders.

Today, radar has a predominant role in the ATC system. Without radar, it would be virtually impossible for ATC to handle the current nationwide volume of traffic. ATC radar facilities provide both VFR and IFR aircraft with a wide range of services, including traffic advisories, vectoring, sequencing, and separation.

RADAR

Radar uses pulses of microwave energy to determine the azimuth and distance of your aircraft from the radar station. **Azimuth** is the direction or angle between the radar site and your aircraft. It is measured clockwise from north in a horizontal plane. There are two types of radar systems — primary and secondary.

Primary radar is a ground-based system with a rotating antenna that sends out pulses of radio energy. These are reflected back to the site, processed, and displayed. Primary radar works on the echo principle. When these pulses of radio energy reach your aircraft, some of the energy is reflected back to the radar antenna. The reflected energy, or echo, is then processed and displayed on a radarscope, which is really a cathode ray tube (CRT). Your distance from the site is determined by measuring the time lapse between the original radar pulse and its echo, or return.

An electron beam (sweep) emanates from the center of the scope and moves in the same direction as the rotating radar antenna. The intensity of the sweep is too low to generate much light on the face of the tube until it reaches a point corresponding to the range and azimuth of your aircraft. At this point, the return echo is intensified to produce a "blip" of light that represents your aircraft. [Figure 2-42]

The ATC radar beacon system (ATCRBS) is the official name for **secondary surveillance radar** or, simply, secondary radar. Secondary radar is a separate system and is capable of operating independently from primary radar. However, in normal air traffic control, they are used together.

Secondary radar requires three components in addition to primary radar. These are a decoder, an interrogator, and a transponder. The decoder is attached to a radarscope console in ATC facilities. The interrogator is mounted on the radar antenna, and the transponder is located in the aircraft. The decoder has two ATC functions. It controls the interrogator, and it interprets the signals received from the transponder. In turn, the interrogator transmits radar pulses and receives replies from the transponder. Both primary and secondary radar returns are usually displayed on the same radarscope. Secondary returns from transponder-equipped aircraft have enhanced presentations. [Figure 2-43]

In spite of its capabilities, primary radar has some serious limitations. One of these is the bending of radar pulses, which can be caused by atmospheric temperature inversions. If the beam is bent toward the ground, extraneous returns, known as "ground clutter," may appear on the scope. If the beam is bent upward, detection range will be reduced.

Another problem with primary radar is that precipitation or heavy clouds can block radar returns, leaving some aircraft undetected. Areas of heavy precipitation are good reflectors of radar energy. Controllers can use a device to eliminate slow-moving objects such as clouds, but they

Because heavy clouds and areas of precipitation can reflect radar energy, primary radar returns from distant aircraft may be completely blocked.

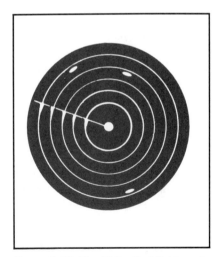

Figure 2-42. The "blips" of light on the screen are called raw radar returns, or skin paints. They are simply the reflected radio energy of the original radar pulse. The controller is then able to interpret both the range and azimuth of your aircraft.

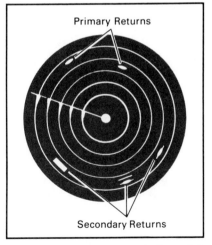

Primary Returns

Secondary Returns

Figure 2-43. The return on the lower left shows what the controller sees when you activate the IDENT feature of your transponder. The return in the lower center shows two control slashes, which result when the transponder and decoder are set to the same code. The return on the lower right represents an aircraft whose transponder code is different from the one the controller is interrogating.

are unable to solve the problem altogether. This is a serious disadvantage for a controller who is trying to help a pilot avoid an area of bad weather such as a line of thunderstorms. A further drawback of primary radar is that the size of the radar return is determined by the reflective surface of the aircraft. Therefore, returns from small aircraft often are intermittent when compared to those of large aircraft, particularly at long range. However, one of the biggest problems with the primary radar system is its inability to easily identify an individual aircraft return. For example, the controller usually asks you for your position from a navaid to establish positive identification. With primary radar, the controller is also unable to determine the altitudes of various aircraft without contacting each pilot. In many situations, this can hamper the controller's ability to provide vertical separation of aircraft.

The strength of secondary radar returns is not dependent on the size of an aircraft's reflective surface.

Secondary radar overcomes most of the limitations of primary radar. Radar returns from secondary radar are much stronger than those from primary radar. This permits controllers to track your aircraft through most weather conditions and extends radar coverage farther than is possible with primary radar. Unlike primary radar, secondary radar returns are independent of an aircraft's reflective surface. Today, controllers depend almost exclusively on secondary radar.

TRANSPONDER

To operate a transponder in controlled airspace, it must be tested and inspected within the preceding 24 calendar months.

A transponder is the airborne portion of the secondary surveillance radar system. The coded signal transmitted by the interrogator causes the aircraft transponder to reply automatically with a specific coded signal. This produces a distinctive return on the controller's radarscope. Since transponder returns are the basis for radar separation, regulations require they be tested and inspected every 24 calendar months for operations in controlled airspace. Regulations further require that if your aircraft is transponder-equipped, you must operate the transponder when you are in controlled airspace, including the Mode C feature (if installed). There are only two exceptions to these transponder operating rules: when the controller instructs you to operate it differently or when your transponder equipment has not been tested and calibrated as required by regulation. If you fly at and above 10,000 feet MSL (except for the airspace at and below 2,500 feet AGL) or within 30 nautical miles of any designated TCA primary airport from the surface to 10,000 feet MSL, you must have and operate a transponder with Mode C capability. Although transponders are relatively simple to use, there are a number of features you need to become familiar with for correct operation. [Figure 2-44]

The function selector of a typical transponder has several positions. They usually include OFF, STY (STANDBY), ON, ALT (ALTITUDE), and TST (TEST). In the **STANDBY** position, the transponder is warmed up and ready for operation but does not reply to interrogations. You usually set your transponder to STANDBY during taxi operations prior to

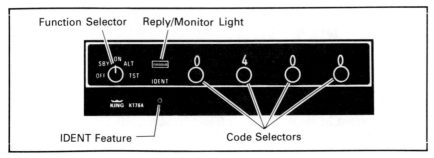

Figure 2-44. A typical transponder has four windows which can be set to any number between zero and seven. This gives a total of 4,096 possible codes. The function selector turns the unit on or off and controls the mode of operation. The reply/monitor light illuminates when you select the test feature to show proper operation. It also flashes when the transponder is replying to interrogation signals or transmitting ident pulses.

departure. Occasionally, during flight, the controller may direct you to "*squawk standby*" for operational reasons. The term **"squawk"** is used by the controller to tell you which transponder function you should select, as well as which four-digit code you should use. [Figure 2-45]

TRANSPONDER PHRASEOLOGY
"*Squawk (Number)*"
Operate your transponder on designated code in Mode A.   *JUST ON*
"*Squawk Standby*"
Switch your transponder to STANDBY position.   *MODE C   ALT*
"*Stop Altitude Squawk*"
Turn altitude reporting switch OFF. If your equipment does not have this capability, turn Mode C OFF.
"*Squawk Altitude*"
Activate Mode C with automatic altitude reporting.
"*Ident*"
Press the IDENT feature of your transponder.
"*Squawk (Number) and Ident*"
Operate your transponder on specified code in Mode A and press the IDENT feature.
"*Squawk Low/Normal*"
Operate your transponder on LOW or NORMAL, as specified. Transponder is operated in NORMAL position unless ATC specifies LOW. ON is used instead of NORMAL on some types of transponders, and many do not have a LOW position.
"*Stop Squawk*"
Switch your transponder OFF.
"*Squawk MAYDAY*"
Operate your transponder in the emergency position, Mode A Code 7700/ Emergency, and Mode C altitude reporting.
"*Squawk VFR*"
Operate transponder on Code 1200.   *VFR Code*

Figure 2-45. Controllers use distinctive phraseology when referring to the operation of your transponder. You should become familiar with this phraseology so you can respond quickly to controller directions. Normally, you must comply with all ATC clearances and instructions, including operation of your transponder.

As a general rule, you should switch the transponder from STANDBY to ON as late as practical on takeoff. Switch to ALTITUDE if your transponder has Mode C automatic altitude reporting equipment. The ON position selects Mode A and is appropriate when your transponder doesn't have Mode C automatic altitude equipment. It is also appropriate when the controller specifies, *"stop altitude squawk."* This means you should turn off Mode C altitude reporting but continue to operate your transponder on Mode A. If the controller subsequently needs your Mode C information, the phrase *"squawk altitude"* will be used. When you land, you should switch your transponder to OFF or STANDBY as soon as practical.

Before using the Mode C information from your transponder for aircraft separation purposes, the controller must make sure your altitude readout is valid. In other words, are you at the altitude your Mode C equipment says you are? For VFR operations where you are in level flight, the controller typically will say, *"verify at 7,500,"* (or other appropriate altitude). If your response is *"affirmative,"* the altitude readout can be used for separation. You also can save the controller some time on your initial callups by stating your exact altitude to the nearest 100 feet.

In cases where your altitude readout differs significantly (300 feet or more) from your reported altitude, the controller will issue instructions such as, *"Stop altitude squawk, altitude differs by 350 feet."* This could mean your Mode C equipment is not calibrated properly or you have an incorrect altimeter setting. The wrong altimeter setting has no direct effect on your Mode C readout, since that equipment is preset to 29.92. However, it would cause your actual altitude to vary from the one assigned by the controller. Be sure to verify that your altimeter setting is correct whenever the controller indicates your Mode C readout is invalid.

The ident feature should not be used unless the controller specifically calls for it.

ATC may ask you to *"squawk ident."* If so, you should press the IDENT button momentarily and release it. This causes the transponder return to "blossom" on the radar screen for a few seconds. The IDENT presentation is the basis for the controller to establish positive radar contact.

Of course, your transponder must be set to the correct code for the IDENT feature to work. The knobs on the face of the transponder are used to select the four-digit numerical codes assigned by the controller. For example, a controller might tell you to *"squawk 1704, and ident."*

Code 1200 is assigned to all VFR aircraft not under radar control, regardless of altitude.

For VFR operations, you normally use code 1200 unless a different code is assigned by a controller. This might happen during an arrival or departure from an airport served by radar facilities. However, when not in a radar environment, you are responsible for correct transponder operation. You should be careful to avoid codes 7500, 7600, and 7700 when you are making routine code changes on your transponder. Inadvertent selection of these codes may cause momentary false alarms at radar facilities. Code 7500 alerts ATC that an aircraft has been hijacked; 7600 is used after the failure of two-way radio communications; and 7700 is used for emergencies. As an example, when switching from code 2700 to code 7200, switch first to 2200, then to 7200; do not switch to 7700 and then to 7200. This procedure also applies to code 7500 and all codes in the 7600 and 7700 series (7600-7677 and 7700-7777).

7500 HIGH JACK
7600 DEAD RADIO
7700 PROBLEMS
1234 FOR DAVE SMUGGLERS

FAA RADAR SYSTEMS

The FAA operates two basic radar systems, referred to as airport surveillance radar and air route surveillance radar. Both of these surveillance systems use primary and secondary radar returns. Both systems also use sophisticated computers and software programs designed to give the controller additional information to help in maintaining aircraft identification and separation. For example, some of these programs provide a readout of aircraft speed and altitude, as well as other information on the radarscope.

AIRPORT SURVEILLANCE RADAR

The direction and coordination of IFR traffic within specific terminal areas is delegated to **airport surveillance radar** (ASR) facilities. These are commonly called approach and departure control. ASR is designed to provide relatively short-range coverage in the airport vicinity and to serve as an expeditious means of handling terminal area traffic. The ASR can also be used as an instrument approach aid.

AUTOMATED RADAR TERMINAL SYSTEM

Most ASR facilities throughout the country utilize the **automated radar terminal system** (ARTS) in one form or another. This system has several different configurations, depending on the computer equipment and software programs used. Usually the busiest terminals in the country have the most sophisticated computers and programs. The type of system installed is designated by a suffix of numbers and letters. For example, an ARTS-IIIA installation can detect, track, and predict primary, as well as secondary, radar returns.

ARTS equipment usually is computer controlled. On a controller's radar screen, it automatically provides a continuous display of an aircraft's actual altitude, groundspeed, position, and other pertinent information. This information is updated continuously as the aircraft progresses through the terminal area. To gain maximum benefit from the system, each aircraft in the area must be equipped with a Mode C transponder and its associated altitude encoding altimeter, although this is not an operational requirement. Direct altitude readouts eliminate the need for time consuming, verbal communications between controllers and pilots

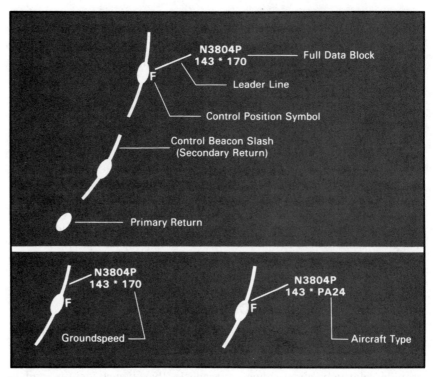

Figure 2-46. The data block at the top shows a call sign of N3804P, an altitude of 14,300 feet, and a groundspeed of 170 knots. The "F" designates the control position handling the traffic, which is the final controller in this case. As shown in the lower portion, additional information is also displayed in the data block on a time-share basis. For example, the groundspeed alternates with aircraft type. An asterisk after the altitude is used when it is not a Mode C readout.

to verify altitude. This helps to increase the number of aircraft which may be handled by one controller at a given time.

An ARTS-III radar display shows primary and secondary returns, as well as computer-generated alphanumerics. The alphanumeric data include the aircraft call sign, the altitude readout, and the groundspeed. [Figure 2-46]

AIR ROUTE SURVEILLANCE RADAR

ARSR is a long range radar system designed primarily to monitor IFR enroute traffic over a large area.

In controlled airspace, the long range radar system that displays traffic in the area is the **air route surveillance radar** (ARSR) system. There are approximately 100 ARSR facilities to relay traffic information to radar controllers throughout the country. Some of these facilities can detect only transponder-equipped aircraft and are referred to as beacon-only sites. Each air route surveillance radar site can monitor aircraft flying within a 200-mile radius of the antenna, although some stations can monitor aircraft as far away as 600 miles through the use of remote sites.

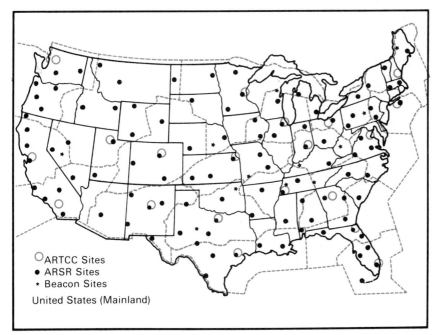

Figure 2-47. ARTCCs are the authority for issuing IFR clearances. There are 20 centers established within the conterminous U.S. Centers also provide services to VFR pilots. If controller workload permits, they will provide traffic advisories and course guidance, or vectors, if requested. Because of their extensive radar coverage, centers can be of assistance to lost and disoriented pilots.

The direction and coordination of IFR traffic in the U.S. is assigned to **air route traffic control centers** (ARTCCs). Each center is responsible for IFR traffic within its assigned geographical area. [Figure 2-47]

VFR RADAR SERVICES

ATC radar facilities routinely provide traffic information to IFR aircraft. Pilots of VFR aircraft may also receive the same service on request. **Radar traffic information service**, also called VFR radar advisory service, is intended to alert you to air traffic that is relevant to your route of flight. When the controller calls out traffic, you should find it much easier to locate, and you will be in a better position to take evasive action, if necessary.

When controllers call out a possible conflict, they will reference the traffic's position relative to yours. For instance, if a controller says, *"traffic at 11 o'clock,"* it means the traffic appears to the controller to be about 30° left of your nose. You should look for the traffic anywhere between the nose (12 o'clock) and left wing (9 o'clock) of your airplane. After you locate the traffic, tell the controller that you have the traffic *"in sight."* You should maintain visual contact with the traffic until it is no longer a factor. If you do not see the traffic, acknowledge the advisory by telling the controller *"negative contact."* [Figure 2-48]

Radar traffic information service is usually available from any ATC radar facility. This includes air route traffic control centers, as well as radar approach and departure control facilities in terminal areas. However, keep in mind that many factors, such as limitations of radar, volume of traffic, controller workload, or frequency congestion, may prevent the controller from providing this service. Even when it is available, it is not intended to relieve you of your responsibility for collision avoidance. When ATC instructs you to follow a preceding aircraft, you are not authorized to comply with any instructions issued to the preceding aircraft.

When you are operating in the radar environment, you should remember that the altitude of the reported traffic may not be known if the aircraft isn't equipped with a Mode C transponder and the pilot is not in communication with ATC. Therefore, the traffic may be well above or below your flight path. In any case, the basic purpose of radar service is to alert you to possible conflicting traffic. VFR pilots must understand that this service is available only as controller workload permits. The controller's first responsibility is to serve the needs of aircraft flying on IFR flight plans.

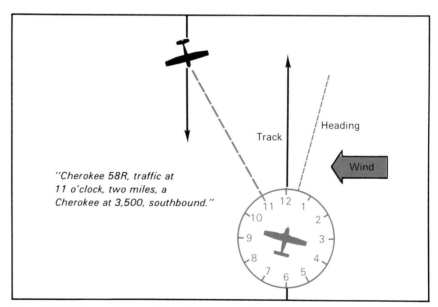

Figure 2-48. When giving traffic alerts, controllers will reference traffic from your airplane as if it were a clock. Since a radar screen can't account for the amount of wind correction you may be using to maintain your track over the ground, you need to take this into account. In this example, the controller thinks that the traffic is at your 11 o'clock position, but your wind correction angle places it at your 10 o'clock position.

VFR RADAR SERVICE IN TERMINAL AREAS

There are different levels of radar service for VFR aircraft operating in terminal areas. The level of service provided depends on the particular terminal area. Usually, the busier the terminal, the higher the level of service. Although these programs are voluntary, you are encouraged to take advantage of the added safety they provide. **Basic radar service** provides you with traffic advisories and limited vectoring. All commissioned terminal radar facilities provide basic radar service on a controller workload-permitting basis.

Basic radar service includes traffic advisories and limited vectoring for VFR aircraft and is available at all terminal radar facilities.

Stage II radar service is provided to adjust the flow of VFR and IFR traffic. Generally, this service provides separation of IFR traffic, but not between VFR and IFR, or VFR traffic. Workload permitting, controllers give traffic advisories to VFR traffic. Normally, VFR pilots also are provided with sequencing service. The purpose of sequencing is to adjust the flow of arriving traffic into the traffic pattern. Departing VFR pilots should request the service through ground control on initial contact. When inbound to a Stage II service area, contact approach control when about 25 miles from the airport. Approach control will assume that Stage II service is requested unless you indicate, "*Negative Stage II.*"

Stage II service should be requested through ground control before departure.

The third type of radar service, Stage III, is available within designated terminal radar service areas (TRSAs). With **Stage III service**, ATC provides traffic separation between participating VFR aircraft and all IFR traffic operating in the TRSA. Additionally, radar vectoring and sequencing are provided for operations to and from the primary airport. This service is not mandatory, but participation is urged. Normally, you will receive Stage II and III radar service, unless you specifically decline it on initial contact with ground or approach control.

ATC radar facilities also issue safety alerts to aircraft under their control when, in the controller's judgment, safety may be compromised. **Safety alerts** are issued when an aircraft is in unsafe proximity to terrain, obstructions, or other aircraft. If terrain or obstructions are involved, the controller will say, "*. . . low altitude alert, check your altitude immediately.*" If other traffic is involved, the controller may say, "*. . . traffic alert, advise you turn right, heading 090 or climb to 8,000 immediately.*" Safety alerts are contingent on the capability of the controller to recognize unsafe situations. These situations often involve uncontrolled aircraft. Safety alerts are not automatic, although an ARTS function called **minimum safe altitude warning** (MSAW) will alert the controller when an aircraft is in unsafe proximity to terrain or obstructions. Another limiting factor is that the primary method of detecting unsafe proximity is through Mode C altitude readouts. Pilots of VFR aircraft may request MSAW monitoring if their aircraft are Mode C equipped.

AIRPORT RADAR SERVICE AREAS

All aircraft flying in an ARSA must be in two-way radio contact with ATC, and their operations must be in compliance with ATC clearances and instructions.

It is mandatory that VFR aircraft participate in ATC radar services within an ARSA. Radar service includes sequencing of all aircraft arriving at the primary airport. Traffic advisories and conflict resolution are provided for IFR and VFR traffic operating in the ARSA. This means that on the controller's screen, aircraft targets do not touch, and vertical separation is at least 500 feet. Between VFR aircraft, traffic advisories and safety alerts are provided. The same services are provided for aircraft operating within the outer area when two-way communications and radar contact are established.

ATC FACILITIES AT CONTROLLED AIRPORTS

Now that you have a basic understanding of transponders, radar, and associated VFR radar services, it's time to consider ATC facilities and services overall. To operate within a larger terminal area, you will need to be familiar with a number of ATC functions that are necessary to coordinate departures and arrivals at controlled airports.

In the following discussion, we will cover the various ATC functions in the normal order you would use them. Departure procedures for a large airport will be covered first. Following that, arrival procedures at the same airport will be described. The airport used in these examples is Phoenix Sky Harbor International Airport, which serves Phoenix, Arizona. This is the primary airport within the Phoenix TCA.

DEPARTURE PROCEDURES

The departure procedures for all controlled airports have certain similarities, since you must always receive permission from a controller to taxi to the active runway and subsequently be cleared for takeoff. You can expect more complex departure procedures at larger airports, because they usually have heavier traffic and require more ATC services. Before contacting ground control, for example, you usually listen to a recording which includes current airport weather and other information, such as the altimeter setting and active runway. The recording may direct you to contact clearance delivery so you can inform them of your destination or direction of flight. Clearance delivery may provide detailed departure instructions and then tell you to contact ground control.

AUTOMATIC TERMINAL INFORMATION SERVICE

ATIS is a noncontrol information service provided by ATC at selected high-activity terminal areas.

At busy airports, it would be difficult and time consuming for controllers to give every aircraft a separate airport advisory. To improve controller effectiveness and to reduce frequency congestion, **automatic terminal information service** (ATIS) is available. ATIS is prerecorded and broadcast on its own frequency. It includes routine, noncontrol information usually available in an airport advisory. At the larger airports, there may be one ATIS frequency for departing aircraft and another one for arriving aircraft.

ATIS, which is broadcast continuously, is updated whenever any official weather is received, regardless of content change. It is also updated whenever airport conditions change. ATIS broadcasts are labeled with successive letters from the phonetic alphabet, such as "Information Alpha" or "Information Bravo." When a new ATIS is broadcast, it is changed to the next letter.

Following the phonetic letter on the broadcast, the ATIS information will state the Zulu time of the current weather report, ceiling, visibility, obstructions to visibility, temperature, dewpoint (if available), magnetic wind direction and velocity, altimeter setting, instrument approach, and runway in use. It will also contain any other pertinent remarks relating to operations on or near the airport, like closed runways or temporary obstructions. If the weather is above a ceiling/sky condition of 5,000 feet and the visibility is five statute miles or more, inclusion of the ceiling/ sky condition, visibility, and obstructions to vision in the ATIS message is optional. You may find it helpful to write down the information that is contained in the ATIS. You may also listen to it as many times as necessary. Here is an example of an ATIS departure broadcast.

"Phoenix Sky Harbor International, Departure Information Delta, 1745 Zulu weather, measured ceiling 5,000 overcast, visibility 10, haze. Temperature 95, wind 280 at 8. Altimeter 29.92. Runways 26L and 26R in use. Notice to Airmen, there are numerous construction cranes in the vicinity of Sky Harbor Airport. Before taxi, all departures contact clearance delivery 118.1. VFR aircraft state destination. All IFR departures contact ground prior to pushback and engine start. Advise on initial contact you have Departure Information Delta."

CLEARANCE DELIVERY

After listening to ATIS, you will contact Phoenix Sky Harbor's **clearance delivery** on a frequency of 118.1 MHz. The clearance delivery facility is established at busy airports mainly for ATC to relay IFR clearances to departing IFR traffic. However, when the ATIS message so indicates, you should contact clearance delivery to inform them of your intentions. This allows departure controllers to improve traffic coordination.

There are several items that you should provide, including your N- number and aircraft type. You should also tell them you are VFR and have listened to the current ATIS. Most important, you should advise them of your destination or direction of flight. Your initial callup to clearance delivery should sound like this, *"Sky Harbor Clearance Delivery, Cherokee 8458R, a 140, with Departure Information Delta, VFR to the southwest."*

The controller will respond and give you a departure clearance, which includes a heading and an altitude, along with a transponder code and the departure control frequency. Your clearance may sound something like this, *"Cherokee 8458R, after departure, fly heading 250, climb and maintain 4,500 feet, squawk 3504, departure frequency will be 123.7, contact ground control 121.9 when ready to taxi."* You should write down the clearance, then read it back to the controller to ensure that you heard everything correctly.

GROUND CONTROL

After talking with clearance delivery, you will call ground control. **Ground control** is an ATC function for directing the movement of aircraft and other vehicles on the airport surface. Before leaving the parking area, you must receive a clearance from ground control to taxi to the active runway. When you call ground control, you should say, *"Phoenix Sky Harbor Ground, Cherokee 8458R, at the general aviation ramp, ready to taxi to runway 26R for departure."* The controller will probably respond with something like, *"Roger 58R, taxi to runway 26R."* When taxiing at unfamiliar airports, inform the controller that you are not familiar with the airport, and you will be given specific instructions.

A clearance to *"taxi to"* your assigned takeoff runway authorizes you to cross any runways (except the active runway) that may intersect your taxi route, but not to taxi onto the departure runway. If you are asked to *"hold short"* of a runway, stop at the hold lines preceding the runway, check for traffic, and continue only after cleared to do so. After taxiing to the departure runway and completing your pretakeoff checklists, taxi up to the hold line, switch to the control tower frequency, and say, *"Phoenix Sky Harbor Tower, Cherokee 8458R, ready for takeoff, runway 26R."* If the final approach path is clear, the controller will say, *"Cherokee 8458R, cleared for takeoff."* You should then make a final check for traffic as you taxi onto the runway for takeoff. You might also be asked to *". . . taxi into position and hold."* This means that you may position yourself on the runway for takeoff while waiting for another aircraft to clear the runway. You will be cleared to take off after the other aircraft is clear.

DEPARTURE CONTROL

The term *"radar contact"* is used by ATC to advise you that your aircraft has been identified and radar flight following will be provided until radar identification has been terminated.

Shortly after you take off, the tower controller will direct you to *". . . contact departure control, 123.7."* When you initiate contact with **departure control**, you can be very brief, since they are familiar with your departure clearance. *"Sky Harbor Departure Control, Cherokee 8458R, climbing through 2,100 for 4,500."* The controller may respond, *"Cherokee 8458R, radar contact, report reaching 4,500."* The term **radar contact** means your aircraft has been radar identified and flight following will be provided. **Flight following** means the controller is observing the progress of your aircraft while you provide your own navigation. Being in radar contact is no guarantee you have or will maintain separation from other aircraft. Radar service in the form of traffic advisories and other instructions normally is provided on a workload-permitting basis as you depart the area. If the controller's workload permits, this will continue until you are clear of the outer area as well. It is important to remember that the controller will not provide terrain and obstruction clearance just because your flight is in radar contact. During departure, terrain and obstruction clearance remains your responsibility until the controller begins to provide navigational guidance in the form of radar vectors. When you are clear of the TCA, the departure controller will inform you that *". . . radar service is terminated, frequency change is approved, squawk 1200."*

ARRIVAL PROCEDURES

When you return to Phoenix, listen to the current ATIS as soon as you can receive it. While you are still outside of the TCA, contact approach control over a designated visual checkpoint or other prominent landmark. **Approach control** is the ATC function that provides separation and sequencing of inbound aircraft. It also provides traffic advisories or safety alerts when necessary.

On your initial contact with approach control, let them know if you are planning other than a full-stop landing. This may determine how you are sequenced into the flow of traffic.

Approach control frequencies are published on sectional charts and broadcast over ATIS. At large terminals, expect different frequencies for approach control, depending on your arrival sector. A typical call to an approach facility might be: *"Phoenix Sky Harbor Approach, Cherokee 8458R, over Avondale, with Sierra, at 4,500 feet, landing."* Usually, approach control will provide a transponder code and ask you to *". . . squawk ident."* After radar contact is established, the controller may say, *". . . radar contact, 15 miles west of Phoenix Sky Harbor Airport, cleared to operate in the TCA, turn right, heading 080 for a left downwind to runway 26L."* The controller will tell you to *". . . contact tower on 118.7"* at the appropriate time. After contacting the tower, continue your approach and follow any other instructions given to you by the tower controller. At tower-controlled airports, you cannot land without permission. On your approach, the tower controller will tell you when you are *". . . cleared to land runway 26L."*

You can obtain approach control frequencies from sectional charts ATIS broadcasts, and the *Airport/Facility Directory*.

On initial contact, ATC will routinely provide you with wind, runway, and altimeter information unless you indicate you have received the ATIS or you use the phrase *"have numbers."* **Have numbers"** means you have already received wind, runway, and altimeter information so the controller does not need to repeat it. The phrase does not indicate you have received ATIS and should not be used for that purpose. There may be times when you want to stay in the traffic pattern to practice landings. You should advise approach control or the tower on initial contact that you will be *". . . remaining in the pattern."* The tower controller may ask you to *". . . make closed traffic . . . ."* This means you should remain in the traffic pattern unless you are otherwise instructed. It is helpful to the tower controllers if you report each time you are on the downwind leg. On your last time around the pattern, request a *"full-stop"* landing. During

The controller will delete wind, runway, and altimeter information on initial contacts when you use the phrase *"have numbers."*

your roll-out, the tower should instruct you to "*. . . turn left on the next available taxiway and contact ground, point niner.*" Ground control, on 121.9 MHz, will provide a taxi clearance to the parking area. You should not switch to ground control before the tower instructs you to do so.

LOST COMMUNICATIONS PROCEDURES

Code 7700 alerts radar controllers to an aircraft with a problem. It is the equivalent of a MAYDAY call on the radio.

As you are aware, establishing two-way radio communications with the control tower is required before you enter an airport traffic area. If your communications radios become inoperative, it is still possible to land at a tower-controlled airport by following the lost communication procedures. If you believe that your radio has failed, set your transponder to 7700 for one minute, then change it to 7600 for 15 minutes or until landing, whichever occurs first. Repeat the cycle, if necessary.

It is possible for only the transmitter or the receiver to fail. For instance, if you are fairly sure that only the receiver is inoperative, you should remain outside or above the airport traffic area until you have determined the direction and flow of traffic. Then, advise the tower of your aircraft type, position, altitude, intention to land, and request to be controlled by light signals. When you are approximately three to five miles away from the airport, advise the tower of your position and join the traffic pattern. From this point on, watch the tower for light signals. And, if you fly a complete pattern, self-announce your position when you are on downwind and/or turning base. [Figure 2-49]

If only your transmitter is not working, follow the same procedure that you would when the receiver is inoperative, but do not self-announce

COLOR AND TYPE OF SIGNAL	MEANING	
	On the Ground	In Flight
Steady Green	Cleared for takeoff	Cleared to land
Flashing Green	Cleared to taxi	Return for landing (to be followed by steady green at proper time) *(go Around)*
Steady Red	Stop	Give way to other aircraft and continue circling
Flashing Red	Taxi clear of landing area (runway) in use	Airport unsafe — do not land
Flashing White	Return to starting point on airport	(No assigned meaning)
Alternating Red and Green	Exercise extreme caution	Exercise extreme caution

Figure 2-49. Located in the cab of the control tower is a powerful light that controllers can use to direct light beams of various colors toward your aircraft. Each color or color combination has a specific meaning for an aircraft in flight, or on the airport surface.

your intentions. Monitor the airport frequency for landing or traffic information, and look for a light signal which may be addressed to your aircraft.

If neither your transmitter nor your receiver are working, you again need to remain outside or above the airport traffic area until you have determined the direction and flow of traffic. Then, join the airport traffic pattern and maintain visual contact with the tower to receive light signals.

If you receive light signals during the daytime, you should acknowledge tower transmission or light signals by rocking your wings. At night, acknowledge them by blinking your landing light or navigation lights to indicate that you understand the light signals and will comply with them.

If there is an uncontrolled airport nearby which may be more convenient to land at than a controlled airport, you may decide to land there instead. If so, you should also determine the landing direction by observing other traffic and the wind direction indicator prior to entering the pattern.

EMERGENCY PROCEDURES

An emergency can be either a distress or an urgency condition. The *Airman's Information Manual* defines **distress** as a condition of being threatened by serious and/or imminent danger and of requiring immediate assistance. An **urgency** situation is a condition of being concerned about safety and of requiring timely, but not immediate, assistance — a potential distress condition. If you become apprehensive about your safety for any reason, you should request assistance immediately.

The frequency of 121.5 MHz is used across the country for transmitting emergency messages. Although range is limited to line-of-sight, it is guarded by military towers, most civil towers, FSSs, and radar facilities. In a distress situation, use of the word "MAYDAY" commands radio silence on the frequency in use. When you hear the words "PAN-PAN," the urgency situation in progress has priority over all other communications and warns other stations not to interfere with these transmissions.

Radar-equipped ATC facilities can provide radar assistance and navigation service to you if you are within an area of radar coverage. Remember that an authorization to proceed in accordance with radar assistance does not constitute authorization for you to violate FARs. The pilot-in-command is still responsible for the airplane and for the safety of the flight.

One of the ways you can be identified easily on radar is to change your transponder to code 7700. This code triggers an alarm, or special indicator, at all control positions in radar facilities. If you are not sure whether

Emergency Message	
Distress or Urgency	*"MAYDAY, MAYDAY, MAYDAY (or PAN-PAN, PAN-PAN, PAN-PAN),*
Name of station addressed	*Denver Radio,*
Identification and type of aircraft	*5674R Cessna 172,*
Nature of distress or urgency	*trapped above overcast,*
Weather	*MVFR,*
Your intentions and request	*request radar vectors to nearest VFR airport,*
Present position and heading	*Newberg VOR, heading 253°,*
Altitude	*6,500,*
Fuel remaining in hours and minutes	*estimate 30 minutes fuel remaining,*
Number of people aboard	*three people aboard,*
Any other useful information	*Squawking 7700."*

Figure 2-50. If you are in distress, your initial communication and any subsequent transmissions should begin with the word *"MAYDAY"* repeated three times. *"PAN-PAN"* should be used in the same manner for an urgency situation. Following this, you need to provide important information about your situation and the assistance you would like to have.

you are within radar coverage, go ahead and squawk 7700, anyway. When you are under radar control already, you usually are in radio contact with ATC. In this case, you should continue squawking the code assigned, unless instructed otherwise. [Figure 2-50]

A VHF transmitter/receiver is the only equipment requried to use VHF/DF facilities.

As we mentioned before, direction finding equipment has been used for many years to locate lost aircraft or to guide aircraft to areas of good weather. The only aircraft equipment required for VHF direction finding assistance is an operable VHF transmitter and receiver. At most DF-equipped airports, DF instrument approaches may be given to aircraft in a distress or urgency situation. Experience has shown that most emergencies requiring DF assistance involve pilots with little flight experience. These approaches are for emergency use only and will not be issued in IFR conditions unless a distress or urgency situation has been declared. Practice DF approaches may be given in VFR weather conditions if they are requested.

Another device that provides emergency aid is the **emergency locator transmitter** (ELT), which is required for most general aviation airplanes. Various types of ELTs have been developed as a means of locating downed aircraft. These electronic, battery-operated transmitters emit a distinctive audio tone on 121.5 MHz. If "armed" and subjected to crash-generated forces, they are designed to activate automatically. The transmitters should operate continuously for at least 48 hours, over a wide range of temperatures. A properly installed and maintained ELT can expedite search and rescue operations and save lives.

As with other equipment, ELTs must be tested and maintained according to the manufacturer's instructions. Required maintenance includes replacing or recharging the battery (for a rechargeable battery) after one-half of the battery's useful life. You should conduct ELT testing only during the first five minutes after the hour, and for no longer than three audible sweeps. Airborne tests of ELTs are not allowed.

An ELT battery must be replaced or recharged (if rechargeable) after one-half its useful life.

Be careful that you do not accidentally activate your ELT in the air or while you are handling it on the ground. Accidental or unauthorized activation generates the emergency signal, leading to expensive and frustrating searches. A false ELT signal can interfere with genuine emergency transmissions and hinder or prevent the timely location of crash sites. Many cases of activation have occurred unintentionally as a result of aerobatics, hard landings, movement by ground crews, and aircraft maintenance. ELT false alarms can be minimized by monitoring 121.5 MHz during flight, prior to engine shut down, and after maintenance.

You are also encouraged to monitor 121.5 MHz while you are flying to assist in identifying possible emergency ELT transmissions. If you do hear an ELT, report your position to the nearest ATC facility the first and last time you hear the signal. Also report your position and cruising altitude at maximum signal strength.

EMERGENCY 121.5

Search and rescue (SAR) is a lifesaving service provided through the combined efforts of federal and state agencies. ARTCCs and FSSs will alert the SAR system when information is received from any source that an aircraft is in difficulty, overdue, or missing. Flight plan information is invaluable to SAR forces for search planning and for executing search efforts. For more information on flight plans, SAR operations, or other emergency procedures refer to the *Airman's Information Manual*.

CHECKLIST ━━━━━━━━━━━━━━

After reading this section, you should have a basic understanding of:

✓ **Primary radar** — How it works and what its limitations are.

✓ **Secondary surveillance radar** — What advantages it has, the additional components needed, and how they operate.

✓ **Transponders** — How they operate, how to select functions and codes, and what code is used for VFR operations.

✓ **Airport surveillance radar** — Where it is used and what type of services it provides.

✓ **ARTS-III** — What the advantages of this automated system are, what equipment is required, and what information it gives the controller.

✓

Air route surveillance radar — What the radar does and how it complements air route traffic control center operations.

✓ **Terminal radar service** — What radar programs are available for VFR aircraft and what types of service they provide.

✓ **Automatic terminal information service** — What ATIS is, what information it provides, and when you will use it.

✓ **Clearance delivery** — What type of service it is and why its use is important.

✓ **Ground control** — When you need clearance to taxi and the types of clearances you can obtain.

✓ **Departure control** — When you will need to contact them and what services they can provide.

✓ **Approach control** — When you should initiate contact and what services they can provide.

✓ **Lost communication procedures** — What procedures you should follow, the transponder codes to use, and what the light gun signals mean.

✓ **Emergency procedures** — Who to talk to on what frequency and what transponder code to use.

CHAPTER 3

AIRCRAFT SYSTEMS AND PERFORMANCE

INTRODUCTION

All airplanes, including the one you will use for your initial training, are designed and equipped to provide safe and reliable service under a wide variety of conditions. In order to do this, airplanes are equipped with a number of instruments and systems that allow you to control and monitor their performance. This chapter discusses the instruments and systems common to most small airplanes. We begin by looking at the flight instruments. Then, we continue with the engine and its supporting systems, including the propeller. Next, you learn about the airplane's electrical and fuel systems. Finally, we conclude with two sections on the calculation of performance information, such as takeoff and landing distances, and the determination of proper airplane loading.

PITOT-STATIC INSTRUMENTS

Since an airplane operates in a three-dimensional atmosphere, you need several special instruments to provide you with necessary flight information. One group of these instruments operates on the principle of pressure differential to provide you with your speed, rate of climb or descent, and altitude. This group is referred to as the pitot-static instruments. [Figure 3-1]

EFFECTS OF ATMOSPHERIC CONDITIONS

Since pressure differential is so important in the operation of the pitot-static instruments, let's consider some basic information about atmospheric pressure and how it varies. The atmosphere is heavier near the earth's surface than it is at higher levels. In fact, at sea level, air exerts an average pressure of 14.7 pounds per square inch (p.s.i.). At 18,000 feet, the pressure decreases to approximately half that much. As pressure

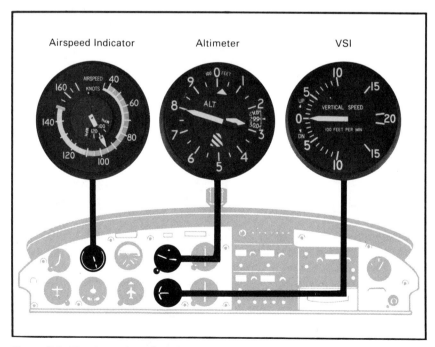

Figure 3-1. The three pitot-static instruments are the airspeed indicator, the altimeter, and the vertical speed indicator (VSI). The other instruments and gauges will be discussed later.

decreases, air density also decreases. In addition, since air expands when it is heated, warm air is less dense than cold air. This means that air density varies with changes in both pressure and temperature. Humidity also affects the density of the air, but to a lesser degree. Humid air is less dense than dry air.

Think of how often these conditions change. Variations are most apparent between seasons, and hourly changes routinely occur. This continuous process of change is one of the most common characteristics of the atmosphere.

INTERNATIONAL STANDARD ATMOSPHERE

To provide a common reference for temperature and pressure, the **International Standard Atmosphere** (ISA) has been established. These standard conditions are the basis for certain flight instruments and most airplane performance data. At sea level, the standard atmosphere consists of a barometric pressure of 29.92 in. Hg (1013.2 mb.) and a temperature of 15°C (59°F). Since both of these values change with altitude, **standard lapse rates** have been established to help you calculate the temperatures and pressures you can anticipate at various altitudes. In the lower atmosphere, the standard pressure lapse rate for each 1,000 feet of altitude change is approximately 1.00 in. Hg, and the standard temperature lapse rate is 2°C (3.5°F). Pressure and temperature normally decrease as altitude increases. For example, the approximate standard pressure and temperature at 2,000 feet MSL are 27.92 in. Hg (29.92 - 2.00) and 11°C (15°C - 4°C).

ISA at sea level equals 29.92 in. Hg, or 1013.2 millibars, and has a temperature of 15°C. Temperature decreases approximately 2°C for each 1,000-foot increase in altitude.

PITOT-STATIC SYSTEM

Pressure-sensitive devices convert pressure supplied by the pitot-static system to instrument indications in the cockpit. The airspeed indicator, altimeter, and vertical speed indicator all use static pressure, but only the airspeed indicator uses pitot pressure.

The static system provides surrounding, or ambient, air pressure to the airspeed indicator, altimeter, and VSI.

Pitot pressure, also called **impact** or **ram** air pressure, is supplied by the pitot tube or head. The **pitot tube** is usually mounted on the wing or on the nose section, so the opening is exposed to the relative wind. This arrangement allows ram air pressure to enter the pitot tube before it is affected by the airplane's structure. Since the pitot tube opening faces forward, an increase in speed increases ram air pressure.

The pitot system provides impact, or ram, air pressure to the airspeed indicator.

Static pressure enters the pitot-static system through a **static port,** which is located in an area of relatively undisturbed air. It is common to have the static port flush-mounted on the side of the fuselage, or it may be com-

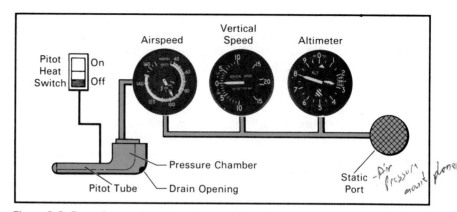

Figure 3-2. Ram air pressure enters the system through a hole in the forward end of the pitot tube. Electrical heating elements may be installed to remove ice from the pitot head, and a drain opening normally is located near the aft portion of the pressure chamber. Ram air pressure is supplied only to the airspeed indicator, while static pressure is used by all three instruments.

bined with the pitot tube. An airplane may have one or two static ports, depending on its design. For simplicity, this discussion references a single port. [Figure 3-2]

AIRSPEED INDICATOR

The airspeed indicator measures the difference between impact and static air pressure and displays the result as an airspeed. The colored arcs denote safe operating ranges for various flight conditions.

The airspeed indicator displays the speed of your airplane through the air by comparing ram air pressure with static air pressure — the greater the differential, the greater the speed. The airspeed indicator is divided into color-coded arcs that define speed ranges for different phases of flight. If you know the significance of each color code, you can easily identify the safe speed ranges for use of flaps, for normal operations, for smooth-air operations (caution range), and for maximum speed. [Figure 3-3]

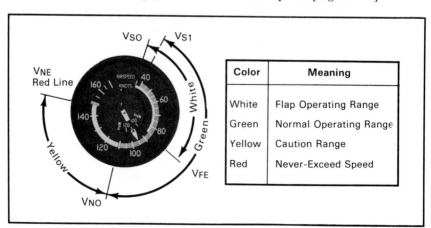

Color	Meaning
White	Flap Operating Range
Green	Normal Operating Range
Yellow	Caution Range
Red	Never-Exceed Speed

Figure 3-3. Besides delineating various speed ranges, the boundaries of the color-coded arcs also identify airspeed limitations.

AIRSPEED LIMITATIONS

Several airspeed limitations, called **V-speeds,** are shown on the airspeed indicator. They are V_{S0}, V_{S1}, V_{FE}, V_{NO}, and V_{NE}. **V_{S0}** is defined as the stalling speed or the minimum steady flight speed in the landing configuration. In small airplanes, this is the power-off stall speed at the maximum landing weight in the landing configuration (gear and flaps down). **V_{S1}** is defined as the stalling speed or the minimum steady flight speed obtained in a specified configuration. For small airplanes, this is the power-off stall speed at the maximum takeoff weight in the clean configuration (gear up, if retractable, and flaps up). You should check the POH for specific information on your airplane. **V_{FE}** indicates the maximum speed with the flaps extended, while **V_{NO}** is the maximum structural cruising speed. Finally, **V_{NE}** denotes the never-exceed speed.

> V-speeds denote important airspeed limitations.

The lower limit of the **white arc** is V_{S0}, and the upper limit is V_{FE}. This arc is commonly referred to as the flap operating range, since its lower limit represents the full flap stall speed and its upper limit provides the maximum flap speed. You will usually fly your approaches and landings at speeds within the white arc. The lower limit of the **green arc** is V_{S1}, and the upper limit is V_{NO}. This is the normal operating range of the airplane. V_{NO} is considered to be the **maximum structural cruising speed**. You should not exceed it except in smooth air. Most of your flying will occur within this range. The **yellow arc**, or caution range, is bounded by V_{NO} and V_{NE}. You may fly within this range only in smooth air and, then, only with caution. Finally, the **red line** is V_{NE}, or the never-exceed speed. Operating above this speed may result in damage or structural failure.

> The white arc is the flap operating range, the green arc is for normal operations, the yellow arc is the caution range, and the red line marks the never-exceed speed.

Although the airspeed indicator presents important airspeed limitations, not all V-speeds are shown. For example, one very important speed not displayed is **V_A,** or maneuvering speed. This represents the maximum speed at which you can stall an airplane or apply full and abrupt control movement without the possibility of causing structural damage. It also represents the maximum speed that you can safely use during turbulent flight conditions. V_A is included in the pilot's operating handbook and is usually on a placard in the cockpit. You should be aware that V_A changes at different aircraft weights for some airplanes. For instance, V_A may be 100 knots when an airplane is heavily loaded and 90 knots when the load is light.

> V_A is the maximum speed for full and abrupt use of the controls without risk of structural damage. It also is the maximum speed for flight in turbulent conditions.

Two additional speeds of importance to you when you are flying a retractable-gear airplane are V_{LO} and V_{LE}. **V_{LO}** is the maximum speed you can safely use while raising or lowering the landing gear. **V_{LE}** is the maximum speed you can safely use with the landing gear in a fully extended position. These speeds are not displayed on the airspeed indicator.

> V_{LO} is the maximum landing gear operating speed, while V_{LE} is the maximum gear extended speed.

Now that you are familiar with airspeed limitations, let's consider the four types of speed you will deal with during flight. They are indicated airspeed, calibrated airspeed, true airspeed, and groundspeed.

As altitude increases, the indicated airspeed at which a given airplane stalls in a specific configuration remains the same.

Indicated airspeed (IAS) is the reading you get directly from the airspeed indicator. Since the airspeed indicator is calibrated to indicate true airspeed under standard sea level conditions, IAS does not reflect variations in air density as you climb to higher altitudes. For example, your indicated stall speed remains the same even though your true airspeed normally increases with altitude. IAS also is uncorrected for installation (position) and instrument errors.

CAS is IAS corrected for installation and instrument errors.

Calibrated airspeed (CAS) is indicated airspeed corrected for installation and instrument errors. Although attempts are made to minimize these errors, it is not possible to eliminate them entirely throughout the full range of operating speeds, weights, and flap settings. To determine calibrated airspeed, read indicated airspeed and then correct it by using the chart or table in the pilot's operating handbook. *Adjusted for instrument error*

TAS is the actual speed of your airplane through the air.

True airspeed (TAS) represents the true speed of your airplane through the air. It is calibrated airspeed corrected for altitude and nonstandard temperature. As altitude or air temperature increase, the density of the air decreases. For a given IAS, this means TAS increases with altitude.

Groundspeed is your actual speed over the ground.

Groundspeed (GS) represents the actual speed of your airplane over the ground. It is true airspeed adjusted for wind. A headwind decreases groundspeed, while a tailwind increases it.

ALTIMETER

The altimeter indicates your flight altitude by measuring ambient air pressure.

The altimeter senses pressure changes and displays altitude in feet. It usually has three pointers, or hands, to indicate the altitude. The longest pointer shows hundreds of feet, the middle-sized pointer indicates thousands of feet, and the shortest pointer shows tens of thousands of feet. It also has an adjustable barometric scale for changes in pressure. [Figure 3-4]

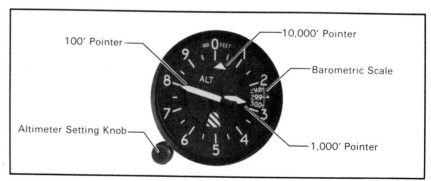

Figure 3-4. This altimeter shows an altitude of 2,800 feet. The barometric scale in the window on the right is set at 29.90 inches of mercury.

Although the altimeter is one of your key flight instruments, it has certain limitations. The basis of its calibration is the International Standard Atmosphere, where pressure, temperature, and lapse rates have fixed values; however, actual atmospheric conditions seldom match these standard values. In addition, local pressure readings within a given area normally change over a period of time, and pressure frequently changes as you fly from one airport to another. As a result, altimeter indications are subject to errors. The extent of the errors depends on how much the pressure, temperature, and lapse rates deviate from standard, as well as how recently you have reset your altimeter.

The best way to minimize altimeter errors is to obtain frequent updated altimeter settings. Then, adjust the barometric scale in the altimeter setting window by turning the knob. In most cases, you use the current altimeter setting of the nearest reporting station along your route of flight. While you can minimize altimeter errors, you cannot entirely eliminate the common inaccuracies caused by nonstandard atmospheric conditions.

A current altimeter setting for the area you are flying over is essential for reliable altitude indications.

ALTITUDE DEFINITIONS

The altimeter measures **altitude**, which is the vertical elevation of an object above a given reference point. The reference may be the surface of the earth, sea level, or some other point. There are several different types of altitude, depending on the reference point used. The five most common types are: indicated, pressure, density, true, and absolute.

Indicated altitude is the altitude you read directly from the altimeter when it is correctly adjusted to the local altimeter setting. This is the altitude you will use most often during flight.

Pressure altitude is displayed when you adjust the altimeter to the standard sea level atmospheric pressure of 29.92 in. Hg. Pressure altitude is used with existing temperature to compute density altitude and other values. Normally, flight computers are used to make these determinations. Flight computers are discussed in Chapter 6.

Density altitude is pressure altitude corrected for nonstandard temperature. It is really a theoretical value which is computed from existing temperature, and it is an important factor in determining airplane performance. Performance charts for many older aircraft are based on density altitude. When density altitude is high (temperatures above standard), aircraft performance is reduced.

True altitude is the actual height of an object above mean sea level. On aeronautical charts, the elevation figures for fixed objects, such as airports, towers, and TV antennas, are true altitudes. You can calculate approximate true altitude with a flight computer, but the computation is based on the assumption that pressure and temperature lapse rates

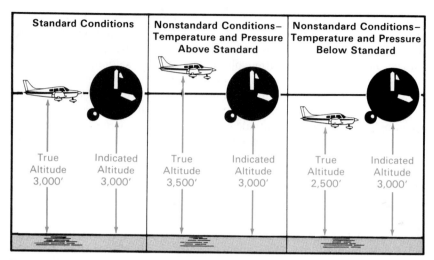

Figure 3-5. During flight, indicated and true altitude are equal only in standard atmospheric conditions. When nonstandard conditions exist, true altitude may be higher or lower than indicated altitude. When atmospheric pressure or temperature is higher than standard, your true altitude is higher than your indicated altitude. When pressure is lower or temperature is colder than standard, your true altitude is lower than your indicated altitude.

match ISA values. Normally, these lapse rates vary from those in a perfectly standard atmosphere. In two cases, however, true and indicated altitude are equal. One occurs during flight, when you have the correct altimeter setting and atmospheric conditions match ISA values. The other occurs on the ground. When you set the altimeter to the local pressure setting, it indicates the field elevation, which is a true altitude. [Figure 3-5]

Absolute altitude is the actual height of the airplane above the earth's surface over which it is flying. This altitude varies with the height of the airplane, as well as the height of the surface. Absolute altitude is commonly referred to as height above ground level (AGL). [Figure 3-6]

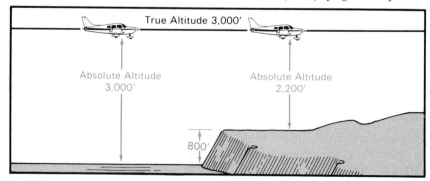

Figure 3-6. Your absolute altitude can change rapidly as you pass over varying terrain elevations.

ALTIMETER ERRORS

The most common altimeter error is also the easiest to correct. It occurs when you fail to keep the altimeter set to the local altimeter setting. For example, assume your altimeter is set to 30.00 in. Hg. and you are flying at a constant altitude of 3,500 feet. If you fly into an area where atmospheric pressure is 29.50 in. Hg, the altimeter will sense this decrease in pressure as an increase in altitude and will display a higher reading. Your response will be to lower the nose of the airplane and descend to maintain your "desired" altitude. [Figure 3-7]

Since you know that atmospheric pressure decreases approximately one inch of mercury for each 1,000 feet of altitude change, you can compute the error. In this example, the altimeter setting decreased from 30.00 to 29.50, a change of 0.50 in. Hg. Since one inch equals 1,000 feet, 0.50 inches equals 500 feet (1000 x .50 + 500). Next, you need to know if you are flying higher or lower than the desired altitude. Since you are flying from an area of higher pressure to an area of lower pressure, your indicated altitude will result in a lower altitude than you intended. A good memory aid is, "When flying from high to low or hot to cold, look out below." The accuracy of altimeters is affected by extreme variations from standard atmospheric pressure and temperature conditions. The *Airman's Information Manual* (AIM) emphasizes the need to exercise caution during flight in conditions with extremely low pressure (below 28.00 in. Hg) or unusually high pressure (above 31.00 in. Hg).

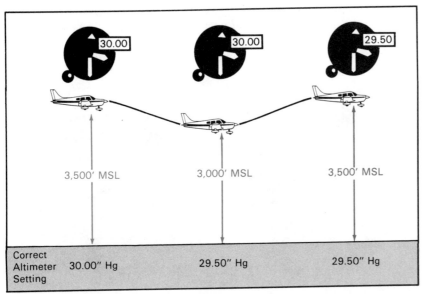

Figure 3-7. If you fly from an area of higher pressure to an area of lower pressure without resetting your altimeter, you will fly at a lower altitude than you had intended. If you reset the altimeter to the correct setting, you will maintain the desired altitude.

VERTICAL SPEED INDICATOR

The VSI measures the change in ambient air pressure as the aircraft climbs or descends. It displays the change as a rate of climb or descent in feet per minute.

The vertical speed indicator (VSI), which sometimes is called a vertical velocity indicator (VVI), is connected to the static system. This instrument measures how fast the ambient air pressure is increasing or decreasing when the aircraft climbs or descends. It then displays the air pressure changes as a rate of climb or descent in feet per minute. [Figure 3-8]

The VSI is capable of displaying two different types of information. One is called trend, and the other is called rate. **Trend** information shows you an immediate indication of an increase or decrease in the airplane's rate of climb or descent. **Rate** information shows you a stabilized rate of change. For example, if you are maintaining a steady 500 f.p.m. climb, and you lower the nose slightly, the VSI will immediately sense this change and display a decrease in the rate of climb. This first indication is called the trend. After a period of six to nine seconds, the VSI will stabilize and display the new rate of climb, which, in this example, would be something less than 500 f.p.m.

BLOCKAGE OF THE PITOT-STATIC SYSTEM

Although pitot-static instruments have some accuracy limitations, usually they are very reliable. Gross errors almost always indicate blockage of the pitot tube, the static port, or both. Blockage may be caused by moisture (including ice), dirt, or even insects.

During preflight, you should make sure the pitot tube cover is removed. Then, check the pitot and static port openings. If they are clogged, the openings should be cleaned by a certificated mechanic. It is also possible for the pitot tube to become blocked during flight through visible moisture when temperatures are near the freezing level. If you are flying in

Figure 3-8. The vertical speed indicator tells you how fast you are climbing or descending. The VSI on the left shows a 300 f.p.m. descent, while the VSI on the right reflects a 300 f.p.m. climb.

visible moisture and your airplane is equipped with pitot heat, you should turn it on to prevent pitot tube icing.

A clogged pitot tube only affects the accuracy of the airspeed indicator, but blockage of the static port affects the altimeter, vertical speed, and airspeed indicators. If the static system clogs and the airplane is equipped with an alternate static source, you should open the alternate source. In most cases, the alternate source is vented inside the cockpit where static pressure is lower than outside static pressure. As a result, its use causes slight errors in pitot-static instrument indications. For example, the airspeed and the altimeter read higher than normal and the vertical speed indicator momentarily shows a climb. Check your pilot's operating handbook for information on use of the alternate static source.

Blockage of the pitot tube affects only the airspeed indicator, but a clogged static system affects all three pitot-static instruments.

Now consider the specific errors caused by pitot-static system blockages, beginning with the airspeed indicator. If the pitot tube clogs and its associated drain hole remains clear, ram air will no longer be able to enter the pitot system. Air already in the system will vent through the drain hole, and the remaining pressure will drop to ambient (outside) air pressure. Under these circumstances, the airspeed indicator reading decreases to zero, because the airspeed indicator senses no difference between ram and static air pressure. In other words, the airspeed indicator acts as if the airplane is stationary on the ramp. The apparent loss of airspeed is not usually instantaneous. Instead, the airspeed generally drops slowly to zero.

If the pitot tube is blocked and its drain hole remains open, the airspeed reading will drop to zero.

If both the pitot tube and the drain hole become clogged in flight, ram air will no longer enter the pitot system, and air in the system will be trapped. This means that no change in ram air pressure occurs as actual airspeed changes; therefore, no change is apparent on the airspeed indicator. If the static port remains clear, however, the airspeed changes with altitude.

If both the pitot tube and the drain hole clog, the airspeed indicator will react like an altimeter.

As altitude increases above the level where the pitot and drain hole clogged, static pressure decreases. This causes an apparent increase in the ram air pressure relative to static pressure, so the airspeed indicator shows an increase in speed. The opposite effect occurs when the airplane descends below the altitude where the blockages occurred.

If the static port clogs and the pitot tube remains clear, the airspeed indicator continues to operate, but it is inaccurate. Airspeed indications are slower than the actual speed when the airplane is operated above the altitude where the static ports clogged. This is because the trapped static pressure is higher than normal for that altitude. Conversely, the airspeed indicates faster than the correct value when you are operating at a lower altitude. This results because the trapped static pressure is lower than normal for that altitude. Remember, if you suspect the static ports are

If the static port clogs, the indicated airspeed increases as the airplane descends and decreases when it climbs.

clogged, you can switch to the alternate static system, if one is available. A blockage of the static system also affects the altimeter, which operates on ambient air pressure. In this case, air pressure in the system will not change and neither will your indicated altitude.

Finally, since the vertical speed indicator is connected to the static system, any blockage of the static system also affects the VSI. When the static system is completely blocked, the VSI continually indicates zero.

CHECKLIST

After studying this section, you should have a basic understanding of:

✓   **International Standard Atmosphere (ISA)** — What ISA values at sea level are and what the standard temperature and pressure lapse rates are.

✓   **Pitot-static system** — How the pitot-static system operates and what instruments are affected.

✓   **Airspeed indicator** — How the airspeed indicator functions; what the differences are between IAS, CAS, TAS, and GS; what V-speeds are; and what the airspeed indicator color codings mean.

✓   **Altimeter** — How the altimeter functions and what the differences are between indicated, pressure, density, true, and absolute altitudes.

✓   **Vertical speed indicator** — How the VSI functions and what the differences are between trend and rate indications.

GYROSCOPIC INSTRUMENTS

In the previous section, you were introduced to the pitot-static instruments. The next group of instruments uses gyroscopic principles to provide you with a pictorial view of the airplane's rate of turn, attitude, and heading. These three instruments are the turn coordinator, attitude indicator, and heading indicator. A fourth instrument, the magnetic compass, is not a gyroscope, but it is used in conjunction with the heading indicator. [Figure 3-9]

Gyroscopic instruments have unique operating principles and power sources. Let's begin by briefly discussing two fundamental concepts that apply to gyroscopes — rigidity in space and precession.

RIGIDITY IN SPACE

Any rotating body exhibits certain gyroscopic properties. One of these properties — **rigidity in space** — means that once a gyroscope is spinning, it tends to remain in a fixed position in space and resists external

A spinning mass tends to remain in a fixed position.

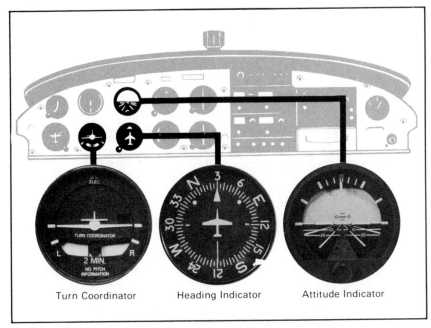

| Turn Coordinator | Heading Indicator | Attitude Indicator |

Figure 3-9. As you climb, descend, or turn, you can cross-check the gyroscopic instruments to confirm your attitude and direction.

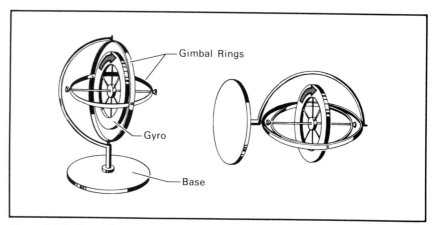

Figure 3-10. Regardless of the position of its base, a gyro tends to remain rigid in space, with its axis of rotation pointed in a constant direction.

forces applied to it. A gyro which is freely, or universally, mounted is set on gimbal rings, which allow the gyro to rotate freely in any direction. [Figure 3-10]

Some gyros, such as those used in turn indicators and some heading indicators, have semirigid mountings and use only two gimbal rings. These gyros have only two planes of rotation.

PRECESSION

A force applied to a gyroscope causes a reaction in the direction of rotation, 90° ahead of the point where the force was actually applied.

Another characteristic of the gyro is **precession,** which is the tilting or turning of a gyro in response to pressure. Unfortunately, it is not possible to mount a gyro in a frictionless environment. A small force is applied to the gyro whenever the airplane changes direction. The reaction to this force occurs in the direction of rotation, approximately 90° ahead of the point where the force was applied. This causes the slow drifting and minor erroneous indications in the gyro instruments. We discussed gyroscopic precession in Chapter 1, with respect to the spinning propeller.

SOURCES OF POWER

The turn coordinator usually is driven by electrical power, while the attitude and heading indicators generally use a vacuum system.

Gyroscopes may be operated either by electrical power or by a vacuum (suction) system. Most small airplanes use a combination of both systems to provide a backup in case one system fails. The turn coordinator typically uses electrical power and may incorporate a small warning flag to indicate a loss of power. The vacuum system includes an engine-driven vacuum pump which powers the attitude and heading indicators. [Figure 3-11]

It is important for you to monitor vacuum pressure during flight, because the attitude and heading indicators may not provide reliable information when suction pressure is low. The vacuum or suction gauge generally is

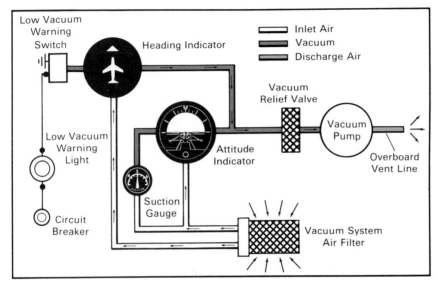

Figure 3-11. Air is first drawn into the vacuum system through a filter assembly. It then moves through the attitude and heading indicators where it causes the gyros to spin. After that, it continues to the vacuum pump where it is expelled. A relief valve prevents the vacuum pressure or suction from exceeding prescribed limits.

marked to indicate the acceptable range. Some airplanes are equipped with a vacuum warning light which illuminates when the vacuum pressure drops below the acceptable level. These airplanes also may be equipped with an electrically driven, standby vacuum pump.

TURN COORDINATOR

The turn coordinator senses yaw and roll movement about the vertical and longitudinal axes. It has two main elements — a miniature airplane to indicate the rate of turn and an inclinometer to indicate coordinated flight. [Figure 3-12]

The turn coordinator shows yaw and roll movement about the vertical and longitudinal axes.

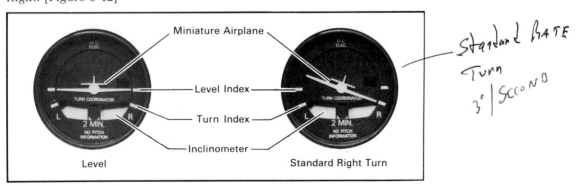

Figure 3-12. When the miniature airplane is level, as shown on the left, the airplane is neither turning nor rolling. When you establish a bank, the miniature airplane also banks. The indicator on the right shows a turn to the right. If the ball is centered in the inclinometer, the turn is coordinated.

In a standard-rate turn, your airplane will complete a 360° turn in two minutes.

When you are rolling into or out of a turn, the miniature airplane banks in the direction the airplane is rolled. A rapid roll rate causes the miniature airplane to bank more steeply than a slow roll rate. You can use the turn coordinator to establish and maintain a **standard-rate turn** by aligning the wing of the miniature airplane with the turn index. This means the turning rate is three degrees per second. At this rate, you will complete a 360° turn in two minutes. You should remember that the miniature airplane of the turn coordinator does not indicate angle of bank. It only indicates the rate at which the airplane is rolled into or out of a turn. After the turn is stabilized, it indicates the rate of the turn itself.

The inclinometer is used to establish and maintain coordinated flight.

The inclinometer is another important part of the turn coordinator. It consists of a liquid-filled, curved tube with a ball inside. The ball actually is a balance indicator, which is used to determine coordinated use of aileron and rudder.

During coordinated, straight-and-level flight, the force of gravity causes the ball to rest in the lowest part of the tube, centered between the reference lines. During a coordinated turn, forces are balanced, which also causes the ball to remain centered in the tube. If forces are unbalanced, such as during a slip or skid, the ball moves away from the center of the tube.

The position of the ball defines the quality of the turn, or whether you have used the correct angle of bank for the rate of turn. In a **slip**, the rate of turn is too slow for the angle of bank, and the ball moves to the inside of the turn. In a **skid**, the rate of turn is too great for the angle of bank, and the ball moves to the outside of the turn.

You maintain coordinated flight by keeping the ball centered. If the ball is not centered, you usually apply enough rudder pressure to center it. To do this, you apply rudder pressure on the side where the ball is deflected. The simple rule, "Step on the ball," may help you remember which rudder pedal to depress. You also may vary the angle of bank to help restore coordinated flight from a slip or skid. To correct for a slip, you should decrease bank and/or increase the rate of turn. To correct for a skid, increase the bank and/or decrease the rate of turn.

Besides maintaining coordination in turns, the inclinometer helps you recognize the need to compensate for engine torque and adverse yaw. For example, when you enter a climb, the nose of the airplane tends to move to the left due to P-factor. This is indicated by the ball of the turn coordinator moving to the right of center. When this occurs, you know the airplane is in uncoordinated flight. To correct this condition, "Step on the ball." In this case, you must depress the right rudder pedal until the ball centers; then, you must maintain sufficient rudder pressure to keep it centered.

ATTITUDE INDICATOR

The attitude indicator is a vacuum-powered instrument which senses pitching and rolling movements about the airplane's lateral and longitudinal axes. It provides you with a substitute horizon, and it is especially useful when the natural horizon is obscured by clouds, reduced visibility, or darkness. The attitude indicator is the only flight instrument that provides both pitch and bank information. It uses an artificial horizon and miniature airplane to depict the position of your airplane. Since it is an extremely precise instrument, you can detect very small changes in pitch and bank. [Figure 3-13]

The attitude indicator displays pitch and roll movement about the lateral and longitudinal axes.

Modern attitude indicators normally are very reliable instruments as long as the correct vacuum pressure is maintained. Some function properly during 360° of roll or 85° of pitch. Gyros in older indicators, however, will "tumble" from their plane of rotation beyond approximately 100° of bank or beyond 60° of pitch.

Although the attitude indicator is a reliable flight instrument, you should remember to cross-check it against outside visual references and other flight instruments. Occasionally, attitude indicators fail gradually without providing obvious warning signals.

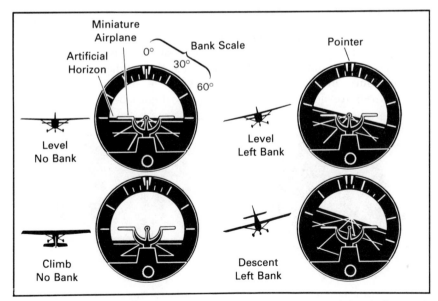

Figure 3-13. The attitude indicator presents you with a view of the airplane as it would appear from an aft position. Prior to flight, you should set the miniature airplane symbol so that it is level with the horizon bar. The angle of bank is shown both pictorially by the relationship of the miniature aircraft to the deflected horizon bar and by the alignment of the pointer with the banking scale at the top of the instrument. Pitch is indicated by the position of the "nose," or center, of the miniature airplane with respect to the horizon bar.

HEADING INDICATOR

The heading indicator
displays yaw movement
about the vertical axis.

The heading indicator, also called a directional gyro (DG), is a vacuum-powered instrument which senses yaw movement of the airplane about the vertical axis. It displays headings based on a 360° azimuth, with the final zero omitted. In other words, "6" indicates 60°, "21" indicates 210°, and so on. When properly set, it is your primary source of heading information. Heading indicators in most training airplanes are referred to as "free" gyros. This means they have no automatic, north-seeking system built into them.

Due to precession, the
heading indicator must
be aligned periodically
with the magnetic com-
pass.

Due to internal friction within the gyroscope, precession is common in heading indicators. Precession causes the selected heading to drift from the set value. For this reason, you must regularly realign the indicator with the magnetic compass and consider the deviation shown on the compass correction card. [Figure 3-14]

Like attitude indicators, the vacuum-powered heading indicator has operating limits in both pitch and roll. If you exceed these limits, the gyro may tumble, which may damage the instrument. If the indicator has tumbled, you must reset it by aligning it with a known heading or with a stabilized indication from the magnetic compass.

MAGNETIC COMPASS

The magnetic compass
is the only direction seeking instrument in most
light airplanes.

The magnetic compass was one of the first instruments to be installed in an airplane, and it is still the only direction seeking instrument in many airplanes. If you understand its limitations, the magnetic compass is a reliable source of heading information. It is a self-contained unit which does not require electrical or suction power. [Figure 3-15]

Figure 3-14. You should align the heading indicator with the magnetic compass before flight and check it at 15-minute intervals during flight. When you do an in-flight alignment, be certain you are in straight-and-level, unaccelerated flight, with the magnetic compass showing a steady indication.

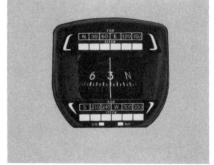

Figure 3-15. The compass doesn't work on gyroscopic principles, but you will use it frequently to help correct for gyroscopic precession in the heading indicator. To use it properly, you need to understand some of the unique characteristics of magnetism.

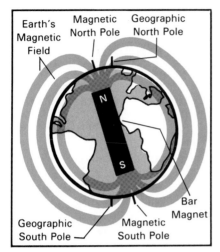

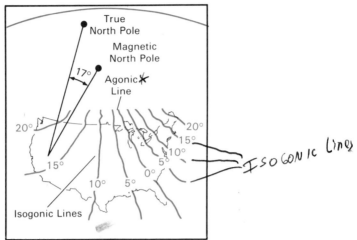

Figure 3-16. The geographic north and south poles form the axis for the earth's rotation. These positions are also referred to as true north and south. Another axis is formed by the magnetic north and south poles, which are referred to as magnetic north and south. A freely mounted bar magnet will align itself with the magnetic axis formed by the north/south magnetic field of the earth.

Figure 3-17. Variation at this point in the western United States is 17°. Since the magnetic north pole is located to the east of the true north pole in relation to this point, the variation is easterly. When the magnetic pole falls to the west of the true pole, variation is westerly. Isogonic lines connect points where the variation is equal, while the agonic line defines the points where the variation is zero.

The only source of power for the magnetic compass is magnetism. It is a simple **bar magnet**, consisting of a metal bar with two poles. Lines of magnetic force flow out from each pole in all directions, and eventually return to the opposite pole. The bar magnet in the compass is mounted so it can pivot freely and align itself automatically with the earth's magnetic field. [Figure 3-16]

VARIATION

When you fly under visual flight rules, you ordinarily navigate by referring to charts which are oriented to true north. Because the aircraft compass is oriented to magnetic north, you must make allowances for the difference between these poles in order to navigate properly. You do this by applying a correction called variation to convert a true direction to a magnetic direction. **Variation** at a given point is the angular difference between the true and magnetic poles. The amount of variation depends on where you are located on the earth's surface. [Figure 3-17]

Variation is the angular difference between magnetic and true direction, as measured at any point on the earth.

DEVIATION

Disturbances from magnetic fields produced by metals and electrical accessories within the airplane itself also produce an error in compass

FOR (MH)	0°	30°	60°	90°	120°	150°	180°	210°	240°	270°	300°	330°
STEER (CH)	359°	30°	60°	88°	120°	152°	183°	212°	240°	268°	300°	329°

RADIO ON [X]   RADIO OFF [ ]

Figure 3-18. On this compass correction card, the deviation varies between 0° and 3°. For example, if you want to fly a magnetic heading (MH) of 060°, the compass heading (CH) also is 060°; to fly 180° magnetic, you must fly a compass heading of 183°.

Deviation is the error caused by the magnetic fields of the airplane and its electronic equipment.

indications. This is referred to as deviation. Although the error cannot be completely eliminated, deviation error can be decreased by manufacturer-installed compensating magnets located within the compass housing. As a pilot, you correct for deviation by using a compass correction card, which is mounted near the compass. The card normally indicates whether the corrections apply with the radio on or off. [Figure 3-18]

COMPASS ERRORS

Although you can apply the appropriate corrections for variation and deviation, additional errors are characteristic of the compass. These errors occur during flight in turbulent air or while you are turning or changing speed. Because of this, your primary heading reference during flight is the heading indicator. The magnetic compass is considered a backup source of heading information.

For the compass to orient itself to magnetic north, it must be able to swing freely within the compass housing. However, this freedom of movement, makes the compass sensitive to in-flight turbulence. In light turbulence, you may be able to use the compass by averaging the readings. For example, if the compass swings between 030° to 060°, you can estimate an approximate heading of 045°. In heavier turbulence, however, the compass is almost useless.

MAGNETIC DIP

Magnetic dip results in turning and acceleration errors.

As we discussed earlier, the compass determines direction through use of a bar magnet which aligns itself with the magnetic field of the earth. These lines of magnetic force are parallel to the surface of the earth at the magnetic equator; however, they deflect increasingly downward as they approach the magnetic poles. Since the compass seeks alignment with these lines, the closer it is to the magnetic poles, the more it deflects downward. This **magnetic dip** results in turning and acceleration/deceleration errors. [Figure 3-19]

ACCELERATION ERROR

Acceleration error is influenced by the amount of magnetic dip. The greater the dip, the greater the error. As you accelerate the airplane, the compass indicates a turn to the north. The compass returns to its pre-

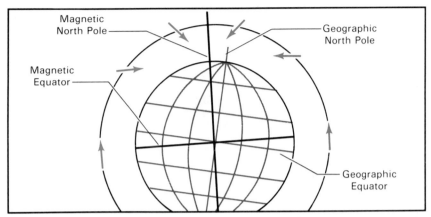

Figure 3-19. The compass is not subject to magnetic dip near the equator, so compass errors are not a factor. Magnetic dip increases gradually as the compass moves closer to the poles, so compass errors increase. Within approximately 300 miles of either magnetic pole, these errors are so great that use of the compass for navigation is impractical.

vious heading as the acceleration subsides. Conversely, as you slow the airplane, the compass shows a turn to the south. Again, when you stop decelerating, the compass returns to an accurate indication. The acceleration/deceleration error is most pronounced when you are flying on headings of east or west, and it decreases gradually as you fly closer to north/south headings. The error doesn't occur when you are flying directly on a north or south heading. The memory aid, ANDS (Accelerate North, Decelerate South), may help you recall this error.

If you accelerate the aircraft in the northern hemisphere, the compass shows a turn to the north; if you decelerate, it indicates a turn to the south.

TURNING ERROR

Turning error is directly related to magnetic dip; the greater the dip, the greater the turning error. It is most pronounced when you are turning to a heading of north or south. In the northern hemisphere, when you begin a turn from a heading of north, the compass initially indicates a turn in the opposite direction. When the turn is established, the compass begins to show the turn, but it lags behind the actual heading. The amount of lag decreases as the turn continues, then disappears as the airplane reaches a heading of east or west.

Turning error causes the magnetic compass to lead or lag the actual magnetic heading of the airplane during turns.

When turning from a heading of east or west to a heading of north, there is no error as you begin the turn. However, as the heading nears north, the compass increasingly lags behind the airplane's actual heading. When you turn from a heading of south, the compass initially indicates a turn in the proper direction but leads the airplane's actual heading. This error also cancels out as the airplane reaches a heading of east or west. Turning from east or west to a heading of south causes the compass to

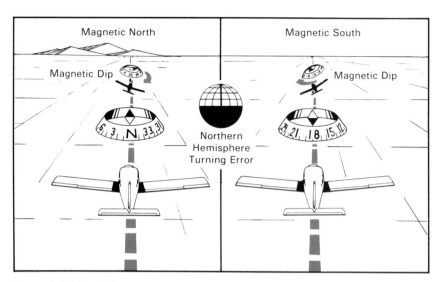

Figure 3-20. The left portion of the figure shows that a right turn from a heading of north initially causes the compass to indicate a left turn. The right portion shows that a turn from a heading of south causes the compass to indicate a turn in the correct direction, but at a much faster rate.

indicate the heading correctly at the start of a turn, but then it increasingly leads the actual heading as the airplane nears a southerly heading. [Figure 3-20]

The amount of lead or lag is approximately equal to the latitude of the airplane. For example, if you are turning from a heading of south to a heading of west while flying at 40° north latitude, the compass will rapidly turn to a heading of 220° (180° + 40°). At the midpoint of the turn, the lead will decrease to approximately half (20°), and upon reaching a heading of west, it will be zero.

The lead and lag errors presented here are only valid for flight in the northern hemisphere. These same types of errors exist in the southern hemisphere, but they act in opposite directions.

MINIMIZING ERRORS

The magnetic compass provides accurate indications only when you are flying in smooth air and in straight-and-level, unaccelerated flight.

If your heading indicator fails and you understand the errors of the magnetic compass, you should still be able to navigate properly. When you are referring to the compass for heading information, remember that it is accurate only when your airplane is in smooth air and in straight-and-level, unaccelerated flight. At other times, you can still minimize compass errors. When you are flying in an area of turbulence, attempt to find smoother flight conditions. Keep in mind that turning errors only exist when you are making a turn; acceleration errors only exist when you are changing speed.

CHECKLIST _____

After studying this section, you should have a basic understanding of:

✓ **Gyroscopic principles** — What rigidity in space and precession are and how these principles affect gyroscopic instruments.

✓ **Turn coordinator** — What the instrument displays and what is meant by a standard-rate turn and coordinated flight.

✓ **Attitude indicator** — What its function is and how it reflects the pitch and bank attitude of an aircraft.

✓ **Heading indicator** — What its function is, why it precesses, and how to keep it properly aligned.

✓ **Magnetic compass** — What its basic operating principles are and how to compensate for its inherent errors.

ENGINE AND PROPELLER

The engine and propeller work in combination to provide thrust. You will often hear an airplane's engine called the **powerplant**. This is an appropriate term, because it not only provides the power to propel the airplane, but it also powers most airplane accessory systems. For example, the electrical system, cabin heating, and windshield defrosting all rely on the energy produced by the engine.

THE ENGINE

There are several types of aircraft engines in use today. This discussion will concentrate on the engines you are most likely to encounter. Training airplanes are normally powered by **reciprocating engines**, which get their name from the back-and-forth movement of their internal parts.

PRINCIPLES OF OPERATION

You can consider each cylinder in a reciprocating engine as a pump for air and fuel. The more air and fuel that is pumped through it in a given time, the more energy it produces. [Figure 3-21]

FOUR-STROKE OPERATING CYCLE

The back-and-forth, or reciprocating, motion of the piston is caused by the ignition and controlled burning of the fuel/air mixture within the cylinder's combustion chamber. This produces mechanical energy by a series of events that occur in a repetitive cycle known as the **four-stroke operating cycle**. [Figure 3-22]

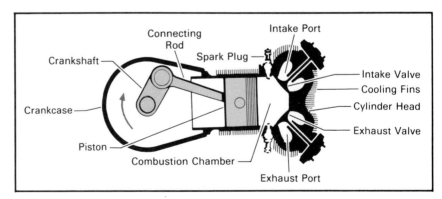

Figure 3-21. The movable piston is attached to the crankshaft by a connecting rod. The crankshaft and the connecting rod change the back-and-forth motion of the piston to rotary, or turning, motion which drives the propeller.

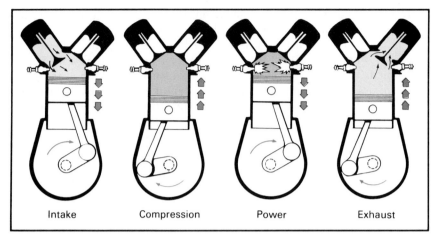

| Intake | Compression | Power | Exhaust |

Figure 3-22. The arrows in this illustration indicate the direction of motion of the crankshaft and piston during the four-stroke cycle.

When the piston moves away from the cylinder head on the intake stroke, the intake valve opens and the fuel/air mixture is drawn into the combustion chamber. As the piston moves back toward the cylinder head, the intake valve closes and the fuel/air mixture is compressed. When compression is nearly complete, the spark plugs fire and the compressed mixture is ignited to begin the power stroke. This is the whole reason for the series of events. The rapidly expanding gases from the controlled burning of the fuel/air mixture drive the piston away from the cylinder head. This provides the power that rotates the crankshaft. Finally, the exhaust stroke expels the burned gases from the chamber through the opened exhaust valve.

Even when the engine is operated at a fairly slow speed, the four-stroke cycle takes place several hundred times each minute. In a four-cylinder engine, each cylinder operates on a different stroke. Continuous rotation of the crankshaft is maintained by the precise timing of the power strokes in each cylinder.

ABNORMAL COMBUSTION

As you might expect, the correct timing of the four-stroke cycle is not the only thing that determines how well the engine operates. Your actions can have a direct impact on its operation. You must be sure the engine is properly serviced and maintained. You also must follow the manufacturer's recommendations for such items as using the recommended fuel grade and keeping engine pressures and temperatures within the specified limits. If you do not observe the recommended procedures, abnormal combustion in the form of detonation or preignition may result.

Detonation occurs when fuel in the cylinders explodes instead of burning smoothly.

With normal combustion, the fuel/air mixture burns in a very controlled and predictable manner. Although the process occurs in a fraction of a second, the mixture actually begins to burn at the point where it is ignited by the spark plugs, then burns away from the plugs until it's all consumed. This type of combustion causes a smooth buildup of temperature and pressure and ensures that the expanding gases deliver the maximum force to the piston at exactly the right time in the power stroke. **Detonation**, on the other hand, is an uncontrolled, explosive ignition of the fuel/air mixture within the cylinder's combustion chamber. It causes excessive temperatures and pressures which, if not corrected, can quickly lead to failure of the piston, cylinder, or valves. In less severe cases, detonation causes engine overheating, roughness, or loss of power.

Detonation may result if you allow the engine to overheat or if you use an improper grade of fuel.

Detonation can happen anytime you allow the engine to overheat. It also can occur if you use an improper grade of fuel. The potential for engine overheating is greatest under the following conditions: use of fuel grade lower than that recommended, takeoff with an engine that is already overheated or is very near the maximum allowable temperature, operation at high r.p.m. and low airspeed, and extended operations above 75% power with an extremely lean mixture. If detonation is suspected on climbout, you can help cool the engine by retarding the throttle and by climbing at a slower rate.

Preignition is the uncontrolled combustion of fuel in advance of normal ignition.

In a properly functioning ignition system, combustion is precisely timed. In contrast, **preignition** takes place when the fuel/air mixture ignites too soon. In extreme cases, it can cause serious damage to the engine in a short period of time. Preignition is caused by residual hot spots in the cylinder. A hot spot may be a small carbon deposit on a spark plug, a cracked ceramic spark plug insulator, or almost any damage around the combustion chamber.

Preignition and detonation often occur simultaneously, and one may cause the other. Inside the aircraft, you will be unable to distinguish between the two, since both are likely to cause engine roughness and high engine temperatures. To avoid these problems, maintain engine temperatures within the recommended limits, maintain a sufficiently rich mixture, and use only the proper grade of fuel.

ENGINE SYSTEMS

Now that you have an idea of how the basic components of an engine work, let's look at the systems that help you control and monitor the engine. These include the throttle and mixture control, as well as the ignition, induction, lubrication, and cooling systems.

ENGINE CONTROLS

In a typical training airplane with a fixed-pitch propeller, there are only two primary engine controls — the **throttle** and the **mixture**. Later in this

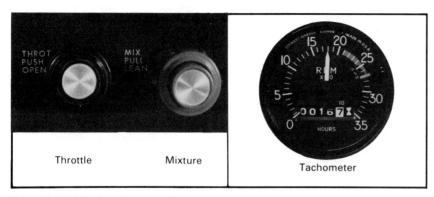

Figure 3-23. The throttle controls engine speed by regulating the amount of fuel and air that flows into the cylinders, while the mixture controls the ratio of the fuel-to-air mixture. A mixture that is too rich contains too much fuel for the existing conditions, and a mixture that is too lean does not contain enough fuel. Engine speed is expressed in revolutions per minute (r.p.m.) and is displayed on the tachometer. The window in the lower part of the instrument keeps a record of engine running time.

section we'll discuss a third control, the propeller control, which applies to airplanes with constant-speed propellers. [Figure 3-23]

IGNITION SYSTEM

The ignition system provides the spark that ignites the fuel/air mixture in the cylinders. It is made up of the magnetos, spark plugs, interconnecting wires, and the ignition switch. [Figure 3-24]

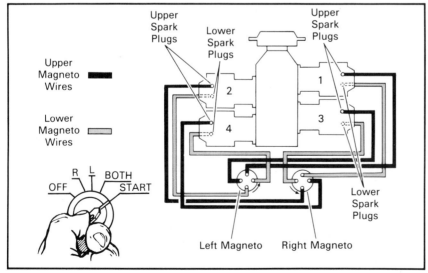

Figure 3-24. Before flight, you use the ignition switch to check each magneto separately. During flight, you use both magnetos. Notice the wires from each magneto are connected to one of the spark plugs in all four cylinders. The numbers in the cylinders indicate firing order.

A **magneto** is a self-contained, engine-driven unit that supplies electrical current to the spark plugs. It uses permanent magnets to generate an electrical current completely independent of the aircraft's electrical system. The magneto generates sufficiently high voltage to jump a spark across the spark plug gap in each cylinder. The system begins to fire as soon as you engage the starter and the crankshaft begins to turn. It continues to operate whenever the crankshaft is rotating.

The dual ignition system on an airplane engine provides improved engine performance.

Use of two magnetos enhances safety and increases reliability of the ignition system. The magnetos operate independently of each other; each fires one of the two spark plugs in each cylinder. The firing of two spark plugs improves combustion of the fuel/air mixture and results in a slightly higher power output. If one of the magnetos fails, the other is unaffected. The engine will continue to operate normally, although you can expect a slight decrease in engine power. The same is true if one of the two spark plugs in a cylinder fails.

You control the operation of the magnetos with the **ignition switch** on the instrument panel. The first four positions are: OFF, RIGHT, LEFT, and BOTH. Some ignition switches also include a START position. When you select the LEFT or RIGHT position, only one magneto is activated. When you select BOTH, the system operates on both magnetos.

You can identify a malfunctioning ignition system during the pretakeoff check by observing the decrease in r.p.m. that occurs when you first move the ignition switch from BOTH to RIGHT, and then from BOTH to LEFT. A small decrease in engine r.p.m. is normal during this check. The permissible decrease is listed in your pilot's operating handbook. If the engine stops running when you switch to one magneto or if the r.p.m. drop exceeds the allowable limit, don't fly the airplane until the problem is corrected. The cause could be fouled plugs, broken or shorted wires between the magneto and the plugs, or improperly timed firing of the plugs.

An engine that continues to run after the ignition switch is turned to OFF may have a disconnected ground wire in the ignition switch.

Although the ignition system is usually trouble free, you still need to be alert for the special problems associated with a magneto. Because the magneto requires no outside source of electrical power, be certain that you turn the ignition switch to the OFF position following engine shutdown. Even with the battery and master switches OFF, the engine can fire and turn over if you leave the ignition switch ON and the propeller is moved. The potential for serious injury in this situation is obvious. In addition, if the ignition switch ground wire is disconnected, the magneto may continue to fire even if the ignition switch is OFF. If this occurs, the only way to stop the engine is to move the mixture lever to the idle cutoff position, then have the system checked by a qualified mechanic. Finally, if you encounter static on the airplane's communications radio, a loose connection in the ignition system or a break in the shielding around the ignition wiring may be the cause.

INDUCTION SYSTEM

The purpose of the induction system is to bring outside air into the engine, mix it with fuel in the proper proportion, and deliver it to the cylinders where combustion occurs. Since it is critically important that an uninterrupted mixture of fuel and air reach the engine, you should be thoroughly familiar with the operation of this system in your airplane.

Outside air enters the induction system through an **intake port** at the front of the engine compartment. This port normally contains an air filter that inhibits the entry of dust and other foreign objects. Since the filter may occasionally become clogged, an alternate source of air must be available. Usually, the alternate air comes from inside the engine cowling where it bypasses a clogged air filter. Some alternate air sources operate automatically, while others operate manually.

The **carburetor** mixes the incoming air with fuel and delivers the fuel/air mixture to the combustion chamber. A float-type carburetor system is used on most light aircraft. When the air enters the carburetor it passes through a venturi. This increases its velocity and decreases its pressure. Fuel enters the carburetor from a float chamber where it is maintained at a nearly constant level by a float device. The float chamber is vented to the outside so that pressure inside remains equal to the atmospheric pressure, even during climbs and descents. [Figure 3-25]

The operating principle of float-type carburetors is based on the difference in pressure at the venturi throat and the air inlet.

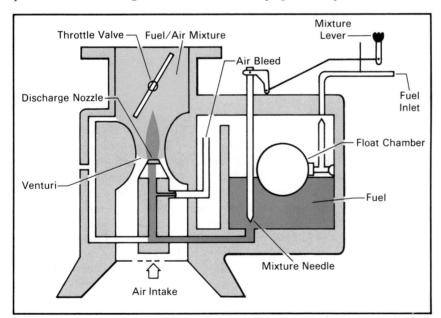

Front View

Figure 3-25. Fuel is drawn from the float chamber past a mixture needle and into the venturi where it mixes with the incoming air. Since the discharge nozzle is located in an area of low pressure created by the venturi, the fuel is forced through the discharge nozzle by the higher atmospheric pressure in the float chamber.

When you lean the mixture, you decrease the fuel flow to compensate for decreased air density.

Carburetors are calibrated at sea level, and the correct fuel-to-air mixture ratio is established at that altitude with the mixture control set in the FULL RICH position. However, as altitude increases, the density of air entering the carburetor decreases while the density of the fuel remains the same. This means that at higher altitudes, the mixture becomes progressively richer. To maintain the correct fuel/air mixture, you must be able to adjust the amount of fuel that is mixed with the incoming air. This is the function of the mixture control. This adjustment, often referred to as **leaning the mixture**, varies from one airplane to another. Refer to the POH to determine specific procedures for your airplane.

You may be able to correct engine roughness during runup at a high-elevation airport by leaning the mixture.

Most mixture adjustments are required during changes of altitude or during operations at airports with field elevations well above sea level. A mixture that is too rich can result in engine roughness. The roughness normally is due to spark plug fouling from excessive carbon buildup on the plugs. This occurs because the excessively rich mixture lowers temperature inside the cylinder, inhibiting complete combustion of the fuel. This condition may occur during the pretakeoff runup at high elevation airports and during climbs or cruise flight at high altitudes. Usually, you can correct the problem by leaning the mixture according to POH instructions.

If you do not adjust the mixture control during descents from high to low altitudes, the fuel/air mixture will be too lean.

If you fail to enrich the mixture during a descent from high altitude, it normally will become too lean. High engine temperatures can cause excessive engine wear or even failure. The best way to avoid this type of situation is to monitor the engine temperature gauges regularly and follow POH guidelines for maintaining the proper mixture.

Carburetor Icing

You should expect carburetor ice when temperatures are below 21°C (70°F) and the relative humidity is high.

The effect of fuel vaporization and decreasing air pressure in the venturi causes a sharp drop in temperature in the carburetor. If the air is moist, the water vapor in the air may condense. When the temperature in the carburetor is at or below freezing, **carburetor ice** may form on internal surfaces, including the throttle valve. Because of the sudden cooling that takes place in the carburetor, icing can occur even on warm days with temperatures as high as 38°C (100°F) and humidity as low as 50%. However, it is more likely to occur when temperatures are below 21°C (70°F) and the relative humidity is above 80%. The likelihood of icing increases as temperature decreases down to 0°C (32°F) and as relative humidity increases. Below freezing, the possibility of carburetor ice decreases with decreases in temperature.

Although carburetor ice can occur during any phase of flight, it is particularly dangerous when you are using reduced power, such as on descents or in the traffic pattern. You may not notice it during a descent until you try to add power. [Figure 3-26]

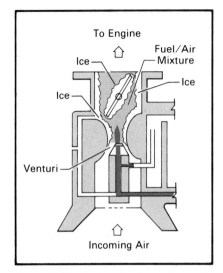

Figure 3-26. Carburetor ice reduces the size of the air passage to the engine. This restricts the flow of the fuel/air mixture and reduces power.

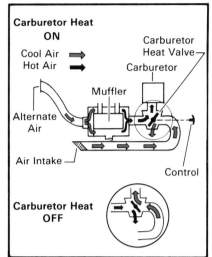

Figure 3-27. When you turn the carburetor heat ON, a valve cuts off air flow from the normal air intake and allows heated air from an alternate source to enter the carburetor.

In an airplane with a fixed-pitch propeller, your first indication of carburetor icing is a decrease in engine r.p.m., followed by engine roughness and possible fuel starvation. In an airplane with a constant-speed propeller, as discussed later in this section, the power changes are reflected by shifts in manifold pressure. The **carburetor heat** system eliminates the ice by routing air across a heat source before it enters the carburetor. [Figure 3-27]

The first indication of carburetor ice in an airplane equipped with a fixed-pitch propeller is a loss of r.p.m.

Generally, you should use full carburetor heat whenever you reduce engine r.p.m. below the normal operating range for your airplane or when you suspect the presence of carburetor ice. Carburetor heat tends to decrease engine output and increase the operating temperature of the engine. Normally, you do not use it continuously when full power is required, particularly during takeoff. Be sure to check your pilot's operating handbook for specific recommendations.

The use of carburetor heat causes a slight decrease in engine power, because the heated air is less dense than the outside air that had been entering the engine. This enriches the mixture. When ice is present in an airplane with a fixed-pitch propeller and you use carburetor heat, there is a slight decrease in r.p.m., followed by a gradual increase in r.p.m. as the ice melts. If ice is not present, the r.p.m. will decrease slightly, then remain constant. Remember that in an airplane with a constant-speed propeller, these power changes are reflected by manifold pressure.

If carburetor ice is present in an airplane with a fixed-pitch propeller, the decrease in r.p.m. caused by the enriched mixture will be followed by an increase in r.p.m. as the ice melts.

Fuel Injection and Turbocharging

Fuel injection and turbocharging are common induction system features for high-performance aircraft used in general aviation. Chances are good that you will encounter both of these systems early in your flying career. Fuel injection is more precise than a float-type carburetor in metering fuel and distributing the fuel/air mixture. Lower fuel consumption, increased horsepower, lower operating temperatures, and longer engine life are some of the advantages of this system. The system also is generally considered less susceptible to icing than a carburetor system. However, starting procedures usually are more complex than for carburetor systems, especially when the engine is hot.

When you operate a reciprocating engine at high altitudes, efficiency of the engine diminishes as a result of lower air density and smaller volume of airflow into the engine. This is a characteristic of any normally aspirated engine, where the fuel/air mixture is not compressed. A turbocharger may be added to the engine to compress the mixture before it enters the cylinders. This compression increases air density so the engine can operate at high altitudes and still produce the same amount of power as it would at sea level. However, turbocharged engines, which usually are also fuel injected, have tight operating parameters, and require careful mixture adjustments and monitoring. Since both turbocharging and fuel injection have unique operating characteristics, you should arrange a checkout with an experienced flight instructor before flying an airplane equipped with these systems.

OIL SYSTEM

Airplane engines depend on circulation of oil for lubrication of internal parts and cooling.

The engine oil system performs two important functions. It lubricates the engine's moving parts and aids in cooling of the engine by reducing friction and removing some of the heat from the cylinders. [Figure 3-28]

The oil filler cap and dipstick for measuring the oil quantity are accessible through a panel in the engine cowling. You should check the oil quantity before each flight. See your pilot's operating handbook or placards near the access panel for the minimum operating quantity, as well as the recommended oil type and weight for your airplane. After engine start, you should use the oil pressure and oil temperature gauges to monitor the system.

Immediately after starting the engine, adjust r.p.m. and check engine instruments for the proper indications.

The oil pressure gauge provides a direct indication of the oil system operation. A below-normal pressure may mean that the oil pump is not putting out enough pressure to circulate oil throughout the engine, while an above-normal pressure may indicate a clogged oil line. You should consider any abnormal indication to mean that vital engine parts are not receiving the necessary lubrication. Under these circumstances, your best course of action is to follow the appropriate instructions in your POH.

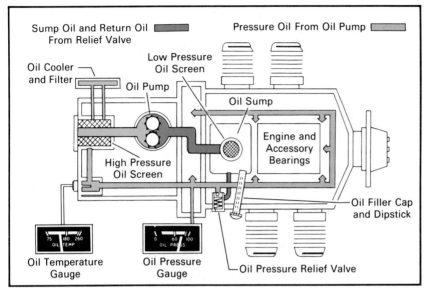

Figure 3-28. The heart of the system is the oil pump, which draws oil from the sump and routes it to the engine. After the oil passes through the engine, it returns to the sump. In some airplanes, additional lubrication is supplied by the rotating crankshaft, which splashes oil onto portions of the engine.

Most manufacturers recommend that you shut down the engine if the oil pressure does not begin to rise within 30 seconds after an engine start in the summer, or 60 seconds in the winter. [Figure 3-29]

The oil temperature gauge is usually located next to the oil pressure gauge. This allows you to check both at the same time. Unlike the oil pressure gauge, which usually reacts quickly to changes in pressure, changes in oil temperature occur more slowly. This is particularly noticeable after starting a cold engine, when it may take several minutes or longer for the gauge to show any increase in temperature. [Figure 3-30]

Excessive engine temperatures can result in loss of power, high oil consumption, and possible engine damage.

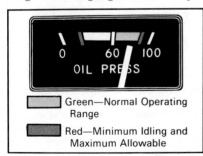

Figure 3-29. This gauge measures the pressure in pounds per square inch (p.s.i.) of the oil supplied to the engine. Green typically indicates the normal operating range, while red indicates the minimum and maximum pressures.

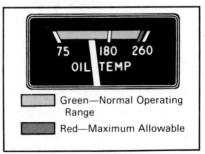

Figure 3-30. The oil temperature gauge measures the temperature of oil as it enters the engine. The green area shows the normal operating range and the red line indicates the maximum allowable temperature.

High engine oil tempera-
tures may be caused by
an oil level that is too
low.

You should check the oil temperature periodically to see if it remains
within the normal operating range. This is particularly important when
you are using a high power setting, since this tends to increase oil
temperatures. Abnormally high indications may also indicate a plugged
oil line, a low oil quantity, or a defective temperature gauge.

COOLING SYSTEM

The burning fuel within the engine's cylinders produces intense heat.
While the engine oil system is essential to internal cooling of the engine,
additional cooling is required to maintain normal temperatures. Much of
the remaining heat is dissipated in the exhaust gases, but outside air is
also used for cooling. [Figure 3-31]

Airplanes equipped with cowl flaps may have a **cylinder head temperature gauge** that provides a direct temperature reading from one of the
cylinders. The cowl flaps are opened when the cylinder head temperature
indicates the engine requires increased cooling. This usually is necessary
during ground operations, when airflow across the engine is at a minimum, and any time during flight when power settings are high and airspeeds are low. [Figure 3-32]

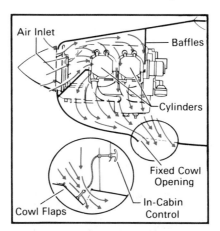

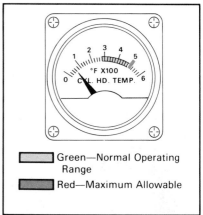

Figure 3-31. Outside air usually enters
the engine compartment through an
inlet behind the propeller hub. Baffles
direct it to the hottest parts of the
engine, primarily the cylinders, which
have fins that increase the area exposed
to the airflow. Some airplanes have fixed
openings in the cowling so outside air
can exit the engine compartment. On
others, cowl flaps provide an adjustable
opening to regulate the airflow around
the engine and to reduce drag.

Figure 3-32. Like the other engine
gauges, the normal range for the cylinder head temperature gauge is marked
in green. You should compare the readings from the cylinder head temperature
and oil temperature gauges. A disparity
between the two may indicate a malfunction in one of the instruments. Oil
and cylinder head temperatures above
the normal operating range may indicate
that you are using too much power with
the mixture set too lean.

Besides using cowl flaps, you can reduce high engine operating temperatures by enriching the mixture. A richer mixture burns at a slightly lower temperature. Other methods for reducing engine temperatures include reducing the rate of climb, increasing the airspeed and, when conditions permit, decreasing the power setting.

Engine temperature may be reduced by enriching the mixture, reducing the rate of climb, increasing the airspeed, or reducing power.

PROPELLER

Although the engine produces the power, the propeller provides the thrust to propel the airplane through the air. The propeller consists of a central hub with two or more blades attached. Each blade is an airfoil that acts like a rotating wing. Since it is an airfoil, the propeller blade is subject to the same aerodynamic factors that apply to any airfoil. [Figure 3-33]

When the propeller rotates through the air, it creates a low pressure area in front of the blade, much like the wing's curvature creates a low pressure area above the wing. However, unlike the wing, which moves through the air at a uniform rate, the propeller sections near the tip rotate at a much greater speed than those near the hub. To compensate for this, each small section of the propeller blade is set at a different angle to the plane of rotation. The gradual decrease in blade angle resulting from this gives the propeller blade its twisted appearance. Blade twist allows the propeller to provide uniform thrust throughout most of the length of the blade.

The overall angle of a propeller's blades affects its operating efficiency. A propeller with a low blade angle, known as a **climb propeller**, provides the best performance for takeoff and climb, while one with a high blade angle, known as a **cruise propeller**, is more adapted to high speed cruise and high altitude flight.

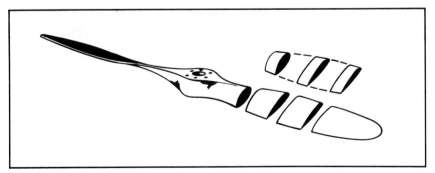

Figure 3-33. The cross sections of this propeller blade illustrate the well-defined airfoil shape. One surface of the blade is cambered, or curved, while the other is comparatively flat. The leading edge is the thick, cambered part of the blade that meets the air during rotation. Notice how the twist of a propeller blade causes the shape of the airfoil cross-sections to change as they move toward the tip of the propeller.

FIXED PITCH

Light airplanes may have either a fixed-pitch or a constant-speed propeller. With a fixed-pitch propeller, blade angle is selected on the basis of what is best for the primary function of the airplane. You cannot change this angle. You shouldn't confuse the term **pitch** as it applies to propeller blades with pitch as it relates to an aircraft's attitude. A propeller's pitch is the number of inches that it would move forward in one revolution if it were moving through a solid medium and did not undergo any slippage or loss of efficiency as it does in air. Pitch is proportional to blade angle (the angle between the chord line of the blade and the propeller's plane of rotation). Because of its direct connection to the crankshaft, the only power control for a fixed-pitch propeller is the throttle, and the only power indicator is the tachometer. [Figure 3-34]

CONSTANT SPEED

A constant-speed propeller allows you to select the blade angle that provides the most efficient performance.

Compared to a fixed-pitch propeller, the constant-speed propeller is much more efficient. It is often referred to as a variable-pitch or controllable-pitch propeller, since you can adjust the blade angle for most efficient operation. The main advantage of a constant-speed propeller is that it converts a high percentage of the engine's power into thrust over a wide range of r.p.m. and airspeed combinations.

With a constant-speed propeller, the throttle controls engine power output, as indicated on the manifold pressure gauge, while the propeller control regulates engine r.p.m.

An airplane with a constant-speed propeller has two power controls — the throttle and the propeller control. The throttle adjusts the power output of the engine, which is directly indicated on the manifold pressure gauge. The propeller control changes the pitch of the propeller blades and regulates the r.p.m. of the engine and the prop, as indicated on the tachometer. [Figure 3-35]

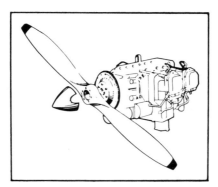

Figure 3-34. A fixed-pitch propeller is connected directly to the engine's crankshaft. Engine power rotates the crankshaft as well as the propeller, and the propeller converts the rotary power into thrust.

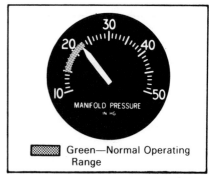

Green—Normal Operating Range

Figure 3-35. The manifold pressure gauge shows the pressure inside the engine in inches of mercury (in. Hg). It usually has color-coded markings to help you identify the normal operating range.

When the engine is not running, the manifold pressure gauge registers atmospheric pressure. When a normally aspirated engine is running, the gauge senses the reduced pressure in the manifold and indicates less than atmospheric pressure. During a climb with a constant power setting, manifold pressure gradually decreases as you gain altitude.

The propeller control permits you to select a low blade angle and high r.p.m. setting for maximum thrust on takeoff. After you reach cruising flight conditions, you can use a higher pitch and a lower r.p.m. setting to maintain adequate thrust for the desired airspeed. This is comparable to using a low gear in your car to accelerate, then using a high gear for cruising speed. Most hydraulic pitch-change mechanisms found on single-engine airplanes use high-pressure oil to oppose the aerodynamic twisting forces acting on the blades. [Figure 3-36]

The governor regulates the oil pressure sent to the pitch-change mechanism to maintain an equilibrium between aerodynamic and hydraulic pitch-changing forces at the selected r.p.m. For a given r.p.m. setting, there is always a maximum allowable manifold pressure. Operating above this level may cause internal stress within the engine. Specific operating instructions are contained in your pilot's operating handbook. As a general rule, you should avoid high manifold pressures with low r.p.m. settings.

With constant-speed propellers, you should avoid low r.p.m. settings with high manifold pressure.

PROPELLER HAZARDS

The propeller is the most dangerous part of the airplane, and you should treat it with caution at all times. You should routinely provide your

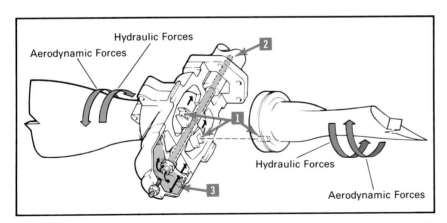

Figure 3-36. A hydraulic piston in the hub of the propeller is connected to each blade by a piston rod. This rod is attached to forks that slide over the pitch-change pin mounted in the root of each blade (item 1). High-pressure oil enters the cylinder from the governor through the center of the propeller shaft and piston rod (item 2). The oil pressure moves the piston toward the rear of the cylinder, moving the piston rod and forks aft (item 3). The forks push the pitch-change pin of each blade toward the rear of the hub, causing the blades to twist toward the high-pitch position.

passengers a thorough briefing regarding propeller hazards and how they can be avoided, stressing the need to stay well clear of the propeller area at all times.

When hand-starting an airplane, a competent pilot must be at the controls.

Occasionally, you may find it necessary to turn the propeller by hand to start the engine. Be sure you have seen a demonstration of the correct procedure before attempting this yourself, since it can be extremely dangerous if done improperly. Always ensure that a qualified pilot is at the controls, and remember that the person hand-propping the airplane is in charge of the starting procedure.

CHECKLIST

After studying this section, you should have a basic understanding of:

✓ **Engine** — What type of engine is used in a typical training airplane and what its general operating principles are.

✓ **Abnormal combustion** — What the causes and indications of detonation and preignition are and what the recommended corrective actions are.

✓ **Ignition system** — What its major components are and how the magnetos operate.

✓ **Carburetor** — What the fuel/air mixture is and how it is controlled, and what hazards are associated with carburetor ice.

✓ **Engine oil system** — How the oil system provides lubrication and cooling for the engine.

✓ **Propeller** — How it produces thrust, and what the differences are between fixed-pitch and constant-speed propellers.

FUEL AND ELECTRICAL SYSTEMS

In previous sections, you were introduced to a variety of instrument and powerplant systems. This section concludes the equipment discussion with a presentation of the airplane's fuel and electrical systems. As you read this section, you will see why correct system operation is so important.

FUEL SYSTEMS

Fuel systems are actually quite complex and include a number of individual components such as tanks, lines, vents, valves, drains, and gauges. There are two general types of fuel systems found in light airplanes — those that require a fuel pump and those that operate on gravity feed. Regardless of the system on the airplane you use for training, you will eventually encounter both systems. [Figure 3-37]

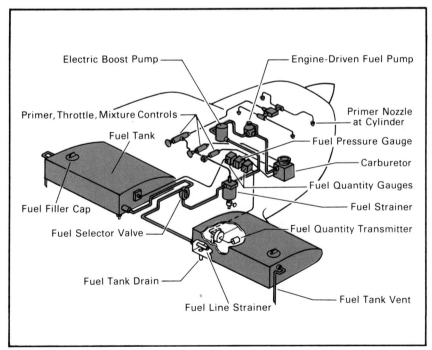

Figure 3-37. A typical fuel-pump system contains the components shown here. Fuel-pump and gravity-feed systems are similar, except the gravity system does not include engine-driven or electric boost pumps and fuel pressure gauges.

The **fuel-pump system** is usually found in low-wing airplanes, where the fuel tanks may be located below the engine. It is also used in most high-performance airplanes with fuel-injected engines. An engine-driven pump provides fuel under pressure from the fuel tanks to the engine. Because the engine-driven pump operates only when the engine is running, an electrically operated **boost pump** provides fuel under pressure for engine starting and as a backup, should the engine-driven pump malfunction. The boost pump is operated by a switch in the cockpit. You should refer to your POH for the correct operating procedures.

If an airplane is equipped with a fuel pump, it will have a **fuel pressure gauge** that allows you to monitor the fuel system. If fuel pressure drops below the normal operating range, indicating a possible malfunction of the engine-driven fuel pump, turning on the fuel boost pump will ensure a steady flow of fuel to the engine.

In a **gravity-feed system**, fuel flows by gravity from the fuel tanks to the engine. It works well in high-wing airplanes where the difference in height between the wing-mounted fuel tanks and the engine allows the fuel to flow under sufficient pressure to meet the requirements of the engine. The gravity-feed system is very common on high-wing airplanes with carbureted engines in the lower horsepower range.

FUEL SYSTEM COMPONENTS

The fuel tanks are usually located in the wings. They are replenished with fuel through a filler cap on top of the wing using a fuel nozzle and hose similar to the one you use to refuel an automobile. However, with airplanes, you should be especially careful not to allow the fuel nozzle spout to project very far into the tank, since you can damage the tank.

Filling fuel tanks after the last flight of the day prevents moisture from condensing by eliminating air in the tanks.

The condensation of moisture in partially filled fuel tanks can result in water entering fuel lines and restricting engine operation. You can minimize this by refilling the tanks following the last flight of the day. Since water and other sediments are heavier than fuel, any foreign material will collect at the bottom of the tank where it can be removed when you open a drain valve during the preflight inspection.

Fuel tanks contain a vent that allows air pressure inside the tank to remain the same as that outside the tank. This prevents the formation of a vacuum which would prevent fuel from flowing out of the tank. The vents may be located in the filler caps, or the tank may be vented through a small tube extending through the wing surface. The tanks also contain an overflow drain that prevents the rupture of the tank due to fuel expansion. The overflow drain may be combined with the fuel tank vent or it may have a separate opening. On hot days, it is not unusual to see a small amount of fuel coming from the overflow drain.

The fuel quantity gauges are located on the instrument panel, where they are usually grouped with engine monitoring gauges such as oil pressure and temperature. The gauges show the amount of fuel measured by a sensing unit in each fuel tank. Newer gauges show the tank capacity in both gallons and pounds. [Figure 3-38]

The fuel selector valve allows you to select fuel from various tanks. A common type of selector valve contains four positions: LEFT, RIGHT, BOTH, and OFF. Selecting the LEFT or RIGHT position allows fuel to feed only from that tank, while selecting the BOTH position feeds fuel from both tanks. Normally, you operate this type of fuel selector in the BOTH position. The LEFT or RIGHT position may be used to balance the amount of fuel remaining in each wing tank. [Figure 3-39]

Another common type of fuel selector switch has three positions: LEFT, RIGHT, and OFF. With this type of system, you must monitor fuel consumption closely to ensure that you don't run a tank completely out of fuel. For one thing, this will cause the engine to stop running. Also, running for prolonged periods on one tank causes an unbalanced fuel load between tanks. Regardless of the type of fuel selector in use, if the airplane is equipped with an engine-driven fuel pump or electrical boost pump, running a tank completely dry may allow air to enter the fuel system and cause a condition known as **vapor lock**. When this situation develops, it may be difficult, or impossible, to restart the engine.

On an airplane equipped with fuel pumps, running a tank completely dry may cause vapor lock.

Proper fuel management requires that you have a detailed knowledge of the airplane's fuel system. Therefore, you should become thoroughly familiar with the specific procedures established in the POH by the manufacturer of your airplane.

Figure 3-38. Do not depend solely on the accuracy of your fuel quantity gauges. Always observe the fuel level in each tank visually during the preflight inspection and then compare it with the corresponding fuel quantity indication.

Figure 3-39. Placards near the fuel selector may show the tank capacity in gallons of usable fuel. There also may be limitations on single tank operations, such as level flight only. Usually, you will find that the BOTH position is required for takeoffs and landings or maneuvering.

After the fuel selector valve, the fuel passes through a strainer before it enters the carburetor. This strainer removes moisture and other sediments that might be in the system. Since these contaminants are heavier than aviation fuel, they settle in a sump at the bottom of the strainer assembly.

It is generally recommended that you drain the fuel strainer before each flight. If the system design will allow it, you should also check the fuel visually to ensure that no moisture is present. Moisture in the sump is hazardous because in cold weather it can freeze and block fuel lines. In warm weather, it can flow into the carburetor and stop the engine. If moisture is present in the sump, it probably means there is more water in the fuel tanks, and you should continue to drain them until there is no evidence of contamination. In any event, never take off until you are certain that all moisture has been removed from the engine fuel system. If you are in doubt, have the system inspected by a qualified mechanic.

The fuel system contains a small hand-operated pump called a primer. It is used to pump fuel directly into the cylinders prior to engine start. The primer is useful in cold weather when fuel in the carburetor is difficult to vaporize. You can often start a cold engine by priming it when it would not start otherwise.

REFUELING

There may be occasions when you will refuel your airplane yourself. Even when it is done by someone else, you should be on hand to ensure it is done properly. While airplane fuel is a hazardous substance, refueling can be safely accomplished if you follow a few simple procedures.

The major refueling hazard is the possible combustion of the fuel by a spark that causes fumes to ignite. The most probable cause of a spark is from static electricity that discharges between refueling equipment and the airplane. The possibility of sparking can be greatly reduced if you make sure that a ground wire from the fuel truck is attached to the airplane before the fuel cap is removed from the tank. The airplane should be grounded throughout the refueling procedure and the fuel truck should be grounded to the airport surface.

FUEL GRADES

In addition to using the proper refueling technique, you must also ensure that you are using the proper grade of fuel. Using an incorrect grade may seriously affect engine performance and it may result in engine damage or failure. This is another reason it is highly recommended that you be present during refueling.

Grade	Color	**AVGAS ONLY**

Figure 3-40. Color coding of fuel and placement of decals near fuel tank filler caps helps ensure that you use the proper grade of fuel.

Airplane engines are designed to operate with a fuel that meets certain specifications. The recommended fuel grade and authorized substitutes are in the pilot's operating handbook for your airplane. Fuel grades are identified according to octane, or performance number, and all fuel of the same grade has been dyed a standard color to assist in identification. [Figure 3-40]

Using a fuel grade lower than specified causes cylinder head and engine oil temperatures to exceed normal operating limits.

In an emergency, using the next higher grade of fuel for a short period of time is not considered harmful, provided the manufacturer authorizes it. On the other hand, using a lower rated fuel may be extremely harmful. If it becomes necessary to mix various grades of fuel, the fuel may lose its characteristic color and become clear. This may cause confusion because turbine fuel also is colorless and reciprocating engines cannot operate on it. You should always use the fuel specified in the POH.

If the recommended fuel grade is not available, you may substitute the next higher grade, if approved by the manufacturer.

ELECTRICAL SYSTEMS

The electrical systems found in light airplanes reflect the increased use of sophisticated avionics and other electrical accessories. Since most operations in today's flight environment are highly dependent on the airplane's electrical system, you need to familiarize yourself with basic features.

ALTERNATORS

On light airplanes, electrical energy is supplied by a 14- or 28-volt direct-current system, which usually is powered by an engine-driven alternator. Some older airplanes may be equipped with generators, but alternators have many advantages for airplanes, just as they do for automobiles. Light weight, lower maintenance, and uniform output, even at low engine r.p.m., are the principal advantages.

Figure 3-40 content:

Grade	Color
80	Red
100LL	Blue
100	Green
Turbine Fuel	Colorless

Grade 100LL   Grade 100

Alternators actually produce **alternating current** (AC) first, and then convert it to **direct current** (DC) for use in the system. Direct current is delivered to a **bus bar** which serves to distribute the current to the various electrical components on the aircraft. [Figure 3-41]

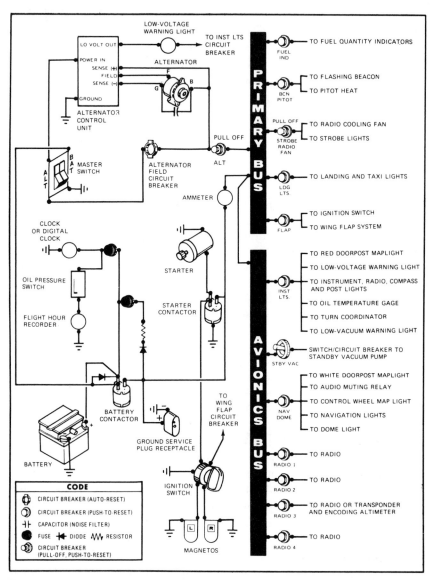

Figure 3-41. An electrical system schematic like this sample is included in most POHs. Notice that the various bus bar accessories are protected by circuit breakers. However, you should still make sure all electrical equipment is turned off before you start the engine. This protects sensitive components, particularly the radios, from damage which may be caused by random voltages generated during the starting process.

Another essential part of the electrical system is the storage battery. Its main purpose is to provide a means of starting the engine. It also permits limited operation of electrical components, such as the radios, without starting the engine. Finally, the battery is a valuable source of standby or emergency electrical power in case of alternator malfunction.

AMMETER

An ammeter is used to monitor the electrical current in amperes within the system. Actually, there are two types of ammeters. One reflects current flowing to or from the battery. The other type simply displays the load placed on the alternator and is often referred to as a loadmeter. [Figure 3-42]

A charging ammeter (needle on the plus side) is normal following an engine start, since the battery power lost in starting is being replaced. After the battery is charged, the ammeter should stabilize near zero and the alternator will supply the electrical needs of the system. A discharging ammeter means the electrical load is exceeding the output of the alternator, and the battery is helping to supply system power. This may mean the alternator is malfunctioning, or the electrical load is excessive. In any event, you should reduce your electrical load to conserve battery power and land as soon as practicable.

With a loadmeter, you can tell immediately if the alternator is operating normally, because it should reflect the amount of current being drawn by the electrical equipment. The POH will tell you the normal load to expect. Loss of the alternator will cause the loadmeter to indicate zero.

Figure 3-42. When the pointer of the ammeter on the left is on the plus side, it shows the charging rate of the battery. A minus indication means more current is being drawn from the battery than is being replaced. The loadmeter type on the right reflects the total load placed on the alternator by the system's electrical accessories. When all electrical components are turned off, it reflects the amount of charging current demanded by the battery.

MASTER SWITCH

The master switch controls the entire electrical system. Turning on the master switch is like turning on the ignition in an automobile. The airplane's ignition system is independent of the electrical system, since magnetos supply current to the spark plugs. However, the engine's starter won't operate unless the master switch is ON because power for the starter comes from the electrical system, not the magnetos. [Figure 3-43]

During normal operations, both sides of the master switch are on. In case of alternator malfunction, it can be isolated from the system. Another use for the split-type master switch is when you want to check equipment on the ground before you start the engine. In this situation, you can select only the battery side.

CIRCUIT BREAKERS AND FUSES

As the electrical system schematic shows, circuit breakers or fuses are used to protect various components from overloads. With circuit breakers, resetting the breaker usually will reactivate the circuit, unless an overload or short exists. If this is the case, the circuit breaker will continue to pop, indicating an electrical problem. [Figure 3-44]

Manufacturers usually provide a holder for spare fuses in the event you need to replace one in flight. In fact, FARs require you to carry extra fuses for night flight. Be sure to familiarize yourself with the electrical system for the airplane you fly. Many airplanes are equipped with low-voltage warning lights which indicate the need for specific corrective actions. The POH provides a thorough description of normal and emergency operations for the electrical system.

Supplies power to RADIO, Lights

Figure 3-43. Most airplanes use a split-rocker type master switch. The right half is labeled "BAT" and it controls all power to the electrical system. The left half is labeled "ALT" and it controls the alternator.

Figure 3-44. As a pilot, you are expected to know the location of the circuit protection device for each electrical component. Normally, the component's name is printed on the circuit breaker panel.

CHECKLIST_____

After studying this section, you should have a basic understanding of:

✓   **Fuel systems** — What the major types are, what components are included, and how they function.

✓   **Fuel grades** — How to recognize fuel grades by color and how to check for fuel contamination.

✓   **Electrical systems** — What the major components are and how they function.

✓   **Master switch** — What it does and how it controls the entire electrical system.

PREDICTING PERFORMANCE

Your ability to predict the performance of an airplane is extremely important. It allows you to determine how much runway you need for takeoff, if you can safely clear obstacles in the departure path, how long it will take you to reach a destination, how much fuel is required, and how much runway you'll need for landing.

In addition to predicting performance, you must also observe the airplane's **operating limitations**. These limits establish the boundaries within which the airplane must be flown. They are often referred to as the flight or performance envelope. Operating within the envelope is safe, while operating outside the envelope may cause structural damage or even failure. If you understand an airplane's operating limitations, you are unlikely to fly outside its performance envelope.

According to FARs, operating limitations may be found in the approved airplane flight manual; approved manual materials, markings, and placards; or any combination of these. For most light airplanes manufactured in the U.S. after March 1, 1979, the pilot's operating handbook is the approved flight manual, and a page in the front of the handbook will contain a statement to that effect. This section emphasizes the performance data and limitations of typical training airplanes. Before you operate any airplane, be sure you consult the pilot's operating handbook or other approved documents for the specific operating limitations, systems information, and performance figures that apply to that airplane.

PERFORMANCE SPEEDS

In determining performance speeds, airplane manufacturers must consider many factors. To compute maximum level flight speed, engine power is compared against total drag. For climbs, excess power and thrust are the important factors; for range and endurance, speeds that result in minimum drag or require minimum power are important.

MAXIMUM LEVEL FLIGHT SPEED

In level flight, the maximum speed of the airplane is limited by the amount of power produced by the engine and the total drag generated by the airplane. If thrust exceeds total drag when you apply full power, the airplane accelerates. This continues until the force of total drag equals the force of thrust. At this point, the airplane is flying at its maximum level flight speed. [Figure 3-45]

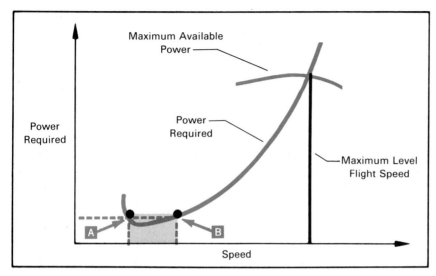

Figure 3-45. The curved power-required line shows the amount of power necessary to maintain level flight at various speeds. The power-available line also is curved, since power available in the typical single-engine airplane is a function of airspeed. The speed at which these two curves cross is where the forces of thrust and drag are in balance and where maximum level flight speed occurs. Note that the power required to operate the airplane at point A is the same as that required at point B, even though the speeds are different. If you were flying at point A, you would be operating on the back side of the power curve, where any decrease in airspeed requires an increase in power. At point A, you are very close to minimum flying speed.

CLIMB SPEEDS

The pilot's operating handbook for the airplane you're flying will list airspeeds for a variety of climbing flight conditions. Two of the most important are the **best angle-of-climb airspeed** (V_X), and the **best rate-of-climb airspeed** (V_Y). [Figure 3-46]

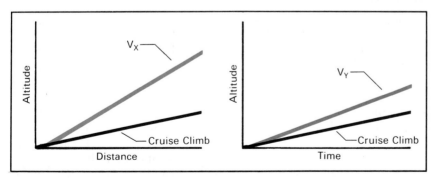

Figure 3-46. Climbing at V_X gives you the greatest gain in altitude for horizontal distance traveled. This airspeed is lower than other climb speeds and results in a fairly steep nose-high pitch attitude. Climbing at V_Y gives you the greatest gain in altitude over a period of time. Best rate-of-climb airspeed is higher than best angle-of-climb airspeed, and provides better forward visibility.

The best angle-of-climb airspeed is normally used immediately after takeoff for obstacle clearance. Because of the increased pitch attitude at V_X, your forward visibility is limited. If you happen to lift off prematurely during takeoff, you should accelerate the airplane while you are still in ground effect to at least the best angle-of-climb airspeed before attempting to climb. This technique is often used by pilots when taking off from soft fields.

Normally, you use V_Y after you have cleared all obstacles during departure. In addition, you may use a **cruise climb** after traffic pattern departure when climbing to cruising altitude. You can also use it during the cruise portion of a flight to climb to a higher cruising altitude. Normally, the cruise-climb speed is higher than V_X or V_Y, and the rate of climb is slower. The advantages of higher indicated climb speed are better engine cooling and improved forward visibility.

Excess power or thrust must be available for the airplane to climb.

Before an airplane can climb, it must have a reserve of power or thrust. At a given speed, more power is required for a sustained climb than for unaccelerated level flight. Since propeller-driven airplanes lose power and thrust with increasing altitude, both the best angle-of-climb and best rate-of-climb speeds change as you climb. When the airplane is unable to climb any further, it will have reached its **absolute ceiling**. Another important altitude, known as the **service ceiling**, refers to the altitude where a single-engine airplane is able to maintain a maximum climb of only 100 feet per minute. This altitude is more commonly used than absolute ceiling, since it represents the airplane's practical ceiling.

As altitude increases, the speed for best angle-of-climb increases, and the speed for best rate-of-climb decreases. The point at which these two speeds meet is the absolute ceiling of the airplane.

CRUISING SPEEDS

In selecting your cruising speed, you usually want to cover the distance to be traveled in the shortest period of time. However, just as an airplane can only fly so fast, it can only go so far and stay up only so long before it runs out of fuel. When range or endurance are important factors, you must select the proper speed for the flight.

Maximum endurance speed is the speed which allows the airplane to remain aloft while using the least amount of power necessary to sustain level flight. The minimum power setting provides the lowest rate of fuel consumption. In contrast, the **maximum range speed** provides the greatest distance for a given amount of fuel. You can think of it as getting the most miles per gallon out of the airplane. To determine this speed, you must consider the speed and rate of fuel consumption for any given power setting. The setting which yields the greatest distance traveled per gallon of fuel burned is the power setting which provides maximum range speed. As you may recall from the discussion of drag in Chapter 1, this speed produces the minimum total drag. It is where the lift-to-drag ratio is greatest, and it is referred to as L/D max. [Figure 3-47]

FACTORS AFFECTING PERFORMANCE

Anything that affects an engine's operating efficiency affects performance. Full power for a normally aspirated engine is based on conditions at sea level in a standard atmosphere. In fact, standard atmospheric conditions are the basis for estimating airplane performance. However, airplanes are rarely flown at sea level and they are almost never operated in weather conditions that exactly duplicate a model of the standard atmosphere. Temperature, pressure, humidity, and wind conditions constantly vary. In addition, the airport elevation, runway slope, and the condition of the runway surface also affect takeoff performance.

DENSITY ALTITUDE

Earlier, you learned that density altitude is pressure altitude corrected for nonstandard temperature. In other words, density altitude at a given level is equal to the pressure altitude only when standard atmospheric conditions exist at that level. You should be concerned about density altitude, because the density of the air directly affects the performance of your airplane. In fact, the primary reason for computing density altitude is to determine aircraft performance. Low density altitude (dense air) is favorable and high density altitude (thin air) is unfavorable. As density

With normally aspirated engines, any increase in density altitude results in a decrease in engine power.

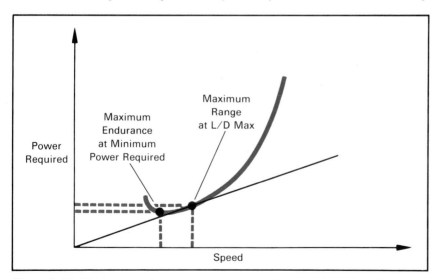

Figure 3-47. Maximum endurance speed occurs at the lowest point on the power-required curve. This is the speed where the lowest power setting will sustain an airplane in steady, level flight. Maximum range speed is a higher indicated airspeed that minimizes total drag.

altitude increases, engine power output, propeller efficiency, and aerodynamic lift decrease. The performance degradation occurs throughout the airplane's operating envelope, but it is especially noticeable in takeoff and climb performance.

One of the ways you can determine density altitude is through the use of charts designed for that purpose. For example, assume you are planning to depart an airport where the field elevation is 1,165 feet MSL, the altimeter setting is 30.10, and the temperature is 70°F. What is the density altitude? [Figure 3-48]

Most modern performance charts do not require you to compute density altitude. Instead, the computation is built into the performance chart

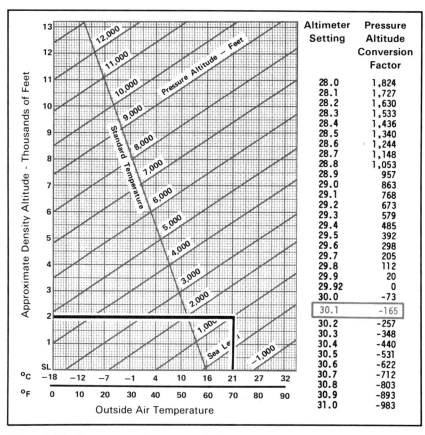

Figure 3-48. First, correct for nonstandard pressure by subtracting 165 feet from the field elevation to obtain the pressure altitude of 1,000 feet. Then, enter the chart at the bottom, just above the temperature of 70°F (21°C). Proceed up the chart vertically until you intercept the diagonal 1,000-foot pressure altitude line, then move horizontally to the left and read the density altitude of approximately 2,000 feet. This means your airplane will perform as if it were at 2,000 feet MSL on a standard day.

itself. All you have to do is enter the chart with the correct pressure altitude and the temperature. Older charts, however, may require you to compute density altitude before entering them. Another way to compute density altitude is with a flight computer, which is covered later in Chapter 6.

HUMIDITY

Humidity refers to the amount of water vapor contained in the atmosphere, and it is expressed as a percentage of the maximum amount of vapor the air can hold. This amount varies with air temperature. As air temperature increases, the maximum amount of water vapor the air can hold increases. At a given temperature, perfectly dry air has a humidity of 0%. When the same air is saturated, it cannot hold any more water vapor at the same temperature, and its humidity is 100%.

Although humidity alone is usually not considered an important factor in reducing airplane performance, it does contribute. It affects performance by taking up airspace that is normally available for vaporized fuel. As humidity increases, less air enters the engine. This has the effect of causing a small increase in density altitude. The moist air also tends to retard even fuel burning in the cylinder. When the relative humidity is very high, the engine power loss may be as high as seven percent, and the airplane's total takeoff and climb performance may be reduced by as much as 10%. Under conditions of high humidity, you should take extra time in setting the mixture control to the manufacturer's specifications to provide the maximum available power.

> You should consider possible effects of high humidity, even though it causes only a small loss of power.

Anytime the humidity or other conditions are apt to increase the density altitude, you should provide yourself with an extra margin of safety by using longer runways and by expecting a decrease in takeoff and climb performance. You also can expect a higher landing speed and a longer landing roll in less dense, humid air. Remember, conditions that cause high density altitude are "high, hot, and humid."

> High humidity causes decreased takeoff and climb performance and a higher landing speed.

SURFACE WINDS

Winds also can have a significant impact on airplane operations. When they are used to your advantage, they reduce takeoff and landing distances. Since surface winds are rarely aligned with the runway in use, you need a method of determining what portion of the wind is acting along the runway and what portion is acting across it. **Headwind** or **headwind component** refers to that portion of the wind which acts straight down the runway toward the airplane. **Tailwind** or **tailwind component** describes that portion of the wind which acts directly on the tail of the airplane. A wind can be either a headwind or a tailwind, but not both. A headwind is desirable for takeoffs and landings, since it decreases takeoff distance and runway length requirements.

A **crosswind** or **crosswind component** refers to that portion of the wind which acts perpendicular to the runway. Most airplanes have a maximum demonstrated crosswind component listed in the POH. Of course, your personal crosswind limit is based on your skill level, as well as any limitations set forth by your instructor during training.

Since headwinds are better for takeoffs and landings, the runway in use normally is a runway that provides some headwind. You can easily compute headwind, as well as crosswind, components by use of a wind component chart. When you use a wind component chart, remember that both the runway number and surface winds are given in magnetic direction.

To use a sample wind component chart, you first need to know the wind direction and the velocity. Next, you find the angle between the runway in use and the wind. For example, assume you are departing on runway 03 and the wind is from 060° at 20 knots. The angle between the runway and the wind is 30° (060 - 030 = 030). In this case, you have a headwind 30° off the runway heading. Since the headwind is from the right, you also have a crosswind component. [Figure 3-49]

WEIGHT

As the weight of the airplane increases, performance decreases. Conversely, as weight decreases, performance increases.

As discussed earlier, the amount of lift required to maintain altitude during flight is directly related to the weight of the airplane. With a constant angle of attack, the airspeed necessary to provide sufficient lift to maintain level fight increases as weight increases. An overloaded airplane must accelerate to a higher-than-normal speed to generate sufficient lift for flight. This means the airplane requires more runway for takeoff, since it must attain a higher speed. The additional weight also reduces acceleration during the takeoff roll, and this adds to the total takeoff distance.

Problems do not end once the airplane is airborne. An overloaded airplane suffers a reduction in climb performance, and its service ceiling is decreased. This is because excess power and thrust are limited. In addition, exceeding the maximum allowable weight may cause the airplane to become unstable and difficult to fly.

For an airplane to be safe, it must be operated within weight limitations. In addition, the weight must be distributed, or balanced, properly. When you operate within weight and balance limitations, you can expect reduced takeoff distances, improved climb performance, and a higher ceiling. If you find you will be unable to safely take off or land at a particular airport at the airplane's maximum allowable weight, you should refer to the pilot's operating handbook. Most performance charts include weight as one variable. By reducing the weight of the airplane,

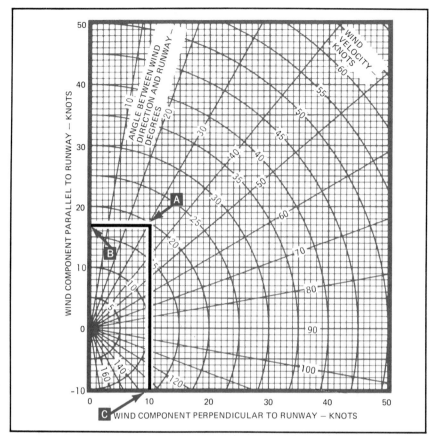

Figure 3-49. To determine the headwind and crosswind components, enter the sample chart at the point where the wind angle and the wind velocity arc meet (point A). Proceed horizontally to the left to find the headwind component of 17 knots (point B). Find the crosswind component by following the vertical lines down from point A to the bottom of the chart. The crosswind component is 10 knots (point C).

usually by carrying less fuel, you may find that you are able to safely take off or land at that airport. If you are in doubt, a better procedure would be to delay your takeoff for more favorable density altitude conditions and, if airborne, land at a nearby airport with a more suitable runway.

RUNWAY CONDITIONS

Runway conditions relating to aircraft performance data generally specify a paved and level runway with a smooth dry surface. If any one of these conditions does not exist for the runway you use, the takeoff and landing distances will not agree with the values listed in the performance charts.

A positive runway gradient adversely affects takeoff performance, but it is beneficial during landing. A negative gradient shortens the takeoff roll, but lengthens the landing distance.

Completely level runways are rare. The **gradient**, or **slope**, of the runway refers to the amount of change in runway height over its length. Gradient is usually expressed as a percentage. For example, a gradient of two percent means the runway height changes two feet for each 100 feet of runway length (100 × 2% = 2). A positive gradient indicates the height of the runway increases, while a negative value means it decreases. A positive gradient is unfavorable for takeoff, because the airplane must take off uphill. However, it is desirable for landings, since landing uphill reduces the landing roll. A negative gradient has the opposite effects on both takeoffs and landings. Runway gradient is listed in the *Airport/Facility Directory* when it is three-tenths of one percent or more.

Mud, water, snow, or grass usually increase takeoff distances.

Runway surface refers to what the runway is made of and what, if anything, is covering it. Generally, any surface that is not hard, smooth, and dry will increase the takeoff roll. This is due to the inability of the tires to roll smoothly along the runway. For example, on soft runways, the tires may sink into the ground and must constantly climb out of small ruts or holes. If a runway is muddy, wet, or covered with grass or snow, the tires must push obstructions out of the way. This reduces the airplane's acceleration. Sometimes, the reduction in acceleration is so great that it may be impossible to accelerate to takeoff speed.

The condition of the runway surface also affects the landing roll. A major concern is braking. **Braking effectiveness** refers to how much braking power you can apply to the runway. It depends, to a large extent, on the amount of friction between the tires and the runway. A great deal of friction and, therefore, braking power is normal on a dry runway. If the runway is wet, however, less friction is available and your landing roll-out will increase. In some cases, you may lose braking effectiveness because of hydroplaning or standing water or slush. **Hydroplaning** is caused by a thin layer of water that separates the tires from the runway. Braking effectiveness also may be completely lost on ice-covered runways. If you must operate in conditions where braking effectiveness is poor or nil, be sure the runway length is adequate and surface wind is favorable.

Although other runway surface conditions, such as mud, grass, and snow reduce the level of friction between tires and runway, in some circumstances they may provide a significant decrease in the landing roll. This occurs because they act as an obstruction to the tires. In extreme cases, this retarding force alone may be strong enough to bring the airplane to a complete stop without use of the brakes.

THE PILOT'S OPERATING HANDBOOK

Originally, airplane manuals did not follow a standardized format, and they often contained minimal information. In an effort to standardize style, format, and content, the pilot's operating handbook (POH) was developed, which includes standardized information. The format divides the POH into several sections and defines the kind of information included in each section. Most light airplanes built after 1975 use this new format. As mentioned earlier, the POHs for most light airplanes built after March 1, 1979, are also designated as the FAA approved flight manual. The typical POH includes the following types of information:

General — Presents basic information of general interest. The information is useful in loading, sheltering, handling, and preflight inspection. Definitions, explanations of symbols, abbreviations, and terminology also are included. In addition, this section contains descriptive data such as principal dimensions, engine type, horsepower rating, propeller type, and fuel specifications.

Limitations — Contains only those limitations required by regulation or necessary for the safe operation of the airplane, powerplant, systems, and equipment. It includes the operating limitations, instrument markings (including color coding), and placards.

Emergency Procedures — Clearly describes the recommended procedures for dealing with various types of emergencies or hazardous situations. Other system malfunctions or situations which, by their nature, are not emergencies may be included in this section or in a separate **Abnormal Procedures** section. Information typically found in the emergency procedures section includes such items as landing with a flat tire, flap and gear malfunctions, and engine and electrical fires. Since procedures contained in this section vary widely from airplane to airplane, you should be certain to become familiar with the procedures listed for the airplane you fly.

Normal Procedures — Presents recommended procedures for the normal operation of the airplane. It also includes airplane checklists and normal procedures to be used with optional equipment or systems. Checklists are guides intended to help you make sure you check all necessary items in a logical sequence. The use of an appropriate written checklist for preflight inspection, engine starting, and other ground procedures is highly recommended.

Performance — Contains all performance information required by the FAA, including performance charts or tables. Additional information, such as a flight planning example, may be included to help you interpret the various performance charts.

Weight and Balance — Presents all information required by the FAA that is necessary to calculate weight and balance.

Airplane Systems — Describes airplane systems in a manner appropriate to the kind of pilot considered most likely to operate the airplane. For advanced airplanes, the manufacturer may assume the pilot has a high degree of knowledge about airplanes in general.

Handling, Servicing, and Maintenance — Presents information to ensure that necessary handling, servicing, and maintenance can be accomplished. It is assumed that the person reading the POH is not a mechanic or technician.

Supplements — Contains operating information for various optional equipment and systems not included on the standard airplane.

In addition to these sections, manufacturers may, at their option, include additional sections. For example, a **Safety and Operational Tips** section or a comprehensive **Alphabetical Index** may be included.

PERFORMANCE CHARTS

Performance charts assume a properly tuned airplane in good condition with good brakes, and the data is based on average piloting abilities.

In developing performance charts, airplane manufacturers must make assumptions about the condition of the airplane and ability of the pilot. They assume the airplane to be in good condition, and that the engine has been properly tuned and is developing its rated power. Also, the brakes are considered to be in good condition. The pilot of the airplane is expected to follow normal checklist procedures and to have average flying abilities. "Average" means the person is not a highly trained test pilot with exceptional reaction time. At the same time, a student pilot or a person who has not flown for a long time is not considered average. In this context, average means a pilot capable of doing each of the required tasks correctly and at the appropriate times.

Performance charts are developed by deriving the data from actual flight tests.

With the aid of these assumptions, the manufacturer develops performance data for the airplane based on actual flight tests. Manufacturers, however, do not test airplanes under each and every condition shown on a performance chart. Instead, they evaluate specific flight data and, based on that data, mathematically derive the remaining data. As a practical consideration, you should remember that the original flight tests were conducted by test pilots flying a new airplane. With this in mind, you should look at performance data with a skeptical eye to ensure yourself a margin of safety. For example, departing on a 2,000-foot runway when performance charts indicate 1,900 feet are required for takeoff is very dangerous and reflects poor judgment.

TYPICAL CHARTS

Keep in mind that all performance charts in this presentation are samples only. They must never be used with any specific airplane you may be flying. When determining performance data for a given airplane, refer only to the POH for that particular airplane. Performance data can vary significantly between similar models or even from one model year to the next. The POH presents numerous charts which allow you to predict the airplane's performance accurately. They pertain to the takeoff, climb, cruise, descent, and landing phases of flight. Some of the typical charts found in the POH include:

Takeoff Distance Chart — Provides the distance required for the airplane to accelerate to takeoff speed and become airborne. These charts usually allow you to determine the actual ground roll distance of the airplane, as well as the total distance required to take off and climb to an altitude of 50 feet.

Maximum Rate of Climb Chart — Helps determine the maximum rate of climb for the airplane under a given set of conditions. This chart is of particular importance when obstructions, such as high terrain, are in the departure path immediately after takeoff.

Time, Fuel, and Distance to Climb — Primarily used as a flight planning tool, this chart allows you to calculate how long it will take the airplane to climb to a selected cruise altitude. You may also determine the fuel required and distance traveled to reach the desired altitude.

Cruise Performance — Provides the speed of the airplane, as well as fuel consumption rate at various altitudes and power settings.

Range Profile — Allows you to determine the maximum distance the airplane can fly at a given power setting. Since this chart typically assumes no wind, be sure to consider its effect.

Endurance Profile — Indicates the maximum length of time the airplane can remain aloft based on the power setting you select. This chart is similar to the range profile chart.

Landing Distance — Allows you to determine how much runway is required to land the airplane safely. This chart, like the takeoff distance chart, usually provides you with the ground roll distance, as well as the distance required to descend over a 50-foot obstacle, land, and bring the airplane to a full stop.

ADDITIONAL CHARTS

The style and content of performance charts vary from one manufacturer to another. You should be familiar with all performance charts in the POH for the airplane you fly. The following additional charts usually are included in the performance section of the POH.

Airspeed Calibration — The airspeed indicator is not a perfect instrument. It cannot accurately display correct readings throughout its entire range, and certain corrections are necessary. You use this chart to correct indicated airspeed (IAS). The result is called calibrated airspeed (CAS).

Fahrenheit/Celsius Conversion — This chart allows you to convert back and forth quickly between degrees Fahrenheit and Celsius.

Stall Speeds — Earlier you learned that the stall speed of an airplane varies with the airplane's weight, angle of bank, and flap setting. The stall speed chart indicates predicted stall speeds at various combinations of weight, bank angle, and flap settings.

Wind Component Chart — You use this chart to determine the headwind (or tailwind) and crosswind components based on current conditions.

Glide Distance Chart — In the event of an engine failure, the airplane will continue to travel in a forward direction as it loses altitude. The glide distance chart tells you how far the airplane can be flown based on the airplane's AGL altitude at the time the engine fails. Some manufacturers include this chart in the emergency section of the POH instead of the performance section.

CHART PRESENTATIONS

Performance charts generally present their information in either a table or a graph format. The table format usually contains several notes which require you to make adjustments for various conditions which are not accounted for in the body of the chart. Graph presentations, though somewhat harder to use, usually incorporate more variables and adjustments may not be required. Almost every chart, whether a table or a graph, will specify a set of conditions under which the chart is valid. For example, a takeoff chart may only be valid for a particular weight and flap setting. Therefore, you should always check the chart conditions before using it.

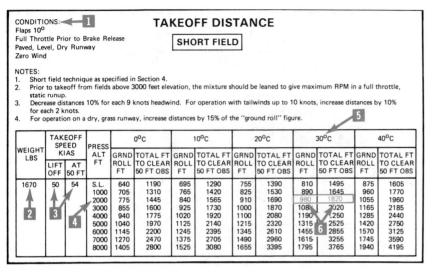

Figure 3-50. A quick check of the conditions (item 1) and the takeoff weight (item 2) indicate you are using the correct chart. Note the takeoff speed of 50 knots and the speed of 54 knots shortly after takeoff at 50 feet (item 3). Enter the tabular data at the pressure altitude of 2,000 feet (item 4) and proceed horizontally to the column for 30°C (item 5). The ground roll distance is 980 feet, and the total distance to clear a 50-foot obstacle is 1,820 feet (item 6).

TAKEOFF CHARTS

For this first sample chart, assume you are planning to depart an airport under the following conditions, and want to determine the ground roll and total distance required to clear a 50-foot obstacle. [Figure 3-50]

Pressure altitude .... 2,000 ft.
Temperature .... 30°C
Flaps .... 10°
Runway .... Paved, level, and dry
Wind ....Calm
Weight .... 1,670 lbs.

In the example, the wind condition was calm, but how would the problem change with a headwind? You can find the answer in the notes listed for the chart. According to note number 3, the distances decrease by 10% for each nine knots of headwind. For example, with an 18-knot headwind, the ground roll is reduced by 20%, to 784 feet (980 – 196 = 784), and total distance is reduced by 20% to 1,456 feet (1,820 – 364 = 1,456). With a dry grass runway surface, note number 4 is applicable. In this case, both distances are increased by 15% of the ground roll figure. This means the actual ground roll increases to 1,127 feet (980 × 15% = 147 + 980 = 1,127). The total distance to clear a 50-foot obstacle also increases to 1,967 feet (1,820 + 147 = 1,967).

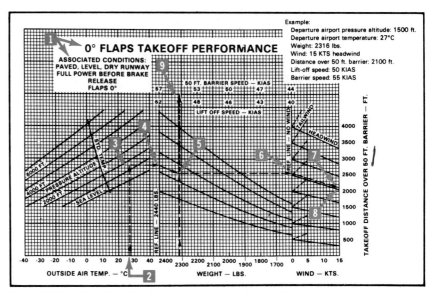

Figure 3-51. After checking the associated conditions (item 1), you can see that this chart is appropriate. Enter the graph at a temperature of 27°C (item 2) and proceed vertically to the pressure altitude of 1,500 feet (item 3). Next, proceed horizontally to the first reference line (item 4), then diagonally down until you intercept the takeoff weight of 2,316 pounds (item 5). Continue across to the second reference line (item 6), and correct for the headwind by paralleling the diagonal line downward until you intercept the 15-knot mark (item 7). You find the takeoff distance of 2,100 feet on the right side of the graph (item 8). To determine the appropriate takeoff and 50-foot barrier speeds, proceed vertically up from the takeoff weight (item 5) to the speeds listed at the top of the chart (item 9). The takeoff speed is 50 knots and the barrier (50-foot obstacle) speed is 55 knots. Note, these speeds are not directly indicated. You have to check the available information carefully and extract the speeds that correspond to the takeoff weight.

For this sample chart, assume you are planning to depart under the following conditions. This time you are only concerned with the distance required to clear a 50-foot obstacle. [Figure 3-51]

Pressure altitude .... 1,500 ft.
Temperature .... 27°C
Flaps .... Up
Runway .... Paved, level, and dry
Wind .... 15 kts. headwind
Weight .... 2,316 lbs.

Since a graphic chart often includes more variables in a single chart, you must use extra care when using it. For example, you generally estimate where two lines meet on the chart. There is also a tendency to "eyeball" the chart. This means that instead of drawing out your lines carefully, you simply select line positions and intersections visually. This can lead to substantial errors.

TIME, FUEL, AND DISTANCE TO CLIMB CHART

This sample chart is a little different from the others. First, you determine the time, fuel, and distance to climb to your cruise altitude, then you apply a credit for departing any airport above sea level. For this example, assume the following conditions, and determine the time, fuel, and distance required to climb from the airport elevation of 2,000 feet to 8,000 feet. [Figure 3-52]

Cruise altitude .... 8,000 ft.
Airport elevation .... 2,000 ft.
Flaps ....Up
Power .... Full throttle
Temperature ....Standard
Weight ....1,670 lbs.

TIME, FUEL, AND DISTANCE TO CLIMB

CONDITIONS:◄——1 **MAXIMUM RATE OF CLIMB**
Flaps Up
Full Throttle
Standard Temperature

NOTES:◄——4
1. Add 0.8 of a gallon of fuel for engine start, taxi and takeoff allowance.
2. Mixture leaned above 3000 feet for maximum RPM.
3. Increase time, fuel and distance by 10% for each 10°C above standard temperature.
4. Distances shown are based on zero wind.

WEIGHT LBS	PRESSURE ALTITUDE FT	TEMP °C	CLIMB SPEED KIAS	RATE OF CLIMB FPM	FROM SEA LEVEL		
					TIME MIN	FUEL USED GALLONS	DISTANCE NM
1670	S.L.	15	67	715	0	0	0
	1000	13	66	675	1	0.2	2
	2000	11	66	630	3	0.4	3
	3000	9	65	590	5	0.7	5
	4000	7	65	550	6	0.9	7
	5000	5	64	505	8	1.2	9
	6000	3	63	465	10	1.4	12
	7000	1	63	425	13	1.7	14
	8000	-1	62	380	15	2.0	17

Figure 3-52. First, check the conditions (item 1). Then, read the time, fuel, and distance to climb to 8,000 feet of 15 minutes, 2.0 gallons, and 17 miles, respectively (item 2). Next, determine the time, fuel, and distance credits to be applied for departing an airport at 2,000 feet. These values are 3 minutes, 0.4 gallons, and 3 miles (item 3). After you subtract the credits, the net values are 12 minutes, 1.6 gallons, and 14 miles. A check of the notes, however, indicates that you must add an additional 0.8 gallons of fuel for the engine start, taxi, and takeoff allowances (item 4). The final values of time, fuel, and distance to climb from 2,000 feet to 8,000 feet are 12 minutes, 2.4 gallons (1.6 + .8), and 14 miles.

CRUISE PERFORMANCE CHART

These charts vary considerably. Before you use a particular chart, make sure you understand how the information is portrayed. Temperatures for cruise may include International Standard Atmosphere (ISA) values, as well as colder and warmer temperatures. For instance, temperature categories may specify ISA −20°C, standard day ISA, and ISA +20°C. Both Celsius and Fahrenheit temperatures may be included. In addition, the temperature figures for some manufacturers may be adjusted for frictional heating of the temperature probe. Assume you are planning a flight under the following conditions, and wish to determine the manifold pressure setting, fuel flow, and cruise true airspeed. [Figure 3-53]

Pressure altitude . . . . 8,000 ft.
Temperature . . . . .ISA −20°C
Power . . . . 2,400 r.p.m.
Weight . . . . 2,600 lbs.

CRUISE POWER SETTINGS - 2400 RPM

65% MCP (or FULL THROTTLE) - 2600 POUNDS *(KNOTS)*

PRESS ALT.	ISA -36°F (-20°C)					STANDARD DAY (ISA)					ISA +36°F (+20°C)				
	IOAT		MAN. PRESS	FUEL FLOW		TAS		IOAT		MAN. PRESS	FUEL FLOW		TAS		IOAT		MAN. PRESS	FUEL FLOW		TAS	

FEET	°F	°C	IN HG	PPH	GPH	KTS	MPH	°F	°C	IN HG	PPH	GPH	KTS	MPH	°F	°C	IN HG	PPH	GPH	KTS	MPH
SL	25	-4	22.3	54	9.0	116	134	61	16	22.9	54	9.0	118	136	97	36	23.5	54	9.0	120	138
1000	21	-6	22.0	54	9.0	117	135	57	14	22.6	54	9.0	119	137	93	34	23.2	54	9.0	121	139
2000	18	-8	21.7	54	9.0	118	136	54	12	22.3	54	9.0	120	138	90	32	23.0	54	9.0	122	140
3000	14	-10	21.5	54	9.0	119	136	50	10	22.1	54	9.0	121	139	86	30	22.7	54	9.0	123	142
4000	11	-12	21.2	54	9.0	119	137	46	8	21.8	54	9.0	122	140	84	29	22.4	54	9.0	124	143
5000	7	-14	20.9	54	9.0	120	138	43	6	21.5	54	9.0	123	142	81	27	22.2	54	9.0	125	144
6000	3	-16	21.7	54	9.0	121	139	41	5	21.3	54	9.0	124	143	77	25	22.0	54	9.0	126	145
7000	1	-17	20.5	54	9.0	122	140	37	3	21.1	54	9.0	125	144	73	23	21.7	54	9.0	126	145
8000	-2	-19	20.3	54	9.0	123	142	34	1	20.9	54	9.0	125	144	70	21	21.5	54	9.0	127	146
9000	-6	-21	20.1	54	9.0	124	143	30	-1	20.7	54	9.0	126	145	66	19	21.3	54	9.0	127	146
10000	-9	-23	19.9	54	9.0	125	144	27	-3	20.5	54	9.0	127	146	63	17	20.8	53	8.8	127	146
11000	-13	-25	19.8	54	9.0	125	144	23	-5	20.1	53	8.8	126	145	59	15	20.1	52	8.7	126	145
12000	-17	-27	19.3	54	9.0	125	144	19	-7	19.3	52	8.7	125	144	55	13	19.3	51	8.5	123	142
13000	-20	-29	18.6	52	8.7	124	143	16	-9	18.6	51	8.5	123	142	52	11	18.6	49	8.2	120	138
14000	-24	-31	17.9	51	8.5	121	139	12	-11	17.9	49	8.2	120	138	48	9	17.9	48	8.0	117	135

NOTES: 1. Shaded area represents operation with full throttle.
2. Full throttle manifold settings are approximate.

Figure 3-53. This sample chart includes data for three sets of temperature conditions: ISA −20°, ISA, and ISA +20°. In this example, the appropriate temperature conditions are ISA −20°C (item 1). Below this subheading proceed down to the line for the cruise pressure altitude of 8,000 feet (item 2). With a temperature 20°C below standard, the indicated outside air temperature (IOAT) at 8,000 feet is −2°F or −19°C (item 3). In this case, the figures do include adjustments for frictional heating of the OAT gauge. The significant values are the manifold pressure of 20.3 in. Hg (item 4), fuel flow of 54 pounds per hour or 9.0 gallons per hour (item 5), and a cruise speed of 123 knots or 142 miles per hour (item 6).

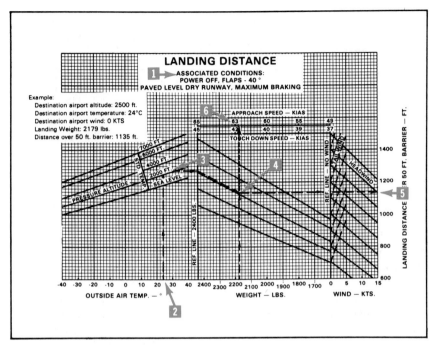

Figure 3-54. First, check the associated conditions listed on the sample chart (item 1). Next, enter the chart at the given temperature of 24°C (item 2) and proceed vertically up to the pressure altitude of 2,500 feet (item 3). Proceed horizontally to the first reference line, then diagonally down to a weight of 2,179 pounds (item 4). Continue horizontally to the right to the second reference line. Note that since the reported wind is calm, no correction is required here for headwind or tailwind. Read the distance required of 1,135 feet on the right side of the chart (item 5). The approach and touchdown speeds are indicated straight up from the landing weight near the top of the chart (item 6). The approximate approach and touchdown speeds are 63 knots and 42 knots, respectively.

LANDING DISTANCE CHART

Landing distance charts are similar to takeoff distance charts. For this sample of a graph-style performance chart, use the following conditions to determine the distance to land over a 50-foot obstacle and bring the airplane to a complete stop. [Figure 3-54]

Pressure altitude .... 2,500 ft.
Temperature .... 24°C
Flaps .... 40°
Runway .... Paved, level, and dry
Wind .... Calm
Weight .... 2,179 lbs.
Braking .... Maximum

WEIGHT LBS	TAKEOFF SPEED KIAS		PRESS ALT FT	0°C		10°C		20°C		30°C		40°C	
	LIFT OFF	AT 50 FT		GRND ROLL FT	TOTAL TO CLEAR 50 FT OBS	GRND ROLL FT	TOTAL TO CLEAR 50 FT OBS	GRND ROLL FT	TOTAL TO CLEAR 50 FT OBS	GRND ROLL FT	TOTAL TO CLEAR 50 FT OBS	GRND ROLL FT	TOTAL TO CLEAR 50 FT OBS
1670	50	54	S.L.	640	1190	695	1290	755	1390	810	1495	875	1605
			1000	705	1310	765	1420	825	1530	890	1645	960	1770
			2000	775	1445	840	1565	910	1690	980	1820	1055	1960
			3000	855	1600	925	1730	1000	1870	1080	2020	1165	2185

Figure 3-55. Looking at the sample takeoff chart excerpt, you can see that the given pressure altitude of 1,500 feet falls between the 1,000- and 2,000-foot pressure altitude values. This means your ground roll distance will fall between 890 and 980 feet. Interpolation is required.

INTERPOLATION

The sample problems you have looked at so far used convenient altitudes and temperatures which permitted you to extract your answers directly. To see how to solve a problem when this is not the case, work another takeoff performance problem. In this example, assume you need to know the ground roll requirement under the given conditions. [Figure 3-55]

Pressure altitude .... 1,500 ft.
Temperature .... 30°C
Flaps .... 10°
Runway .... Paved, level, and dry
Wind .... Calm
Weight .... 1,670 lbs.

Interpolation refers to the process of finding an unknown value between two known values. Often this is necessary when you use charts with tabular information. In this case, you know the ground roll figures for 1,000 and 2,000 feet and want to determine the ground roll for 1,500 feet. The first step in interpolation is to compute the differences between known values.

	Pressure Altitude	**Ground Roll**
	2,000 ft.	980 ft.
	1,000 ft.	890 ft.
Difference	1,000 ft.	90 ft.

The 1,500-foot airport pressure altitude is 50% of the way between 1,000 and 2,000 feet. Therefore, the ground roll also is 50% of the way between 890 and 980 feet. The answer then, is 935 feet (90-foot difference × .5 + 890 feet = 935 feet).

In practice, pilots often round off values derived from table charts to the more conservative figure. This practice gives you a good estimate of performance data, and it also provides a margin of safety.

CHECKLIST ━━━━━━━━━

After studying this section, you should have a basic understanding of:

✓ **Performance speeds** — How maximum level speed, best angle-of-climb, and best rate-of-climb speeds are determined.

✓ **Service and absolute ceilings** — What they are and how they are determined.

✓ **Cruising airspeeds** — How maximum range and maximum endurance airspeeds are determined.

✓ **Factors affecting performance** — How density altitude, humidity, winds, and runway conditions affect airplane performance.

✓ **The pilot's operating handbook (POH)** — How this publication is organized and the type of information included in each section.

✓ **Performance charts** — What some of the more common performance charts are and how they are used.

SECTION F

WEIGHT AND BALANCE

In previous sections, you learned about airplane design and how the location of the airplane's center of gravity (CG) directly affects stability. This section expands the center of gravity concept by providing you with some of the terminology and techniques you use in determining weight and balance. Keep in mind that the weight and balance charts, graphs, and tables in this presentation are samples only. They must never be used with any specific airplane you may be flying. When determining the weight and balance condition for a given airplane, refer only to the POH for that airplane.

AIRPLANE WEIGHT

The empty weight of an aircraft always includes unusable fuel and optional equipment.

You are already aware that weight is caused by the downward pull of gravity and varies with several factors. These factors include the weight of the basic airplane, installed equipment, passengers, cargo, and fuel. You also know that the effective weight varies when you maneuver the airplane in flight. This is called load factor. In this section, however, we are concerned primarily with the weight of the airplane and its contents when at rest. The starting point for weight computation is the weight of the airplane before passengers, cargo, and fuel are added. The term **basic empty weight** includes the weight of the standard airplane, optional equipment, unusable fuel, and full operating fluids including full engine oil. Older airplanes might use the term **licensed empty weight**, which is similar to basic empty weight except that it does not include full engine oil. Instead, it includes only the weight of undrainable oil. If you fly an airplane that lists a licensed empty weight, be sure to add the weight of oil to your computations.

One gallon of avgas equals 6 pounds; one gallon of oil equals 7.5 pounds.

Standard weights are used for computing the weight of aviation gasoline (avgas) and engine oil. Avgas weighs 6 pounds per gallon, while oil weighs 7.5 pounds per gallon. Remember that engine oil capacity is usually given in quarts; therefore, you must convert it to gallons before determining its weight.

Another term, **payload**, refers to the weight of the flight crew, passengers, and any cargo or baggage; **useful load** is the difference between maximum takeoff weight and basic empty weight. Useful load includes payload and usable fuel. **Usable fuel** is the fuel available for the flight. It does not include **unusable fuel**, which is the quantity of fuel that cannot be safely used during flight. The following summary should help you understand how various weights are calculated:

	Basic Empty Weight
+	Payload
=	Zero Fuel Weight
+	Usable Fuel
=	Ramp Weight
−	Fuel Used for Start, Taxi, and Engine Runup
=	Takeoff Weight
−	Fuel Used During Flight
=	Landing Weight

WEIGHT LIMITATIONS

Some weight and balance terms may be preceded by the word **maximum**. When this word is used, it indicates a limitation which must not be exceeded. For example, the **maximum ramp weight** is the maximum weight approved for ground operations, while **maximum takeoff weight** is the maximum weight approved for the start of the takeoff roll. Weight limitations are necessary to guarantee the structural integrity of the airplane, as well as enable you to predict airplane performance accurately. For example, airplanes certified in the normal category usually are capable of withstanding a positive load factor of 3.8 G's and have an additional safety factor built in. Regardless of the safety factor, you should never intentionally exceed the limit loads for which an airplane is certificated. These structural limitations are based on an airplane operated at or below the maximum weight. Operating the airplane above this weight could result in structural deformation or failure during flight if you encounter excessive load factors, strong wind gusts, or turbulence. Operating in excess of the maximum weight also affects performance. It results in a longer takeoff roll, reduced climb performance, reduced cruising speed, an increase in fuel consumption, an increase in stall speed, and an increase in the landing roll.

Operating above the maximum weight limitation compromises the structural integrity of the airplane and adversely affects performance.

DETERMINING EMPTY WEIGHT

The airplane's weight and balance records contain essential data for the airplane, including a complete list of all optional equipment that has been installed. You use these records to determine the weight and balance condition of the empty airplane. From time to time, the owner or operator of an airplane may have equipment removed, replaced, or additional equipment installed. These changes must be made to the weight and balance records. In addition, major repairs or alterations to the airplane itself also must be recorded by a certificated mechanic. When the revised weight and moment are recorded on a new form, the old record is marked with the word "superseded" and dated with the effective date of the new record. In this way, you can easily determine which is the latest version.

Weight and balance information for each airplane can be found in the airplane's weight and balance records.

AIRPLANE BALANCE

Airplanes must be loaded within acceptable CG limits before flight and the distribution of the load must be maintained during flight.

The center of gravity of an airplane is defined as the theoretical point where all of the airplane's weight is considered to be concentrated. As you learned in Chapter 1, the location of this point is critical to an airplane's stability and stabilator (or elevator) effectiveness. Improper balance of the airplane's load can result in serious control problems. Fortunately, you can avoid these problems by taking the time to determine the location of the CG prior to flight and then comparing the computed location to the acceptable limits prescribed by the manufacturer. If the CG is located within these limits, the airplane can be flown safely. However, if it is located outside of these limits, you will have to relocate fuel, passengers, or cargo in order to move the CG within acceptable limits. It is equally important to maintain this distribution of weight during flight, since any movement of passengers or cargo will change the location of the CG.

WEIGHT AND BALANCE CONTROL

Whenever practical, ask your passengers for their actual weights and use a scale to weigh baggage.

There are three different methods commonly used in determining weight and balance. They include the computational, graph, and table methods. It is important to note that each method is only as accurate as the information you provide. Therefore, you should ask passengers what they weigh and add a few pounds to cover the additional weight of clothing, especially during the winter months. The weight of baggage should be determined by the use of a scale, if practical. If a scale is not available, be conservative and overestimate the weight. When estimating weights, you can use certain standard weights designated by the FAA. A person of average stature is considered to weigh 170 pounds, and a child between 2 and 12 years of age is considered to weigh 80 pounds. However, if the aircraft is loaded near a weight and balance limit, or a passenger's weight is obviously different from these standard weights, you should use actual weights.

The reference datum is an arbitrarily fixed vertical plane.

Balance is determined by the location of the CG, which is usually described as a given number of inches aft of the reference datum. The **reference datum** is an imaginary vertical plane, arbitrarily fixed somewhere along the longitudinal axis of the airplane, from which all horizontal distances are measured for weight and balance purposes. There is no fixed rule for its location. It may be located on the nose of the airplane, the firewall, the leading edge of the wing, or even at a point in space ahead of the airplane. The location of the datum is established by the manufacturer and is defined in the POH or in the airplane's weight and balance papers. The horizontal distance from the datum to any component of the airplane or to any object located within the airplane is called the **arm**.

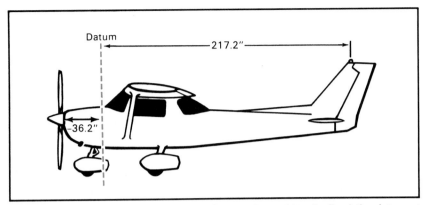

Figure 3-56. For this airplane, the manufacturer has arbitrarily fixed the datum at the front face of the firewall. The arm of the propeller spinner is –36.2 inches (36.2 inches ahead of the datum plane). The rotating beacon, located on the tail, has an arm of 217.2 inches aft of the datum plane.

Another term which can be used interchangeably with arm is **station**. If the component or object is located to the rear of the datum, it is measured as a positive number and usually is referred to as inches aft of the datum. Conversely, if the component or object is located forward of the datum, it is indicated as a negative number and is usually referred to as inches forward of the datum. [Figure 3-56]

If the weight of an object is multiplied by its arm, the result is known as its **moment**. You may think of moment as a force which results from an object's weight acting at a distance. Moment is also referred to as the tendency of an object to rotate or pivot about a point. The farther an object is from a pivotal point, the greater its force. The concept of weight, arm, and moment can be shown with a teeter-totter. [Figure 3-57]

Moment = Weight × Arm

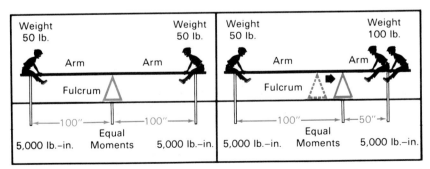

Figure 3-57. The teeter-totter on the left shows that each child is exerting a moment of 5,000 lb.-in. (50-pound weight times 100-inch arm). As long as each child maintains the same distance from the fulcrum, their moments are balanced. The teeter-totter on the right shows that unequal weights also can be balanced if the distance from the fulcrum is adjusted. In this case, 100 pounds at 50 inches exerts the same moment as 50 pounds at 100 inches.

Just like the children on the teeter-totter, each component of an airplane, as well as each object it carries, exerts a moment proportional to its weight and distance from the designated reference datum. By totaling the weights and moments of all components and objects carried, you can determine the point where a loaded airplane would balance on an imaginary fulcrum. This is the airplane's CG.

COMPUTATIONAL METHOD

With the computational method, you use simple mathematics to solve weight and balance problems. The first step is to look up the basic empty weight and total moment for the particular airplane you fly. If the center of gravity is given, it should also be noted. The empty weight CG can be considered the "arm" of the empty airplane. As mentioned earlier, this information is contained in the airplane's weight and balance records. You should record it as the first item on the weight and balance form. [Figure 3-58]

Next, the weights of the fuel, pilot and passengers, and baggage are recorded. Since avgas weighs six pounds per gallon, multiply the gallons of usable fuel by six to get the total fuel weight. For example, 38 gallons of avgas weighs 228 pounds. Use care in recording the weight of each

WEIGHT and BALANCE FORM			
ITEM	WEIGHT (pounds)	ARM (inches)	MOMENT (pound-inches)
BASIC EMPTY WT.	1,437	38.75	55,684
FUEL		48.0	
PILOT & PASSENGER		37.0	
REAR PASSENGERS		73.0	
BAGGAGE		95.0	
TOTAL			

CG = _____ INCHES

Figure 3-58. In this example, the airplane's weight of 1,437 pounds is recorded in the first column, its CG or arm of 38.75 inches in the second, and its moment of 55,684 pound-inches in the last. Notice that the weight of the airplane multiplied by its CG equals its moment. Also, note the arm for each of the other items has already been recorded by the manufacturer. However, some manufacturers require you to look up and record this information yourself.

item, since some airplanes have several rows of seats and baggage compartments. Recording each weight in its proper location is extremely important to the accurate calculation of a CG. Once you have recorded all of the weights, add them together to determine the total weight of the loaded airplane.

Now, check to see that the total weight does not exceed the maximum allowable weight under existing conditions. If it does, you will usually reduce the amount of fuel you are carrying and plan an extra fuel stop. Once you are satisfied that the total weight is within prescribed limits, multiply each individual weight by its associated arm to determine its moment. Then, add the moments together to arrive at the total moment for the airplane. Your final computation is to find the center of gravity of the loaded airplane by dividing the total moment by the total weight. [Figure 3-59]

$$CG = \frac{\text{Total Moment}}{\text{Total Weight}}$$

After determining the airplane's weight and center of gravity location, you need to determine if the CG is within acceptable limits. This is usually done by consulting the airplane's center of gravity limits graph. If the CG falls outside of acceptable limits, you will have to adjust the loading of the airplane. To determine if the center of gravity is within limits, plot the point at which the airplane's total weight and CG meet. If

WEIGHT and BALANCE FORM			
ITEM	WEIGHT (pounds)	ARM (inches)	MOMENT (pound-inches)
BASIC EMPTY WT.	1,437	38.75	55,684
FUEL (38 gal.)	228	48.0	10,944
PILOT & PASSENGER	340	37.0	12,580
REAR PASSENGERS	280	73.0	20,440
BAGGAGE	15	95.0	1,425
TOTAL	2,300		101,073
CG = 43.9 INCHES			

Figure 3-59. Here is an example of a completed weight and balance form. The appropriate weight is recorded next to each item. Notice that the amount of fuel in gallons also has been recorded on the fuel line. The CG, filled in at the bottom of the form, is determined by dividing the total moment of the airplane by its total weight.

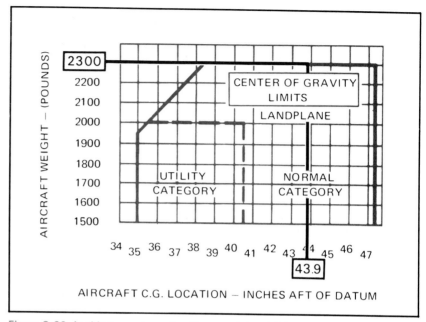

Figure 3-60. In this example, notice that a weight of 2,300 pounds and a CG location of 43.9 inches are within acceptable limits for operations in the normal category. However, the airplane is too heavy and is loaded with the CG too far aft for operations in the utility category.

this point is within the approved limits on the graph, the airplane is considered to be properly loaded. [Figure 3-60]

GRAPH METHOD

The graph method is a simplification of the computational method. Instead of multiplying weight times arm to determine moment, you simply use a graph supplied by the manufacturer. In addition, when a manufacturer uses this method, the center of gravity limits graph usually reflects weight and moment instead of weight and CG.

The graph method uses the same first step as the computational method. Record the basic empty weight of the airplane, along with its total moment. (The CG, if provided, is not required.) Remember to use the actual weight and moment of the airplane you will be flying. Next, record the weights of the fuel, pilot, passengers and baggage on the weight and balance worksheet. Then, determine the total weight of the airplane.

If the airplane is too heavy for the flight, you must leave some fuel, baggage, or a passenger behind.

If this weight exceeds the maximum allowable weight, you will have to make some adjustments to fuel, baggage, or passengers. For example, assume the maximum allowable weight for the airplane is 2,400 pounds and the total weight of the loaded airplane comes to 2,550 pounds. In this situation, the airplane is 150 pounds over its maximum allowable weight.

To make this flight, you will need to carry 25 gallons less fuel (25 gal. × 6 lb./gal. = 150 lb.) or leave 150 pounds of baggage behind. Another option is to leave behind a passenger who weighs 150 pounds or more. Once you have determined the weight to be within prescribed limits, compute the moment for each weight and for the loaded airplane. You do this using a loading graph provided by the manufacturer. For example, let's assume the pilot and front seat passenger have a combined weight of 340 pounds. [Figure 3-61]

Reduction factors are commonly used to reduce the size of large numbers to manageable levels. In most cases, you need not be concerned with a

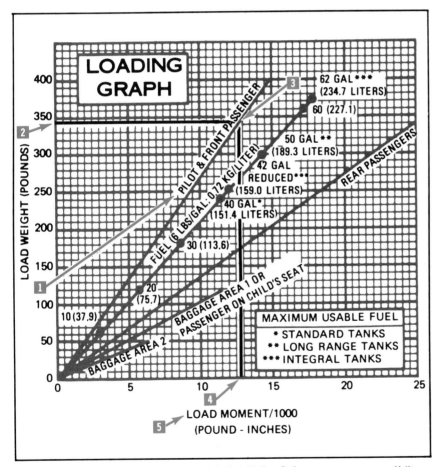

Figure 3-61. First, find the line that is labeled "pilot & front seat passenger" (item 1). Now, enter the graph from the left side at a weight of 340 pounds (item 2), and proceed horizontally to the appropriate line (item 3). Next, drop straight down and read the moment of 12.6 (item 4). Notice that numbers on this scale represent the load moment/1,000 (item 5). This is referred to as a reduction factor. In this case, the moment of 12.6 actually represents a moment of 12,600 pound-inches.

SAMPLE LOADING PROBLEM	SAMPLE AIRPLANE		YOUR AIRPLANE	
	Weight (lbs.)	Moment (lb.-ins. /1000)	Weight (lbs.)	Moment (lb.-ins. /1000)
1. Basic Empty Weight	1467	57.3	1,522	56.2
2. Usable Fuel (At 6 Lbs./Gal.) Standard Tanks (40 Gal. Maximum)	240	11.5	240	11.5
3. Pilot and Front Passenger (Station 34 to 46)	340	12.6	340	12.6
4. Rear Passengers	340	24.8		
5. *Baggage Area 1 or Passenger on Child's Seat (Station 82 to 108, 120 Lbs. Max.)	20	1.9		
6. *Baggage Area 2 (Station 108 to 142, 50 Lbs. Max.)				
7. RAMP WEIGHT AND MOMENT	2407	108.1	2,102	80.3
8. Fuel allowance for engine start, taxi, and runup	-7	-.3	-7	-.3
9. TAKEOFF WEIGHT AND MOMENT (Subtract Step 8 from Step 7)	2400	107.8	2,095	80.0

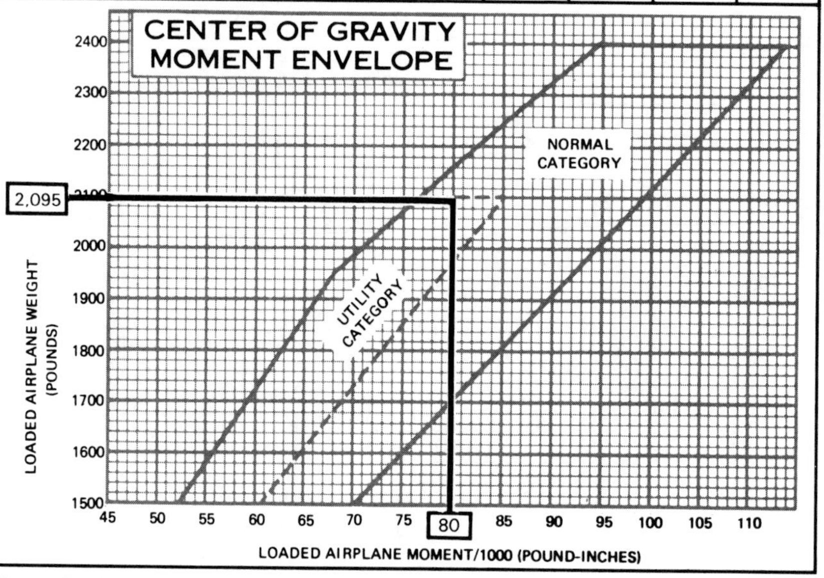

Figure 3-62. After recording the basic empty weight and moment of the airplane, and the weight and moment for each item, total and record all weights and moments. Notice that you apply a weight and moment credit for fuel used during engine start, taxi, and runup. Next, plot the listed takeoff weight and moment on the sample moment envelope graph. Based on a weight of 2,095 pounds and a moment/1,000 of 80 pound-inches, the airplane is properly loaded for flight in the utility category.

reduction factor. This is because the CG moment envelope chart normally uses the same reduction factor. [Figure 3-62]

TABLE METHOD

The table method is a further refinement of the computational and graph methods. Using this method, you locate a given weight on the appropriate table, then look up its corresponding moment. Often, however, the exact weight you are looking for is not found on the table. In these situations, look up two smaller weights which add up to the total weight you want, and add their corresponding moments. Assume you need to determine the moment for the third and fourth seat occupants whose combined weight is 340 pounds. Also, assume this airplane has a bench seat. [Figure 3-63]

After the weight and balance worksheet is complete, you must check to see if the airplane is loaded within acceptable limits for flight. You have already seen one method of doing this — consulting a center of gravity moment envelope. Another method is to check a "moment limit versus weight table" provided by some manufacturers. To use this table, first find the loaded weight of the airplane. Then, check to see if the loaded

	FRONT SEATS			3RD AND 4TH SEATS	
	FWD POS.		AFT POS.	BENCH SEAT	SPLIT SEAT
	ARM 104	ARM 105	ARM 112	ARM 142	ARM 144
WEIGHT	MOM 100	MOM 100	MOM 100	MOM 100	MOM 100
120	125	126	134	170	173
130	135	137	146	185	187
140	146	147	157	199	202
150	156	158	168	213	216
160	166	168	179	227	230
170	177	179	190	241	245
180	187	189	202	256	259
190	198	200	213	270	274
200	208	210	224	284	288

Figure 3-63. Note that this table uses a reduction factor of 100 and the highest weight given is 200 pounds. To determine the moment/100 for 340 pounds, look up the moments for 200 pounds and 140 pounds (200 lb. + 140 lb. = 340 lb.). In this case, the moment/100 is 483 pound-inches (284 lb.-in. + 199 lb.-in.).

ITEM	WEIGHT	MOM/100
1. BASIC EMPTY CONDITION	1,728	1,912
2. FRONT SEAT OCCUPANTS	340	357
3. 3rd & 4th SEAT OCCUPANTS	340	483
4. 5th & 6th SEAT OCCUPANTS		
5. BAGGAGE	100	167
6. CARGO		
7. SUB TOTAL	2,508	2,919
8. FUEL LOADING (40 gal.)	240	281
9. SUB TOTAL RAMP CONDITION	2,748	3,200
10. *LESS FUEL FOR START, TAXI, AND TAKE-OFF	-8	-9
11. SUB TOTAL TAKE-OFF CONDITION	2,740	3,191
12. LESS FUEL TO DESTINATION	162	189
13. LANDING CONDITION	2,578	3,002

*Fuel for start, taxi and take-off is normally 8 lbs at an average mom/100 of 9.

MOMENT LIMITS vs WEIGHT

Weight	Minimum Moment 100	Maximum Moment 100
2500	2775	2958
2510	2788	2969
2520	2801	2981
2530	2814	2993
2540	2828	3005
2550	2841	3017
2560	2854	3028
2570	2867	3040
2580	2880	3052
2590	2894	3064
2600	2907	3076
2610	2920	3088
2620	2933	3099
2630	2947	3111
2640	2960	3123
2650	2973	3135
2660	2987	3147
2670	3000	3159
2680	3013	3170
2690	3027	3182
2700	3040	3194
2710	3054	3206
2720	3067	3218
2730	3081	3230
2740	3094	3241
2750	3108	3253

Figure 3-64. On the left is a completed weight and balance worksheet using given values for a sample flight. Note the takeoff weight of 2,740 pounds and moment/100 of 3,191 pound-inches. Using the table on the right, for a weight of 2,740 pounds, the minimum acceptable moment/100 is 3,094 pound-inches and the maximum is 3,241 pound-inches. Since our moment is well within these limits, the airplane is safely loaded for flight.

moment falls within the minimum and maximum values given for that weight. [Figure 3-64]

WEIGHT SHIFT

Often during weight and balance computations, you will find that either the weight of the airplane or its CG location is beyond acceptable limits.

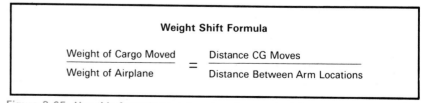

Weight Shift Formula

$$\frac{\text{Weight of Cargo Moved}}{\text{Weight of Airplane}} = \frac{\text{Distance CG Moves}}{\text{Distance Between Arm Locations}}$$

Figure 3-65. Use this formula to determine changes in CG when weight must be shifted. An easy way to remember this formula is to note that the small values are on top of the formula and the large values are on the bottom.

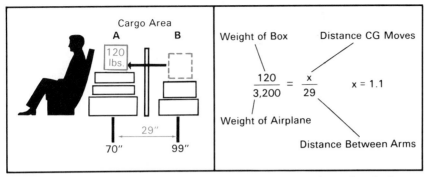

Figure 3-66. As shown in this illustration, the first step is to determine the known values. For example, the distance between cargo areas "A" and "B" is 29 inches. Next, insert the other known values into the formula and solve for the unknown. In this case, the unknown value is the distance the CG moves forward when the weight is shifted. Solving this equation results in the answer of 1.1 inches.

Usually, decreasing weight is a fairly simple matter, especially if you accomplish it before the airplane's CG is calculated. However, if you change the load in order to adjust the CG, the computations are somewhat more complex. [Figure 3-65]

Perhaps the easiest way to see how to apply this formula is to work two different weight shift problems. In the first, assume a loaded airplane weight of 3,200 pounds and a CG of 45.6 inches. A box weighing 120 pounds is moved from cargo area "B" which has an arm of 99 inches, to cargo area "A," whose arm is 70 inches. How many inches will the CG move when this weight is shifted? [Figure 3-66]

For the next example, assume the CG is located aft of acceptable limits and you need to determine the amount of weight to be shifted from the aft cargo area to the forward one. Again, the same formula is used; the only difference is which value is unknown. [Figure 3-67]

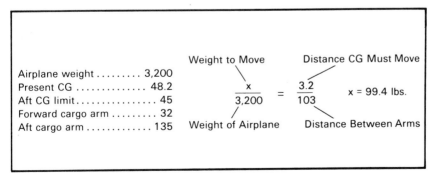

Figure 3-67. As with the previous problem, insert the known values into the formula. In this case, you are solving for the weight of the cargo to be moved. Solving this equation results in an answer of 99.4 pounds.

CHECKLIST ——————————————————

After studying this section, you should have a basic understanding of:

✓ **Airplane weight** — What terms are used to describe various weights and what the hazards of overloading an airplane are.

✓ **Empty weight** — What the difference is between basic empty weight and licensed empty weight.

✓ **Airplane balance** — What the terms arm, moment, and CG mean; how they are determined; and what the effects of operating an airplane outside prescribed CG limits are.

✓ **Determining weight and balance** — How the weight and balance condition of an airplane can be determined and what three methods are used.

✓ **Weight shift** — What the weight shift formula is and how to use it.

METEOROLOGY FOR PILOTS

CHAPTER
4

INTRODUCTION

Weather is one of the most important factors that influence airplane performance and flying safety. In this chapter, we will discuss the way weather affects the operation of your airplane. In Section A, we'll explain basic weather theory regarding the composition of the atmosphere and the cause of winds. In Section B, we'll see how weather patterns develop and how you can anticipate their movement. Finally, in Section C, we will look at aviation weather hazards and how you can avoid them. After completing the chapter, you should have a good understanding of how weather influences your daily flying activity.

BASIC WEATHER THEORY

Weather conditions take on new meaning when you soar above the earth. There's more at stake now than deciding whether to take your umbrella. When you fly, you are literally inside the environment that ruled you on the ground. You move with it in much the same way that a balloon does as it drifts through the air. To fully appreciate weather, you will need to evaluate day-to-day elements like clouds, wind, and rain, so you can determine their impact on your flying. This isn't a difficult task if you start with a solid understanding of weather and its causes. This section provides a basic framework for that understanding.

THE ATMOSPHERE

The earth's atmosphere is a mixture of gases that is in constant motion. If you could see it, it might look like the ocean, with swirls, eddies, rising and falling air, and waves that travel for great distances.

COMPOSITION OF THE ATMOSPHERE

Water is constantly being absorbed and released in the atmosphere. This action is responsible for major changes in the weather.

If you could capture a cubic foot of typical atmosphere and analyze it, you would find it is composed of about 78% nitrogen and 21% oxygen. The remaining 1% is made up of several other gases, primarily argon and carbon dioxide. This cubic foot of atmosphere also contains some water vapor, but the amount can vary from almost zero to about five percent by volume. This relatively small amount of water vapor is responsible for major changes in the weather. [Figure 4-1]

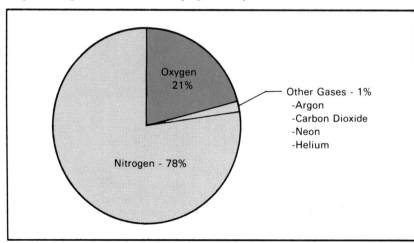

Figure 4-1. The atmosphere is a mixture of gases that exists in fairly uniform proportions up to approximately 30 miles above the earth.

ATMOSPHERIC LEVELS

The atmosphere is divided into layers, or spheres, according to the characteristics of each layer. The **troposphere** is the one closest to the earth, extending from the surface to an average altitude of about six or seven miles.

The **tropopause** is a thin layer of the atmosphere at the top of the troposphere. It acts as a lid to confine most of the water vapor. This, in turn, keeps most of the weather below the tropopause.

Above the tropopause are three more atmospheric layers. The first is the **stratosphere,** which extends to a height of approximately 19 to 22 miles. It has much the same composition as the troposphere and is important to you because certain types of clouds occasionally extend into it. Above the stratosphere are the **mesosphere** and the **thermosphere,** which have little practical influence over weather. [Figure 4-2]

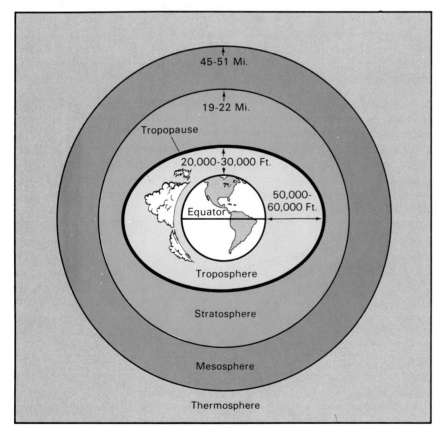

Figure 4-2. The height of the troposphere varies. It slopes upward from about 20,000 feet at the poles to 60,000 feet at the equator. It is also higher in the summer than it is in the winter. Of the various atmospheric layers, the troposphere has the greatest impact on weather.

ATMOSPHERIC CIRCULATION

Now that you've looked at the basic features of the atmosphere, let's consider the factors that set it in motion. This information will provide you with an understanding of the phenomenon we call wind, including the reasons for its speed and direction.

CONVECTION

Uneven heating of the earth's surface causes variations in air temperature and density.

The uneven heating of the earth's surface is the major force that sets the atmosphere in motion. This movement is generally referred to as **circulation**. It occurs through a process known as **convection**, which is defined as the circular motion that results when warm air rises and is replaced by cooler air.

To understand the convection process, it helps to know what happens to air when it warms up and cools off. When air is heated, its molecules spread apart. As the air expands, it becomes less dense and lighter than the surrounding air. As air cools, the molecules become packed more closely together, making it denser and heavier than warm air. As a result, the cool, heavy air tends to sink and replace warmer, rising air. You may have noticed the effect of this convection process when you've felt a cold draft along the floor, or encountered warmer air near the ceiling while working on a ladder.

Although atmospheric circulation is the result of several factors, it will be easier to understand if we initially assume that it is caused only by convection. In this convection-only model, the earth is warmed by energy radiating from the sun. This solar energy strikes equatorial regions in much greater concentrations, resulting in much higher temperatures than at the poles. As a result, cold, dense air from the poles sinks and flows toward the equator, where it displaces rising air that is warmer and less dense. [Figure 4-3]

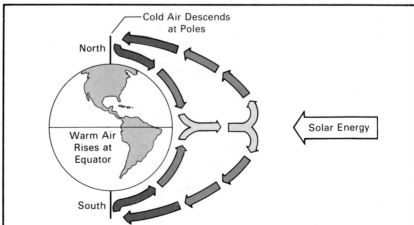

Figure 4-3. If the earth did not rotate, a huge convective circulation pattern would develop as air flowed from the poles to the equator and back again.

ATMOSPHERIC PRESSURE

As we have seen, the unequal heating of the surface modifies air density and creates circulation patterns. It also causes changes in pressure. This is one of the main reasons for differences in altimeter settings between weather reporting stations. Meteorologists plot these pressure readings on weather maps and connect points of equal pressure with lines called **isobars**. Isobars are measured in millibars and are usually drawn at four-millibar intervals. The resulting pattern reveals the **pressure gradient**, or change in pressure over distance. When isobars are spread widely apart, the gradient is considered to be weak, while closely spaced isobars indicate a strong gradient. Isobars also help to identify pressure systems, which are classified as highs, lows, ridges, troughs, and cols. A **high** is a center of high pressure surrounded on all sides by lower pressure. Conversely, a **low** is an area of low pressure surrounded by higher pressure. A **ridge** is an elongated area of high pressure, while a **trough** is an elongated area of low pressure. A **col** can designate either a neutral area between two highs and two lows, or the intersection of a ridge and a trough. [Figure 4-4]

Air flows from the cool, dense air of highs into the warm, less dense air of lows. The speed of the resulting wind depends on the strength of the pressure gradient. A strong gradient tends to produce strong wind, while a weak gradient results in lighter winds. The force behind this movement is caused by the pressure gradient and is referred to as **pressure gradient force**.

Variations in altimeter settings between weather reporting points are primarily caused by the unequal heating of the earth's surface.

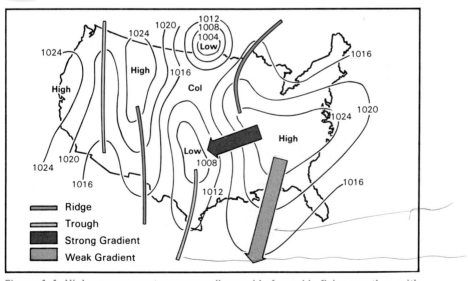

Ridge
Trough
Strong Gradient
Weak Gradient

A high pressure ride

lo pressure trough

Figure 4-4. High pressure systems generally provide favorable flying weather, with good visibility, calm or light winds, and few clouds. Ridges also normally present good weather. In the area of a low, on the other hand, you can anticipate generally poor weather with possible low clouds, poor visibility, precipitation, gusty winds, and turbulence. Weather may be very violent in the area of a trough.

CORIOLIS FORCE

If the earth did not rotate, pressure gradient force would propel wind directly from highs to lows. Instead, the earth's rotation introduces another force, called Coriolis, that affects air circulation.

Coriolis is a deflective force that is created by the difference in rotational velocity between the equator and the poles. To complete one revolution, a point on the equator must travel faster than a point near the poles. In fact, the velocity of the earth's surface varies from about 900 knots at the equator to zero at the poles. As long as air remains stationary over one position on the surface of the earth, gravity tends to hold it in place. However, once air begins to migrate in its normal circulation patterns, it moves into areas of different surface velocity. Coriolis force deflects this air to the right in the northern hemisphere and to the left in the southern hemisphere. This principle can be shown using the turntable of a record player. [Figure 4-5]

Now let's apply this principle to the rotating earth, concentrating on the northern hemisphere. As the earth rotates from west to east, air migrating toward the north passes over surface areas that are moving slower than the source region. Similarly, air moving toward the south passes over surface areas that are moving faster. [Figure 4-6]

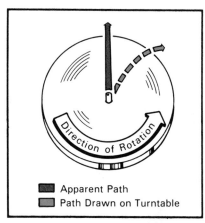

Apparent Path
Path Drawn on Turntable

Figure 4-5. The rotating turntable causes the same type of deflection as the earth's rotation. You can demonstrate this phenomenon by using a piece of chalk and a ruler. First, visualize the nearly stationary center of the turntable as the north pole, and the fast-moving outer edge as the equator. Next, draw a straight line from the center of the rotating turntable to the outer edge. When you stop the turntable you will see that your "straight" line is really curved.

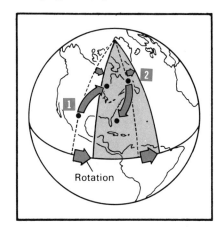

Rotation

Figure 4-6. As a parcel of air moves northward (item 1), the surface speed of the earth below it is progressively slower. Because of this, the movement of air seems to be directed to the east. When air moves south (item 2), it passes over a faster-moving surface and is deflected westward. No matter which direction air moves, Coriolis force always deflects it to the right in the northern hemisphere and to the left in the southern hemisphere.

The amount of deflection produced by Coriolis force varies with latitude. It is zero at the equator and increases toward the poles. It also is proportional to the speed of the airmass. The faster the air moves, the greater the deflection.

WIND

Pressure gradient and Coriolis forces work in combination to create wind. Pressure gradient force causes air to move from high pressure areas to low pressure areas. As the air begins to move, Coriolis force deflects it to the right in the northern hemisphere. This results in a clockwise flow around the high. The deflection continues until pressure gradient force and Coriolis force are in balance, and the wind flows roughly parallel to the isobars. As the air flows into the low pressure area, it moves counterclockwise around the low. The speed of the resulting wind is proportional to the pressure change — the stronger the pressure gradient, the stronger the wind.

Winds in the northern hemisphere flow clockwise around highs and counterclockwise around lows.

Within about 2,000 feet of the ground, friction caused by the earth's surface slows the moving air. This diverts the wind from its path along the isobars. [Figure 4-7]

Friction causes a wind shift near the earth's surface.

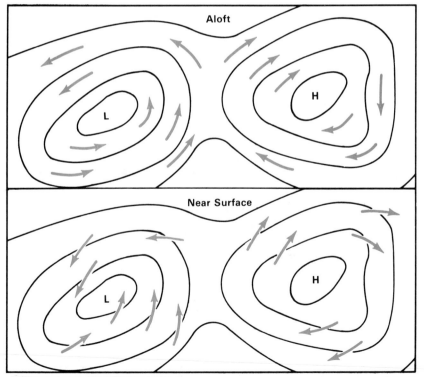

Figure 4-7. As surface friction retards the airflow, Coriolis force is weakened. This allows pressure gradient force to shift the airflow toward areas of lower pressure, causing the wind to blow at an angle across the isobars.

GLOBAL WIND PATTERNS

When Coriolis force is applied to the global circulation pattern, the simple, convection-only model is modified. As tropical air rises and flows northward, it is deflected to the right by Coriolis. Around 30° north, the flow is eastward, causing air to pile up at this latitude. This creates a semipermanent high pressure area. At the surface, air flows back toward the equator. This low-level southerly flow is deflected to the right again and creates the northeast trade winds common to areas like the Caribbean. [Figure 4-8]

The low-level air flowing northward from the high pressure at 30° also is deflected to the right by Coriolis. This creates the prevailing westerlies common to the mid section of North America.

The cold polar air that flows southward is deflected to the right to create the polar easterlies. As this cold air meets the relatively warmer air from the prevailing westerlies, it piles up to create another semipermanent high pressure area around 60° north latitude. This blocks the cold polar air and forms the polar front.

LOCAL WIND PATTERNS

Our discussion so far has centered on the circulation of winds on a global scale. Of greater practical importance to you as a pilot are the winds in

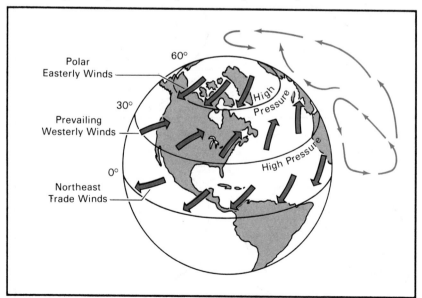

Figure 4-8. In the northern hemisphere, Coriolis force produces a three-cell circulation pattern around two semipermanent high pressure areas at 30° and 60° north latitude. The deflection of air within each cell creates prevailing wind patterns.

the area where you will be flying. These localized wind patterns are caused by terrain variations such as mountains, valleys, and water. The force behind these winds — cool air replacing warm air — is the same as it is for global wind patterns, but on a much smaller scale.

SEA AND LAND BREEZES

If you have ever wondered why waves striking a beach increase in size throughout the day, the sea breeze provides the answer. Land surfaces warm or cool more rapidly than water surfaces; therefore, land is warmer than water during the day. This creates the **sea breeze,** a wind that blows from the cool water to the warmer land. As afternoon heating increases, so does the sea breeze. At night, land cools faster than water, and a **land breeze** blows from the cooler land to the warmer water.

VALLEY AND MOUNTAIN WINDS

Local wind patterns also develop near hilly or mountainous terrain. In the daytime, as mountain slopes are warmed by the sun, air adjacent to them also is heated. A **valley wind** is created as the cooler air over the valley sinks and air close to the mountain flows upward. At night, the surface of the slope cools rapidly, lowering the temperature of the air close to the surface. The cooler air flows down the slope and displaces the air in the valley. This is called a **mountain wind.**

KATABATIC WINDS

A katabatic wind is the name given to any wind blowing down an incline. As you can see from the preceding discussion, a mountain wind is one type of katabatic wind. Depending upon local conditions, katabatic winds may have a dramatic effect on temperature. They occur when cold, dense air spills over a mountain and flows down the slope, displacing the air ahead of it. If this continues over sufficient altitude, the descending air is warmed by compression until it is warmer than the air it is displacing. A warm descending wind is called a **foehn wind**, but may also be referred to locally by other names, such as the **Santa Ana** in California and the **chinook** in the Rockies.

Occasionally, a descending airmass will be so cold that, even though it is warmed during the descent, it is still colder than the air it displaces. This is known as a **fall**, or **gravity**, **wind**.

MOISTURE

Weather is very dependent upon the moisture content of the air. If the air is dry, the weather usually will be good. If the air is very moist, poor or even severe weather can occur. This section looks at the basic properties and characteristics of moisture, and provides you with information that is important in the safe operation of your aircraft.

CHANGE OF STATE

Every physical process of weather is accompanied by a heat exchange.

Water is present in the atmosphere in three states: solid, liquid, and gas. All three states are found within the temperature ranges normally encountered in the atmosphere, and the change from one to another happens readily. Changes in state occur through the processes of evaporation, condensation, sublimation, melting, and freezing. As water changes from one physical state to another, an exchange of heat takes place.

Water vapor is added to the atmosphere by evaporation and sublimation.

Evaporation is the changing of liquid water to invisible water vapor. As water vapor forms, heat is absorbed from the nearest available source. For example, as perspiration evaporates from your body, you feel cooler because some of your body heat has been absorbed by the water vapor. This heat exchange is known as the **latent heat of evaporation.** The reverse of evaporation is **condensation.** It occurs when water vapor changes to a liquid, as when water drops form on a cool glass on a warm day. When condensation takes place, the heat absorbed by water vapor during evaporation is released. The heat released is referred to as the **latent heat of condensation**. It is an important factor in cloud development.

Sublimation is the changing of ice directly to water vapor, or of water vapor to ice. In sublimation, the liquid state is bypassed. Melting and freezing are well known to you. **Melting** is the change of ice to water. **Freezing** is the reverse process. The heat exchange in each of these processes is small and has relatively little affect on weather.

HUMIDITY

The amount of moisture in the air depends on air temperature. Dewpoint is the temperature at which air becomes saturated.

Since the amount of water vapor in the air is of such importance, scientists have developed several ways to measure and describe it. **Humidity** simply refers to moisture in the air; for example, on warm, muggy days when you perspire freely, the air is said to be humid. **Relative humidity** is the actual amount of moisture in the air compared to the total amount that could be present at that temperature. **Dewpoint** is the temperature at which air reaches a state where it can hold no more water. When the dewpoint is reached, the air contains 100% of the moisture it can hold at that temperature, and it is said to be **saturated**. Note that each of these terms relates moisture to temperature, two inseparable features of our weather. [Figure 4-9]

VISIBLE MOISTURE

Clouds, fog, or dew always form when water vapor condenses.

As air cools to its saturation point, the processes of condensation and sublimation change invisible water vapor into states that are readily seen. Most commonly, this visible moisture takes the form of clouds or fog. [Figure 4-10]

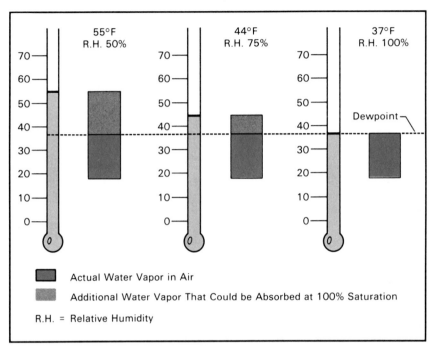

Figure 4-9. Three parcels of air can be used to show the relationship between relative humidity, temperature, and dewpoint. The parcel of air on the left at 55°F (13°C) contains only half the water vapor it could hold, so its relative humidity is 50%. If the temperature of the same parcel drops to 44°F (7°C), it can hold less water vapor than at 55°F, increasing its relative humidity to 75%. The parcel on the right shows the air at 37°F (3°C) to be completely saturated with a relative humidity of 100%.

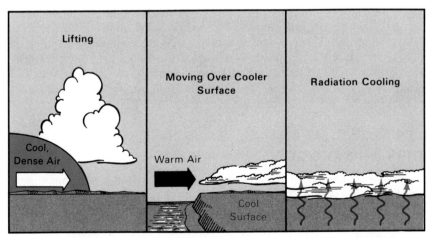

Figure 4-10. Air can be cooled by lifting it, by moving it over a cooler surface, or by cooling the underlying surface. Depending upon the temperature of the air, water vapor may condense into visible water droplets or sublimate into snow.

CLOUDS AND FOG

A small and decreasing temperature/dewpoint spread indicates conditions are favorable for the formation of fog.

Clouds are one of the most fascinating forms of visible moisture. They are composed of very small droplets of water or, if temperature is low enough, ice crystals. The droplets condense or sublimate on very small particles of solid matter in the air. These particles, called **condensation nuclei**, can be dust, salt from evaporating sea spray, or products of combustion. When clouds form near the surface, they are referred to as fog.

Clouds and fog usually form as soon as the air becomes saturated. You can anticipate the formation of fog or very low clouds by monitoring the difference between surface temperature and dewpoint, usually referred to as the **temperature/dewpoint spread**. When the spread reaches 4°F (2°C) and continues to decrease, the air is nearing the saturation point and the probability of fog and low clouds forming increases.

PRECIPITATION

Drizzle, rain, snow, hail, ice pellets, and ice crystals are all forms of **precipitation**. They occur when the particles of moisture in a cloud grow to a size where the atmosphere can no longer support their weight and they fall from the atmosphere.

Water droplets that remain liquid fall as drizzle or rain. Precipitation that forms by sublimation falls as snow, provided the temperature of the air remains below freezing. As precipitation falls, it may change its state due to the temperature it encounters. For example, falling snow may melt to form rain. Rain that remains liquid even though its temperature is below freezing is considered to be **supercooled**, and is referred to as **freezing rain**. Rain may also freeze as it falls, striking the ground as **ice pellets**. In clouds with strong upward currents and cold temperatures, water droplets may freeze. As they rise and fall, they increase in size from collisions with other freezing water droplets. Eventually they become too large for air currents to support, and they fall as **hail**.

DEW AND FROST

Frost forms on aircraft surfaces when the surface is at or below the dewpoint of the surrounding air and the dewpoint is below freezing.

On cool, still nights, surface features and objects may cool to a temperature below the dewpoint of the surrounding air. Moisture then condenses out of the air in the form of dew, which explains why grass is often moist in the early morning. If the temperature of the surrounding air is below freezing, moisture sublimates out of the air and forms frost. From late fall through early spring, you may frequently encounter frost on your airplane on early morning flights.

CHECKLIST _____

After studying this section, you should have a basic understanding of:

✓ **Characteristics of the atmosphere** — What its composition is and the names and features of its layers.

✓ **Hemispherical convection currents** — What causes convection currents and how they affect global circulation.

✓ **Atmospheric pressure** — What atmospheric pressure is, why it varies from one location to another, and how it affects wind.

✓ **Coriolis force** — What it is and how it affects wind direction.

✓ **Local wind patterns** — What causes them and how they influence local weather.

✓ **Moisture in the atmosphere** — How it is measured, under what conditions moisture in the atmosphere will increase, and how it affects weather.

✓ **Change of state** — What the physical states of moisture are in the atmosphere and the processes involved in change of state.

✓ **Clouds and fog** — How clouds and fog are formed, what their relationship is to condensation nuclei, and how temperature/dewpoint spread can be used to predict cloud formation.

✓ **Dew and frost** — What conditions are favorable for the formation of dew and frost. At what time of day their formation would usually occur.

SECTION B

WEATHER PATTERNS

In the previous section, we looked at the basic weather principles and the influence of temperature, pressure, and moisture. This section begins with a discussion of how these conditions combine to cause stable or unstable weather. It then examines the cause, development, and interaction of large airmasses. As we proceed, you will begin to broaden your view of what is happening in the atmosphere, based on your own observations and those you receive from a weather briefer.

ATMOSPHERIC STABILITY

In order to have a good understanding of weather, you must have a thorough knowledge of atmospheric stability. If you understand stability, including the properties of stable and unstable air, you will be much better prepared to evaluate weather conditions and to make intelligent decisions about the operation of your airplane.

Stability is the atmosphere's resistance to vertical motion. Put another way, the stability of air determines whether it will rise or descend in relation to the air around it. This is very important, because stable air resists vertical motion and tends to inhibit cloud formation, precipitation, and severe weather. Unstable air has a tendency to move vertically. This can lead to significant cloud development, turbulence, and hazardous weather. To determine whether a parcel of air is stable or unstable, you need to know about its temperature and moisture content.

TEMPERATURE AND MOISTURE

A major factor affecting the stability of air is its temperature. As we learned in Section A, the uneven heating of the earth's surface creates variations in the density of the overlying air. These variations produce convective currents in which warm air rises and is replaced by cooler, denser air. Moisture is another factor affecting stability. Water vapor is lighter than air. Therefore, as moisture is added to air, its density decreases and it tends to rise. Conversely, as moisture decreases, air becomes denser and it tends to sink. [Figure 4-11]

The combined effects of temperature and moisture determine the stability of the air and, to a large extent, the type of weather produced. You can see that the greatest instability occurs when the air is both warm and

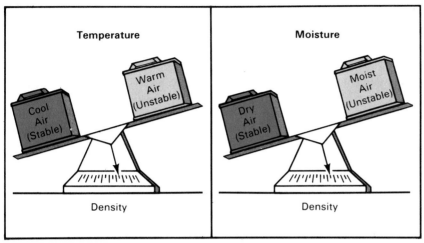

Figure 4-11. The stability of a parcel of air is determined by its density. Air that is warm or moist is unstable; air that is cool or dry is stable.

moist. Tropical weather, with its almost daily thunderstorm activity, is a perfect example of weather that occurs in very unstable air. Air that is both cool and dry resists vertical movement and is very stable. A good example of this can be found in arctic regions in winter, where stable conditions often result in very cold, generally clear weather. Now that you understand why air rises and falls, let's see what takes place within a parcel of ascending or descending air.

RISING AND DESCENDING AIR

Air that moves upward expands due to lower atmospheric pressure. When air moves downward, it is compressed by the increased pressure at lower altitudes. As the pressure of a given portion of air changes, so does its temperature. The temperature change is caused by a process known as **adiabatic heating** or **cooling**, which is a change in the temperature during expansion or compression when no energy is added to or removed from the air.

The adiabatic process takes place in all upward and downward moving air. When air rises into an area of lower pressure, it expands to a larger volume. As the molecules of air expand, the temperature of the air lowers. As a result, when a parcel of air rises, pressure decreases, volume increases, and temperature decreases. When air descends, the opposite is true.

The rate at which temperature decreases with an increase in altitude is referred to as its **lapse rate**. As you ascend through the atmosphere, the average rate of temperature change is 2°C (3.5°F) per 1,000 feet. The adiabatic lapse rate of a parcel of air that is lifted depends on the amount of

You can use the actual lapse rate to determine the stability of the atmosphere.

moisture present in the air. The dry adiabatic lapse rate (unsaturated air) is 3°C (5.4°F) per 1,000 feet. The moist adiabatic lapse rate varies from 1.1°C to 2.8°C (2°F to 5°F) per 1,000 feet. However, it is always less than the rate for dry air.

When you compare the adiabatic lapse rates, you can see that they can be used to indicate the stability of the air. For example, moist air is less stable than dry air, because it cools at a slower rate. This means that moist air must rise higher before its temperature cools to that of the air around it.

When warm, moist air begins to rise in a convective current, cumulus clouds often form at the altitude where its temperature and dewpoint reach the same value. When lifted, unsaturated air cools at about 5.4°F per 1,000 feet, and the dewpoint temperature decreases at about 1°F. Therefore, the temperature and dewpoint converge at about 4.5°F per 1,000 feet.

The lapse rate and the temperature/dewpoint spread can be used to calculate cloud bases.

You can use these values to estimate cloud bases. For example, if the surface temperature is 80°F and the surface dewpoint is 62°F, the spread is 18°F. This difference, divided by the rate that the temperature approaches the dewpoint (4.5°F), will help you judge the approximate height of the base of the clouds in thousands of feet (18 ÷ 4.5 = 4 or 4,000 feet AGL).

TEMPERATURE INVERSIONS

A stable layer of air and a temperature increase with altitude are features of a temperature inversion.

Although temperature usually decreases with an increase in altitude, the reverse is sometimes true. When temperature increases with altitude, a **temperature inversion** exists. Inversions are usually confined to fairly shallow layers and may occur near the surface or at higher altitudes. They act as a lid for weather and pollutants. Visibility is often restricted by fog, haze, smoke, and low clouds. Temperature inversions occur in stable air with little or no wind and turbulence.

One of the most familiar types of inversion is the one that forms just above the ground on clear, cool nights. As the ground cools, it lowers the temperature of the adjacent air. If this process continues, the air within a few hundred feet of the surface may become cooler than the air above it. An inversion can also occur when cool air is forced under warm air, or when warm air spreads over cold. Both of these are called frontal inversions.

OBSERVING STABLE AND UNSTABLE AIR

Moist, unstable air causes the formation of cumuliform clouds and showers.

With a little practice, you can easily tell the difference between areas of stable and unstable air. By observing features such as cloud types, precipitation, and visibility, you should be able to distinguish between stable and unstable air and predict other weather conditions, such as turbulence and icing. Turbulence and aircraft icing will be discussed in detail in the next section. [Figure 4-12]

CLOUDS

Clouds are your weather signposts in the sky. They provide a visible indication of the processes occurring in the atmosphere. To the astute observer, they give valuable information about current and future conditions. Your understanding of how weather affects your flight will be greatly improved if you are able to read and interpret these signposts.

TYPES OF CLOUDS

Clouds are visible moisture that has condensed or sublimated onto condensation nuclei such as dust, salt, or combustion particles. Individual condensation nuclei are extremely small, as are the water or ice particles that adhere to them. Before precipitation can occur, these particles must grow in size. They do this by constantly colliding and merging with other particles, a process most apparent in the strong updrafts of cumulus

CHARACTERISTICS OF STABLE AND UNSTABLE AIR		
	Stable Air	**Unstable Air**
Clouds	Wide areas of layered clouds or fog; gray at low altitude, thin white at high altitude	Extensive vertical development; bright white to black; billowy
Precipitation	Small droplets in fog and low-level clouds; large droplets in thick stratified clouds; widespread and lengthy periods of rain or snow	Large drops in heavy rain showers; showers usually brief; hail possible
Visibility	Restricted for long periods	Poor in showers or thundershowers, good otherwise
Turbulence	Usually light or nonexistent	Moderate to heavy
Icing	Moderate in mid-altitudes; freezing rain, rime, or clear ice	Moderate to heavy clear ice
Other	Frost, dew, temperature inversions	High or gusty surface winds, lightning, tornadoes

Figure 4-12. Stable air is generally smooth, with layered or stratiform clouds. Visibility is usually restricted, with widespread areas of clouds and steady rain or drizzle. Unstable air is usually bumpy, with good surface visibility outside of scattered rain showers.

Family	Altitude (Middle Latitude)	Cloud Type
Low	Bases range from the surface to 6,500 ft. AGL	Cumulus Stratocumulus Stratus
Middle	Bases range from 6,500 ft. AGL to 23,000 ft. AGL	Altocumulus Altostratus Nimbostratus
High	Bases usually range from 16,500 ft. AGL to 45,000 ft. AGL	Cirrus Cirrocumulus Cirrostratus
Clouds with Extensive Vertical Development	Bases range from 1,000 ft. AGL or less to 10,000 ft. AGL or more; tops sometime exceed 60,000 ft. MSL	Towering Cumulus Cumulonimbus

Figure 4-13. Cumulus clouds form in unstable air, while stratus clouds form in stable air. The term ''nimbus'' describes clouds that produce rain.

clouds. Clouds are divided into four basic groups, depending upon their characteristics and the altitudes where they occur. [Figure 4-13]

LOW CLOUDS

Low clouds extend from near the surface to about 6,500 feet AGL. A surface-based cloud most people are familiar with is **fog.** Low clouds usually consist almost entirely of water but sometimes may contain supercooled water which can create an icing hazard for aircraft.

Stratus clouds form in stable air.

Stratus clouds are layered clouds that form in stable air near the surface due to cooling from below. Although turbulence in these clouds is low, they usually restrict visual flying due to low ceilings and visibility. Icing conditions are possible if temperatures are at or near freezing. Stratus clouds may form when stable air is lifted up sloping terrain, or when warm rain evaporates as it falls through cool air. [Figure 4-14]

Stratocumulus clouds are white, puffy clouds that form as stable air is lifted. They often form as a stratus layer breaks up or as cumulus clouds spread out. [Figure 4-15]

Cumulus clouds form in convective currents resulting from the heating of the earth's surface. They usually have flat bottoms and dome-shaped tops. Widely spaced cumulus clouds that form in fairly clear skies are called fair weather cumulus and indicate a shallow layer of instability. You can expect turbulence, but little icing and precipitation.

Figure 4-14. Stratus clouds have a gray, uniform appearance and generally cover a wide area.

Figure 4-15. These are mainly strato-cumulus clouds. A few cumulus clouds indicate an area with slightly more con-vective currents than the surrounding areas.

MIDDLE CLOUDS

Middle clouds have bases that range from about 6,500 to 23,000 feet AGL. They are composed of water, ice crystals, or supercooled water. They may contain moderate turbulence and potentially severe icing.

Altostratus clouds are flat, dense clouds that cover a wide area. They are a uniform gray or gray-white in color. Although they produce minimal turbulence, they may contain moderate icing. **Altocumulus clouds** are gray or white, patchy clouds of uniform appearance that often form when altostratus clouds start to break up. They may produce light turbulence and icing. [Figure 4-16]

Nimbostratus clouds are gray or black clouds that can be more than several thousand feet thick and contain large quantities of moisture. If temperatures are near or below freezing, they may create heavy icing. [Figure 4-17]

HIGH CLOUDS

These clouds have bases that range from about 16,500 to 45,000 feet AGL. They are generally white to light gray in color and form in stable

Figure 4-16. Altocumulus clouds extend over a wide area and may contain highly supercooled water droplets.

Figure 4-17. Nimbostratus clouds pro-duce widespread areas of rain or snow. Although they are classified as middle clouds, they may merge into low stratus or stratocumulus.

air. They are composed mainly of ice crystals and seldom pose a serious turbulence or icing hazard.

Cirrus clouds are thin, wispy clouds that usually form above 30,000 feet. White or light gray in color, they often exist in patches or narrow bands that cross the sky. They are sometimes blown from the tops of thunderstorms or towering cumulus clouds. [Figure 4-18]

Cirrostratus clouds also are thin, white clouds that often form in long bands or sheets against a deep blue background. Although they may be several thousand feet thick, moisture content is low and they pose no icing hazard. In contrast, **cirrocumulus clouds** are white patchy clouds that look like cotton. They form as a result of shallow convective currents at high altitude and may produce light turbulence.

CLOUDS WITH EXTENSIVE VERTICAL DEVELOPMENT

The bases of vertically developed clouds are found in altitudes associated with low to middle clouds, and their tops extend into the altitudes associated with high clouds. Frequently, these cloud types are obscured by other cloud formations. When this happens, they are said to be **embedded**.

Vertical cloud development and turbulence result from the lifting of unstable air.

Towering cumulus clouds are similar to cumulus clouds, except they have more vertical development. They look like large mounds of cotton with billowing cauliflower tops. Their color may vary from brilliant

Figure 4-18. Cirrus clouds form in stable air at high altitudes. In some cases, they are an advance warning of approaching bad weather.

white at the top to gray near the bottom. Towering cumulus clouds indicate a fairly deep layer of unstable air. They contain moderate to heavy turbulence with icing and often develop into thunderstorms. [Figure 4-19]

Cumulonimbus clouds, which are more commonly called thunderstorms, are large, vertically developed clouds that form in very unstable air. They are gray-white to black in color and contain large amounts of moisture. Many flying hazards are linked with cumulonimbus clouds. These hazards are discussed in Section C.

Cumulonimbus clouds form when moist, unstable air is lifted.

AIRMASSES

Now that you have a good understanding of atmospheric stability and the types of clouds that are produced, let's look at airmasses and the way they influence weather. An **airmass** is a large body of air with fairly uniform temperature and moisture content. It may be several hundred miles across and usually forms where air remains stationary or nearly stationary for at least several days. During this time, the airmass takes on the temperature and moisture properties of the underlying surface.

SOURCE REGIONS

The area where an airmass acquires the properties of temperature and moisture that determine its stability is called its **source region.** An ideal source region is a large area with fairly uniform geography and temperature. A source region is usually located where air tends to stagnate. The best areas for airmass development are in the regions where atmospheric circulation has caused the buildup of semipermanent areas of high pressure. Some excellent areas are snow and ice covered polar regions, tropical oceans, and large deserts. The middle latitudes are poor source

Figure 4-19. Towering cumulus clouds develop in unstable air and often contain strong vertical currents.

regions because of the strong westerly winds and the continual mixing of tropical and polar airmasses.

CLASSIFICATIONS

Airmasses are classified according to the regions where they originate. They are generally divided into polar or tropical to identify their temperature characteristics and continental or maritime to identify their moisture content. A continental polar airmass, for example, originates over a polar land mass and contains cold, dry, and stable air. A maritime tropical airmass originates over water and contains warm, moist, and unstable air. [Figure 4-20]

MODIFICATION

As an airmass moves out of its source region, it is modified by the temperature and moisture of the area over which it moves. The degree to which an airmass is changed depends on several factors:

1. Its speed
2. Nature of the region it moves over
3. Temperature difference between the airmass and the new surface
4. Depth of the airmass

WARMING FROM BELOW

Warming from below decreases airmass stability.

As an airmass moves over a warmer surface, its lower layers are heated and vertical movement of the air develops. Depending on temperature and moisture levels, this can result in extreme instability. [Figure 4-21]

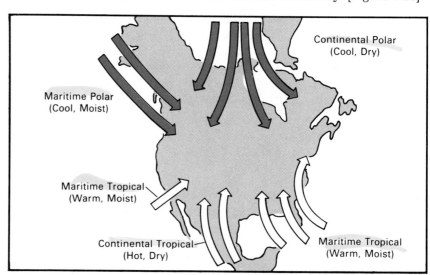

Figure 4-20. Airmass source regions surround North America. As airmasses move out of their source regions, they often converge and give birth to the continent's major weather systems.

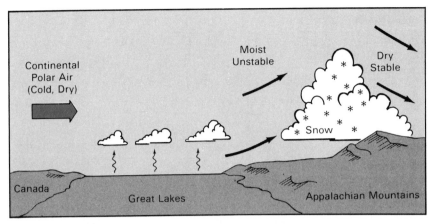

Figure 4-21. The Great Lakes do much to modify continental polar airmasses moving out of Canada. In early winter, the lakes heat and moisten air near the surface, creating very unstable air. This often results in large quantities of snow over the Great Lakes and downwind of them.

COOLING FROM BELOW

When an airmass flows over a cooler surface, its lower layers are cooled and vertical movement is inhibited. As a result, the stability of the air is increased. If the air is cooled to its dewpoint, low clouds or fog may form. This cooling from below creates a temperature inversion and may result in low ceilings and visibility for long periods of time. [Figure 4-22]

Cooling from below may cause smooth air and poor visibility.

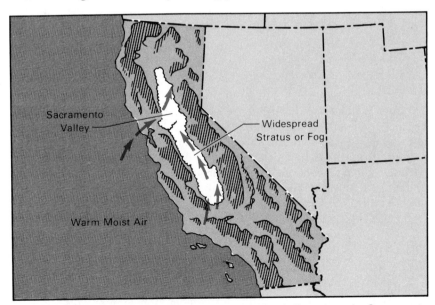

Figure 4-22. In winter months, warm, moist Pacific air flows into the Sacramento Valley of California and is cooled from below. As its temperature drops, its stability increases. Prolonged cooling causes the air to cool to its dewpoint, often resulting in widespread stratus clouds or fog that may persist for weeks.

FRONTS

Fronts are boundaries be-
tween airmasses.

When an airmass moves out of its source region, it comes in contact with other airmasses that have different moisture and temperature characteristics. The boundary between airmasses is called a **front**. Since the weather along a front often presents a serious hazard to flying, you need to have a thorough understanding of this weather.

TYPES OF FRONTS

Fronts are named according to the temperature of the advancing air relative to the temperature of the air it is replacing. A **cold front** is one where cold air is moving to displace warmer air. In a **warm front,** warm air is replacing cold air. A **stationary front** has no movement. Cold fronts are usually fast moving and often catch up to and merge with a slower moving warm front. When cold and warm fronts merge, they create an **occluded front**.

FRONTAL DISCONTINUITIES

When you cross a front, you move from one airmass into another airmass with different properties. The changes between the two may be very abrupt, indicating a narrow frontal zone. On the other hand, the changes may occur gradually, indicating a wide and, perhaps, diffused frontal zone. These changes can give you important cues to the location and intensity of the front.

TEMPERATURE

A change in the temperature is one of the easiest ways to recognize the passage of a front. At the surface, the temperature change is usually very noticeable and may be quite abrupt in a fast-moving front. With a slow-moving front, it usually is less pronounced. When you are flying through a front, you can observe the temperature change on the outside air temperature gauge. However, the change may be less abrupt at middle and high altitudes than it is at the surface.

WIND

When you are flying across a front, you will notice a change in wind direction. Wind speed also may change.

The most reliable indications that you are crossing a front are a change in wind direction and, less frequently, wind speed. Although the exact new direction of the wind is difficult to predict, the wind always shifts to the right in the northern hemisphere. When you are flying through a front at low to middle altitudes, you will always need to correct to the right in order to maintain your original ground track.

PRESSURE

As a front approaches, atmospheric pressure usually decreases, with the area of lowest pressure lying directly over the front. Pressure changes on the warm side of the front generally occur more slowly than on the cold side. When you approach a front toward the cool air, pressure drops slowly until you cross the front, then rises quickly. When you are crossing toward the warm air, pressure drops abruptly over the front and then rises slowly. The important thing to remember is that you should update your altimeter setting as soon as possible after crossing a front.

FRONTAL WEATHER

The type and intensity of frontal weather depend on several factors. Some of these factors are the availability of moisture, the stability of the air being lifted, and the speed of the frontal movement. Other factors include the slope of the front and the moisture and temperature variations between the two fronts. Although some frontal weather can be very severe and hazardous, other fronts produce relatively calm weather. Before beginning a flight that will penetrate a front, you should obtain a complete weather briefing on the conditions you might encounter.

COLD FRONTS

A cold front separates an advancing mass of cold, dense air from an area of warm, lighter air. Because of its greater density, the cold air moves along the surface and forces the less dense, warm air upward. In the northern hemisphere, cold fronts are usually oriented in a northeast to southwest line and may be several hundred miles long. Movement is usually in an easterly direction. The speed of a cold front usually dictates the type of weather associated with the front. However, there are some general weather characteristics that are found in most cold fronts. These include:

1. Cumulus clouds
2. Turbulence
3. Showery precipitation
4. Strong, gusty winds
5. Clearing skies and good visibility after the front passes

FAST-MOVING COLD FRONTS

Fast-moving cold fronts are pushed along by intense high pressure systems located well behind the front. Surface friction acts to slow the movement of the front, causing the leading edge of the front to bulge out and to steepen the front's slope. These fronts are particularly hazardous

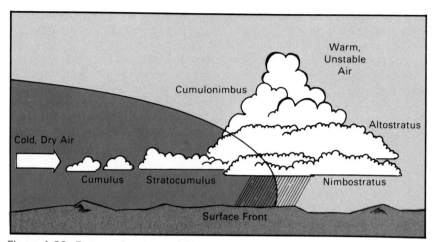

Figure 4-23. Fast-moving cold fronts force warmer air to rise. This causes wide-spread vertical cloud development along a narrow frontal zone if sufficient moisture is present. An area of severe weather often forms well ahead of the front.

because of the steep slope and wide differences in moisture and temperature between the two airmasses. [Figure 4-23]

When a cold front pushes into extremely moist, unstable air, a **squall line** often forms ahead of the front itself. The squall line is an area of severe weather characterized by extensive vertical cloud development and turbulence. It often develops 50 to 300 miles ahead of the front and frequently contains weather more severe than that found along the front.

The weather usually clears quickly behind a cold front. You will often notice reduced cloud cover, improved visibility, lower temperatures, and gusty surface winds following the passage of a fast-moving cold front.

SLOW-MOVING COLD FRONTS

The leading edge of a slow-moving cold front is much shallower than that of a fast-moving front. This produces clouds which extend far behind the surface front. A slow-moving cold front meeting stable air usually causes a broad area of stratus clouds to form behind the front. When a slow-moving cold front meets unstable air, large numbers of vertical clouds often form at and just behind the front. Fair weather cumulus clouds are often present in the cold air, well behind the surface front. [Figure 4-24]

WARM FRONTS

Steady precipitation with little turbulence usually precedes a warm front.

Warm fronts occur when warm air overtakes and replaces cooler air. They usually move at much slower speeds than cold fronts. The slope of a warm front is very gradual, and the warm air may extend up over the

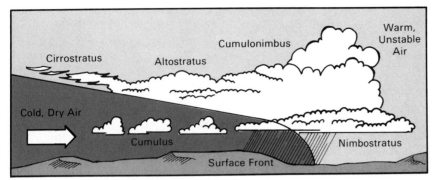

Figure 4-24. As a slow-moving cold front meets unstable air, cumulonimbus and nimbostratus clouds may develop near the surface front, creating hazards from icing and turbulence.

cool air for several hundred miles ahead of the front. Some of the common weather patterns found in a typical warm front include:

1. Stratus clouds, if the air is moist and stable
2. Little turbulence, except in an unstable airmass
3. Precipitation ahead of the front
4. Poor visibility with haze or fog
5. Wide area of precipitation

The stability and moisture content of the air in a warm front determines what type of clouds will form. If the air is warm, moist, and stable, stratus clouds will develop. If the air is warm, moist, and unstable, cumulus clouds will develop. [Figure 4-25]

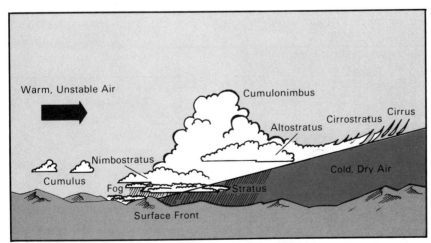

Figure 4-25. Stratus clouds usually extend out ahead of a slow-moving warm front. Vertical clouds sometimes develop along and ahead of the surface front, depending on the stability and moisture content of the warm air. When ice pellets are reported at the surface, you can expect freezing rain at a higher altitude.

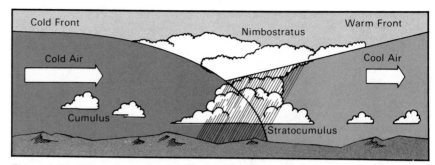

Figure 4-26. When the air being lifted by a cold front occlusion is moist and stable, the weather will be a mixture of that found in both a warm and cold front.

STATIONARY FRONTS

Stationary fronts have qualities of both warm and cold fronts.

When the opposing forces of two airmasses are relatively balanced, the front that separates them may remain stationary and influence local flying conditions for several days. The weather in a stationary front is usually a mixture of that found in both warm and cold fronts.

FRONTAL OCCLUSIONS

A frontal occlusion occurs when a fast-moving cold front catches up to a slow-moving warm front. The difference in temperature within each frontal system is a major factor that influences which type of front and weather are created. A **cold front occlusion** develops when the fast-moving cold front is colder than the air ahead of the slow-moving warm front. In this case, the cold air replaces the cool air at the surface and forces the warm front aloft. [Figure 4-26]

A **warm front occlusion** takes place when the air ahead of the slow-moving warm front is colder than the air within the fast-moving cold front. In this case, the cold front rides up over the warm front, forcing the cold front aloft. [Figure 4-27]

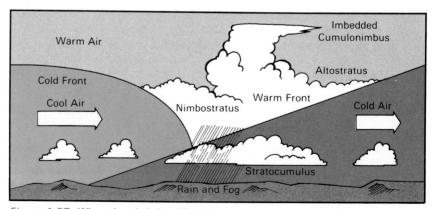

Figure 4-27. When the air being lifted by a warm front occlusion is moist and unstable, the weather will be more severe than that found in a cold front occlusion.

CHECKLIST _____

After studying this section, you should have a basic understanding of:

✓   **Stability** — What it is and what determines whether air is stable or unstable.

✓   **Effect of moisture and temperature** — How they influence stability.

✓   **Lapse rates** — What they represent and their relationship to stability.

✓   **Temperature inversions** — What they are and what kind of weather is associated with them.

✓   **Characteristics of stable and unstable air** — What cloud types, precipitation, visibility, and turbulence you can expect to encounter in stable and unstable air.

✓   **Clouds** — How clouds are classified and the characteristics associated with each class.

✓   **Airmasses** — What they are, where they come from, and how they influence weather.

✓   **Fronts** — What the types of fronts are and their associated weather.

WEATHER HAZARDS

Weather hazards come in many forms. Often, they are plainly visible, but serious hazards can also exist in clear skies and at times when you least expect them. It is important to understand these hazards and to know how to avoid them. We will begin our discussion with thunderstorms, since they produce a number of dangerous weather elements.

THUNDERSTORMS

Thunderstorm formation requires unstable conditions, a lifting force, and high moisture levels.

Three conditions are necessary to create a thunderstorm — air that has a tendency toward instability, some type of lifting action, and relatively high moisture content. The lifting action may be provided by several factors, such as rising terrain (orographic lifting), fronts, or heating of the earth's surface (convection).

LIFE CYCLE

The three stages of a thunderstorm are cumulus, mature, and dissipating.

Thunderstorms progress through three definite stages — cumulus, mature, and dissipating. You can anticipate the development of thunderstorms and the associated hazards by becoming familiar with the characteristics of each of these. [Figure 4-28]

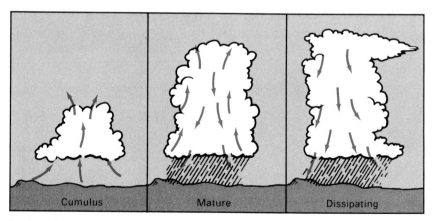

Cumulus   Mature   Dissipating

Figure 4-28. These distinctive cloud shapes signal the stages of a thunderstorm. Although not every cumulus cloud develops into a thunderstorm, all storms do begin at the cumulus stage. You should be aware that other weather phenomena may prevent you from seeing these characteristic shapes. For example, a cumulonimbus cloud may be embedded, or obscured, by massive cloud layers. There may also be a number of thunderstorms in an area, all in different stages of development.

In the **cumulus stage**, a lifting action initiates the vertical movement of air. As the air rises and cools to its dewpoint, water vapor condenses into small water droplets or ice crystals. If sufficient moisture is present, heat released by the condensing vapor provides energy for continued vertical growth of the cloud. Because of strong updrafts, precipitation usually does not fall. Instead, the water drops or ice crystals rise and fall within the cloud, growing larger with each cycle. Updrafts as great as 3,000 feet per minute (f.p.m.) may begin near the surface and extend well above the cloud top.

> The cumulus stage is characterized by continuous updrafts.

As the drops in the cloud grow too large to be supported by the updrafts, precipitation begins to fall. This creates a downward motion in the surrounding air and signals the beginning of the **mature stage**. The resulting downdraft may reach a velocity of 2,500 f.p.m. The down-rushing air spreads outward at the surface, producing a sharp drop in temperature, a rise in pressure, and strong, gusty surface winds. The leading edge of this wind is referred to as a **gust front**, or the **first gust**. As the thunderstorm advances, a rolling, turbulent, circular-shaped cloud may form at the lower leading edge of the cloud. This is called the **roll cloud.** Early in the mature stage, the updrafts continue to increase up to speeds of 6,000 f.p.m. The adjacent updrafts and downdrafts cause severe turbulence. The most violent weather occurs during this phase of the life cycle.

> Thunderstorms reach the greatest intensity during the mature stage, which is signaled by the beginning of precipitation.

As the mature stage progresses, more and more air aloft is disturbed by the falling drops. Eventually, the downdrafts begin to spread out within the cell, taking the place of the weakening updrafts. Because upward movement is necessary for condensation and the release of the latent energy, the entire thunderstorm begins to weaken. When the cell becomes an area of predominant downdrafts, it is considered to be in the **dissipating stage.** During this stage, the upper level winds often blow the top of the cloud downwind, creating the familiar anvil shape. The anvil, however, does not necessarily signal the storm's dissipation; severe weather can still occur well after its appearance.

> A dissipating thunderstorm is characterized by downdrafts.

Occasionally, a thunderstorm doesn't dissipate in the typical manner. If winds become markedly stronger with altitude, the upper portion of the cloud may be "tilted," or blown downwind. In this case, precipitation falls through only a small portion of the rising air, or it may fall completely outside the cloud. As a result, the mature stage can be prolonged as the updrafts continue, until their source of energy is exhausted. This is commonly referred to as a **steady-state** thunderstorm, which can produce very severe weather.

TYPES OF THUNDERSTORMS

Thunderstorms usually have similar physical features, but their intensity, degree of development, and associated weather do differ. They are generally classified as airmass or frontal storms. **Airmass thunderstorms**

> Airmass storms are usually caused by convection or orographic lifting.

generally form in a warm, moist airmass and are isolated or scattered over a large area. They are usually caused by solar heating of the land, which results in convection currents that lift unstable air, and are most common during summer afternoons or in coastal areas at night. Airmass storms can also be caused by orographic lifting. Although they are usually scattered along individual mountain peaks, they may cover large areas. They may be embedded in other clouds, making them difficult to identify when approached from the windward side of a mountain. Nocturnal thunderstorms can occur in late spring and summer during the late night or early morning hours when relatively moist air exists aloft. They are usually found from the Mississippi Valley westward. Nocturnal storms cover many square miles, and their effects may continue for hours at a given location.

Frontal thunderstorms can be associated with any type of front. Those which occur with a warm front are often obscured by stratiform clouds. You should expect thunderstorms when there is showery precipitation near a warm front. In a cold front, the cumulonimbus clouds are often visible in a continuous line parallel to the frontal surface. Occlusions can also spawn storms.

A squall line is a non-frontal band of thunderstorms that contains the most severe types of weather-related hazards.

A **squall line** is a narrow band of active thunderstorms which normally contains very severe weather. While it often forms 50 to 300 miles ahead of a fast-moving cold front, the existence of a front is not necessary for a squall line to form.

THUNDERSTORM HAZARDS

The cumulonimbus is the type of cloud that produces the most severe turbulence.

Thunderstorms typically contain many severe weather hazards, and may include lightning, hail, turbulence, gusty surface winds, or even tornadoes. These hazards are not confined to the cloud itself. For example, you can encounter turbulence in VFR conditions as far as 20 miles from the storm. It might help to think of a cumulonimbus cloud as the visible part of a widespread system of turbulence and other weather hazards. In fact, the cumulonimbus cloud is the most turbulent of all clouds. Now, let's look at some of the associated weather elements separately.

Lightning is always associated with thunderstorms.

Lightning is one of the hazards which is always associated with thunderstorms. While it rarely causes crew injury or substantial damage to the aircraft structure, it can cause temporary loss of vision and puncture the aircraft skin or damage electronic navigation and communications equipment.

Hail can occur at all altitudes within or outside a storm. You can encounter it in flight, even when no hail is reaching the surface. In addition, large hailstones have been encountered in clear air several miles downwind from a thunderstorm.

Thunderstorm turbulence develops when air currents change direction or velocity rapidly over a short distance. The magnitude of the turbulence depends on the differences between the two air currents. Within the thunderstorm cloud, the strongest turbulence occurs in the shear between the updrafts and downdrafts. Near the surface, there is a low-level area of turbulence which develops as the downdrafts spread out at the surface. These create a **shear zone** between the surrounding air and the cooler air of the downdraft. The resulting area of gusty winds and turbulence can extend outward for many miles from the center of the storm.

Severe turbulence often exists in a thunderstorm.

Funnel clouds are violent, spinning columns of air which descend from the base of a cloud. Wind speeds within them may exceed 200 knots. If a funnel cloud reaches the earth's surface, it is referred to as a **tornado.** If it touches down over water, it is called a **waterspout.**

TURBULENCE

We discussed turbulence briefly with relation to thunderstorms. Now, let's take a closer look at this dangerous weather phenomenon. There are many causes of turbulence, including wind shear, convective currents, obstructions to wind flow, clear air turbulence, and wake turbulence. Its effect can vary from occasional light bumps to severe jolts which can cause personal injury to occupants and/or structural damage to the airplane. To avoid or minimize the effects of turbulence, you must understand its causes and know where it is likely to be found. If you enter turbulence or expect that you will encounter it, slow the airplane to maneuvering speed or less, maintain attitude, and accept variations in airspeed and altitude.

If you encounter turbulence, establish maneuvering speed and try to maintain a level flight attitude.

WIND SHEAR

Wind shear is a sudden, drastic shift in wind speed and/or direction that may occur at any altitude in a vertical or horizontal plane. It can subject your aircraft to sudden updrafts, downdrafts, or extreme horizontal wind components, causing loss of lift or violent changes in vertical speeds or altitudes.

Wind shear can exist at any altitude and may occur in a vertical or horizontal direction.

You should anticipate wind shear when frontal systems and thunderstorms are in the area. It also may occur during a temperature inversion when cold, still surface air is covered by warmer air which contains winds of 25 knots or more. A low-level wind shear alert system (LLWAS) is installed at some airports. If the system indicates a significant difference between the surface wind at center field and peripheral sensors, tower controllers will alert you by advising you of the wind velocities at two or more of the sensors.

Wind shear often exists near the surface when there is a frontal system, thunderstorm, or temperature inversion with strong upper winds in the area.

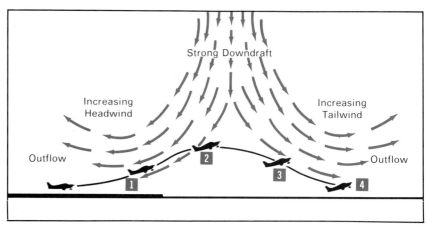

Figure 4-29. As this aircraft inadvertently takes off into a microburst, it first experiences a headwind which increases performance (position 1). This is followed rapidly by decreased performance as the downdraft is encountered (position 2) and the wind shears to a tailwind (position 3). This may result in terrain impact or operation dangerously close to the ground (position 4).

MICROBURSTS AND DOWNBURSTS

A microburst is an intense downburst which covers only a small area and has a very short life cycle. However, a downburst covers a larger area and may last up to 30 minutes.

A **microburst** is an intense, localized downdraft which spreads out in all directions when it reaches the surface. This creates severe horizontal and vertical wind shears which pose serious hazards to aircraft, particularly those near the surface. A microburst typically covers less than two and a half miles at the surface, with peak winds as high as 150 knots and lasting only two to five minutes. Any convective cloud can produce this phenomenon. Although microbursts commonly occur during heavy precipitation in thunderstorms, they often are associated with **virga**, or streamers of precipitation that trail beneath a cloud but evaporate before they reach the ground. If there is no precipitation, your only cue may be a ring of dust at the surface. If you suspect the presence of microbursts in your local area, don't fly. A related phenomenon is the **downburst** which can cover an area up to 10 miles in diameter and last up to 30 minutes. [Figure 4-29]

CONVECTIVE CURRENTS

When sufficient moisture is present, cumulus clouds indicate the presence of convective turbulence.

Convective turbulence is caused by currents which develop in air heated by contact with the warm surface below. This heating can occur when cold air is moved horizontally over a warmer surface or when the ground is heated by the sun. The strength of the convective currents depends on the type of substance being heated and the intensity of the heat. For example, rocky or barren land heats more quickly than areas covered by heavy vegetation. In addition, the strongest convective currents are found on hot summer afternoons. Generally, the effect of these currents decreases with altitude. When the air is moist, the currents are marked by the cumulus clouds which form near their tops. Some of these clouds may grow into towering cumulus clouds and develop into thunderstorms.

OBSTRUCTIONS TO WIND FLOW

When obstacles like buildings or rough terrain interfere with the normal wind flow, turbulence develops. This phenomenon, referred to as **mechanical turbulence**, is often experienced in the traffic pattern when the wind blows around or over hangars and causes eddies to form.

Mechanical turbulence also occurs when strong winds flow nearly perpendicular to mountain ridges. If the air is unstable, expect turbulence on the windward side of the mountain. If the air is both moist and unstable, orographic thunderstorms may develop. As the unstable air spills down the leeward side, violent downdrafts may develop. These downdrafts can exceed the climb capability of an aircraft.

In contrast, when stable air crosses a mountain barrier, the airflow is smooth on the windward side. Wind flow across the barrier is laminar —that is, it tends to flow in layers. The barrier may set up waves, called **mountain waves**. Mountain wave turbulence is possible as the stable air moves across a ridge and the wind is 40 knots or greater. The wave pattern may extend 100 miles or more downwind, and the crests may extend well above the highest peaks. Below the crest of each wave is an area of rotary circulation, or a **rotor**, which forms below the mountain peaks. Both the rotor and the waves can create violent turbulence. If sufficient moisture is present, characteristic clouds will warn you of the mountain wave. [Figure 4-30]

> Mountain wave turbulence can be anticipated when the winds across a ridge are 40 knots or more, and the air is stable.

The following discussion presents only general information about flying near mountains. It does not preclude the need for a thorough mountain checkout by a qualified flight instructor. You should anticipate some mountain wave activity whenever the wind is in excess of 25 knots and is blowing roughly perpendicular to mountain ridges. As wind speed increases, so does the associated turbulence. When conditions indicate a possible mountain wave, recommended cruising altitudes are at least

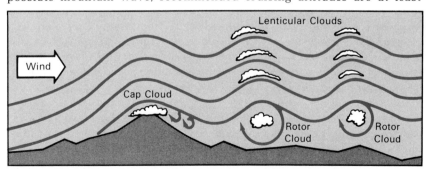

Figure 4-30. The crests of the waves may be marked by lens-shaped, or lenticular, clouds. These clouds form in the updrafts and dissipate in the downdrafts so they do not move as the wind blows through them. Because of this, they are sometimes referred to as standing lenticulars. Rotor clouds may also form in the rotors, and cap clouds may obscure the mountain peaks.

3,000 to 5,000 feet above the peaks. You should climb to the selected altitude while approximately 100 miles from the range, depending on wind and aircraft performance. Approach the ridge from a 45° angle to permit a safer retreat if turbulence becomes too severe. If winds at the planned flight altitude exceed 30 knots, the FAA recommends against flight over mountainous areas in small aircraft.

CLEAR AIR TURBULENCE

Clear air turbulence (CAT) is commonly thought of as a high altitude phenomenon; however, it can take place at any altitude and is often present with no visual warning. Clear air turbulence may be caused by wind shear, convective currents, or obstructions to normal wind flow. It often develops in or near the **jet stream**, which is a narrow band of high altitude winds near the tropopause.

WAKE TURBULENCE

Wingtip vortices are created when an airplane generates lift.

Whenever an airplane generates lift, air spills over the wingtips from the high pressure areas below the wings to the low pressure areas above them. This flow causes rapidly rotating whirlpools of air called **wingtip vortices**, or **wake turbulence**. The intensity of the turbulence depends on aircraft weight, speed, and configuration.

The greatest vortex strength occurs when the generating aircraft is heavy, slow, and in a clean configuration. Wingtip vortices tend to sink below the flight path of the aircraft which generated them and are most hazardous during light, quartering tailwind conditions.

The greatest wake turbulence danger is produced by large, heavy aircraft operating at low speeds, high angles of attack, and in a clean configuration. Since these conditions usually exist on takeoff and landing, be alert for wake turbulence near airports used by large airplanes. In fact, wingtip vortices from commercial jets can induce uncontrollable roll rates in smaller aircraft. Although wake turbulence settles, it persists in the air for several minutes, depending on wind conditions. In light winds of three to seven knots, the vortices may stay in the touchdown area, sink into your takeoff or landing path, or drift over a parallel runway. The most dangerous condition for landing is a light, quartering tailwind. It can move the upwind vortex of a landing aircraft over the runway and forward into the touchdown zone. [Figure 4-31]

Wake turbulence can be extremely hazardous, particularly to pilots of small aircraft taking off or landing behind large aircraft.

If you are in a small aircraft approaching to land behind a large aircraft, controllers must ensure a separation of four miles (six miles behind a heavy jet). However, if you accept a clearance to follow an aircraft you have in sight, the responsibility for wake turbulence avoidance is transferred from the controller to you. On takeoff, controllers provide a two-minute interval behind departing heavy jets (three minutes for intersection takeoffs or takeoffs in the opposite direction on the same runway). You may waive these time intervals if you wish, but this is not a wise procedure.

Jet engine blast is a related hazard. It can damage or even overturn a small airplane if it is encountered at close range. To avoid exhaust velocities in excess of 20 knots, you must stay several hundred feet behind a jet with its engines operating, even when it is at idle thrust.

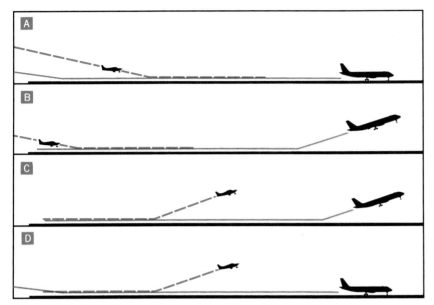

Figure 4-31. To avoid turbulence when landing behind a large aircraft, stay above the large airplane's glide path and touch down beyond its touchdown point (part A). If a large airplane has just taken off as you approach to land, touch down well before the large aircraft's liftoff point (part B). When taking off behind a large aircraft, lift off before the large airplane's rotation point and climb out above or upwind of its flight path (part C). When departing after a large aircraft has landed, lift off beyond its touchdown point (part D).

REPORTING TURBULENCE

You are encouraged to report encounters with turbulence, including the frequency and intensity. Turbulence is considered to be "occasional" when it occurs less then one-third of a given time span, "moderate" when it covers one-third to two-thirds of the time, and "continuous" when it occurs more than two-thirds of the time. You can classify the intensity using the following guidelines:

Light — Slight erratic changes in altitude or attitude; slight strain against seat belts. **Light chop** is slight, rapid bumpiness without appreciable changes in altitude or attitude.

Moderate — Changes in altitude or attitude occur, but aircraft remains in positive control at all times; usually changes in indicated airspeed; definite strains against seat belts. **Moderate chop** is rapid bumps or jolts without appreciable changes in altitude or attitude.

Severe — Abrupt changes in altitude or attitude; usually large variations in indicated airspeed; aircraft may be momentarily out of control; occupants forced violently against seat belts.

Extreme — Aircraft practically impossible to control; may cause structural damage.

ICING

Visible moisture is necessary for structural icing to form, and freezing rain usually produces the highest accumulation rate.

Structural icing can occur during flights in areas of visible moisture, when the temperature of the aircraft surface is 0°C or colder. Ice can build up on any exposed surface of an aircraft, causing a loss of lift, an increase in weight, and control problems. There are two general types of ice — rime and clear. Mixed icing is a combination of the two. **Rime ice** normally is encountered in stratus clouds and results from instantaneous freezing of tiny water droplets striking the aircraft surface. It has an opaque appearance caused by air being trapped in the water droplets as they freeze instantly. A major hazard is its ability to change the shape of an airfoil and destroy its lift. Since rime ice freezes instantly, it builds up on the leading edge of airfoils, but it does not flow back following the basic curvature of the wing and tail surfaces. **Clear ice** may develop in areas of large water droplets which are in cumulus clouds or in freezing rain beneath a warm front inversion. The highest accumulation rate generally occurs in freezing rain. When the droplets flow over the aircraft structure and slowly freeze, they can glaze the aircraft's surfaces. Clear ice is the most serious form of ice because it adheres tenaciously to the aircraft and is difficult to remove.

If frost is not removed from the wings before flight, it may decrease lift and increase drag, preventing the aircraft from becoming airborne.

Frost is a related element which poses a serious hazard during takeoffs. It interferes with smooth airflow over the wings and can cause early airflow separation, resulting in a loss of lift. It also increases drag and, when combined with the loss of lift, may prevent the aircraft from becoming airborne. Always remove all frost from the aircraft surfaces before flight.

RESTRICTIONS TO VISIBILITY

Up to this point, most of the hazards we have discussed occur at altitude. Let's complete our discussion with a look at some ground-based weather hazards which can restrict visibility.

Radiation fog forms in moist air on clear, calm nights.

Fog is classified according to the way it forms. **Radiation fog**, also known as **ground fog**, is very common. It forms over fairly level surfaces on clear, calm, humid nights. As the surface cools by radiation, the adjacent air is also cooled to its dewpoint. Radiation fog usually occurs in stable air associated with a high pressure system. As early morning temperatures increase, the fog begins to lift and usually "burns off" by mid-morning. If higher clouds layers form over the fog, visibility will improve more slowly.

Advection and upslope fog require a wind for formation.

Advection fog is caused when a low layer of warm, moist air moves over a cooler surface. It is most common under cloudy skies along coastlines where sea breezes transport air from the warm water to the cooler land. Winds up to about 15 knots will intensify the fog. Above 15 knots, turbulence creates a mixing of the air, and it usually lifts sufficiently to form low stratus clouds. **Upslope fog** forms when moist, stable air is forced up a sloping land mass. Like advection fog, upslope fog can form in moderate to strong winds and under cloudy skies.

Precipitation-induced fog may form when warm rain or drizzle falls through a layer of cooler air near the surface. Evaporation from the falling precipitation saturates the cool air, causing fog to form. This fog can be very dense, and usually it does not clear until the rain moves out of the area. **Steam fog**, which is often called sea smoke, occurs as cold, dry air moves over comparatively warmer water. It rises upward from the water's surface and resembles rising smoke. It is composed entirely of water droplets that often freeze quickly and fall back into the water as ice particles. Low-level turbulence can occur and icing can become hazardous in steam fog.

Low-level turbulence and icing are associated with steam fog.

Haze, smoke, smog, and blowing dust or snow can also restrict your visibility. **Haze** is caused by a concentration of very fine salt or dust particles suspended in the air. It occurs in stable atmospheric conditions with relatively light winds. Haze is usually no more than a few thousand feet thick, but it may occasionally extend to 15,000 feet. Visibility above the haze layer is usually good; however, visibility through the haze can be very poor. Smoke is usually much more localized; it is generally found in industrial areas and is a hazard only when it drifts across your intended landing field. On the other hand, **smog**, which is a combination of fog and smoke, can spread very poor visibility over a large area. Blowing dust and blowing snow present similar problems. They occur in moderate to high winds and can extend to an altitude of several thousand feet.

CHECKLIST _____

After studying this section, you should have a basic understanding of:

✓ **Thunderstorms** — What the conditions are for their formation, and what the types, characteristics, and hazards of thunderstorms are.

✓ **Turbulence** — What the various types are and the hazards associated with them.

✓ **Structural icing** — What the types of structural icing are, how each type forms, and the hazards associated with each.

✓ **Restrictions to visibility** — What they are, what causes their formation, and what their associated hazards are.

CHAPTER 5

INTERPRETING WEATHER DATA

INTRODUCTION

While a basic knowledge of weather theory and weather hazards is essential, your ability to interpret weather data is equally important. You need to know what kind of information is available, how it is presented, and where it can be obtained. This chapter concentrates on weather information for pilots, including printed reports and forecasts, graphic weather charts, and a variety of telephone, TV, and in-flight weather information services. Printed reports and forecasts are covered in the first section, followed by a presentation of graphic weather charts. The final section describes various sources of weather information for preflight briefings, as well as in-flight advisories.

PRINTED REPORTS AND FORECASTS

Before beginning any flight as pilot-in-command of an aircraft, you are required to familiarize yourself with all available information concerning that flight. For a flight not in the vicinity of an airport, that information must include the latest or most current weather reports and forecasts. Aviation weather services are designed to provide you with the necessary information. To take advantage of these services, you need to know enough about them to ask the right questions. For short, local flights, you may need to know only the general weather conditions. For extended cross-country flights, you need more detailed information.

SURFACE AVIATION WEATHER REPORTS

An observation of surface weather which is reported and transmitted is called a **surface aviation weather report** (SA). Learning the common weather abbreviations, symbols, and word contractions will help you understand this type of report, as well as others that are important for flight planning. After a little practice, you will discover the SA is relatively easy to read. A surface aviation weather report may contain as many as 10 separate elements, which are discussed in the following paragraphs. [Figure 5-1]

STATION DESIGNATOR

Each report begins with a three-letter location identifier. A list of station designators usually is available at an FSS or NWS office. You can also use the *Airport/Facility Directory* to decode the identifiers.

TYPE AND TIME OF REPORT

The two basic types of weather reports are the scheduled **record observation** (SA), which is taken on the hour, and the special report. A **special report** (SP) may be an unscheduled special observation indicating a significant change in one or more elements, or it may be a scheduled record observation that also qualifies as a special, so it is called a **record special** (RS). After the type of report, the time of the observation is given in UTC or Zulu.

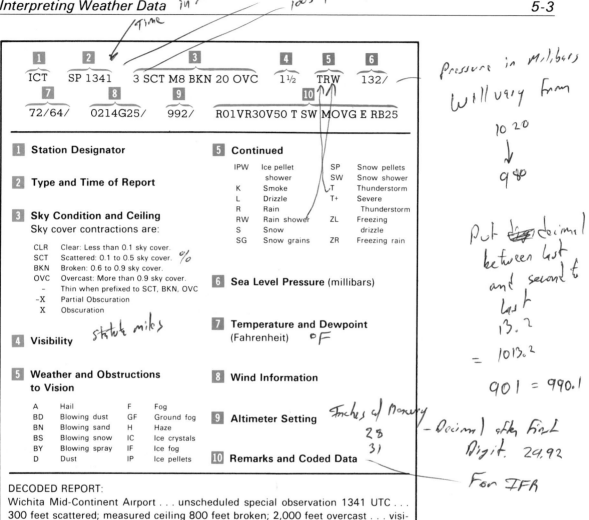

Figure 5-1. The surface aviation weather report usually contains most of these elements. When an element that should be included is missing, the letter "M" appears in its place. An item also may be omitted if it is not occurring at observation time or is not pertinent. It may be helpful to refer back to this example as you read the description of each element.

SKY CONDITION AND CEILING

The height of clouds or obscuring phenomena is reported in hundreds of feet above ground level (AGL). To determine the cloud height, you add two zeros to the number given in the report. When more than one layer is present, the layers are reported in ascending order. However, the sky

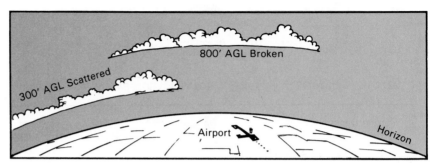

Figure 5-2. Note that the upper layer is reported as broken, even though that layer by itself covers less than 0.6 of the horizon. If the total coverage did not exceed 0.5, the upper layer would be reported as scattered.

cover condition for any higher layers represents total sky coverage, which includes any lower layer. [Figure 5-2]

For a layer of clouds to be classified as a ceiling, it must be reported as broken or overcast and not classified as thin.

A **ceiling** is the AGL height of the lowest layer of clouds or obscuring phenomena that is reported as broken, overcast, or obscured, but is not classified as scattered, thin, or partial. In general terms, a ceiling exists when more than half of the sky is covered. The term **thin** means the cloud cover is predominantly transparent and does not constitute a ceiling. This condition is indicated by a minus sign (-) preceding the sky cover symbol.

You should realize that a ceiling may be either a layer of clouds or an **obscuration** which is surface-based, such as precipitation, fog, dust, or blowing snow. To be classified as a ceiling, an obscuration must hide all of the sky. If it covers only part of the sky, it is termed a **partial obscuration** and it does not constitute a ceiling.

The ceiling figure in an aviation weather report is always preceded by a code letter such as "M" for measured, "E" for estimated, and "W" for indefinite. No code letter precedes a nonceiling cloud layer.

A **measured** ceiling is usually determined with an electronic device called a rotating beam ceilometer. Measured ceilings may also be determined by other means, such as a ceiling light, cloud detection radar, or by the unobscured portion of a landmark that rises into the ceiling layer.

Estimated ceilings are determined by pilot reports, balloons, or other measurements that do not meet the criteria for measured ceilings. When a ceiling is estimated from a pilot report, the MSL altitude reported by the pilot is converted to an AGL height. Balloon-estimated ceilings are based on the time it takes for the balloon to ascend, and they may be inaccurate because of convective air currents. Other measurements include estimates by meteorologists who must rely on experience and knowledge of cloud formations.

An **indefinite** ceiling means that a surface-based obscuration is covering all of the sky. The ceiling height is the vertical visibility into the obscuration. A partial obscuration has no height value, since it is not a ceiling. For example, "-X M7 OVC" indicates the sky is partially obscured, with a measured ceiling of 700 feet overcast.

> The height value for an indefinite ceiling is the vertical visibility into a surface-based obscuration which covers the entire sky.

If a ceiling is **variable**, the letter "V" is included after the ceiling height. The range of variability is specified in the remarks section at the end of the report. For example, "M12V OVC" means there is a measured ceiling at 1,200 feet AGL with a variable overcast. In the remarks, "CIG 10V13" means the ceiling is variable between 1,000 and 1,300 feet AGL.

VISIBILITY

Prevailing visibility is the greatest distance an observer can see and identify objects through at least 180° of the horizon. It follows the sky condition and ceiling, and is given in statute miles and fractions. The letter "V," included as a suffix, shows variability, and the remarks explain it further. Variable visibility is reported only when it is critical to aircraft operations. For example, "1½V" indicates a variable visibility of one and one-half statute miles. In remarks, "VSBY1V3" means the visibility is variable between one and three statute miles.

> In SA reports, visibility is given in statute miles.

WEATHER AND OBSTRUCTIONS TO VISION

When weather or obstructions to vision are present at the time of the observation, you will find them immediately after the visibility. The term "weather" as used in this SA element includes all forms of precipitation, as well as thunderstorms, tornadoes, funnel clouds, and water spouts. Weather symbols are used for all types of precipitation, followed by intensity levels: light (-), moderate (no sign), and heavy (+). No intensity level is reported for hail or ice crystals. A **severe thunderstorm** (T+) has surface winds of at least 50 knots and/or surface hail at least three-quarters of an inch in diameter. Tornadoes, funnel clouds, and water-spouts are spelled out in the SA to avoid the possibility of misinterpretation. Obstructions to vision refer to general atmospheric phenomena other than precipitation. No intensities are given for these items.

SEA LEVEL PRESSURE

Sea level pressure is reported to the nearest tenth of a millibar, using three digits and no decimal point. Actually, this is local station pressure converted to the equivalent sea level pressure. Since sea level pressure is usually greater than 960.0 millibars and less than 1050.0 millibars, you must prefix the reported figures with a 9 or a 10, whichever brings it closer to 1,000.0 millibars. For example, "132/" is decoded as 1013.2 millibars. A slash after the sea level pressure separates it from the next item.

> Decode sea level pressure by prefixing a 9 or 10, whichever brings the value closer to 1,000.

TEMPERATURE AND DEWPOINT

Temperature and dewpoint are reported in degrees Fahrenheit and are separated by a slash. For example, "72/64" indicates a surface temperature of 72°F and a dewpoint of 64°F. The dewpoint is followed by another slash.

WIND INFORMATION

The first two digits in wind information indicate wind direction in tens of degrees, while the second two represent its speed.

Wind information follows the dewpoint and uses four digits to indicate the average wind direction and speed observed over a one-minute period. The first two digits represent the direction from which the wind is blowing. It is reported in tens of degrees, referenced to true north. To decode, you add a zero to the two-digit number. The second two digits show the speed in knots. A calm condition is reported as "0000." If the speed is 100 knots or greater, 50 is added to the direction code and the hundreds digit of speed is omitted. For example, "5908" means the wind is blowing from 090° (59 – 50 = 9) at a speed of 108 knots (08 + 100 = 108).

In addition to direction and speed, the character, or type, of wind may be reported. A **gust** (G) is a variation in wind speed of at least 10 knots between peaks and lulls. A **squall** (Q) is a sudden increase in speed of at least 15 knots which results in a sustained speed of 20 knots or more that lasts for at least one minute. [Figure 5-3]

ALTIMETER SETTING

Decode the altimeter setting by prefixing a two or three, whichever brings the values closer to 30.00.

The altimeter setting, also separated by a slash, is reported in inches of mercury. Only the last three digits are transmitted and the decimal point is omitted. To decode, prefix the three-digit figure with either a two or a three, whichever brings it closer to 30.00 inches. For example, when "992" is prefixed with a two and the decimal point is added, the altimeter setting is 29.92 in. Hg. Altimeter settings reflect local station pressure converted to sea level.

REMARKS AND CODED DATA

Certain remarks are routinely reported, while others may be included when they are considered significant. Some of the most important information in a weather report often is in the remarks. In most cases, you

Coded Data	Explanations
0000	Calm
2014	Wind from 200° at 14 knots
1510G25	Wind from 150° at 10 knots, gusts to 25 knots
2212Q35	Wind from 220° at 12 knots, squalls with peak speeds to 35 knots
7610	Wind from 260° at 110 knots

Figure 5-3. This figure shows several examples of wind information as it appears on surface aviation weather reports. The decoded wind direction, speed, and character are shown to the right.

will notice more remarks when the weather is bad and the airport is approved for IFR operations.

Some IFR airports have special equipment to measure the visibility. When the visibility at these airports is near or below VFR minimums, the first remark should be runway visibility value or runway visual range. **Runway visibility value** (RVV) is measured in miles or fractions of miles along a given runway. RVV usually is determined by an electronic instrument called a transmissometer. **Runway visual range** (RVR) is always measured by a transmissometer, and it pertains to a specific instrument runway. RVR is the maximum horizontal distance you can expect to see high intensity runway lights down that runway. It is always reported in hundreds of feet.

When RVV or RVR is reported in the SA, the remark begins with the actual runway number and the abbreviation VV or VR, as appropriate. Both RVV and RVR are for the 10-minute period preceding the observation time. When visibility is variable, the 10-minute extremes are reported. For example, "R01VR30V50" means runway 01 has a visual range of 3,000 variable to 5,000 feet. When runway visual range is greater than 6,000 feet, it is shown as 60+. An RVR less than the minimum value that the transmissometer can detect is followed with a minus sign. For example, an RVR of less than 1,000 feet is reported as "10-." Even though RVV and RVR remarks are primarily for IFR operations, they provide VFR pilots with information on runway conditions. The second part of the remarks usually contains information which clarifies or expands on other elements of the report. This information is presented in abbreviated format. [Figure 5-4]

Freezing level data are available at airports where upper air observations are taken. You can identify this information by the letters "RADAT" in the remarks, followed by a coded group of numbers.

Coded Data	Explanations
ACSL SW–NW	Standing lenticular altocumulus southwest to northwest*
BINOVC	Breaks in overcast
CB N MOVG E	Cumulonimbus north moving east*
CIG 14V 19	Ceiling variable between 1,400 and 1,900 feet
CUFRA W APCHG STA	Cumulusfractus clouds west approaching the station
FK4	Fog and smoke obscuring 4/10 of the sky
FQT LTGCG	Frequent lightning cloud to ground
PRESFR	Pressure falling rapidly
SB15E40	Snow began at 15 and ended 40 minutes past the hour
RB 12	Rain began at 12 minutes past the hour
WSHFT 30	Wind shifted at 30 minutes past the hour

Figure 5-4. Examples of coded remarks are shown in the left column, with the corresponding explanations on the right. The asterisks indicate highly significant cloud types that the observer should always report. You should also report these cloud types to an FSS if you observe them in flight.

RADATs are added to the first record report after the information becomes available, usually twice each day. They contain information on the relative humidity at the freezing level or levels. Up to three freezing levels (low, medium, and high) may be reported. "RADAT 87045," for instance, means the relative humidity is 87 percent and the freezing level is at 4,500 feet MSL. Later in this chapter, you will see that freezing level information is also indicated on some weather forecasts and charts.

Notices to airmen (NOTAMs) may be added to the end of the SA report or transmitted as separate lines of information. NOTAMs report changes in the status of airports or airway facilities that could affect your decision to make a flight. They include such information as runway closures, obstructions in the approach and departure paths to airports, and outages or curtailed operation hours of navaids and ATC facilities.

Pilot reports (PIREPs) of current weather conditions often confirm such information as the height of bases and tops of cloud layers, in-flight visibility, icing conditions, and turbulence, which are not routinely available from other observation sources. When you encounter unexpected weather conditions, you are encouraged to make a pilot report. If the ceiling is at or below 5,000 feet, or visibility is at or below five miles, ATC facilities are required to solicit PIREPs. If you make a PIREP, the ATC facility or the FSS can add your report to the distribution system, and it can be used to brief other pilots or to provide in-flight advisories. [Figure 5-5]

RADAR WEATHER REPORTS

General areas of precipitation, especially thunderstorms, are observed by radar on a routine basis. Most radar stations issue **radar weather reports** (RAREPs) each hour, with intervening special reports as required. These reports are routinely transmitted on weather service circuits and some are included in FSS weather broadcasts.

Radar weather reports describe areas of precipitation along with information on the type, intensity, and trend.

RAREPs not only define the areas of precipitation, they also provide information on the type, intensity, and trend. In addition, these reports normally include movement (direction and speed) of the precipitation areas, as well as maximum height. When the clouds extend to high levels, thunderstorms are likely. This means you can expect turbulence and the possibility of hail.

TERMINAL FORECASTS

Terminal forecasts tell you what weather you may expect in the future at specific airports.

A prediction of surface weather expected at an airport is a **terminal forecast** (FT). It is one of your best sources for predicting what the weather will be in the future at a specific terminal. The forecast conditions pertain to an area within five nautical miles of the center of the runway complex. The term "VCNTY" covers an additional area extending from 5

PIREP Elements	Explanations
UA or UUA	Type of report — UA is routine PIREP; UUA is urgent PIREP
/OV	Location — In relation to VOR or route segment (station identifier, radial, DME)
/TM	Time — Coordinated Universal Time (UTC)
/FL	Altitude — Above mean sea level (MSL)
/TP	Type of aircraft — Example, CE172
/SK	Sky cover — Cloud bases and tops (both MSL), amount of coverage (scattered, broken, overcast)
/WX	Weather — Precipitation, visibility, restrictions to vision
/TA	Temperature — Degrees Celsius
/WV	Wind — Direction in degrees magnetic, speed in knots
/TB	Turbulence — Light, moderate, severe, as appropriate
/IC	Icing — Trace, light, moderate, severe, as appropriate
/RM	Remarks — To clarify the report or for additional information

Coded PIREP: UA/OV OKC 063064/TM 1522/FL 080/TP CE172/TA -04/WV 245040/TB LGT/RM IN CLR

Decoded PIREP: Routine pilot report . . . 64 n.m. on the 63° radial from Oklahoma City VOR . . . at 1522 UTC . . . flight altitude 8,000 ft . . . type of aircraft is a Cessna 172 . . . outside air temperature is minus four degrees Celsius . . . wind is from 245° magnetic at 40 kts . . . light turbulence and clear skies.

Figure 5-5. PIREPs are made up of several elements, as indicated in the upper portion of this figure. The lower part provides a sample PIREP and its plain-language interpretation. Notice that MSL altitudes are used. Although PIREPs should be complete and concise, you should not be overly concerned with strict format or terminology. The important thing is to forward the report so other pilots can benefit from it.

to 25 nautical miles beyond the center of the runway complex. For example, "TRW VCNTY" means thunderstorms are expected to occur between 5 and 25 miles from the center of the airport.

FTs generally are issued three times each day and are valid for a 24-hour period. The first part of the forecast covers expected weather for an 18-hour period. This is followed by a six-hour categorical outlook. The categories include four types of weather conditions:

1. LIFR (Low IFR) — Ceiling less than 500 feet and/or visibility of less than one mile
2. IFR — Ceiling 500 to less than 1,000 feet and/or visibility one to less than three miles
3. MVFR (Marginal VFR) — Ceiling 1,000 to 3,000 feet and/or visibility three to five miles, inclusive
4. VFR — No ceiling or ceiling greater than 3,000 feet and visibility greater than five miles

Remarks, expected changes, and the six-hour categorical outlook are important parts of the FT. When necessary, remarks describe variations

[handwritten annotations: "25th of Month", "10", "today to tomorrow", "10", "From 16 Greenwich"]

```
    1        2        3    4   5      6              7
STL FT   251010   C5 X  ½  S-BS   3325G35   OCNL C0 X 0S+ BS.
                          8
```

```
16Z C30 BKN 3BS 3320 CHC SW-. 22Z 20 SCT 3315. 00Z CLR.
    9
```

```
04Z VFR WND . .
```

1 Station Identifier

2 Date-time Group — The date-time group specifies the day of the month and the valid times.

3 Sky and Ceiling — The letter "C" always identifies a forecast ceiling layer. Cloud heights are AGL.

4 Visibility — The absence of a visibility entry indicates the visibility is more than six statute miles.

5 Weather and Obstructions to Vision

6 Wind — Omission of the wind entry indicates wind less than six knots. Winds are given in relation to true north.

7 Remarks

8 Expected Changes

9 Six-hour Categorical Outlook — The double period signifies the end of the report.

DECODED REPORT:

Terminal forecast for St. Louis, MO . . . valid beginning on the 25th day of the month at 1000Z until 1000Z on the 26th . . . ceiling 500 feet; sky obscured . . . visibility ½ statute mile . . . light snow and blowing snow . . . wind from 330° (true) at 25 knots gusting to 35 knots . . . occasional conditions of ceiling zero, sky obscured . . . visibility zero . . . heavy snow and blowing snow . . . by 1600Z, ceiling 3,000 feet broken . . . visibility three miles . . . blowing snow . . . wind from 330° at 20 knots . . . chance of light snow showers . . . by 2200Z, 2,000 scattered . . . visibility more than six miles (implied) . . . wind from 330° at 15 knots . . . by 0000Z, sky clear . . . visibility more than six miles (implied) . . . wind less than six knots (implied) . . . outlook from 0400Z to 1000Z . . . ceiling more than 3,000 feet or more . . . visibility greater than five miles (VFR) . . . wind 25 knots or stronger.

Figure 5-6. The codes used in this forecast are very similar to those shown for surface aviation weather reports. Exceptions are noted, when appropriate.

from the prevailing conditions. The contraction "OCNL" (occasional) in the remarks means the conditions are expected to occur less than half of the time during the period between 1000 and 1600Z. The probability of these occurrences, however, is greater than 50 percent. [Figure 5-6]

When prevailing conditions are forecast to change, the original conditions are followed by a period before the time and conditions of the expected change. For example, ". 23Z CFP C100 BKN 250 OVC 3215G25" means a cold front is forecast to pass the station by 2300Z. After frontal passage and also by 2300Z, prevailing conditions are forecast to change. The ceiling should be 10,000 feet broken and 25,000 feet overcast, with wind from 320° at 15 knots, gusting to 25 knots. Often, the expected change is much different than the original prevailing condition. Frontal passage is important because it always indicates a shift in wind direction, and usually affects the ceiling and visibility. If the contraction "WND" is added to a VFR outlook, it means that winds of 25 knots or stronger are expected during the outlook period. Six-hour categorical outlooks for conditions below VFR always include a reason. For example, "MVFR CIG H K" indicates the outlook is for marginal VFR due to low ceilings and the visibility is restricted by haze and smoke.

AREA FORECASTS

An area forecast (FA) covers general weather conditions over a wide area and is a good source of information for enroute weather. It also helps you determine the conditions at airports that do not have terminal forecasts. FAs are issued three times a day in the 48 mainland states and Alaska, twice a day for the Gulf of Mexico, and four times a day in Hawaii. [Figure 5-7]

To determine forecast weather conditions between reporting stations, refer to the area forecast.

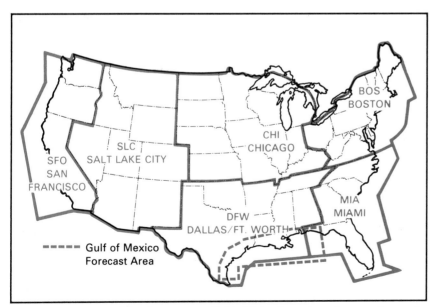

Figure 5-7. The 48 mainland states are divided into six regions for area forecasts. FAs are issued by the National Aviation Weather Advisory Unit in Kansas City, MO. A specialized Gulf of Mexico FA is issued by the National Hurricane Center in Miami, Florida.

FAs provide a 12-hour forecast plus an additional six-hour outlook. The forecasts are arranged in two sections which describe specific weather phenomena: Hazards/Flight Precautions (H), and Synopsis and VFR Clouds/Weather (C). [Figure 5-8]

HAZARDS/FLIGHT PRECAUTIONS

The hazards and flight precautions section outlines the type and general location of weather hazards within the forecast area.

In the heading "SLCH FA 191140," the "SLC" identifies the Salt Lake City forecast area, "H" indicates the hazards/flight precautions section, "FA" means area forecast, and "191140" tells you this forecast was issued on the 19th day of the month at 1140 Zulu. Since these forecasts are rounded to the nearest full hour, the valid time is from 1200Z on the 19th to 0000Z on the 20th day of the month. Flight precautions are indicated for IFR conditions, mountain obscurations, icing, and turbulence with the affected states listed using standard two-letter abbreviations.

Standard notes in each hazard section remind you that thunderstorms imply possible severe or greater turbulence, severe icing, low-level wind shear, and instrument conditions. Non-MSL heights are noted by the letters AGL (above ground level) or CIG (ceiling). All heights are expressed in hundreds of feet.

SYNOPSIS AND VFR CLOUDS/WEATHER

This section contains an 18-hour synopsis and a 12-hour specific forecast. The synopsis is followed by a 6-hour (18-hour in Alaska) categorical outlook giving a total forecast period of 18 hours (30-hours in Alaska).

The location and movement of fronts and pressure systems is described in the synopsis.

The synopsis describes the location and movement of fronts and pressure systems. When significant weather systems are not present, airmass descriptions may be used. In the example, the synopsis is valid for an 18-hour period, until 0600 Zulu on the 20th. A surface low pressure cell is located in northern Arizona with a cold front moving south into Mexico, and another cold front moving southeast into western Texas. The low will remain stationary through 0600 Zulu with the Arizona cold front rotating eastward into western Texas and to the south into northern Mexico. The other cold front will drift to the southeast. This airmass will contain moisture in the central and southern portions of the area in the vicinity of the low pressure cell.

Cloud conditions and areas of marginal VFR (MVFR) for affected areas are described under VFR clouds/weather.

The VFR Clouds/Weather portion lists by state, cloud conditions, weather, and/or visibility that are marginal VFR (MVFR) or better. For Idaho, south of a line between Boise, ID and Jackson, WY, clouds are 8,000 to 10,000 MSL broken to overcast with layers up to 18,000 MSL. There are isolated areas of visibility between 3 to 5 miles in snow and light fog. By 1800 Zulu

1 {

SLCH FA 191140
HAZARDS VALID UNTIL 200000
ID MT WY NV UT CO AZ NM

.
FLT PRCTNS. . . IFR. . . WY UT CO AZ NM
          . . . MTN OBSCN. . . ID WY NV UT CO AZ NM
          . . . ICG. . . WY NV UT CO AZ NM
          . . . TURBC. . . ID MT WY NV UT CO AZ NM

.
TSTMS IMPLY PSBL SVR OR GTR TURBC SVR ICG LLWS AND IFR CONDS.
NON MSL HGTS ARE DENOTED BY AGLE OR CIG.
. . . .

}

2 {

. . .
SLCC FA 191140
SYNOPSIS AND VFR CLDS/WX
SYNOPSIS VALID UNTIL 200600
CLDS/WX VALID UNTIL 200000 .OTLK VALID 200000-200600

.
SYNOPSIS. . . SFC LOW NRN AZ WITH ONE CDFNT SWD INTO MEX AND
ANOTHER SEWD INTO WRN TX LOW WILL RMN QSTNRY THRU
06Z WITH AZ CDFNT ROTATG EWD INTO WRN TX SWWD INTO NRN MEX
AND THE OTHER CDFNT DRFTG SEWD. AMS WILL CONT MOIST CNTRL
AND SRN PTNS OF AREA VCNTY OF LOW.

.
ID
S OF A BOI-JAC LINE. . . 80-100 BKN-OVC LYRD TO 180 ISOLD 3-5SW-F.
18Z 80-100 SCT SCT CI. OTLK. . . VFR.
N OF A BOI-JAC LINE. . . CLR. OTLK. . . VFR.

}

1 Hazards/Flight Precautions   **2** Synopsis and VFR Clouds/Weather

Figure 5-8. You should notice that each of the two sections in the area forecast has a unique heading identifier which includes the valid time. This permits amendments or corrections to separate sections without changing the entire forecast. Area forecasts contain standard abbreviations and word contractions. The information in this sample forecast is interpreted in the accompanying paragraphs.

clouds will be scattered from 8,000 to 10,000 MSL along with scattered cirrus clouds. The outlook is forecasting VFR conditions. Clear conditions are forecast north of the same line between Boise, ID and Jackson, WY. The outlook for this area is also forecast to be VFR.

GULF OF MEXICO AREA FORECAST

Gulf of Mexico FA is unique since it is intended to support offshore helicopter operations. The Gulf FA includes in-flight advisories and marine precautions. Each section describes the phenomenon impacting each area and will always have an entry. If no hazardous weather is expected, a statement such as "NONE EXPCD" will be included.

AMENDMENTS

Amendments to individual sections are issued whenever the weather significantly improves or deteriorates based upon the judgment of the forecaster. Each SIGMET, Convective SIGMET, or AIRMET affecting the area also amends the FA. The contraction "AMD" (amend) and the amendment number since the last scheduled issuance and/or the contraction "COR" (correction) followed by the correction number is included after the date-time group of the amendment and/or correction in the heading. The date and time given in the heading is the issuance time of the amendment or correction.

WINDS AND TEMPERATURES ALOFT FORECASTS

Winds aloft are forecast in true direction and knots.

Winds and temperatures aloft forecasts provide an estimate of wind direction in relation to true north, wind speed in knots, and the temperature in degrees Celsius for selected altitudes. Depending on the station elevation, winds and temperatures are usually forecast for nine levels between 3,000 and 39,000 feet. [Figure 5-9]

The FD does not include levels within 1,500 feet of the station elevation, and temperatures are not forecast for the 3,000-foot level or for a level within 2,500 feet of the station elevation. At Denver (DEN), for example, the forecast for the lower two levels is omitted, since the station elevation at Denver is over 5,000 feet.

The wind information included in the body of the FD is presented almost like it is on other reports and forecasts. The first two numbers indicate the true direction from which the wind is blowing. For example, "2736-02" indicates the wind is from 270° at 36 knots and the temperature is -2°C. Quite often you must interpolate between the two levels. For instance, if you plan to fly near Joliet (JOT) at 7,500 feet, you must interpolate between 6,000 and 9,000 feet. In this case, your planned flight altitude is

```
┌─────────────────────────────────────────────────────────────────────┐
│                              ┌─┐                                      │
│                              │1│                                      │
│                           ───┴─┴───────────────                       │
│   FD    KWBC      161640                                              │
│   DATA BASED ON 161200Z                                              │
│   VALID 161800Z       FOR USE 1700-2100Z    TEMPS NEG ABV 24000      │
│                              ┌─┐                                      │
│                              │2│                                      │
│                          ────┴─┴──────────────────                    │
│   FT    3000       6000       9000     12000      18000      24000    │
│                                                                       │
│   DEN                        2315+04   2519+00    2519-16    2523-27  │
│   HOU   2619      2728-01     2635-05   2641-09    2654-21    2665-32  │
│   JOT   2526      2736-02     2642-06   2649-11    2662-22    2674-33  │
│                                                                       │
│   ┌─┐                              ┌─┐                                │
│   │1│  Heading Data                │2│  Body of Forecast             │
│   └─┘                              └─┘                                │
└─────────────────────────────────────────────────────────────────────┘
```

Figure 5-9. Heading information includes the type of forecast, the day of the month, and time of transmission. The second line tells you the forecast is based on observations at 1200Z and is valid at 1800Z on the 16th. It is intended for use between 1700Z and 2100Z on the same day. Since temperatures above 24,000 feet are always negative, a note indicates that the minus sign is omitted for 30,000 feet and above. The column on the left lists the FD location identifiers. The columns to the right show forecast information for each level appropriate to that location. This excerpt shows winds only to the 24,000 foot level.

midway between them. A good estimate of the wind is 265° at 39 knots with a temperature of –04°C.

Wind speeds between 100 and 199 knots are encoded so direction and speed can be represented by four digits. This is done by adding 50 to the two-digit wind direction and subtracting 100 from the velocity. For example, a wind of 270° at 101 knots is encoded as "7701" (27 + 50 = 77 for wind direction, and 101 – 100 = 01 for wind speed). A code of 9900 indicates light and variable winds (less than five knots).

When wind speeds are 100 to 199 knots, decode by subtracting 50 from the first two digits and adding 100 to the next two digits. The code 9900 means light and variable.

SEVERE WEATHER REPORTS AND FORECASTS

Although most weather gathering activity is concerned with routine reports and forecasts, considerable effort is devoted to monitoring and reporting severe weather conditions. The National Hurricane Center in Miami, FL, issues hurricane advisories; the National Severe Storms Forecast Center in Kansas City, MO, also issues special forecasts and reports for severe weather conditions. These include convective outlook forecasts and severe weather watch bulletins.

The **convective outlook** (AC) forecasts general thunderstorm activity for the next 24-hour period. ACs are used by meteorologists to prepare graphic charts. You may use the data for planning flights within the forecast period. A **severe weather watch bulletin** (WW) is a weather report that defines areas of possible severe thunderstorms or tornadoes. WWs are issued on an unscheduled basis and are updated as required. Satellite photos have improved the accuracy of forecasting severe weather phenomena. Normally, you will know about severe weather conditions well in advance of the actual occurrence. Since severe weather forecasts and reports may affect the general public, as well as pilots, they are widely disseminated through all available media.

CHECKLIST

After studying this section, you should have a basic understanding of:

✓ **Surface aviation weather report (SA)** — What the basic types are, the main information elements they provide, and how they are interpreted.

✓ **SA remarks** — How remarks pertain to the basic report and the types of information that may be included.

✓ **Pilot Reports (PIREPs)** — What they are and the types of information typically included.

✓ **Radar weather reports (RAREPs)** — What information they provide.

✓ **Terminal forecast (FT)** — What they are, where they apply, and what information they contain.

✓ **Area forecast (FA)** — What information the various sections contain and how to interpret the information.

✓ **Winds and temperatures aloft forecasts (FDs)** — What the basic format is and how to interpret it.

✓ **Severe weather reports and forecasts** — What their significance is and what types are available.

GRAPHIC WEATHER PRODUCTS

Besides printed weather reports and forecasts, the National Weather Service also produces a variety of graphic weather charts which are available at flight service stations and weather service offices. These charts give you a pictorial view of large-scale weather patterns and trends.

SURFACE ANALYSIS CHART

The surface analysis chart, also referred to as a surface weather chart, shows weather conditions as they existed a few hours ago. By reviewing this chart, you can get a picture of atmospheric pressure patterns at the earth's surface. More importantly, you also can see the locations of high and low pressure systems and associated fronts. Although this chart is transmitted every three hours, the time needed to generate the chart makes the data at least two hours old when you first see it. [Figure 5-10]

The surface analysis chart shows pressure patterns, high and low pressure areas, fronts, and station models.

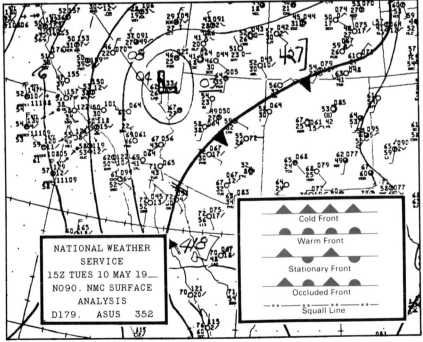

Figure 5-10. The box at the lower left of this excerpt reflects the date and time of the plotted observations. In this case, they were made at 1500Z on May 10. An inset at the lower right shows the symbols that represent various types of fronts, as well as squall lines. The symbols for cold, warm, and occluded fronts point in the direction of frontal movement.

Weather briefers often color code fronts and squall lines.

Weather briefers often color code fronts and squall lines for quick identification. The cold front is blue; the warm front is red. Stationary fronts are both blue and red, since they represent both warm and cold fronts. Occluded fronts and squall lines are purple.

A station model reflects the weather at a given reporting point.

The surface analysis chart also provides surface weather observations for a large number of reporting points throughout the United States. Each of these points is illustrated by a **station model**. To interpret these models, you first need to become familiar with the symbols that are used. [Figure 5-11]

Wind direction is shown relative to true north, and wind velocity is given in knots.

Symbols extending out from the station circle give wind information. The symbol shows the general true direction the surface wind is blowing from and gives the velocity in knots. The absence of a wind symbol and a double circle around the station means calm wind. True wind direction is shown by the orientation of the wind pointer. Velocity is indicated by barbs and/or pennants attached to the wind pointer. One short barb is five knots, a longer barb is 10 knots, and a pennant is 50 knots. For example, the wind pointer in the sample station model shows the wind is from the northwest at 15 knots.

Low cloud symbols are placed below the station model, while middle and high cloud symbols are placed immediately above it. A typical station model may include only one cloud type; seldom are more than two included. Decoding information for these symbols is available in various FAA publications and at flight service stations.

Temperature is given in degrees Fahrenheit, while pressure is given in millibars.

Temperatures are shown in degrees Fahrenheit; pressure is given in millibars. For example, the temperature at the sample station is 34°F, and the atmospheric pressure is 1014.7 millibars. Just below the station pressure, the number "28" indicates the pressure at this station has increased 2.8 millibars in the past three hours and is now steady. The ".45" below the pressure change tells that 45-hundredths of an inch of precipitation fell within the past six hours.

WEATHER DEPICTION CHART

For flight planning, the weather depiction chart is most useful for determining general weather conditions and quickly locating areas of adverse weather.

The weather depiction chart may be thought of as a simplified version of the surface weather chart. It is an excellent source to help you determine general weather conditions during flight planning. Information plotted on this chart is derived from surface aviation weather reports.

Like the surface chart, the weather depiction chart is also prepared and transmitted by computer every three hours. Unlike the surface chart, pressure patterns and wind information are not provided. However, frontal activity and abbreviated station models are included. Symbols for

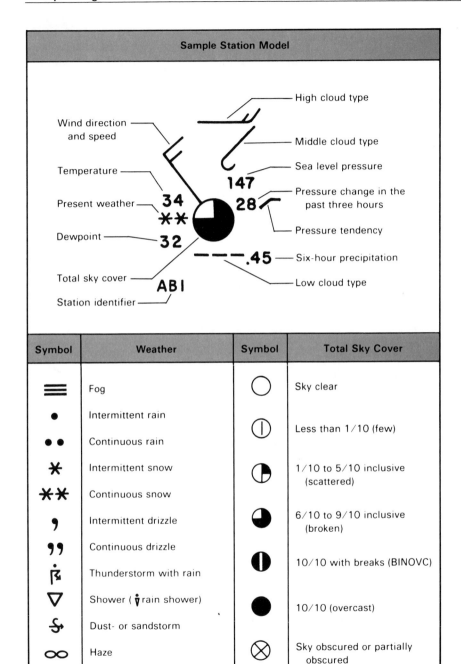

Figure 5-11. A sample station model is shown at the top of the illustration. The table at the lower left presents some common weather symbols used for current weather. According to the sample station model, continuous snowfall is in progress. The table at the lower right explains the symbols used for sky cover. The sample station indicates a broken sky cover.

fronts are the same as those used with surface charts. The most distinctive and useful feature of the weather depiction chart is that you can immediately locate areas of adverse weather simply by scanning it. [Figure 5-12]

The station model used for the weather depiction chart is a simplified version of the one used for the surface weather chart.

Weather depiction charts also feature simplified station models. Sky cover symbols are the same as those used for the surface analysis chart. The number directly below the station is the height of the cloud layer in hundreds of feet. In the sample station model, the ceiling is 500 feet overcast. To the left of the station, the visibility is provided in statute miles

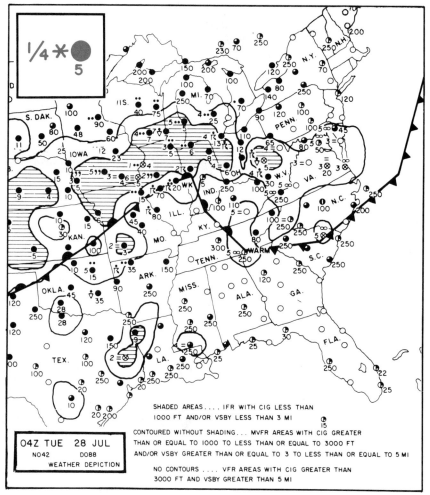

Figure 5-12. This excerpt of a weather depiction chart covers the eastern United States. The legend at the lower right gives the definitions and symbols for IFR, marginal VFR, and VFR weather areas shown on the chart. The inset at the upper left shows a sample of the station model. You may wish to refer back to this illustration during the following discussion.

or fractions of a mile if it is six miles or less. The reason for the obstruction to vision also may be given. In this case, the reported visibility is one-quarter mile in intermittent snow.

IFR, represented by enclosed shaded areas, means the ceiling is less than 1,000 feet AGL and/or the visibility is less than three statute miles. Marginal VFR is indicated by enclosed areas without shading. Marginal means the ceiling is 1,000 to 3,000 feet AGL inclusive and/or the visibility is three to five miles. In VFR conditions which are located outside enclosed areas, the ceiling is greater than 3,000 feet AGL and the visibility is greater than five miles.

RADAR SUMMARY CHART

The radar summary chart provides a graphic illustration of certain types of weather phenomena that special weather radar systems can detect. Pulses of radar energy are transmitted in a specific direction by a rotating antenna. When the signals encounter precipitation, they are reflected back to the antenna. The reflected signals, also called echoes, are then presented on a radar display which shows the strength and location of the radar return.

Computers prepare radar summary charts from these radar observations. The charts show the size, shape, and intensity of returns, as well as the intensity trend and direction of movement. As you examine the chart, keep in mind that the intensity of the radar returns increases as storms become more severe. In addition, the chart provides echo heights of the tops and bases of associated precipitation areas. However, the absence of echoes does not guarantee clear weather. Radar only detects precipitation, either in frozen or liquid form; it does not detect all cloud formations. For instance, fog is not displayed, and actual cloud tops may be higher or lower than the precipitation returns indicate.

Radar summary charts display only precipitation that can be detected by weather radar.

While the radar summary chart is a valuable preflight briefing aid, it has certain limitations. Keep in mind that it is an observation of conditions that existed at the valid time. Since thunderstorms develop rapidly, you should examine other weather sources for current and forecast conditions that may affect your flight.

Thunderstorms develop rapidly, so be sure to check other reports and forecasts for the latest weather conditions.

Intensity is shown on the chart by **contours**. The six levels displayed on a radar display are combined into three contours which are printed on the radar summary chart. The first contour represents levels one and two (light to moderate precipitation), the second shows levels three and

The radar summary chart displays precipitation in one of three contour levels representing precipitation intensity.

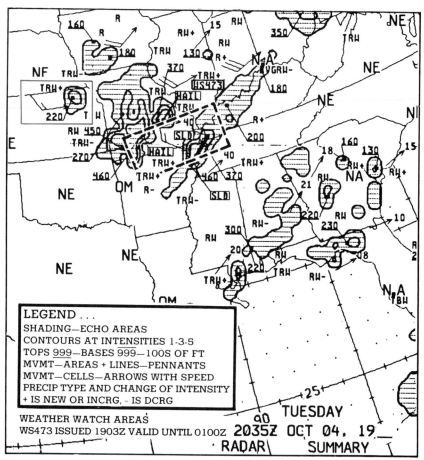

Figure 5-13. This excerpt of a radar summary chart covers the southeastern United States. The highlighted section represents one area of precipitation. Within the second contour, the radar returns correspond to level three or four (heavy to very heavy precipitation). The number "220" to the lower left indicates the top of a single cell within this area to be 22,000 feet MSL. The line from the number into the return area marks the location of the cell. You may wish to refer back to this illustration during the following discussion.

four (heavy to very heavy precipitation), and the third outlines levels five and six (intense to extreme precipitation). [Figure 5-13]

There are several other symbols you need to be familiar with when interpreting a radar summary chart. For example, the arrow pointing to the right indicates an area of precipitation is moving to the east at 15 knots. The letters "TRW+" tell you that a new thunderstorm, or one that is in progress, is building in intensity. A rectangular dashed-line box denotes a severe weather watch area. In this case, the notation "WS473" appears above the upper right corner of the box. The letters "WS" iden-tify this as a severe thunderstorm watch area. The numbers "473" mean

Symbol	Meaning	Symbol	Meaning
	Intensity level 1-2 Weak and moderate	$\frac{240}{80}$	Echo top 24,000' MSL Echo base 8,000' MSL
	Intensity level 3-4 (second contour) Strong and very strong	+	Intensity increasing or new echo
	Intensity level 5-6 (third contour) Intense and extreme	–	Intensity decreasing
		SLD	Solid, over 8/10 coverage
		LEWP	Line echo wave pattern
[---]	Dashed lines define areas of severe weather	HOOK	Hook echo
		HAIL	Hail
▭	Area of echoes	⌐WS999¬	Severe thunderstorm watch
		⌐WT999¬	Tornado watch
↗	Line of echoes	NE	No echos
→20	Cell moving east at 20 knots	NA	Observation not available
		OM	Equipment out for maintenance
⇗	Line or area is moving east at 20 knots (10 knot barbs)	STC	STC on-all precipitation may not be seen

Figure 5-14. Here are some of the symbols which may appear on the radar summary chart, along with brief explanations of their meanings.

this is the 473rd severe weather watch to be issued during the year. According to the notation at the lower left margin of the chart, this watch area was issued at 1903Z and is valid until 0100Z. [Figure 5-14]

A line of echoes is often shown on the chart. If there is at least 8/10 coverage, the line is labeled "SLD" at both ends. A **hook-shaped echo** (HOOK) may be associated with a tornado. In a **line echo wave pattern** (LEWP), one portion of a squall line bulges out ahead of the rest producing strong, gusty winds. **Sensitivity time control** (STC) is a radar feature which diminishes nearby echoes to enhance reception of more distant returns. This may mask some echoes or distort their relative intensities.

LOW-LEVEL SIGNIFICANT WEATHER PROG

The three charts we have discussed so far — the surface analysis, weather depiction, and radar summary charts — are all based on weather observations of the conditions that existed at a particular time. The next chart is a forecast chart instead of an observation chart. The U.S. low-level significant weather prognostic chart is valid from the surface up to the 400-millibar pressure level (24,000 feet). It is, therefore, designed for use in planning flights below this altitude. A prognostic chart is usually referred to as a "prog" chart. [Figure 5-15]

The significant weather prog chart provides a 12- and 24-hour forecast.

Low-level prog charts are issued four times each day. The valid time is printed on the lower margin of each panel. Since the two panels on the left forecast the weather 12 hours from the issue time and the two panels on the right forecast 24 hours, you can compare the two sets of panels and note expected changes between the two time frames.

SIGNIFICANT WEATHER PANELS

The symbols used to mark areas of IFR and MVFR differ from those on the weather depiction chart.

The upper panels show areas of IFR and marginal VFR weather, turbulence, and freezing levels. These panels of the prognostic chart help you determine areas to be avoided. Smooth lines enclose areas of forecast IFR weather; scalloped lines represent marginal VFR. As shown by the legend information, IFR areas have ceilings less than 1,000 feet and/or visibility less than three statute miles. Scalloped lines enclose marginal VFR (MVFR) ceilings from 1,000 to 3,000 feet and/or visibilities of three to five miles inclusive. Although the definitions of IFR and MVFR for this chart are the same as the weather depiction chart, the symbols for portraying the areas are different.

Low-level progs are designed to help you plan to avoid areas and altitudes where the most significant turbulence and freezing level are forecast.

Low-level progs provide turbulence and icing forecasts. Dashed lines enclose areas of moderate or greater turbulence. Numbers within these areas give the height of the turbulence in hundreds of feet MSL. Figures below a line show the expected base, while figures above a line represent the top of the turbulence. For example, 180 indicates turbulence from the surface to 18,000 feet MSL. Since thunderstorms always imply moderate or greater turbulence, areas of possible thunderstorm turbulence are not outlined. **Freezing level height contours** are drawn at 4,000-foot intervals with dashed lines. These contours are labeled in hundreds of feet MSL. A dotted line labeled "32°F," or "SFC," shows the surface location of the freezing level.

Since graphic weather charts cover large areas of the United States, they are most useful as aids during the planning phase of a cross-country flight. They should also be used as a starting point when you obtain a preflight weather briefing, since they allow you to get the "big picture" of the weather likely to affect your flight.

SURFACE PROG PANELS

The two lower panels are the surface prog panels. They contain standard symbols for fronts and pressure centers. Direction of pressure center movement is shown by an arrow; the speed is listed in knots. Areas of

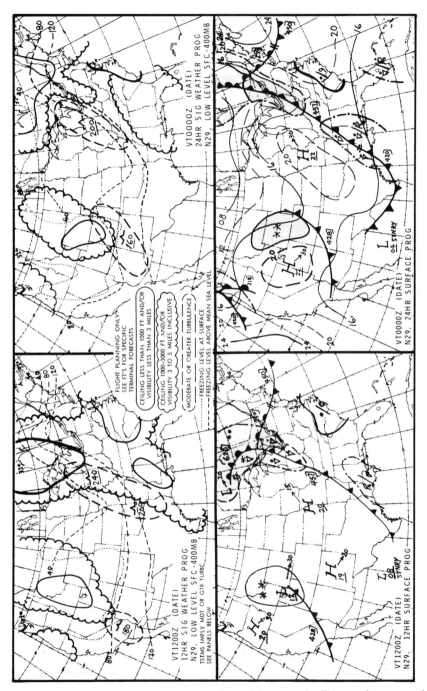

Figure 5-15. A low-level prog chart consists of four panels. The two lower panels are 12- and 24-hour forecasts of surface weather conditions, while the two upper panels are 12- and 24-hour forecasts of weather between the surface and 24,000 feet. Legend information is included between the two upper panels.

Symbol	Meaning	Symbol	Meaning	Symbol	Meaning
 (R/✦)	Showery precipitation (thunderstorms/rain showers) covering half or more of the area	⚆	Rain shower	⌃	Moderate turbulence
(••)	Continuous precipitation (rain) covering half or more of the area	⚇	Snow shower	⌃	Severe turbulence
(✱)	Showery precipitation (snow showers) covering less than half of the area	R	Thunderstorms	Ѱ	Moderate icing
		∿	Freezing rain	Ѱ	Severe icing
(❞)	Intermittent precipitation (drizzle) covering less than half of the area	ϭ	Tropical storm	●	Rain
		ϭ	Hurricane (typhoon)	✳	Snow
				❞	Drizzle

NOTE: Character of stable precipitation is the manner in which it occurs. It may be intermittent or continuous. A single symbol means intermittent and a pair of symbols means continuous.

Figure 5-16. An area which is expected to have continuous or intermittent (stable) precipitation is enclosed by a solid circle. If only showers are expected, the area is enclosed with a dot-dash pattern. When precipitation covers one-half or more of the area, it is shaded.

forecast precipitation, as well as thunderstorms, are outlined. Prog charts also have several unique symbols that are used to forecast weather conditions. [Figure 5-16]

CHECKLIST _____

After studying this section, you should have a basic understanding of:

✓ **Surface analysis charts** — How they represent atmospheric pressure patterns and weather at reporting stations across the country.

✓ **Weather depiction charts** — How you can use these charts to determine areas of IFR and marginal VFR weather.

✓ **Radar summary charts** — How these charts show thunderstorm activity based on radar returns from precipitation.

✓ **Low level significant weather progs** — How you can use these charts to forecast weather conditions 12 to 24 hours in the future.

SOURCES OF WEATHER INFORMATION

Now that you are able to interpret printed reports and forecasts and weather charts, you also need to become familiar with sources of weather information. Aside from your primary contacts with FSS and NWS telephone briefers, there are several other sources of supplemental weather information. This section will explain how to obtain a formal weather briefing from FSS or NWS personnel, as well as how to use supplemental weather sources effectively.

PREFLIGHT WEATHER BRIEFINGS

Flight service stations are your primary source for preflight and in-flight weather information. In areas not served by an FSS, Weather Service Offices (WSOs) may provide pilot weather briefings and also supply backup service to the FSS network. Telephone numbers for these outlets are available in the *Airport/Facility Directory* (A/FD). You also may find them in the telephone directory within the U.S. Government listings. Look under the Department of Transportation for the FAA or the Department of Commerce for the NWS.

When you request a briefing, you need to identify yourself as a pilot and supply the briefer with the following background information: type of flight planned (VFR or IFR), aircraft number or pilot's name, aircraft type, departure airport, route of flight, destination, flight altitude(s), ETD, and ETE.

When you contact a weather briefer, identify yourself as a pilot flying VFR and provide relevant background data for the flight.

The briefer can then proceed directly with the briefing and concentrate on weather affecting your flight. FSS personnel are certificated by the NWS as pilot weather briefers. While they do not make original forecasts, they do translate and interpret reports and forecasts into terms that describe the weather conditions you can expect along your route of flight and at your destination. Generally, there are three types of preflight weather briefings, and you should request the appropriate one when you contact the briefer. These include the standard, abbreviated, and outlook briefings.

STANDARD BRIEFING

Whenever you are planning a trip and have not had the opportunity to obtain preliminary weather or a previous briefing, you should request the **standard briefing**. This is the most complete weather briefing, since it assumes you have no basic familiarity with the overall weather picture.

The standard briefing provides the most information concerning weather for your flight.

When you request the standard briefing, the briefer automatically provides certain types of information in sequence.

A standard briefing includes the items in the following list, provided they are applicable to your proposed fight. The first three items may be combined in any order when, in the briefer's opinion, it will help to describe conditions more clearly to you.

1. **Adverse Conditions** — This includes the type of information that might influence you to alter your proposed route or cancel the flight altogether. Examples include such things as hazardous weather, closed runways, or navigation aids out of service.

2. **VFR Flight Not Recommended** — This statement means that, in the briefer's judgment, it is doubtful that you can complete the flight under VFR. Although the final decision to conduct the flight rests with you, this advisory should be taken very seriously.

3. **Synopsis** — The briefer will provide you with a broad overview of the major weather systems or airmasses that affect the proposed flight.

4. **Current Conditions** — This information is a rundown of existing conditions, including pertinent hourly, pilot, and radar reports. If your proposed departure time is beyond two hours, this item is omitted unless you specifically request it.

5. **Enroute Forecast** — This is a summary of forecast conditions in a logical order along the proposed route.

6. **Destination Forecast** — The briefer will provide the forecast for your destination at the ETA and also include any significant changes within +/- one hour.

7. **Winds Aloft** — The briefer will provide you with a summary of forecast winds for your route and interpolate wind direction and speed between levels and stations for your planned cruising altitude(s).

8. **Notices to Airmen** — You will receive pertinent NOTAM information from the briefer. However, information which has already been published in the *Notices to Airmen* publication will not be included unless you specifically request it.

9. **ATC Delays** — You will be advised of any known air traffic control delays that might affect your proposed flight.

The briefer will provide you with other information upon request. Examples include MOA and MTR activity within 100 n.m. of the FSS, a review of the *Notices to Airmen* publication, and approximate density altitude. Other "on-request" items include information concerning ATC services and rules, as well as customs and immigration procedures.

ABBREVIATED BRIEFING

When you need to update weather information that you obtained from mass dissemination sources, a previous briefing, or when you need only one or two specific items, you should request an **abbreviated briefing**. Tell the briefer the source of the prior information and the time you received it, plus any other pertinent background information. This allows the briefer to limit the conversation to information you did not receive, plus any significant changes in weather conditions. Usually, the sequence of information will follow that of the standard briefing. If you request only one or two items, you still will be advised if adverse conditions are present or forecast. If they are, you should request clarifying details.

Request an abbreviated briefing to update weather information you receive from mass dissemination sources, or an earlier briefing.

OUTLOOK BRIEFING

Whenever your proposed departure time is six or more hours away, it is appropriate to request an **outlook briefing**. The briefer will provide forecast information appropriate to the proposed flight, which will help you make an initial judgment about the feasibility of the trip. As your departure time draws near, you will need to request either a standard or abbreviated briefing to receive current conditions and the latest forecasts.

You should request an outlook briefing when your proposed departure is six or more hours away.

Following the briefing, feel free to ask for any information you or the briefer may have missed. It helps to save your questions until the briefing has been completed. This allows the briefer to present the information logically and lessens the chance that items will be overlooked.

SUPPLEMENTAL WEATHER SOURCES

As you might expect, the high volume of flight operations generates a tremendous demand for weather information. Because of this, many FSSs provide recorded data. By listening to the recordings, you can obtain preliminary weather and decide whether you need to talk to a briefer for more detailed information. In many instances, recorded weather briefings may be sufficient for local flights. In other cases, you can use them to help develop an overall picture of the weather for a proposed trip. You may use this preliminary information to make an initial decision on the feasibility of the trip, much as you would do with an outlook briefing.

One type of continuous weather recording is the **pilots automatic telephone weather answering service** (PATWAS). Normally, it provides a summary of data for an area within 50 n.m. of the parent station, although some locations also provide route-oriented information. PATWAS is not considered a substitute for a formal weather briefing. It is

PATWAS recordings provide preliminary briefing information for making a go/no-go decision.

highly recommended as a preliminary briefing tool because it helps you make a go/no-go decision. Since PATWAS is given a high operational priority to ensure the information is current and accurate, you can expect frequent updates. However, it is not broadcast over navaids, so it cannot be used for in-flight purposes.

TWEB recordings are broadcast over selected VORs and NDBs. Usually they include specific route forecasts, as well as winds aloft information.

Another type of recorded weather information is the **transcribed weather broadcast** (TWEB), which is broadcast continuously over selected low frequency NDBs (190-535 kHz) and/or VORs. Frequencies are published on aeronautical charts. The broadcasts are made from a series of individual tape recordings, and changes are transcribed into the tapes as they occur. At some locations, telephone access to the recording is provided (TEL-TWEB). The information in a TWEB varies with the type of recording equipment that is available. Generally, the broadcast includes route-oriented data with specially prepared National Weather Service forecasts, in-flight advisories, winds aloft, and preselected information such as weather reports, NOTAMs and special notices.

At some locations, the information is broadcast over the local VOR only and is limited to items such as the hourly weather for the parent station and up to five adjacent stations, local NOTAM information, terminal forecast for the parent station, adverse weather conditions, and other potentially hazardous conditions.

TWEBs are designed primarily for preflight and inflight planning. As is true with PATWAS, a TWEB should not be considered as a substitute for a formal weather briefing. Phone numbers for both PATWAS and TWEB are listed in the *Airport/Facility Directory*.

In addition to these automated weather information sources, you can also use TOUCH-TONE® phones to access a complete menu of recorded weather information from an **automated flight service station** (AFSS). When you reach the FSS, you will hear an informational recording telling you how to access further information or how to go directly to a weather briefer. **Telephone information briefing service** (TIBS), for example, provides a continuous recording of meteorological and/or aeronautical information. These automated systems are easy to use and they provide local and route-oriented information. After you have selected the recordings you need, you can transfer directly to a briefer if you need more detailed information.

Because of FSS consolidation, you may often find yourself at airports which are beyond local calling distance. To counter this problem, many FSSs have toll-free telephone numbers. To use these numbers, dial "1 + 800" and the number. Check the *Airport/Facility Directory* for further details. Another method of calling an FSS is through a "direct line," which is often available at a local airport or FBO.

At selected FSSs, you can also use the **fast-file flight plan system** to file your VFR flight plan. This is appropriate when you have already received your weather briefing and just want to file. After reaching the special telephone number, you file your flight plan using recorded instructions. VFR flight plans are transcribed and retained at the FSS for activation by the pilot. When you use this system, remember to speak at a normal rate and avoid lengthy pauses between items, since the system will automatically disconnect eight seconds after you stop speaking. Also, remember to file at least 30 minutes in advance of your proposed departure time.

Since weather briefing and flight plan filing procedures are subject to new technology, make sure you check the *Airman's Information Manual* or the *Airport/Facility Directory* for the latest systems descriptions. For example, with the **direct user access terminal** (DUAT) system, you can file flight plans and receive weather briefings directly. You access DUAT through toll-free numbers and a personal computer. Finally, don't overlook your local TV weather programs or the A.M. Weather telecast on the PBS network. They can help you size up the general weather picture a day or two before a flight.

IN-FLIGHT WEATHER SERVICES

As you already know, forecasting is still an inexact science, and weather conditions can change rapidly in the course of a few hours. During flight, you need to update your weather information on a continual basis. You may do this by contacting an FSS. In other situations, you can receive in-flight weather broadcasts by monitoring appropriate FSS radio frequencies. TWEBs are also available from selected NDBs and VORs.

ENROUTE FLIGHT ADVISORY SERVICE

An FSS service specifically designed to provide timely enroute weather information upon pilot request is referred to as **enroute flight advisory service** (EFAS). You can usually contact an EFAS specialist from 6 A.M. to 10 P.M. anywhere in the conterminous U.S. The discrete EFAS frequency, 122.0 mHz, is established for pilots of aircraft flying between 5,000 feet AGL and 17,500 feet MSL. Different frequencies are allocated for each ARTCC area for operations above 18,000 feet MSL.

> The frequency for EFAS below FL180 is 122.0 mHz.

The weather advisories you receive are tailored to the type of flight you are conducting and are appropriate to your route and cruising altitude. In addition, EFAS is a central collection and distribution point for pilot reports (PIREPs), so you normally receive very current or real-time weather information. This includes any thunderstorm activity along your route.

> EFAS facilities provide actual weather, including any thunderstorm activity that might affect your route.

When you wish to contact EFAS, use the words *"Flight Watch."* A flight watch facility usually serves a large geographic area through remote communications outlets (RCOs). Because of this, you should make your initial callup to the controlling or parent facility, then give your aircraft identification and the name of the VOR nearest your position. For example, *"Denver Flight Watch, Cherokee 141FS, Casper VOR."* This way, the briefer will know which RCO to use for the reply. Since sectional charts do not show flight watch outlets or parent facilities, there may be times when you won't know your flight watch area. In these situations, you can make your initial callup as follows: *"Flight Watch, Cherokee 141FS, Casper VOR."* The flight watch briefer then responds with the name of the parent facility. The A/FD contains charts depicting the locations of flight watch control stations (parent facilities) and the outlets they use.

All flight watch facilities and many other FSSs have the **radar remote weather display system** (RRWDS). This system is designed to provide real-time radar weather information from a national network of radar sites. The radar units use color to display weather returns, which makes them easier to interpret. This information is available for preflight as well as in-flight briefings.

Keep in mind that flight watch is not intended for matters relating to flight plans, position reports, preflight briefings, or to obtain weather reports or forecasts unrelated to your flight. For these items, you should contact an FSS on other published frequencies. On the other hand, pilot participation is essential to the success of flight watch, and you are encouraged to make pilot reports of the flight conditions you encounter, whether favorable or unfavorable.

IN-FLIGHT WEATHER ADVISORIES

The purpose of in-flight advisories is to notify pilots of the possibility of encountering hazardous flying conditions which may not have been forecast at the time of the preflight briefing. Whether or not the conditions may be hazardous to a flight is something that you, as the pilot, must evaluate on the basis of experience and the operational limits of the airplane. The first advisories to be discussed are called AIRMETs and SIGMETs. **AIRMET** is an acronym for "airman's meteorological information," and **SIGMET** means "significant meteorological information."

AIRMETs and SIGMETs

AIRMETs warn of weather hazards which mainly concern light aircraft.

AIRMETs (WAs) are issued every six hours with amendments issued, as necessary, for weather phenomena which are of operational interest to all aircraft. These weather conditions are potentially hazardous to aircraft having limited capability because of lack of equipment, instrumentation, or pilot qualifications. AIRMETs concern weather of less severity than that covered by SIGMETs. They are of particular concern to pilots of light aircraft. AIRMETs are issued for moderate icing, moderate turbulence, sustained winds of 30 knots or more at the surface, ceilings less than 1,000 feet and/or visibility less than three miles affecting over 50 percent of an area at any one time, and extensive mountain obscurement.

Nonconvective SIGMETs (WSs) are issued for hazardous weather (other than convective activity) which is considered significant to all aircraft. SIGMET criteria include severe icing, severe and extreme turbulence, volcanic eruptions and duststorms, sandstorms, or volcanic ash lowering visibility to less than three miles.

SIGMETs warn of weather hazards which concern all aircraft.

WSs are issued whether or not the conditions were included in the area forecast. Both SIGMETs and AIRMETs are identified by an alphanumeric designator. AIRMETs use Zulu for icing and freezing levels, Tango for turbulence, strong surface winds, and low level wind shear, and Sierra for IFR and mountain obscuration. Nonconvective SIGMETs use consecutive alphanumeric designators November through Yankee excluding those designators reserved for scheduled AIRMETs. [Figure 5-17]

Convective SIGMETs (WSTs) are issued for hazardous convective weather significant to the safety of all aircraft. They always imply severe or greater turbulence, severe icing, and low-level wind shear, so these items are not specified in the advisory. They may be issued for any convective situation which the forecaster considers hazardous to all categories of aircraft and include any of the following phenomena: tornadoes, severe thunderstorms, lines of thunderstorms, thunderstorms over an area of at least 3,000 square miles and hail greater than or equal to 3/4 of an inch in diameter.

Convective SIGMETs include tornadoes, thunderstorms, and hail.

DFWP UWS 051710 SIGMET PAPA 1 VALID UNTIL 052110 AR LA MS FROM MEM TO 30N MEI TO BTR TO MLU TO MEM OCNL SVR ICING ABV FRZLVL EXPCD. FRZLVL 080 E TO 120 W. CONDS CONTG BYD 2100Z.	MIAT WAS 151900 ARIMET TANGO FOR TURBC VALID UNTIL 160100 AIRMET TURBC. . . GA FL FROM SAV TO JAX TO CTY TO TLH TO SAV MDT TURBC BLO 100 EXPCD CONDS IPVG AFT 160000Z

Figure 5-17. The first issuance of a SIGMET, as shown on the left, is labeled UWS (Urgent Weather SIGMET). PAPA 1 means it is the first issuance for a SIGMET phenomenon; PAPA 2 would be the second issuance for the same phenomenon. In the example on the right, AMD 2 means this is the second AIRMET issuance of the phenomenon (moderate turbulence) identified as TANGO. The alphanumeric designator stays with the phenomenon even when it moves across the country.

MKCC WST 221655	MKCC WST 221655
CONVECTIVE SIGMET 17C	**CONVECTIVE SIGMET 18C**
KS OK TX	SD NE IA
VCNTY GLD—CDS LINE	FROM FSD TO DSM TO GRI TO BFF
NO SGFNT TSTMS RPRTD	TO FSD
FCST TO 1855Z	AREA TSTMS WITH FEW EMBDD
LINE TSTMS DVLPG BY 1755Z WILL	CELLS MOVG FROM 2725 TOPS 300
MOV EWD 30-35 KT THRU 1855Z	FCST TO 1855Z DSPTG AREA WILL
HAIL TO 1 1/2 IN PSBL.	MOV EWD 25 KT.

Figure 5-18. WST in the header identifies these reports as convective SIGMETs. The designators 17C and 18C indicate they are consecutive issuances for the Central U.S. One forecasts a line of thunderstorms with possible hail, while the other forecasts embedded thunderstorms over a large area.

Convective SIGMETs are issued for the Eastern (E), Central (C), and Western (W) United States. Individual convective SIGMETs are numbered sequentially for each area (01-99) each day. [Figure 5-18]

SEVERE WEATHER FORECAST ALERTS

An unscheduled message which is issued to alert forecasters, briefers, and pilots that a severe weather watch bulletin is being issued is called a **severe weather forecast alert** (AWW). These preliminary messages define areas of possible severe thunderstorms or tornado activity. [Figure 5-19]

CENTER WEATHER ADVISORIES

An unscheduled weather advisory issued by an ARTCC to alert pilots of existing or anticipated adverse weather conditions within the next two hours is called a **center weather advisory** (CWA). A CWA may supplement an existing in-flight advisory and is intended primarily for IFR traffic. It may also alert pilots when a SIGMET has not been issued, but conditions meet those criteria based on current pilot reports. CWAs are one of the most current sources for existing or forecast hazardous weather.

Flight service stations broadcast AIRMETs, SIGMETs, Convective SIGMETs, AWWs, and CWAs during their valid period when they pertain to the area within 150 n.m. of the FSS. This is one reason you should

```
MKC AWW 241817
WW 256 TORNADO NE 241900Z - 250000Z
AXIS. . 70 STATUTE MILES EAST AND WEST OF LINE. .
55SSW EAR/KEARNEY NE/ — 65NNW CFK/NORFOLK NE/
HAIL SURFACE AND ALOFT. . 2 1/2 INCHES. WIND GUSTS. . 70 KT.
MAX TOPS TO 550. MEAN WIND VECTOR 260/35.
```

Figure 5-19. "AWW" in the header identifies this report as a severe weather forecast alert. This message warns of possible tornado activity in Nebraska and defines the watch area. Hail and high winds also are possible. A detailed severe weather watch bulletin (WW) immediately follows the alert message.

always monitor FSS frequencies while enroute. The broadcast schedule is as follows:

1. **AIRMETs, SIGMETs, and CWAs** — Upon receipt and at 30-minute intervals at H+15 and H+45 for the first hour after issuance.

2. **AWWs and Convective SIGMETs** — Upon receipt and at 15-minute intervals at H+00, H+15, and H+30 and H+45 for the first hour after issuance.

Beginning with the second hour, a summarized alert notice is broadcast. It simply states that the particular advisory is current and briefly describes the weather phenomenon and the area affected. If you hear an alert notice and have not received the advisory, you should contact the nearest FSS for more detailed information, since it might be pertinent to your flight. Affected ARTCCs and terminal control facilities also make a single broadcast on all normal frequencies when a SIGMET, AWW, or CWA is issued. In terminal areas, local control and approach control may limit these broadcasts to weather occurring within 50 n.m. of the airspace under their jurisdiction.

HAZARDOUS IN-FLIGHT WEATHER ADVISORY SERVICE

A program for broadcasting hazardous weather information on a continuous basis over selected VORs is called **hazardous in-flight weather advisory service** (HIWAS). The broadcasts include summarized AIRMETs, SIGMETs, convective SIGMETs, AWWs, CWAs and urgent PIREPs. In areas where HIWAS is implemented, you should be aware that ARTCC, terminal ATC, and FSS facilities have discontinued their normal broadcasts of in-flight advisories. However, FSSs and ARTCCs announce updates to HIWAS information on all normal frequencies. While HIWAS is an additional source of hazardous weather information, it is not a replacement for preflight or in-flight briefings or real- time weather updates from flight watch. VORs used for HIWAS broadcasts can be found in the A/FD. Since HIWAS is a developing program, check the *Airman's Information Manual* and NOTAMs publication for the latest information.

> HIWAS continuously broadcasts summaries of in-flight advisories and PIREPs.

AUTOMATED WEATHER OBSERVING SYSTEM

Another source of weather is an automated unit which can make surface weather observations and transmit them directly to you during flight. This unit is the **automated weather observing system** (AWOS), which uses various sensors, a voice synthesizer, and a radio transmitter to provide real-time weather data. AWOS transmissions can usually be received within 25 n.m. of the site, at or above 3,000 feet AGL. Most units transmit a 20- to 30-second weather message updated each minute. These minute-by-minute weather messages can be accessed via telephone at most AWOS sites. Locations where AWOS is installed are published in the A/FD.

You should be aware that AWOS sensors have some limitations which are related to the configuration of individual systems. Refer to the *Airman's Information Manual* for a description of specific limitations.

CHECKLIST

After studying this section, you should have a basic understanding of:

✓ **Preflight weather briefings** — What the three types are and which type you should request.

✓ **Supplemental weather sources** — What the various sources are, including PATWAS, TWEB, VRS, TIBS, and DUAT, and how to access them.

✓ **In-flight weather services** — What the various sources of in-flight weather services are, including EFAS, and how to contact them.

✓ **In-flight advisories** — What the criteria for issuance of AIRMETs, SIGMETs, convective SIGMETs, AWWs, and CWAs are and how to receive them in flight.

✓ **HIWAS** — What it is and how you can benefit from it during flight.

✓ **AWOS** — What it is and how you can use it.

CHAPTER 6

BASIC NAVIGATION

INTRODUCTION

Eventually, you will leave the training area at your airport and venture off on a cross-country flight with your instructor. Finding your way from one airport to another requires you to develop basic navigational skills. Our initial discussion will cover interpretation of VFR aeronautical charts. Next, we will look at different types of flight computers used in flight planning. A third area of study will involve navigating by pilotage and dead reckoning. Finally, we will look at various sources of flight information which you will find useful in planning your cross-country flights.

SECTION A

AERONAUTICAL CHARTS

Whenever you fly away from your home base airport, you will need aeronautical charts to help you navigate accurately. The charts you will be using provide a detailed portrayal of the topography of the covered area and also include aeronautical information. Because you will navigate initially with visual reference to objects or landmarks on the surface, topographical information will be very useful. The National Ocean Service (NOS) publishes several charts which supply an abundance of information for pilots operating under visual flight rules.

SECTIONAL CHARTS

The charts most commonly used for VFR flight are **sectional charts**. They cover all of the 48 mainland states, plus Alaska, Hawaii, Puerto Rico, and the Virgin Islands. To allow for greater detail, each chart shows a section of the country and is given the name of a primary city within its coverage.

Sectional aeronautical charts use a scale of 1:500,000.

Topographical information includes relief features (such as terrain contours), cities, towns, rivers, highways, railroads, and other distinctive landmarks which you can use as visual checkpoints. Along with airport depictions, sectionals also contain aeronautical information pertaining to navigation and communication facilities, as well as airspace and obstructions. The scale of a sectional chart is 1:500,000. This means that each inch on the sectional chart represents 500,000 actual inches. This translates to one inch on the sectional equaling approximately seven nautical or eight statute miles on the earth's surface. Most sectionals are revised every six months, but some outside the 48 mainland states are on an annual revision schedule. [Figure 6-1]

The chart index on the front panel of a sectional tells you the names of the adjoining charts. If your route of flight is near the edge of a chart, you should always take along appropriate adjoining charts. The back panel contains detailed legend information which will receive special coverage later in this section.

Aeronautical charts are folded for easy handling, storage, and identification during flight. Most are printed on both sides in order to reduce the total number of charts required. When you look at the front panel of a sectional, you will notice arrows labeled "North" and "South." When you unfold the chart, these arrows direct you to the northern and southern portions of the covered area.

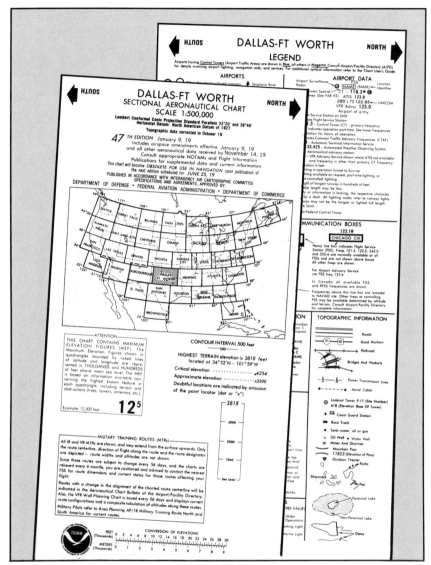

Figure 6-1. You can easily identify a sectional chart by the name or title printed on the front and back panels. Below the title, dates are provided to tell you when the chart is effective, and when it is scheduled to become obsolete for navigation.

Important terrain information is shown on the front of each chart. The colors, or gradient tints, assigned to each thousand feet of elevation are shown by a graph. Colors range from green at sea level to brown for elevations above 12,000 feet MSL. The contour intervals appearing on the sectional are also shown on the front. These contour lines connect areas of equal elevation, and are a good reference for determining the mean sea level elevations of the terrain you're flying over. The front panel also

Contour lines connect points of equal elevation.

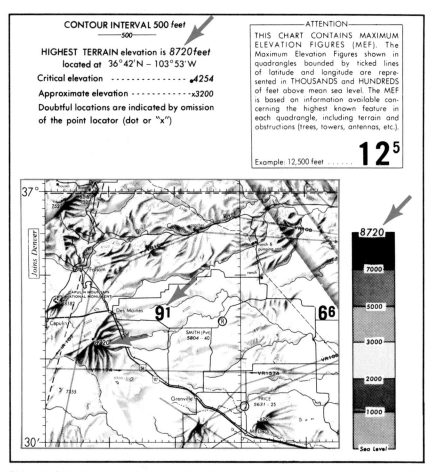

Figure 6-2. In this example, a chart inset has been placed over the front panel. The inset shows the location of the highest elevation for this sectional, which is 8,720 feet MSL. Near the center of the inset, the maximum elevation figure (MEF) is shown by "91" (9,100 feet MSL).

contains information concerning the highest terrain and other known features for the entire area of the chart, including **maximum elevation figures** (MEFs). MEFs are rounded to the next 100-foot level and adjusted upward approximately 100 to 300 feet, depending on the nature of the terrain and/or obstacles. [Figure 6-2]

VFR TERMINAL AREA CHARTS

VFR terminal area charts use a scale of 1:250,000.

Whenever you're flying VFR in or around terminal control areas, **VFR terminal area charts** will help significantly with orientation and navigation. These charts have a large scale (1:250,000) and give you a more detailed display of topographical features than sectional charts. VFR terminal charts are revised every six months. [Figure 6-3]

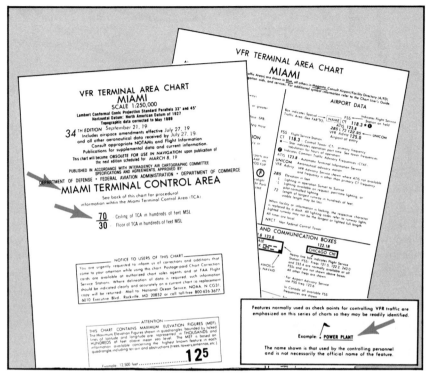

Figure 6-3. The title block of the terminal area chart clearly identifies the terminal control area location. The symbology used to designate ceilings and floors within the TCA is also shown on the front panel. Legend information on the back panel is the same as you will find on sectional charts. VFR checkpoints used to identify your position upon initial callup to a TCA facility are shown by a magenta flag.

Terminal area charts show the lateral limits of the various sections of the TCA. The lateral boundaries are marked by a heavy blue line which encircles the terminal area. Ceilings and floors are designated in hundreds of feet MSL. On sectional charts, the availability of a terminal area chart is indicated by a wide, blue band which encloses the terminal area and reflects the boundaries of the terminal area chart.

Bold numbers above and below a horizontal line indicate the ceilings and floors of TCAs.

You will find the most efficient means of avoiding major controlled traffic flows in and out of a terminal control area is to refer to the VFR flyways which are shown on the reverse side of TCA charts. **VFR flyway planning charts** depict multiple routes for use by VFR pilots as alternatives to flight within an established TCA. They are not intended to discourage requests for VFR operations within TCAs, but are designed to aid pilots planning to avoid heavily congested areas, such as IFR arrival and departure routes. Flyway charts omit most of the terrain features and geographic information found on TCA charts because they are for planning, not navigating. However, major landmarks are shown as visual aids to orientation. Although these routes go through areas of reduced air traffic congestion,

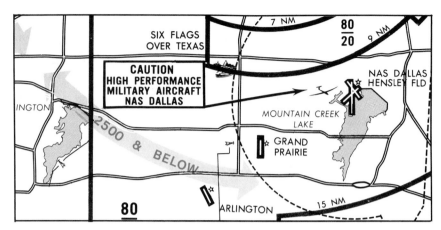

Figure 6-4. Flyways are marked by wide blue arrows and show the recommended VFR altitudes to fly. Although you are not required to use the flyways when operating VFR, you will find they usually are convenient routes between frequently traveled areas.

you should be aware that flying through them does not mean that you have separation from other aircraft. [Figure 6-4]

WORLD AERONAUTICAL CHARTS

WAC charts use a scale of 1:1,000,000.

A **world aeronautical chart** (WAC) is similar to a sectional, but it uses a scale of 1:1,000,000. At this scale, approximately 14 nautical miles, or 16 statute miles, are represented by one inch on the map. The symbols are basically the same as those found on sectionals, but some of the detail is omitted due to the smaller scale. [Figure 6-5]

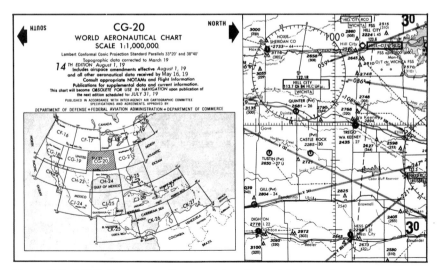

Figure 6-5. WAC charts are often used by pilots of high-performance airplanes, since they fly at higher altitudes and airspeeds. WAC charts not only reduce the total number of charts needed, but also reduce the need to change charts frequently.

In addition to the contour intervals and elevation information, the front shows a map index of the charts which can be placed together to incorporate the total network. The date at which the chart becomes effective is shown, as well as the date it is expected to become obsolete for navigation. Usually, this date is keyed to the publication schedule of the next edition. Most WAC charts are revised on a yearly basis.

LATITUDE AND LONGITUDE

Because the key to navigation is knowing where you are at a given moment, a system was established to reference the exact location of any point on the earth. This system is based on latitude and longitude.

The equator is the imaginary line which circles the earth midway between the north and south poles. To aid in determining locations on a map, a system of lines parallel to the equator was established. These lines are called **lines of latitude**. As a reference point, the equator is labeled as 0° of latitude. The parallel lines north of the equator are numbered from 0° to 90°, with 90° north latitude positioned at the north pole. Parallels in the southern hemisphere are also numbered from 0° to 90°, with 90° south latitude representing the south pole. You can locate a position north or south of the equator by using lines of latitude.

The location of an airport can be determined by the intersection of lines of latitude and longitude.

Meridians, or **lines of longitude**, are imaginary lines which extend from the north to the south pole. Because they connect the poles, lines of longitude are always given in a direction of true north and south. Just as the equator is designated 0° of latitude, the **Prime Meridian**, which passes through Greenwich, England, is labeled 0° of longitude. [Figure 6-6]

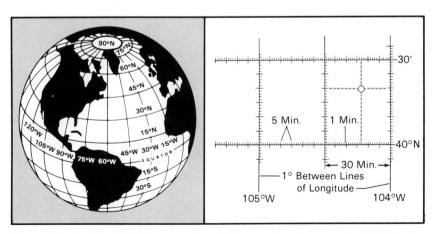

Figure 6-6. The lines of latitude and longitude are printed on aeronautical charts, with each degree subdivided into 60 equal segments called minutes. By knowing the geographic coordinates (or the intersection of the lines of latitude and longitude), you can locate any position on the earth. In this example, the airport is located at 40°20'N, 104°13'W.

There are a total of 360° of longitude encompassing the earth, with 180° on the east and 180° on the west side of the Prime Meridian. The line of 180° of longitude is on the opposite side of the earth from the Prime Meridian. The International Date Line approximately corresponds with the 180° line of longitude, although segments of the Date Line actually vary as much as 20°. When you locate a position east or west of the Prime Meridian, you will be determining a position in reference to a line of longitude.

PROJECTIONS

Navigating with reference to latitude and longitude could be done by using a globe. However, this procedure would be very impractical, since you would have to use an extremely large globe to show the required detail. For convenience, the spherical surface of the earth is "flattened" on aeronautical charts. Since this is like pressing a section of orange peel on a flat surface, some distortion ultimately occurs in this process.

Projections are used for transferring a section of the earth's surface onto a flat chart. Two of the most common types of projections are the Mercator and the Lambert Conformal Conic. The **Lambert Conformal Conic** is frequently used on aeronautical charts because it minimizes distortion. **Mercator** charts are usually used as wall maps. Their distortion increases with distance from the equator. [Figure 6-7]

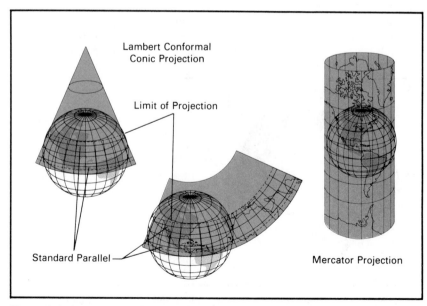

Figure 6-7. Sectional, VFR terminal, and world aeronautical charts are all Lambert projections. The overall scale inaccuracies which you obtain when comparing nautical miles on a Lambert chart to actual miles on earth are small enough that you can consider them negligible on a single chart.

LEGEND

Besides the topographical elevation information given on the front of the chart, the **legend** supplies an abundance of information to help you understand chart symbols. Symbols used in the legend include: airports, airport data, radio aids to navigation and communication, airspace information, topographical information, obstructions to flight, and other miscellaneous symbols.

AIRPORT SYMBOLOGY

As you study a sectional chart, you will notice several types of airport diagrams. Information provided in the legend will help answer questions you might have concerning a specific airport. There are thousands of airports identified by symbols on sectional charts. Because of the variety of airport types, shapes, and sizes, these symbols help you picture the actual airport being illustrated. [Figure 6-8]

Tick marks extending from airport symbols show that fuel is available, and that the airport is attended during normal working hours.

Airports having control towers are shown in blue, while all others are identified by a magenta color. Although the color blue signifies an airport with a control tower, it does not mean that the control tower operates

Airports with control towers are shown in blue; uncontrolled airports are shown in magenta.

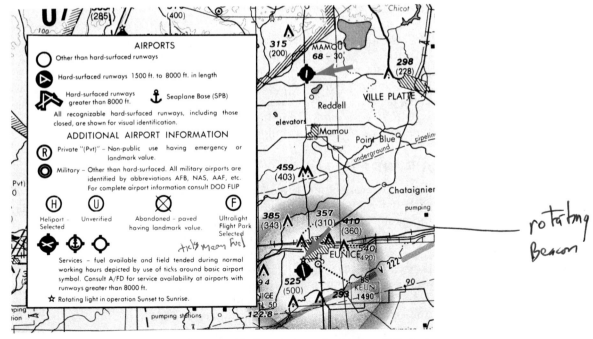

Figure 6-8. The airport portion of the legend helps you to understand and interpret the symbols used. The tick marks extending from the airport diagram at Mamou indicate that fuel is available and that the field is attended, at least during normal working hours. The star that appears next to the diagram at Eunice marks an airport beacon which normally operates from sunset to sunrise.

continuously. The chart margin on an inside panel of the sectional will give you information about the hours of operation of a particular control tower.

Circular symbols are used to represent most airports. If an airport has at least one hard-surfaced runway 1,500 to 8,000 feet long, the runway will be shown inside the circle. It also will be oriented to reflect its approximate magnetic direction.

Runways are not enclosed in a circle at larger airports where at least one runway is longer than 8,000 feet. However, the outline of the runways will still be shown to reveal the general layout. If you were flying over the airport, you could recognize all hard-surfaced runways, since they would show the same pattern as the chart. Even hard-surfaced runways that are closed will be shown to aid in identification.

Private airports have landmark value and practical use in an emergency.

When an open circle is used and no runway pattern is shown, the airport does not have a hard-surfaced runway. Private airports appear as the letter "R" enclosed in an open circle. Although landing at a private airport requires the owner's permission, you could use one in an emergency, and they also have landmark value in navigation.

Military airports have the same appearance as civilian airports and are identified by abbreviations such as AFB, NAS, and AAF. Military airports with other than hard-surfaced runways are shown as one circle inside another. Other miscellaneous types of aerodromes, such as seaplane bases, heliports, ultralight flight parks, and unverified airports, are shown by additional symbols. A circle with an "X" superimposed over it represents a closed or abandoned airport.

AIRPORT DATA

The MSL elevation is shown underneath the name of the airport.

A second portion of the sectional legend explains the data printed near each individual airport. While the amount of information available is limited at some of the smaller, remote airports, you can obtain an abundance of facts from the airport data at larger airports. [Figure 6-9]

When applicable, the control tower frequency will be listed, following the letters "CT," as part of the airport data. Any time the tower is not in operation continuously, a star is placed after the frequency. Non-Federal control towers are marked by the abbreviation NFCT.

If automatic terminal information service is available at the airport, the designation "ATIS" is printed in this section, along with the frequency used to obtain it. If UNICOM is available, the frequency will be shown at the end of the airport data.

Figure 6-9. The airport data portion of the legend helps you to interpret information about a particular airport. The letters "FSS" tell you there is a flight service station on the field at the Eagle County Regional Airport, 122.95 MHz is the UNICOM frequency, and the letter "C" following the frequency 123.6 MHz indicates the CTAF. The number "6538" shows the airport elevation above sea level, and the "L 80" to the right of the elevation indicates lighting and the length of the longest runway in hundreds of feet (8,000).

The common traffic advisory frequency (CTAF) at uncontrolled airports is indicated on sectional charts in the airport data. For example, if the data for an airport doesn't list a frequency, the CTAF should be the MULTICOM frequency of 122.9 MHz. If only a UNICOM frequency is shown, that will be the designated CTAF unless there is an FSS on the field. When an FSS is located on the field, 123.6 MHz is usually the CTAF. At controlled fields where the tower operates part time, the tower frequency normally is used as the CTAF after the tower closes.

When a part-time tower is closed, the CTAF is normally the tower frequency.

Airport data also tells you if lighting is available at an airport. A capital "L" designates lighting that is in operation at the airport from sunset to sunrise. Lighting available on request, part-time lighting, or pilot-controlled lighting is shown by an "L" with an asterisk next to it.

NAVIGATION AIDS

For cross-country planning and flight, you will find a significant amount of sectional chart information concerning navigation and communication facilities. An area of the legend has been set aside to help you interpret information in these navaids. [Figure 6-10]

Rectangular boxes printed on charts provide data on navaids and communication frequencies. These boxes are placed near the appropriate navaid, and include the name, frequency, and Morse code identifier of the navaid. VHF radio frequencies are colored blue, while low- and medium-frequency facilities are printed in magenta. [Figure 6-11]

The frequencies for an FSS are printed on the top of the communications box. Usually, you can transmit and receive on the same frequency when you are communicating with an FSS. In some cases, though, the navigation facility may be located a long way from the flight service station. In this situation, you may need to transmit to the FSS on 122.1 MHz and receive a reply on the navaid frequency. When the FSS can receive only on a given frequency, the letter "R" follows the frequency listing.

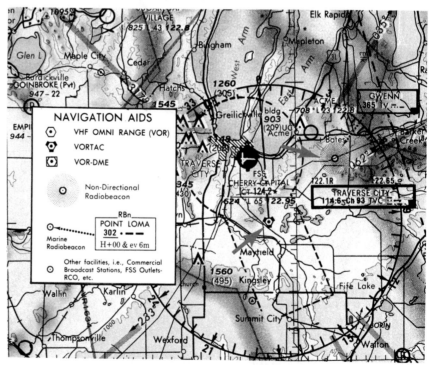

Figure 6-10. The triangular symbol marks a VORTAC facility located south of the Cherry Capital Airport. The circular dot pattern east of the airport represents a non-directional radio beacon (NDB). The insert shows the symbols for these and other navaids that you will become familiar with in Chapter 7.

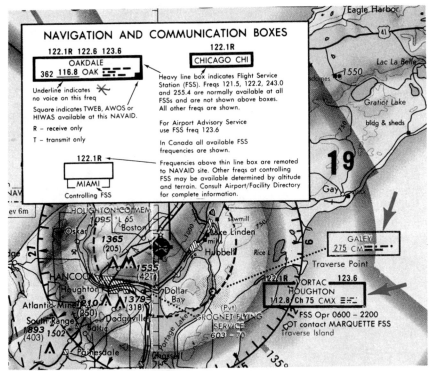

Figure 6-11. Information about the Galey NDB is printed in a magenta box. The underlined frequency indicates there is no voice capability on the frequency, and only the Morse code identifier is audibly transmitted. The heavy-lined box containing the Houghton VORTAC data tells you that a flight service station is located on the field.

At an airport with an FSS, the two-way frequency of 123.6 MHz usually is shown. The FSS uses this frequency to provide you with airport advisories concerning known traffic, winds, altimeter setting, and recommended runway. The emergency frequency, 121.5 MHz, and the two-way frequency, 122.2 MHz, are normally available at all FSSs and are not listed on the chart.

The common FSS frequency for airport advisory service is 123.6 MHz.

Enroute navigation facilities can provide you with a wide variety of in-flight weather updates. Whenever a square is located in the bottom right-hand corner of a communications box, either TWEB, AWOS, or HIWAS is available at the navaid. Enroute flight advisory service (EFAS) can be obtained by contacting Flight Watch on 122.0 MHz.

A square in the lower right corner of a communications box shows the availability of TWEB, AWOS, or HIWAS.

AIRSPACE

Special-use airspace and some types of controlled airspace are shown by distinctive symbols on aeronautical charts. Because of the regulatory requirements for flying through the various classifications of airspace, you must be able to identify them and apply the appropriate flight rules.

A flag symbol marks a recommended visual checkpoint for identifying your position on initial callup.

Some symbols simply alert you to special information, such as the flag which is used to designate recommended checkpoints for initial callup. [Figure 6-12]

Although permission is not required to fly through a military operations area, you should exercise extreme caution if military aircraft are using it. You can determine military activity within an MOA by contacting the nearest FSS. To help you locate this type of special-use airspace, a solid magenta line is printed on sectionals, with crosshatched lines extending into the MOA. [Figure 6-13]

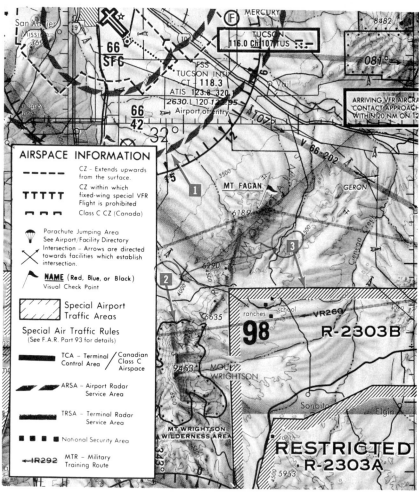

Figure 6-12. The boundary of the Tucson ARSA appears as a heavy dashed magenta line (item 1). The edge of a prohibited, restricted, alert, or warning area is marked by a blue crosshatched line (item 2). Certain areas regulated by the National Park Service, U.S. Fish and Wildlife Service, and the U.S. Forest Service are illustrated by a line and dot pattern (item 3). You are requested to maintain an altitude of at least 2,000 feet above these areas. Other designations are shown in the legend excerpt.

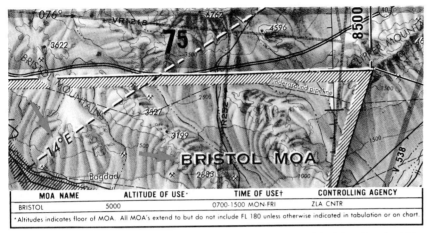

MOA NAME	ALTITUDE OF USE*	TIME OF USE†	CONTROLLING AGENCY
BRISTOL	5000	0700-1500 MON-FRI	ZLA CNTR

*Altitudes indicates floor of MOA. All MOA's extend to but do not include FL 180 unless otherwise indicated in tabulation or on chart.

Figure 6-13. The name of the MOA, such as the "Bristol MOA," is printed within the boundaries. The margin of the sectional provides a table listing the name, altitude of use, time of use, and controlling agency for all MOAs shown on the chart. The dashed line and symbol "14°E" represent an isogonic line used to determine the magnetic variation for this area of the chart.

Military training routes, or MTRs, also are shown on sectional charts by gray lines labeled with identifiers, such as "VR1218" or "IR252." VR or IR followed by a three-digit number means the route includes one or more segments above 1,500 feet AGL. Four digits mean the VR or IR route is flown at or below 1,500 feet. Regardless of your cruising altitude, you should always remain alert when crossing an MTR.

MTRs with operations above 1,500 feet AGL are given three-digit identifiers, while those at or below 1,500 feet AGL are designated with four digits.

The limits of controlled airspace are shown by tint bands which are color coded. The 700-foot floor of a transition area is colored magenta, while blue indicates a floor 1,200 feet above the surface. The outer limits of controlled airspace are shown by a dark edge, and the color dissolves into the controlled portion. [Figure 6-14]

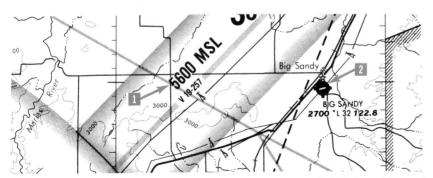

Figure 6-14. Although Federal airways normally begin at 1,200 feet AGL and extend up to 18,000 feet MSL, the floor of the V-19-257, in this example, is 5,600 feet MSL (item 1). Big Sandy Airport (item 2) lies in uncontrolled airspace extending from the surface up to 14,500 feet MSL, the base of the continental control area.

The lateral limits of a control zone appear as a blue dashed line encircling an airport. Sometimes extensions for instrument approaches and departures are included. [Figure 6-15]

Normally, there is no symbol for an airport traffic area. By definition, an airport traffic area exists at locations where a control tower is in operation. A few airports have such unique operational requirements that special airport traffic areas are designated by regulation. On sectional charts, these airports are enclosed by solid blue lines with blue cross-hatched marks and notes alerting you that special air traffic rules apply.

Wherever an ADIZ is located, it will be marked by a blue line with dotted shading. The name of the zone, such as "Atlantic Coastal Air Defense Identification Zone," will appear in bold letters. In the interest of national security, you should pay close attention to these areas on sectionals and follow the procedures outlined in the *Airman's Information Manual* when you are penetrating them.

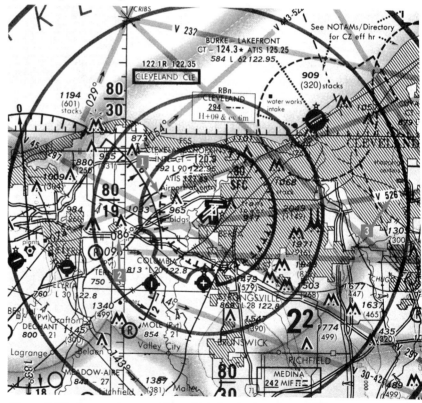

Figure 6-15. A control zone within which fixed-wing special VFR flight is prohibited is depicted by a series of ''T's'' surrounding the affected airspace (item 1). Victor airways are displayed as light blue lines connecting VOR, VOR/DME, or VORTAC facilities. The radial, or magnetic course, of the airway is shown (item 2), as well as the airway number, such as V-526 (item 3).

OBSTRUCTIONS

Besides being concerned with the terrain elevations, you must also be aware of man-made obstructions to flight. While some structures may extend only several feet above the ground, others may rise more than 1,000 feet and impose a hazard to aircraft in flight. Sectional charts provide information about the locations and heights of obstructions. [Figure 6-16]

Groups of obstructions are marked by two symbols placed side by side. Two elevation figures may be located next to the symbol and represent the MSL and AGL heights of the obstacle. While obstructions impose hazards to flight, they can also be good references in identifying your position.

When two elevation figures are used to specify an obstacle's height, the bold number indicates MSL height and the figure in parentheses denotes AGL height.

TOPOGRAPHICAL INFORMATION

With the help of contour lines, spot elevations, and the elevations of obstructions, you can choose a safe cruising altitude. You can also determine whether or not you will be more than 3,000 feet AGL and will need to use the required VFR cruising altitudes.

You can choose a safe and appropriate VFR cruising altitude by referring to topographical information.

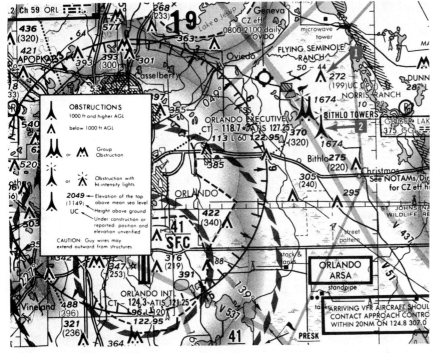

Figure 6-16. Item 1 represents an obstruction that is less than 1,000 feet AGL. Item 2 marks an obstruction that stands 1,000 feet or more above the ground. The symbol atop the figure indicates that high intensity lighting is used for collision avoidance. The dot below each symbol shows the actual location of the structure.

The locations of natural and man-made features are shown as reference points for navigation. Features such as lakes, rivers, railroads, roads and highways are clearly represented. Miscellaneous symbols also help you locate areas of parachuting and heavy glider and ultralight activity. [Figure 6-17]

Finally, changes in aeronautical data that could affect your flight might occur between chart revisions. For this reason, you should consult the *Airport/Facility Directory* prior to flight and review the "Aeronautical Chart Bulletin" contained in the *Notices to Airmen*. A discussion of these sources of flight information will follow later in this chapter.

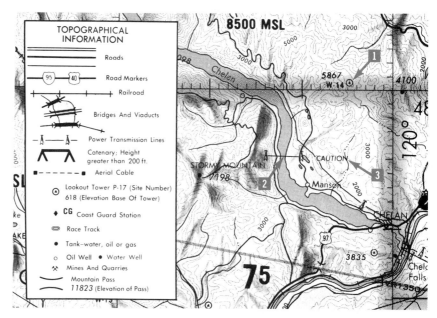

Figure 6-17. Another topographical symbol is the one for a lookout tower (item 1). The site number, such as "W-14," is painted on the tower and can be seen from the air. The elevation at the base of the tower is 5,867 feet MSL. Power transmission lines are shown by thin black lines connecting symbols for their supporting towers (item 2). The word "caution" in this example, alerts you to the existence of powerlines which cross bodies of water (item 3).

CHECKLIST ───────────────

After studying this section, you should have a basic understanding of:

   ✓   **Aeronautical charts** — The differences between sectional charts, world aeronautical charts, and VFR terminal area charts.

   ✓   **Terrain information** — How contour lines, gradient tints, and elevation figures help you determine your altitude above the ground.

✓ **Latitude and longitude** — How the location of an airport can be determined from its geographic coordinates.

✓ **Airport data** — How to interpret printed information about each airport, including symbols, frequencies, length of the longest runway, airport elevation, and the availability of lighting.

✓ **Radio aids to navigation and communication** — The symbols used for various navigational facilities, as well as information concerning communications with flight service stations.

✓ **Airspace symbology** — How symbols on aeronautical charts alert you to various types of airspace along your route.

✓ **Obstructions** — How to interpret the symbols used to mark the locations and heights of hazardous obstructions.

✓ **Topographical information** — How natural and man-made features are shown on charts as reference points for navigating.

FLIGHT COMPUTERS

This section introduces you to mechanical and electronic flight computers. Both of these computers allow you to solve most of the navigation problems you will encounter during flight planning and in-flight operations. The first part of this section discusses the theory behind some of these calculations. Next, depending on what calculator you are using, you should review the appropriate set of problems and solutions. One set is based on the mechanical slide graphic computer (CSG) and one is for the Avstar electronic flight computer. Although this section offers theory and practice on the use of both types of computers, it is intended only as an introduction. For complete information on the features and operation of your unit, be sure to study the computer manual carefully.

NAVIGATION THEORY

Perhaps the best way to understand the problem-solving capabilities of a flight computer is to analyze some of the computations required to plan a typical cross-country flight. Some of your objectives are to determine the heading which will compensate for the effects of wind, and to estimate groundspeed, time enroute, and fuel requirements.

COMPENSATING FOR WIND

Whenever you fly in wind, your aircraft's performance is affected. The wind direction and speed have a direct impact on your aircraft's direction of flight and groundspeed. This may be easier to visualize if you first think of a balloon as it drifts freely in the wind. [Figure 6-18]

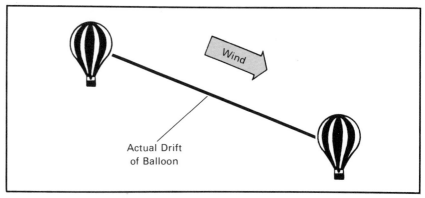

Figure 6-18. A balloon simply moves with the wind and drifts above the terrain in the same direction and at the same speed as the wind.

The effect of wind on a moving object, such as an airplane, is somewhat different. It deflects the object from its intended path (course) and alters its speed over the ground. That portion of the wind which causes the airplane to drift off course is called the **crosswind component,** while the **headwind** or **tailwind component** decreases or increases the airplane's forward speed. [Figure 6-19]

In order to compensate for the effects of wind, it is important to understand the terms course, heading, and wind correction angle. **Course** is the intended flight path, or direction of travel, over the surface of the earth with respect to north. **Heading** is the direction in which the longitudinal axis of the airplane is pointing in relation to north. In a no-wind situation (or with a direct headwind or tailwind), course and heading are the same. **Wind correction angle** (WCA) is the difference between the heading of an airplane and the desired course. It tells you how much you need to adjust your heading to maintain the desired course. [Figure 6-20]

Wind correction angle is applied to course to determine heading.

With the mechanical slide graphic computer, you solve for wind correction angle first; then you apply the correction to your course. The electronic flight computer eliminates a step in the wind problems by automatically applying the WCA to the course. It solves directly for the heading necessary to maintain course.

Another way you look at the wind problem is that your course, corrected for wind, equals your heading. When the wind is blowing from the left, you subtract the WCA from your desired course. When it is blowing from the right, you add the WCA to your course.

The WCA is subtracted from the course for a left crosswind and added to the course for a right crosswind.

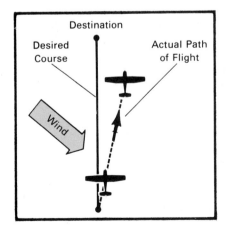

Figure 6-19. In this example, the wind pushes the airplane off course to the right and retards the airplane's forward motion.

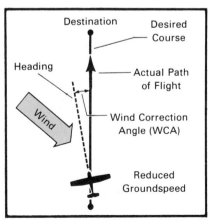

Figure 6-20. In this case, to maintain your desired course, you must adjust your heading to the left, into the wind.

Let's take a moment and review the information you need to solve wind problems. First, you need the direction you intend to fly. This is your course which is usually obtained by direct measurement from your aeronautical chart. You also must know how fast you intend to fly. This is the actual speed of the airplane through the air, or true airspeed, as found in the pilot's operating handbook. Next, you need the predicted wind direction and speed. As you learned in Chapter 5, this information is obtained from the winds and temperatures aloft forecast.

With these four variables — course, true airspeed, wind direction, and wind speed — you can use a slide graphic flight computer to determine the wind correction angle and resultant groundspeed. By applying the wind correction angle to the course, you will find the appropriate heading that compensates for the wind. An electronic computer uses the same four variables to solve the problem. However, the electronic computer applies the wind correction angle and solves directly for heading and groundspeed.

TIME AND FUEL REQUIRED

Based on the computed groundspeed and the distance to the destination, you can use the flight computer to determine how long the flight will take. Next, you will want to calculate the amount of fuel required. You will also need to consult the pilot's operating handbook to determine the fuel consumption rate. With this figure and the estimated time enroute, you can use the flight computer to determine fuel requirements for the trip. After adding required reserves, you can tell if the airplane carries sufficient fuel to make the flight nonstop.

IN-FLIGHT CALCULATIONS

The flight computer also provides several important in-flight calculations, such as true airspeed and actual winds aloft. You can then compare these values to the estimated true airspeed and the winds aloft forecast used to plan the flight. For example, if the actual true airspeed is slower than the speed used in planning, it will take longer to reach your destination and will require additional fuel. This may necessitate a fuel stop at some intermediate airport.

TRUE AIRSPEED

To compute true airspeed during flight, you need to know your pressure altitude, outside air temperature, and calibrated airspeed. You determine pressure altitude by temporarily resetting the altimeter to 29.92 and reading pressure altitude directly off the altimeter. Remember to note the original setting, so you can reset the altimeter after you have read the pressure altitude.

You can read the air temperature directly off the outside air temperature gauge found in most airplanes. The temperature read off this gauge is called **indicated air temperature**. Due to the friction of the air passing over the temperature probe, the indicated temperature is slightly higher than the actual, or static, air temperature. At speeds below 200 knots, however, this error is negligible and may be disregarded.

To determine calibrated airspeed, read the indicated airspeed off the airspeed indicator, then correct it using the airspeed correction table found in the pilot's operating handbook. With pressure altitude, temperature, and calibrated airspeed established, you then use the flight computer to determine actual true airspeed.

ACTUAL WINDS ALOFT

Another in-flight computation you will find useful is to determine the actual winds aloft and compare them to the forecast winds used during flight planning. To do this, you will need to know the planned course (from flight planning calculations), the actual heading being used to maintain the planned course (read off the heading indicator), actual true airspeed (determined by your flight computer), and actual groundspeed (determined from groundspeed checks). The flight computer uses these variables to calculate the actual wind direction and speed.

During cross-country flights, you will soon realize that actual winds are seldom the same as forecast. As a result, you can usually expect your actual groundspeed to vary somewhat from that estimated. If your groundspeed is faster than planned, you will use less fuel, so your reserve will be more than adequate. It is when your groundspeed is significantly slower than planned that you can have fuel problems. The additional time needed to complete the flight will translate directly into fuel consumed.

MECHANICAL FLIGHT COMPUTERS

In this segment, we will work through several typical computations you normally perform before and during cross-country flights. The mechanical flight computer used in this discussion is referred to as a slide graphic computer (CSG). The operations presented here apply to many of the more common mechanical computers available on the market. However, since we are providing only introductory material, be sure to consult your computer manual for any differences in operation or additional features.

CSG computers have two sides which are referred to as the calculator side and the wind side. The calculator side uses two circular discs which are fastened together in the center. The top disc usually has windows or cutouts. The two discs are mounted so you can rotate the top disc, using the windows to align various values on the three scales which are printed on the two discs. Since the top disc is smaller than the bottom disc, you can align an "index pointer" on one scale to a value or pointer

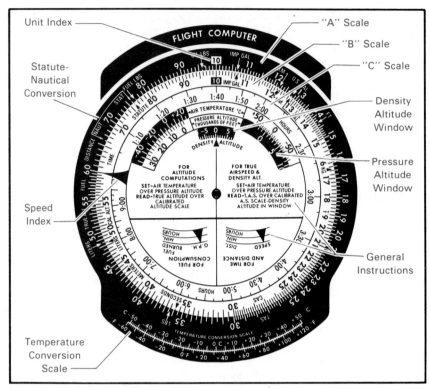

Figure 6-21. The main portion of the calculator side of the flight computer consists of two discs, three windows, and three separate scales. The outer "A" scale, printed on the bottom disc, is fixed. Scales "B" and "C" are printed on the top disc, which is free to pivot over the bottom disc.

on the other. The **"A" scale** may be used to represent speed, distance, fuel, or other units, depending on the problem being worked. The **"B" scale** also may represent speed, distance, or fuel, as well as time. The **"C" scale** is used almost exclusively to represent time. [Figure 6-21]

A number on the computer scales can represent that number to any power of ten.

A single number on the "A" or "B" scale can represent that number to any power of ten. For example, the number "40" can stand for .04, .4, 4, 40, 400, etc. For any given problem, you must use common sense to determine which value is correct. If a short distance is involved, 25 on the "A" scale might be read as 2.5 miles. If a long distance is involved, zeros are added to the 25 to get the proper answer. For instance, 25 might be 250 or 2,500 miles.

Notice also that the graduations between all the values are not equal. On the "A" and "B" scales, for example, there are 10 graduations between 14 and 15, and 5 between 15 and 16. Graduations on the "C" scale can reflect increments of 5 or 10 minutes. Therefore, you should always use care to determine the value of each graduation.

TIME-SPEED-DISTANCE

This type of problem involves three variables: elapsed time, speed (usually groundspeed), and distance. When any two of the three variables are known, you can use your flight computer to determine the third. For example, when speed and distance are known, rotate the disc until the **speed index** pointer is on the specified speed. Then, locate the distance on the "A" scale and read the required time in hours and minutes on the "C" scale. You can also read time in minutes on the "B" scale. [Figure 6-22]

Speed × Time = Distance

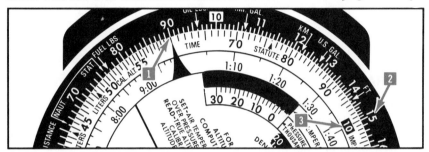

Figure 6-22. In this example, you want to know how long it will take to fly 150 miles at 90 knots. First, place the speed of 90 knots opposite the speed index pointer (item 1). Next, find the distance of 150 miles on the "A" scale (item 2) and directly opposite it read the time required of 100 minutes on the "B" scale (item 3). You also can read the time of 1 hour, 40 minutes (1:40) on the "C" scale.

FUEL CONSUMPTION

Fuel consumption and time-speed-distance problems are very similar. Both types of problems have the same mathematical relationships. However, when solving fuel problems, "gallons per hour" is used instead of knots, and "gallons of fuel consumed" is used instead of distance traveled.

Fuel Flow × Time = Fuel Consumed

FUEL REQUIRED

Suppose you want to determine how much fuel you will need, based on a known fuel consumption rate and flight time. To accomplish this, place the fuel consumption rate opposite the speed index and read the fuel required ("A" scale) opposite the flight time ("B" or "C" scales). [Figure 6-23]

Remember to consider required reserves whenever you are determining the amount of fuel needed.

Figure 6-23. Assume a fuel consumption rate of 8.5 g.p.h. and a flight time of 1:40. First, place the consumption rate opposite the speed index pointer (item 1). Next, find the flight time on the "C" scale (item 2) and read the fuel requirement of 14.2 gallons on the "A" scale (item 3).

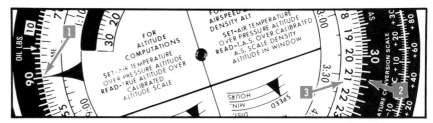

Figure 6-24. Assume a fuel quantity of 31.5 gallons and a consumption rate of 9 g.p.h. To solve this problem, place the fuel consumption rate of 9 g.p.h. opposite the speed index (item 1). Now locate the fuel quantity of 31.5 gallons on the "A" scale (item 2) and read the endurance of 210 minutes on the "B" scale or 3:30 on the "C" scale (item 3).

ENDURANCE

Endurance refers to the amount of time you can remain aloft, based on a known fuel quantity and consumption rate. Since a fuel consumption rate is rarely constant for an entire flight, think of endurance as an approximation and not as an absolute value. [Figure 6-24]

ACTUAL CONSUMPTION RATE

After completing a flight, you may wish to determine the actual fuel consumption rate, based on the total amount of fuel used. You can then compare this figure against the original fuel consumption rate and take it into consideration for future flight planning. [Figure 6-25]

DENSITY ALTITUDE

Solving for density altitude requires you know the pressure altitude and outside air temperature. You may read the pressure altitude directly off the altimeter when it is set to 29.92. Temperature is usually determined by reading the outside air temperature gauge or by using reported surface temperature for the airport. Since most computers use temperature

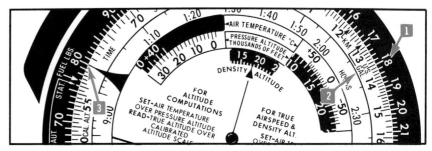

Figure 6-25. For this example, assume that 18 gallons of fuel were consumed over a 2:15 flight. To solve this problem, place the fuel consumed on the "A" scale (item 1) over the elapsed time on the "C" scale (item 2). You can then read the fuel consumption rate of 8.0 g.p.h. opposite the speed index pointer (item 3).

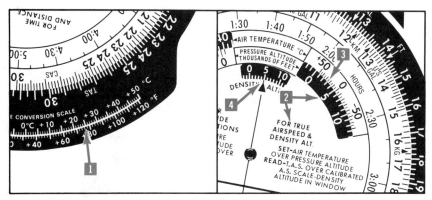

Figure 6-26. Assume the pressure altitude is 3,000 feet and the temperature is 77°F. First, use the scale at the bottom of the computer to determine that 77°F is equal to 25°C (item 1). Next, use the window for true airspeed and density altitude computations (item 2), and set the pressure altitude opposite the temperature (item 3). Read the density altitude of approximately 4,800 feet in the density altitude window (item 4).

in degrees Celsius for this computation, you must convert Fahrenheit values to Celsius. [Figure 6-26]

AIRSPEED CALCULATIONS

You can use the flight computer to determine true airspeed (TAS), based on calibrated airspeed (CAS), or you can determine calibrated airspeed if you know true airspeed. To solve either of these problems, you must know the pressure altitude and outside air temperature. [Figure 6-27]

Using your CSG, you can solve for TAS if CAS is known, or vice versa.

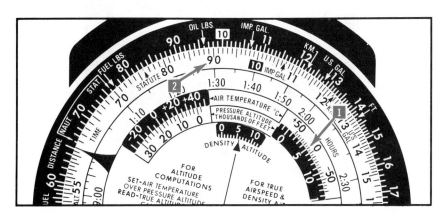

Figure 6-27. Assume you wish to determine your true airspeed using a pressure altitude of 5,000 feet, an outside air temperature of 10°C, and a calibrated airspeed of 90 knots. Use the true airspeed and density altitude window for this problem and place the pressure altitude opposite the outside air temperature (item 1). Read the true airspeed of 98 knots on the "A" scale opposite the calibrated airspeed of 90 knots on the "B" scale (item 2). You can also use true airspeed and pressure altitude to solve for calibrated airspeed. Using the same settings, 98 knots true airspeed equals 90 knots calibrated airspeed.

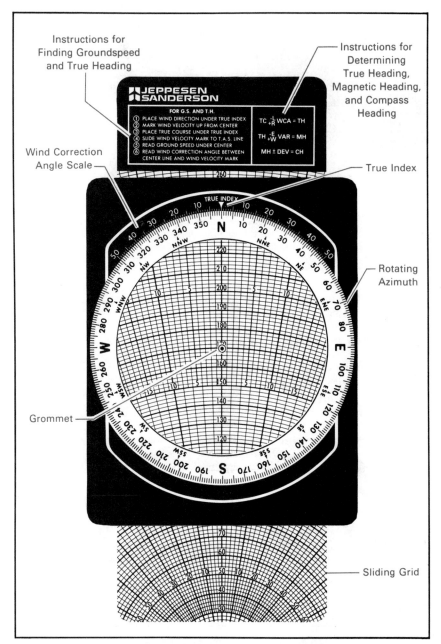

Figure 6-28. The components of the wind side include the rotating azimuth and the sliding grid. The sliding grid is a section of a graduated circle. The straight lines represent degrees right or left of the centerline and the curved lines represent speed. The sliding grid of this computer has two sides, a high speed side and a low speed side. The azimuth circle rotates freely and is graduated into 360°. The transparent portion is frosted so you can write on it with a pencil. In the center is a small circle called the grommet, which moves directly over the centerline of the grid.

WIND PROBLEMS

As discussed in navigation theory, wind problems involve six variables: course, true airspeed, wind direction, wind speed, heading, and groundspeed. During the flight planning process, you typically want to determine the wind correction angle and apply it to the course. This gives you the heading needed to compensate for the predicted winds. You also need to know your groundspeed to compute the estimated time enroute and fuel requirements. Wind problems are calculated using the wind side of the flight computer. [Figure 6-28]

Wind problems involve solving for heading and groundspeed based on course, true airspeed, wind direction, and wind speed.

HEADING AND GROUNDSPEED

For this example, assume a planned course of 239° and a true airspeed of 98 knots. According to the winds and temperatures aloft forecast, the winds at your cruising altitude are 100° at 15 knots. The first step in this type of wind problem is to plot the predicted wind. Once the wind has been plotted, your next step is to place the planned course under the true index and position the wind dot based on the predicted true airspeed. Then read the wind correction angle and groundspeed. Finally, you must apply the WCA to the course to determine heading. [Figure 6-29]

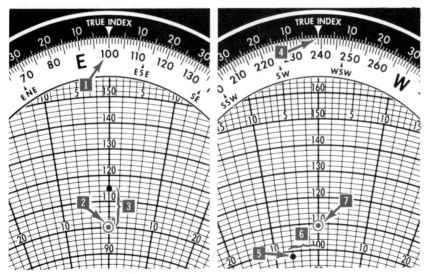

Figure 6-29. The left illustration shows the first step, which is to set the wind direction of 100° under the true index located at the top of the computer (item 1). Next, place the center grommet over a convenient point, such as 100 knots (item 2), and plot the wind speed up from this point. In this case, the wind speed is 15 knots, so the wind dot is placed a distance equal to 15 knots above the grommet (item 3). The right illustration shows the second step, which is to rotate the azimuth until the course of 239° is set under the true index (item 4). Next, slide the scale to place the wind dot on the true airspeed line of 98 knots (item 5). The wind correction angle of 6° is indicated by the distance between the wind dot and centerline (item 6). Since the wind dot is to the left of center, the WCA should be subtracted from the course to determine the heading of 233°. The groundspeed of 109 knots is read directly under the grommet (item 7).

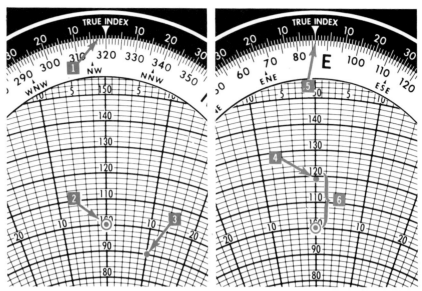

Figure 6-30. The left illustration shows how this problem is set up. The course of 320° is placed at the top of the flight computer under the true index (item 1). Next, slide the grid until the grommet is directly over the groundspeed of 100 knots (item 2). Now place a dot at the point where the true airspeed of 90 knots meets a right wind correction angle of 10° (item 3). Then, rotate the azimuth until the wind dot is above the grommet and directly on the centerline, as shown in the right illustration (item 4). The wind direction of 86° is read under the true index (item 5) and wind speed is equal to the distance between the grommet and the wind dot. In this case, the wind speed is 19 knots (item 6).

UNKNOWN WIND

To determine the actual winds aloft, you need to know true airspeed, groundspeed, course, and heading. Remember, the wind correction angle is the difference between the course and the heading being used to maintain that course. For this example, assume a true airspeed of 90 knots, a groundspeed of 100 knots, a course of 320°, and a heading of 330°. In this case, the wind correction angle is determined to be +10° (330 - 320 = 10). Once you have determined these values, enter them in the appropriate positions on the wind side of the flight computer. [Figure 6-30]

MOST FAVORABLE WINDS

Wind speed and direction typically change as altitude changes. This causes a change in groundspeed.

One of the factors you consider in selecting an altitude is the effect of wind on groundspeed. However, wind direction and speed usually change with altitude, so it is difficult to tell which altitude will result in the best groundspeed. The flight computer offers a fairly simple method of determining which altitude offers the most favorable winds for a given course. The first step is to plot the forecast wind direction and speed for each altitude. [Figure 6-31]

The next step is to rotate the azimuth until the course to be flown is directly under the true index. By measuring the distance between the grommet and each wind dot, you can select the best wind. For this example, assume you intend to fly a course of 250°. [Figure 6-32]

Based solely on the forecast winds aloft, the winds at 3,000 feet are most advantageous to the flight. Of course, other considerations, such as terrain or weather conditions, may affect your final choice of cruising altitudes.

CONVERSIONS

Flight computers incorporate many different conversion scales. In fact, you have already used one of these — the temperature conversion scale located at the bottom of the CSG. Other conversion scales are located directly on the "A" and "B" scales of the flight computer.

STATUTE TO NAUTICAL

Converting between statute and nautical miles is relatively easy. To see how this works, let's complete two conversions — one from nautical

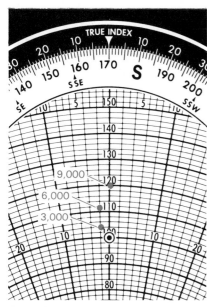

Figure 6-31. The winds plotted here are 130° at 5 knots for 3,000 feet, 150° at 12 knots for 6,000 feet, and 170° at 20 knots for 9,000 feet.

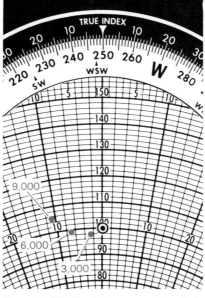

Figure 6-32. On this course, the winds at 3,000 feet provide a 2-knot tailwind; the winds at 6,000 feet have almost no effect on groundspeed; and the winds at 9,000 feet produce a 6-knot headwind.

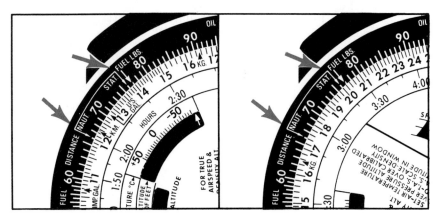

Figure 6-33. To convert 120 nautical miles to statute, place the 12 on the "B" scale directly under the "NAUT." arrow on the "A" scale (left illustration). Read the distance of 138 statute miles on the "B" scale directly under the "STAT." arrow. Next, convert 200 statute miles to nautical. This time, place the 20 on the "B" scale directly under the "STAT." arrow (right illustration), and read the answer of 174 nautical miles under the "NAUT." arrow.

miles to statute and the other from statute to nautical. Both conversions use the "NAUT. STAT." arc found on the "A" scale of the flight computer. [Figure 6-33]

OTHER CONVERSIONS

In weight and balance you learned that one gallon of aviation gasoline (avgas) weighs six pounds. Most flight computers allow you to directly convert avgas between gallons and pounds. [Figure 6-34]

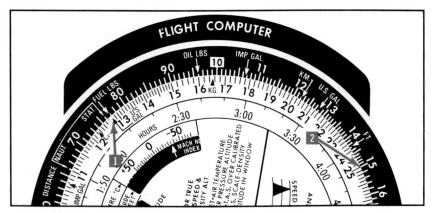

Figure 6-34. For this conversion, align the "FUEL LBS." index pointer on the "A" scale with the "U.S. GAL." index pointer on the "B" scale (item 1). You can then read pounds on the "A" scale opposite gallons on the "B" scale. For example, 25 gallons of avgas weigh 150 pounds (item 2). See your computer manual for other useful conversions.

ELECTRONIC FLIGHT COMPUTERS

This section presents the solutions to several problems using the Avstar electronic flight computer. Avstar is a multi-function calculator with memory, which has been especially designed by pilots, for use by pilots. Its ease of operation and extreme accuracy greatly simplify flight planning and in-flight calculations. Since this segment provides only introductory material on Avstar's operation, be sure to consult your operator's manual for additional features and computations. [Figure 6-35]

TIME-SPEED-DISTANCE

When any two of the three time, speed, and distance variables are known, the flight computer can be used to solve for the third. Note that with Avstar, you can enter or compute time in the hours, minutes, and seconds format. For example, assume it took 1 hour, 30 minutes (1:30:00) to cover 210 n.m. To solve for groundspeed, proceed as follows:

Always remember to CLEAR the flight computer before starting any new problem.

Press	Display	Comments
ON/c	0	Clear display
TSD	0	Select time-speed-distance mode
1 T:	1-00	
30	1-30	Enter time
TIME	1-30-00	
210 Ds/F	210	Enter the distance flown
CMP G/ft	140.0	Groundspeed = 140 knots

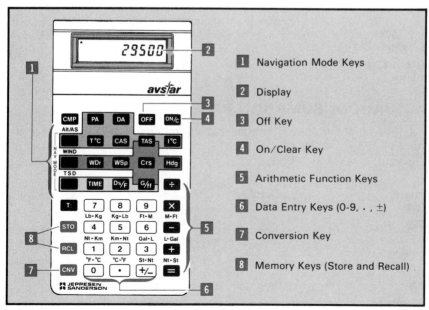

Figure 6-35. The keyboard of the Avstar flight computer is shown here. Study the manual to familiarize yourself with the locations and functions of the various keys.

FUEL REQUIRED

Remember, fuel consumption and time-speed-distance problems use the same mathematical relationships.

For this example, assume a flight time of 2:32:15 and a fuel consumption rate of 8.5 g.p.h. To determine the fuel required for this flight, proceed as follows:

Press	Display	Comments
ON/C	0	Clear display
TSD	0	Select time-speed-distance mode
2 T:	2-00	
32 T:	2-32-00	Enter time
15 TIME	2-32-15	
8.5 G/ff	8.5	Fuel consumption rate
CMP Ds/F	21.6	Fuel required = 21.6 gallons.

ENDURANCE

The airplane you are using carries 45 gallons of fuel. You intend to operate at a power setting which will cause fuel to be consumed at the rate of 9 g.p.h. How long can you remain aloft? This problem is solved as follows:

Press	Display	Comments
ON/C	0	Clear display
TSD	0	Select time-speed-distance mode
45 Ds/F	45	Enter fuel quantity available
9 G/ff	9	Enter fuel consumption rate
CMP TIME	5-00-00	Time = 5 hours

ACTUAL CONSUMPTION RATE

For this example, you determine that 80 gallons of fuel has been consumed over a 2:30:00 time period. To compute the actual fuel consumption rate, proceed as follows:

Press	Display	Comments
ON/C	0	Clear display
TSD	0	Select time-speed-distance mode
2 T:	2-00	
30	2-30	Enter time
TIME	2-30-00	
80 Ds/F	80	Fuel consumed
CMP G/ff	32.0	Actual fuel consumption rate = 32 g.p.h

DENSITY ALTITUDE

You are departing from an airport with a pressure altitude of 2,000 feet and a true temperature of 25°C. To find the density altitude for this airport, follow these steps:

Press		Display	Comments
ON/c		0	Clear display
Alt/AS	A	0	Select altitude/airspeed mode
2000 **PA**		2000	Enter pressure altitude
25 **T°C**		25	Enter true temperature in °C
CMP **DA**		3607	Density altitude = 3,607 feet

STANDARD TEMPERATURE

While planning a flight, you need to determine the standard temperature at a pressure altitude of 4,000 feet. Standard temperature is determined as follows:

Press		Display	Comments
ON/c		0	Clear display
Alt/AS	A	0	Select altitude/airspeed mode
4000 **PA**		4000	Enter the pressure altitude
CMP **T°C**		7	Standard temperature = 7°C

TRUE AIRSPEED

You are flying at a pressure altitude of 12,000 feet, with a calibrated airspeed of 121 knots. The temperature on the outside air temperature gauge is -6°C. To determine the true airspeed of the airplane, use the following steps:

Press		Display	Comments
ON/c		0	Clear display
Alt/AS	A	0	Select altitude/airspeed mode
12000 **PA**		12000	Enter the pressure altitude
6 **+/−**		-6	Change 6°C to -6°C
I°C		-6	Enter temperature as indicated air temperature
121 **CAS**		121	Enter CAS
CMP **TAS**		145	TAS = 145 knots

In the preceding example, notice the temperature was entered as an indicated air temperature. This allows Avstar to adjust the temperature automatically to compensate for the effects of friction. As noted earlier, friction causes the indicated air temperature to read slightly warmer than its actual value. Although this small rise in temperature can normally be disregarded at speeds under 200 knots, entering it here allows Avstar to provide you a more precise answer.

For in-flight calculations, enter the outside air temperature as indicated air temperature, not as true air temperature.

HEADING AND GROUNDSPEED

During flight planning, you determine that the forecast winds aloft at your cruising altitude are 080° at 20 knots. Your course and true airspeed will be 030° and 170 knots, respectively. Using Avstar, you compute the true heading and groundspeed as follows:

Press		Display	Comments
ON/c		0	Clear display
WIND	B	0	Select wind mode
80 WDr		80	Enter wind direction
20 WSp		20	Enter wind speed
30 Crs		30	Course
170 TAS		170	True airspeed
CMP Hdg		35	True heading = 035°
CMP G/ff		156	Groundspeed = 156 knots

UNKNOWN WIND

For this example, you want to calculate the actual winds aloft using a course of 175°, actual heading of 160°, true airspeed of 180 knots, and actual groundspeed of 144 knots. Now apply these factors to solve for wind direction and wind speed:

Press		Display	Comments
ON/c		0	Clear display
WIND	B	0	Select wind mode
175 Crs		175	Enter the course
160 Hdg		160	Enter the heading
180 TAS		180	The true airspeed in knots
144 G/ff		144	Groundspeed in knots
CMP WDr		118	Wind direction = 118°
CMP WSp		55	Wind speed = 55 knots

CONVERSIONS

The Avstar flight computer incorporates the most common conversions used in aviation. These conversions can be addressed regardless of Avstar's operating mode. Here are two examples.

A distance of 124 statute miles is converted to nautical miles as follows:

Press	Display	Comments
124 CNV	124	Enter 124 s.m. and select the convert function
St-Nt	107.75305	124 s.m. = 108 n.m.

A temperature of 81°F is converted to Celsius as follows:

Press	Display	Comments
81 CNV	81	Enter 81°F
°F-°C	27.222222	81°F = 27°C

MULTI-PART PROBLEMS

Often a series of interrelated problems is required for a final solution. This is known as a multi-part problem. A good example of this is the following problem, which allows you to find the fuel required for an anticipated flight. The true airspeed is determined first, followed by the groundspeed and time enroute and, finally, the fuel required.

Given:

Pressure altitude .... 7,500 ft.
Temperature ....15°C (True)
Calibrated airspeed .... 105 kts.
Wind direction .... 035°
Wind speed .... 12 kts.
Course .... 270°
Distance .... 256 n.m.
Fuel consumption rate .... 11.5 g.p.h.

Press	Display	Comments
ON/c	0	Clear display
Alt/AS	A 0	Select altitude/airspeed mode
7500 PA	7500	Enter pressure altitude
15 T°C	15	Enter true air temperature °C
105 CAS	105	Enter CAS
CMP TAS	121	TAS = 121 knots
WIND	B 120.5534	Select wind mode
TAS	120.5534	TAS entered from display
35 WDr	35	Enter wind direction
12 WSp	12	Enter wind speed
270 Crs	270	Enter course
CMP G/ʜ	127	Groundspeed = 127 knots
TSD	127.03484	Select time-speed-distance mode
G/ʜ	127.03484	GS entered from display
256 Ds/F	256	Enter distance
CMP TIME	2-00-55	Time enroute = 2:00:55
11.5 G/ʜ	11.5	Enter fuel consumption rate
CMP Ds/F	23.2	Fuel consumed = 23.2 gallons

CALIBRATED AIRSPEED

Occasionally you will find a problem that requires you to compute the CAS needed to maintain a given TAS. To solve this problem, use the altitude/airspeed mode and enter the known values of pressure altitude and temperature. Then, enter the CAS choices until you find one that gives the given TAS. For example, to maintain a TAS of 200 knots with a pressure altitude of 7,000 feet and a temperature of 5°C, what is the CAS? (1) 170 knots (2) 179 knots (3) 186 knots (4) 192 knots

Press		Display	Comments
ON/c		0	Clear display
Alt/AS	A	0	Select altitude/airspeed mode
7000 PA		7000	Enter pressure altitude
5 T°C		5	Enter true air temperature °C
170 CAS		170	Enter first answer choice CAS
CMP TAS		190	Does not equal 200 knots; try again with data overwrite
179 CAS		179	Enter second answer choice
CMP TAS		200	200 knots TAS = 179 knots CAS

CHECKLIST ─────────────────────

After studying this section, you should have a basic understanding of:

✓   **Time-speed-distance problems** — How to determine any one of the three values if the other two are given.

✓   **Fuel problems** — Why fuel problems have the same relationships as time-speed-distance problems.

✓   **Density altitude problems** — How to compute density altitude when you know pressure altitude and temperature.

✓   **Standard temperature** — How to solve for standard temperature from pressure altitude.

✓   **Airspeed calculations** — How to compute true airspeed and what values are required.

✓   **Wind problems** — How to determine most favorable winds, as well as heading and groundspeed, during flight planning. What values are required for computation of actual wind speed and wind direction during flight.

✓   **Conversions** — How to perform conversions, including Fahrenheit to Celsius temperatures and nautical to statute distances.

PILOTAGE AND DEAD RECKONING

There are several methods of navigating from one point to another. In this section we will discuss two of the most common ones — pilotage and dead reckoning. Although pilotage and dead reckoning usually are presented as two different means of VFR navigation, you will find that they are normally used together.

PILOTAGE

In the early days of flight, pilots would find their way by following landmarks such as rivers, streams, or railroads. They also flew from one town to the next, using any prominent objects or structures in the area for guidance. This method, called **pilotage**, is a form of navigation by visual reference to landmarks. Today, flying by pilotage is accomplished by comparing symbols on aeronautical charts with their corresponding features on the earth's surface. Sectional charts are recommended for pilotage because of their detailed portrayal of terrain and man-made features.

Pilotage is navigation by reference to checkpoints.

Flying by pilotage requires that you select an altitude that allows you to identify the chosen landmarks, or checkpoints, on your route of flight. Obviously, if you fly at too high an altitude, the selected references may be so small that you can't identify them. On the other hand, flying too low also presents problems. Aside from the dangers of tall obstructions, flying too low gives you a poor perspective for identifying landmarks. Selection of a cruising altitude depends on the terrain you are flying over, as well as the types of checkpoints available. Of course, above 3,000 feet AGL, you also must comply with the east/west cruising altitude rules.

One of the advantages of pilotage is that, once you have received training and acquired experience, it is relatively easy to perform and does not require special instruments. The most basic airplane will enable you to navigate by pilotage. On the other hand, pilotage has a number of disadvantages. In areas where few prominent landmarks are present, pilotage can be difficult. A direct course may be impractical if there are few good landmarks. You are also limited by visibility. If your visibility is reduced by haze, smoke, or fog, your ability to navigate by pilotage diminishes.

SELECTING CHECKPOINTS

You should select checkpoints which are easy to identify from the air.

The checkpoints used to determine your position along a route of flight are useful only if they can be positively identified. When selecting checkpoints, you must attempt to pick those with distinctive features which will be easily recognizable from the air. Training and experience will help you evaluate chart symbology and select checkpoints that are useful in navigating.

There are no specific rules to follow when selecting checkpoints, since each route you travel is different. However, one general guideline is to avoid using any single landmark as a sole reference, if possible. For example, you should not rely solely on a water tower to identify a small town, since other small towns in the area may have water towers, too. When flying by pilotage, it is important to take a look at the "whole picture." Whenever possible, compare your selected checkpoint against a combination of ground features so you can identify your position positively. Another guideline is to fly with current aeronautical charts, even when flying over familiar territory. Man-made structures are always changing, and an out-of-date chart could be a deceptive tool when you are trying to identify your position.

Intersecting lines, such as highways, railroad tracks, powerlines, or rivers normally provide good references for position identification. However, it is important to compare them with the surrounding terrain and landmarks. [Figure 6-36]

Although primary roads are usually good checkpoints, secondary roads can be deceiving. Aeronautical charts do not print every road, although those shown are generally obvious when viewed from the air. You should also remember that new roads and highways are continuously under construction. This brings up an important point regarding aeronautical charts — they do not portray all of the surface details on the earth.

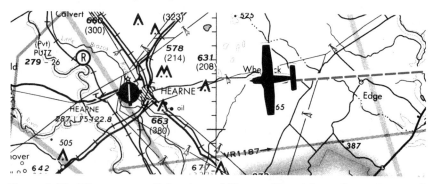

Figure 6-36. When you are flying toward Hearne Airport from the east, several checkpoints are available, including primary roads, railroad tracks, and powerlines that merge into the city. The position of the airport, on the west side of the city, also makes an excellent visual checkpoint.

Rivers often provide excellent landmarks, especially when they have significant bends or curves. However, they may be somewhat deceptive. Some rivers have numerous tributaries, and the main body may be difficult to follow. During a flood stage, the appearance from the air may be significantly different from the chart pattern. During a drought, on the other hand, the body of water shown on a sectional may actually be a dried-up river bed. Lakes usually provide good references for determining your position. As with rivers, certain cautions must be exercised. In many parts of the country, hundreds of small lakes exist within close proximity, and identifying a particular one can be extremely difficult. What appears to be a small lake on a chart may actually be a pond that has dried up.

Cities can have excellent landmark value. The yellow pattern printed on charts provides you with a good representation of the actual shape of the city when viewed from the air. You should be careful when using small towns and villages as checkpoints, though, because they often resemble one another from aloft.

Small towns and villages may not be good checkpoints, because they tend to look similar from the air.

FOLLOWING A ROUTE

There are two basic approaches to flying by pilotage. The first is to follow a major topographical feature, such as a river or highway. As the direction of the landmark changes, you simply alter your course to fly along its route. Although this is an easy means of navigating, a primary disadvantage is that a direct flight is usually impossible, so the length of your flight is increased. An alternative to meandering along an indirect route is to draw a straight line on your chart between the departure and destination airports. Instead of following a major topographical feature or flying from one particular landmark to another, you select checkpoints along a direct route of flight. A straight-line course not only decreases your time enroute, but also allows you to perform more accurate time, speed, and distance calculations.

ORIENTATION

Because pilotage is a visual means of navigation, maintaining an accurate orientation between your intended and actual routes of flight is fundamental. If you become disoriented over unfamiliar or featureless terrain, determining your position can be difficult. The key to preventing disorientation is in taking the time to plan your flight adequately.

Preparation for a cross-country flight by pilotage begins by studying the charts for the area you will be flying over. Use a straightedge to lay out a direct course between your departure and destination airports. With the course line drawn, you can select suitable checkpoints along your route. As you select them, mark them on the chart so you will remember them when airborne. This is important even for short routes. As you acquire

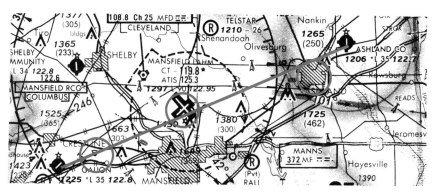

Figure 6-37. The outdoor theater northeast of Galion Airport between the two primary roads is a good selection for the first checkpoint. The Mansfield Lahm Airport
is also a good checkpoint. The airport data alerts you to the fact that an airport
traffic area exists when the tower is in operation. The city of Ashland makes a final
checkpoint before you land.

cross-country experience, you will be able to use fewer checkpoints and
still maintain orientation to your route. [Figure 6-37]

**You should always make
a detailed study of your
planned route of flight.**

After laying out your course and marking your checkpoints, carefully
study the entire route. One of the most significant items in the example is
the airport traffic area at Mansfield Lahm Airport. Since the field elevation is 1,297 feet MSL, you should overfly the airport at no less than
5,500 feet MSL. This is because you normally should avoid airport traffic
areas except for the purpose of taking off or landing. In turn, you must
comply with the east/west cruising altitude rules, and 5,500 feet is the
lowest appropriate altitude for your easterly course. This means you
must climb more than 4,000 feet for this relatively short route. This may
be reason enough to alter your planned course, depending on the performance capability of your airplane. For example, you could fly north
beyond the city of Shelby, then turn east to avoid passing through the
airport traffic area. Of course, you also could contact the tower and
request permission to transit the area. If you do this, you should consider
the implications of the control zone, shown by the dashed line on the
chart. These are some of the things you should analyze when you study
your planned route of flight.

DEAD RECKONING

**Dead reckoning allows
you to predict the move-
ment of your aircraft
along the planned route.**

A second means of navigating cross-country stems from mathematical
computations. **Dead reckoning** is a technique of navigation based on calculations of time, speed, distance, and direction. From the previous section on flight computers, you know the four variables required to solve
for heading and groundspeed. They are TAS, course, wind direction, and
wind speed. These values allow you to predict the movement of your
airplane along your intended route of flight. However, before you can use
the flight computer to solve for heading and groundspeed, you need to
determine your course with a navigation plotter.

NAVIGATION PLOTTER

A navigation plotter is usually made of clear plastic, so that chart details can be seen through it. The **plotter** is a simple instrument which features a straightedge for drawing a course line, a protractor for measuring the direction of flight, and scales for measuring distance. Normally, the distance scales allow you to measure in either nautical or statute miles. In addition, most plotters provide scales for sectional, WAC, and VFR terminal area charts.

The plotter functions as a straightedge, protractor, and distance measuring device.

FLIGHT PLANNING

The first step in dead reckoning is to draw a line on the chart between your departure and destination airports. Then, use a plotter to determine the distance between them. It is important to make sure that you're using the correct scale on the plotter for this measurement. Your next step is to measure the true course. Actually, there are several ways to do this. The most common way is to place the small hole in the center of the plotter directly over one of the longitude lines printed on the chart. It is most accurate to select a line of longitude which is near the midpoint of the route. Then align the upper or lower edge of the plotter with the course line, and read your course where the line of longitude intersects the plotter azimuth. [Figure 6-38]

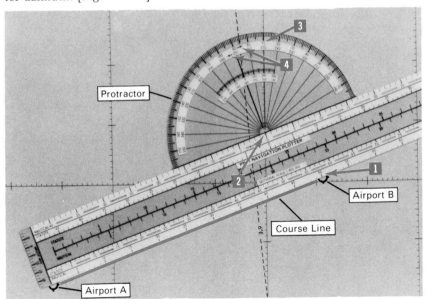

Figure 6-38. A course line has been drawn between airport "A" and airport "B." The distance between them is 50 n.m. (item 1). Notice that the grommet in the center of the protractor (item 2) is directly over the line of longitude, and the course line is aligned with the lower edge of the plotter. The true course between airports "A" and "B" is 70° (item 3). The inner scale provides the true course between "B" and "A," which is 250°. The directional arrows (item 4) signify that easterly courses are measured on the outside scale and westerly courses use the inside scale.

Sometimes, you will draw a course line that does not cross a meridian. Instead of extending the line until it finally crosses a line of longitude, you can use a parallel of latitude instead. The small north/south scale printed on the protractor allows you to do this. Now, let's look at an example of this, using an actual chart excerpt. [Figure 6-39]

Another problem you may encounter occurs when your departure and destination airports are on opposite sides of the same chart. Since the north and south sides of a chart depict adjacent areas, occasionally you will have to draw your course line from one side to the other. In order to

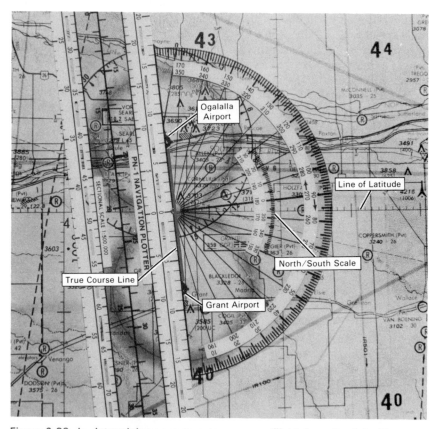

Figure 6-39. In determining your true course on a flight from Ogallala Airport to Grant Airport, the small hole on the plotter is placed directly over an intersection of the true course and a line of latitude. Your true course of 174° is read off the inner scale, which provides for northerly and southerly courses. You can see that the special north/south scale has two sets of numbers. The inner set of numbers, 210° decreasing to 150°, is for plotting courses to the south. The second set of numbers is for plotting courses to the north. For example, the northerly true course in the opposite direction from Grant Airport to Ogallala Airport is 354°. This is indicated on the outer portion of the special north/south scale.

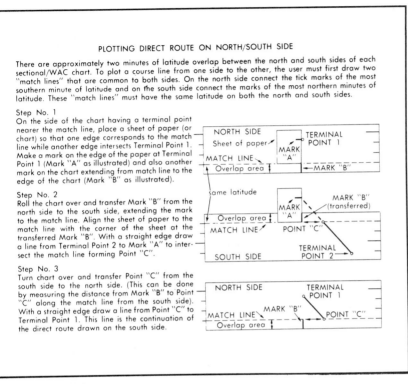

PLOTTING DIRECT ROUTE ON NORTH/SOUTH SIDE

There are approximately two minutes of latitude overlap between the north and south sides of each sectional/WAC chart. To plot a course line from one side to the other, the user must first draw two "match lines" that are common to both sides. On the north side connect the tick marks of the most southern minute of latitude and on the south side connect the marks of the most northern minutes of latitude. These "match lines" must have the same latitude on both the north and south sides.

Step No. 1
On the side of the chart having a terminal point nearer the match line, place a sheet of paper (or chart) so that one edge corresponds to the match line while another edge intersects Terminal Point 1. Make a mark on the edge of the paper at Terminal Point 1 (Mark "A" as illustrated) and also another mark on the chart extending from match line to the edge of the chart (Mark "B" as illustrated).

Step No. 2
Roll the chart over and transfer Mark "B" from the north side to the south side, extending the mark to the match line. Align the sheet of paper to the match line with the corner of the sheet at the transferred Mark "B". With a straight edge draw a line from Terminal Point 2 to Mark "A" to intersect the match line forming Point "C".

Step No. 3
Turn chart over and transfer Point "C" from the south side to the north side. (This can be done by measuring the distance from Mark "B" to Point "C" along the match line from the south side). With a straight edge draw a line from Point "C" to Terminal Point 1. This line is the continuation of the direct route drawn on the south side.

Figure 6-40. Special instructions provide step-by-step procedures for plotting north/south routes that start on one side of a chart and end on the other.

help you extend this line accurately, an instruction guide is printed in the chart margin. [Figure 6-40]

After plotting your true course, the next step in flight planning is to determine the effects of wind on your airplane at your planned flight altitude. Use forecast winds to determine your true heading and groundspeed. During the weather briefing prior to your flight, obtaining the winds aloft forecast will enable you to perform this calculation. As an example, assume you are making a flight between Kimball Airport and Sidney Airport. Use the following values for calculating your true heading and groundspeed:

True airspeed .... 105 kts.
True course .... 099°
True wind direction .... 310°
Wind speed .... 15 kts.

Solving the wind problem with a flight computer results in a true heading of 095° for your trip. This is the true course minus the wind correction angle. Your groundspeed is 118 knots.

Check Points (Fixes)	VOR Ident Freq.	Course (Route)	Altitude	Wind Dir.	Vel.	CAS	TC	TH	MH		Dist.	GS	Time Off	GPH
				Temp.		TAS	-L +R WCA	-E +W Var.	± Dev.	CH	Leg Rem.	Est. Act.	ETE ATE	ETA ATA	Fuel Rem.
Kimball	↗	7,500		310 20°C	15	105	099 -4°	095						
Sidney														

Figure 6-41. The navigation log enables you to record the known values and compute the unknown values. Recording the winds aloft, true airspeed, and true course enables you to solve the wind problem and determine a wind correction angle (item 1). In this example, the WCA is subtracted from the true course to determine a true heading of 095° (item 2).

NAVIGATION LOG

To help with your flight planning and enroute calculations, use a navigation log to record data pertaining to your trip. The **navigation log** allows you to list information in a systematic fashion and also helps you to keep track of the progress of your flight. [Figure 6-41]

TRUE AND MAGNETIC VALUES

True values corrected for magnetic variation equal magnetic values.

Because the course line drawn on a chart is in relation to true north and you normally fly by magnetic reference, you will need to correct for the variation between the two. You can do this by adjusting true course for variation to get magnetic course, or by adjusting true heading for variation to get magnetic heading. Typically, you solve for true heading first, since winds aloft forecasts are given in true direction and you know the true course. Then, you apply variation to true heading to get magnetic heading.

The isogonic line of variation printed next to the true course from Kimball to Sidney is 11° east. The memory aid "east is least and west is best," tells you whether to add or subtract the variation. [Figure 6-42]

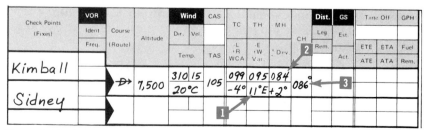

Figure 6-42. Subtracting the 11° easterly variation (item 1) from the true heading gives you a magnetic heading of 084° (item 2). The magnetic deviation noted from the compass correction card for this magnetic heading is added, and a compass heading of 086° will be flown between the two checkpoints on the first leg.

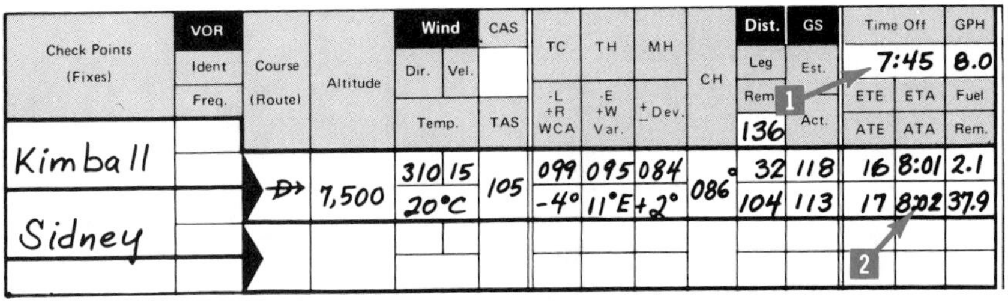

Check Points (Fixes)	VOR Ident / Freq	Course (Route)	Altitude	Wind Dir / Vel. — Temp.	CAS / TAS	TC — -L +R WCA	TH — -E +W Var.	MH — ±Dev.	CH	Dist. Leg / Rem — Est. / Act.	GS Est. / Act.	Time Off / ETE / ATE	GPH / Fuel / Rem.
Kimball		⟶ 7,500		310 15 — 20°C	105	099 — -4° WCA	095 — 11°E+2°	084	086	32 — 136	118	7:45 — 16 — 8:01	8.0 — 2.1
Sidney										104	113	17 — 8:22	37.9

Figure 6-43. By noting your departure time (item 1), you can determine differences in the estimated time of arrival (ETA) and your actual time of arrival (ATA) (item 2).

The navigation log is an excellent tool for determining your time enroute. By knowing the distance between checkpoints, along with your anticipated groundspeed, you can calculate the estimated time enroute (ETE) between them. While airborne, you can calculate your actual time enroute (ATE) and compare it to your estimated time to keep track of your flight's progress. If the actual winds aloft are substantially different than forecast, you can use your flight computer to recalculate your estimated time enroute and the fuel needed to reach your destination. [Figure 6-43]

During flight, the navigation log permits you to compare your estimates with the actual time enroute.

The key to computing ETE and fuel required during flight is an accurate groundspeed check. You can do this anywhere along a direct route. All you have to do is accurately record how long it takes to fly a known distance. For instance, if you fly 10 nautical miles in six minutes while maintaining a constant heading and indicated airspeed, your groundspeed is 100 knots.

Because of high terrain or weather conditions, you may find that a direct route to your destination is impractical. In these situations, you can plan your flight to include additional "legs." A leg may be any segment of a cross-country flight, such as the distance between checkpoints, intermediate stops, or course changes. In flight planning, legs often refer to any straight-line segment of a flight. Navigation logs are designed to accommodate multiple-leg flights, as well as direct flights. Depending on the total length of your trip, you may designate any number of checkpoints. Each checkpoint may be an entry on the navigation log. If your trip is not direct, you will need to solve a wind problem for each separate leg. The "Totals" line at the bottom of the navigation log allows you to add distances, times, and fuel consumption for multiple-leg flights. [Figure 6-44]

FUEL REQUIREMENTS

The total fuel requirement of 16.3 gallons includes an allowance for the time to climb to 2,500 feet MSL and time to enter the traffic pattern at the destination. FARs also require that day VFR flights carry enough fuel to fly to the first point of intended landing at normal cruise speed, and to fly after that for an additional 30 minutes. A reserve of 45 minutes is required for night flights.

FARs require a minimum of 30 minutes reserve fuel for day VFR flights.

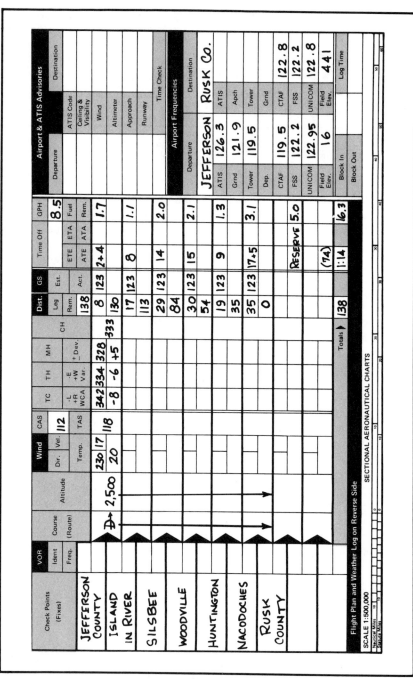

Figure 6-44. This is a completed navigation log for a direct flight. Notice the trip distance of 138 n.m. will require 1 hour, 14 minutes, at a groundspeed of 123 knots. Also note that the frequency box has been completed to provide easy access to this information during the flight.

FLIGHT PLAN

Aside from its value for preflight planning and its obvious use during flight, the navigation log also permits you to extract pertinent information you will need to complete an FAA flight plan. For convenience, the flight plan form is included on the reverse side of some navigation logs. [Figure 6-45]

Flight plan forms have several blocks for recording data pertinent to your flight. The information which follows describes the data appropriate to each numbered block on the flight plan form.

1. **Type of Flight Plan** — Mark "VFR" in this block, since you will be flying under visual flight rules. Only instrument-rated pilots can file "IFR" flight plans. Use "DVFR" when your flight will transit an ADIZ/DEWIZ area. You can find more information on DVFR flight plans in the *Airman's Information Manual.*
2. **Aircraft Identification** — Use the full identification number of the aircraft, such as N5246R.
3. **Aircraft Type and Special Equipment** — Enter the designator for the aircraft, followed by a slash (/) and the transponder and DME code letter; for example, PA-28/A. If the designator is unknown, use the manufacturer's name. You can find the equipment code letters in the *Airman's Information Manual* and at the bottom of the Jeppesen Sanderson flight plan form.

U.S. DEPARTMENT OF TRANSPORTATION
FEDERAL AVIATION ADMINISTRATION

FLIGHT PLAN

(FAA USE ONLY) ☐ PILOT BRIEFING ☐ VNR ☐ STOPOVER | TIME STARTED | SPECIALIST INITIALS

1 TYPE	2 AIRCRAFT IDENTIFICATION	3 AIRCRAFT TYPE/ SPECIAL EQUIPMENT	4 TRUE AIRSPEED	5 DEPARTURE POINT	6 DEPARTURE TIME PROPOSED (Z)	6 DEPARTURE TIME ACTUAL (Z)	7 CRUISING ALTITUDE
X VFR / IFR / DVFR	N5246R	PA28/A	118 KTS	BPT	1500		2500

8 ROUTE OF FLIGHT: DIRECT

9 DESTINATION (Name of airport and city)	10 EST. TIME ENROUTE HOURS	10 EST. TIME ENROUTE MINUTES	11 REMARKS
F12 RUSK COUNTY HENDERSON, TX	1	14	

12 FUEL ON BOARD HOURS	12 FUEL ON BOARD MINUTES	13 ALTERNATE AIRPORT(S)	14 PILOT'S NAME, ADDRESS & TELEPHONE NUMBER & AIRCRAFT HOME BASE	15 NUMBER ABOARD
4	30		MAX GROSS 1114 FOX, BEAUMONT, TX. (409) 355-0159, AIRCENTER 1 17 DESTINATION CONTACT/TELEPHONE (OPTIONAL): (214) 643-2267	2

16 COLOR OF AIRCRAFT: WHITE/RED

CIVIL AIRCRAFT PILOTS. FAR Part 91 requires you file an IFR flight plan to operate under instrument flight rules in controlled airspace. Failure to file could result in a civil penalty not to exceed $1,000 for each violation (Section 901 of the Federal Aviation Act of 1958, as amended). Filing of a VFR flight plan is recommended as a good operating practice. See also Part 99 for requirements concerning DVFR flight plans.

CLOSE VFR FLIGHT PLAN WITH Ft. Worth FSS ON ARRIVAL

Figure 6-45. After completing your navigation log, you should fill out a flight plan and file it with the nearest FSS.

4. **True Airspeed** — Give this figure in knots, based on the estimated TAS at the planned flight altitude.

5. **Departure Point** — Enter the departure point/airport identifier code or the name, if the identifier is unknown. Identifier codes are listed in the *Airport/Facility Directory*.

6. **Departure Time** — This is the proposed departure time stated in Coordinated Universal Time (UTC), or Zulu time. The use of Zulu time eliminates confusion when you cross time zone boundaries during a flight.

7. **Cruising Altitude** — On a VFR flight plan, enter only the initial VFR cruising altitude to assist briefers in providing weather and wind information.

8. **Route of Flight** — Define your proposed route using identifiable points of reference, particularly those which will mark a change in direction. This will assist search and rescue in retracing your route in the event of an emergency. These points may be navaids, airways, or prominent geographic features. When you are not flying on published airways, use the term "direct" to describe a straight-line course between two points.

9. **Destination** — Enter the destination airport identifier code or the name, if the identifier code is unknown. Include the city and state, if the airport name alone might be confused with another.

10. **Estimated Time Enroute** — Enter the total estimated time from takeoff to landing in hours and minutes, based on the latest forecast winds.

11. **Remarks** — Use this block to enter remarks pertinent to ATC or to clarify other flight plan information. This information could include a stopover at an intermediate airport to pick up a passenger or to refuel. You can also use this block to request customs service at an airport of entry.

12. **Fuel on Board** — Enter the total usable fuel on board the aircraft in hours and minutes.

13. **Alternate Airport(s)** — If you desire, specify an alternate airport.

14. **Pilot's Name, Address, Telephone Number, and Aircraft Home Base** — Specify a telephone number where someone will answer who is knowledgeable about your flight. For aircraft home base, include the name of the FBO (if appropriate), as well as the airport name.

15. **Number of Persons Aboard** — Enter the total number of persons on board, including yourself and any other crewmembers.

16. **Color of Aircraft** — List the major color or colors.

17. **Destination Contact/Telephone (Optional)** — Specify the telephone number for the place where you can be reached at the destination to assist search and rescue should you fail to report or cancel your flight plan within one-half hour after your ETA. Use the last line at the bottom of the flight plan to record the name of the FSS that serves your destination airport.

Whether you file the flight plan in person or by telephone, it gives you the opportunity to make a final check of the weather. In cases where no telephone is available, you can still file it over the radio after departure. However, this practice is discouraged unless it is absolutely necessary, because of frequency congestion.

After the flight plan has been filed, you should activate it once you are airborne by calling the FSS and informing them of your actual time of departure. If your flight plan has not been activated, it will be kept on file by the FSS for one hour after your proposed departure time, after which you must refile. When you know your departure will be delayed beyond one hour, you should advise the FSS by phone. When a stopover flight is anticipated, the FAA recommends that you file a separate flight plan for each "leg" if the stop is expected to be more than one hour.

After the flight plan is activated, the flight service station sends a flight notification message to the FSS nearest the destination. Normally, you close the flight plan after you arrive at the destination. You may elect to close the flight plan with a flight service station other than the one serving your destination. However, you should inform the departure FSS of this decision when the flight plan is filed. If you land at an alternate airport, or any airport that is not your filed destination, you should inform the FSS of your original destination when you close.

When the estimated time of arrival has changed significantly, it is important for you to extend the flight plan through any flight service station within radio range. You can see that it is extremely important to close the flight plan by contacting the destination flight service station when the flight is complete. You can do this by radio, if necessary, or by telephone after you have landed. In situations where an FSS is not available, you may request any ATC facility to relay your cancellation to an FSS. Remember that VFR flight plans are never opened or closed automatically by control towers or FSSs.

If you fail to report or to cancel your flight plan within 30 minutes after your ETA, your aircraft is considered overdue. If your flight plan is not closed, the FSS will begin a telephone search to locate your overdue aircraft. If the FSS is unable to locate your aircraft, costly search-and-rescue procedures will be started.

Don't forget to close your flight plan.

POSITION REPORTS

During the flight, you should make periodic position reports to flight service stations (or other ATC facilities) along the route. Although position reports are not required on VFR flight plans, they permit significant information to be passed to you by the FSS. They also mark the progress of your flight if, for some reason, you do not reach your destination.

Making position reports on VFR flight plans is a good operating practice.

When you make a position report, it should sound like this: "*Lufkin Radio, Cherokee 5246R, over Lufkin at 1650 Zulu, VFR flight plan, 2,500, Beaumont to Henderson.*"

FLYING OVER HAZARDOUS TERRAIN

In some parts of the country, regularly traveled VFR routes often cross large bodies of water, swamps, and mountains. Selected FSSs provide Hazardous Area Reporting Service. The locations where this service is available are indicated in the *Airman's Information Manual.* These areas are mainly in the northeastern section of the country (including the Great Lakes), while some are located in the swamplands of Florida. When you request this service, you are expected to make frequent radio contacts with the FSS. Refer to the AIM for specific information on each location where the service is available.

Mountain flying and flight over open water are potentially hazardous operations from several standpoints. To be conducted safely, they require specialized training from experienced instructors who are familiar with the area over which the flights will be conducted. Appropriate survival gear is an absolute necessity. Mountain flying and flight over open water are usually beyond the scope of private pilot training depending on where you learn to fly. Before undertaking these types of operations, be sure to obtain a local checkout. Mountain flying, in particular, carries numerous hazards for the inexperienced. High density altitude, turbulence, rapidly changing weather, and difficulty in identifying landmarks are just a few of the challenges facing you on a mountain flight.

You can see that pilotage and dead reckoning complement each other in VFR navigation. You use pilotage to maintain your orientation to the planned route of flight and to identify the landmarks you have selected for checkpoints. The use of dead reckoning computations during flight planning provides an estimate of the heading necessary to maintain course. You also know what groundspeed to expect and can calculate your estimated time enroute, as well as fuel requirements. By recording this information on a navigation log, you can compare your estimated time between checkpoints with your actual time during flight. The navigation log also provides information needed to fill out your FAA flight plan.

CHECKLIST ━━━━━━━━━━━━━━━━━━━━

After studying this section, you should have an understanding of:

✓ **Pilotage** — How it is performed and what the advantages and disadvantages of this form of navigation are.

✓ **Orientation** — The importance of maintaining an orientation between your intended and actual routes of flight and how adequate flight planning will help to prevent disorientation.

✓ **Dead reckoning** — How performing calculations of time, speed, distance, and direction will help you to predict movement of your airplane along your intended route of flight.

✓ **Navigation plotter** — How its scales are used for measuring distance, and how its protractor is used to determine a true course.

✓ **Navigation log** — How it is used for flight planning and for in-flight calculations concerning the progress of your flight.

✓ **Flight plan** — How to fill one out and how to open and close it.

SOURCES OF FLIGHT INFORMATION

The need for current flight information has been a concern of cross-country pilots since the earliest days of aviation. As a pilot, you need to know when airports or runways are temporarily closed or when navigation aids are shut down for maintenance. You also need to be aware of new procedures and factors affecting flight safety as they are developed. While you study this section, you will find that aeronautical charts do not always provide the most current flight information. Updating and disseminating flight information on a timely basis is essential to safe flight operations. In this section, we will briefly summarize several important sources of flight information. These include the *Airport/Facility Directory* (A/FD), *Airman's Information Manual* (AIM), *Notices to Airmen* (NOTAMs), *Advisory Circulars* (ACs), and the *Jeppesen Airport and Information Directory* (J-AID).

AIRPORT/FACILITY DIRECTORY

The *Airport/Facility Directory* contains all airports, seaplane bases, and heliports open to the public.

During your training, you will soon become familiar with one of the most comprehensive sources of flight information — the **Airport/Facility Directory**. Published by the National Ocean Service, it contains a descriptive listing of all airports, heliports, and seaplane bases which are open to the public. [Figure 6-46]

Figure 6-46. The *Airport/Facility Directory* consists of several volumes which are divided for regional coverage. The entire directory is reissued several times a year and is designed to be used in conjunction with aeronautical charts. The effective dates are shown on the cover of each volume, so you will know if you have the most recent issue.

Figure 6-47. The information provided in the A/FD includes the location of the airport, which is four miles east of the city (item 1). "Rgt. tfc." means you should fly a right-hand traffic pattern when landing on runway 25 (item 2). The letters "VHF/DF" indicate the FSS has direction finding equipment to aid in determining your direction from the station (item 3). The TCA designation notifies you of mandatory radar sequencing and separation for the aircraft in the TCA (item 4). The approach and departure control frequency is 128.35 MHz (item 5).

DIRECTORY LEGEND

The airports presented in the *Airport/Facility Directory* are listed alphabetically by state, and then by the city associated with the airport. In order to help you interpret the abundance of information, there is a directory legend in the front of each regional volume. This sample gives you a thorough breakdown of all of the information in the booklet, including data pertaining to the airport's location, runways, lighting, ground services, communications facilities, and navigation aids. As well as showing the general sequence of the data, the legend also provides a detailed explanation of how to interpret each of the items. [Figure 6-47]

The directory legend gives a detailed description of each item in an airport listing.

OTHER FLIGHT PLANNING INFORMATION

Although airport listings make up the bulk of the directory, there are several other sections that contain essential information. Many of these pertain to VFR flight operations.

In the Special Notices section, you will find information concerning changes that affect the airspace system, as well as important miscellaneous items. Another section provides telephone numbers for the flight

---

1 **SPECIAL NOTICES**

NATIONAL PARK AREAS
VOLUNTARY OVERFLIGHT PRACTICES

As expressly encouraged by FAA Advisory Circular (AC) 91-36C, Visual Flight Rules (VFR) Near Noise-Sensitive Areas, *2,000 feet above the surface* of National Park areas (including Parks, Forests, Primitive Areas, Wilderness Areas, Recreational Areas, National Seashores, and National Wildlife Refuge and Range Areas).

NOTE: — AC 91-36C defines the *surface* of a National Park Areas as: the highest terrain within 2,000 feet laterally of the route flight, **or** the upper-most rim of a canyon or valley.

---

2 **FAA AND NWS**

TELEPHONE NUMBERS

★ PATWAS
■ TWEB
◆ Restricted Number for Aviation Weather Information
§§ Fast File (Flight Plan Filing Only)

Location and Identifier		Area Code	Telephone
Cedar Rapids CID	FSS	(319)	364-7127
Davenport (via Moline, Ill.)	WS	(309)	762-8347
Dubuque	WS	(319)	582-3171
Fort Dodge	FSS	(800)	WX-BRIEF ★§§

---

3 **VOR RECEIVER CHECK POINTS**

	111.6/FHU	G	210		On runup area rwy 02.
Prescott (Ernest A. Love Fld)	114.1/DRK	A/7000	124	5.0	Over apch end rwy 29.
Scottsdale Muni	115.6/SRP	A/7500	343	12.0	Over rwy 21 thld.
Tucson (Tucson Intl)	116.0/TUS	G	305	2.4	On int Twy A and 02 on apron.
		G	298	2.7	On west ramp at Twy B.

VOR TEST FACILITIES (VOT)

Facility Name (Airport Name)	Freq.	Type VOT Facility	Remarks
Phoenix Sky Harbor Intl.	109.0	G	

---

4 **PARACHUTE JUMPING AREAS**

LOCATION	DISTANCE AND RADIAL FROM NEAREST VOR/VORTAC	MAXIMUM ALTITUDE	REMARKS
Cedar Rapids	14 NM; 047° Cedar Rapids	15,000 AGL	3 NM Radius. Continuous
(c) **Dallas Center, Husband Field**	25 NM; 305° Des Moines	12,800	3 NM radius. Weekends and holidays
Davenport	13 NM; 258° Davenport	12,500	2 NM radius. Daily
Decorah Arpt	15 NM; 264° Waukon	7,000 AGL	Summer. Tue-Thu 1700-SS, Sat-Sun 1000-SS. Winter. 1000-SS Sat, Sun.

---

5 **AERONAUTICAL CHART BULLETIN**

WICHITA SECTIONAL
37th Edition, November 20, 19_

Add obst 4275'MSL (315'AGL)UC 36°01'55"N 102°27'32"W Add obst 3403'MSL (448'AGL)UC 36°03'12"N 100°48'07"W Add obst 1649'MSL (499'AGL)UC 37°03'33"N 97°05'41"W Add obst 1615'MSL (272'AGL) 37°34'35"N 97°29'44"W
Delete arpt SCHULZ FIELD 38°02'37"N, 98°46'36"W Add UNICOM 122.95" to SALINA MUNI 38°47'30"N 97°38'59"W

Figure 6-48. Other information contained in the *Airport/Facility Directory* includes Special Notices (item 1), FAA and NWS Telephone Numbers (item 2), VOR Receiver Check Points (item 3), Parachute Jumping Areas (item 4), and the Aeronautical Chart Bulletin (item 5).

service stations and National Weather Service outlets located in the region. In addition, numbers for PATWAS and TWEB are listed to provide you with recorded information. [Figure 6-48]

If you are planning to use VOR navigation, you may wish to consult the lists of ground and airborne checkpoints you can use to test the accuracy of your VOR receiver. If a symbol printed on the aeronautical chart alerts you to a parachute jumping area along your route of flight, you can check the A/FD for the location, maximum altitude, and pertinent remarks about those activities.

The A/FD provides information concerning parachute jumping areas.

The Aeronautical Chart Bulletin provides you with major changes in aeronautical information that have occurred since the last publication date of each sectional, VFR terminal area, and WAC chart. It includes changes affecting airports, obstructions, and communications and navigation facilities. By consulting this listing, you can obtain current information that could affect your flight.

Consult the Aeronautical Chart Bulletin before your flight for changes to aeronautical charts.

A variety of miscellaneous information is also provided in the *Airport/ Facility Directory*, which includes the address and phone number for each General Aviation District Office (GADO) and Flight Standards District Office (FSDO) in the region. A map showing stations that provide enroute flight advisory service is also furnished. Additional information of special interest to IFR pilots includes a regional list of sector frequencies for ARTCCs, as well as preferred IFR routes.

AIRMAN'S INFORMATION MANUAL

Your official guide to basic flight information and ATC procedures is the *Airman's Information Manual*. It is revised several times a year, and it furnishes a detailed description of the national airspace system, including the procedures necessary to conduct flight operations in the United States. The AIM also includes items of special interest to pilots, such as medical facts and other flight safety information. [Figure 6-49]

The AIM contains information necessary for flight in the U.S.

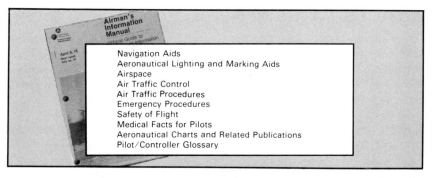

Figure 6-49. The AIM covers the general topics shown here. A comprehensive table of contents and an alphabetical index help you locate specific subjects. In addition, each new issue provides an explanation of major changes.

The AIM describes the various air navigation aids available to both VFR and IFR pilots. This information includes the capabilities, components, and procedures required for the use of each type of navaid. It also contains a discussion of radar services and procedures available to pilots, as well as information about the capabilities and limitations of radar. In addition, the AIM provides a comprehensive description of the many types of airport lighting and marking aids available.

It is a good idea to review airspace requirements and ATC procedures periodically. The AIM provides a means of doing this. It covers the various forms of controlled, uncontrolled, and special use airspace, as well as weather minimums and VFR cruising altitudes. A thorough discussion of the air traffic control system is also provided. This includes a description of the facilities and services available to pilots, such as air route traffic control centers, control towers, flight service stations, and aeronautical advisory stations. Because of the importance of the link between the pilot and controller in the ATC system, a discussion is devoted to radio communications phraseology and techniques. A related area, the Pilot/Controller Glossary, is intended to promote a common understanding of the terms used in the air traffic control system. International terms that differ from the FAA definitions are listed after their U.S. equivalents.

You can also find important information on emergency services available to you, such as radar, transponder operation, and VHF/DF instrument approach procedures. In addition, the AIM covers distress and urgency messages, as well as procedures for two-way radio communications failure. Numerous weather services available for your preflight and enroute operations are detailed in the Safety of Flight section. It discusses altimeter settings, wake turbulence avoidance, and potential flight hazards, as well as safety, accident, and hazard reporting procedures. Other areas outline pertinent medical factors and list the various aeronautical charts and publications available from the government.

NOTICES TO AIRMEN

NOTAMs supply time-critical changes in aeronautical information to pilots.

Often, changes which affect the national airspace system are not known far enough in advance to be included in the most recent aeronautical chart or *Airport/Facility Directory*. The National Notices to Airmen System provides you with time-critical flight planning information. Each notice is categorized as a NOTAM-D, a NOTAM-L, or an FDC NOTAM.

A NOTAM which is given distant, as well as local, dissemination is a **NOTAM(D)**. This information is provided for all public use airports, seaplane bases, and heliports listed in the *Airport/Facility Directory*, and for all navigational facilities that are part of the National Airspace System. These NOTAMs concern aeronautical data relating to IFR operations, such as primary runway closures, approach light systems out of service, runway

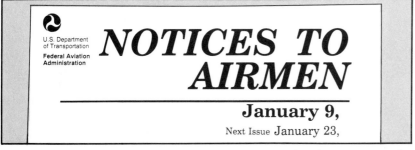

Figure 6-50. *Airport/Facility Directory* listings include the associated FSS and NOTAM file identifiers. At Fort Smith Landing Strip, the FSS is Billings and the airport NOTAM file identifier is "BIL." The same NOTAM identifier is used for radio aids.

lengthening, navigation aid frequency changes, and changes in operation of a control tower. NOTAM(D)s are distributed automatically, appended to the hourly weather reports. FSSs have access to the nationwide data base of these NOTAMs. In contrast, **NOTAM(L)** information includes local items like taxiway closures, construction activities near runways, and airport lighting, such as VASI, that does not affect instrument approach criteria. This information is disseminated locally only, and is not attached to the hourly weather reports. A separate file of local NOTAMs is maintained at each FSS for facilities in their area. You must specifically request NOTAM(L)s for other FSS areas. [Figure 6-50]

FDC NOTAMs are issued by the National Flight Data Center. They contain regulatory information such as temporary flight restrictions or amendments to instrument approach procedures and other current aeronautical charts. FDC NOTAMs are available through all air traffic facilities with telecommunications access.

An important part of your preflight planning should be a review of the *Notices to Airmen* publication. It is issued every 14 days and contains all current NOTAM-Ds and FDC NOTAMs available in time for publication. When NOTAM-D information is printed in this publication, it is taken off the distribution circuits and will not be provided during pilot briefings unless you request it. Data of a permanent nature are sometimes printed in the NOTAM publication as an interim step prior to publication on the appropriate aeronautical chart or in the A/FD. [Figure 6-51]

You should always check the *Notices to Airmen* publication prior to flight.

Figure 6-51. In addition to alerting you to changes in the airway system, the NOTAM publication details information about individual airports and is alphabetized by state, city, and airport name.

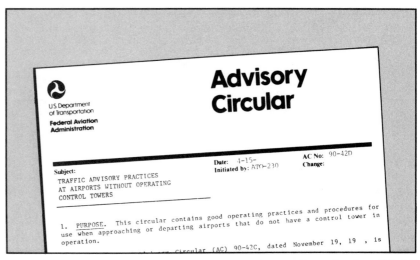

Figure 6-52. The subject of this advisory circular is identified in the heading. This AC defines the concept of a common traffic advisory frequency (CTAF).

ADVISORY CIRCULARS

ACs are informational in nature and present non-regulatory material of interest to pilots.

The Federal Aviation Administration has developed a systematic means of providing pilots with nonregulatory information of interest. These **advisory circulars** (ACs) are normally issued to provide you with guidance and information in a variety of subject areas, or to show a method acceptable to the Administrator for complying with Federal Aviation Regulations. Unless incorporated into a regulation by reference, the contents are not binding. [Figure 6-52]

Advisory circulars are divided into subjects by numbers. For example, ACs covering Airspace are issued under subject number 70.

Advisory circulars are divided into a variety of subjects, and are identified by numbers corresponding to the different part numbers of the Federal Aviation Regulations. Some of the subject areas are:

00	General	70	Airspace
10	Procedural Rules	90	Air Traffic Control
20	Aircraft		and General Operating Rules
60	Airmen	150	Airports

FAA advisory circulars are available to all pilots. They may be ordered through the Department of Transportation, U.S. Government Printing Office.

You may find that a series of circulars exists for a given subject. When this happens, the general area of information is subdivided into specific areas. For example, within the 150 series pertaining to airports, *Advisory Circular 150/5340-1E* describes marking of paved areas on airports. Periodically, the *Advisory Circular Checklist (AC-00-2)* is revised and reissued to inform you of the current status of ACs. The checklist also provides you with pricing and ordering information. Some ACs are free and others are available at cost. You can order either type through the Department of Transportation, U.S. Government Printing Office.

J-AID

One means of obtaining the most current aeronautical and airport information available is through the **Jeppesen Airport and Information Directory**. You will find data pertaining to VFR and IFR operations, as well as an airport directory.

The J-AID includes material covered in the *Airman's Information Manual* and the *Airport/Facility Directory*. Because of the extensive coverage of material and the frequency of revisions, FAR Part 135.81 authorizes air taxi and commercial operators to use the J-AID as a substitute for the AIM and the A/FD. Because of its convenient looseleaf format and ease of revision, many airlines and air taxi operators prefer it. [Figure 6-53]

The Radio Aids section is designed to help you understand the variety of air navigation aids in use today. Besides presenting you with a detailed description of navigation aids, each navaid within the U.S. is listed by name, identifier, frequency, class, and geographic coordinates. A list of commercial broadcast stations and VOR receiver check signals also is given.

You'll find the Meteorology section to be an excellent source of information for a variety of weather-related topics. It supplies addresses and telephone numbers of U.S. flight service stations and National Weather Service outlets. It also contains a description of weather services available for your preflight planning and enroute operations. Because of the importance of PIREPs, a portion of this section explains procedures for reporting items such as cloud heights, visibility, airframe icing, turbulence, and wind shear.

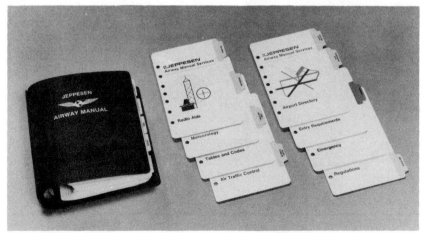

Figure 6-53. The J-AID is divided into a number of different subject areas. You will find sections covering Radio Aids, Meteorology, Tables and Codes, Air Traffic Control, Regulations, Entry Requirements, Emergency Procedures, and an Airport Directory.

A number of conversion tables and commonly used codes are presented in the J-AID. You'll find tables for converting inches of mercury to millibars, temperatures from Celsius to Fahrenheit, and various other metric conversions. Wind component tables, sunrise, sunset, and twilight tables also are included.

Much of the information found in the *Airman's Information Manual* is contained in the Air Traffic Control section, including the Pilot/Controller Glossary. Other topics include aeronautical lighting and airport marking aids, airspace, services available to pilots, radio communications phraseology and techniques, airport operations, ATC clearance/separation, safety of flight, and information concerning wake turbulence and medical facts for pilots.

J-AID AIRPORT DIRECTORY

The Airport Directory lists the public use airports contained in the *Airport/Facility Directory*. The J-AID Airport Directory is divided into geographic areas, which are arranged alphabetically by state, city, and airport name. A legend is shown to help you interpret the information presented. [Figure 6-54]

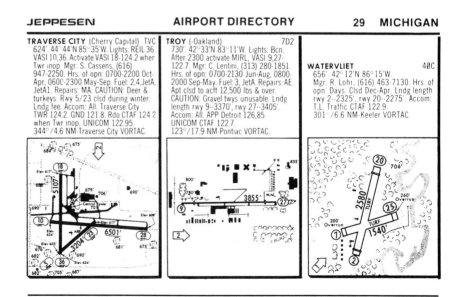

JEPPESEN   **AIRPORT DIRECTORY**   **29   MICHIGAN**

TRAVERSE CITY (Cherry Capital) TVC
624'. 44°44'N 85°35'W. Lights: REIL 36.
VASI 10,36. Activate VASI 18-124.2 when
Twr inop. Mgr: S. Cassens, (616)
947-2250. Hrs. of opn: 0700-2200 Oct-
Apr, 0600-2300 May-Sep. Fuel: 2,4,JetA,
JetA1. Repairs: MA. CAUTION: Deer &
turkeys. Rwy 5/23 clsd during winter.
Lndg fee. Accom: All. Traverse City
TWR 124.2. GND 121.8. Rdo CTAF 124.2
when Twr inop. UNICOM 122.95.
344°/4.6 NM-Traverse City VORTAC.

TROY (-Oakland)   7D2
730'. 42°33'N 83°11'W. Lights: Bcn.
After 2300 activate MIRL, VASI 9,27-
122.7. Mgr: C. Lentini, (313) 280-1851.
Hrs. of opn: 0700-2130 Jun-Aug, 0800-
2000 Sep-May. Fuel: 3, JetA. Repairs: AE.
Apt clsd to acft 12,500 lbs & over.
CAUTION: Gravel twys unusable. Lndg
length rwy 9--3370', rwy 27--3405'.
Accom: All. APP Detroit 126,85.
UNICOM CTAF 122.7.
123°/17.9 NM-Pontiac VORTAC.

WATERVLIET   40C
656'. 42°12'N 86°15'W.
Mgr: R. Lohr, (616) 463-7130. Hrs. of
opn: Days. Clsd Dec-Apr. Lndg length
rwy 2--2325'; rwy 20--2275'. Accom:
T.L. Traffic CTAF 122.9.
301°/6.6 NM-Keeler VORTAC.

Figure 6-54. There is an airport diagram for each airport contained in the J-AID, including the name, elevation, and geographic coordinates. Other information relates to runways, lighting, services available, and communication frequencies, as well as the distance and direction from a local navaid to the airport.

A reprint of current Federal Aviation Regulations includes FAR Parts 1, 61, 91, 121, 125, 135, and 141. The hazardous materials regulations contained in Part 175 is presented, as well as the National Transportation Safety Board (NTSB) Part 830.

The Entry Requirements section covers the U.S. regulations concerning entry, transit and departure of civil aircraft on international flights. A listing of airports of entry and customs services is provided to help answer questions you might have when you plan an international flight.

The J-AID also supplies you with information that you, as pilot-in-command, should know in the event of an emergency. Among the items covered are communications failure, transponder operation, search and rescue, emergency locator transmitters, and radar services for VFR aircraft in difficulty.

CHECKLIST ──────────────

After studying this section, you should have a basic understanding of:

✓ *Airport/Facility Directory* — How it is used in conjunction with aeronautical charts, and how to interpret the information contained in each regional volume.

✓ *Airman's Information Manual* — What basic flight information and ATC procedures it contains.

✓ *Notices to Airmen* — How NOTAM-Ds, NOTAM-Ls, and FDC NOTAMs are used to update changes to information contained in the *Airport/Facility Directory*, the *Airman's Information Manual*, and aeronautical charts.

✓ **Advisory circulars** — What they are, how they are indexed, and how you can obtain them.

✓ **J-AID** — The variety of topics it contains, and how it provides you with current aeronautical and airport information.

RADIO NAVIGATION SYSTEMS

CHAPTER 7

INTRODUCTION

One way to expand your basic navigation skills is to become familiar with radio navigation. This chapter covers a variety of radio navigation systems available for your use during cross-country flights. Our initial discussion will cover the VOR system, which forms a network of navaids and airways covering the entire country. Then we will show you how to navigate using the automatic direction finder, which relies on nondirectional radio beacons as well as commercial broadcast stations. The last section provides an overview of advanced navigation which is designed to familiarize you with the capabilities of several systems, including area navigation and LORAN.

VHF OMNIDIRECTIONAL RANGE

Course guidance, automatic wind correction, and magnetic heading information are useful features of the VOR navigation system.

Of the many types of navigation systems available to you, the **very high frequency omnidirectional range** (VOR) system is the one you will probably use most frequently. A basic VOR system provides course guidance, automatic wind correction, and magnetic headings. The VOR system actually uses three different types of ground facilities to help you navigate through the sky. The basic VOR station provides you with course guidance, while VOR/DME and VORTAC facilities provide both course and distance information. Since all three of these facilities help you follow a course, your first step will be to learn how to use this feature.

PRINCIPLES OF OPERATION

A VOR station transmits radio beams, called **radials**, outward in every direction. Actually, there is an infinite number of radials, but you will be concerned with the 360 which are numbered clockwise from magnetic north. [Figure 7-1]

VORs are depicted on sectional charts, as discussed in Chapter 6. The compass rose surrounding the station helps you to visualize the radials

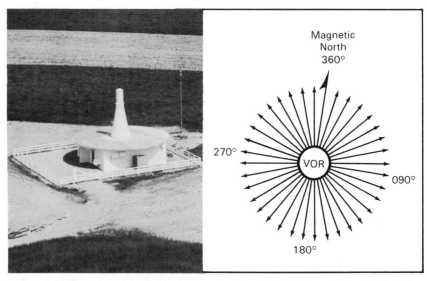

Figure 7-1. The ground-based component of the VOR system is the VOR station shown on the left. It transmits radials throughout 360° of azimuth starting at magnetic north. During flight, you will use these radials to determine your position relative to the station.

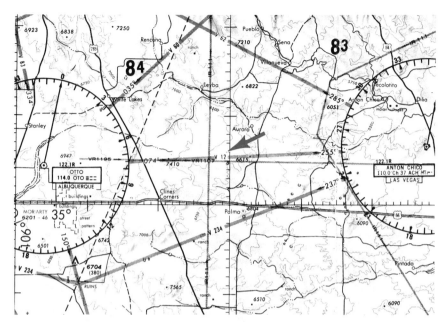

Figure 7-2. Victor 12 connects the Otto VOR and the Anton Chico VORTAC. The airway is defined by the 074° radial of Otto and the 255° radial of Anton Chico. When navigating between two stations you typically change from one station to the next at the midpoint.

as they travel outward. Many VOR stations are connected by specific radials, which form direct routes called Victor airways. [Figure 7-2]

The VOR signals are transmitted in the very high frequency range of 108.00 through 117.95 MHz. They travel on a line-of-sight basis. Any obstacle, such as a mountain or the curvature of the earth, can reduce the reception distance of the signal. In certain situations, terrain features can render the signals unusable for navigation purposes. You can find these exceptions published in the *Airport/Facility Directory* under the individual VOR listings. The reception range also varies with altitude. At low altitudes you must be very close to the station to receive the signal. As your altitude increases, you can use the VOR at greater distances from the station.

> Reception range for VOR signals is limited by line of sight.

VOR AIRBORNE EQUIPMENT

Your airborne equipment consists of an antenna, a receiver, and an indicator. VOR signals are received through the antenna. Next, they are relayed to the VOR receiver, which interprets the signals and sends the information to the VOR indicator. Although most airborne VOR equipment is similar in appearance and operation, you should familiarize

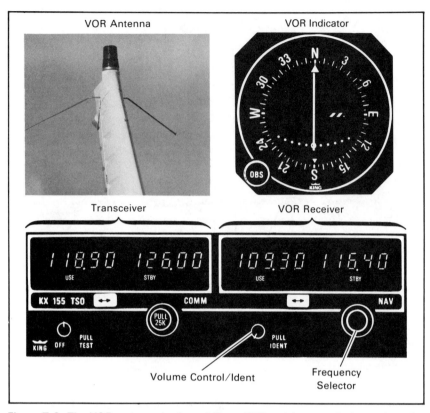

Figure 7-3. The VOR antenna is shaped like a "V" and is normally located on the vertical stabilizer or on top of the fuselage. The VOR indicator displays course information required for navigation. This VOR receiver has 50 kHz spacing which provides 200 navigation channels. By pulling the volume control knob out, you access the ident feature which permits you to identify the station.

yourself with the particular make and model you are using. Information normally is available in the POH or in separate publications from the radio manufacturer. [Figure 7-3]

VOR NAVIGATION

VOR is simple to use once you understand its basic principles. To navigate effectively with it, you must complete certain preliminary steps. The first is to obtain the VOR frequency from the appropriate aeronautical chart and enter it into the VOR receiver with the frequency selector. Next, you need to identify the station to ensure that you have picked the right frequency. You must also determine that the station is operating properly, and that you have a reliable navigation signal.

The VOR indicator has three different components which give you related navigation information. The components are the course deviation

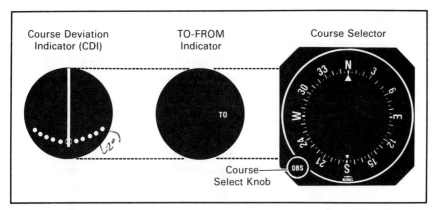

Figure 7-4. The CDI needle shows you whether you are on or off course. When it is centered, you are on course. If it swings to either side, you are off course. The TO-FROM indicator tells you whether your selected course will take you to or from the station. The course selector, also called the omnibearing selector (OBS), allows you to choose a particular radial by setting it under the course index.

indicator (CDI), the TO-FROM indicator, and the course selector. They work together to help you navigate along the course you have selected. [Figure 7-4]

COURSE INFORMATION

It is important to remember that radials travel outward from the VOR station. If you are flying away from the VOR on a given radial, your heading and the VOR course will be approximately the same. If you are going to the station, your heading will be 180° different than the radial you are following. Of course, wind can cause some heading variation, but assume a no-wind condition for this example. [Figure 7-5]

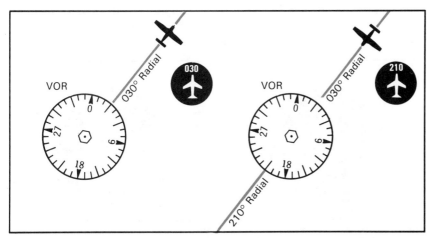

Figure 7-5. When you are flying away from a VOR station on the 030° radial (in a no-wind condition), your heading indicator will read 030°. On the other hand, if you fly inbound to the station on the 030° radial, your heading will be 210°.

If you wish to follow a particular radial to or from the station, simply set the desired course under the index at the top of the indicator. The reciprocal, or reverse course, appears under the index at the bottom of the indicator. When you are off course, the CDI points toward the desired course. The scale underneath the needle shows how far you are off course, with each dot on the scale representing a course deviation of two degrees. For example, if your CDI is deflected two dots to the left of center, your desired course is four degrees to your left. [Figure 7-6]

You should always identify a VOR station before using it for navigation.

In order to receive reliable course information, you must always identify a station before using it for navigation. A station may be identified by a three-letter Morse code signal or by a combination of code and a repetitive voice transmission that gives the name of the VOR. You can monitor the station identifier by selecting the ident feature on the VOR receiver. If you don't hear the identifier, it may mean that the station is not operating or that you are out of range of the facility. When a station is shut down for maintenance, it may radiate a T-E-S-T code (− · ··· −), or the identifier may be removed. In any case, do not use a station for navigation unless you can identify it.

TO-FROM INDICATIONS

The TO-FROM indicator helps you maintain your sense of orientation with respect to the station. With the course selector properly set, a FROM indication is shown when you are flying away from the station. When you are flying toward the station, it shows TO.

The TO-FROM indicator can also help you determine which course will provide the most direct route to a VOR station. For example, assume you are in the vicinity of a VOR and would like to fly directly to the station. After you tune and identify the station, simply turn the course selector until the TO-FROM indicator shows TO. Continue turning the selector until the CDI centers. The reading under the index is your magnetic

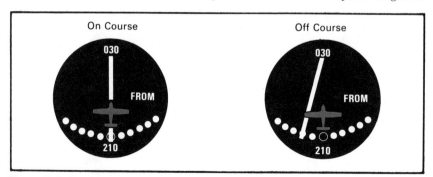

Figure 7-6. To aid in orientation, picture your airplane at the bottom of the VOR indicator. If the CDI overlaps the airplane, as it does on the left, you are on the selected course. If your airplane and the CDI are not aligned, you are off course, as shown on the right side of the illustration.

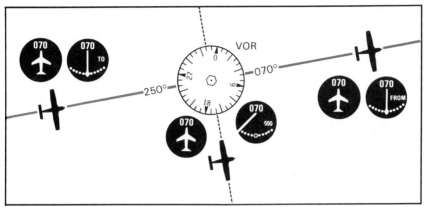

Figure 7-7. Besides signaling your position over the station, the OFF or NAV indication appears briefly when you are abeam, or 90° to either side of, your desired course. The FROM indication appears as you continue past the abeam position, even if you don't pass directly over the station.

course to the station. As you fly over the station, the TO indication disappears, and is replaced briefly by an OFF or NAV indication. On some equipment, a red flag is displayed momentarily. If these indications appear at times other than station passage, it means the VOR signal is too weak for reliable navigation. As you leave the station behind, the indicator reads FROM, meaning you are traveling away from the station. [Figure 7-7]

It is important for you to remember that the aircraft's heading has no direct relationship to the course selected in the VOR indicator. The VOR indicator reflects your position relative to the station you are receiving, regardless of the direction you are flying. However, when you actually navigate with VOR, the headings you fly will be in general agreement with your selected course. [Figure 7-8]

You can have many different magnetic headings for a single set of VOR indications.

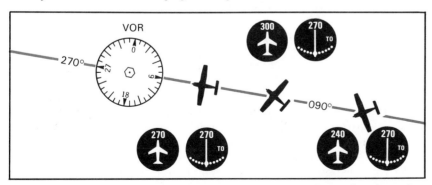

Figure 7-8. Even though the aircraft are heading in three different directions, they are all located on the 090° radial (inbound course of 270°) and have the same VOR indications. However, only the airplane nearest the station will remain on the 090° radial, provided wind is not a factor. The headings of the other two airplanes will carry them away from the course selected.

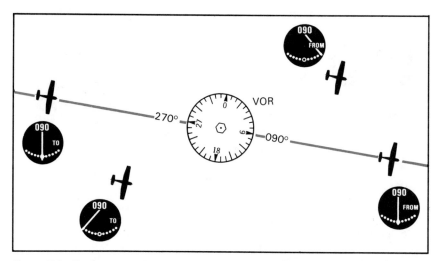

Figure 7-9. Since you are flying to the station, a magnetic course of 090° is entered in the course selector, and a TO indication is displayed. As you fly left or right of course, the CDI is deflected accordingly. When you have passed over or abeam the station, the TO indication switches to FROM.

PRACTICE PROBLEM

As an example, assume you are on a cross-country flight and want to travel to a VOR, which you will approach from the west. You intend to fly inbound on the 270° radial. Your first step is to tune and identify the station using the frequency from the sectional chart. [Figure 7-9]

If you are flying away from the station in a no-wind situation, your aircraft heading will be the same as the course selected on the VOR indicator. However, if you experience wind, your wind correction will make your heading different from the selected course.

USING VOR NAVIGATION

Wind correction is normally required to maintain course and fly a straight line to or from a VOR station.

The most common VOR navigation you will perform is flying from one station to another during cross-country flights. You will use a process called tracking to accomplish this. Tracking involves entering a course in the course selector and maintaining that course by keeping the CDI centered. To stay on track if you are experiencing a crosswind, you will use a technique called bracketing. In a crosswind situation, the wind causes you to drift off course, so you need to make a series of corrections to regain your desired course and then maintain it. [Figure 7-10]

VOR ORIENTATION

Determining your position with respect to VOR navaids is called **VOR orientation**. You have learned how to determine the magnetic course to a

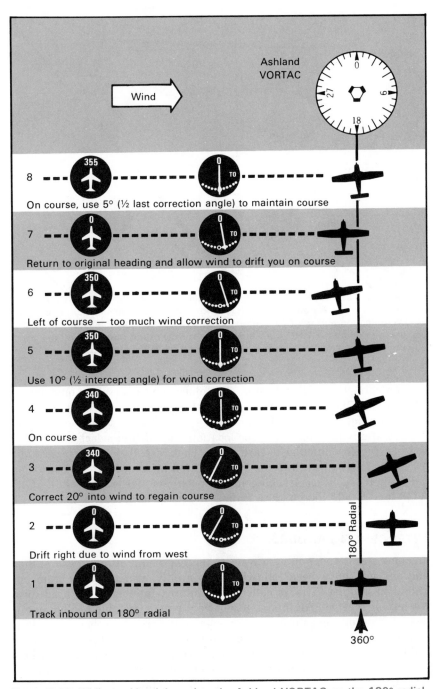

Figure 7-10. While tracking inbound to the Ashland VORTAC on the 180° radial, assume you begin to drift right of course due to a crosswind. This example shows the bracketing procedure required to regain the course and determine a heading that will compensate for wind.

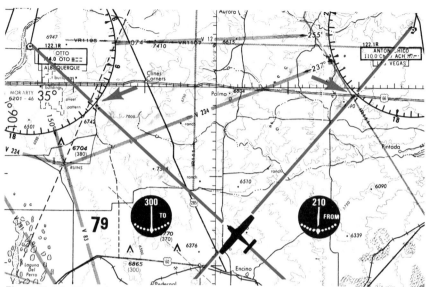

Figure 7-11. First, draw a line from Otto, following the 120° radial. After tuning and identifying the Anton Chico VORTAC, turn the course selector until you get a FROM indication and the CDI centers. In this case, the VOR indicator shows that you are located on the 210° from Anton Chico. By plotting that radial on the chart, you can see that your position is the point where the lines intersect.

You can determine your exact position on a chart using two VOR stations.

station using the VOR indicator. This places you somewhere on a particular radial. One of the ways you can tell your distance from the station on that radial is to cross-check it with a second VOR. When you use two VOR stations to determine your location, you should select radials that are nearly perpendicular to each other. That way, they will intersect at a 90° angle, and you can locate your position more accurately. For example, assume you are tracking inbound on the 120° radial of the Otto VOR, and would like to know your exact location. [Figure 7-11]

INTERCEPTING RADIALS

In some situations, you may want to navigate on a different radial than the one you have been following. Essentially, you must fly from one radial to another. This is called intercepting. Intercepts are used for a variety of reasons. An intercept will help you get established on an airway following departure for a cross-country trip. Another example is when you need to position your aircraft over a VFR checkpoint for initial callup to a TCA or ARSA. To use an intercept, you must visualize where you are from the station, and where you want to go. The intercept angle you use depends on how close you are to the station. It may range from 20° through 90°, depending on your position. The radials are closest together at the facility, much as spokes are closest together at the hub of a wheel. [Figure 7-12]

VOR CAUTIONS

There are two aspects of VOR navigation with which you should exercise caution. The first concerns unusual CDI fluctuations. Certain propeller r.p.m. settings can cause the CDI to fluctuate as much as six degrees. By varying the propeller r.p.m. slightly, you normally will eliminate this problem. The second aspect concerns a situation called reverse sensing.

The CDI may fluctuate with certain propeller r.p.m. settings.

Reverse Sensing

When your course selector is in general agreement with your heading indicator in an off-course situation, the CDI will be deflected toward the selected course. Therefore, if you want to get on course, all you need to do is correct toward the CDI. However, if you mistakenly set your course selector to the reciprocal of the desired course, your CDI will be deflected away from the course you want to follow. This situation is known as **reverse sensing**. It can be very confusing, because following the normal procedure of correcting toward the needle will actually take you farther off course. When you track to the station, you must set the VOR course selector to the reciprocal (180° opposite) of the radial you want to follow inbound.

If the course selected in your VOR indicator is in general agreement with your heading indicator, the CDI off-course indication will be in the direction of the desired course.

To illustrate this point, assume you want to track inbound on the 090° radial. In the course selector, you mistakenly enter a course of 090° and then take up a magnetic heading of 270° to get to the station. Your heading indicator now differs from the course selected by about 180°. In addition, you have a FROM indication, even though you are inbound to the station. This is a reverse sensing situation. [Figure 7-13]

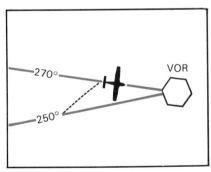

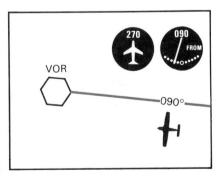

Figure 7-12. While tracking inbound on the 250° radial with a course of 070°, you decide to intercept the 270° radial inbound. After turning left to establish an intercept angle, enter the new inbound course (090°) into the course selector. When the CDI begins to center, turn right and track inbound.

Figure 7-13. Your CDI is deflected toward the left, indicating that a turn to the left will bring you on course. However, with reverse sensing, this will take you farther from course. In this situation, you should enter the desired course of 270° into the course selector so you will have a TO indication and correct sensing.

VOR ADVANTAGES

VOR has many advantages that make it popular and easy to use. Its frequency range is relatively free from precipitation static and other annoying interference caused by storms and various weather occurrences. Since it is omnidirectional (radiates in all directions), you have many possible courses to choose from. The VOR is accurate to plus or minus one degree. By keeping the needle centered, you automatically compensate for wind drift during flight. Since VOR compass roses on sectional charts are oriented toward magnetic north, you can use magnetic headings to maintain course. The following illustration provides a review of the principles of VOR navigation. [Figure 7-14]

VOR TEST SIGNALS

Before you navigate using VOR, you should check your equipment to ensure it is functioning accurately. **VOR test facilities** (VOTs) enable you to make VOR accuracy checks regardless of your position in relation to the VOT. This is possible because they broadcast the signal for only one specific radial — 360°. The first step is to get the frequency for the check from the *Airport/Facility Directory* and set it in the VOR receiver. You should also note if the VOT is for ground or airborne checks, or both. Next, check the VOT for proper operation by verifying the aural signal, which should be a series of dots or a continuous tone.

A VOT check using a course of 180° should center the CDI and give you a TO indication. Using 0° should center the CDI and give you a FROM indication.

Now you are ready to set a course of either 0° or 180° in the VOR indicator. If the course selector is set at 0°, the CDI should center and the TO-FROM indicator should read FROM. If the course selector is set at 180°, the CDI should center and the TO-FROM indicator should read TO. If the CDI doesn't center, determine the magnitude of error by rotating the course selector until the needle does center. The new course should not vary from the test course (0° or 180°) by more than four degrees.

OTHER VOR CHECKS

You can also determine the accuracy of your VOR using ground or airborne checkpoints. On the ground, you can taxi your aircraft to a specific point on the airport designated in the "VOR Receiver Check" section of the *Airport/Facility Directory* and check your VOR course reading. Then, compare this reading to the published course. The maximum permissible error is plus or minus four degrees.

Airborne checkpoints are also listed in the directory and are usually located in the immediate vicinity of airports. These checkpoints are usually placed over easily identifiable terrain or man-made features on the ground. With this type of check, the maximum permissible course error is plus or minus six degrees.

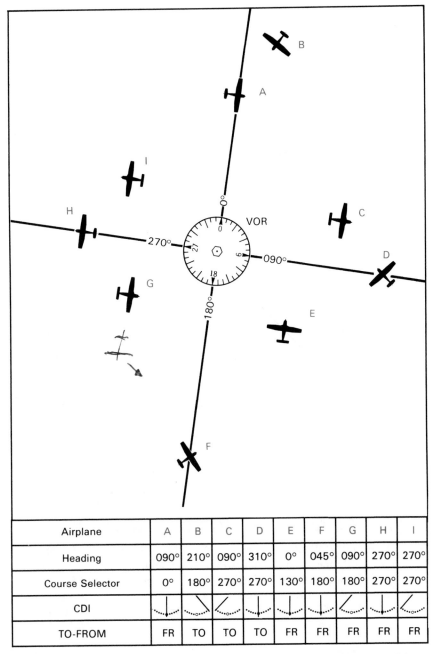

Turn them to
the course
selection
to decide
needle direction

Airplane	A	B	C	D	E	F	G	H	I
Heading	090°	210°	090°	310°	0°	045°	090°	270°	270°
Course Selector	0°	180°	270°	270°	130°	180°	180°	270°	270°
CDI									
TO-FROM	FR	TO	TO	TO	FR	FR	FR	FR	FR

Figure 7-14. You can see that there are many possible combinations of aircraft position, heading, and VOR indications. For example, airplane A is directly north of the station on the zero degree radial with a magnetic heading of 090°. With zero degrees set in the VOR indicator, the CDI will be centered with a FROM indication. Study the other airplane positions, headings, and CDI indications so you are sure you understand VOR navigation.

Another airborne check uses the VOR airways. Because the VOR airway system is tested to plus or minus one degree, you can obtain a very accurate test of your VOR. To do this, select a VOR radial that defines the centerline of a VOR airway. On this route, select a prominent terrain feature, preferably 20 miles or more from the VOR facility. Maneuver your aircraft directly over the point and note the course reading on the VOR indicator. The permissible difference between the published radial and the indicated course is six degrees. You can also conduct a VOR check by using two VOR systems which are independent of each other. If your aircraft is equipped with two VOR radios, set both to the same VOR facility and note the indicated readings on each. When you check one against the other, the maximum difference should not be greater than four degrees.

The tolerances that have been discussed regarding VOR accuracy actually are specified for IFR operations in FAR Part 91. Although regulations do not require specific VOR accuracy for VFR operations, it is appropriate to follow the IFR guidelines.

CLASSES OF VOR FACILITIES

During your flying career, you will use three classes of VOR facilities. They are the **terminal VOR** (TVOR), the **low altitude VOR** (LVOR), and **high altitude VOR** (HVOR). Each class has a different function for navigation purposes. The TVOR provides terminal guidance and, as such, should not be used farther than 25 n.m. from the station or above 12,000 feet AGL. You may use an LVOR reliably up to 40 n.m. from the station at altitudes between 1,000 and 18,000 feet AGL. At altitudes above 18,000 feet AGL, interference from other VORs with the same frequency may exist. HVOR is effective to various ranges, depending on the altitude. Many of the airways you will fly on are defined by HVORs that have a maximum reception range of 130 n.m. The class designation of a VOR facility can be found in the *Airport/Facility Directory*.

DISTANCE MEASURING EQUIPMENT (DME)

DME provides distance information in nautical miles.

VOR/DME and VORTAC facilities provide you with an added capability to course guidance — distance. **Distance measuring equipment** (DME) provides a distance reading in nautical miles from a VOR/DME or VORTAC site. Without DME, the only way to get an accurate position is to use two VOR facilities and plot your location on a chart. With DME, you need only one navaid to achieve the same result. [Figure 7-15]

DME THEORY

DME operates on a UHF frequency band of 962-1213 MHz and, like VOR, is subject to line-of-sight restrictions. Your aircraft first transmits an interrogation signal to the station. The ground station receives this signal and transmits a reply back to the aircraft. The airborne DME records the round trip time of this signal exchange and computes distance values in terms of nautical miles and groundspeed values in knots. Many DME units also provide **time to station**, which is the time it will take you to reach the station at the computed groundspeed. These values are displayed on your cockpit indicator. With enough altitude, you should be able to receive reliable signals at 199 n.m. DME normally is accurate to less than one-half a mile or three percent of the distance, whichever is greater.

USING DME

There are two things you need to be cautious about when using DME. The groundspeed reading is accurate only when you are traveling directly to or from the station. Flight in any other direction will give you an unreliable reading. Also, DME measures slant range distance, not horizontal distance. Slant range distance is the result of two components, the horizontal distance and the vertical distance. Slant range error is not considered significant if the aircraft is one mile or more from the station for every 1,000 feet of altitude. [Figure 7-16]

Slant range error is greatest when you are at a high altitude and close to the station.

DME IDENTIFICATION

When you are using both VOR and DME, it is important to ensure both systems are working properly. This is done by first entering the navigation frequency of the VORTAC into the VOR receiver. Most general aviation VOR and DME receivers have paired frequencies. When you tune

The absence of the single-coded identification signal every 30 seconds means the DME is not operational.

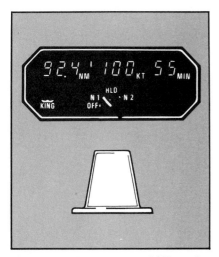

Figure 7-15. The airborne DME equipment consists of a transceiver and a "shark's fin" antenna. You will usually find the antenna on the underside of the aircraft.

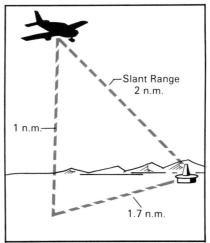

Figure 7-16. If you are flying at an altitude of 1 n.m. at a horizontal distance of 1.7 n.m. from the station, your DME will register a distance of 2 n.m. The difference is due to slant range error which is greatest directly over the station.

the VORTAC frequency, you will automatically receive DME information. Then, listen for the synchronized coded signals or voice identifications. The VOR identifier is repeated three or four times for each DME identifier. If one of the systems is not working, you will notice a gap in transmissions. A single-coded identification transmitted approximately every 30 seconds indicates the VOR is inoperative. The absence of the single-coded identification every 30 seconds indicates the DME is inoperative.

CHECKLIST

After studying this section, you should have a basic understanding of:

✓ **VOR operation** — How it works and what advantages it offers.

✓ **VOR components** — What the air and ground components are and how to check them.

✓ **VOR indicator** — What it is and the information it provides.

✓ **VOR navigation** — How to set up your equipment for proper operation, how to track by bracketing, and how to intercept radials.

✓ **Reverse sensing** — What it is, when it occurs, and how to avoid it.

✓ **DME** — What it is, how it works, and the information it provides.

✓ **Slant range error** — How it affects you and when it is greatest.

AUTOMATIC DIRECTION FINDER

Another navigation system, and one which you could use as a backup to VOR, is the **automatic direction finder** (ADF). Unlike VOR, ADF does not rely on line-of-sight transmissions. This allows reliable navigation at lower altitudes than VOR and, depending on the facility, may also provide greater reception range. Your airborne ADF equipment is capable of receiving radio signals from ground facilities called **nondirectional radio beacons** (NDBs), as well as commercial broadcast stations.

ADF equipment allows you to navigate using NDBs and commercial broadcast stations.

ADF EQUIPMENT

ADF equipment in the aircraft permits L/MF signals to be received through the antenna, relayed to the ADF receiver where they are processed, and then sent to the ADF indicator. Although most automatic direction finders have similarities in appearance and operation, you should familiarize yourself with the make and model installed in the airplane you plan to use. Consult the POH or other publication provided by the radio manufacturer. [Figure 7-17]

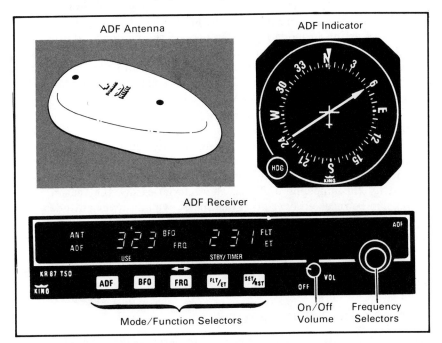

Figure 7-17. The ADF airborne equipment consists of a combined loop and sense antenna, a receiver, and an indicator. When properly tuned, the bearing pointer of the ADF indicator points to the station selected.

ADF RECEIVER

Your ADF receiver has an on/off/volume control, selectors for entering the station frequency, and several function or mode selectors. The ANT, ADF, and BFO modes are typical of most ADF receivers. Normally, you tune and identify a station with the ANT mode, since it provides maximum sensitivity to radio signals. After you enter the charted NDB or broadcast station frequency into the receiver, you typically increase the volume until you can hear background noise, then readjust it for comfortable listening volume. Always identify the station positively by listening to the Morse code identification. You may also use the ANT mode to monitor voice transmissions such as weather broadcasts. The bearing pointer of the ADF indicator does not function in this mode.

The BFO (beat frequency oscillator) mode is for tuning and identifying CW (continuous wave) signals. CW signals are unmodulated compared to normal NDB signals. While tuning in the BFO mode, you determine maximum signal reception by the strength of the audio tone; that is, a maximum signal provides the strongest audio. Within the conterminous U.S., the BFO system usually is not required for station identification.

Always use the test function to verify that the bearing pointer is responding to a reliable signal.

Once you have tuned and identified the station, place the switch in the ADF mode, which allows the receiver to send navigation information to the ADF indicator. You should then notice the needle on the bearing indicator starting to move as it searches for the station's relative position. Once a strong signal from the station is found, the needle will stop searching and steady itself. At this time, you should use the ADF test function to ensure the signal is reliable. Check your operator's handbook to see how this function works on the ADF you will be using.

NDBs transmit ground and sky waves in the low and medium frequency ranges.

NDBs are shown on aeronautical charts and can be used for either VFR or IFR operations. They transmit low/medium frequency (L/MF) signals in the frequency range of 190 to 535 kHz. These signals travel both as ground waves that penetrate obstacles and as sky waves that are refracted by the ionosphere. These characteristics are the reason L/MF waves can be received over great distances, even at lower altitudes.

Selected commercial broadcast stations of the AM class are also shown on aeronautical charts. AM radio stations use the frequency range from 535 to 1605 kHz. However, their use is restricted to VFR operations, since they are required to identify themselves only once each hour.

ADF BEARING INDICATORS

An ADF bearing reflects the horizontal direction, or angle, between your aircraft and the station.

With L/MF facilities, bearings are used to describe your position rather than radials. A **bearing** is the horizontal direction to or from any point, which is measured clockwise through 360° from magnetic north. A bearing indicator gives you the horizontal direction, or angle, between your aircraft and the L/MF station. Actually, there are two types of bearing indicators — the fixed card and the movable card. Initially, we will discuss the fixed-card indicator. You will learn more about the movable card later in this section.

The fixed-card bearing indicator measures **relative bearing** — the number of degrees between the nose, or longitudinal axis, of your aircraft and the station. If you wish to fly directly to the station, you must add your magnetic heading to your relative bearing. This value is called **magnetic bearing**; it will take you directly to the station. Stated in formula terms, magnetic heading (MH) + relative bearing (RB) = magnetic bearing (MB). If the total is more than 360°, you will need to subtract 360° to find the magnetic bearing to the station. [Figure 7-18]

According to the ADF formula, MH + RB = MB.

HOMING

A procedure where you always keep the nose of the aircraft pointing directly to the station is called **homing** to the station. You do this by keeping the fixed-card bearing pointer on the aircraft's nose, or at 0°. In a no-wind situation, the magnetic heading will remain constant as you fly inbound to the station. However, in a crosswind situation, the wind will push you off course, and you must adjust the magnetic heading to keep the nose of the aircraft pointing toward the station. [Figure 7-19]

Homing to the station results in a curved flight path in crosswind condition.

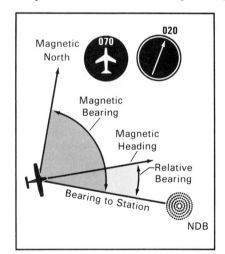

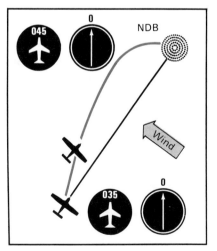

Figure 7-18. In this sample problem, the ADF bearing indicator is pointing 020° to the right of the aircraft's nose. This is a 020° relative bearing. To find the magnetic bearing to the station, read the magnetic heading of 070° from the heading indicator, then use the formula to determine the magnetic bearing: MH (070°) + RB (020°) = MB (090°). This means you should maintain a course of 90° to get to the station.

Figure 7-19. The curved, blue line represents your flight path while homing to the station in a right crosswind. When using this method, your flight path over the ground is uncertain; and the distance you travel can vary greatly, depending on the wind velocity and the distance to the station. In a no-wind situation, your flight path would follow the black line.

ORIENTATION

Assume you want to locate your position on a chart. To do this, you will need to determine the **reciprocal bearing**, which is the bearing from the station. First, add your relative bearing and your magnetic heading to determine your magnetic bearing to the station. Next, you will need to find the reciprocal bearing by adding 180° to or subtracting 180° from the magnetic bearing. If the magnetic bearing is less than 180°, add 180°; if it is more than 180°, subtract 180° to get the reciprocal. For example, if your magnetic bearing to the station is 090°, the reciprocal bearing is 270° (090° + 180° = 270°). If your magnetic bearing is 210°, the reciprocal is 30° (210° - 180° = 30°).

Some people find it easier to determine the reciprocal of the magnetic bearing by using the 200/20 rule. If the magnetic bearing is less than 180°, add 200 to the number and subtract 20. If the number is greater than 180°, subtract 200 and add 20 to find the reciprocal of the magnetic bearing.

To plot your position on a chart, convert the magnetic bearing to true bearing.

The magnetic bearing reciprocal would be easy to plot if the station on the chart had a magnetic compass rose surrounding it. However, since a chart depiction of an NDB does not have a compass rose, you will have to plot your azimuth with reference to grid lines. Since grid lines are referenced to true north instead of magnetic north, you will have to convert your magnetic values to true values. If you remember from Chapter 6, this is accomplished by adding or subtracting variation. However, when you convert magnetic values to true values, you add easterly variation and subtract westerly variation. After you have made this final computation, the result is called **true bearing**, which is your horizontal direction from the station with respect to true north. Now, plot this line by placing the edge of your plotter on the NDB and rotating it until the compass rose intersects a line of longitude at the same angle as your true bearing. By drawing this line on the chart, you will have narrowed your position down to some point on that line. To find your exact location, you can use a second navaid, as discussed in the VOR section. You may also locate your position with respect to identifiable landmarks or terrain beneath you.

TRACKING

The best way for you to get to or from a station is in a straight line, which requires tracking if any wind is present. The tracking procedure you learned in VOR is similar to the procedure used for ADF. It involves flying into the wind to compensate for its effect on your flight path. However, fixed-card ADF does not provide an automatic wind correction angle. Bracketing is required to determine the WCA, and then a corresponding bearing is used to maintain a steady track. [Figure 7-20]

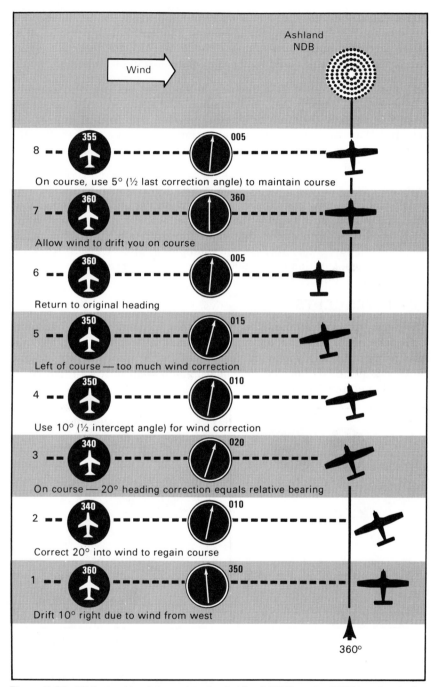

Wind

Ashland
NDB

8 — On course, use 5° (½ last correction angle) to maintain course

7 — Allow wind to drift you on course

6 — Return to original heading

5 — Left of course — too much wind correction

4 — Use 10° (½ intercept angle) for wind correction

3 — On course — 20° heading correction equals relative bearing

2 — Correct 20° into wind to regain course

1 — Drift 10° right due to wind from west

360°

Figure 7-20. While tracking inbound to the Ashland NDB on the 360° bearing to the station, assume you begin to drift right of course due to a crosswind. This example shows the bracketing procedures necessary to regain course and determine a heading that will correct for wind.

When you are on course, the wind correction angle should be exactly equal to the number of degrees the bearing indicator points left or right of the aircraft's nose. For example, if your WCA is 10° left, the station will be 10° to the right, and the bearing pointer will also indicate 10°.

ADF station passage is indicated when the needle shows either wingtip position or settles at or near the 180° position.

As you pass over the station, the needle tends to fluctuate. You are cautioned not to "chase" the needle, since many of the indications are erroneous close to the station. When the needle stabilizes at or near the 180° position, you have passed the station. If you do not pass directly over the facility, station passage occurs when the needle is steady and points to either wingtip position.

You can track outbound the same way you tracked inbound. With outbound tracking, however, the wind correction angle should be exactly equal to the number of degrees the station is located to the left or right of the aircraft's tail. Remember, the tail of the aircraft is the 180° position on the fixed-card indicator. As an example, assume you are tracking outbound from a station on the 090° bearing and experience a crosswind from the north. [Figure 7-21]

ADF INTERCEPTS

ADF intercepts are accomplished in a manner similar to those required for bracketing procedures, but the angles used are much greater. Use the ADF formula to help you with this procedure. Assume you are located southwest of an NDB on the 250° bearing and want to track inbound to the station on the 270° bearing. [Figure 7-22]

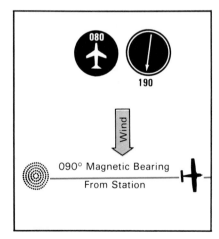

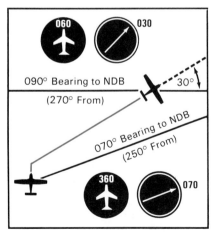

Figure 7-21. After you regain the course, take up a heading of 080° and notice the relative bearing remains at 190°. Use the ADF formula to determine the magnetic bearing to the station (80° + 190° = 270°). This means that 80° should result in a straight line course outbound from the station.

Figure 7-22. A heading of 060° will give you an intercept angle of 30° to the 090° bearing to the station (270° from). When the bearing pointer indicates 30°, you will know you have intercepted the 90° bearing to the station (270° from), and you can turn inbound.

MOVABLE-CARD INDICATORS

The movable-card bearing indicator is almost identical to the fixed-card indicator. The only difference is that you can rotate the movable card manually to reflect the aircraft heading at the top of the instrument. By putting the magnetic heading value under the top index of the ADF indicator, the bearing pointer will directly indicate magnetic bearing to a station. In addition, the number under the tail of the needle indicates magnetic bearing from the station.

The movable card reduces your workload in the cockpit, since it does not require you to use the ADF formula to find the magnetic bearing. In the next section, you will see that movable-card indicators have some of the same capabilities as the radio magnetic indicator (RMI).

ADF CAUTIONS

You should be aware of the limitations concerning L/MF navigation. First of all, the VFR reception range for L/MF facilities can vary greatly, depending on transmitter power, atmospheric conditions, and time of day. The ADF indicator does not have an OFF flag, so the tendency may be to use it when the signals are unreliable. A proper identification and test will counter this problem. You also should continuously monitor the station's ident feature, keeping in mind that commercial broadcast stations may not identify themselves regularly. The ident information for NDBs can be found in the associated frequency box on sectional charts. You also can find NDBs within the airport listings in the *Airport/Facility Directory*. These listings include the NDB name, power classification, and frequency.

The ADF indicator has no provision to warn you of unreliable signals.

You should also be aware that reliable ADF navigation is dependent upon the accuracy of the heading indicator. If the heading indicator has precessed 10°, tracking procedures and intercepts will be in error by 10°. Although this may not be very significant during inbound tracking, during outbound tracking over large distances, the error is multiplied. You can be miles off course and yet be completely unaware of your predicament. Be sure your heading indicator is in agreement with the magnetic compass.

The remaining limitations concern L/MF radio waves in general. Sometimes the signals are refracted by the ionosphere and return to earth 30 to 60 miles or more from the station. This leads to needle fluctuations on the ADF indicator. The phenomenon is called **twilight effect**, so named because the occurrence is most pronounced during the period just before and just after sunrise or sunset. To minimize the effect, you can average the fluctuations or fly higher. You also can select a station transmitting on frequencies lower than 350 kHz, since twilight effect has little impact on this portion of the frequency range.

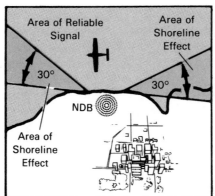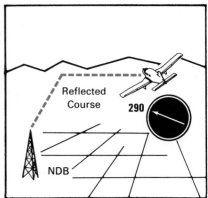

Figure 7-23. Shorelines can refract low frequency radio waves when they cross at small angles. However, radio waves that pass from land to water at angles greater than 30° have little or no shoreline effect. You can minimize this phenomenon by using stations where the signals cross the shoreline at angles greater than 30°. Terrain effect normally occurs in mountainous areas, since mountains have the ability to reflect radio waves. This can cause large fluctuations in bearing indications, as well as false courses. You should use only stations that give you strong steady signals while flying near mountainous areas.

Near thunderstorms, the bearing pointer may respond to lightning flashes. This is known as **thunderstorm effect**. You can compensate for it by disregarding the ADF indications during lightning flashes. Another problem can be interference from **precipitation static**, which is caused by a buildup of static electricity on an aircraft flying in rain, snow, or clouds. In severe cases, the bearing indicator may wander aimlessly, and you may not be able to identify the station properly. Two other problems associated with L/MF navigation include **shoreline effect** and **terrain effect**. [Figure 7-23]

CHECKLIST ━━━━━━━━━━━━━━━━━━━━

After studying this section, you should have a basic understanding of:

✓ **L/MF facilities** — What types there are and the advantages they offer.

✓ **ADF components** — What the air and ground components are and how to use them.

✓ **Bearing** — What the different types are and how they are measured.

✓ **ADF navigation** — How to determine position, what the homing procedure is, how to bracket a bearing, and how to intercept a predetermined bearing and track inbound or outbound.

✓ **ADF cautions** — What they are and how to counter them.

ADVANCED NAVIGATION

As your flying career progresses, you will see more and more advanced navigation systems and equipment in the airplanes you fly. This discussion is designed to give you an overall view of the capabilities of some of these navigation systems; it is not intended to make you operationally proficient. If you need detailed information, refer to the POH or manufacturer's description for the particular equipment in question.

VORTAC-BASED RNAV

So far, you have become familiar with VOR and ADF, which are the systems you will probably use most frequently in the beginning. The next step for many pilots is area navigation. **Area navigation** (RNAV) allows you more lateral freedom in navigating, because it does not require you to track directly to or from navigation facilities. RNAV systems which utilize VOR/DME or VORTAC sites are referred to as VORTAC-based. **VORTAC-based area navigation** provides you with both course and distance information and allows you to fly to a predetermined point without overflying VOR/DME or VORTAC facilities. You benefit in many ways with this capability, since direct routing saves time, improves fuel economy, and lowers operating expenses. [Figure 7-24]

RNAV allows you to fly a straight path directly to your destination.

RNAV OPERATION

With RNAV, you have complete flexibility for determining the course you want to fly. VORTAC-based RNAV uses a **courseline computer** (CLC) which permits you to create "phantom stations" for use in navigation. Basically, the computer relocates, or offsets, the navigation aid to the desired radial and distance from the original location. You use a control panel to enter the amount of offset you want. The computer uses this

VORTAC-based RNAV allows you to offset a ground station to a specified distance along any desired radial from the facility.

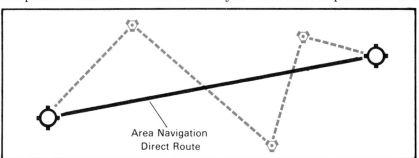

Area Navigation
Direct Route

Figure 7-24. With VOR routes, you typically travel from facility to facility. With RNAV capability, you can eliminate the zigzag flight path and fly in a straight line.

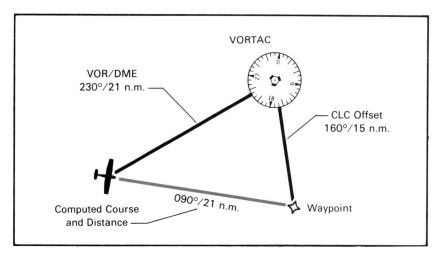

Figure 7-25. Your courseline computer compares the angle and distance between your aircraft and the VORTAC to the angle and distance between the VORTAC and the waypoint. By doing this, it knows two sides of a triangle and continuously solves for the third side, giving you angle and distance information from your position to the waypoint.

information to create the phantom stations, or **waypoints**. For a long cross-country flight, you will have a series of waypoints which collectively define an RNAV route. [Figure 7-25]

Another desirable RNAV feature is that you navigate using the VOR indicator. With RNAV, the needle deflections still indicate course displacement, but the deviation scale is in nautical miles and not degrees. Each dot on the horizontal scale represents a given value, such as .5 n.m. or 10 n.m., depending on what the manufacturer has set. When you are using RNAV, the DME will show the correct distance from you to the waypoint, but the groundspeed information also depends on the manufacturer. Some groundspeed readouts indicate the groundspeed in relation to the original facility, not the waypoint. Be sure to study the information supplied by the manufacturer for the RNAV equipment you are using.

LORAN

Long range navigation, or **LORAN,** is a leading navigation system. The popularity of LORAN is based on its capabilities, simplicity of operation, and low cost. LORAN was first used for navigation by the maritime industry in boats and ships. Early models of LORAN equipment were so heavy and cumbersome they were impractical for light aircraft, but technological advances in microprocessors and miniature circuitry led to lightweight versions suitable for aviation. As a result, more and more LORAN receivers are being found in the general aviation aircraft of today, and chances are good you will fly a plane that has LORAN in it.

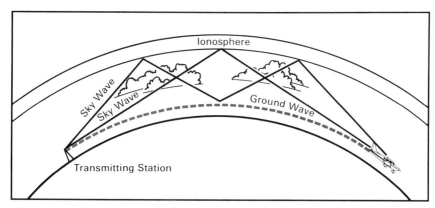

Figure 7-26. Since low frequency ground waves follow the contour of the earth, the reception range of LORAN signals is great (often 600 to 1,200 n.m. over land), and the transmitters can be located several hundred miles apart. Sky waves are also formed by LORAN signals but are not considered as reliable for navigation as ground waves.

The LORAN receiver you use will get its position information from a chain of low frequency (LF) transmitters. The chain transmits a synchronized signal on a frequency of 100 kHz in the form of ground and sky waves. [Figure 7-26]

You will find there are many types of LORAN receivers on the market with very different capabilities and operating requirements. The various receivers are differentiated primarily by the software programs or data bases they use. Generally, the more sophisticated a receiver is, the more capability it has, and the more extensive its data base. [Figure 7-27]

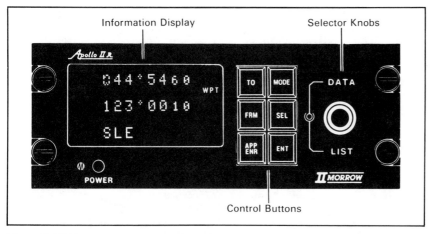

Figure 7-27. Although individual LORAN units vary considerably, this one has typical controls and display features and includes a major data base. Among other features, the data base contains the latitude, longitude, and identifier for over 2,500 waypoints, including all federally designated airports and VORs in the continental United States.

A typical LORAN receiver can compute bearing and distance from your present position to your intended destination. However, some data bases can give you navigation information, such as wind direction and velocity, fuel consumption, nearest airports in case of an in-flight emergency, audible warnings before you enter special use airspace, radio frequencies, and phone numbers. This is why it is so important to study the manufacturer's handbook to determine the capabilities of the particular LORAN set you are using.

LORAN OPERATION

In a typical LORAN chain, one transmitter is the master and two or more others are called secondaries. The master station transmits a group of coded pulses first; then, each secondary station transmits at a specific time interval after the master pulse. The time interval between one master pulse and the next is referred to as a **group repetition interval** (GRI). A GRI of 9940 means the master station pulses every 99,400 microseconds (millionths of a second). The GRI is unique to each chain and, in fact, identifies the chain. You use the GRI when you select a particular LORAN chain.

LORAN determines your position by measuring differences in radio signal arrival time.

Next, you need to determine your location. Your LORAN receiver does this by measuring the **time difference** (TD) between a master station's signal and that of a secondary station. In other words, how long did it take for the master station's signal to reach you compared to the secondary signal? If this time difference were plotted on a chart, it would produce a **line of position** (LOP). [Figure 7-28]

The LORAN receiver automatically calculates your LOP fix, translates it into latitude and longitude values, and continuously updates your present position as you travel. Once the receiver has determined where you are, you can enter the coordinates of your destination, as well as other

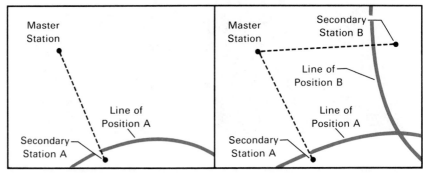

Figure 7-28. The line of position (LOP) in the left illustration represents all points with the same time difference (TD) between the master and one secondary. Your position is somewhere on this line. For the LORAN receiver to pinpoint your location, a second LOP needs to be determined using another secondary. Your present position is where the two LOPs intersect, as shown in the right illustration.

waypoints. The receiver will calculate the course and distance to the point you specified, and continually update this information as you progress along your flight path. Most receivers will also give your groundspeed, as well as distance and time remaining to the destination.

LORAN CAUTIONS

Although LORAN is a popular navigation system, it does have some drawbacks. Since LORAN uses a low frequency AM radio signal, electrical disturbances such as thunderstorms and precipitation static can cause interference. It is not unusual to experience signal loss when you are flying in areas of electrical activity or heavy precipitation. An aircraft passing through rain, ice, or snow builds up a static charge which degrades signal reception. Static discharge wicks on airfoil trailing edges, fuselage grounding, and special antenna coatings are used to combat precipitation static.

A major limitation of LORAN deals with characteristics of the radio signals themselves. Even though they are very accurate (especially over water), they have a tendency to travel over land at different speeds. Surface type, foliage, seasonal changes, and weather can affect the speed of the radio waves and, consequently, their accuracy. You can use LORAN for enroute navigation, since this problem isn't significant. However, these problems and current specification requirements prohibit the use of LORAN as an instrument approach aid. Many LORAN receivers are classified as "VFR Only" because of these and other concerns.

Surface type, foliage, seasonal changes, and weather affect LORAN signals.

ADVANCED NAVIGATION INDICATORS

You have already become familiar with the VOR and ADF systems and their associated navigation indicators. More advanced indicators have come into the marketplace, with the aim of simplifying navigation by providing more information on a single indicator. This is usually done by combining two or more instrument indicators into one. You will see these indicators more and more in the airplanes you fly. In the remaining discussion, you will become familiar with two of them.

RMI

The **radio magnetic indicator** combines the heading indicator with two bearing pointers. One functions like an ADF bearing indicator, while the other points to VOR stations. An RMI usually has a single-bar needle and a double-bar needle superimposed over a slaved compass card that is referenced to magnetic north. The single-bar needle normally points to a VOR station, while the double-bar needle may use either a VOR or an NDB facility, depending on the manufacturer. This provides you with constant position orientation, since the needles indicate magnetic bearing to their respective stations. The number under the tail of each needle indicates magnetic bearing from the appropriate station. Whereas the

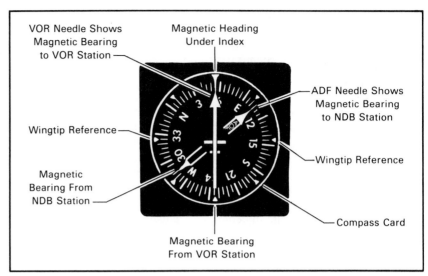

Figure 7-29. According to this RMI, you are located on the 235° radial of a VOR and are tracking inbound on a heading of 055°. You are also on the 105° bearing to an NDB facility. If you want to track inbound to the NDB, turn directly to the station (heading 105°) and apply wind correction, as needed.

fixed-card ADF indicator requires you to use the ADF formula to find the magnetic bearing, the movable card in the RMI indicator displays magnetic bearings directly. This reduces your workload in the cockpit.

Navigating with RMI is much like navigating with VOR or ADF, depending on which needle and ground facility you use. The advantage of RMI is the combination of two navigation instruments on a properly oriented heading indicator. As you track inbound toward one facility, you can monitor your progress with the other indicator. Also, with two needles at your disposal, you can plot your position on a chart very easily. You should remember to consider variation when you plot your ADF bearing on sectional and WAC charts, since the charts are oriented toward true north. [Figure 7-29]

During a VOT check, the needle of an RMI should point to 180°, plus or minus four degrees.

Since the VOR pointer in the RMI depends on the VOR equipment, you need to check it for accuracy. The VOT check for an RMI is slightly different than the check for a VOR. When your VOR receiver is properly tuned to the VOT frequency, the RMI needle should indicate 180°, plus or minus four degrees.

HORIZONTAL SITUATION INDICATOR

VOR course deviation, magnetic heading, and glide slope data are shown on an HSI.

You will find that many high-performance airplanes are equipped with a **horizontal situation indicator** (HSI). The HSI combines the functions of the heading indicator and the VOR indicator in one display. This provides you with an accurate navigation picture on a single instrument.

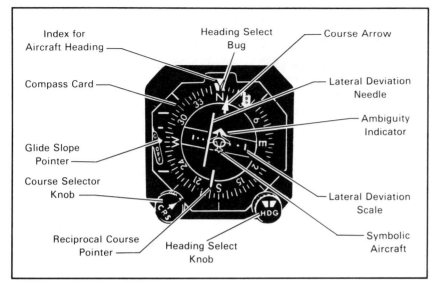

Figure 7-30. The course arrow and the reciprocal course pointer move when you turn the course selector knob. Notice the symbolic aircraft in the center, which represents your aircraft's position with respect to the desired course. Three OFF flags are usually incorporated in the HSI display to alert you to unreliable signals or equipment malfunctions.

The HSI also presents glide slope information, which can be used by instrument pilots during ILS approaches. [Figure 7-30]

The HSI has several components that help you navigate. The compass card provides you with the magnetic heading under the index at the top of the instrument. The heading select bug is used with an autopilot and automatically turns the aircraft to a newly selected heading. The HSI also incorporates the VOR course indications. The lateral deviation needle performs the same function as the CDI in a basic VOR indicator, depicting how far you are off course. When you are on course, the lateral deviation needle is aligned with the course arrow and the reciprocal course pointer.

The display shows the course selected, as well as its reciprocal. You will benefit from having a reverse course readily available during navigation. Another benefit for you is the ambiguity indicator, which does the same thing as the TO-FROM indicator on the conventional VOR. The arrowhead shifts to point rearward when you cross over a VOR station. Glide slope information is also displayed on the HSI. The glide slope pointer indicates aircraft position in relation to the ILS glide slope. If the pointer is above the center position, the aircraft is below the glide slope, and vice versa.

CHECKLIST ━━━━━━━━━━━━━━━━━━━━

After studying this section, you should have a basic understanding of:

✓ **VORTAC-based RNAV** — What it is, how it operates, and the advantages of using it.

✓ **LORAN** — How it operates and what information it provides.

✓ **RMI** — What it is, how it works, and the advantages it provides.

✓ **HSI** — What information you get from it and how it relates to VOR.

CHAPTER 8

AVIATION PHYSIOLOGY

INTRODUCTION

An understanding of how your body and mind work when you fly is just as important as knowing how the systems and equipment work in your airplane. You are, in fact, the most important element in the airplane, and how well you function has a direct influence on flight safety. What you learn in this chapter can help you deal with the limitations of both your body and the environment in which you operate. Section A discusses the eye and how your vision works in bright sunlight, as well as at night. It also covers some of the common visual illusions and how you can counteract them. Section B looks at spatial disorientation and some of the confusing sensory inputs encountered in flight. Section C covers the effects of flying in reduced atmospheric pressure and what happens when your normal respiration is changed. The subject of Section D is human performance and how it is affected by alcohol and drugs. When you finish this chapter, you should have a better understanding of how your body functions and reacts to the various environmental situations encountered during flight.

VISION IN FLIGHT

Vision is by far the most important sense that we have, and flying is obviously impossible without it. Nearly everything that we perceive is visual or heavily supplemented by vision. The visual sense is especially important in collision avoidance and depth perception. Our vision sensors are our eyes, and they are not perfect in the way they function or see objects. Our eyes are not always able to see all things at all times: illusions and blindspots occur. The more you understand the eye and how it functions, the easier it will be to compensate for these illusions and blindspots.

THE EYE

Vision is primarily the result of light striking a photosensitive layer, called the **retina**, at the back of the eye. The retina is made of light-sensitive cones and rods. The cones in your eye perceive an image best when the light is bright, while the rods work best in low light. Your brain interprets what an image looks like by the pattern of light that strikes the cones and rods. Some information, such as movement and basic shapes, is actually processed on the retina itself, while other key features are sent by the optic nerve to the brain for processing there. [Figure 8-1]

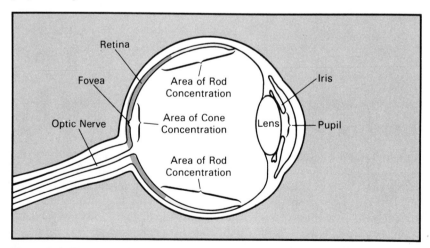

Figure 8-1. The eye works in much the same way as a camera. Both have an adjustable opening, or iris, to allow light in; a lens that focuses the image; and something to receive and record the image. The receptor in a camera is film; in the eye the receptors are rods and cones. These receptors instantly record the image and transmit it through the optic nerve to the brain for interpretation. Your eyes are like a camera with a never-ending roll of film.

CONES

Cones are concentrated around the center of the retina. They gradually diminish in number as the distance from the center increases. Cones allow you to perceive color by sensing red, blue, and green light. Directly behind the lens on the retina is a small, notched area called the **fovea**. This area contains only a high concentration of cone receptors. When you look directly at an object, the image is focused mainly on the fovea. The cones, however, do not function well in darkness, which explains why we cannot see color as vividly at night as we can during the day. [Figure 8-2]

RODS

The rods are our dim light and night receptors and are concentrated outside the fovea area. The number of rods increases as the distance from the fovea increases. Rods "see" only in black and white. Because the rods are not located directly behind the pupil, they are responsible for much of our peripheral vision. Images that move are perceived more easily by the rod areas than by the cones in the fovea. If you have ever seen something move out of the corner of your eye, it was most likely detected by your rod receptors.

Since the cones do not see well in the dark, you may not be able to see an object if you look directly at it. The concentration of cones in the fovea can make a night blindspot at the center of your vision. To see an object

Off-center viewing should be used at night. This helps compensate for the night blindspot in the center of your vision.

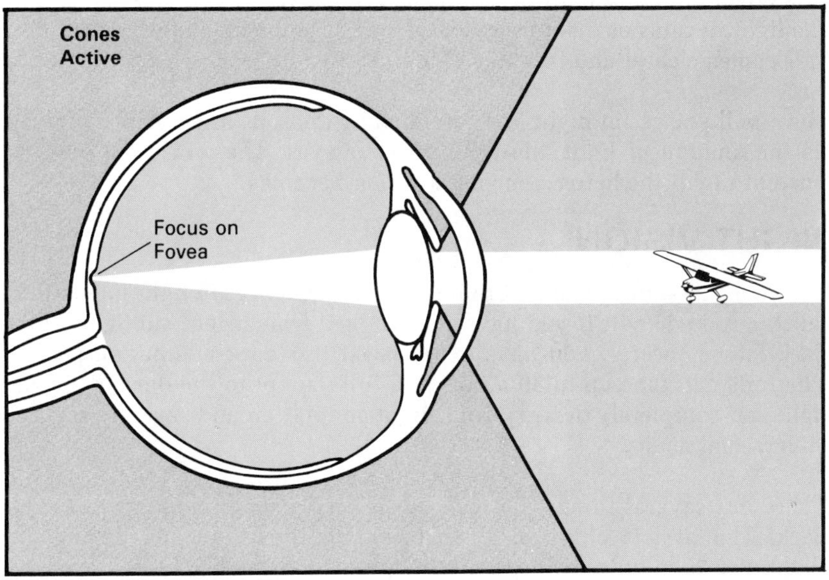

Figure 8-2. The best vision in daylight is obtained by looking directly at the object. This focuses the image on the fovea, which "sees" detail best.

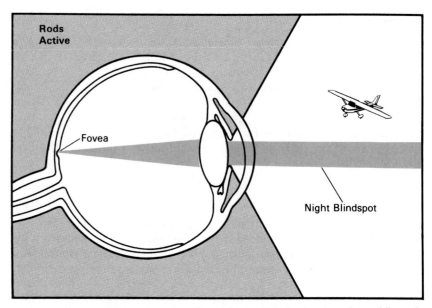

Figure 8-3. In low light, the cones lose much of their visual acuity, while rods become more receptive. The eye sacrifices sharpness for sensitivity. Your ability to see an object directly in front of you is reduced, and you lose much of your depth perception, as well as your judgment of size.

clearly, you must expose the rods to the image. This is accomplished by looking 5° to 10° off center of the object you want to see. You can try out this effect on a dim light in a darkened room. When you look directly at the light, it dims or disappears altogether. If you look slightly off center, it becomes clearer and brighter. [Figure 8-3]

How well you see at night is determined by the rods in your eyes, as well as the amount of light allowed into your eyes. The wider the pupil is open at night, the better your night vision becomes.

NIGHT VISION

The cones in your eyes adapt quite rapidly to changes in light intensities, but the rods do not. If you have ever walked from bright sunlight into a dark movie theater, you have experienced this dark adaptation period. The rods can take up to 30 minutes to fully adapt to the dark. A bright light can completely destroy your night adaptation and severely restrict your visual acuity.

Bright lights should be avoided for at least 30 minutes before a night flight.

There are several things you can do to keep your eyes adapted to the dark. The first is obvious; avoid bright lights before and during the flight. For 30 minutes before a night flight, avoid any bright light sources such as headlights, landing lights, strobe lights, or flashlights. If you encounter a bright light, close one eye to keep it light sensitive. This will allow you to see again once the light is gone. Light sensitivity also can be gained by using sunglasses if you will be flying from daylight into an area of increasing darkness.

Red cockpit lighting also helps preserve your night vision. But, red light severely distorts some colors, especially those found on aeronautical charts. A dim white light or carefully directed flashlight can enhance your night reading ability. While flying at night, keep the instrument panel and interior lights turned up no higher than necessary. This helps you see outside visual references more easily. If your eyes become blurry, blinking more frequently will often help.

> Red cockpit lighting enhances dark adaptation, while regular white light, such as that from a flashlight, impairs your night adaptation.

Your diet and general physical health have an impact on how well you can see in the dark. Deficiencies in vitamins A and C have been shown to reduce night acuity. Other factors, such as carbon monoxide poisoning, smoking, alcohol, certain drugs, and a lack of oxygen also can greatly decrease your night vision.

NIGHT SCANNING

Good night visual acuity also is needed for collision avoidance. Night scanning is much like the day scanning technique discussed in Chapter 2. Unlike day scanning, however, off-center viewing is used to focus objects on the rods rather than the fovea blindspot.

> When scanning for traffic at night, move your eyes slowly and in small sectors. Use off-center viewing and avoid staring in one place for too long.

When you look at an object, avoid staring at it too long. If you stare at an object without moving your eyes, the retina becomes accustomed to the light intensity and the image begins to fade. To keep it clearly visible, new areas in the retina must be exposed to the image. Small, circular eye movements help eliminate the fading. You also need to move your eyes more slowly from sector to sector than during the day to prevent blurring.

AIRCRAFT LIGHTING

In order for us to see other aircraft more clearly, regulations require that all aircraft operated during the night hours have special lights and equipment. The requirements for operating at night are found in FAR Part 91. In addition to aircraft lighting, the regulations also provide a definition of nighttime, currency requirements, fuel reserves, and necessary electrical systems.

Position lights enable you to see where an aircraft is, as well as its direction of flight. The approved aircraft lights for night operations are a green light on the right wingtip, a red light on the left wingtip, and a white position light on the tail. In addition, flashing aviation red or white

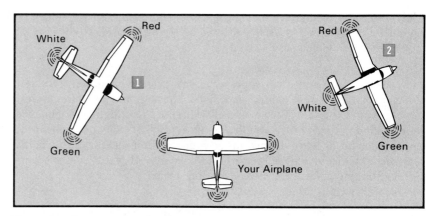

Figure 8-4. By interpreting the position lights on other aircraft, you can determine whether the aircraft is flying away from you or is on a collision course. If you see a red position light to the right of a green light, such as shown by aircraft number 1, it is flying toward you. You should watch this aircraft closely and be ready to change course. Aircraft number 2, on the other hand, is flying away from you, as indicated by the white position light.

anticollision lights are required for night flights. These flashing lights can be in a number of locations, but are most commonly found on the wingtips or tail. [Figure 8-4]

VISUAL ILLUSIONS

There are many different types of visual illusions. You can experience them at any time, day or night. The next few paragraphs cover some of the illusions that commonly occur at night and some that you may encounter during the approach and landing.

AUTOKINESIS

Autokinesis is caused by staring at a single point of light against a dark background, such as a ground light or bright star, for more than a few seconds. After a few moments, the light will appear to move on its own. If you attempt to align the aircraft in sole relation to the light, you can lose control of the airplane. Guard against this situation by keeping a normal visual scan and referring frequently to the instruments.

NIGHT MYOPIA

Another problem associated with night flying is night myopia, or night-induced nearsightedness. It is similar to empty field myopia, but is more pronounced because of the lack of visual references. With nothing to focus on, your eyes automatically focus on a point three to six feet in front of you. This happens less frequently to pilots who are more than 40 years old. Searching out and focusing on distant light sources, no matter how dim, will help prevent the onset of night myopia.

LANDING ILLUSIONS

Landing illusions occur in many forms. Above featureless terrain or at night, there is a natural tendency to fly a lower-than-normal approach. Elements that cause any type of visual obscuration such as rain, haze, or a dark runway environment also can cause low approaches. Bright runway lights, steep surrounding terrain, and a wide runway can produce the illusion of being too low, and there is the tendency to fly a higher-than-normal approach. [Figure 8-5]

Your landing approaches at night should be made the same as during daytime to reduce the possibility of landing illusions.

Another type of landing illusion is produced by a sloping runway. It's not uncommon to find public airports that have runways with a grade, or slope, of three percent or more. On a 6,000-foot runway, a three percent grade means a 180-foot elevation difference between the approach and departure ends. There are many private airports that have even more grade. These runways appear very steep and give a very strong landing illusion. If you are aware of the contributing factors that lead to these types of visual illusions you will be able to identify them long before they become problems. For advance warning of conditions that could cause visual illusions, consult the aeronautical chart and *Airport/Facility Directory* for your destination airport. When available, take advantage of a visual approach slope indicator system to verify your landing approach.

Using the information supplied by a visual approach slope indicator system helps to verify approach height and descent rate and eliminates many of the visual landing illusions.

APPROACH ILLUSIONS		
Situation	**Illusion**	**Result**
Upsloping Runway or Terrain	Greater Height	Lower Approaches
Narrower-Than-Usual Runway	Greater Height	Lower Approaches
Featureless Terrain	Greater Height	Lower Approaches
Rain on Windscreen	Greater Height	Lower Approaches
Haze	Greater Height	Lower Approaches
Downsloping Runway or Terrain	Less Height	Higher Approaches
Wider-Than-Usual Runway	Less Height	Higher Approaches
Bright Runway and Approach Lights	Less Distance	Higher Approaches
Penetration of Fog	Pitching Up	Steeper Approaches

Figure 8-5. A variety of atmospheric and terrain conditions can produce visual illusions. When you encounter these situations, you must be able to recognize them and use all the resources available to counteract them.

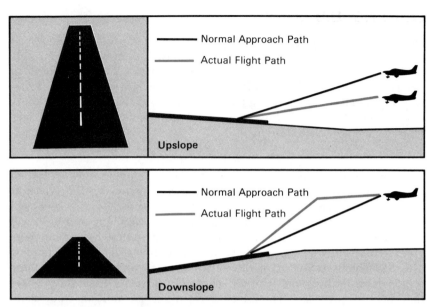

Figure 8-6. When approaching a sloped runway, the tendency is to position the airplane so the runway appears as it would for a normal, flat runway. On a runway that slopes uphill, this produces a dangerously low approach. For a downhill runway, it produces a high approach with the possibility of overshooting the runway. The runways depicted to the left show how normal three-degree approaches might look for upslope and downslope runways.

In addition, look for other clues, such as steep or featureless surrounding terrain. If you suspect an illusion, fly a normal traffic pattern and avoid long, straight-in approaches. [Figure 8-6]

As a pilot, you will not always be able to eliminate the visual illusions that you may encounter. Understanding the various types and how they occur, and taking preventative measures when appropriate, will go a long way toward making a safer flight.

CHECKLIST _____

After studying this section, you should have a basic understanding of:

✓ **The eye** — The structure and the components, and how day and night vision differ.

✓ **Blindspots** — Where they are, when they occur, and what methods can be used to counteract them.

✓ **Night vision** — How night scanning is used and what factors can increase night visual acuity.

✓ **Dark adaptation** — The amount of time required for the adaptation and what you can do to preserve it.

✓ **Aircraft position lights** — What color they are, where they are located, and how they are used in collision avoidance.

✓ **Visual illusions** — What the different types are and what causes them. What the effects of each illusion are and how they are avoided.

SECTION B

SPATIAL DISORIENTATION

Your body is designed to live and work in a one-G environment. Orientation with the world around you is easily maintained when your feet are planted firmly on the ground. However, when you enter the three-dimensional realm of flight, your body can be put into positions that are totally in conflict with what you see and feel. To deal effectively with these unrealistic sensations, you must know how they are created and what illusions are produced. Your awareness of your body's position is a result of input from three main senses: vision, vestibular, and kinesthetic.

VISUAL SENSE

As you have seen in Section A, vision helps you maintain balance and your position relative to objects around you. When other sensory input is contradictory or confusing, the brain relies primarily upon sight to determine orientation. In darkness or limited visibility, when few outside visual references are available, you need to rely heavily on your visual sense to interpret the flight instruments for accurate information.

VESTIBULAR SENSE

The semicircular canals and the vestibule (sometimes referred to as the static organ), located in your inner ear, are primarily responsible for your vestibular sense. This sense tells you when you are turning, climbing, descending, speeding up, or slowing down. It also senses gravity and G-loads created by centrifugal force. The **semicular canals** sense angular acceleration such as roll, pitch, and yaw. The three semicircular canals are filled with fluid and are located so that each canal lies along a specific axis. At the base of each canal are small hair cells that detect movement when they are displaced. When you maneuver the airplane or move your head, the semicircular canals move too, while the fluid remains temporarily stationary. This deflects the sensory hairs and sends a nerve impulse to the brain, which interprets the "movement" as motion around an axis. [Figure 8-7]

The vestibular organs in the inner ear are easily deceived by slow or gradual movement.

The semicircular canals may not be able to sense a slow rate of rotation. They also are unable to sense movement after prolonged periods of uniform movement. If you maintain a prolonged turn without outside visual reference, it will seem normal after a while. This feeling is a result of fluid in the inner ear "catching up" to the rest of the ear; movement is no longer perceived by the small hairs.

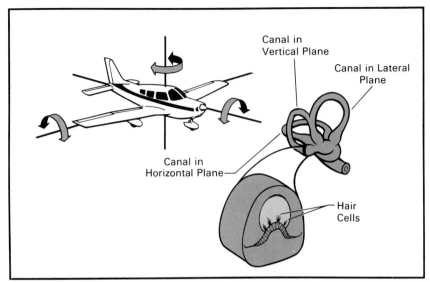

Figure 8-7. The semicircular canals lie in three planes that correspond approximately to those of an airplane. As you change the pitch attitude, an angular acceleration is created in the canal lying along the vertical axis. The brain interprets this acceleration by the deflection of tiny hair cells located at the base of the vertical canal. A roll into a turn is detected by the lateral canal, and a yawing movement is sensed by the horizontal canal.

The **utricle** and **saccule** organs within the **vestibule** are responsible for the perception of linear acceleration, which is movement forward and back, side to side, and up and down. One of the major problems with this sensory organ is its inability to tell the difference between gravity caused by the earth and G-loads caused by centrifugal force. [Figure 8-8]

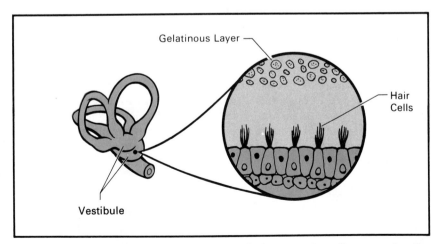

Figure 8-8. A gelatinous layer within the vestibule responds to linear acceleration forces. This, in turn, moves small hair cells that create the sensation of movement.

KINESTHETIC SENSE

When your awareness of position is obtained from the nerves in your skin, joints, and muscles, it is called the kinesthetic sense. Using this sense is sometimes called "flying by the seat of your pants," and this is literally what you are doing. Kinesthetic sense is unreliable, however, because the brain cannot tell the difference between input caused by gravity and that of maneuvering G-loads.

DISORIENTATION

When the brain receives conflicting messages from your sensory organs, a confused condition called spatial disorientation can occur. **Spatial disorientation** is an incorrect mental image of your position, attitude, or movement in relation to what is actually happening to your airplane.

Vertigo is the feeling that you are spinning, or that the world is spinning or tumbling about you. It is usually caused by a physical disorder in the inner ear, and can be completely incapacitating. Vertigo should not be confused with spatial disorientation. Although they are sometimes used interchangeably, spatial disorientation normally is caused by misinterpretation of outside stimuli, while vertigo is the result of a physiological problem.

Spatial disorientation is most common at night and during times of restricted visibility.

In good weather and daylight, you obtain your orientation primarily through your vision. Because of this, spatial disorientation rarely occurs during the day in good weather conditions. At night or in marginal weather conditions, visual cues are fewer, and you rely upon the vestibular and kinesthetic senses to supplement your visual sense. However, neither of these senses is as reliable for perceiving motion, and they can give false cues about your orientation. The probability of spatial disorientation occurring is quite high during these times. Correctly interpreting your flight instruments is extremely important, because they are your only sources of accurate information under these conditions.

Relying on the instruments and believing what they tell you, regardless of "how it feels," are the keys to maintaining spatial orientation.

Everyone is subject to spatial disorientation; even experienced pilots have felt its effects in one form or another and in varying degrees. Some situations are more disorienting than others. An awareness of the conditions that are more likely to produce spatial disorientation and the illusions they create will help you guard against their occurrence. Remember, you can avoid misinterpreting visual and spatial information by referring frequently to the flight instruments.

SPATIAL ILLUSIONS

The majority of the illusions presented here have one thing in common; they occur when visibility is restricted, either by darkness or by weather. Weather conditions can change very rapidly, and what was marginal VFR (MVFR) one moment can be IFR the next. Predicting when this change will occur can be difficult, if not impossible. It takes many hours of training and experience before a pilot is competent to fly an aircraft solely by reference to instruments. Each year, many fatalities result from non-instrument rated pilots continuing flight into deteriorating weather conditions.

GRAVEYARD SPIRAL

A prolonged, constant-rate turn may produce a graveyard spiral. During this type of turn, the fluid in the semicircular canals eventually stops moving. This can create the illusion that you are no longer turning. A loss of altitude in this situation may be interpreted as a wings-level descent, which can lead you to increase elevator back pressure. This action only tightens the turn and increases the altitude loss. A recovery to wings-level flight may produce the illusion that the airplane is in a turn in the opposite direction, resulting in a reentry of the spiral. This "feeling" must be fought until the fluid in your semicircular canals quits moving again.

CORIOLIS ILLUSION

Another illusion that occurs in a prolonged, constant-rate turn is the Coriolis illusion. If you tilt your head down to change a fuel tank or pick up a pencil, the rapid head movement puts the fluid in motion in more than one semicircular canal. This creates an overwhelming sensation of rotating, turning, or accelerating along an entirely different plane. An attempt to stop the sensation by maneuvering the airplane may put it into a dangerous attitude. Because this type of illusion is so overwhelming, it is considered to be one of the most deadly. To avoid it, do not move your head too fast in limited visibility or darkness. A simple wing-leveling autopilot can help overcome the temporary and sometimes overpowering feelings of spatial disorientation.

Since spatial disorientation can occur along more than one axis, use slow, deliberate head movements when performing cockpit functions.

LEANS

One of the most common types of spatial disorientation is called the leans. It occurs when an abrupt recovery or a rapid correction is made to a bank. If you make such a recovery, your semicircular canals sense a roll in the opposite direction. This may cause you to reenter the original attitude. When you return the aircraft to a wings-level condition, you will tend to lean in the direction of the incorrect bank until the semicircular canal fluids return to normal. Maintaining a level attitude for a minute or two generally will stop the leans.

SOMATOGRAVIC ILLUSION

A rapid acceleration or deceleration can cause a somatogravic illusion. An acceleration can produce the illusion that you are in a nose-high attitude, even though you are still in straight-and-level flight. This may prompt you to lower the nose and enter a dive. A deceleration, such as rapidly retarding the throttle, produces the opposite effect. You may think you're in a dive and raise the nose. If you raise the nose too far, a stall may be produced.

INVERSION ILLUSION

An abrupt change from a climb to straight-and-level flight can produce an inversion illusion. This illusion creates the feeling that you are tumbling backward. The effect may cause you to lower the nose abruptly, which may intensify the illusion.

FALSE HORIZONS

Another illusion, that of a false horizon, occurs when the natural horizon is obscured or not readily apparent. It can be generated by confusing bright stars and city lights. [Figure 8-9]

A false horizon can occur while you are flying toward the shore of an ocean or a large lake. Because of the relative darkness of the water, the lights along the shoreline can be mistaken for the stars in the sky. [Figure 8-10]

Flying above a sloping cloud deck can produce another illusion of a false horizon. The natural tendency, in this case, is to level the aircraft with the clouds.

FLICKER VERTIGO

A light flickering at a frequency of 4 to 20 flashes per second can produce flicker vertigo. Although rare, it can lead to convulsions, nausea, or

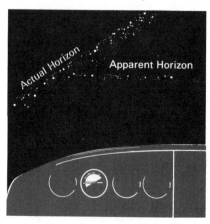

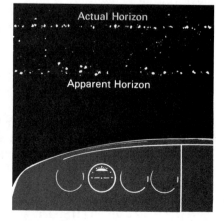

Figure 8-9. You can place your aircraft in an extremely dangerous flight attitude if you align the aircraft with the wrong lights. Here, the aircraft is aligned with a road and not the horizon.

Figure 8-10. In this illusion, the shoreline is mistaken for the horizon. To correct for the apparent nose-high attitude, you may lower the nose of the aircraft and attempt to fly "beneath the shore."

unconsciousness. It most frequently occurs when you are looking through a slow-moving propeller (240-1,200 r.p.m.) toward the sun. It can also happen when the sun is behind you, reflecting off the propeller. This situation can occur during descent, while landing, or while taxiing. The best way to prevent flicker vertigo is to avoid looking at a light source through a propeller for any length of time. Making frequent but minor changes in propeller r.p.m. can also decrease your susceptibility to flicker vertigo.

Fatigue, anxiety, heavy pilot workloads, and the intake of alcohol or other drugs increase your susceptibility to spatial disorientation and visual illusions. These factors increase response times, inhibit decision-making abilities, and cause a breakdown in scanning techniques and night vision. Reducing your workload with the use of a simple autopilot and improving your cockpit management skills help prevent "pilot overload" and the possibility of spatial disorientation.

The effects of spatial disorientation can be duplicated with the use of a vertigo simulator. All you need is a blindfold, a swivel chair, and some friends. With the blindfold on, tilt your head to one side. Then, have someone spin the chair at a constant rate for 30 to 60 seconds. The chair should then be brought to a gradual stop. When the chair has stopped, you will be told to raise your head. This action should produce the illusion of spinning or rotating. The simulation of spatial disorientation is so realistic that you should have someone close by to catch you if you fall out of the chair.

MOTION SICKNESS

Motion sickness, or airsickness, is caused by the brain receiving conflicting messages about the state of the body. The same types of factors that cause spatial disorientation also bring on airsickness. Passengers are more susceptible to motion sickness than pilots, because they often focus their attention inside the aircraft rather than outside. Airsickness comes in many forms. The most common symptoms are dizziness, nausea, and sweating. Other symptoms include general discomfort, paleness, and vomiting.

Specific remedies for airsickness can vary among people, but there are some actions that generally seem to help. You can suggest that your passengers put their heads back and attempt to relax. Most people are susceptible to the up-and-down motion common to flying in turbulent air. With the head reclined, passengers are better able to tolerate this up-and-down motion. Since anxiety and stress can contribute to motion sickness, keep unsure or nervous passengers informed on how the flight is progressing, and explain unusual noises such as flap or landing gear retraction and power changes. Opening the fresh-air vents and allowing cool, fresh air into the cabin also can improve the comfort level of your passengers.

Another suggestion that can reduce the possibility of airsickness is having passengers focus on objects outside the plane. A common road map can be very useful in this situation. Have passengers "follow along" and pick out various landmarks they can recognize. Avoiding warm, turbulent air and using earplugs also can reduce the likelihood of motion sickness. Keep in mind that most passengers are not used to steep banks or quick maneuvers, so be gentle.

CHECKLIST

After studying this section, you should have a basic understanding of:

✓ **Visual sense** — What information it provides and its limitations.

✓ **Vestibular sense** — What parts of the body provide this sense, how it functions, and its limitations.

✓ **Kinesthetic sense** — Where this sense comes from and its limitations.

✓ **Spatial disorientation** — How it is produced, where it is most frequently encountered, and how it differs from vertigo.

✓ **Spatial illusions** — What types of illusions are created, where they are frequently encountered, and how you can prevent them from occurring.

✓ **Flicker vertigo** — What causes it, and when does it occur. What precautionary measures can be taken to guard against it.

✓ **Motion sickness** — What causes it, and what can be done to prevent or reduce it.

RESPIRATION AND ALTITUDE

Your body needs energy to survive. We all know the body begins to deteriorate when it is deprived of food and water for very long, but we rarely consider the energy obtained from the oxygen we breathe. Since the body cannot store oxygen as easily as it does food energy, changes begin to occur rapidly when you are deprived of oxygen. This section covers the normal respiration cycle and looks at what happens when this process is interrupted or breaks down. It also includes a discussion of the effects on your body of changing atmospheric pressure.

RESPIRATION

To understand the respiration cycle, it is important to know how the atmosphere is constructed as it relates to the air you breathe. Each breath you inhale is a fairly uniform mixture of gasses. Life-sustaining oxygen makes up only about 21% of each breath, while 78% is nitrogen and 1% is other gasses, such as carbon dioxide and argon.

Your body uses only the oxygen in the air. Inhaled oxygen is diffused through the lungs into the bloodstream, where it attaches to hemoglobin. When the oxygen reaches individual cells, it acts upon certain compounds in the cells and causes them to release energy. This process creates a waste product called carbon dioxide (CO_2). Carbon dioxide is returned through the bloodstream to the lungs, where it is exhaled back into the atmosphere.

Although the mixture of air you breathe remains relatively uniform as altitude increases, the pressure or density of the air is less. This means there is less oxygen reaching the cells in your body as you climb. The altitude at which your body becomes starved for oxygen depends upon your level of activity. The higher the activity level, the lower the altitude.

HYPOXIA

Hypoxia occurs when the tissues in the body do not receive enough oxygen, regardless of the cause. There are two types of hypoxia that are common to flying: hypoxic hypoxia and anemic hypoxia.

Hypoxia is a state of oxygen deficiency in the body.

HYPOXIC HYPOXIA

Hypoxic hypoxia occurs when there is a lack of available oxygen in the atmosphere. It is considered to be the most lethal factor of all physiological causes of accidents. It can occur very suddenly at high altitudes during rapid decompression, or it can occur slowly at lower altitudes when you are exposed to insufficient oxygen over an extended period of time. The symptoms of hypoxia vary with the individual. Some of the common symptoms include:

1. An increase in breathing rate
2. Lightheaded or dizzy sensation
3. Headache
4. Sweating
5. Tingling or warm sensation
6. Blue fingernails and lips
7. Reduced visual field
8. Sleepiness or frequent yawning
9. Impaired judgment
10. A slowing of decision-making processes
11. A feeling of euphoria
12. Changes in personality traits

One of the first symptoms of hypoxia is impaired judgment. Don't wait for the symptoms; anticipate them and use supplemental oxygen.

Your individual response to hypoxia can be safely experienced in an altitude chamber; however, some pilots have the misconception that it is possible to learn the early symptoms of hypoxia so they can take corrective action whenever they occur. This is an extremely dangerous assumption, because an early symptom is impaired judgment. When the onset of hypoxia is rapid, your judgment may be impaired before you have a chance to recognize other symptoms. Normally, the part of the body that is first affected by oxygen deprivation is the retina of the eye. The effectiveness of the retina begins to show signs of a loss of night visual acuity as low as 5,000 feet MSL. At higher altitudes, though, the first symptom can be unconsciousness.

USEFUL CONSCIOUSNESS

When you fly on an airliner and listen to the flight attendant's announcement concerning the sudden loss of cabin pressure, do you wonder just how long you really have to get the oxygen mask over your face, or what will happen if the mask doesn't come down?

Life expectancy at high altitudes without oxygen is a matter of minutes, and the time of useful consciousness is even less. The **time of useful consciousness** is the maximum time you have to make a rational, life-saving decision and carry it out following a lack of oxygen at a given altitude. If you go beyond this time, you may not be able to place an oxygen mask over your face, even if you try. [Figure 8-11]

TIME OF USEFUL CONSCIOUSNESS		
Altitude	**While Sitting Quietly**	**During Moderate Activity**
40,000 Ft.	30 Sec.	18 Sec.
35,000 Ft.	45 Sec.	30 Sec.
30,000 Ft.	1 Min. and 15 Sec.	45 Sec.
25,000 Ft.	3 Min.	2 Min.
22,000 Ft.	10 Min.	5 Min.
20,000 Ft.	12 Min.	5 Min.

Figure 8-11. Your amount of exertion can dramatically affect the time of useful consciousness. Although you may remain conscious for three or four minutes at 35,000 feet, you are receiving less than 30% of the oxygen your body needs, and you will be able to function less than a minute without supplemental oxygen.

Recovery from hypoxia usually occurs rapidly after a person has been given oxygen. If you have suffered severe hypoxia, your mental and physical performance may be reduced for several hours.

ANEMIC HYPOXIA

When your blood is not able to carry a sufficient amount of oxygen to the cells in your body, a condition called anemic hypoxia occurs. As the name implies, this type of hypoxia is a result of a deficiency in the blood (anemia), rather than a lack of inhaled oxygen. Anemia can occur as a result of excessive bleeding, a stomach ulcer, or a diet deficiency. It also can occur when oxygen is not able to attach itself to hemoglobin.

CARBON MONOXIDE

The most common cases of anemic hypoxia come from carbon monoxide poisoning. Carbon monoxide (CO) attaches itself to the hemoglobin about 200 times more easily than does oxygen. In fact, carbon monoxide prevents oxygen from attaching to the hemoglobin and can produce anemic hypoxia. It can take up to 48 hours for the body to dispose of carbon monoxide. The symptoms are very similar to hypoxic hypoxia, and can produce the loss of muscle power, a headache, and dizziness. If the poisoning is severe enough, it can result in death.

Carbon monoxide robs the body of oxygen by attaching to the hemoglobin and reducing the oxygen-carrying capacity of the blood. Large accumulations of CO result in a loss of muscular power.

Because carbon monoxide poisoning is a form of hypoxia, you are more susceptible to its effects as altitude increases. Carbon monoxide poisoning can result from a faulty aircraft heater. If you suspect carbon monoxide poisoning, you should turn off the heater immediately, open the fresh air vents or windows, and use supplemental oxygen if it is available.

Susceptibility to carbon monoxide poisoning increases as altitude increases.

Smoking also causes a mild case of CO poisoning. The effects of cigarette smoke are especially apparent by a reduction in visual acuity during a night flight. Smoking three cigarettes during a night flight can dramatically reduce the sharpness of your vision.

BLOOD DONATION

Another type of anemic hypoxia can be caused by the loss of blood that occurs during a blood donation. Your blood can take several weeks to return to normal following a donation. Although the effects of the blood loss are slight at ground level, there are risks when flying during this time. Therefore, you are advised not to give blood prior to flying.

SUPPLEMENTAL OXYGEN

To avoid the effects of hypoxia, do not fly for prolonged periods above 10,000 feet MSL during the day or 5,000 feet MSL at night without breathing supplemental oxygen.

Since judgment and rationality can be impaired when you are suffering from hypoxia, prevention is the best approach. There are two ways to prevent hypoxia. First, you can fly at low altitudes where hypoxia will not be a factor. This, of course, is not always practical. The most effective way to prevent hypoxia is through the use of supplemental oxygen.

Federal regulations specify when you must use supplemental oxygen. If you are planning a flight with a cruise altitude over 12,000 feet, you should consult these regulations. As a general rule, consider using supplemental oxygen when you fly above 10,000 feet during the day or above 5,000 feet at night.

Use only aviator's breathing oxygen to fill aircraft oxygen cylinders.

Aircraft oxygen systems should always be filled with aviator's breathing oxygen. Medical oxygen contains too much moisture, which can collect in the valves and lines of the system and freeze. This may stop the flow of oxygen.

HYPERVENTILATION

Rapid or extra deep breathing can cause hyperventilation. It can occur even while breathing supplemental oxygen.

Hyperventilation is the term used to describe a breathing rate that is too rapid and too deep. This process forces too much carbon dioxide from your body and creates a chemical imbalance in the blood. In severe cases it can lead to unconsciousness. It is possible to suffer from hyperventilation even if you are using supplemental oxygen.

Hyperventilation is most likely to result when you are experiencing emotional tension, anxiety, or fear.

Hyperventilation usually is an involuntary response to a stressful situation. Your body's natural attempt to maintain a normal breathing rate can be overcome when you are tense, anxious, apprehensive, fearful, or overworked. Since many of the symptoms of hyperventilation are similar to those of hypoxia, it is important to correctly diagnose and treat the proper condition. If you are using supplemental oxygen, check the equipment and flow rate to ensure you are not suffering from hypoxia. Some of the symptoms of hyperventilation include:

1. Dizziness
2. Tingling of the fingers and toes
3. Muscle spasms
4. Coolness
5. Drowsiness
6. Weakness or numbness
7. Rapid heart rate
8. Apprehension and mental confusion
9. Finally, loss of consciousness

The treatment for hyperventilation involves restoring the proper carbon dioxide level in the body. Breathing normally is both the best prevention and the best cure for hyperventilation. In addition to slowing the breathing rate, you also can breathe into a paper bag or talk aloud to overcome hyperventilation. Recovery is usually rapid when the breathing rate is returned to normal.

PRESSURE EFFECTS

As you climb or descend, changes in atmospheric pressure affect many parts of your body. Since half of the atmospheric pressure lies below 18,000 feet, you can experience a fairly large pressure change within this realm. Air trapped in the ears, sinus cavities, gastrointestinal tract, and teeth can cause pain and discomfort as the outside pressure changes. [Figure 8-12]

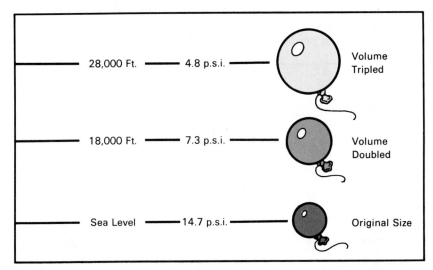

28,000 Ft.	4.8 p.s.i.	Volume Tripled
18,000 Ft.	7.3 p.s.i.	Volume Doubled
Sea Level	14.7 p.s.i.	Original Size

Figure 8-12. As a balloon ascends, atmospheric pressure decreases and the air within the balloon expands in an attempt to equalize itself with the surrounding pressure. The same thing happens with the air trapped in your body.

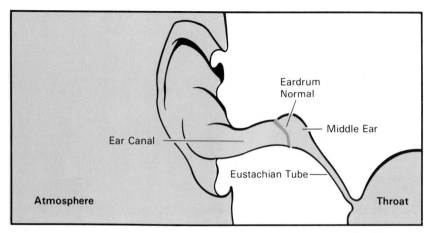

Figure 8-13. Normally, the eustachian tube keeps the pressure equalized between the ear canal and the middle ear. When the pressure is equal, the eardrum is not distended.

EARS

The ears are probably the most common area affected by changes in pressure. The pain you feel generally is the result of air trapped in the middle ear. When the air pressure in the middle ear is equal to the pressure in the ear canal there is no plugged feeling or pain. [Figure 8-13]

When you ascend, the pressure in the ear canal decreases. Usually, the increased pressure in the middle ear will open the eustachian tube and escape, thus equalizing the pressure in the middle ear. If the tube does not open, you may feel a fullness in the ear and experience a slight hearing loss and discomfort. This is because the eardrum is distended and cannot vibrate as freely as before. [Figure 8-14]

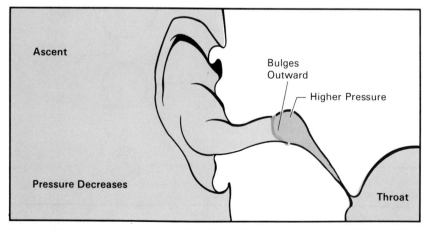

Figure 8-14. When the eustachian tube does not open during an ascent, the positive air pressure in the middle ear pushes the eardrum outward toward the ear canal.

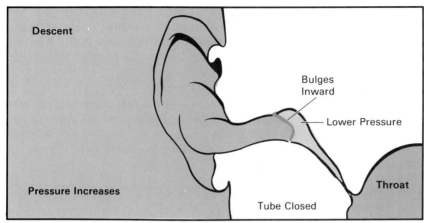

Figure 8-15. During a descent, the pressure inside the ear canal increases, while lower pressure air remains in the middle ear. If the eustachian tube remains closed, the eardrum bulges inward causing severe pain.

During a descent, the opposite condition exists. The outside pressure in the ear canal will become higher than the pressure in the middle ear. This situation is harder to correct, because the eustachian tube opens more easily to let positive pressure out than it does to allow air back into the middle ear. Because of this, your ears seem to "plug" more easily when descending. [Figure 8-15]

Most people are aware of the pressure imbalance during descent. Sometimes you can open the eustachian tube by yawning, swallowing, or chewing. Air can also be forced into the middle ear by holding your nose and mouth shut and attempting to blow air gently into your nostrils. This is called the Valsalva technique, and it forces positive pressure into the eustachian tube and middle ear. This equalizes the pressure in the middle ear. [Figure 8-16]

Clearing your ears is more difficult when you are descending into higher pressure. You may have to gently force the eustachian tube open if an imbalance in pressure exists.

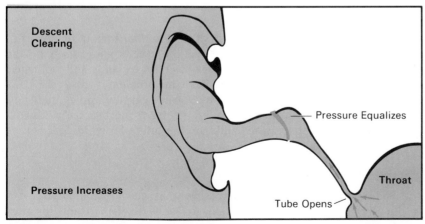

Figure 8-16. During times of descent, the inner ear may have to be reinflated manually to allow the pressure to equalize between the middle ear and the throat.

When the eardrum is pushed too far by the pressure imbalance, it can become very painful. If you have a cold, an ear infection, or a sore throat, you may not be able to equalize the pressure in your ears. A flight in this condition can be extremely painful, as well as very dangerous. You should avoid flying when you cannot clear your ears.

If you are experiencing minor congestion, nose drops or nasal sprays may reduce the chance of a painful ear blockage. Before you use any medication, check with an aviation medical examiner to make sure it will not affect your ability to fly. Slow descent rates can also help prevent or reduce the severity of ear problems.

Another preventive measure is associated with long-term hearing loss. Your ability to hear gradually diminishes with prolonged exposure to excessive noise levels. Most older pilots have experienced some loss of hearing, especially in the higher frequency ranges. The damaging exposure to noise is cumulative, but it can be minimized by the simple preventive measure of wearing noise attenuating headsets or ear plugs.

SINUSES

Your sinus cavities can sometimes cause problems during pressure changes. If you have an inflammation of the sinuses or nose from an allergy or a cold, you may experience discomfort from trapped air. As with the ears, using the Valsalva technique can help equalize the pressure.

TEETH

Trapped air in a cavity can expand and cause pain. Imperfect fillings, damaged root canals, and abscesses also can produce pain at altitude. A descent to a lower altitude may bring relief, but good dental care is the best way to prevent problems such as these.

GASTROINTESTINAL TRACT

At any given time, your gastrointestinal tract contains about one quart of gas. Most of this is swallowed air, and the rest is gas caused by the digestion process. As altitude increases, this gas expands and can cause abdominal pain. You are less likely to have this problem if you avoid foods that produce excess gas, such as onions, cabbage, raw apples, radishes, beans, cucumbers, melons, and any food that tends to "disagree" with you. A good diet and regular eating habits are important in avoiding this type of problem.

SCUBA DIVING

Flying and scuba diving don't mix well. Decompression sickness can develop in those who fly too soon after diving.

The reduction of atmospheric pressure that accompanies flying can produce a number of physical problems for scuba divers. Probably the most well known is decompression sickness, more commonly referred to as the "bends." Decompression sickness occurs when the nitrogen absorbed during a scuba dive comes out of solution and forms bubbles in the tissues and bloodstream, much like uncapping a bottle of soda. The condition is very serious and can produce extreme pain, paralysis and, if severe enough, death. Even though you may finish a dive well within the no-decompression limits, the reduced atmospheric pressure of flying can cause the onset of decompression sickness. If you plan to fly following one or two days of no-decompression diving and your total accumulated bottom time for both days is less than two hours, wait at least 12 hours before flying. Wait 24 hours if your total bottom time is more than two hours in two days, if you have more than two days of diving, or after a dive requiring a decompression stop. Transporting a diver who is suffering from decompression sickness can be very hazardous to the diver. You should maintain as low an altitude as practical when flying divers to medical help.

CHECKLIST ⎯⎯⎯⎯⎯⎯⎯⎯⎯⎯⎯⎯⎯

After studying this section, you should have a basic understanding of:

✓ **Respiration** — What the normal respiration processes are, how oxygen is used, and how carbon dioxide is produced.

✓ **Hypoxia** — What the types of hypoxia are, how they are caused, and what the symptoms are.

✓ **Time of useful consciousness** — What it represents, and how it is affected by activity level and altitude.

✓ **Carbon monoxide** — Where it comes from, and how it affects the body.

✓ **Supplemental oxygen** — What type of oxygen should be used and when you should use it.

✓ **Hyperventilation** — What it is and how it affects your body.

✓ **The effects of pressure** — How the body is affected by pressure changes and what can be done to minimize the effects.

ALCOHOL, DRUGS, AND PERFORMANCE

Good health and safe flying go hand-in-hand. Your physical and mental skills must be in top shape when you are at the controls. Alcohol dulls these senses and can reduce your performance to a dangerous level. Illness and disease also can affect the functioning and performance of your body, as can the drugs that are meant to fight these illnesses. The purpose of this section is to explain the hazardous effects of alcohol and the way seemingly harmless drugs can sometimes cause serious problems in the flying environment.

Various drugs are used to help fight illnesses, diseases, or to reduce the severity of their symptoms. A drug is a substance that is used to promote health or to treat a disease. It is not a food, but a chemical that alters the structure or function of the body. Among other things, drugs are used to eliminate pain (aspirin), satisfy a habit (nicotine), and produce "good feelings" (alcohol). In this section, alcohol is treated as a drug, since its effects are similar to depressant drugs.

One of the most complicated aspects of drugs is that they can produce side effects that can be completely unexpected or unrelated. Because of this, many of them cannot be used while flying. There are thousands of drug compounds available to the public. This section, obviously, cannot look at them all, but there are several common drugs, both prescription and over-the-counter, that we will examine as they relate to flying.

Either the use of a drug or the illness itself can prohibit safe flight. Both these factors need to be considered before you fly.

There are two things you should consider before flying while using a drug. First, what is the condition you are treating and, second, what are the side effects of the drug used to treat the condition. Some conditions are serious enough to prohibit flying, even if the illness is being treated successfully with drugs. When you take a drug, it is an indication that you are not well. Your main concern is whether the illness itself is severe enough to influence flight safety. In many cases, your decision to fly will end with the answer to these questions. In addition, many doctors prescribe medication without knowing that you are a pilot. Always let your physician know you are a pilot and ask about the side effects of the medication. You should also consult an aviation medical examiner (AME) about any medication that you suspect will adversely affect your ability to pilot an aircraft.

In this section, we have divided some common drugs into three basic categories according to their primary use or potential side effects. These are depressants, stimulants, and analgesics. Although all the drugs listed under each category may not be manufactured primarily for that purpose, they may have side effects that produce those responses.

DEPRESSANTS

Depressants are drugs that reduce the body's functioning in many areas. They lower blood pressure, reduce mental processing, and slow motor and reaction responses. There are several types of drugs that can cause a depressing effect on the body. The most common of these is alcohol.

Depressants slow your motor responses and mental processes.

ALCOHOL

Ethyl alcohol is the most widely used and abused drug. Although some alcohol is used for medicinal purposes, the majority of it is consumed as a beverage.

When you drink alcohol, it is not digested the same way as food; rather, it passes through your liver and is absorbed into your bloodstream. This produces a depressing effect on your nervous system and acts like a general anesthetic. The rate at which alcohol is absorbed into the body varies with the percentage of alcohol in the drink, the rate at which it is consumed, the amount and type of foods you have eaten, and the length of time you have been drinking.

Unlike many depressants, alcohol may increase your heart rate and blood pressure while depressing your central nervous system. Shortly after consumption, the blood vessels in the skin dilate, which increases the blood flow to the skin. When combined with the stimulant reaction on the heart, a sensation of warmth and stimulation is created. Under the influence of alcohol, you experience a dulling of the senses, a decrease in good judgment, and a reduced sense of responsibility. You begin to feel less fatigued and may experience a feeling of emotional and physical well-being. Sensory perception is diminished, as well as skilled responses, intellectual functioning, memory, and vision.

ALCOHOL AND ALTITUDE

Alcohol reduces the amount of oxygen absorbed into your bloodstream. It affects you in much the same way as a climb to a higher altitude. Therefore, when you drink, your "physiological altitude" is much higher than your actual altitude. The effect of alcohol on physiological altitude is much greater than that of smoking. Also, the body cannot metabolize alcohol as easily at higher altitudes. At sea level, the average person takes about three hours to metabolize an ounce of alcohol. After consuming one ounce of alcohol at 12,000 feet, the average person will take nearly four times longer to metabolize it as compared to sea level.

BLOOD ALCOHOL

Federal regulations require that your blood alcohol level be below .04% and that at least eight hours pass between "bottle and throttle."

Intoxication is determined by the amount of alcohol in the bloodstream. This is usually measured as a percentage by weight in the blood. The FARs require that your blood alcohol be less than .04% and that eight hours pass between drinking alcohol and piloting an aircraft. If you have a blood alcohol level of .04% or greater after eight hours, you cannot fly until your blood alcohol falls below that amount. Even though your blood alcohol may be well below .04%, you cannot fly sooner than eight hours after drinking alcohol. Although the regulations are quite specific, it is a good idea to be more conservative than the FARs. Most pilots allow a minimum of 12 hours from the last drink to flying; commercial airlines generally require their pilots to wait 24 hours.

There are several regulations that apply to offenses involving alcohol. You should be familiar with the regulations in Parts 61 and 91 that relate to alcohol violations and testing requirements. Any violation or refusal to submit to an alcohol test may result in the denial of the application for a pilot certificate or the suspension or revocation of a pilot certificate.

HANGOVER

If you have a hangover, you are still under the influence of the drug. Flying with a hangover is just as dangerous as flying while intoxicated.

A greatly underestimated hazard is the hangover. When you have a hangover, you are still under the influence of alcohol, even though you may think that you are functioning normally. The degrading effects on motor and mental responses still remain. The possibility of committing errors while under the influence of a hangover is increased. Considerable amounts of alcohol can remain in the body for over 16 hours, so you should be cautious about flying too soon after drinking.

TRANQUILIZERS

Taking tranquilizers or relaxants is extremely hazardous when you are flying. Sleeping pills and other types of tranquilizers, whether prescription or nonprescription, can greatly reduce motor response, coordination, attentiveness, and judgment. Decision making is inhibited to a point where risks and information are not appropriately weighed. The effects of tranquilizers increase as altitude increases. In no case should they be used in conjunction with flying activities unless you have gotten the approval of an aviation medical examiner.

MOTION SICKNESS MEDICATION

Although Dramamine and other types of motion sickness remedies can be very helpful for airsick passengers, you should not use them when piloting an aircraft. These types of drugs often contain sedatives that can cause drowsiness and decreased alertness. You should not fly for at least 24 hours after taking them.

STOMACH MEDICATION

The antacids used for minor indigestion or an upset stomach are generally considered safe to use when flying. If repeated or painful indigestion occurs for more than a few weeks, you should stop using antacids and see a physician. You may have a more serious condition that would affect your ability to safely pilot an aircraft.

Drugs that help alleviate the stomach problems associated with a nervous or hyperactive digestive tract usually contain anticholinergics. These drugs reduce the activity of the nervous system that controls the levels of acid and digestive fluid going to the stomach and small intestine. This helps reduce stomach distress and the growth of ulcers. Many of these drugs contain sedatives which can cause blurred vision and reduce your ability to respond and function in a fully alert state. You should consult an aviation medical examiner for specific information about any drug you may be taking for this and related purposes. In many cases, if you suffer from a peptic ulcer, you are considered unfit to fly.

DECONGESTANTS AND ANTIHISTAMINES

There are many forms of decongestants and antihistamines available over the counter. Most are designed to alleviate cold and allergy symptoms. These drugs often cause drowsiness and slowed motor response, and can be very hazardous to use when flying. Antihistamines can also cause a stimulant reaction in some people. Nasal decongestants that are taken for clearing sinuses and ears should be used in moderation. You can get a good idea of whether a specific antihistamine produces side effects by looking at the precautions printed on the container. If you are in doubt, ask an AME about taking the drug before flying. A cold or allergy, whether treated or not, may be severe enough to preclude safe flying. When using any drug, always familiarize yourself with its effects before you fly.

STIMULANTS

Stimulants are drugs that stimulate the central nervous system and produce an increase in alertness and activity. Some of the common uses of these drugs include appetite suppression, fatigue reduction, and mood elevation. These drugs can produce anxiety and drastic mood swings, both of which are very dangerous when you fly. Some drugs cause a stimulant reaction, even though this reaction is not their primary function. Amphetamines, caffeine, and nicotine are all forms of stimulants.

Stimulants generally excite the central nervous system and can be hazardous when mixed inappropriately with flying. Amphetamines, caffeine, and nicotine are all stimulant drugs.

AMPHETAMINES

Amphetamines may be used in the form of pep pills, uppers, and appetite suppressants. Some common brand names include Dexedrin, Benzedrin, Methedrin, and Drinamyl. Flying under the influence of amphetamines can be very dangerous. They can produce restlessness, anxiety, mood swings, panic, cardiac disturbances, paranoia, hallucinations, convulsions, and coma. Consult an aviation medical examiner for information concerning the specific drug and its side effects.

CAFFEINE

Caffeine is a very common stimulant. It is found in soda, coffee, tea, some pain killers, and some antihistamines. Caffeine is used every day by millions of people as a quick "pick-me-up." It begins to show up in the bloodstream within five minutes of ingestion, and its effects can last for as long as 14 hours. Too much caffeine can lead to nervousness and sleep disturbances. Other symptoms of a caffeine overdose are increased mental fatigue, muscle tremors, and occasional stomach irritation. Although caffeine use is not prohibited by the FARs, you should use it in moderation to avoid the side effects.

NICOTINE

Nicotine, which is the active ingredient in tobacco, has several side effects that are hazardous to your health. It stimulates the nervous system and can cause a sensation of lessened fatigue and euphoria in some people. Within 20 to 30 minutes after taking nicotine, it begins to wear off and the user experiences feelings of fatigue and of slowing down. Nicotine withdrawal may produce irritability, aggression, or hostility. Although nicotine and cigarette smoking are addictive, they are not prohibited under Part 67 of the FARs. However, many of the long-term health conditions caused by smoking are medically disqualifying. Your aviation medical examiner can give you the details on the risks and effects of smoking and flying.

Smoking increases the level of carbon monoxide in your bloodstream and increases the chance of hypoxia.

If you are a regular smoker, you carry a carbon monoxide level of about five percent in your bloodstream. This raises your physiological altitude from sea level to about 7,000 feet. A smoker is much more susceptible to hypoxia and will feel the effects of hypoxia at lower altitudes.

PASSIVE SMOKING

Cigarette smoke is also hazardous to others flying with you. Smoke from the lit end of a cigarette has twice the amount of carbon monoxide as does exhaled smoke. This can cause hypoxia in passengers and can increase their overall discomfort and susceptibility to air sickness. Smoking can harm your aircraft as well. The gyroscopic instruments have sensitive bearings and filters which can become gummed by tar and other chemicals contained in cigarette smoke. This tar also clogs outflow valve movement in aircraft pressurization systems and is the most common cause of pressurization system failure.

PAIN KILLERS

Pain killers can be grouped into two broad classes: analgesics and anesthetics. Analgesics are drugs that decrease pain such as aspirin and codeine. Anesthetics are drugs that deaden pain or cause a loss of consciousness. These drugs are commonly used for dental and surgical procedures.

ANALGESICS

There are many over-the-counter analgesics available for the relief of pain. The majority of the drugs that contain acetylsalicylic acid (Aspirin), acetaminophen (Tylenol), and ibuprofen (Advil) have few side effects when taken in the correct dosage. Flying usually is not restricted when you take these drugs. However, some people are allergic to these analgesics or may suffer from stomach irritation. Other drugs, such as an antihistamine, may be added to relieve other symptoms. These additives may restrict flying because of their side effects.

Prescription analgesics, such as Darvon, Percodan, Demerol, and codeine, have a wide variety of side effects that usually preclude flying while using them. They are used for the reduction of moderate to severe pain and can be prescribed for extensive dental and surgical procedures. Codeine is also found in several types of cough syrups. These prescription drugs may cause mental confusion, dizziness, a headache, nausea, and vision problems. You should consult an aviation medical examiner before using any prescription drug when you are flying.

LOCAL ANESTHETICS

Most local anesthetics used for minor dental and outpatient procedures wear off within a relatively short period of time. The anesthetic itself may not limit flying so much as the actual procedure and subsequent pain. You should carefully weigh all factors when determining whether to fly soon after any procedure requiring a local anesthetic. Your physician and AME can assist you in making an informed decision concerning your specific case.

OTHER PROBLEM DRUGS

Other types of drugs can also have adverse effects on flying. These drugs can neither be classified as stimulants nor depressants; however, they can produce perceptual errors in balance and vision.

ANTIBIOTICS

Some forms of antibiotics can produce dangerous side effects, such as balance disorders, hearing loss, nausea, and vomiting. Other antibiotics are safe for use while flying. As a general rule, you should consult your aviation medical examiner before using an antibiotic. Certain infections require specific antibiotics, and the infection itself often will prohibit safe flight. Generally, at least two days should elapse between last taking these antibiotics and flying.

When you are not feeling well or are taking medication, you should ask yourself several key questions to determine your flying status. If you have an illness, does the condition present a hazard to safe flight? If you are taking a drug for an illness and it wears off during a flight, will it cause an unsafe condition? If you are taking a drug, can the drug produce any side effect that would influence your motor, perceptual, or psychological condition? If the answer to any of these questions is "Yes" or "I don't know," consult with an AME before flying.

CHECKLIST

After reading this section, you should have an understanding of:

✓ **Drugs** — What they are and how they can present hazards to flight.

✓ **Depressants** — What they are and what effects they have on the body's system. What different types of drugs fit into this category.

✓ **Alcohol** — What the effects of alcohol on the body are, what blood alcohol is, and what regulations pertain to alcohol use and flying.

✓ **Stimulants** — What the different types are and what effects they have on the body.

✓ **Smoking** — What the hazards of smoking are and its ill effects on the pilot, the passengers, and the aircraft.

✓ **Pain Medicine** — What the general rule of use is, and the different types available.

FLIGHT PLANNING
AND
DECISION MAKING

INTRODUCTION

Section A provides a summation of several subject areas you have already studied throughout the text. It relates to the planning process you should use each time you prepare for a cross-country flight. Section B introduces you to factors that affect the way you make decisions. You will develop new insights into the subtle effects your own attitudes can have on the decision-making process. Since flying involves a continual series of decisions, a knowledge of these factors will benefit you directly. Good decision-making skills and flight safety go hand in hand.

PLANNING AND ORGANIZING FLIGHTS

By now you should have a good idea of what the flight planning process involves. This section brings together several subject areas from previous sections, including aeronautical charts, flight publications, weather, navigation, communications, performance, and regulations. Preflight planning puts all of this information to practical use and helps to build an extra margin of safety into every flight you make. It is important to develop a definite pattern of preflight activities so you will not omit essential items. As you gain experience, you should also strive to refine your planning skills. To provide an overview of the process, we have selected a cross-country flight between two small airports in Nebraska. Although the route selected is intentionally short for purposes of illustration, it requires the same steps you would use for longer cross-country flights.

INITIAL PLANNING

Normally, you should make a preliminary check of the weather ahead of time to see if the planned flight is feasible. Unfortunately, an FSS usually is unable to issue a forecast beyond 24 to 36 hours. You can, however, assess the current national weather situation in terms of pressure systems and fronts and decide if adverse weather is likely. When you need a long-range forecast, it is best to contact the NWS. Forecasters there can provide reasonably accurate predictions of general weather patterns up to five days into the future. They also can provide a 6- to 10-day outlook, but keep in mind that the longer the forecast period, the less accurate the information.

There are several other sources that you can use for getting an overall picture. In many areas, there are local cable channels that are devoted to weather; the "AM Weather" on the local public service station is another useful program. Regardless of what preliminary source you use, be sure to get a standard weather briefing from an FSS specialist before you complete your flight planning on the day of the flight.

Another preliminary step is selecting current sectional charts for the trip. The Omaha Sectional covers the area of the planned flight from York Municipal to Stefan Memorial Airport at Norfolk, Nebraska. [Figure 9-1]

After drawing the course line on the chart, you should select checkpoints which will be easy to identify. In this example, they are Stromsburg Airport, the road and railroad near the town of Oconee that intersect

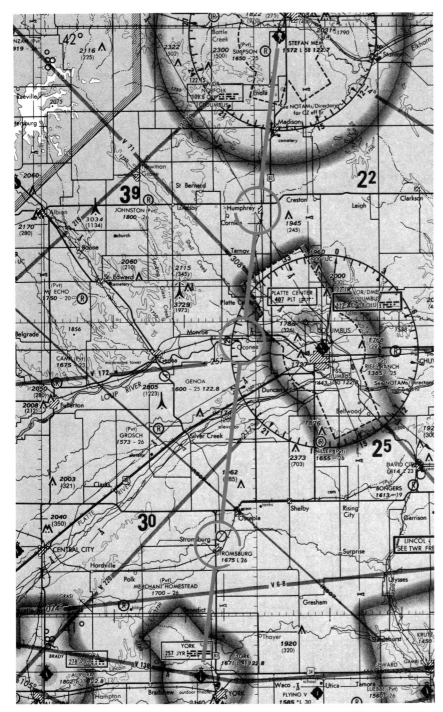

Figure 9-1. For this flight, you will follow a direct route between York and Norfolk. You may want to refer back to this excerpt during the following discussion.

with the 272° radial from the Columbus VOR/DME, and the town of Humphrey. Don't forget to look over the surrounding area for other prominent landmarks that will help you maintain your orientation.

Direct routes are not the best choices for every situation.

Keep in mind that terrain, special use airspace, or the availability of checkpoints may influence your route selection. Sometimes, a direct course may not be the best choice because of terrain, performance limitations, or navigation equipment. Although a longer route may take more time, it may be the most practical choice. Another factor you should consider is the necessity for an intermediate fuel stop. A direct route is appropriate for this example, since the terrain is relatively flat and the available fuel is adequate.

Note the checkpoints on the navigation log as individual legs. Remember from Chapter 6 that a leg may be any segment of a cross-country flight, such as the distance between checkpoints, intermediate stops, or course changes. Since this flight is direct, your estimates of heading, ground-speed, and wind correction angle will be the same for each leg.

Take the time to study your route of flight carefully. You can begin by looking at the different types of airspace in the area. IR507, an MTR, crosses your course just north of the Stromsburg Airport. Remember that a three-digit identifier means the MTR has segments which may be flown above 1,500 feet AGL. When receiving the standard weather briefing on the day of the flight, ask the weather briefer if it will be in use. Also, make a mental note to be especially alert for traffic arriving at or departing from the airport at Columbus when you pass through the area.

Always check the types of airspace along your route of flight.

Since the flight to Stefan Memorial will be conducted in controlled airspace, appropriate VFR cloud clearance and visibility requirements will be considerations the day of the flight. Three statute miles visibility and a 1,000-foot ceiling are required for landing at Stefan Memorial because of the control zone surrounding the airport. As you can see by the special use airspace boundary, there is an MOA to the west of Norfolk. This could become a factor if you needed to make a diversion to the west. When you receive your preflight weather briefing, check to see if the MOA will be active. If so, you may need to consider other alternatives if a diversion becomes necessary.

Use the plotter to determine the total distance, the distance between checkpoints, and the true course. The distance between York Municipal and Stefan Memorial Airport is 66 nautical miles, with legs of 14, 21, 13, and 18 nautical miles. The true course is 7°. Although the variation is not shown on this chart excerpt, it is 7° east. Note these items on the nav log.

You can also give some consideration to your cruising altitude ahead of time. After checking the terrain and obstruction heights, select an approximate altitude. Remember that the VFR cruising altitudes are based on your magnetic course. For the example, the true course minus the variation is 0°. This makes a cruising altitude of 5,500 feet appropriate, although winds aloft and cloud cover the day of the flight will be the final determining factors.

Above 3,000 feet AGL, use odd thousands plus 500 feet cruising altitudes for magnetic courses from 0° to 179°.

This is an appropriate time to check pertinent flight publications, such as the *Airport/Facility Directory* and NOTAMs. Along with the airport elevation, a description of services available, and runway information, the A/FD gives valuable data about communications facilities and radio aids to navigation. [Figure 9-2]

Another item to check in the A/FD is the aeronautical chart bulletin to see if there are any changes to the Omaha Sectional since its publication

---

AIRPORT/FACILITY DIRECTORY

NORFOLK

KARL STEFAN MEM   (OFK)   3 SW   UTC-6(-5DT)   41°59′08″N 97°26′05″W   **OMAHA**
  1572   B   S4   FUEL 100LL, JET A   CFR Index Ltd   **H-1D, 3A, L-11B**
  RWY 01-19: H5800X150 (ASPH-PFC)   S-75, D-192, DT-360   HIRL   .7% up S   **IAP**
  RWY 01: MALSR. Tree.
  RWY 19: VASI(V4L)—GA 3.0°TCH 39.3′. Antenna.
  RWY 13-31: H5800X150 (ASPH–PFC)   S-75, D-192, DT-400 +   MIRL   .4% up SE
  RWY 13: VASI(V4L)—GA 3.0°TCH 39.3′. Railroad.   **RWY 31:** VASI(V2L)—GA 3.0°TCH 27′. Ground.
  AIRPORT REMARKS: Attended Nov-May 1400-2400Z‡, May-Nov 1400-0200Z‡, other times call 371-1783. ACTIVATE
    MALSR Rwy 01, VASI Rwy 19, 13 and 31—122.7. Ultralight activity on and in vicinity of arpt. CLOSED to air carrier
    ops with more than 30 passenger seats except PPR call arpt manager 402–371-7210. Control Zone effective
    continuously.
  COMMUNICATIONS: CTAF/UNICOM 122.7
    COLUMBUS FSS (OLU) Toll free call Dial 1–800–WX–BRIEF. NOTAM FILE OLU.
    NORFOLK RCO 122.15 (COLUMBUS FSS)
  RADIO AIDS TO NAVIGATION: NOTAM FILE OLU.
    WOLBACH (H) VORTAC 114.8   OBH   Chan 95   41°22′33″N 98°21′12″W   038°55.1 NM to fld. 2010/10E.
    NORFOLK (L) VORW 109.6   OFK   41°59′17″N 97°26′03″W   at fld. NOTAM FILE OFK.
      VOR unusable beyond 35 NM below 3000′ and 200°-230° beyond 35 NM below 3400′.
    ILS 111.5 I-OFK Rwy 01 Unmonitored.

NOTAMS	**NORFOLK**
	Karl Stefan Memorial
	FDC 6/3418 /OFK/KARL STEFAN MEMORIAL, NORFOLK, NE.
	ILS RWY 1 AMDT 1 ALTERNATE MINIMUMS NA.
	Norfolk VOR/DME
	(OFK) DME UNUSABLE 130-190 BYD 25 NM BLO 4000 FT; 190-240 BYD 20 NM BLO 5000 FT; 240-255 BYD 25 NM BLO 4000 FT; 280-130 BYD 30 NM BLO 3500 FT. (6/)

Figure 9-2. The A/FD excerpt shows that the Norfolk VOR/DME has several restrictions, depending on your altitude and distance from the station. From this, you can conclude that the VOR signals may not be reliable during the descent into the Norfolk area. In addition, NOTAMs issued since the last A/FD issue indicate further restrictions involving the DME portion of the navaid. This demonstrates the importance of checking all available information for the flight.

date. You can also use a map in the back of the A/FD to locate flight watch facilities. This check reveals the Columbus FSS does not provide EFAS, but Grand Island has a remote flight watch outlet from Huron, South Dakota. You can use this facility for an enroute weather update on your way to Norfolk.

To complete your navigation log, enter the appropriate radio frequencies and use the pilot's operating handbook to find the fuel flow, true air-speed, and power setting for the cruise portion of the flight. These should be entered on the navigation log in the appropriate spaces. [Figure 9-3]

Be sure you have the necessary equipment and supplies gathered up in advance. Having a well-equipped flight case can aid in cockpit management during cross-country flights. Typical items you may want to include are a fuel sampler, clipboard, flight computer, plotter, charts, a flashlight, and a small first aid kit. No one likes to consider that the airplane may develop mechanical problems or that an emergency landing will have to be made. In fact, these occurrences are rare. As a precautionary measure, however, you may want to assemble a survival kit for long flights, flights over remote areas, or flights over large bodies of water.

FINAL PLANNING STAGE

Always obtain a weather briefing prior to departure.

An hour or so before you are scheduled to leave, call the FSS and get a complete weather briefing. For the flight to Norfolk, the standard weather briefing is obtained through the Columbus Flight Service Station. FSS phone numbers are usually included in the communications section of airport listings in the A/FD. They are also listed in the back of the A/FD in a section called "FAA and NWS Telephone Numbers."

Check Points (Fixes)	VOR Ident	Course	Altitude	Wind Dir.	Wind Vel.	CAS	TC	TH	MH	CH	Dist. Leg	GS Est.	Time Off ETE	Time Off ETA	GPH Fuel
	Freq.	(Route)		Temp.	TAS		-L +R WCA	-E +W Var.	± Dev.		Rem. 66	Act.	ATE	ATA	Rem.
YORK						07°					14				
STROMSBURG AIRPORT	D→	5,500						-07°			52				
272° RADIAL COLUMBUS VOR	OLU 112.2					07° 114		-07°			21 31				
HUMPHREY						07° 114		-07°			13 18				
STEFAN MEMORIAL	OFK 109.6					07° 114		-07°			18 0				

Figure 9-3. As you complete your advanced planning, your navigation log will look similar to this. After you receive your weather briefing on the day of the flight, the remaining calculations will take a relatively small amount of time.

When you call for your standard briefing, you should tell the FSS special-ist that you are a student or private pilot, as appropriate, and that you will be flying VFR. Include the type and registration number of the plane you will be flying, your intended cruising altitude, and your estimated time of departure. The weather section on the back of a navigation log can serve as a guide as you write down the information given to you by the briefer. It enables you to record the weather with the rest of your flight planning information. It also helps you to locate specific weather data needed for your remaining calculations or for later in-flight refer-ences. [Figure 9-4]

After receiving the briefing, you may have unanswered questions. If you need more detailed information, don't hesitate to ask for it. For example, an inquiry about special use airspace and MTRs reveals that IR507 is in use until 10 p.m., and the O'Neill MOA will be active during the after-noon. You may also need weather for any alternate airports that you have chosen.

With the information from the weather briefing, you can finish the naviga-tion log by computing your wind correction angles, magnetic headings, groundspeed, estimated time enroute, estimated time of arrival, and the total fuel requirements. You should also calculate your takeoff distance; the time, fuel and distance to climb; and your landing roll for the destina-tion airport. Although it is not a requirement, it is highly recommended

WEATHER LOG

| | Ceiling, Visibility, and Precipitation | | Winds Aloft | Icing and |
	Reported	Forecast		
Departure	70 SCT 120 SCT VIS.20 WIND 220/7	120 SCT VIS.20 TRW AFTN	270/10 TEMP. +14	N/A
En Route	60 SCT 120 SCT VIS.20	120 SCT VIS.20 TRW AFTN		
Destination	50 SCT 100 SCT VIS.20 WIND 330/10	120 SCT VIS.20 TRW AFTN		
Alternate				

Figure 9-4. This weather log excerpt reflects the information from the briefing. Generally, current conditions show scattered clouds at 5,000 to 12,000 feet with visibilities 20 miles throughout the area. The forecast shows no adverse weather except for some thundershower activity by late afternoon or evening. Winds at 6,000 feet are expected to be from 270° at 10 knots.

FLIGHT PLAN

1. TYPE	2. AIRCRAFT IDENTIFICATION	3. AIRCRAFT TYPE/ SPECIAL EQUIPMENT	4. TRUE AIRSPEED	5. DEPARTURE POINT	6. DEPARTURE TIME		7. CRUISING ALTITUDE
VFR / IFR / DVFR	N773PR	PA 28/A	114 KNOTS	YORK MUNI (JYR)	PROPOSED (Z) 1700Z	ACTUAL (Z)	5,500

8. ROUTE OF FLIGHT

DIRECT

9. DESTINATION (Name of airport and city)	10. EST. TIME ENROUTE		11. REMARKS
STEFAN MEMORIAL NORFOLK (OFK)	HOURS 0	MINUTES 40	STUDENT PILOT

12. FUEL ON BOARD		13. ALTERNATE AIRPORT(S)	14. PILOT'S NAME, ADDRESS, TEL. NO. & AIRCRAFT HOME BASE	15. NUMBER ABOARD
HOURS 5	MINUTES 25	NONE	B. BRAND, 614 COWEN ST., YORK, NE (402) 362-1234, YORK MUNI	1

16. COLOR OF AIRCRAFT	17. DESTINATION CONTACT/TELEPHONE (OPTIONAL)
GREEN ON WHITE	(402) 371-4321

CLOSE VFR FLIGHT PLAN WITH COLUMBUS FSS ON ARRIVAL

SPECIAL EQUIPMENT SUFFIX		
A – DME TRANSPONDER WITH ALTITUDE ENCODING	C – RNAV, TRANSPONDER WITH NO ALTITUDE ENCODING	T – TRANSPONDER WITH NO ALTITUDE ENCODING
B – DME, TRANSPONDER WITH NO ALTITUDE ENCODING	D – DME, NO TRANSPONDER	U – TRANSPONDER WITH ALTITUDE ENCODING
	R – RNAV, TRANSPONDER WITH ALTITUDE ENCODING	W – RNAV, NO TRANSPONDER
		X – NO TRANSPONDER

Figure 9-5. After completing the flight plan, call and file it with Columbus FSS. You may use the "Fast File" system, which records the information from your flight plan as you give it. Normally, the flight service specialist transmits essential parts of the flight plan to the destination FSS. For this flight, however, Columbus FSS serves both departure and destination airports.

that you file a flight plan with an FSS before departure. All of the information that you need to file can be taken from the navigation log. [Figure 9-5]

Always perform a walk-around inspection using a written checklist before you fly an airplane.

Before any flight, you should always perform a walk around inspection of the airplane. Using the appropriate checklist for the preflight and other operations is highly recommended to ensure that all necessary items are checked in a logical sequence. During the preflight, it is extremely important to verify that the airplane has been serviced with the correct grade and amount of fuel for the flight. Don't assume the oil level has been checked just because the airplane was refueled. If the oil quantity is low, have it filled too. You may even want to take an extra quart or two with you so that, if you need to add oil, you will be using the same type. If any portion of the trip will be taken at night, make a visual inspection of the position, anti-collision, and landing lights.

Remember, if you do not open your flight plan within one hour of the departure time you gave to the FSS, they will usually delete it from the system. In the event of an unexpected delay, be sure to call the FSS and amend your departure time.

Even if the airplane was hangared and ready to fly the night before, a preflight inspection will allow you to check on possible fuel contamination from condensation or other conditions that may have changed overnight. In cases where an aircraft has been stored for an extended period of time, be especially alert for damage or obstructions caused by animals, birds, or insects.

Check for damage caused by animals, birds, or insects when you preflight an airplane coming out of storage.

As pilot-in-command, you are responsible for determining the airworthiness of the airplane. One of the factors involved with this is ensuring that the maintenance for the airplane is up to date. Remember, the airworthiness certificate for the airplane remains valid only so long as the airplane is maintained and operated according to FARs.

An airworthiness certificate is not valid unless the aircraft is maintained according to FARs.

COCKPIT MANAGEMENT

Disorganization can complicate the simplest of flights, so keep your sectional charts and nav log within easy reach. Other flight-related items in your flight case can be kept next to you. By keeping everything organized, your attention won't be as easily diverted from flying the airplane.

Actually, cockpit management for a flight begins with the first planning activity. One of the largest safety margins you can build into your flight is the use of thorough preflight procedures. "Inadequate preflight planning" remains a frequent causal factor in aircraft accidents year after year. Your conscious effort to think and plan ahead is your best guarantee of safety. As you prepare for departure, always ask yourself this question, "Have I considered the alternatives if the flight cannot be completed as planned?"

CHECKLIST _____

After studying this section, you should have a basic understanding of:

✓ **The planning process** — What it entails and what sequence to follow.

✓ **Route consideration** — How to select a route based on airplane performance, terrain, and weather conditions.

✓ **Weather briefing** — How to assess weather conditions in advance and determine the feasibility of the flight.

✓ **Navigation log** — Why it is essential and how it helps you complete the flight plan.

✓ **Cockpit management** — How a well-planned flight and an orderly cockpit contribute to flight safety.

SECTION B

FACTORS AFFECTING DECISION MAKING

In recent years, the FAA, General Aviation Manufacturer's Association, and Transport Canada have conducted studies concerning decision making. Various other aviation groups also participated in or contributed to these studies. The following section is a summary of the results of this research.

THE DECISION-MAKING PROCESS

Flying requires a continuous stream of decisions about yourself, your airplane, and the environment.

Flying is a combination of events which requires you to make a continuous stream of decisions. The events in this process are interrelations between people, the aircraft, and the environment which occur over time. They can be placed in five subject areas:

1. **Pilot** — As a pilot, you are continually making decisions about your own competency, state of health, level of fatigue, and many other variables.
2. **Aircraft** — Your decisions are frequently based on evaluations of the aircraft, such as its power, equipment, or airworthiness.
3. **Environnment** — This encompasses many of the items not included in the two previous categories. It can include such things as weather, air traffic control, and runway length or surface.
4. **Operation** — The interaction of you, your aircraft, and the environment is influenced by the purpose of each flight operation. You must evaluate the three previous areas to decide on the desirability of undertaking or continuing the flight as planned. Is the trip worth the risks?
5. **Situation** — Situational awareness is the accurate perception of the conditions affecting you and your aircraft during a specific period of time. More simply, it is knowing what is going on around you. [Figure 9-6]

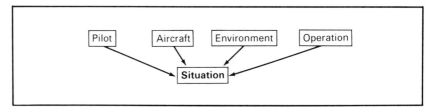

Figure 9-6. Any given situation is affected by the pilot, aircraft, environment, and operation subject areas. There is a direct relationship between your awareness of the situation and safety. The higher your situational awareness, the safer you are as a pilot.

In conventional decision making, the need for a decision is normally triggered by the recognition that something has changed or that an expected change did not occur. Once you have recognized the need for a decision, your selection of the proper response depends on several elements. Your level of skill, knowledge, experience, and training all influence your ability to make the best choice. If you fail to search for and recognize the change, you reduce your chance of controlling it. As time passes, your available alternatives may decrease. For example, if you have already entered an area of hazardous weather, your alternative to circumnavigate the weather is automatically lost.

It is important to recognize a change, then take action to control it.

Aeronautical decision making (ADM) builds on the foundation of the conventional process, but enhances it to decrease the probability of pilot error. It can be defined as:

* The ability to search for and establish the relevance of all available information regarding a flight situation, to specify alternative courses of action, and to determine expected outcomes from each alternative
* The motivation to choose and authoritatively execute a suitable course of action within the time frame permitted by the situation

The first portion of this definition refers to intellectual capabilities. It relies on your abilities to sense, store, retrieve, and integrate information. This part of decision making is purely rational. If used alone, it would allow problem solving in much the same manner as a computer. The second portion implies that, in part, your decisions are based on tendencies to use other than safety-related information when choosing courses of action. For example, you might consider such items as job demands, convenience, monetary gain, and self-esteem before taking action. Ideally, this non-safety information can be eliminated and your decisions can be directed by a more rational process.

The decision-making process is quite complex; however, it can be condensed into six elements, using the acronym DECIDE. The steps in the DECIDE process are as follows:

The steps in the DECIDE process are detect, estimate, choose, identify, do, and evaluate.

* **D**etect the fact that a change has occurred.
* **E**stimate the need to counter or react to the change.
* **C**hoose a desirable outcome for the success of the flight.
* **I**dentify actions which could successfully control the change.
* **D**o the necessary action to adapt to the change.
* **E**valuate the effect of the action.

Several elements are involved in good decision making. These include: identifying personal attitudes which are hazards to safe flight, developing risk assessment skills, learning to recognize and cope with stress, learning behavior-modification techniques, and evaluating the effectiveness of your ADM skills. First, lets look at the role your attitudes play in decision making.

HAZARDOUS ATTITUDES

The five hazardous attitudes are anti-authority, impulsivity, invulnerability, macho, and resignation.

There are five hazardous attitudes which affect pilot decision making. It is important to understand them as they apply to your flying. The *Private Pilot Exercise Book* contains a self-assessment inventory to give you personal insight into these attitudes.

1. **Anti-authority:** "Don't tell me!" — People with this attitude may resent having someone tell them what to do, or they may just regard rules, regulations, and procedures as silly or unnecessary. (Remember, though, it is always your prerogative to question authority if you feel it is in error.)
2. **Impulsivity:** "Do something — quickly!" — This is the thought pattern of people who frequently feel the need to do something — anything — immediately. They do not stop to consider what they are about to do so they can select the best alternative; they do the first thing that comes to mind.
3. **Invulnerability:** "It won't happen to me!" — Many people feel that accidents happen to others but never to them. Pilots who think this way are more likely to take chances and run unnecessary risks.
4. **Macho:** "I can do it." — These people are always trying to prove that they are better than anyone else by taking risks and by trying to impress others. While this pattern is thought to be a male characteristic, women are equally susceptible.
5. **Resignation:** "What's the use?" — People with this attitude do not see themselves as making a great deal of difference in what happens to them. When things go well, they think, "That's good luck." When things go badly, they attribute it to bad luck or feel that someone is "out to get them." They leave the action to others — for better or worse. Sometimes, such an individual will even go along with unreasonable requests just to be a "nice guy."

ANTIDOTES FOR HAZARDOUS ATTITUDES

There are ways to overcome the five major hazardous attitudes which contribute to poor pilot decision making. One way is to become thoroughly aware of them by studying the preceding paragraphs and completing the self-assessment inventory in the *Exercise Book*. Another is to use **antidotes**. By telling yourself something to counteract the hazardous attitude, you're "taking an antidote." Learn to recognize a hazardous attitude, correctly label the thought, and then say its antidote to yourself. [Figure 9-7]

RISK ASSESSMENT

To enjoy safe flying, you must learn to identify and deal with the elements of risk.

Every aspect of life involves some element of risk, regardless of whether you drive a car, ride a motorcycle, or fly an airplane. You must learn to cope with the risks associated with flying to ensure years of safe flying. The five subject areas discussed earlier — pilot, aircraft, environment,

HAZARDOUS ATTITUDE	ANTIDOTE
Anti-authority: "Don't tell me!"	"Follow the rules. They are usually right."
Impulsivity: "Do something—quickly!"	"Not so fast. Think first."
Invulnerability: "It won't happen to me!"	"It could happen to me."
Macho: "I can do it."	"Taking chances is foolish."
Resignation: "What's the use?"	"I'm not helpless. I can make a difference."

Figure 9-7. To overcome hazardous attitudes, you must memorize the antidotes for each of them. Know them so well that they will automatically come to mind when you need them.

operation, situation — are also the five elements of risk. Let's look at each of these separately.

As a pilot, your performance may be affected in many ways during a flight. The risk raisers, or things that affect you by raising the degree of risk, are called **stressors**. The three types of pilot stressors are:

1. **Physical stress** — Conditions associated with the environment, such as temperature and humidity extremes, noise, vibration, and lack of oxygen
2. **Physiological stress** — Your physical condition, such as fatigue, lack of physical fitness, sleep loss, missed meals (leading to low blood sugar levels), and illness
3. **Psychological stress** — Social or emotional factors, such as a death in the family, a divorce, a sick child, a demotion at work, or the mental workload of in-flight situations

The risk element of the aircraft focuses on its equipment, condition, and suitability for the intended purpose of the flight. The best time to make this assessment is on the ground during preflight planning. However, it also needs to be done continuously during flight, since conditions can change at any time. For example, winds aloft may increase your anticipated flight time, making available fuel a factor to be analyzed.

The environment is a far-reaching risk element which includes situations outside the aircraft that might limit, modify, or affect the aircraft, pilot, and operational elements. Weather is a common environmental risk raiser. Density altitude, runway length, obstacles, and related factors can also create environmental concerns.

In terms of the purpose of the flight operation, you must evaluate the interaction of you, your aircraft, and the environment. When determining the desirability of undertaking or continuing the flight as planned, be sure to consider all available information.

The combination of these first four risk elements leads into the fifth — the overall situation which you must evaluate continuously. Remember, to become a safer pilot, you should increase your situational awareness.

To assess risk effectively, you must be aware of risk raisers and the possibilities for risk accumulation so you can determine the need to neutralize or balance these factors. One way to become aware of risk is to look at statistics to see what types of flight activities are most likely to result in accidents. The National Transportation Safety Board (NTSB) has conducted studies of accident rates for the various types of flying in general aviation (1982 data). They reveal that aerial application operations have the highest accident rate, followed by personal and business flying.

Poor decision-making skills are often a factor in aircraft accidents.

You should also be aware that the accident rate for single-engine airplanes is the highest for all general aviation airplane operations. More importantly, studies of the most common cause/factors of accidents in fixed-wing aircraft show that most accidents were the result of an unsafe outcome of the pilot's decision-making process. In fact, 85% of all general aviation accidents can be attributed, at least in part, to pilot error. Some common causes were: failure to maintain directional control, failure to maintain airspeed, misjudged distance, fuel exhaustion, inadequate preflight preparation and/or planning, selection of unsuitable terrain, and inadequate visual lookout.

The NTSB also evaluated the phase of operation in which accidents occurred. The results indicate that the largest number (27.1%) occurred during landing, while 21.5% occurred during takeoff.

Other statistics concern accident rates for pilots without instrument ratings flying single-engine airplanes at night' in VFR conditions. The night VFR accident rate is high for pilots with less than 51 hours. [Figure 9-8]

Unless all five risk elements indicate ''go,'' you should reconsider your decision to make a flight.

Good aeronautical decision making requires a continuous assessment of whether to start a particular flight or to continue a flight as planned. You can use the five risk elements to help you make a "go/no go" decision. Unless all five indicate "go," you should reevaluate your decision to make a flight. A good decision maker in aviation does not act hastily

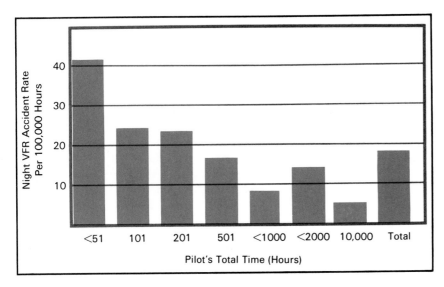

Figure 9-8. The accident rate decreases by nearly 50% once a pilot obtains 100 hours, and continues to decrease until the 1,000-hour level. The data suggest that, for the first 500 hours, pilots flying VFR at night should establish higher personal limits than are required by the regulations and apply instrument flying skills in this environment.

upon "gut" feelings. With an accurate assessment of the risks associated with each of the five elements, you are best able to arrive at decisions that ensure a safe conclusion to a flight, even if it means not taking off.

STRESS REDUCTION

Stress can be defined as the body's response to any demand made on it by physical, physiological, or psychological factors known as stressors. Anything that is perceived as a threat to the body's equilibrium causes a reaction as the body marshals its resources to cope with it. These reactions include the release of chemical hormones (such as adrenalin) into the blood and the speeding of the metabolism to provide energy to the muscles. Blood is shunted away from the stomach and digestive tract to supply the muscles in the arms and legs with more oxygen. Blood sugar is increased. Heart rate, respiration, blood pressure, and perspiration all increase. Other hormones improve the blood's ability to clot. The result prepares the body to fight or flee.

Stress is the body's re-action to demands.

The factors that may cause this type of stress are also the five elements of risk discussed in "Risk Assessment." During flight, it is common to have to deal with many stressors simultaneously. For instance, on a cross-country flight, you realize you are much lower on fuel than you expected. The clouds ahead appear to be building. Static is interfering with your radio. You are off course and can't locate your current position on the sectional chart. On top of all this, you are tired, and hungry. The cabin heater isn't working, and you have to contend with turbulence. You begin to worry about arriving at your destination on time and missing an important appointment. You contemplate a forced landing and begin to worry about damaging your aircraft. What if your insurance won't cover it? Can you afford the deductible? What about injury to yourself or your passengers? Your palms are sweating, your mouth is dry, and your heart is pounding! At this point, you feel a growing sense of urgency and tension. You may give too much attention to "what if" questions which should be ignored. You are reaching (or have reached) a state of stress overload. You begin to use poor judgment that results in a series of bad decisions, such as pressing on into deteriorating weather or overflying good landing areas, until you are almost out of fuel. The stage is set for panic and disaster.

Your performance level decreases rapidly when stress levels exceed your ability to cope.

A certain amount of stress is good for you. It keeps you on your toes and prevents complacency. However, stress effects are cumulative and can eventually add up to an intolerable burden, unless you cope with them adequately. Performance generally increases with the onset of stress, but peaks and then begins to fall off rapidly as stress levels exceed your ability to cope. [Figure 9-9]

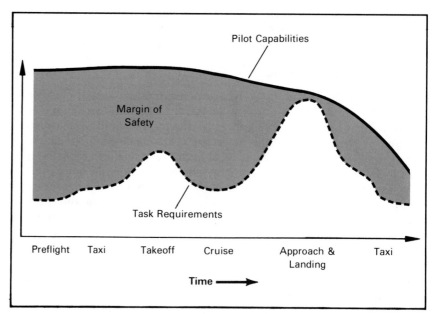

Figure 9-9. Accidents often occur when flying task requirements exceed pilot capabilities. The difference between these two factors is called the margin of safety. Note that in this idealized example, the margin of safety is minimal during the approach and landing. At this point, an emergency or distraction could overtax pilot capabilites, causing an accident.

Stress-handling techniques vary considerably. An individual's personal strategies for dealing with stress may be healthy and adequate, or they may be inappropriate and lead to an increased burden through self-imposed stress. Individuals who are not coping with stress adequately often show symptoms in three ways: emotional, physical, and behavioral. These symptoms differ, depending upon whether aggression is focused inward or outward.

Those individuals who typically turn their aggressive feelings inward often demonstrate the emotional symptoms of depression, preoccupation, sadness, and withdrawal. Physical symptoms may show up as headaches, insomnia, appetite changes, weight gain or loss, indigestion, and so on. Behavioral symptoms can include hypochondria, self-medication, a reluctance to accept responsibility, tardiness, absenteeism, and poor personal appearance.

On the other hand, those individuals who typically take out their frustrations on other people or objects will show few physical symptoms. However, emotional symptoms may show up as overcompensation, denial, suspicion, paranoia, agitation, restlessness, defensiveness, excess sensitivity to criticism, argumentativeness, arrogance, and hostility. The behavioral symptoms can include episodes of desperate acting out or temper tantrums.

You need to be able to recognize the symptoms of stress overload in yourself and to learn how to manage your stress. There are several techniques which can be applied to help prevent the accumulation of life stresses. The first involves a program of physical fitness. Second, learn to recognize and avoid the heavy pressures imposed by getting behind schedule and not meeting deadlines. Plan your schedule to accomplish those tasks that are important and necessary, and don't worry about those that are not. Allow time in your schedule for relaxation. Third, take a realistic assessment of yourself. What are your capabilities and limitations? Strengths and weaknesses? Set your goals accordingly. Fourth, whenever possible, avoid stressful situations and encounters. If driving in traffic raises your blood pressure, join a car pool or ride the bus. If crowds add to your frustration, avoid them whenever possible. Finally, be aware of other, more specialized techniques that can help you cope with stress, such as biofeedback and meditation. Most are designed to evoke what psychologists call the relaxation response. These techniques have been used successfully by athletes, businessmen, and others in high tension professions to maximize performance and minimize the effects of stress.

Learn to recognize the signs of stress overload in yourself and develop techniques for dealing with stress.

The "I'm Safe" Checklist	
Illness?	Do I have any symptoms?
Medication?	Have I been taking prescription or over-the-counter drugs?
Stress?	Am I under psychological pressure from the job? Worried about financial matters, health problems, or family discord?
Alcohol?	Have I been drinking within eight hours? Within 24 hours?
Fatigue?	Am I tired and not adequately rested?
Eating?	Am I adequately nourished?

Figure 9-10. Check yourself as carefully as you check your airplane before flight. If in doubt, don't go.

SELF-ASSESSMENT

Use the "I'm Safe" checklist before each flight.

Most pilots give their aircraft a thorough preflight, yet many forget to preflight themselves. You should use the "I'm Safe" checklist before you decide to fly. [Figure 9-10]

If an emergency occurs, stay calm and maintain a safe airspeed.

If an emergency does occur, be calm — think for a moment, weigh the alternatives, then act. Remember that fear and panic are your greatest enemies during an in-flight emergency. Be sure you maintain a safe airspeed as you determine your course of action. Don't hesitate to declare an emergency, when necessary, or to let other people (including passengers) know about your situation. Don't delay until it is too late.

Your greatest tool for combating fear and panic is to familiarize yourself thoroughly with your aircraft, its systems, and emergency procedures, along with the navigation/communications frequencies along your route of flight. Above all, maintain proficiency in your aircraft, because proficiency builds confidence. Know and respect your own personal limits. Always have a plan and an alternate plan — leave yourself an out! Finally, if flying is adding to your stress, then you had better quit. But, if it helps you cope with your life by providing an enjoyable means of earning a living or a hobby that takes your mind off everyday cares, then relax and enjoy.

CHECKLIST ━━━━━━━━━━━━━━

After studying this section, you should have a basic understanding of:

✓   **The decision-making process** — What it is and what factors influence it.

✓   **Hazardous attitudes** — What they are and how you can combat them.

✓   **Risk** — How to assess it and reduce it.

✓   **Stress** — What its symptoms are and how you can relieve them.

CHAPTER 10

AVIATION HISTORY

INTRODUCTION

Mankind's quest for flight has evolved from a dream, inspired by the soaring of birds, to successful space travel. Volumes have been written on this subject, and it would require an extensive library to adequately cover all of the exploits undertaken to overcome the obstacles to flight. This chapter is intended to acquaint you with some of the key events of aviation history. This historic coverage concentrates on our efforts to fly within the earth's atmosphere; the historical significance of rockets and spacecraft developments have been purposely omitted, since they are covered in Chapter 12.

SECTION A

THE QUEST FOR FLIGHT

Throughout history, men have tried to copy the flight of birds. Many notable efforts to achieve flight have been recorded. Although not lacking in courage, imagination, or desire, most early attempts ended abruptly, often in disastrous failure.

According to ancient Greek mythology, Daedalus was the first to master the art of flying like a bird. Supposedly, this occurred before the Trojan War, about 1200 B.C. Centuries later, around 8 A.D., the Roman poet, Ovid, revived and immortalized the old Greek legend in *"The Metamorphoses."* This poem describes how Daedalus and his son, Icarus, escaped from an island prison by descending from a high cliff and flying over the heads of their guards. They used bird-like wings covered with feathers and held together by flax, twine, and wax.

The legend explains how Icarus failed to heed his father's advice to "wing your course along the middle air." He flew too high, and the sun melted the wax that held the feathers in place. Icarus plunged to his death in the sea near an island which now bears his name, but Daedalus flew on safely to Sicily, where he lived for many years. Although the story of Daedalus is fiction, it symbolizes man's early attempts to conquer the mystery of flight.

Leonardo da Vinci (1452-1519) was an Italian artist, engineer, and inventor.

Centuries later, the first recorded scientific experiments were conducted by Leonardo da Vinci. Although best known for his paintings of *The Last Supper* and the *Mona Lisa*, da Vinci's 15th century manuscripts contained about 160 pages of descriptions and sketches of flying machines, including discussions about the center of gravity, center of pressure, and streamlining. The progress of aviation was perhaps hampered by the fact that his writings were not published until three hundred years after his death. [Figure 10-1].

Figure 10-1. Like many of his predecessors, da Vinci concentrated his efforts on making sketches of machines which were propelled by flapping wings.

BALLOONS

In the 17th century, ideas began to change into scientific theories and experiments. A number of significant discoveries were made about our atmosphere and its characteristics. For example, scientists agreed that the atmosphere is a fluid and that pressure decreases with increases in altitude. This understanding, coupled with the discovery of various gases and their properties, led to experiments with lighter-than-air flight in balloons.

The Montgolfier brothers of France are generally credited with sending the first passengers aloft in a balloon. After several experiments, they developed a paper and linen bag, or envelope, to contain hot air which was heated through an opening at the bottom. In a demonstration for King Louis XVI and Marie Antoinette on September 19, 1783, the Montgolfiers attached a cage to their balloon with the first living passengers — a sheep, a rooster, and a duck. The first men to ascend in the Montgolfier lighter-than-air balloon were a young physician and an infantry officer. [Figure 10-2]

The Academie des Sciences became interested in the experiments of the Montgolfiers and invited the brothers to demonstrate their balloon in Paris. The Academie, impressed with the demonstration, hired J. A. C. Charles to conduct more research into balloons. He added an important

Figure 10-2. On November 21, 1783, Jean-Francois Pilatre de Rosier and the Marquis d'Arlandes became the first to fly in a hot-air balloon. The flight lasted about 25 minutes and covered a distance of a little more than five miles.

contribution when he substituted hydrogen for hot air to obtain lift in the balloons he constructed.

The French balloonist, Jean Pierre Blanchard, and an American physician, Dr. John Jeffries, became the first to cross the English Channel in a balloon. During the flight from Dover, England, to Calais, France, they had problems with altitude control and were forced to dump unnecessary items overboard, including Blanchard's trousers.

Two other Americans, John Haddock, a newspaper editor, and John La Mountain, a balloonist, departed Watertown, New York, for what was intended to be a short demonstration flight. They ascended to about 15,000 feet where they evidently encountered strong winds and descended some distance north of Ottawa, Canada, into the middle of the Canadian woods. When the pair returned to Watertown after their four-hour, 300-mile journey, they received a hero's welcome.

In 1859, John Wise startled the world by riding cross-country in a balloon from St. Louis, Missouri, to Henderson, New York, in a little more than 19 hours. The balloon used for the trip was 60 feet in diameter and 100 feet high. Wise had optimistically named this balloon the "Atlantic," hoping to prove that a west-to-east Atlantic crossing was possible. Although Wise never succeeded in crossing the ocean, his 19-hour, 804-mile journey to Henderson, New York, set a distance record that remained unbroken for half a century.

Another balloonist who had dreams of crossing the Atlantic was Thaddeus S. C. Lowe. His expedition was equipped with a balloon large enough to carry a small crew and a steam-powered lifeboat. The lifeboat had both a screw to propel it through water and an aerial propeller to provide locomotion in the air. Before Lowe could attempt the Atlantic crossing, his balloon was destroyed while being inflated for the journey.

During a second attempt, the winds proved less favorable than he had expected, and the balloon was forced down in South Carolina. Unfortunately, this occurred just before the Civil War, and Lowe was held as a prisoner. However, he was able to convince his captors to release him before the actual fighting began.

After returning to the North, Lowe helped develop a Balloon Corps for the Union Army. Their main job was to observe a nearby Confederate army during several battles. A reasonably efficient mode of field operation was established by the reconnaissance group. A portable gas generator was set up in the field behind Union lines to inflate the envelope with hydrogen. The balloon was kept captive by a strong rope and was allowed to go high enough to observe the Confederate troop movements and yet be out of the range of enemy weapons fire. [Figure 10-3]

Telegraph communications also were set up so that Lowe or one of the observers in the team could relay information to the Union Army headquarters below. Although this method of observation proved to be successful, the Balloon Corps did not receive adequate funding or support, and it was disbanded in 1863 after the first two years of the Civil War.

Figure 10-3. This is an example of a captive balloon that was used as an elevated observation post. The term captive balloon means the balloon is restrained from free flight by cables or tethers. A free balloon, in contrast, is one that is untethered and free to ascend or descend and move over the surface with the wind. The Montgolfier balloons were free balloons.

AIRSHIPS

The main disadvantages of balloons were their lack of an effective means of directional control and the absence of a propulsion system. During the latter half of the 19th century, several balloonists began experimenting with lighter-than-air designs that included these features.

The dirigible was the natural offspring of the balloon. A **dirigible** was a lighter-than-air aircraft that was engine-driven and steerable. Dirigibles were normally designed in the shape of a fat cigar, rather than in the spherical shape of a balloon. Designers of the first dirigibles included a number of French and German experimenters, as well as Thomas Baldwin in the United States, and the Brazilian heir to a coffee fortune, Alberto Santos-Dumont. However, the most notable designer was Count Ferdinand von Zeppelin.

Count Ferdinand von Zeppelin (1838-1917) was the German pioneer who developed giant airships.

Count von Zeppelin was a German army officer by profession. His name is probably the most famous of all the lighter-than-air advocates. Count von Zeppelin served as an observer in the Union army during the U.S. Civil War where he is reported to have made several limited ascents in Lowe's captive balloons. He was also a witness to the successful use of the balloon for observation during the Franco-Prussian War. After his retirement from the German army in 1891, he turned his full attention to his lighter-than-air designs and built a construction site at Friedrichshafen in southern Germany.

By 1900, Count von Zeppelin had completed a giant airship, the LZ-1. It was 419 feet long and 38 feet in diameter. The design incorporated most of the desirable features that other designers had experimented with during the previous 50 years. These features included a powerplant, a controllable rudder, and a device that functioned like an elevator. However, one of the most distinctive characteristics was the rigid steel framework that contained the hydrogen gas.

The term **airship** has been used commonly in reference to large dirigibles. Airships are broadly categorized as rigid, nonrigid (or flexible), and semi-rigid. A **rigid airship** maintains the same basic shape regardless of the pressure of the gas within. A **nonrigid airship** requires gas pressure to maintain its shape. In a **semi-rigid airship**, the shape or form is maintained by a rigid or jointed keel and gas pressure. Since the von Zeppelin design was a rigid airship, the name Zeppelin is practically synonymous with rigid airships.

The rigid airship design gained recognition when Count von Zeppelin's LZ-1 was test flown in July, 1900. This event was the beginning of a long period of German dominance in the development of large, rigid airships. In fact, they became known as "Zeppelins." Count von Zeppelin continued to build improved versions of his design, and in 1910, the LZ-7 became the world's first commercial airship. Between 1910 and the beginning of World War I, the Zeppelins flew over 100,000 miles and carried approximately 34,000 passengers.

During World War I, Germany pressed all Zeppelins into military service, primarily for long-range bombing. The Zeppelin was not successful for this purpose. Since its gas bag was filled with highly flammable hydrogen, it was extremely vulnerable to enemy attack. Machine guns and bombs had to be carried below the main structure for balance, and the massive structure, which was almost impossible to conceal, became easy prey for Allied fighter pilots.

At this time, Germany did not have access to nonflammable helium, which was subsequently used for airships. The southwestern United States was the only place in the world where helium was available in quantities sufficient to be extracted from the earth. The first commercial airship to use helium was the Goodyear blimp, "Pilgrim," which was built in 1925. [Figure 10-4]

Figure 10-4. The development of the Zeppelin reached its peak during the 1930's with the construction of the "Hindenburg." This huge airship was filled with hydrogen. In 1937, following one of its many transatlantic crossings, it was destroyed while attempting to land at Lakehurst, New Jersey. The actual cause of the explosion of this magnificent machine is still a matter of conjecture. The "Hindenburg" tragedy marked the end of the Zeppelin era.

GLIDERS

Sir George Cayley (1773-1857), an Englishman, was one of the first pioneers in heavier-than-air flight.

Although advances in gliders lagged behind the development of the balloon, Sir George Cayley began experiments with **aeronautics** (heavier-than-air flight) in 1796 at the age of 23. At first, he built helicopter-like devices with a whirling arm to test airfoil concepts. By 1809, Cayley had designed, built, and flown several small, fixed-wing gliders. In spite of these early successes, gliding did not continue to develop as rapidly as **aerostatics** (lighter-than-air flight) in balloons and airships.

Ballooning was more popular, since it generally was witnessed by a greater number of people. Anyone with enough funds could have a balloon constructed that could gain enough altitude to impress spectators and stay in the air for a considerable length of time. Flying skill was not considered essential and, consequently, ascending in a balloon required little experience or training. A glider, on the other hand, was extremely difficult to control, because little was known about heavier-than-air flight. Glider flights of 10 seconds were considered successful.

Since early glider flights were seldom witnessed by more than a few spectators, verification of many claims are difficult to substantiate. However, official documentation indicates that Cayley successfully flew a full-sized glider with no one on board. The glider was flown like a kite with lines attached to it. In 1809, he published an essay based on his theories and experiments. This information was reprinted several times and widely used as a handbook throughout the 19th century.

Until his death in 1857, Cayley maintained his passion for flight and was able to leave behind a number of important contributions. While observing birds in flight, he made the discovery which may be his greatest contribution. He noted that birds could soar great distances by twisting and dipping their extended, arched wings, rather than by flapping them. This observation led to his design of a fixed-wing glider. In other experiments, Cayley identified the forces of lift, drag, and thrust. He tested the behavior of air pressure on various types of wings and recognized the importance of camber and streamlining, as well as the necessity of a tail for longitudinal stability and control. He also saw the need for a light engine for propulsion and the significance of the power-to-weight ratio. Cayley is considered by many historians to have been ahead of his time. Although he never succeeded in flying a powered aircraft, his research and scientific papers proved to be of great value to those who followed him.

Otto Lilienthal (1848-1896) was a German engineer and inventor who has been called the "father of modern aviation."

Otto Lilienthal was the next pioneer in the field of gliding. With his engineering background, he was able to combine theory with practical flight. By 1891, when Lilienthal and his brother Gustav succeeded in

Figure 10-5. Lilienthal launched his gliders by running down an artificial hill, constructed for that purpose, and building up enough speed to sustain flight. When airborne, he relied on body movement for control, a technique similar to that used by modern hang gliders. In five years, Lilienthal made over 2,000 glides, but accumulated only five hours of total flight time.

making short flights, heavier-than-air machines had gained some respect. Despite this fact, both the Lilienthal brothers risked considerable ridicule for their activities. [Figure 10-5]

In 1896, Lilienthal attached an engine to a biplane which was patterned after a double-winged glider he had designed and flown. Before his attempt to fly the powered biplane, he was killed while practicing in his glider.

The activities of the Lilienthal brothers became known over much of the western world through favorable recognition of the German press. Their work inspired many other pioneers of aviation. With the development of photography, Otto Lilienthal was able to include pictures of aircraft in his writings. One pioneer who benefitted from his work was Octave Chanute, a French-born engineer who was an established expert on railroad construction in the United States.

Octave Chanute (1832-1910) was a French-American civil engineer and inventor who is best known for sharing information and promoting progress in heavier-than-air flight.

Like others before him, Chanute carefully studied the flight of birds. However, he went a step further and categorized the methods of flight of various species. He began experimenting with aeronautics rather late in

Figure 10-6. The Chanute gliders ranged from structures with as many as six tiers of wings down to the more effective models like the one shown here. Control depended on body movement of the occupant who was called a "birdman."

life. In fact, he was nearly 64 when he immersed himself in experiments with manned gliders. Some of the principles and structural techniques he discovered became the standard for future airplanes. [Figure 10-6]

Not all of the pioneers conducting experiments were as eager as Chanute to share information, however. By the late 19th and early 20th centuries, heavier-than-air flight was being taken much more seriously by the general public and, in many cases, keen rivalry existed between builders. Because of this, the exchange of information was curtailed, and the mistakes of one competitor were often duplicated by others.

Samuel Langley (1834-1906) was an American aviation pioneer who held positions with several eastern universities and was an official of the Smithsonian Institution.

Samuel Langley also participated in numerous gliding experiments during this period. He maintained that by building a small working model before constructing a larger one, you could complete inexpensive tests before risking a full-sized version. Langley painstakingly labored with small models of hundreds of designs but actually achieved little success with his work. He remained optimistic, however, and continued to experiment with gliders, and later with powered flight.

In gliding, the work of the Wright brothers cannot be discounted. They built a series of gliders, attempting to devise some type of control system. One method they used was flying a glider like a kite. They attached cables to the experimental control surfaces, and then manipulated them from the ground. Their approach to flight was to first develop an aircraft that was controllable, and then add an engine and a propeller.

POWERED FLIGHT

The lack of a suitable powerplant was a major obstacle in the progress of powered flight. Thanks to discoveries of Nikolaus Otto and refinements by Gottlieb Daimler, the internal combustion engine was fairly reliable, but the power-to-weight ratio was the main drawback to its use in an airplane. By the turn of the century, a powerplant specifically for aircraft had not yet been developed.

One of the first to experiment with such an engine was Sir Hiram Maxim, the American-born British subject who invented an early version of the machine gun. Another was a French electrical engineer named Clement Ader.

As the 19th century drew to a close, Maxim was already rich and famous. After many experiments with wing shapes and propellers, he proceeded to build a giant flying machine. Maxim approached the problem on a grand scale. He constructed several steam engines that developed more than 300 horsepower to be used in a heavier-than-air flying machine.

By 1894, Maxim had designed and built a huge three and one-half ton aircraft that was 104 feet long and was powered by two 180-horsepower steam engines. Maxim also designed a long track for the engine-driven flying machine to move on. The tracks were constructed so that the huge aircraft was captive to the track. While testing the machine, Maxim gradually increased the steam pressure until the aircraft attained enough speed to lift off. Then, the control surfaces, consisting of two elevator-like devices, were moved to a lifting position. [Figure 10-7]

Figure 10-7. On the third trial run, when Maxim had attained considerable speed, he pulled back on the controls; the aircraft developed so much lift that it tore itself loose from the tracks. Maxim immediately reduced power to prevent the machine from going further, and it crashed to the ground. Luckily, the inventor's life was spared in the accident.

Although Maxim's efforts were generally considered unsuccessful, he did demonstrate two of the requirements for powered flight — sufficient power and lift. However, he did not achieve a third requirement — control. The experiments by Ader met with a similar fate. He also used a steam-powered machine, but during trials before French officials in 1897, the craft failed to leave the ground. Financial backing was withdrawn, and Ader terminated his experiments.

Samuel Langley, previously mentioned in relation to gliding activities, was another who worked diligently to build a powered heavier-than-air machine. He used the same method of experimentation that he had used with gliders — the practice of scaling. [Figure 10-8]

While associated with the Smithsonian Institution, Langley succeeded in obtaining a government grant of $50,000 for the construction of a flying machine, provided that it met certain criteria. Once again, a major problem was finding a suitable engine. The government required that the machine include a gasoline-powered engine which could develop 12 horsepower and not exceed 100 pounds in weight.

Initially, Langley had difficulty finding someone who would accept the job of constructing an engine to government specifications. A Cornell engineer named Charles M. Manley agreed to take on the task and became Langley's chief engineer and pilot. He not only succeeded in constructing such an engine, but also produced a radial design engine that weighed 207.45 pounds and developed 52.4 horsepower. A **radial engine** consists of a row, or rows, of cylinders arranged around a central crankcase. Manley's engine was bench-run three times for 10 hours each time

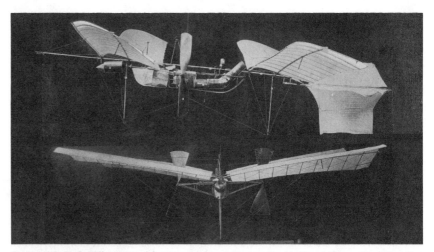

Figure 10-8. Small steam-driven models were constructed and flown to determine flying characteristics for a passenger-carrying model. Some of the models built were actually rather large, with wingspans of up to 12 feet.

without a major mechanical failure; however, the airframe of Langley's airplane, which he called the "aerodrome," did not measure up in quality to the engine produced by Manly. The tail assembly was fixed, and two wings were mounted on the open fuselage in tandem rather than in a biplane configuration. Directional control was provided by a rudder located behind the two large pusher propellers. The aerodrome was to be launched by a catapult from the top of a houseboat anchored in the Potomac River.

During a test flight on October 7, 1903, the aerodrome was catapulted into the Potomac River with Manly at the controls. The aircraft and Manly were retrieved and repairs and modifications were made to the aircraft. A final attempt was made on December 8, 1903, this time before the press and government officials. Again, the aerodrome plunged to the bottom of the Potomac. Newspaper reporters observing the accident used the opportunity to discredit Langley and the United States Government for wasting money and for getting involved in such a foolhardy scheme. Although Langley's attempts ended in failure, Glenn Curtiss flew this model in 1914 after making a few modifications.

Two of history's more renowned pioneers in heavier-than-air flight differed in many ways from their predecessors. They were not engineers, held no academic degrees, and they did not possess fortunes to follow their aeronautical pursuits. However, they were among the most successful in applying theories, including lift and drag formulas, to practical use. These two men were Orville and Wilbur Wright. Sons of a clergyman, they owned a small bicycle manufacturing shop in Dayton, Ohio. Heavier-than-air flight had excited the Wright brothers since mid-1890.

The Wright brothers are the best known of the heavier-than-air pioneers. Wilbur was born in 1867 and died in 1912; Orville was born in 1871 and died in 1948.

To his credit, Octave Chanute was very supportive of the efforts by the Wright brothers. They wrote to Chanute before they achieved notable success in gliding and, characteristically, he aided them in every way he could. After considerable correspondence, Chanute even went to Kill Devil Hills, North Carolina, to help conduct gliding experiments with the Wrights. Kill Devil Hills was selected by the Wrights after carefully checking with the U.S. Weather Bureau in Washington. This site was likely to have the most suitable winds for gliding experiments.

In September 1903, the Wrights were ready to begin testing their powered airplane, which closely resembled their gliders. The wings were light and fragile, with wires or cables attached to the tips so that one or the other of the wings could be warped. They could make coordinated turns by manually warping the wing in conjunction with rudder deflection. Unlike today's conventional airplanes, the Wright's "Flyer" had the elevator ahead of the aircraft and the rudder behind.

Although the Wright brothers had no previous experience in power-plants, they designed and built a lightweight, four-cylinder, water-cooled gasoline engine that produced about 12 horsepower. The engine was assembled in the Wright's bicycle shop in Dayton, Ohio, with the help of one of their machinists. In view of the state of engine development in the early 1900's, this alone was a remarkable feat.

Next, they built two pusher propellers which were unique because they were designed with a profile like a wing. The propellers were connected to the engine by bicycle chains and turned in opposite directions to counteract torque. The Wright brothers realized that propeller efficiency was essential because of the limited engine power. They also were aware of other critical factors, including the distribution of weight and the controllability of their fragile aircraft.

Generally, the Wrights did not seek news coverage of their activities. They lived very frugally, did not drink or smoke, and were considered rather colorless personalities. Perhaps the bad publicity from the Langley failures made them shy away from the press even more. [Figure 10-9]

The takeoff was effective without the aid of a catapult or other booster device. These aids were not incorporated by the Wright brothers until 1904. It is interesting to note that the length of the first flight was actually shorter than the wingspan of a Boeing 747.

Figure 10-9. The Wright brothers' first flight on December 17, 1903, was not witnessed by reporters. Several people who were at the remote sites of a nearby life-saving station and a nearby village telegraphed reports to the press. The reports were so exaggerated, however, that their credibility was questionable.

The Wrights' success was not met with immediate acclaim. Some Dayton papers ran the announcement, but it was not headline news. Most papers throughout the country dismissed the flight as a hoax. In 1904, the Wrights moved their flying activities to a pasture near Dayton and continued experimenting to improve their machine.

In March, 1903, the Wrights had applied for a patent of the unique features of the airplane, particularly the wing-warping device. It was not until they demonstrated their achievement in 1906 that the patent was granted. The Wrights were also met with rejection when they tried to sell their airplane to the United States Government. After exhausting every possibility to sell their ideas in the United States, the Wrights concentrated on France. Wilbur Wright went to France in 1907, taking one airplane with him, while Orville took care of matters at home. Negotiations dragged on in France, possibly because some of the Europeans were having limited success in developing their own airplanes during this period.

In late 1907, the United States finally became interested in purchasing an airplane. Considering the state of technological development and the time involved in filing a bid, the required specifications were very rigid. The aircraft was to have a minimum speed of 36 miles per hour, and it was to carry two persons and enough fuel to fly 125 miles.

While Orville was building a new airplane for the U.S. Army tests, Wilbur performed exhibition flights in France for European governments and businessmen. This proved to be rewarding financially, as well as in the honors received. In March 1908, Wilbur signed a $100,000 contract to form a French company for the purpose of building airplanes using the Wright's patented ideas. In September, 1908, Orville made a series of public demonstration flights at Fort Meyer, near Washington, D.C. To climax a generally successful year, Wilbur won the 20,000-franc Michaelin Prize in France for remaining aloft for 2 hours, 20 minutes during a flight of 77 miles.

While Orville and Wilbur Wright were trying to sell their airplane, another pioneer, Glenn Curtiss, began experimenting with aviation. Curtiss also had a background in the bicycle business and he advanced the bicycle by adding an engine. Since all motorcycle engines traditionally produced high power for their weight, they were exactly what airplane designers needed. The first aircraft engine that Curtiss produced was actually for a lighter-than-air ship. The powerplants he designed were based on his motorcycle-building experience. In addition to being powerful and lightweight, they were also dependable.

Glenn Curtiss (1878-1930), like the Wrights, had a background in the bicycle business.

In 1907, Curtiss and Alexander Graham Bell, the inventor of the telephone, founded the Aerial Experiment Association for the purpose of

Figure 10-10. The innovation of ailerons eliminated the need for wing-warping and gave better control stability and greater rigidity to the wings.

developing and building airplanes. Curtiss provided most of the engines for the various airships and airplanes designed and built by this experimental group. While working as an engine builder for the group, Curtiss also learned a considerable amount about building airframes. He was a person who could visualize a completed project and was extremely good at making improvements to existing models and methods of construction.

The first airplane he built and designed for the association contained many important improvements. One of the most significant was the addition of ailerons as separate control surfaces located between the wings of his biplane design. [Figure 10-10]

EXHIBITION AND RECORD FLIGHTS

After the third airplane was constructed, Curtiss left the Aerial Experiment Association and began to demonstrate his airplane before public groups. These public displays were the start of a long rivalry between Curtiss and the Wright brothers.

After 1909, the Wright brothers abandoned much of their developmental work to become involved in a series of lawsuits regarding the patent rights. The Wrights could not patent the idea of heavier-than-air controlled flight, but did succeed in using their patent for a wing-warping device to demand royalties and licensing fees from manufacturers of other airplanes. They violently disapproved of using airplanes for exhibition flying, which they considered to be a "circus performance." Perhaps because the Wrights were unwilling to give adequate demonstration flights, the public began to turn against them.

Glenn Curtiss, who was their only really important competitor, presented a different public image. Friendly and outgoing, Curtiss made arrangements for many exhibition flights and entered numerous competitions with the airplanes his company constructed. He helped start one of the first schools of flying in the United States and he worked to see that others had an opportunity to purchase airplanes for exhibition purposes.

Curtiss took his airplane abroad. After competing with considerable success in several air meets in France, he returned to the United States to accomplish a feat which had great impact in America. He flew from Albany to New York City in an airplane of his own design to win a prize of $10,000.

In 1910, Curtiss flew exhibition flights in St. Louis and Chicago as publicity for his airplane. Later that year, he organized a team of flyers whose purpose it was to tour the country, providing rural America with its first glimpse of an airplane. It was not long before the Wright brothers followed suit and formed their own team. The pilots who made up these teams were hired more for their daring than for their technical knowledge of airplanes. They performed a variety of crowd-pleasing stunts and tried to outdo each other during each performance. As a result of this type of competition, much was learned about aerodynamics; records of speed, distance, and time spent in the air were continuously broken. Many pilots became famous while flying with the exhibition teams. Lincoln Beachey, who flew with the Curtiss team, was considered by Orville Wright to be "the greatest aviator of all." He is perhaps best known for setting an altitude record of 11,600 feet by completely filling his gas tank and climbing until he ran out of fuel, then gliding down to a successful power-off landing.

During these early years of flying, it was not considered "proper," or "lady-like" for women to fly. For these reasons, Glenn Curtiss expressed his reluctance when Blanche Stuart Scott, 19, asked him to teach her to fly. Her persistence convinced Curtiss, and on September 2, 1910, she became the first American woman to solo. [Figure 10-11]

Figure 10-11. Although Blanche Stuart Scott never received her pilot's license, she went on to become an exhibition pilot.

By the end of 1910, the range of airplanes increased significantly. This increase resulted more from the persistence of pilots than from improvements in engine design. Overwater flights, mountain crossings, and long distance cross-country flights soon became the goal of many pilots.

On July 25, 1909, Louis Bleriot of France overcame a number of problems, including an overheated engine and rainy weather, to be the first person to cross the English Channel in an airplane. The first woman to accomplish this same feat was Harriet Quimby on April 26, 1912. [Figure 10-12]

The first successful crossing of the Alps was accomplished by a Peruvian, Gene Bielovucio, on January 25, 1911. Although he was not the first to fly across this mountain range, Bielovucio was the first to land safely after the crossing.

In the United States, William Randolf Hearst offered a $50,000 prize to any pilot who could fly from New York to California in 30 days. A motorcycle enthusiast, Calbraith P. Rodgers, set out on September 17, 1911, on a flight from New York to Pasadena. Rodgers was forced to make numerous unscheduled stops for repairs, but finally completed the flight on November 5, 1911. Although he was 19 days too late to collect

Figure 10-12. Harriet Quimby was the first American woman to receive a pilot's license.

the prize, Rodgers was greeted by a crowd of 20,000 people who cheered him for being the first to complete a coast-to-coast flight. Unfortunately, Rodgers did not have long to enjoy the public adulation. He was killed four months later in a crash in the Pacific Ocean while performing an exhibition flight.

Another development in 1911 was the introduction of the first practical seaplane by Glenn Curtiss. For water takeoffs and landings, he simply added a large float to the center section of his standard landplane and attached two smaller floats to the wings.

Ruth Law Oliver became one of America's more colorful early barnstormer pilots. Because of her background, she was billed as "The Flying Debutante." In 1915, Mrs. Oliver established an altitude record for women. A year later, on November 19, she participated in a record nonstop flight of 512 miles (from Chicago to New York) in 5 hours and 40 minutes. [Figure 10-13]

Between 1911 and 1917, a number of significant changes were made in the design of airplanes. One of the major changes was moving the location of the ailerons from a position between the wings to the trailing edge of the wings. Wing-warping, as developed by the Wrights, was virtually abandoned by 1918. By 1914, another significant change had

Figure 10-13. Like Scott and Quimby, Ruth Law Oliver later became famous for her exhibition and aerobatic flying.

Figure 10-14. This arrangement, shown here on the Curtiss Jenny, provided for simpler fuselage construction, better protection for the pilot, and improved weight distribution. After 1914, a tandem seat for passengers was another feature of many airplanes.

appeared. Engines were being mounted in a tractor (forward) position rather than a pusher position. [Figure 10-14]

A continuing problem for airplane designers was finding strong enough lightweight materials for the airframe while, at the same time, eliminating many components which produced drag. In addition to a tandem seat for the passenger, the elevator was moved from the front of the aircraft to the tail. With the empennage, fuselage, and other changes, the airplane began to take on the appearance that prevailed for many years.

Progress in aircraft design, however, was hampered because the builders had to contend with the threat of legal action by the Wright brothers. Because of this, the scientific community in the United States began to turn away from the Wright brothers. The last scientific award received by the Wrights was the Collier Trophy Award in 1913, the year after Wilbur died of typhoid fever. During this period, the Smithsonian Institution refused to give the Wright brothers adequate recognition and went so far as to hire Glenn Curtiss, their main competitor, to fly the Langley aerodrome which had been carefully stored in Hammondsport, New York. The Smithsonian contended that the Langley aerodrome was capable of sustained flight, and it was only due to the unfavorable circumstances that Langley encountered which allowed the Wright brothers' model to succeed before the Langley model. [Figure 10-15]

Figure 10-15. Curtiss equipped his Langley aerodrome with floats, made a series of changes to provide for better structural integrity, and succeeded in flying the machine.

The controversy between Orville Wright and Glenn Curtiss continued. Orville was unwilling to have the Wright airplane of 1903 exhibited in this country and made arrangements to send the airplane to London to be exhibited in the South Kensington Museum. It was not until after Orville's death in 1948 that the Wright airplane was returned to the United States and exhibited in the Smithsonian Institution, where it is to this day. The label on this airplane reads, "The World's First Power-Driven Heavier-Than-Air Machine in Which Man Made Free, Controlled, and Sustained Flight."

In addition to the legal problems, historians can cite many reasons for the slow development of the airplane before World War I. These include major technical problems, limited funding, resistance to new concepts, and the lack of a practical way to use the airplane. Shortly after the beginning of World War I, the circumstances changed dramatically. Public interest and Congressional action were accelerated. In the short span of a few years, the United States was destined to become the world's major producer of aircraft.

CHECKLIST ━━━━━━━━━━━━━━━━━━━━━

After studying this section, you should have a basic understanding of:

✓ **Balloons** — How balloons were developed, what the two common types are, and what some of the limitations are.

✓ **Airships** — How airships differ from balloons, what the main characteristics and types are, and how they have been used.

✓ **Gliders** — Who the early heavier-than-air pioneers were, and how they contributed to the future of aviation.

✓ **Powered flight** — What the main obstacles were, who the major figures were, and how they succeeded.

✓ **Exhibition and record flights** — How the airplane was displayed to the public and what some of the early record-setting achievements were.

✓ **Problems in development of the airplane** — What the main obstacles to growth of airplane utilization were and what steps were initially taken to overcome these obstacles.

SECTION B

WORLD WAR I

History shows that war, or the threat of war, speeds up technological development. This was especially true in the case of the airplane during World War I and, later, in World War II. In 1914, the airplane was barely 10 years old, and its practical use was limited. This situation was soon to change.

PREWAR STATUS OF AVIATION

Before World War I, the success of men like the Wright brothers and Glenn Curtiss attracted many people who wished to make a name for themselves by demonstrating their aircraft or flying abilities. Flying contests and exhibitions, which were held throughout the world, provided a stage where performers could entertain crowds of spectators. Even though these exhibitions led to improvements in aircraft design and the flying ability of pilots, the airplane was still considered a novelty.

Among the first to find a practical use for an airplane was the famed magician, Harry Houdini. In 1910, he bought a French-made Voisin and began flying it from one theatrical engagement to another. During the next few years, a number of money-making ventures were attempted by a variety of businessmen. Although most of these initial attempts were unsuccessful, others later succeeded with the same ideas.

The first experiments that used an airplane to deliver mail were in 1911.

A French pilot named Paquet made the first mail run as part of the All-India Exposition on February 18, 1911. Later the same year, Earle L. Ovington dropped mail from his monoplane onto the sidewalk in front of the Mineola Post Office in Long Island. This first U.S. experiment in airmail delivery was a daily attraction of the Sheepshead-Long Island Air Meet which lasted nine days. Several more airmail experiments were conducted the following year. While the Post Office cooperated by supplying the mail and granting permission for the experimental delivery, it did not help with the costs.

In November 1912, Anthony Jannus started a one-man air freight and passenger service between Omaha, Nebraska, and New Orleans, Louisiana. His service, which was limited to carrying lightweight merchandise, mail, and an occasional passenger, lasted for a little over a month. About one year later, on January 1, 1914, Jannus opened a new passenger service operating between St. Petersburg and Tampa, Florida. The "flying boat" he used could carry only one passenger. Jannus had trouble finding enough people who were willing to pay the high fares necessary to make the venture profitable; he abandoned the operation after three months.

Skywriting was introduced in Seattle, Washington, by Milton J. Bryant on July 19, 1913. Although originally a stunt, skywriting developed into a form of advertising and became popular at large gatherings, such as circuses and fairs. About two years later, another use for the airplane was discovered. On June 22, 1915, while flying over a wooded area in Wisconsin, forest ranger E. M. Griffiths and pilot Jack Vilas became the first to use an airplane for spotting forest fires.

While these early experiments proved that the airplane could be useful, they also indicated it would be difficult to make a profit. As a result, governments and businessmen were seldom willing to invest the money needed to establish a long-standing service. After war was declared in Europe in 1914, much of the doubt about the utility of the airplane began to disappear.

CIVIL AVIATION DEVELOPMENTS (1914-1918)

Not long after the Wright brothers' first flight, a number of city and state laws were passed to govern the operation of airplanes. They varied from prohibiting flying on Sundays to registration of aircraft. In 1915, President Woodrow Wilson established the **National Advisory Committee for Aeronautics** (NACA). Its purpose was to "supervise and direct the scientific study of the problems of flight, with a view of their practical solution." The NACA was an independent agency with 17 unpaid members who were appointed by the President and reported directly to him. They established policy and planned research that eventually was conducted by 8,000 scientists, engineers, and support personnel in unique research facilities throughout the United States. The NACA was absorbed by the **National Aeronautics and Space Administration** (NASA) which was created in 1958.

The NACA, which was established in 1915, developed into the agency known today as NASA.

In 1916, Congress allocated $50,000 for airmail service, but the development was curtailed by World War I. Two years later, Congress appropriated an additional $100,000 for establishment of experimental airmail routes. Two of the key figures in organizing the first route were Captain Benjamin Lipsner of the United States Army Signal Corps and Otto Praeger, who served as the Second Assistant Postmaster General between 1915 and 1921.

Praeger was able to persuade the U. S. Army to provide four Curtiss Jenny training airplanes and Army pilots to fly the initial route. It went between Washington, D.C. and New York City, with a planned stop in Philadelphia. The inaugural flight took place on May 15, 1918. During

The first experimental airmail route in the United States was established May 15, 1918.

this first attempt, there were a few unplanned diversions, but the experimental flight was completed later that same day by Army Lieutenants Webb and Culver without serious incident.

The experimental route remained in effect until August 10, 1918. Two days later, the Post Office Department started the world's first permanent civilian airmail service. The Standard Aircraft Company of Elizabeth, New Jersey, had delivered six custom-built airplanes to the Postal Service. Army pilots were replaced with experienced civilian pilots and a number of routes were established between cities. Lipsner resigned his Army commission and became the first Aerial Mail Superintendent. Aviation historians generally consider the beginning of regular airmail service as the key event in the development of air transportation in this country.

When regularly scheduled airmail service was established in August 1918, it marked the real beginning of air transportation in the United States.

DEVELOPMENT OF AIR WARFARE

Most of the major European nations had formed some type of military flying service by 1914. However, in the United States, the single Wright airplane purchased in 1908 remained the Army's only airplane until 1911 when Congress allocated funds to buy five more. By the beginning of 1914, only 19 of the 28 airplanes purchased by the U.S. Army remained. Of the 40 trained pilots, 11 had been killed in crashes.

At the beginning of 1914, the U.S. Army had only 19 airplanes and 29 pilots.

Until 1917, the United States maintained a neutral position and did not enter the war. However, many young men did not wait; they volunteered their services before 1917. Some flew with England's Royal Flying Corps, and many others joined American flying units in France — the most famous of which was the Lafayette Escadrille. This unit of the French Air Service was made up of American personnel.

American pilots flew in combat before the U.S. entered the war in April 1917. At that time, the most famous American flying unit was the Lafayette Escadrille.

When Americans first volunteered, they had to find a way to get around a French law that required all pilots to be French-born citizens. Most dealt with this requirement by joining the French Foreign Legion as infantrymen, then eventually being assigned to a flying unit. This arrangement was not satisfactory, and influential French and American citizens petitioned to have the law changed. In July 1915, the law was changed so Americans could be assigned directly to various units for flight training. The first all-American unit was initially called Escadrille Americaine. When the German ambassador in Washington, D.C. complained that the American unit was in violation of the U.S. neutral position, the name was changed to the Lafayette Escadrille in honor of the French general who fought on the side of the Americans during the Revolutionary War.

When the United States entered the war in April 1917, the total number of planes that had been delivered to the military services was probably less than 200. Considering that many of these airplanes had been destroyed and others were obsolete, the number of aircraft available for combat was much lower. It was difficult to build an air service, because no facilities existed for mass production of airplanes and pilot training programs were not established.

During this period, airplanes were built by hand as individual units. The advantages of mass production and interchangeable parts, already in use in the automobile industry, had not been implemented in aircraft manufacturing. To add to the problem, no support industries had been established to complement the production of airplanes. Machine guns, flight instruments, and aviation camera equipment had not been developed in the United States.

As of May 12, 1917, there were standing orders for 334 aircraft to be delivered by 16 different manufacturers. These aircraft included 10 different types and 32 separate designs. The largest order placed with a single manufacturer, the Curtiss Airplane and Motor Company, was for 126 airplanes. To speed up delivery times, mechanical designers and engineers were sent to Europe to study the latest types of aircraft. Models of these aircraft were purchased and brought to McCook Field at Dayton, Ohio, to be studied in detail.

Licensing agreements were made with European manufacturers to produce successful designs, rather than to begin experimenting with unproven American designs. A group known as the Joint Army and Navy Technical Board recommended a program calling for the production of 22,000 airplanes by July 1, 1918. Of course, the underdeveloped state of aircraft manufacturing in the United States made this task impossible. By the end of the war, not a single American-designed airplane saw action.

Airplanes for military use became available in Europe at a much faster rate. During the prewar years, Europeans experienced the same problems as those that existed in the United States — convincing political leaders that airplanes were necessary and that governments must provide funding. Several countries were able to overcome these problems and began building airplanes before the war. Rough estimates indicate that France entered the war with about 300 airplanes, Britain with about 250, and Germany with about 1,000 aircraft.

When the war began in Europe in August 1914, airplanes were still not widely accepted for military use. Although balloons had been used in the Civil War and in Europe during the Franco-Prussian War, airplanes had been used in combat on only a limited basis by the Italian Army over Turkey. Many people could not foresee the potential of the airplane in combat. World War I provided a test of the airplane's usefulness in warfare.

Initially, pilots flew small, light airplanes over enemy positions to observe enemy defenses and troop movements. The only contact that pilots of one side had with pilots of the other side was an occasional wave of the hand if they flew close enough for visual contact. This casual attitude did not last long, however. In the two-place observation planes, or "ships" as they were sometimes called in imitation of the naval term, the observers began arming themselves with pistols. At first, air-to-air encounters amounted to no more than the exchange of a few pistol shots at long-range, but this soon led to closer and more deadly engagements.

When pilots first flew over enemy positions, the troops in the trenches sometimes responded with small arms fire. Pilots and observers, in turn, dropped grenades and fired hand-held weapons. Initially, these aerial attacks by "observation" airplanes were discouraged. Before long, though, pilots or observers began dropping hand-armed bombs from their airplanes.

Within a few months, air warfare broadened. Light machine guns were mounted at the rear of the observer's cockpit to fire at airborne enemies. Bomb racks were added to the wings so loose bombs would not roll around the cockpit and explode accidentally during flight maneuvers.

The first long-range strategic bombing mission was flown by the British in 1914.

In November 1914, the British attempted what is generally considered the first long-range strategic bombing mission in the history of aviation. They sent three Avro 504's to bomb Zeppelin bases in southern Germany. During this time, Germany also had formed a bomber squadron called the "Carrier Pigeons." By January 1915, German pilots were raiding Dunkirk, France, behind Allied lines. Surprisingly, they flew at night and in formation.

Soon, pilots were assigned the task of driving off intruders and air-to-air combat intensified. Airplanes on both sides were quickly modified to counteract enemy advances. At first, existing observation planes were fitted with armaments, but designs specifically for air combat were introduced by 1915. [Figure 10-16]

By the end of 1914, many efforts were being made to mount a fixed, forward-firing gun. The main problem was the obstacle created by the spinning propeller, which was in a forward position on most airplanes. [Figure 10-17]

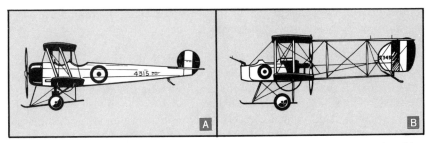

Figure 10-16. The Avro 504 (airplane A) was used in the first long-range bombing mission. It was a biplane with the propeller mounted in the "tractor" (forward) position. Over 8,000 of these legendary British fighters were built. One of the first airplanes equipped with a machine gun was the Vickers F.B. 5 (airplane B). It also was a British biplane, but the propeller was mounted in the "pusher" position, behind the engine. The "F.B." was an abbreviation for "fighting biplane"; however, the F.B. 5 was usually called the "Gunbus."

FAMOUS COMBATANTS

In February 1915, the pilot of a German observation airplane was surprised when a French fighter, flown by Roland Garros, attacked head-on. Garros had modified his forward-firing Morane-Saulnier by bolting steel wedges to his propeller blades directly in front of the gun barrel. When he fired through the propeller arc, most of the bullets missed the spinning blades. Those that hit the blades ricocheted off the deflector device. With this crude and dangerous deflector, Garros shot off several propellers, but he was successful in downing six enemy aircraft within three weeks. The French people awarded him the title of "ace" after he shot down the fifth enemy airplane.

Five "victories" or "kills" became the standard requirement for a fighter pilot to become an ace. The advantage Garros gained with his forward-firing gun lasted until April 19, 1915, when engine trouble forced him to land behind enemy lines. Although Garros later escaped, his airplane remained in Germany. The Germans immediately assigned the task of

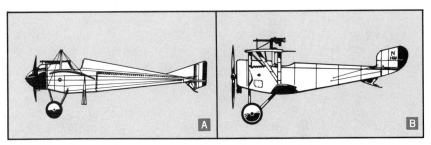

Figure 10-17. The first Allied fighter to be equipped with a fixed, forward-firing gun was the French Morane-Saulnier (airplane A), with the gun mounted directly behind the propeller. Another arrangement was the French Nieuport 11 biplane (airplane B), with the gun mounted on the high wing, above the propeller.

improving the Garros gun design to a brilliant Dutch airplane designer, Anthony Fokker. [Figure 10-18]

With the forward-firing, synchronized gun mounted on their Fokker Eindecker, a monoplane, the Germans gained a huge advantage. The first Fokker Eindecker equipped with the new gun was assigned to Lieutenant Oswald Boelcke, a former school teacher, who was then Germany's leading ace. The second went to Max Immelmann who was already famous for the aerial combat maneuver that is named for him. The Immelmann is now a standard acrobatic maneuver.

Because of Fokker's ingenuity, the Germans were dominant in the air for several months. The Allies, however, countered with their own forward-firing designs, such as the British Vickers F.B. 5 (Gunbus) with its pusher propeller and the French-designed Nieuport with a gun mounted at the top of the upper wing. While these arrangements provided a forward-firing capability, the Nieuport was slowed by increased drag from the gun; the Vickers Gunbus, however, was more evenly matched against the Fokker Eindecker.

Since the Germans were afraid that the enemy would capture and copy the new design, they initially flew Fokkers equipped with these guns only over their own lines. Eventually, a German pilot became lost in the fog and mistakenly landed in Allied territory. The plane was captured and the gun was examined and copied. As a result, the Germans lost their advantage.

One of the most notable German aces was Baron Manfred von Richthofen, better known as the **Red Baron**. Richthofen earned a reputation for being a relentless hunter who seldom missed his mark. [Figure 10-19]

As squadron commander, the Red Baron identified his plane by painting it brilliant red. Later, each plane in his squadron sported a different color. As a result, Richthofen's troop was called the Flying Circus. Richthofen also used formation flying with his squadron in a V-formation of six or more planes. This tactic provided mutual support and hindered enemy aircraft from positioning themselves above or behind him. He also used tactics such as superior force and surprise which were developed earlier by Oswald Boelcke.

On April 21, 1918, a British Royal Air Force pilot, Captain Arthur Royal Brown, came upon the Red Baron chasing another British plane. All three planes flew toward the British lines with Brown shooting at Richthofen's airplane. Richthofen was flying a Fokker with pastel lavender wings instead of his usual red Fokker. Brown was assisted by ground fire from an Australian machine-gun crew. The Fokker crashed behind Allied lines, though it is not known whose bullet actually killed the Red Baron.

Figure 10-18. Fokker succeeded in perfecting a method of shooting through the propeller by synchronizing the gun with the propeller shaft so the bullets completely missed the propeller blades.

Figure 10-19. Richthofen used Fokker's forward-firing machine gun to bring down 80 enemy planes in less than 15 months.

In recognition of his daring as a fighting man, the British buried Richthofen with full military honors.

"Ace of Aces" was a term bestowed on fighter pilots like Richthofen who downed more aircraft than any other pilot in his country. This honor was also held by Rene Fonck of France with 75 kills, England's Edward Mannock with 73, Canada's Billy Bishop with 72, Italy's Francesco Barrac with 36, Belgium's Willy Coppens with 34, Edward V. Rickenbacker of the United States with 26, and Russia's Alexander Kazakov with 17.

Other top American aces included Frank Luke Jr. with 18 kills and Raoul Lufbery of the Lafayette Escadrille with 17. Like Rickenbacker, Luke was awarded the Congressional Medal of Honor. Luke Air Force Base in Arizona was named for him. Lufbery, an American of French ancestry, was decorated by Great Britain, France, and the United States. He was the top ace of the Lafayette Escadrille. All together there were 100 American aces in World War I; 20 flew with British flying units and 80 were assigned to French or U.S. units in France.

In spite of the prestige enjoyed at home by the war-time pilots, most of them came to the front lines with only a brief period of training. Many entered combat with less than 10 hours total flying time, half of which was dual instruction. They were fortunate to be able to get their airplanes off the ground and back in one piece, let alone fly against a relatively well-trained enemy in combat.

Most pilots in World War I went into combat with very little flying experience.

Training was not the only problem. Pilots were also troubled by aircraft of poor structural design, particularly during the early part of the war.

The airplanes of World War I were, for the most part, rushed to the front without adequate testing. They often had poor flying characteristics, and several models had serious quality control problems. Wings warped with changes in humidity and fabric ripped from wings. Control surfaces, and even wings, sometimes came off entirely. It was not unusual for only a few airplanes to return from a mission because the rest were forced down by mechanical failures.

IMPROVED DESIGNS

During the war, tremendous advances were made in the design of airplanes, engine technology, and the use of armament. This evolution came about because of the changing role airplanes played in the war. They were first used for observation, and were designed to fly slow and remain stable so the pilot or observer could study or photograph the ground.

Most of the observation planes were based on prewar designs. Examples include the British BE-2, designed by Captain Geoffrey de Havilland, the Bristol Scout, and the Sopwith Tabloid. These were steady and reliable reconnaissance airplanes. The French initially used Morane-Saulnier monoplanes and Nieuport biplanes for scouting and a slower Farman pusher biplane for observation. Several heavy biplanes were used by the Germans for artillery spotting and reconnaissance. They used others, like the Albatross biplane and the Taube "Dove" monoplane for scouting.

After the first crude form of air-to-air combat between observation pilots, the need for arms and for faster, more maneuverable airplanes was recognized. At the start of the war, the airplanes had an average speed of 70 to 80 m.p.h. and a ceiling, or maximum flight altitude, of about 10,000 feet. By the end of the war, the average speed increased to 140 to 150 m.p.h. and the ceiling to 24,000 feet. [Figure 10-20]

The S.E. 5a became Britain's best fighter. It was a favorite of many aces, including Edward Mannock and Billy Bishop. Mannock, the top British ace who downed 73 planes, scored 50 of his kills while flying the S.E. 5a. Aces who flew the Spad included France's Fonck and America's Rickenbacker. The Fokker Dr.1, a triplane, is closely linked with the legendary Baron von Richthofen and his Flying Circus. The Junkers CL-1 appeared late in the war and only about 45 of them were completed by November, 1918. Although few of these aircraft reached the front, the design was an indicator of the fighter airplane of the future.

Bombers also evolved from the small reconnaissance planes capable of dropping a few hand-held bombs to airplanes which could carry up to 6,000 pounds of bombs. British, French, and Russian airplanes were designed especially for bombing. In 1916, the Germans introduced the first of the famous Gotha bombers. It carried three machine guns and

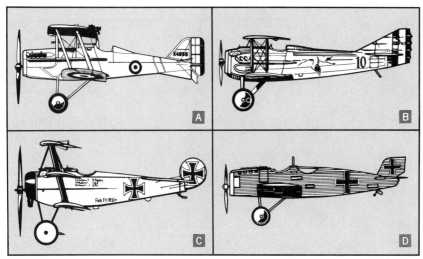

Figure 10-20. The faster and more maneuverable fighters toward the end of the war included the S.E. 5a (airplane A), France's Spad VII (airplane B), Germany's Fokker Dr.1 (airplane C), and the world's first all-metal, low-wing monoplane — the Junkers CL-1 fighter (airplane D).

1,000 pounds of bombs. The British used a series of de Havilland bombers and later the Handley Page 0/400 models. French designs included the Voisin Pusher, the Cuadron G-IV, and the Breguet 14. The most successful Russian bomber produced in World War I was the Ilya Mourometz (Giant) which was built by pioneer designer, Igor Sikorsky. Because of their heavy armor, only two were lost out of approximately 75 that were built.

Improvements in airplane speed and load capacity could not have been made without similar advances in engine design. Early engines averaged less than 100 horsepower, and 80 hours between overhauls was considered excellent performance. Britain's D.H. 2 was powered by a 100-horsepower, pusher-type Gnome engine; the Sopwith Tabloid was powered by an 80 horsepower Gnome rotary engine. A 70-horsepower, Renault pusher engine was used on the French Farman "Shorthorn." Early German airplanes were powered by Argus or Mercedes 100-horsepower, water-cooled engines. By the end of the war, horsepower increased significantly, as did the time between overhauls. The D.H. 4, first flown by Britain in 1917, was powered by a 375-horsepower, liquid-cooled Rolls Royce engine. The Liberty Engine, first tested on July 4, 1917 by America's Packard Motor Company, was a 400-horsepower, V-12 engine with the cylinders in two blocks.

By November 1918, pilots on both sides were flying fast, heavily armed fighters. Multiplane aerial battles, called dogfights, were common with whole squadrons engaged in deadly combat. Reconnaissance airplanes were able to photograph and report on practically every movement of ground forces. They also directed artillery fire. Bombers ranged

By the end of World War I, airplanes were used widely for varied combat missions.

over great distance, dropping high-explosive and fire bombs on troop concentrations as well as industrial targets. Torpedo planes had been developed and were successful against ships at sea. Long-range flying boats roamed far out to sea while guarding against the submarine threat.

Along with these developments, the aircraft industry grew from a few, scattered workshops to a large network of manufacturers. For example, by 1918, the aircraft industry in Britain employed approximately 350,000 men and women. By war's end, they were able to produce about 30,000 warplanes a year. Comparable expansion of the aircraft industry also occurred in the other major countries which produced warplanes during this period.

CHECKLIST

After studying this section, you should have a basic understanding of:

✓ **Prewar status of aviation** — How the airplane was displayed and used in the U.S. before World War I.

✓ **Civil aviation developments (1914-1918)** — How significant events during this period promoted civil aviation.

✓ **Development of air warfare** — How the role of airplanes changed from observation to active combat.

✓ **Famous combatants** — Who some of the most well-known pilots of World War I were, and what their accomplishments were.

✓ **Improved designs** — How airplane design, engine development, and the use of armament evolved during World War I.

THE GOLDEN AGE

Many historians refer to the period between approximately 1919 and 1939 as "the golden age" of aviation. During this 20-year period, there were many dramatic and exciting exploits by aviators. New speed and altitude records were set, only to be broken and reset over and over again. Continents and oceans were crossed and each accomplishment encouraged others to try and do it better or faster. By the end of this period, the airplane changed from a slow, fabric-covered biplane to a fast, all metal monoplane.

In the period immediately after World War I, the prosperity, spurred by wartime production, created a false sense of optimism. By 1919, thousands of airplanes were available at bargain prices because they were declared war surplus. In addition, associated spare parts, including brand new engines, were plentiful. For example, an airworthy JN-4, "Jenny," in good condition, could be purchased for as little as $200. Unfortunately, the glamour of civil aviation had been dampened by the war, and few were able to take advantage of the low purchase cost because of a postwar recession.

THE FLYING CIRCUS AND BARNSTORMING

The main challenge for aviation was to convince the public that the airplane was still exciting and, more importantly, useful. Since the mere sight of an airplane in flight was no longer enough to attract a crowd, flying circuses were organized.

At first, these events could draw crowds by giving extended aerobatic shows. In a short time, though, even mock World War I dogfights could no longer fill the stands. Next, acrobats were suspended from trapezes under airplanes. Women and children were used as acrobats to draw even larger crowds. Finally, wing walkers were attached to the top of biplanes where they stayed in the same position while the airplanes went through aerobatic maneuvers. Plane-to-plane transfers became popular, and plane-to-automobile transfers followed. Aerial acrobatic teams began touring the country. One team, the Five Blackbirds, was a group of black aerial acrobats who thrilled the crowds with their death-defying stunts.

In addition to scheduled air shows like the flying circuses, barnstorming also attracted public attention. Generally, **barnstorming** consisted of brief, unscheduled stops by pilots performing stunt flying and sometimes offering rides to passengers. Usually, the barnstormers traveled across

Figure 10-21. Although military aviation was reduced by about 95% shortly after World War I, interest in aviation was kept alive by barnstormers. Charles Lindbergh was one of the most daring of the early barnstormers.

the United States, often making their stops in rural areas. Barnstorming provided a training ground for many famous pilots of the period. Among these were Art Gobel, Roscoe Turner, and Charles Lindbergh. [Figure 10-21]

THE OCEAN BARRIER

While the barnstormers did much to promote aviation, attempts to span the Atlantic Ocean provided an even greater stimulus. The natural barriers, such as mountain ranges and oceans, remained to be conquered. Some of the record flights were made to collect prize money, while others were flown by military pilots to demonstrate or test new airplanes.

The first successful flight across the Atlantic Ocean was completed in May 1919 by Lieutenant Albert C. Read of the U.S. Navy. Although this was not a nonstop flight, it was an historic event in aviation history.

In May 1919, the United States Navy made the first attempt to fly across the Atlantic Ocean. The flight was planned in four stages with three Curtiss flying boats. The long, critical leg was from Trepassey, Newfoundland, to the Azores, which is an island off the coast of Portugal. This leg of the flight was about 1,200 miles over open water. Of the three flying boats that began the trip, only one actually completed it. One did not reach the Azores, although the crew was rescued. The second had to land short of the Azores and taxi the last 205 miles. Due to rough seas, this second airplane was damaged and unable to continue. The third flying boat, commanded by Lieutenant Read, completed the leg of the trip from Newfoundland to the Azores. From there, it flew triumphantly to Portugal and then to Plymouth, England, where the Mayflower had embarked more than 300 years earlier. [Figure 10-22]

In 1913, the London Daily Mail newspaper offered 10,000 pounds, which was approximately $10,000 at that time, for a nonstop flight between the

Figure 10-22. Although this first attempt was nearly a disaster, it did prove the feasibility of flying across the Atlantic. The total time for the single NC-4 that completed the four-leg trip was more than 50 hours.

New World and the British Isles. The offer was still unclaimed after World War I when Captain John Alcock and Lieutenant Arthur Brown accepted the challenge. They were veterans of the Royal Air Force and both had outstanding war records. After lengthy preparations and weather delays, they finally took off from St. John's, Newfoundland, in July 1919. Their aircraft was a British Vickers-Vimy bomber, converted for this flight. The two 350-horsepower Rolls-Royce engines were barely adequate for the heavyweight takeoff. The huge open-cockpit biplane was loaded with 856 gallons of fuel and it weighed 13,500 pounds at liftoff. After 16 hours, 12 minutes, much of it in heavy fog, they attempted to land in what appeared to be an open meadow. The field actually was an Irish bog, and the airplane was substantially damaged upon landing. However, Alcock and Brown survived uninjured and collected the prize after their history-making flight.

During this same period shortly after the first World War, the U.S. Post Office continued trying to organize airmail service. By the summer of 1919, a service was established between New York and Chicago — but not without a price. Pilots flying rebuilt warplanes with open cockpits referred to the route over the stormy Allegheny Mountains as the "graveyard run." Of the first 40 pilots hired by the Post Office, 31 were killed before the operation was turned over to private airlines.

In spite of the problems with eastern airmail routes, the Post Office opened new routes in the west and contracted with private aviators for others. In Seattle, Edward Hubbard was successful in running a route across Puget Sound to Victoria, British Columbia. He made his initial

The first nonstop flight across the Atlantic was completed in 1919 when John Alcock and Arthur Whitten Brown covered 1,880 miles in a little over 16 hours — a ground-speed of almost 120 miles per hour.

flight in 1919 in a pontoon-equipped biplane which was built at the new Seattle factory of William E. Boeing.

THE ERA OF BILLY MITCHELL

General William "Billy" Mitchell (1879-1936), the son of a U.S. Senator, became America's chief advocate of military air power.

The hard-earned interest created by the barnstormers, the record setters, and the airmail pioneers did not completely overcome the depressed state of postwar aviation. However, Brigadier General "Billy" Mitchell, who in 1919 was the Assistant Chief of the Army Air Service in Washington, D.C., remained a driving force behind military air progress. [Figure 10-23]

In the 1920's, some serious interservice rivalries existed. Following the impact of the book, *The Influence of Sea Power Upon History, 1660-1783,* by Captain Alfred Mahan, the United States Navy was given priority over the other military services. The basic point of the book was that the most powerful nations in the world, historically, had risen to greatness largely because of their sea power. In order to support such a force on a worldwide basis, Mahan stated that it was necessary to have colonies to use as naval bases all over the world. Even though this book was published in 1890, its influence was particularly strong after the close of World War I.

General Mitchell, one of the foremost proponents of a powerful military air service, challenged Mahan's basic idea of an invincible Navy. As the result of this battle with the Navy and members of Congress, his appointment as Assistant Chief of the Air Services was not renewed. He reverted to his permanent rank of Colonel and was assigned to Fort Sam Houston, Texas. This got him far away from Washington, but did not quiet his tongue. It was from Fort Sam Houston that he issued a blistering 6,000-word statement in response to the Navy's abortive California-to-Hawaii flight and the crash of a Navy dirigible, the "Shenandoah." The most controversial part was his public accusation that the War and Navy Departments were guilty of "incompetency, criminal negligence, and almost treasonable administration of the national defense." It was this statement made in September 1925 that eventually resulted in his court martial.

This furor actually began much earlier. Mitchell's support of air power as a separate military service received tremendous support when Mitchell's bombers sunk the German battleship, "Ostfriesland." On July 21, 1921, Mitchell's pilots carefully dropped specially prepared, 2,000-pound bombs alongside the battleship, and the resulting underwater reverberations ruptured the hull. The "unsinkable" vessel, which had been the pride of the German Navy, turned over and went down 25 minutes later. In 1923, a further demonstration achieved a similar result. Two old U.S. battleships — the "Virginia" and the "New Jersey" — were sunk by Martin MB-2 bombers. [Figure 10-24]

Figure 10-23. Brigadier General William "Billy" Mitchell rekindled the interest in military aviation after World War I.

Figure 10-24. The sinking of the giant battleship, "Ostfriesland," in 1921 left no doubt that air power would play a dominant part in future warfare at sea.

Although General Mitchell had demonstrated the effectiveness of aircraft against large warships, the Navy secured the backing of some influential Congressmen in condemning his outspoken criticism of defense policy. In December 1925, an Army court martial convicted General Mitchell of insubordination and sentenced him to suspension from rank and duty for five years.

After the controversial court-martial, President Coolidge attempted to lighten the punishment by restoring a portion of Mitchell's pay and allowances. Mitchell replied by resigning from the Army. Free of the military shackles on his speech, he carried on his crusade as a private citizen. He set out on a lecture tour and pointed out that the major mission of military aviation was first to destroy the military air forces of the enemy country. When this was accomplished and control of the skies was assured, the next step was to attack the centers of enemy warmaking capability. The forerunner to the concept of strategic bombing was carried one step further when he insisted that the most important and vulnerable area of the United States extended from the Chesapeake Bay to Boston and from Chicago to New York.

Before resigning from the Army, General Mitchell had toured postwar Europe and was convinced that the Germans were already planning to develop air power for a future war. A visit to the Far East also left him critical of U.S. defenses in that region of the world, especially at Pearl Harbor. General Mitchell's prediction of a surprise attack in the Pacific was considered ridiculous during his court martial, but it later proved to be remarkably accurate.

Although General Mitchell did not succeed in his efforts to establish a separate air service during his lifetime, the Air Corps Act was passed by Congress in July 1926. The law changed the name of the air service to the Army Air Corps and created the post of Assistant Secretary of War for Aeronautics. Similar provisions were made for the Navy, and five-year expansion plans were authorized for both services. The resulting new orders for military planes helped establish the U.S. aircraft industry. General Mitchell died in 1936, but Congress gave him special recognition in 1946. A year later, a separate U.S. Air Force was created.

RECORD FLIGHTS

Charles A. Lindbergh (1902-1974), one of the best known figures in aviation history, is remembered most for his solo flight across the Atlantic.

An offer that renewed interest in transatlantic flight was the Orteig Prize of $25,000 offered to the pilot who successfully completed a non-stop flight from New York to Paris. Three American attempts were planned by Commander Richard Byrd, Clarence Chamberlin, and Charles Lindbergh. The first two entries in the contest had almost unlimited funds at their disposal; Charles Lindbergh, on the other hand, had very limited resources. Lindbergh originally proposed the idea of flying over the Atlantic to Paris to several airplane manufacturers. They agreed that it was an excellent idea and offered to allow him to take part in preparation for such a flight. They would not, however, agree to allow him to be the pilot in command on such a venture. [Figure 10-25]

Lindbergh personally negotiated for the airplane which was built by Ryan Aircraft of California. It was constructed in 60 days. [Figure 10-26]

Figure 10-25. Lindbergh approached a group of businessmen in St. Louis to sponsor a transatlantic flight. They agreed on the condition that the name of the airplane contain the name of the sponsoring city, thus the "Spirit of St. Louis."

Figure 10-26. After a few test flights, the airplane was flown to the east coast with a stop in St. Louis. On May 20, 1927, Lindbergh, encouraged by a favorable weather forecast, took off for France with a huge load of fuel. Although bad weather prevailed initially, he continued, and the weather improved. In just over 33 hours, Lindbergh reached Paris.

Without modern radio navigation aids and with only one very reliable engine, he succeeded alone in doing what at the time was thought to be impossible. He completed the flight from New York to Paris, and the Orteig Prize of $25,000 was his. This exploit in 1927 stirred the imagination of the public throughout the United States and Europe. If this young man was able to make such a trip with a minimum of equipment, could it be that transatlantic air transportation for the public could become a reality?

Byrd and Chamberlin decided to continue with their respective plans for an Atlantic crossing. Although both succeeded in flying across the Atlantic, neither was able to do so without damaging his airplane. Byrd ditched his trimotor just off the French coast without injury to the crew, and Chamberlin made a forced landing in Germany, damaging his airplane. Lindbergh had succeeded where others had failed.

After the successful completion of Lindbergh's flight to Paris, another ocean barrier became the primary challenge. In August 1927, James Dole, president of the Hawaiian Pineapple Company, offered a prize of $25,000 to the first pilot who flew nonstop from the mainland of the United States to Honolulu. The second successful completion would net the pilot $10,000. The overwater stretch to be covered by this flight was about 2,400 miles, while the longest overwater stretch that Lindbergh had faced earlier was 1,800 miles.

Dole's offer sparked other offers of prize money for various attempts at distance records. For example, challenges included a round-trip flight from the mainland to Hawaii and a flight to Tokyo from Dallas with a maximum of three fuel stops. None of the newly announced prizes were great enough to attract Lindbergh. They did, however, attract many others. [Figure 10-27]

Figure 10-27. Art Gobel, flying a Travel Air named ''Woolaroc'' (after the ranch in Oklahoma owned by the sponsor, Frank Phillips) won the race to Honolulu and was followed on landing by another monoplane, the ''Aloha,'' piloted by Martin Jensen. After the two had landed, news of the disasters of the race reached them. When the final toll was taken, 10 of the 13 entrants had lost their lives.

Amelia Earhart (1898-1937) was the best known of several women pilots during the 1920's and 1930's.

On June 17, 1928, Amelia Earhart became the first woman passenger to cross the Atlantic. She accompanied Wilbur Stultz and Louis Gordon on this flight. By May 1932, she was ready to make the transatlantic crossing by herself. She took off from Grace Harbor, Newfoundland. Despite stormy conditions, an altimeter malfunction, and an exhaust stack burning through the weld and causing vibrations, she landed safely in Londonderry, Ireland. This made her the first woman ever to fly the Atlantic. She received the Distinguished Flying Cross from the United States Government and various foreign awards for this flight. [Figure 10-28]

Five years later, Amelia Earhart disappeared over the Pacific during an attempt to fly around the world. She and her navigator, Fred Noonan, took off from Lae, New Guinea, on July 1, 1937, bound for Howland Island in the Pacific. About 7,000 miles remained in their around-the-world venture, but this hop to Howland Island was the most difficult since it entailed flying 2,556 miles over open water. The last radio transmission sent by Amelia Earhart did not clearly indicate her position. This message was of little help to the U.S. Navy personnel who searched over 262,281 square miles of the Pacific Ocean. Much speculation remains to this day concerning her disappearance.

Women set many records in the ensuing years of aviation development. Ruth Nichols flew a transcontinental cross-country in less than 17 hours in 1930, and set a women's cross-country speed record. A year later, she set a women's altitude record of 28,743 feet and, in the same year, flew at more than 210 m.p.h. to set the women's speed record. Phoebie Omlie, an exhibition stunt flyer turned racer, won three events in the 1930 National Air Races and advanced ahead of 80 men and women in the field to win the National Sweepstakes Race in 1931. [Figure 10-29]

Figure 10-28. Amelia Earhart was the first person to fly solo from Hawaii to California and from Mexico City to New Jersey.

Figure 10-29. Amy Johnson, at 26, took only 19½ days to fly solo from England to Australia in 1930. This British pilot ranks among the top women in aviation. She was killed when her aircraft crashed during a flight over England in 1941.

AIR COMMERCE ACT

Prior to these record-setting attempts, the United States government passed an Air Commerce Act. After the bill was signed into law in 1926 by President Coolidge, the Secretary of Commerce was given authority to "foster air commerce, designate and establish airways, establish, operate, and maintain aids to navigation (except airports), arrange for research and development to improve such aids, license pilots, issue airworthiness certificates for aircraft and major components, and investigate accidents."

The Air Commerce Act of 1926 designated the Secretary of Commerce as the authority responsible for promoting and regulating civil aviation.

As 1926 ended, the Department of Commerce had taken on new regulatory functions connected with civil aviation. By this time, regulations required that airplanes engaged in private and commercial flying be registered and carry proper identification markings, and that all pilots in interstate commerce be required to have the proper license. Mechanics were also required to be licensed under the same provisions.

Government appropriation for the new Aeronautics Branch of the Department of Commerce increased rapidly until the middle years of the depression. In 1927, the new agency received an appropriation of $550,000; and in 1928, $3,791,000. The high appropriation for the period was $10,362,300 in 1931. By 1936, the depression budget for this new office was reduced to a little over $5,000,000. With the small appropriations received by this agency during the mid-1930's, it is amazing how it was so successful in enforcing so many of its programs.

AIRMAIL AND PASSENGER SERVICE

A daylight airmail system spanning the United States was in operation by 1920, and a transcontinental route to be used at night as well as in the daytime was also set up by the Post Office Department. This route was not set up on a radio navigation aids system as we know it today. Instead, a series of lights, spaced about 25 miles apart, extended from one town to another along the route running all the way from the east coast to the west coast of the United States.

By 1924, a regularly scheduled service was completed so an airplane with mail could leave the west coast of the United States the morning of one day and arrive at its destination on the east coast the evening of the following day. With the passage of the Air Mail Act of 1925, the Post Office Department was relieved of the responsibility of supplying equipment and pilots for the mail service. Under this act, which was known as the Kelly Act, private companies were to compete on a bid basis for the right to carry air mail across the country.

The Kelly Act was significant because it encouraged manufacturers to develop airplanes that could be used for passenger service.

The Air Mail, or Kelly, Act brought several important changes. The new operators were not compelled to use war surplus airplanes to carry the mail. This encouraged designers and manufacturers to develop an airplane for a specific purpose. The second important result of the Kelly Act was that a passenger service could be practically subsidized by the government. Since a company could be paid for carrying mail, why then would it not be possible to carry passengers for additional revenue? [Figure 10-30]

By 1929, another attempt was made to put a regular passenger service into operation. The unique thing about this service was its planned operation as a transcontinental airline/railroad combination. Passengers could leave New York City's Pennsylvania Station by train and travel to Columbus, Ohio. On arrival in Columbus, the train was switched to a siding near the Columbus airport, and the passengers were chauffeured a short distance to board Ford Trimotor transports for a flight to Waynoka, Oklahoma. There, the passengers were driven to a train equipped with Pullman cars. At Clovis, New Mexico, the passengers were taken to more waiting Ford Trimotors to complete the trip to the west coast by air. This service reduced the travel time from the east coast to the west coast from 72 hours to 48 hours. By this arrangement, the passengers traveled only two of the four legs of the trip by airplane. Even though

Figure 10-30. The mail/passenger concept led to a number of designs which could be used for this dual purpose. Usually, the combination-type airplane had a single engine, an open pilot's cockpit, and a small cabin for the mail and two or three passengers.

this combination system lost millions of dollars in its first year of operation, the experiment led to a series of developments of dependable transportation using multi-engine airplanes.

Glenn Curtiss had designed a successful twin-engine airplane that saw limited service for short hops to various places in the United States. This airplane had a major drawback — it was built by outdated construction methods using old-type materials. [Figure 10-31]

It soon became apparent that a new design was needed. One breakthrough that made many new designs possible was the ability to manufacture large quantities of the metal alloy, duralumin. Duralumin was the trademark for a light, strong alloy of aluminum, copper, manganese, and magnesium. When this metal became available, the Ford Motor Company of Dearborn, Michigan, was just beginning work in the research and development of a transport plane. It is unclear if the famous World War I Dutch airplane designer, Anthony Fokker, first came up with the idea of installing three engines on a large, high-winged monoplane, or if the idea was originated by the Ford designers. It may be

Figure 10-31. The Curtiss twin-engine passenger airplane was a large biplane constructed of wood, metal tubing, and fabric. Its single-engine performance was not adequate, and its appearance did not inspire confidence.

possible that technological development reached a stage where the ideas and designs came about simultaneously. [Figure 10-32]

Fokker held to the idea of using plywood skins over a wooden structure for the wings of his airplane for a lighter, smoother surface. Ford, on the other hand, used corrugated duralumin for the outer surface of his trimotor models. Since this metal was suggestive of the walls of chicken houses, the name "Tin Goose" became firmly attached to the aircraft during this period.

Luckily, before the stock market crash in the fall of 1929, the aircraft industry underwent considerable financial consolidation. Had it not been for the interest of such large companies as General Motors, Ford, Curtiss Wright, and others, the aircraft manufacturers would not have approached the stock market crash with sufficient financial health to weather the storm. Revenues in this growing transportation industry declined during the early 1930's, but not to the same degree as revenues in other industries.

Boeing Aircraft, a company which had concentrated mainly on building single-engine planes, entered the competition to build a passenger airplane in the early 1930's with something almost entirely new to offer to the airlines — the Boeing 247. [Figure 10-33]

Figure 10-32. In any case, this trimotor airplane produced by Fokker (airplane A) was very similar in appearance and performance to the Ford Trimotor (airplane B); however, construction techniques were different.

Figure 10-33. The Boeing 247 was of all-metal construction with twin engines. It carried 10 passengers and 400 pounds of mail with a cruising speed of 155 m.p.h. The difference in comfort and performance between this Boeing model and the Ford Trimotor was extraordinary.

During this same period, Douglas Aircraft was given specifications by Trans World Airlines to design and build an airplane that would satisfy the real needs of air transportation. Douglas met the challenge by surpassing the specifications by a considerable margin and produced the first of the DC series. The DC-1 was built as the prototype for the series, and the Douglas factory immediately came out with an improved version, the DC-2. This airplane was similar in many ways to the airplane that succeeded it — the DC-3. The DC-3, which first flew in 1935, soon became the most successful aircraft of that era. It is credited with putting the world in the air. Many versions were built, including thousands for military use. The military version was called the C-47 and nicknamed the "Gooneybird." [Figure 10-34]

By the late 1930's, the Douglas DC-3 was used by nearly all civilian airlines in the world.

Figure 10-34. The DC-3 design was far ahead of its time. By 1940, roughly 90% of all airline passengers were carried in it. Many DC-3's are still in service.

THE LIGHT AIRPLANE

By the mid-1920's, Henry Ford had succeeded, through mass production techniques, in producing automobiles at a cost low enough to "put America on wheels." With the developing technology in aviation, some manufacturers saw the day when they would be able to produce and sell small airplanes the same way. On the surface, such an assumption would appear to have been a safe one; but in the final analysis, it was wrong. The market for light airplanes was much smaller than that of the automobile. It was, however, large enough to make profits for the manufacturer.

It is not surprising that construction of the early airplanes was of wood and fabric. Wood was a material that was easily worked by hand, and technology of woodworking skills and tools had developed to a very high level. [Figure 10-35]

This dope was applied over balloon cloth, linen, or cotton fabric. If constructed properly with a sufficient number of coats of dope, the airplane, with proper care, would last for years. The cloth, as it absorbed and acquired coat after coat of dope, became almost the equal of a smooth metal surface. The major advantage of this method of construction was that no sophisticated tools were necessary. Most of the airplanes of World War I were built in this way, as were the light planes of the 1920's and 1930's which followed.

Figure 10-35. Fabric could be applied with ease and shrunk on the wood structure for the fuselage assembly. It could be installed in a similar manner over the wooden ribs of the wings. The material used for this shrinking process was a "dope" made of nitrate or butyrate base.

Figure 10-36. Fabric was installed as an outer covering to seal out moisture. It was found that, as long as the moisture content of a properly selected aircraft grade wood was sealed, it lasted almost indefinitely. Additional moisture or excessive drying destroyed the structural integrity of the wood.

A substitute for fabric and dope on wings that came into limited use during this period was borrowed from small boat construction techniques. Large pieces of plywood could be steamed to form skins for wings and fuselage structures. When the skins were installed properly on formers, much of the weight of the inner structural members was eliminated. [Figure 10-36]

With the beginning of the use of metal for structures during the 1920's, it is interesting to note that many pilots and manufacturers feared that metal tubing (steel) would rust. To combat this problem, the steel tubing in many of the early airframes was filled with oil so that rusting could not occur. However, manufacturers soon discovered that the tubing structure had no more inherent weaknesses than the wood structure.

Before long, methods were devised to replace plywood skin over wooden formers with metal skins (aluminum alloy) over metal tubing and formers. Techniques in welding and machining metals moved forward at a rapid pace in the 1930's, making metal airplanes far more desirable to the public than aircraft made of wood and fabric. [Figure 10-37]

The use of metal on outer surfaces boosted public confidence in airplanes.

Figure 10-37. Although the all-metal design was costly, it immediately became popular. This is a Beech Model 18.

Figure 10-38. Walter Beech was an advocate of the biplane and probably carried the design to the ultimate in light airplanes with the advent of his Beechcraft Model 17 (Staggerwing) that was first introduced in 1933.

Another major consideration of design for light airplanes at the end of the 1920's was whether a plane should be constructed with one or two wings. The biplane had been used more frequently up to that time, but the monoplane was gaining in popularity. The proponents of the biplane claimed that its extra lifting surface made it safer to fly and easier to handle with a shorter takeoff and landing roll. The proponents of the monoplane believed that a biplane had too much drag and an unnecessarily large area of lifting surface. In Wichita, Kansas, the arguments about the two designs actually caused old companies to break up and new ones to be formed. [Figure 10-38]

Clyde Cessna, on the other hand, defended the monoplane and did an extraordinary job in the middle and late 1930's of designing a high-wing, light plane called the Airmaster. [Figure 10-39]

Figure 10-39. The Cessna Airmaster achieved almost unbelievable efficiency at that time by providing one mile per hour for each horsepower the engine developed.

The Beechcraft Staggerwing, with the addition of a more powerful engine, matched the performance of some of the medium-priced, single-engine airplanes being offered today. In its final model, it could cruise at 200 m.p.h. Both the Beech Staggerwing and the Cessna Airmaster were excellent performers. Neither, however, could be considered an "economy" airplane suitable for training and light personal use, since they were expensive for their day. What, then, did the industry have to offer in the area of light, economical trainers and personal airplanes?

Before organization of the Aeronautical Branch of the Department of Commerce, anyone who had the necessary skill could build a light airplane and fly it. No inspection or license was needed. All that was required was an airframe that could accommodate a Model "T" automobile engine or some other left-over powerplant, and the courage to fly it.

After the Aeronautics Branch was formed, much of this type of activity was curtailed. Engines were required to have a dual ignition system, and airframes had to meet certain construction safety requirements. Components for aircraft were manufactured under government supervision. As a result, many dreams of building cheap airplanes were abandoned.

The major problem in building a low-cost airplane was not the problem of manufacturing an airframe that was suitable, but of finding a good, reliable, and licensable engine to power it. During the 1920's, several suitable powerplants were produced, but none in sufficient quantity to ensure delivery to airframe manufacturers. [Figure 10-40]

It was not until the designs produced by Continental and Lycoming in the late 1930's that the light plane powerplant problem was solved. These engines were not expensive to purchase and maintain, and they did not require excessive amounts of fuel or oil. [Figure 10-41]

Figure 10-40. Larger engines had been perfected by the time Lindbergh made his famous flight to Paris but, unfortunately, they were bulky, air-cooled radials which required a large, heavy airframe.

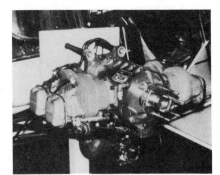

Figure 10-41. The new Continental and Lycoming designs were small, lightweight, horizontally opposed engines. They developed 40-70 horsepower with four cylinders.

Through a combination of circumstances and with the right people behind the ideas and designs, a light plane at moderate cost became a reality. In 1929, a man named G. C. Taylor designed a lightweight airplane which was eventually to be one of the most famous and popular light airplanes in history. Having failed at the time of the depression to get his small craft into production, an oil man named William T. Piper bought Taylor's share in the company. In 1937, the factory was moved to Lock Haven, Pennsylvania, where the 40-horsepower, Piper J-2 Cub was built. [Figure 10-42]

In 1939, a $4,000,000 appropriation was allocated by Congress to establish the **Civilian Pilot Training Program**. This new program was for training 10,000 pilots in 460 colleges throughout the United States. Funds were also made available to teach aeronautics in high schools. The Piper J-3 Cub accounted for 75% of all the airplanes used in this program. As a result, thousands of the Piper Cub models were built and sold in the United States and abroad. This one act of Congress put Piper on the map of the aviation industry with an airplane that became a standard training craft for many years thereafter. In spite of the benefit to Piper, other companies shared in the appropriations to some extent. [Figure 10-43]

Simplicity was an important feature of these new light airplanes. The dependable starting system consisted of the strong arm of the pilot or flight line helper. They had no electrical system, no hydraulic system, or anything else that required expensive maintenance. The engines, with proper care, could run as long as 1,000 hours between major overhauls.

At this stage of light plane development in aviation, World War II brought mixed blessings. For the first time, money was available for extensive research, but the idea of manufacturing light planes for public use had to be curtailed until the end of the war.

Figure 10-42. In a short time, the famous Piper J-3 Cub was put into limited production. The J-3 Cub was based on the design of the J-2.

Figure 10-43. Aeronca, which came out with its original "flying bathtub" featuring a two-cylinder engine of its own design, started manufacturing a series of heavier and more popular models. Among these was the Aeronca Champion.

Light plane manufacturers had to change their thinking. The armed forces needed heavier and more sophisticated training airplanes to help make the transition to more powerful single-engine fighter or multi-engine bombers easier. Orders from overseas also dictated changes for most light plane manufacturers. As the war continued, many stopped production of complete airplanes because they found it more profitable to manufacture components for some of the larger companies.

CHECKLIST _____

After studying this section, you should have a basic understanding of:

✓ **Flying circuses and barnstorming** — How pilots maintained public interest in aviation after World War I by staging public exhibitions.

✓ **Conquering the ocean barrier** — How the first attempts to fly across the Atlantic Ocean succeeded or failed and who the main figures were.

✓ **Billy Mitchell** — Who he was, what he advocated, and how his beliefs were accepted.

✓ **Record flights** — What some of the major flight records were, and who accomplished them.

✓ **Air Commerce Act** — What was significant about this legislative action.

✓ **Airmail and passenger service** — How this service contributed to improved airplane designs and promoted the growth of aviation.

✓ **The light plane** — What some of the main advances in light plane design were.

WORLD WAR II

The progress of commercial aviation in the 1930's provided the technical and industrial base for further advances in airplane development during World War II. In fact, the airplane developed faster between 1939 and 1945 than in any other comparable period in the history of aviation. Airpower was destined to play a dominant role in the future. This section covers some of the key events and developments during and shortly after World War II.

PRELUDE TO WAR

While most of the leading industrial nations were engaged in peaceful activities between the two World Wars, by the early 1930's some were concentrating on developing weapons of war. The worldwide depression, which had created economic and political chaos, helped military leaders solidify their control of governments in Germany, Italy, and Japan. These leaders had promised full employment, and for the most part, they achieved it by a military buildup.

During the 1920's, the German aircraft industry expanded rapidly and pilot training programs were established.

The Treaty of Versailles, which ended World War I, prohibited Germany from developing military aircraft; but after the first six months, there was no restriction on building civilian airplanes. By the early 1920's, the German aircraft industry began to thrive. Several German companies established subsidiaries in neighboring countries. At the same time, a number of civil aviation organizations were formed. Aviation sport clubs and schools for glider pilots provided a pool of future pilots. The Ministry of Transport also increased pilot training by providing crews to Lufthansa, the state-operated airline. Additional trainees were secretly sent to a Russian military school for airmen at Lipetz, U.S.S.R.

The pilots being trained in Germany during the 1920's and early 1930's were part of a secret air force.

The pilot training programs with Lufthansa and glider schools produced a cadre of future pilots for the German Air Force, the **Luftwaffe**. They were part of what was called the "secret air force." Other elements of this secret air force included a network of aircraft production facilities and civilian airplanes that could easily be converted to military use. By 1932, there were 1,500 trained pilots and another 3,000 trainees in the secret air force. When Adolph Hitler took over the German government in 1933, the military buildup became obvious. In 1935, the Luftwaffe was officially formed and the pretense of peaceful intentions ended.

The Germans planned carefully. Long before German military aircraft production became a threat, they had made detailed plans outlining which type of airplane was to be manufactured in which plant. In many cases, the factories had not even been built. The Germans claimed they could build a factory and begin production of advanced fighter planes in six months. Although few people believed the claim, it turned out to be a very accurate prediction.

The Spanish Civil War of the mid-to-late 1930's provided Germany with an opportunity to test their new equipment in combat. Germany, in support of General Francisco Franco, began using combat aircraft in Spain in August 1936. Italy also aided General Franco in his armed bid to take over the Spanish Republic.

Italy began warlike actions even before 1936 under the rule of Benito Mussolini. Generally, the countries that Italy invaded were not prepared to defend themselves against a hostile and well-armed enemy. Italian successes were mainly in Africa where Mussolini hoped to reestablish the glory that once was Rome. Most of the airplanes used by the Italian forces were not as advanced in design as those of Germany.

In the Far East, Japan became increasingly aggressive. Following an undeclared war with Russia at the turn of the century, the Japanese began to exert their power. First they took control of Korea. Then, in the 1930's, they gained control of Northern China (Manchuria). By 1937, Japanese forces had succeeded in gaining control of most Chinese coastal areas. The conquests of the late 1930's would not have been possible without air power.

During this period in the 1930's, the United States was still recovering from the effects of the depression. Although some Americans volunteered to fight against the Germans and Italians in Spain, and against the Japanese in China, most agreed with the wait-and-see policy that prevailed at the time. Only after the attack on Poland had begun and Czechoslovakia had fallen, did the citizens of the United States realize that they might become involved in a war of survival.

In September 1939, Germany succeeded in destroying the Polish air force in two days and began a bombing attack on the major Polish cities. General Mitchell, in testimony before a Congressional committee in 1921, had stated that future wars would use aircraft as offensive weapons. This proved to be true with Germany's attack on Poland. With air supremacy established, the offensive might of air power was demonstrated against Poland. Only a few weeks passed before all of Poland was in German control. By June 20, 1940, France had surrendered, and most of Western Europe had fallen to Germany. The lightning war, or **blitzkrieg**, as it was called, consisted of sudden thrusts by air and armored forces to destroy defenses and to permit rapid movement deep into enemy territory.

The offensive use of air-power became a reality in the attacks on Poland in 1939 and on France in 1940.

THE BATTLE OF BRITAIN

In July of 1940, Germany turned its attention to air attacks against England, although the blitzkrieg tactics were not used. Instead of attacking enemy airfields first to gain air superiority immediately, the Germans restrained the use of airpower during July and early August. The initial air strikes were limited to southern British ports and shipping targets. Some historians have speculated that Hitler was still hopeful of a truce with the British government. During this first phase of the "Battle of Britain," the Royal Air Force (RAF) inflicted heavy losses on the Luftwaffe. In the latter part of August 1940, the Germans changed their tactics. They began to use fighter escorts to protect their bomber formations, and the main targets became airfields and airplane factories. This targeting strategy indicated an attempt to gain control of the air and was consistent with the blitzkrieg doctrine.

The use of radar by the RAF during the Battle of Britain was one of the key factors in the first major defeat of the Luftwaffe.

While the air battle raged on into September, losses on both sides mounted. The RAF was perilously close to defeat, but the Germans did not know how serious the situation was. The British antiaircraft units and the RAF always seemed to be able to muster strong defensive forces. The secret weapon of the British was radar. They used it effectively to detect attacking formations and to direct the RAF fighters into visual contact. To the Germans, the strength of the RAF opposition indicated more airplanes and pilots than were actually available.

In an effort to cut down their losses, the Germans again changed their tactics. They began using night raids to bomb industrial targets and the city of London. The heavy night attacks continued into 1941 and became known as the "Blitz of London." More than 43,000 civilians were killed and 56,000 more were injured. Although British losses were heavy, the RAF and antiaircraft units were able to defend Britain and deplete the strength of the Luftwaffe.

Before the end of 1940, our allies, mainly Great Britain, desperately needed military aircraft, but the costs were so great that they could not afford them. The Battle of Britain had destroyed many industries which manufactured goods for export to earn Britain's livelihood in the world economy. Britain could no longer pay cash.

It was in the best interest of the United States to assure that a German land invasion of Britain did not take place. President Roosevelt's Lend-Lease Plan, was put into operation. After a debate in Congress, seven billion dollars was set aside for war materials for our allies, including the Soviet Union.

By 1944, the United States was producing 96,000 airplanes a year.

The Lend-Lease program directly affected the aircraft industry. The yearly output of aircraft in the U.S. in 1940 totaled 6,000. By 1941, this production total was increased to 19,000. By the time the United States was in the War in 1942, the total reached 48,000 airplanes; and by 1944, the United States was producing 96,000 airplanes a year for the war effort. The aviation industry has not seen production like this at any time — before the war, or since.

PEARL HARBOR

After France fell in 1940 and a new government was formed at Vichy, the time was right for Japan to occupy French Indochina. (Viet Nam is a part of this old French colonial holding.) On December 7, 1941, the Japanese surprise air attack on the United States military base at Pearl Harbor, Hawaii, brought America into the war. The attack came at 7:55 a.m. on a Sunday morning. In one hour and five minutes, over 350 Japanese carrier-based airplanes had killed more than 2,000 Americans, destroyed most of the United States Pacific Fleet, and destroyed about half of the 169 naval aircraft in the vicinity. Of the 231 army aircraft, only 79 were serviceable at the end of that "infamous" day. Most U.S. aircraft never even got off the ground. The Japanese lost 28 airplanes in this attack. A second decisive air attack came later that same day at Clark Field in the Philippines. With another surprise attack, the Japanese destroyed half of the 35 B-17's at Clark Field. Once again a prophecy of Billy Mitchell came true. [Figure 10-44]

On December 7, 1941, the United States was forced to enter the war by the Japanese attack on Pearl Harbor.

COMBAT AIRCRAFT

In time of war, the necessity for overcoming the enemy leads to many technological developments that would otherwise require years of research and development. World War II was no different. During that period, great advancements were made in aviation; one of the most notable of which was the introduction of jet aircraft.

Figure 10-44. The December 1941 attack achieved complete surprise and firmly established the importance of offensive airpower.

GERMANY

Although the first turbo-jet engine was developed by an Englishman, Frank Whittle, the first jet aircraft was the German Heinkel He 178.

An Englishman named Frank Whittle is generally recognized as the designer of the first turbojet engine for use in aircraft. He began ground testing the engine in 1937. It was not until 1941 that England tested its first jet airplane; but by this time, Germany had tested and flown the He 178 jet aircraft and was in the process of developing the more advanced jet, the Messerschmitt, Me 262.

Many advances also were taking place in the design of propeller-driven aircraft. In 1934, Willy Messerschmitt produced a four-place, all-metal, low-winged monoplane with retractable gear. It could fly as slow as 38 m.p.h. and as fast as 189 m.p.h. The model designation for this airplane was Bf 108 Taifun. [Figure 10-45]

With experience in building only the Taifun, Messerschmitt entered a competition to design a fighter aircraft for Germany. The result was the Me 109 series. This basic design started with a 695-horsepower Rolls-Royce engine. By the time the war in Europe ended, the same basic design had a Mercedes Benz, liquid-cooled, inverted V-12 engine of 1,800-horsepower. During its production in Germany from 1936 to the end of World War II, 33,000 of these fighters were produced.

The Focke-Wulf 190 was an excellent fighter that was flown by many German war aces.

Another famous and effective fighter used by Germany in World War II was the Focke-Wulf 190. Its design work was started in 1928; in 1939, the first prototype was completed. The production model, an all-metal fighter airplane, was powered by a 1,600-horsepower BMW radial air-cooled engine. It was first used in combat against the RAF in 1941 and was a successful match for the British Spitfire. More than 20,000 of this model were built. [Figure 10-46]

The Germans also developed the first operational jet aircraft used in combat. The Allies had nothing that could compare with this airplane. The Me 262 jet aircraft, mentioned earlier, was roughly 100 m.p.h. faster than any Allied fighter. However, those in the Luftwaffe who supported

Figure 10-45. The Bf 108 proved to be an outstanding design which led to the development of Germany's most widely used fighter, the Me 109.

Figure 10-46. Development of the Focke-Wulf 190 continued throughout World War II. By 1945, it was capable of over 470 m.p.h. at altitudes up to 41,000 feet.

Figure 10-47. With two jet engines and four powerful guns, the Me 262 was a formidable aircraft; but it was not for novice pilots. Many inexperienced German pilots were killed in the Me 262 during the last few months of the war.

the new Me 262 were unable to get approval to speed up production in time to use it effectively. Its use was also clouded. Apparently, Hitler preferred to see the Me 262 used as an attack bomber rather than as a fighter. At the end of the war, hundreds of these airplanes were found in Germany, fresh from the factory and ready for combat. [Figure 10-47]

The fighter designs of the German aviation industry were noteworthy, but the bombers were not as successful. A few four-engine models were produced, however, most German bomber aircraft were twin-engine models. They were not particularly fast nor were they noted for great accuracy in high altitude bombing.

JAPAN

Some of the designs originated by the Japanese for military aircraft were impressive. The Zero was designed by a Japanese who gained much of his training while studying and working in aircraft manufacturing plants in the United States. Altogether about 11,000 were built. In 1944 and 1945, the Japanese, in desperation, began using some Zero's for one-way suicide missions. These missions, known as **kamikaze attacks**, were flown by young pilots with only very limited training. The tactics they used consisted of diving their airplane, which was loaded with bombs, into Allied ships. [Figure 10-48]

Figure 10-48. This highly maneuverable aircraft first flew in 1939 and became the most effective Japanese fighter in the Pacific.

ALLIED COMBAT AIRCRAFT

At the outbreak of the war in Europe, Britain had one excellent fighter, the Spitfire. This airplane was based on a design that won the Schneider Trophy for England in 1931 with a speed of 340.08 m.p.h. The Spitfire was a more-than-even match for the Me 109 and an even match for the FW-190. During the war, the Spitfire went through many modifications to keep ahead of German developments and remained the main airplane used by British fighter squadrons. At the time of the Battle of Britain, a small number of Spitfires succeeded in defending Britain. [Figure 10-49]

The fighters produced in the United States were generally heavier than those produced in Britain, Germany, or Japan. The P-47 is an example of a fighter that was built for a specific purpose — to protect bombers to the target and back to their home base. Before the introduction of this type of fighter, the Allies had nothing with enough range to stay with the bombers. As a result, bomber losses were high, and raids within Germany were infrequent.

Following the P-47, the United States produced one of the best fighters of World War II, the P-51 Mustang. The development of the P-51 was achieved in record time — going from the design stage to the production of a prototype in a little over 100 days. It was powered by a 12-cylinder, liquid-cooled, Packard-built, Rolls Royce Merlin engine and became one of the war's most successful fighters. [Figure 10-50]

The famed 332 Fighter Group flew their missions in this aircraft. The unit, commanded by Colonel Benjamin O. Davis, Jr., was awarded the Distinguished Unit Citation following a raid on Berlin in which they flew as escort. In a fierce battle with German Me 109's and Me 262's, they succeeded in protecting the bombers. In the Italian campaign, not a single U.S. bomber was lost during 200 escort missions flown by the 332nd.

Figure 10-49. The Spitfire was Britain's best known aircraft, and it remained in production until after the war. Approximately 20,000 were built.

Figure 10-50. The famous P-51 Mustang was originally designed for the RAF, but after many modifications, it became the primary fighter of the U.S. Army Air Force.

Figure 10-51. Known as the Flying Fortress, the B-17 was heavily armed and capable of strategic bombing missions deep in enemy territory.

Although the United States developed some very good fighters during World War II, probably the most significant achievements were in the design of the big bombers. Generally, the bombers produced by the United States were well suited to the concept of strategic bombing. The airplanes for this type of mission were, in some cases, derived from transport designs. For example, the B-17 Flying Fortress was based on research in the development of the Boeing 247 transport. [Figure 10-51]

Another airplane manufactured in the U.S. was the B-24 Liberator. It was used in raids against Central European targets such as the oil fields at Ploesti, Rumania. The B-25 twin-engine bomber is associated with the dramatic Doolittle raid against Tokyo.

Jimmy Doolittle was already a renowned aviator before the war. As a Lieutenant in the U.S. Army in 1925, he won the international Schneider Trophy at a race in Cowles, England. The following year he won the Mackay Trophy race, and in 1929, he received the Harmon Trophy for aeronautical achievement in pioneering all-weather flying. The Tokyo raid was launched from a U.S. carrier, the "Hornet," and it provided a tremendous boost to Allied morale when it was most needed.

In contrast to the first raid on Tokyo with only 16 aircraft, pilots later flew B-29's in formations numbering in the hundreds and dropped millions of tons of bombs on Japan. The two final blows against the Japanese cities of Hiroshima and Nagasaki were delivered by B-29s named the "Enola Gay" and the "Bock's Car." [Figure 10-52]

The use of long-range bombers against strategic targets helped turn the tide in World War II.

On April 18, 1942, Colonel James H. "Jimmy" Doolittle led a flight of 16 Mitchell B-25 medium bombers on the first air attack against Tokyo.

Figure 10-52. The B-29 Superfortress made its first flight in September 1942. It was the largest bomber used in World War II.

Along with the atomic bomb, and the judicious use of fighters, strategic bombing helped end the war in 1945. The use of airpower was enhanced by the ability of the United States to produce the right aircraft at the time they were needed. As a result, the Allies were able to dictate the terms of unconditional surrender.

POSTWAR AVIATION

Postwar aviation continued rapid advances in technology, not only in military aircraft but also civilian aircraft. Supersonic flight, which is covered in the next section, became a reality in 1947. At the same time, the prospect of the general public using airplanes for recreation and travel led to the design of many new light airplanes. Commercial airlines were beginning to develop and expand their services. One of the events that highlighted the capabilities of air transportation was the Berlin Airlift.

BERLIN AIRLIFT

The Berlin Airlift, which began in 1948, demonstrated airlift capability under adverse conditions.

The Berlin airlift proved it was possible to move large amounts of essential supplies by air. In June 1948, Russia blockaded West Berlin from the rest of West Germany. All of the highways, railroads, and waterways passing through Russian-occupied East Germany were closed. This cut off ground transportation of supplies to the citizens of West Berlin, but one access remained — three air corridors, each 20 miles wide. [Figure 10-53]

On June 26, 1948, the massive airlift began using C-47 transports and, later, various other aircraft. By the end of July, over 2,000 tons of supplies were flown into West Berlin daily; and by September, over 5,000

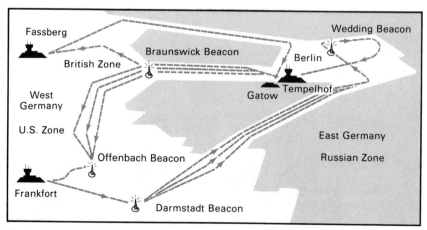

Figure 10-53. The narrow air corridors leading to West Berlin left little margin for error. However, the airlift continued in all types of weather and proved to be successful.

tons daily. The blockade ended in May of 1949; but by that time, over 277,000 flights had been made and over two million tons of supplies had been transported by around-the-clock flight operations.

CIVIL AVIATION DEVELOPMENTS

Before the United States entered the war, two important designs for airline use were developed — the Boeing 307 Stratoliner (the first pressurized commercial airliner) and the Douglas DC-4. They carried more passengers than previous land-based airplanes and had the safety and reliability of four engines.

The race to develop pressurized transport aircraft which would fly faster and carry more passengers continued during the war. In 1943, the first of the 300 m.p.h. Lockheed Constellation series flew. By 1950, it was one of the main airplanes used by airlines in the United States. Boeing came out with a transport in 1949 based on the B-29 and the follow-on B-50 bomber series that carried 75 passengers. This two-level airplane, the Stratocruiser, had a lounge and a bar on the lower level. The DC-4 four-engine series was fitted with new engines and redesigned until it became the DC-6, which is one of the last four-engine, piston-driven airplanes developed. [Figure 10-54]

With the end of the war and the release of most of the pilots in the United States military, market analysts believed the aviation industry should begin producing small, light airplanes of the two- and four-seat type on a large scale. Cessna, which had built thousands of T-50 and UC-78 models, came out with the 120 and 140 series in 1946. These were two-place, and each was powered with an 85-horsepower Continental engine. In 1947, Cessna added the five-place 190 and 195 models powered by radial engines ranging from 220- to 300-horsepower. By 1948, Cessna had reentered the four-place market with the 170 model, which was similar in

Figure 10-54. The Boeing Stratocruiser on the left and the Douglas DC-6 on the right proved to be successful airliners but were soon replaced by jet aircraft.

Figure 10-55. Postwar aircraft produced by Cessna were successful and helped increase the public's interest in smaller airplanes. The five-place 195 model is shown here.

appearance to the 140 and powered by a six-cylinder, 145-horsepower Continental engine. [Figure 10-55]

Piper continued production of its Cub series with several power options, ranging from 65-horsepower up to an eventual 150-horsepower. Other models were added to the Piper line such as the Pacer, a side-by-side two-seater with a 65-horsepower engine, and the Super Cruiser powered with the new 108-horsepower Lycoming engine. [Figure 10-56]

Figure 10-56. The Pacer on the left and Super Cruiser on the right were two of the successful aircraft produced by Piper.

Figure 10-57. The Aeronca Chief is shown here on the left and the Mooney Mite is illustrated on the right.

Swift came out with an all-metal, two-place airplane with retractable gear. It was powered by a variety of engines, ranging from 85- to 145-horsepower. Aeronca, which had been involved in military production, began producing the Aeronca Chief and Super Chief with 65-and 85-horsepower respectively. Mooney probed the low-cost, single-place airplane market with the Mooney Mite which was powered with a 40-to 50-horsepower Crosley engine. [Figure 10-57]

Another airplane on the market was the Ercoupe with its non-spin design and no-rudder-pedal control system. Beechcraft continued to build, for a short time, its famous Model 17 Staggerwing biplane with 450-horsepower; and a new V-tail model, the Bonanza. [Figure 10-58]

North America Aviation built the four-place Navion, a single-engine airplane based to some degree on its successful fighter, the P-51. One of the most successful of the immediate postwar airplanes was the Stinson Voyager, a four-place airplane. It was fabric-covered and powered with a 150-horsepower Franklin engine. Its four-place capacity appealed to business people and started the airplane market trend for business usage. Another postwar airplane was the Luscombe Silvair, a two-place airplane powered with a 65-horsepower Continental engine. This airplane

Figure 10-58. The twin-tail Ercoupe and V-tail Bonanza were two departures from standard airplane design.

Figure 10-59. The Stinson Voyager on the left proved popular because of its four-place capability and the Luscombe Silvair on the right used all metal technology.

was the first all-metal light airplane in the two-place market. The all-metal technology developed during World War II soon was adopted by other light aircraft manufacturers. [Figure 10-59]

The number and variety of airplanes manufactured and those conceived on the drawing board are too numerous to mention. Although many were built, the manufacturers discovered that they had overestimated the market. As a result, some of the companies merged and others closed. Only the most productive and successful manufacturers remained in business within a few years.

During the 1950's, many businesses found that, by using airplanes for their sales staff and executives, key personnel could cover territory in a fraction of the travel time required by automobile or public transportation. At the same time, more and more people began to learn to fly and to use their own airplanes for both business and pleasure. Some of the airplanes manufactured after World War II were still available at bargain prices on the used market so that it was possible for more people to learn to fly and own an airplane.

The light planes that were manufactured at the end of the war usually were constructed of fabric over metal airframes. By 1950, most of the fabric airplanes were on the way out. Cessna, which had been constructing fuselages of all-metal design since the end of the war, changed the wings from fabric to metal. Later, Piper replaced its Pacer series with the new all-metal Cherokee series. By the mid 1960's, only a few fabric-covered models were still manufactured. Among these were the Piper Super Cub, the Maule airplanes, and the Bellanca which retained a wooden, fabric-covered wing.

The more recently manufactured light airplanes are sleeker, faster, and more comfortable. The use of turbocharging has increased performance both in speed and altitude capabilities. Pressurization in many models has increased passenger comfort and provided a wider operational range. [Figure 10-60]

Figure 10-60. The Cessna Centurion (left) and the Beech Baron (right) are examples of light, general aviation airplanes with pressurization.

CHECKLIST _____

After studying this section, you should have a basic understanding of:

✓ **The prelude to war** — What countries were preparing for war, how they did it, and what some of the consequences were.

✓ **Battle of Britain** — What strategies were used by the Luftwaffe and how the RAF defended Britain.

✓ **Pearl Harbor** — The date it occurred, the significance of this event, and the losses sustained by the United States.

✓ **Combat aircraft** — What some of the aircraft used by Germany, Japan, Britain, and America were and how well these aircraft were suited to their combat missions.

✓ **Postwar aviation** — Why the Berlin Airlift was necessary, what it achieved, and what caused the postwar boom in the development of civil aircraft.

THE JET AGE

As you learned in the last section, the first operational jet airplane flew during World War II. The potential of jet power brought new challenges to the aviation industry. Shortly after the war, the race was on to see who could produce the fastest and most useful jet airplanes.

JET ENGINES

The jet engine produces power according to the principle of Newton's Third Law of Motion which states, "for every action, there is an equal and opposite reaction." Hot gas in the combustion chamber exits at a high velocity through the exhaust, which is the open end of the engine, as it pushes with equal force against the opposite, or closed, end of the engine. The common example of this principle is air escaping from the neck of a balloon.

Actually, jet and rocket engines function the same way, and are often referred to as reaction engines. The main difference is that a jet engines need air from the atmosphere to mix with the fuel for combustion. Because of this, a jet engine will work only within the atmosphere. In contrast, rocket engines, which are covered in Chapter 12, have their own source of oxygen and can operate in space, beyond the Earth's atmosphere. [Figure 10-61]

The turbine, which is in the path of the heated air, acts like a windmill. It captures much of the energy of the high velocity heated air and trans-

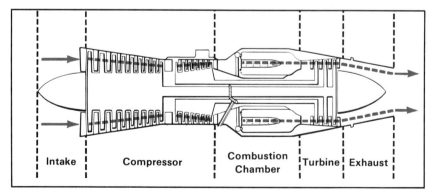

| Intake | Compressor | Combustion Chamber | Turbine | Exhaust |

Figure 10-61. This simplified illustration shows that a basic turbojet engine is essentially a tube where thrust is produced by a four-stage process: intake, compression, combustion, and exhaust. Outside air enters at the intake and is directed to the compressor where it accelerates. Then, the air mixes with fuel in the combustion chamber, ignites, and exits through the turbine section and the exhaust.

mits its spin to the compressor by means of a connecting shaft. The remaining heated air is expelled through the exhaust, or tail pipe. The greater the volume and speed of the hot gaseous air escaping through the exhaust, the greater the thrust.

Compared to reciprocating engines, jet engines have many advantages — fewer working parts, less maintenance, and cheaper fuel are a few. From an operational point of view, greater operating speeds, altitudes, and climb rates offer increased capabilities. Jet engines also require less warmup time, torque is practically nonexistent, and the higher operational altitudes allow flights above most weather systems.

The jet engine made it possible for airplanes to fly faster and higher.

The first operational jets were "pure jets" with simple gas turbine engines. A pure jet engine, or **turbojet,** creates thrust by drawing air from the atmosphere, compressing and burning it, and expelling the burned gas at high velocity. A **turboprop** is a variation that accelerates air in the same way (by compression and combustion), but it uses the exhaust gas to drive a propeller. The turboprop is sometimes referred to as a "prop jet." The **turbofan,** a later development, uses the same process (compression, combustion, and exhaust), but a large amount of the air bypasses the combustion and compression chambers. Then, the lower velocity, unburned air mixes with the hot gas in the exhaust stream and thrust is increased while fuel requirements are minimized. Some of the newer developments in jet engines are covered later in this section.

In the years shortly after World War II, jet engine technology advanced rapidly. Before long, England and the United States were flying test aircraft that were on the verge of flying faster than the speed of sound, which is referred to as Mach 1. Mach is associated with Ernest Mach (1838-1916), a physicist and philosopher, who was a professor at the University of Vienna in Austria. **Mach number** is the ratio of an aircraft's speed to the local speed of sound. For instance, a speed of eight-tenths of the speed of sound is Mach .8.

Mach number refers to the ratio of the speed of an aircraft to the speed of sound.

As speed increased with improved jet engines, test pilots began to encounter what they described as a "brick wall." The air no longer flowed smoothly around the aircraft. It began to compress and flow in strange patterns which caused vibration and control problems. Pilots found that controls became reversed or totally ineffective at very high speeds. These problems were caused by **compressibility**, which refers to an increase in air density as velocities approach Mach 1. The range of airspeeds where compressibility occurs varies with different airplanes, but it generally begins below Mach .75 in straight-wing airplanes. Airflow patterns associated with compressibility include air which is **subsonic** (below Mach 1) as well as **supersonic** (above Mach 1). When the airflow pattern around an aircraft is both subsonic and supersonic, the aircraft is in the region of flight called **transonic**. The transonic range for a particular aircraft depends on its design, but it is usually considered to be between about Mach .75 and Mach 1.2. **Hypersonic** refers to speeds above Mach 5.

BREAKING THE SOUND BARRIER

During World War II, pilots of airplanes such as the Submarine Spitfire and the Lockheed Lightning experienced the effects of compressibility as they approached the speed of sound during high speed dives. Although the jet engine made higher speeds possible, research was needed to determine the effects of speeds approaching Mach 1 and beyond.

Captain (later General) Charles E. "Chuck" Yeager, while flying an X-1 experimental aircraft in 1947, was the first to fly faster than the speed of sound.

The first supersonic design was by the Miles Company in England in 1946. The British, however, cancelled their research program the same year, stating that manned flight at such a speed was too dangerous. Approximately a year later, on October 14, 1947, Chuck Yeager broke the sound barrier in the Bell X-1, reaching a speed of 670 m.p.h. at an altitude of 42,000 feet. At that time, Yeager was a U.S. Air Force test pilot. Previously, he had been a combat pilot in Europe. During World War II, Yeager was shot down over Germany, but escaped with the aid of the French underground. After returning to action, he became a double ace by destroying more than 10 enemy airplanes.

The first woman to break the sound barrier was Jacqueline Cochran.

Yeager's female counterpart in breaking the sound barrier was Jacqueline Cochran, who is one of the most well known women in aviation. Her achievements span several decades. In the 1930's she became the first woman to compete in the Bendix transcontinental air race. After placing third among all pilots in 1937, she won the 1938 race from California to Ohio. Then, she continued on to the East Coast and established a transcontinental speed record of 10 hours, 27 minutes, and 55 seconds. During World War II, she served with the British Air Transport Auxiliary before becoming the Director of the U.S. Women's Air Force Service Pilots (WASPs) in 1942. In 1953, flying a Canadian-built F-86 Sabre, Cochran became the first woman to fly faster than the speed of sound. She also was the first woman to land a jet airplane on a carrier and to fly at twice the speed of sound (Mach 2).

The same year that Jacqueline Cochran broke the sound barrier, Yeager established a new speed record. On December 12, 1953, he reached Mach 2.42 in an improved version of the X-1. [Figure 10-62]

Research continued and designs capable of even higher speeds and altitudes followed. The Bell X-2 and the North American X-15 are two examples of aircraft that began to probe the fringes of space. Military aviation benefited from the research, and the Korean conflict brought the first extensive use of jet aircraft in combat.

Figure 10-62. The X-1 series of research aircraft had a straight wing and was rocket, rather than jet, powered. To save fuel, they were carried aloft by a B-29 and air-launched.

JET AIRCRAFT AND THE KOREAN CONFLICT

When the Korean conflict began in June of 1950, the F-80 Shooting Star was the most advanced fighter in the U.S. Air Force. It was a straight-wing subsonic design which first flew in January 1944. At the end of the war, orders for several thousand were cancelled, and only 1,717 were built. The F-80 was not as advanced as the Russian-built MIG-15. With its German-designed swept wing and powerful Rolls Royce-designed turbojet engine, the MIG-15 could fly faster and higher. Even though Chinese and Korean pilots were not as well trained as American pilots, the F-80 was no match against the MIG. Because of this, the F-80 was mostly used for ground-attack missions.

America's first successful jet fighter was the Lockheed P-80 Shooting Star. The designation P-80 was later changed to F-80.

The more advanced North American F-86 Sabre went into service in Korea in December of 1950. It was faster and better suited for combat against the MIG-15 even though the MIG maintained an advantage in climb rate and maximum operating altitude. The F-86 became the standard fighter in the air services of over 30 countries around the world. [Figure 10-63]

Figure 10-63. The F-86 was one of the 1950's most successful fighters. Including all models, a total of about 5,800 airplanes were produced.

The North American F-100 Super Sabre was developed when the Korean conflict showed a need for larger and faster fighters. In May of 1953, the first F-100 flew. It eventually became the first production airplane capable of sustained supersonic flight. The F-100 did not see service in Korea, and it was not involved in armed conflict until the 1960's in Vietnam.

The F-100 was only the first of the U.S. "Century-series" fighters. Others which first flew in the 1950's were the F-101 Voodoo (1953), F-102 Delta Dagger (1953), the F-104 Starfighter (1954), the F-105 Thunderchief (1955), and the F-106 Delta Dart (1956). Although all of these aircraft were supersonic, they exhibited poor slow-flight characteristics. Long, well-maintained runways were necessary because of high takeoff and approach speeds. Most of these post-Korean fighters required an approach speed of approximately 170 knots (196 m.p.h.) and a similar speed for heavyweight takeoffs. However, by the late 1950's, the F-4 and the F-111 were being developed with improved designs that permitted slower takeoffs and landings.

The B-52 has been the primary long-range bomber of the U.S. Air Force for over 30 years.

Military aviation also needed an advanced bomber. This led to the design and production of several long-range strategic aircraft, including the B-47, B-58, and the B-52. The Boeing B-52 Stratofortess has been the most durable. Design work on the B-52 began in the 1940's, and the first one flew in 1952. At the time, it was the largest, most advanced bomber in production, with a wing span of 185 feet and a weight of up to 250 tons when fully loaded. Although some models are obsolete, later models of the B-52 are still in use.

JETS FOR COMMERCIAL AVIATION

Commercial aviation was also progressing, especially during the early 1950's. A change was taking place in the development of engines for transport airplanes. The airlines and industry were constantly searching for a quieter, more vibration-free engine with a greater time between overhauls. The British thought they had the answer with the de Havilland Comet 1 which began passenger service in 1952. With this pure jet, British Overseas Airways Corp. was the envy of all the airlines. The success of this airplane, however, was short-lived. Between May 1953 and April 1954, three of the Comets broke up in the air. The third accident ended commercial passenger-carrying service in the Comet 1. What followed was one of the most thorough accident investigations in history. Metal fatigue from repeated pressurization cycles had caused the catastrophic structural failures. [Figure 10-64]

In 1954, the first Boeing 707 flew. By 1958, it was in airline service, and scheduled five-hour flights across the continent became a reality. In 1959, Douglas put its first jet transport — the DC-8 — into service. [Figure 10-65]

Figure 10-64. The de Havilland Comet 1 was years ahead of its time in appearance and performance, but the pressurized cabin was structurally flawed.

Figure 10-65. The Boeing 707 and Douglas DC-8 proved to be comfortable transport airplanes. Both are still in service, although many have improved engines and other modifications.

During the 1960s, the French designed the Caravelle, a medium jet which met with great success around the world. The Soviets equipped their airline, Aeroflot, with new turboprops and the pure jet TU-104. The British also designed several new jet airplanes for airline use. Among these models were an improved Comet 4 and the BAC 1-11 jet. [Figure 10-66]

The use of turbojets and turboprops for business travel has become an important part of general aviation. Beech, Cessna, Gates Learjet, and Gulfstream produce popular jets for use by the business community. Sud Aviation of France produces the Falcon, which is a slightly larger series of business jets. North American Aviation, now Rockwell, marketed the

The introduction of the business jet has changed the way many corporations transport personnel.

Figure 10-66. The BAC 1-11 was a successful British design used by airlines on every continent. It entered commercial service in 1965.

Figure 10-67. Two of the successful business jets are the Learjet on the left and the Falcon on the right.

Sabreliner, which is a successful business jet based on a military aircraft design. Many other companies are also designing and producing business jets and turboprops. [Figure 10-67]

VIETNAM

The use of air power in Vietnam was restricted to achieve only limited objectives.

American involvement in Vietnam actually started in the 1950's after the French defeat near the town of Dien Bien Phu. By 1964, U.S. forces were actively engaged in the conflict. Air power was used primarily between 1964 and 1973. Even though it was a limited, guerilla war, air power was effective in supporting ground forces in South Vietnam. For the most part, the restrained use of air power also achieved limited objectives against military targets in North Vietnam, Laos, and what was then Cambodia.

Although several new aircraft and weapons were employed in Vietnam, the most important development was the expanded role of helicopters. In addition to their traditional missions of support, supply, and rescue, helicopters were used as offensive weapons for the first time. Jet engine technology provided long-range, reliable, turbine-powered engines for helicopters like the UH-1 Huey and AH-1 Cobra, as well as the larger CH-47 Chinook and the CH-54 Skycrane. Not only were these turbine engines reliable, they were also rugged and easy to maintain. [Figure 10-68]

Figure 10-68. Attack helicopters, or "gunships," like the UH-1 Huey also offered mobility to ground forces. It has been said that the helicopter was used in Vietnam like the jeep was used in World War II. Often gunships carried soldiers into battle, provided fire support, resupply, and then evacuated them when the operation was over.

A second achievement of the Vietnam conflict was development of an effective close air support system. U.S. air power was committed to support ground forces to a greater extent than in other conflicts. One advantage was that an adequate number of airplanes was available. By 1966, the U.S. Air Force, Navy, and Marines all had fighter aircraft in place in South Vietnam or on carriers.

A communications network was set up so ground force units could contact a Tactical Air Control Center (TACC) and request air support any place within the 43 provinces of South Vietnam. The TACCs then directed fighter aircraft to the target area. In an emergency, aircraft already airborne were diverted. Usually, fighters were over the troubled area within 15 minutes.

In most cases, fighters were able to provide close air support for ground forces anywhere in South Vietnam within 15 minutes.

Another major air activity in Vietnam was interdiction in North Vietnam and along the Ho Chi Minh Trail. The objective of **interdiction** is to destroy, cut, or damage enemy lines of supply and communication. The Ho Chi Minh Trail, which was named for the leader of the North Vietnamese, was one of the major supply routes from the north into South Vietnam. This supply route extended into Laos and Cambodia along the western boarders of Vietnam.

CONTINUED DEVELOPMENT

Experience gained in the Korean conflict, several Middle East confrontations, and Southeast Asia highlighted the need for improved airlift for the armed forces. Since U.S. commitments extended around the world, a capability was required to move large numbers of personnel and their equipment in a short time to distant points. These military needs and the growing airline passenger traffic led to the development of "jumbo jets." The size of these huge jet transports required advances in manufacturing techniques and facilities, redesign of ground support equipment, and even new passenger terminal facilities.

The need for advancement in military transports helped lead to the development of larger aircraft for civilian use.

These large aircraft benefited from advanced technology in metals, improved engine combustion chambers which were designed to reduce air pollution, and new navigation systems. One example is the enormous Lockheed C-5 developed for the U.S. Air Force. It is big enough to hold six buses in the cargo compartment with room to spare.

AIRLINERS

Passenger travel also benefited from the introduction of the mammoth Boeing 747. The cabin has a width of 20 feet and a ceiling height of 8 feet, 4 inches. Side walls are 6 feet high, allowing most passengers to stand erect even at the window seats. In some models, the rear of the first-class cabin contains a spiral staircase leading to an upper level. The interior of the aircraft is divided into "salons" to prevent any long, auditorium-like

Figure 10-69. Aircraft like the Lockheed L-1011 on the left and the Douglas DC-10 on the right have greatly increased passenger comfort and the capacity for carrying large cargo loads.

appearance. Two other wide-body jets — the Lockheed L-1011 and the Douglas DC-10 — are also in commercial service. [Figure 10-69]

The Boeing 747SP (Special Performance) is a shorter and lighter version of the Boeing 747. This aircraft has a much greater range, and it can fly faster and higher than the 747. With its 10-abreast seating and two-level design, the 747SP can carry approximately 305 passengers. [Figure 10-70]

Interest in fuel efficiency and noise level reductions have influenced airplane manufacturer's designs and new aircraft.

For general use, however, a trend in passenger transport is toward more fuel efficient engines with reduced noise levels, large seating capacities, and improved safety features. The Boeing 757 and 767 are typical of this new generation. The international Airbus A300 is another example of improved design and better overall efficiency for specific types of routes. In addition, several manufacturers are modifying previous models to make them more competitive in the airline market. Some examples

Figure 10-70. The Boeing 747SP evolved from the 747 to fill the need for a smaller airplane with the same passenger comforts and longer range.

Figure 10-71. The use of turbofan engines and improved aerodynamic designs have led to the introduction of transports such as the Boeing 757 on the left and the Boeing 767 on the right.

include the Boeing 747-300, 737-300, 727-200, as well as the McDonnell Douglas DC-8 70 series and the DC-9 Super 80 and MD 80 and 90. [Figure 10-71]

The SST (supersonic transport) is the most advanced transport in terms of performance capability for high speed and high altitude flight; however, it presents many problems. The principal ones are cost, noise, and sonic booms. Although the Anglo-French Concorde has been in service since 1976, these problems have not yet been resolved. As a result, the Concorde has limited access to many of the world's major air terminals, and routes must be carefully selected and approved by international agreement. [Figure 10-72]

The Soviet Union also developed an SST, the Tupolev TU-144. Both the Concorde and the TU-144 were designed to operate above 50,000 feet at twice the speed of sound (Mach 2). U.S. plans for a Mach 3 variable geometry (swing-wing) SST were abandoned in 1971 because of the expense and the environmental questions.

Figure 10-72. The advanced design of the SST has provided super-sonic travel for civilian aviation. Because of its limited size, the passenger-carrying capacity and comfort is less than that of the wide-bodied jets.

STOL AND VTOL

Research and development continues for airplanes that fly higher and faster, but another requirement is aircraft that can take off and land in shorter distances. This capability reduces the need for airports with long runways and improves the overall versatility of aircraft. Research on **STOL**, short-field takeoff and landing, and **VTOL**, vertical takeoff and landing, aircraft led to many new design concepts.

The helicopter is an example of a VTOL aircraft; however, other methods for vertical takeoff without using rotors are technologically feasible. The most successful has been the use of vectored thrust from jet engines. An example of this type aircraft is the British Hawker Siddeley Harrier, which first flew in 1966. [Figure 10-73]

The use of VTOL aircraft has been limited by the large amount of power and fuel needed for vertical ascent and descent.

Other methods of vertical takeoff also have been used, such as separate engines to provide lift only, engines that swivel, and wing structures that can be tilted for vertical or horizontal thrust. Tests also have been done on aircraft that have conventional wings and engines but which use rotors for takeoff. A disadvantage of this type of aircraft is that the vertical takeoff and landing requires so much power and fuel that the operational range and useful load are limited.

STOL aircraft have generally been more successful than VTOL. The STOL aircraft is much like a conventional aircraft except the takeoff and landing distance is less because the design of the airfoil produces more

U.S. Navy Photograph

Figure 10-73. The Harrier was the first operational V/STOL (vertical/short takeoff and landing) fighter. It flew in the British RAF in 1969 and entered service with the U.S. Marine Corps in 1971. The U.S. Marine Corps version shown here is the 8V-8C.

lift at slower airspeeds. The additional lift required for slow speed flight is obtained in different ways, depending on the design of the aircraft. One method is leading edge flaps or slats which, together with conventional trailing edge flaps, increase the wing camber and area and provide more lift at slow airspeeds. Another method of increasing lift is **boundary layer control** where compressed air from the engine(s) is blown over the leading edge of the wing. This prevents the airflow from breaking away from the wing surface at slow speeds and high angles of attack. Other methods include the use of extra long wings, increased camber built into the wings, and improved wing designs.

SWING-WING DESIGN

The necessary design requirements of aircraft used for short takeoff and landing often reduce the ability to reach high speeds in flight. One method developed to make an airplane capable of low, as well as high, speeds was the variable geometry or swing-wing. When extended, this wing provides the low-speed flight characteristics of a straight-wing aircraft; when swept, it provides the high-speed characteristics of a swept-wing design. The wing can rotate to a forward position for takeoff, landing, and low-speed flight or to a swept position for high speeds. The swing-wing provides maximum aerodynamic efficiency through a larger speed range, which improves fuel economy and widens the flight envelope.

The swing-wing design is now used on military aircraft. The first to become operational was the General Dynamics F-111 tactical fighter in the 1960's. Other operational U.S. airplanes with this design include the Grumman F-14 Tomcat and Rockwell International B-1 long-range, supersonic bomber. [Figure 10-74]

The swing-wing design provides good slow speed and high speed flight characteristics in the same airplane.

U.S. Navy Photograph

Figure 10-74. The F-14 was developed for the U.S. Navy. First flown in 1970, the Tomcat is a multipurpose aircraft capable of speeds well in excess of Mach 2. It is used primarily as an air superiority fighter to protect naval forces.

FLY-BY-WIRE

The F-16 is the first production airplane using the fly-by-wire system for flight control.

Further developments in aerodynamic and system design came with the General Dynamics F-16. It is the first production aircraft with a "fly-by-wire" system. This system uses direct electrical circuits to servo-actuators to operate the flight controls. There is no mechanical linkage between the pilot and the flight controls as a backup system. Instead, there are four separate electrical systems to provide control in the event one system fails. The F-16 also is designed with a center of gravity much farther aft than normally would be possible without a special electronic system which simulates normal stability. This decreases drag and permits the use of smaller wings because the tail section supports part of the weight. [Figure 10-75]

STEALTH TECHNOLOGY

Another new military development is the Northrop B-2 advanced technology bomber. Its flying-wing design closely resembles Northrop's YB-49 "Flying Wing" of the 1940's. The B-2, also called the **Stealth Bomber**, is designed to make radar detection difficult. Design features include contoured shapes, no prominent vertical surfaces, and composite, radar-absorbent materials. It is powered by four non-afterburning General Electric engines. The engine inlets and exhausts are buried in the main aircraft body to inhibit infrared detection. [Figure 10-76]

The Lockheed F-117 is another stealth aircraft with low-observable characteristics. Nicknamed the "Stealth Fighter," it has been operational for several years, and its performance in special mission activities has been highly successful.

Figure 10-75. The F-16 uses many new developments in control system technology. It is capable of speeds close to Mach 2 and is one of the most maneuverable airplanes ever produced.

Figure 10-76. The B-2 is 17 feet high, 69 feet long, and the wingspan is 172 feet. It will have a range exceeding 6,000 nautical miles and operate at subsonic speeds up to altitudes of 50,000 feet.

CANARD

At first glance, the canard appears to be a revolutionary design of the late twentieth century, but a further look into its development indicates it was used by the Wright Brothers. In recent years, research and development of the canard design continue to demonstrate its merit. Canards are now being used on many aircraft, from ultralights to transports and fighters.

With a canard design, the horizontal stabilizer, normally located at the rear of the airplane, is moved to the front. This design gives an airplane better stall characteristics because, at high angles of attack, the canard stalls before the wing, pitches the nose over, and returns the aircraft to normal flight. This characteristic makes an airplane with a canard very hard to stall or spin. Another advantage is that the canard acts like a wing, providing positive lift instead of negative lift as a tail-mounted horizontal stabilizer does.

The canard will stall before the wing, pitch the nose down, and break the stall.

The American reincarnation of the canard design has been greatly influenced by Burt Rutan, an aerospace engineer. He has concentrated on designs for many amateur-built and experimental airplanes using the canard configuration. One of his most well-known aircraft, the Voyager, was made almost entirely of lightweight, highly flexible, composite materials. After extensive testing and several modifications, Rutan was ready to attempt a record-setting flight. In December of 1986, his brother, Dick, and Jeana Yeager flew around the world nonstop.

Airplane manufacturers are also building new models using the canard concept. The Beechcraft Starship, made of composite materials and powered by two pusher-type turboprop engines, is an example. The

Starship design also solves one of the major problems of canard design — flap pitching moment. This is accomplished by making the canard (also called the forward wing) variably swept. With the main wing flaps extended, the forward wing is straight, producing enough lift to cancel the flap pitching moment. When the flaps are retracted the forward wing sweeps aft, generating less lift so that the canard will stall before the main wing. The certified Starship has a top speed of 336 knots and a range of 1,670 nautical miles.

COMPOSITE MATERIALS

Composite materials are becoming widely used in the manufacture of aircraft.

Composite is a term used to describe a variety of materials, such as thermoplastic, polyimides, and polycarbonates. They are changing the way airplanes are made. Generally, composites are much lighter and stronger than the metals currently used in aircraft production. Because of this, they can be used for almost any aircraft component, including internal structures, such as wing spans, and even turbine engine parts. Since the use of composites reduces weight, they improve overall performance and provide greater fuel economy.

SPORT AVIATION

At the other end of the spectrum, new recreational planes are evolving at the same time as these high technology concepts. The availability of small engines and new lightweight materials, as well as the rising cost of owning most airplanes, has led to many new designs. Some, like the first ultralights, resemble hang gliders. They are made of aluminum tubing, wire supports, and sailcloth. With their lightweight design, two-cycle engines, and simplified controls, the ultralights are reminiscent of the earliest powered airplanes. [Figure 10-77]

Figure 10-77. Although thousands of ultralights have been assembled, they have not been fully accepted in some segments of the aviation community. Lack of ultralight certification requirements and pilot certification standards have been cited as the main objections to ultralights.

Figure 10-78. The lightweight Gossamer Albatross, on the left, was pedaled 22 miles across the English Channel on June 12, 1979, by pilot Bryan Allen in 2 hours, 49 minutes. The Solar Challenger, on the right, was piloted by Steven Ptacek. On July 7, 1981, he successfully completed a 5 hour, 22 minute, sun-powered flight of 180 miles. This flight also extended over the English Channel.

Other designs for sport aviation have taken many forms, ranging from inexpensive, prefabricated kit models to experimental aircraft. Some designs are replicas of classic airplanes of the past. In the experimental area, there have been some unusual successes. These include the innovative Gossamer Albatross and Solar Challenger. Both were designed and developed by a team led by Paul MacCready. [Figure 10-78]

AIRCRAFT OF THE FUTURE

Airplanes have progressed from flimsy machines that would barely fly to a highly reliable mode of transportation for millions of people. Some phases of progress have been painfully slow while others occurred within a few years. The jet engine was only one of the technological developments that accelerated progress. Refinement in jet engines now have made them more fuel efficient, quieter, and even cleaner. No one knows for sure what the next technological breakthrough will be, but improved powerplants, new wing designs, and the space plane are certainly possibilities.

A recent development in turbine-engine progress is the **ultra high bypass propfan**. This concept is similar to the turbofan; however, the fan is outside of the engine like a propeller. The turbojet portion of the engine provides the power to drive the large external fan. This type of system may have bypass ratios of 60:1 or greater and, potentially, it can provide fuel savings of 25% to 30%. NASA and several engine manufacturers are testing and refining this new engine.

The X-29, designed and built by the Grumman Corp., is a radical forward-swept wing design being tested by NASA and the U.S. Air

Figure 10-79. The Grumman X-29 research aircraft has conclusively demonstrated the forward-swept wing is a workable concept that can improve fighter-type aircraft performance. Transport aircraft could also benefit from the design.

Force. It has a unique three-surface control system, incorporating fly-by-wire technology, canards, and double-hinged wing control surfaces that provide variable camber. According to program engineers, wind tunnel tests indicate that this aircraft with forward-swept wings can demonstrate significant control improvements over the aft-swept wing designs of current tactical aircraft. [Figure 10-79]

NASA and the Air Force also have successfully tested a variable-camber, mission adaptive wing (MAW). Using a General Dynamics F-111 as the testbed aircraft, the MAW can be flown in both manual (pilot-selectable) and automatic modes. Automatic modes of the MAW enable computer-commanded adjustments to the wings' camber and curvature by altering leading and trailing edge surfaces to match existing flight conditions. For example, minimum drag shapes are used for cruise flight and an optimum lift-to-drag ratio camber is used for high-G maneuvers. Performance gains of up to 20% in range and maneuvering capability have been demonstrated.

Advanced engineering concepts also are evident in helicopter development. The Bell-Boeing V-22 Osprey tilt-rotor design is an example. The aircraft is equipped with wing-mounted rotors/propellers that allow it to take off and land vertically like a helicopter, but cruise at higher speeds like a fixed-wing turboprop airplane. The V-22, which is still in the

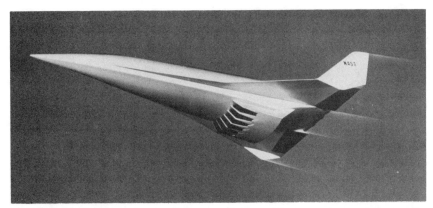

Figure 10-80. Like the shuttle, the space plane could also perform military tasks, retrieve or repair satellites, carry out high-altitude reconnaissance, and so forth.

development stage, is fabricated primarily from graphite/epoxy composite materials and has a triple-redundant fly-by-wire flight control system.

The space plane is already in development. It is also known as the National Aerospace Plane, the hypersonic (greater than Mach 5) airplane, the transatmospheric vehicle, and the "Orient Express." According to Thomas O. Paine, former administrator of NASA, such an aircraft "would probably do to today's jumbo jets and supersonic transports what airplanes did to ocean liners." Most supporters of the space plane see it as a logical successor of the shuttle orbiter. It would be able to take off and land like a normal airplane. After takeoff, it might continue its ascent into a low-Earth orbit and perform missions similar to those of the shuttle orbiter, or it could arc back to Earth and land at a distant airport halfway around the world. [Figure 10-80]

Several difficult problems remain to be solved in the development of this aircraft. The first is to find satisfactory propulsion systems. For acceleration beyond Mach 6, the space plane will need special combustion chambers, as well as a fuel like liquid hydrogen that burns very quickly. Then, to accelerate into orbit, some form of rocket engine will probably be needed. Besides the powerplant, new materials, combining great strength and light weight, must be developed to withstand the unusual stresses of hypersonic flight in the region of Mach 25. Another problem is the cost; the first phase of development, alone, is estimated to be billions of dollars. This is certain to become a major hurdle.

Technical advances have made the space plane feasible, and Japanese, European, and American research programs are moving ahead. The first phase in the U.S. is a secret military program under the Department of

Defense and NASA. It includes use of the experimental X-30 aircraft to test the concept. The timetable calls for the first test flight of the X-30 by the mid-1990's.

CHECKLIST

After studying this section you should have a basic understanding of:

✓ **The jet engine** — How it produces thrust, what some of its advantages are, and what the main types are.

✓ **The sound barrier** — What the terms associated with high-speed flight are, and how this barrier was broken.

✓ **Jet aircraft in the Korean era** — What some of the first successful military jet aircraft were, including those that flew later in the 1950's.

✓ **Jets for commercial aviation** — What some of the first civilian jets were, and how they were developed.

✓ **Vietnam** — How the role of the helicopter expanded, and how air power was used.

✓ **Continued development** — What some of the major advances in air transportation were, including wide-bodied jets, fuel efficient engines, SSTs, STOL/VTOL aircraft, swing-wing, fly-by-wire, stealth technology, canard, and composite designs.

✓ **Sport aviation** — What types of aircraft are used in recreational flying, and what some of the unusual experimental aircraft designs are.

✓ **Aircraft of the future** — What some of the new design innovations are and what capabilities are projected for the space plane.

THE NATURE OF SPACE

INTRODUCTION

For thousands of years, people have looked up from Earth in an attempt to uncover the mysteries that lie beyond in the vast environment of space. In recent years, our knowledge of this fascinating and mysterious expanse has increased significantly through the use of both manned and unmanned explorations. This chapter begins with a discussion of the elements of the atmosphere surrounding our planet. From there, we'll concentrate on the characteristics of interplanetary space and the planets associated with our solar system. Finally, we'll look at the galaxies far beyond our own.

THE EARTH'S ATMOSPHERE

In Chapter 4, we looked briefly at the various atmospheric layers and their effect on the Earth's weather. Space exploration has expanded our knowledge of the atmosphere because we pass through the layers as we travel to and from our planet. By understanding the composition of these layers, we can see how we're affected during flight through them.

ATMOSPHERIC LAYERS

Nearly all of the Earth's weather occurs in the troposphere.

The **troposphere** is the lowest region of the atmosphere. It varies in depth from an average of approximately five miles over the poles to over 10 miles above the equator, with a greater depth in the summer than winter.

The troposphere contains about 75% of the Earth's atmosphere by weight, and it is within this layer of air that almost all clouds and weather occur. The upper boundary of the troposphere, called the **tropopause**, serves as the boundary between the troposphere and stratosphere. [Figure 11-1]

Cabin pressurization or a pressurized space suit is essential for travel in the stratosphere.

The atmospheric layer above the tropopause is called the **stratosphere**. The altitude of the top of this layer varies from 19 to 22 miles above the Earth. Approximately 99% of the Earth's atmosphere lies below the outermost reaches of the stratosphere. The temperature is constant from the tropopause up to about 12 miles, where it increases toward the top of the stratosphere. This region is further characterized by the near absence of

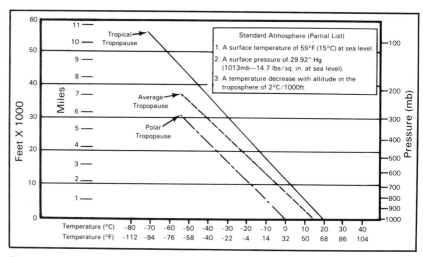

Figure 11-1. As altitude increases, there is a steady decrease in temperature within the troposphere up to the tropopause, where the average temperature stabilizes at approximately –70° Fahrenheit.

water vapor and clouds. In addition to a lack of oxygen in the stratosphere, there is almost no atmospheric pressure. When pressure falls below three pounds per square inch (above approximately 40,000 feet), some type of environmental protection is necessary. An unprotected space traveler could not live because of the extremely low atmospheric pressure in the stratosphere. Therefore, a pressurized cabin or pressurized space suit is imperative for operations in this atmospheric region. The composition of the stratosphere is nearly the same as that of the troposphere, although it contains a substantially higher amount of ozone. An ozone layer, which is near the middle of the stratosphere, is vital to us since it absorbs most of the deadly ultraviolet rays from the sun.

The next atmospheric region, called the **mesosphere**, extends to about 250,000 feet, or approximately 50 miles. The high concentration of ozone in this region helps to shield the Earth from ultraviolet rays and causes the temperature of the thin atmosphere to increase. At about 30 miles from the Earth's surface, the outside temperature begins to decrease until it reaches about –135°F near the top of this zone.

The **thermosphere** is also called the **ionosphere** because of its intense electrical activity. The base of the ionosphere actually begins in the mesosphere and extends upward through the thermosphere. [Figure 11-2]

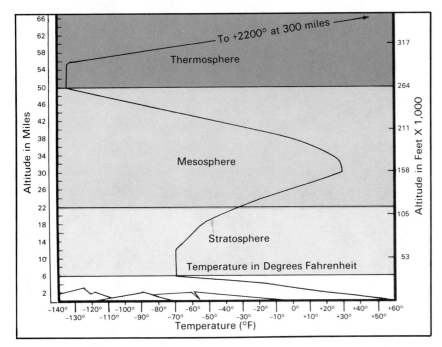

Figure 11-2. The thermosphere extends up to approximately 300 miles; however, all but one millionth of the atmosphere lies below 60 miles. The atmosphere is so thin in this region that no sound is transmitted. From the low temperature of –135°F, the temperature curve goes up again, reaching +2,200°F at 300 miles.

Solar disturbances can alter the thermosphere's ability to reflect radio waves back to Earth.

Atoms and molecules in this layer are bombarded by solar radiation and become electrified or **ionized**. The thermosphere is important in long distance radio communications because of its ability to reflect radio waves back to the surface. The greatest concentration of electrons is found at approximately 75 miles from the Earth's surface. Disturbances on the sun often result in an excessive emission of electrons, which in turn, varies the strength of the ionospheric layers. When these electrons reach the ionosphere, the molecules of ionized atmospheric gases absorb the speeding electrons. The gases, therefore, lose their electrical charge and reflective properties. The radio waves pass through the ionosphere and long distance radio communication fade outs are experienced on the sunlit side of the Earth. [Figure 11-3]

The upper limits of the **exosphere** blend into outer space somewhere between 500 and a 1,000 miles. The gas molecules in this region are so few in number that they do not collide until they return to a lower level of the atmosphere. In fact, some of these particles may escape the Earth's gravitational pull and disperse into space. [Figure 11-4]

Courtesy of Robert Bumpas, National Center for Atmospheric Research/National Science Foundation

Figure 11-3. Another phenomenon resulting from ionospheric storms is the aurora borealis, or northern lights. Particles emitted from the sun are attracted by the magnetic poles of the Earth. Light energy is released as they stream in from space and collide with gas molecules in the upper atmosphere. This light produces the beautifully colored display commonly observed by people in the northern latitudes. When these lights are observed in the southern hemisphere, they are called aurora australis.

BEYOND THE ATMOSPHERE

The region found beyond the atmosphere is the beginning of the road to the moon. This region is called **near space** in celestial terms. An arbitrary limit of near space is drawn at about 10,000 miles from Earth.

Well beyond the limits of the atmosphere, the area between the Earth and the moon is often termed **cislunar space**. This area covers the approximately 239,000-mile distance to the Earth's nearest neighbor in the sky. The vast distance beyond the moon is as yet unexplored except by instrument space probes. For purposes of definition, this area out to a 1,000,000-mile limit is called **translunar space**. [Figure 11-5]

The enormous distances between individual stars in the galaxy of the Milky Way are referred to as **interstellar space**. The almost incomprehensible distances between individual groups of stars, called galaxies, are referred to by most authorities as **intergalactic space**. It is within this region that new and somewhat unfamiliar terms must be used to describe the enormous distances involved. These terms will be developed and explained later in this chapter.

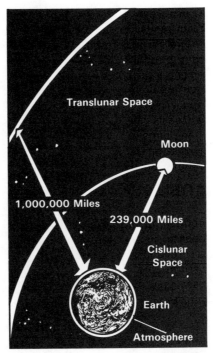

Figure 11-4. Satellites orbiting in the exosphere are slowed very little by air friction.

Figure 11-5. Translunar space marks the start of interplanetary travel. The conquest of this vast region will require the application of mankind's most advanced knowledge and technology.

CHECKLIST _____

After studying this section, you should have a basic understanding of:

✓ **Troposphere** — What its limits are and how much of the Earth's weather occurs in this region.

✓ **Stratosphere** — How the low atmospheric pressure in this layer affects travel within it.

✓ **Mesosphere** — What the concentration of ozone in this region does to shield the Earth from cosmic rays.

✓ **Thermosphere** — Why it is also called the ionosphere, and how it affects long distance radio communications.

✓ **Exosphere** — What the limited air friction does to satellites orbiting in this region.

CHARACTERISTICS OF SPACE

In the previous section, you learned about the various atmospheric layers surrounding the Earth. You were also introduced to the regions outside our atmosphere. This section introduces you to the features of space that exist as you venture past the Earth's atmosphere into near space and beyond.

VACUUM

Probably the most significant characteristic of space is the sparse distribution of matter. Space is often compared to a vacuum, although it is not a perfect one. Even interstellar space contains large amounts of widely distributed dust and gas particles. However, most of the universe can be described as nearly empty space with most of the matter clustered into vast systems called galaxies. One of the consequences of the sparse distribution of matter is that sound cannot be transmitted. Sound originates from vibrations of matter which is in contact with an elastic medium such as air, water, or even metal. The vibrations set up wave motions in the medium which transmit the sound. The term "sound" actually refers to the sensation of sound as we hear and interpret vibrations transmitted by the medium. In space, there is no medium for the transmission of sound waves.

Space contains no medium for the transmission of sound waves.

TEMPERATURE

Another consequence of the sparse distribution of matter in space is extremely low temperatures. Since temperature actually is a measure of the molecular motion or vibration of particles of matter, space itself is devoid of heat because it contains only minute quantities of matter. This has significant implications for objects journeying through space. For example, bodies like the moon, which have no protective atmosphere, are subjected on one side to the intense heat and other forms of radiation streaming from the sun. The other side facing away from the sun is not subjected to the sun's heat and, consequently, temperatures near **absolute zero** (−459.67°F or −273.15°C) are the rule. Absolute zero is a hypothetical temperature completely void of any heat. A spacecraft is subjected to the same large variations in temperature.

RADIATION HAZARDS

As already indicated, outer space is not really empty. Streams of electromagnetic radiation of all wave lengths, as well as electrons, protons, and other particles flow through it. Cosmic rays also are present.

The solar wind is a stream of charged particles from the sun.

Although these phenomena are often referred to as rays, they are actually showers of high energy protons, **alpha particles** (helium nuclei), and the nuclei of heavier elements such as iron. The so-called "solar wind" consists mostly of protons and electrons flowing outward from the sun. The solar wind becomes a solar storm as the quantity of particles increases during periods of high sunspot activity. [Figure 11-6]

VAN ALLEN BELTS

The possibility of electrically charged solar particles becoming entrapped in the external magnetic field of the Earth was first shown theoretically by the Norwegian mathematician Karl Stoermer in 1907. However, the actual existence of **radiation belts** was not discovered until early 1958. These belts are actually zones surrounding the Earth where the charged particles collect and become trapped.

The Van Allen belts help to shield the Earth from solar radiation.

The Van Allen radiation belts are found within the magnetic field surrounding the Earth. The belts are named in honor of Dr. James Van Allen, who, with his colleagues at the University of Iowa, was responsible for the interpretation of data from the Explorer series of satellites. The data was used to map particles trapped by the Earth's magnetic field. The magnetic field had been previously visualized as a pattern similar to the assemblage of iron filings around a bar magnet. Dr. Van Allen found that the magnetic field is shaped more like a teardrop. The belts are usually divided into two zones. This division is made on the basis of different particle characteristics within the zones. [Figure 11-7]

The radiation belts present a health hazard to manned space flight because radiation can severely disrupt the chemical processes within a living cell and also interfere with normal cell division. There is very

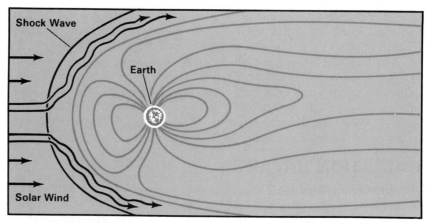

Figure 11-6. As the solar wind passes around the Earth, the planet's magnetic field is compressed on the side nearest the sun, and stretched on the other side, creating its teardrop form.

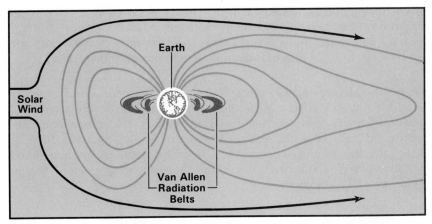

Figure 11-7. Although the Earth is protected from solar radiation by the magnetic field surrounding it, some of the charged atomic particles are not deflected, and are then caught in the Van Allen radiation belts. These particles eventually diffuse back into space.

little, if any, danger below altitudes of 250 miles, but an extremely hazardous area is found at an altitude of 1,500 miles above the equatorial regions.

Adequate radiation protection for astronauts requires very heavy shielding. For this reason, manned flights have normally been restricted to altitudes below 250 miles or to a rapid crossing of the radiation belts, as was done in the Apollo Lunar Missions. It's fortunate that increased levels of radiation, such as those common during the high levels of sunspot activity associated with solar storms, can be forecast some time in advance.

Mission planners can adjust the space flight schedule to a time when the radiation hazard is at a minimum.

METEOROID HAZARD

One of the dangers that was discussed prior to actual manned space flight was the possibility of a collision between the spacecraft and a meteoroid traveling at thousands of miles per hour. Experience has shown, however, that there is practically no danger from pebble-sized meteoroids. Some concern was also expressed that micrometeoroids, which are sand grain size and smaller, would seriously erode the metal surfaces, and damage the complex equipment aboard a spacecraft. When Mariner II journeyed to Venus, only two impacts were recorded during the whole mission. A later journey by Mariner IV to Mars recorded 200 impacts from micrometeoroids, none of which were considered serious. A special layer of material in the Apollo astronauts' spacesuits protected them from micrometeoroids while they explored the moon's surface.

Meteoroids pose little danger to space travel.

MICROGRAVITY

Just as a total vacuum does not exist in space, there is no such thing as gravity-free space. Terms such as **zero-G** and **weightlessness** have been used to describe an environment in which the forces of gravity are so small or are sufficiently in balance with other forces that the effects of gravity can generally be disregarded. The term **microgravity** more correctly describes the true nature of this environment. [Figure 11-8]

Before the Mercury space flights, many people were concerned about the possible adverse effects of prolonged microgravity on the astronauts. Most of these concerns were proven false. However, Mercury flights and continued research with Gemini, Apollo, and Skylab missions did indicate some loss of muscle tissue (muscle atrophy) and a condition known as "lazy heart." The latter is a result of the heart being given a vacation from the pull of gravity.

In a microgravity environment, the heart does not have to pump blood against the pull of gravity and, therefore, it does not have to work as hard. Fortunately, both muscle atrophy and the "lazy heart" condition appear to be manageable by incorporating regular exercise programs into the mission schedule. The Space Shuttle missions indicated no serious adverse effects from microgravity; however, space flights of a year or more still raise unanswered questions about the long term effects of microgravity. Now let's look at the element of time as it relates to space travel.

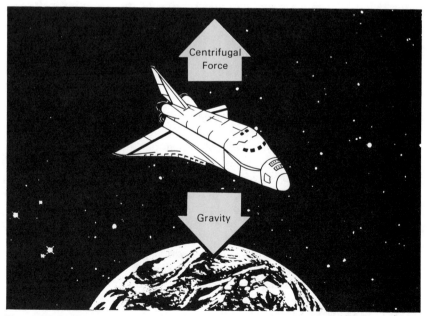

Figure 11-8. In orbit, the downward pull of gravity is balanced by the outward centrifugal force generated as the spacecraft orbits the Earth. In this situation, the occupants of the spacecraft will experience microgravity.

TIME

One of the consequences of Albert Einstein's **Special Theory of Relativity** may be expressed as a characteristic relating to space travel. Within Einstein's frame of reference, time and space are relative terms, not absolute, and vary depending on the state of motion of the person observing them. Accordingly, if the speed of an object is changed, time will also change; as speed increases, time slows down.

To understand time as it relates to space travel, imagine an astronaut in a spacecraft traveling near the speed of light, while an observer on Earth witnesses the movement. From the observer's viewpoint, it will take much longer for the spacecraft to move than is witnessed by the astronaut inside. This relativity of time becomes important as we look at the possibility of someday being able to send astronauts into space at the tremendous speeds approaching that of light. For instance, imagine sending an astronaut to the galaxy of Andromeda and back at this speed. While the astronaut might age only 56 years, the Earth would have aged approximately four million years.

The theory of relativity as it pertains to time and space travel is more than a wild dream. There is experimental evidence that very short-lived subatomic particles, known as mesons, take longer to undergo radioactive decay when moving at extremely high speed than when in relatively slow motion. In other words, their life span is stretched out, just as an astronaut's would be, when traveling at speeds near that of light.

CHECKLIST _____

After studying this section, you should have a basic understanding of:

✓ **Vacuum** — Why it exists in space and how it affects the transmission of sound.

✓ **Temperature** — How it is a measure of molecular motion and how space and the bodies within it are affected by the sun's heat.

✓ **Radiation hazards** — How the solar wind affects the Earth as well as other bodies in the solar system.

✓ **Van Allen belts** — Where they exist and how they help to shield the Earth from solar radiation.

✓ **Meteoroid hazards** — How meteoroids affect space flight and how astronauts are protected from micrometeoroids.

✓ **Microgravity** — Why it occurs, and how astronauts limit the adverse effects of this condition.

THE SOLAR SYSTEM

The solar system is tiny compared to the universe, but it is an area of tremendous magnitude when you consider it in relation to familiar Earth references. In this section, we'll study the sun, which is the primary body of the solar system, as well as the planets that revolve around it. The planets are held in their orbits by the sun's gravitational pull. They all move in the same direction around the sun, and except for Pluto, their orbits lie in nearly the same plane. [Figure 11-9]

THE SUN

The sun represents more than 99% of the total mass of the solar system.

The sun is really a star located at the center of our solar system. Over 99% of the mass of the solar system is contained in the sun. Its mass is

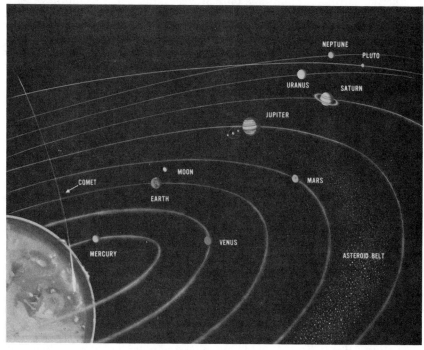

Figure 11-9. Orbital speeds are generally higher near the sun. Mercury, the planet nearest the sun, completes one circuit in 88 days. Pluto, on the other hand, takes 248 Earth-years to make one circuit around the sun.

330,000 times that of Earth, and its diameter is 109 times greater. A familiar characteristic of the sun is the dark **sunspots** that appear on its surface. They appear to be related to magnetic activity. The number of sunspots reaches a maximum every 11 years. [Figure 11-10]

Solar eruptions and solar flares occur frequently. The energy released from each violent eruption produces definite effects on Earth, including ionospheric disturbances, magnetic storms, interruptions of radio communications, and unusual auroral displays.

Besides sunspots and solar flares, scientists are studying numerous other solar features, such as the solar wind and the **photosphere**, which is the visible disc of the sun on which sunspots occur and from which solar flares leap forth. Also under study are streams of luminous condensed gas, called **prominences**, that rise above the sun's surface and reach temperatures of 18,000°F. [Figure 11-11]

Sunspots occur on the photosphere.

Other areas of study include the sun's core and the **chromosphere**, which is a transition layer of gas between the relatively cool photosphere and the extremely hot corona. The temperature at the center of the sun is estimated to be about 27,000,000°F. Thermonuclear reactions in this region convert hydrogen to helium, and to enormous amounts of energy emitted as radiation. This radiation includes visible light and other radiation in the form of rays and particles. The study of the sun is important to space flight because it controls the motion of the Earth and the other bodies in the solar system, and it produces part of the radiation that we must consider during space travel.

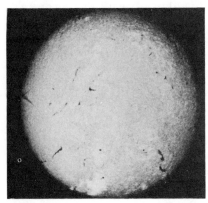

Figure 11-10. During periods of maximum sunspot activity, the sun shows marked increases in the production of short wave length radiation, particularly X-rays and ultraviolet rays.

Figure 11-11. Scientists are studying the sun's corona, or solar atmosphere, which is visible during eclipses. Temperatures in this region soar to 2,700,000°F.

THE MOON

The moon is the Earth's only natural satellite. It revolves about our planet from west to east in slightly more than 27 days. The distance varies several thousand miles between **perigee**, or the point nearest to Earth, and **apogee**, which is the point farthest from Earth. The average distance is more than 238,000 miles. Its orbital speed averages 2,287 miles per hour. Because it rotates in nearly the same length of time that it takes to revolve around the Earth, it constantly presents the same side toward Earth.

By Earth standards, the moon's atmosphere is a high vacuum.

The moon is approximately 2,160 miles in diameter, although data has revealed that it is somewhat lopsided because the center of its mass and geometrical center are not the same. Its surface is about one-fourth that of Earth, and its atmosphere is thin and scarcely measurable. Tiny amounts of argon, helium, and neon have been detected by instruments aboard the Apollo spacecraft. This heavenly body has no region of charged particles such as those in the Earth's ionosphere and Van Allen radiation belts, and it has no magnetic field, although lunar rocks show weak magnetism. This is evidence that the rocks were magnetized ages ago, probably due to a molten iron core creating a magnetic field that has since disappeared.

Temperature variations are a significant part of the moon's environment. Because it rotates on its axis once each 27.3 days, each area of the moon's surface, except near the poles, is in the sunlight for about 14 days, followed by 14 days of darkness. The temperature of the surface on the side facing the sun reaches 250°F, while the side away from the sun may dip below -280°F. The Apollo temperature probes showed that surface variations in temperature disappear at a depth of eight feet. The temperature increases with depth, due to a flow of heat from the moon's interior. Results from seismic soundings have led scientists to suspect that the moon has at least a partially molten core.

The moon's gravity, which is one-sixth that of the Earth, was once thought to present difficult problems in walking. However, astronauts found the adjustment to be much less than anticipated, and they had very little difficulty moving about on the moon. [Figure 11-12]

Because of the moon's low gravitational pull, it is not capable of retaining an atmosphere; therefore, wind and sound do not exist in the usual sense. Also, without the protection of an atmosphere, astronauts exploring its surface were subjected to radiation and to the hazards of micrometeoroids. [Figure 11-13]

From an observer's standpoint, the Earth's atmosphere gives the moon its characteristic yellow or sometimes orange color, but the first Apollo astronauts found the area where they had landed to be gray. [Figure 11-14]

Figure 11-12. The astronauts found it easy to work on the moon because of the reduced gravity.

Figure 11-13. Because there is no atmosphere on the moon to diffuse light, the sky is black, even in the daytime, and shadows are much darker than on Earth.

The surface of the moon is strewn with rocks and craters of all sizes. According to Apollo astronauts, the lunar soil is very fine, with a consistency similar to sticky wet beach sand. Probably the most significant surface feature of the moon is the vast number of huge basins that range from 650 miles across and 18,000 feet deep to small craters only an inch or two across. Large craters, which are much more common in the highlands than in the plains, are marked with medium-sized craters which, in turn, are pitted with smaller ones.

Figure 11-14. Orange soil was discovered when Apollo 17 astronauts surveyed the moonscape in the lunar rover. Studies have revealed that this coloration comes from the composition of the soil which includes microscopic glass beads tinted by titanium. They probably were formed 3.7 billion years ago when a volcano or meteorite threw molten rock skyward.

Some craters are shaped like shallow bowls with sharp rims and edges extending above the surface around them. Others have more rounded edges, often without raised rims. Some of the largest craters have flat floors similar to the plains area. Many have brilliant streaks, called rays, radiating from them across the lunar surface. Other lunar features are low domes and long valleys that extend for miles across the plains.

MOON ROCKS

An analysis of the rocks returned by Apollo astronauts and the unmanned Soviet spacecraft in the Luna series has revealed exciting knowledge about the Earth's nearest neighbor. At first glance, the rocks look very much like those found on Earth, but a closer look shows them to be unlike anything found here. Some are pitted with small glass-lined scars, and others are covered with spatters of glass that form whitish patches on the surface. The samples brought back to Earth are composed of orange, green, and red glass, as well as pieces of gray basalt and speckled chunks of breccia. More than one-third of the lunar material is soil, half of which is glass. In contrast, very little glass is found naturally in Earth soil.

Some lunar rocks contain minerals not found on Earth.

Researchers have found that lunar rocks contain elements in different proportions than Earth rocks. For example, the moon has a high proportion of elements with high melting points, such as calcium and titanium, but is lacking in elements that vaporize easily, such as lead or sodium. Carbon, iron, and granite are also rare on the moon. An examination of the samples has revealed some extraordinary minerals never seen before on Earth. Their uniqueness is partially due to a lack of oxygen that would otherwise have combined with minerals when they were formed.

Lunar rocks contain bits of the sun itself. These atomic particles are thought to have come from the solar wind. Since the moon is not shielded by an atmosphere or magnetic field, these particles strike the lunar surface, and a fraction of them are imbedded there. Scientists are learning a great deal about the chemical composition of the sun from an analysis of the solar particles within these rocks.

Examination of the lunar rocks has shown them to be older than most scientists had expected. While 99% of the rocks on the Earth's surface are less than 3.1 billion years old, Apollo 12 brought back pieces of rock ranging from 3.16 billion to 4.6 billion years old. The oldest piece is thought to date back to the origin of the solar system. It is believed to have been blasted down from the highlands of the moon. Rock samples from Apollo 14 that were taken directly from the lunar highlands confirmed that rocks dating from the origin of the solar system are intact on the surface of the moon.

Bioscientists have uncovered some unusual reactions to lunar soil samples. Certain bacteria were exposed to four lunar samples. Three of the samples had no effect, but soil taken one foot beneath the lunar surface killed the bacteria. Investigators believe the bacteria were killed by a poison in the soil. A further puzzle is the strange effect of lunar soil on plants. Certain lower plants, including several kinds of ferns, some liverworts, and mosses grow greener and, in some cases, larger when exposed to the lunar material.

MERCURY

Mercury is the closest planet to the sun. It is roughly two-thirds of the distance from the Earth to the sun. Mercury does not have an atmosphere because of its low gravity and extreme temperature. Without an atmosphere to protect it from meteoroids, Mercury's cratered landscape resembles the moon's.

Mercury is the innermost planet in the solar system.

Mariner 10 flew past Mercury in March 1974 and then entered a solar orbit that gave it two additional flybys in September 1974 and March 1975. The mission revealed significant differences between Mercury and our moon. Mercury has relatively smooth areas between its craters and basins, whereas the moon's highlands are marked with densely packed craters which overlap each other. The moon has a lot of craters that are much larger in diameter than those found on Mercury. The prominent features on Mercury are scalloped cliffs which run for hundreds of miles. The cliffs are a geologic characteristic not found on the moon.

For many years, astronomers thought Mercury always kept the same side toward the sun. It was thought that the sun's gravitational pull slowed down the rotation speed of the planet to the point where it revolved on its axis in the same amount of time it takes to circle the sun, which is 88 days. However, Mariner 10 photographs and further radar observations confirmed that Mercury rotates around its axis once every 59 days. Therefore, it rotates three times while circling the sun twice.

VENUS

The first actual unmanned probe of Venus occurred on December 14, 1962, when Mariner 2 passed the planet at a distance of 21,648 miles. Since that time, numerous American and Soviet spacecraft have ventured to Venus to help us uncover the mysteries that lie beneath this planet's cloud cover. Analysis of data from various expeditions has revealed that Venus is quite different than Earth. The atmosphere is composed primarily of carbon dioxide, along with traces of nitrogen,

Venus is always entirely covered by clouds.

oxygen, sulfur dioxide, and water vapor. The atmospheric pressure at the surface is 90 times greater than Earth's. [Figure 11-15]

Ground-based radar studies have provided evidence that, while it takes only 225 Earth-days for Venus to revolve around the sun, it takes roughly 244 Earth-days for the planet to complete one rotation about its axis. [Figure 11-16]

Ordinarily, because of Venus' indicated slow rotation, its night side should get very cold and its day side very hot. However, findings do not show any appreciable temperature differences at various locations on the planet's surface. This suggests that the atmosphere is circulating vast quantities of heat from the day to the night side. This massive heat transfer generates searing upper level winds that blow at an estimated 200 miles per hour or more.

Although the first four Venera probes sent to Venus by the Soviets were crushed by the pressure of the atmosphere as they parachuted toward the surface, later spacecraft were able to make it through the thick atmosphere and land. Before they overheated and stopped functioning, they were able to transmit photographs and additional information back to Earth. Scientists were surprised to see the extended visibility and vivid detail apparent in the photographs. They formerly thought that the surface would be dark, due to little sunlight being able to penetrate the vast cloud cover. However, light readings taken in the Venusian clouds

Figure 11-15. The temperature on Venus approaches 900°F, which is hot enough to melt lead and precludes the possibility of life like that found on Earth.

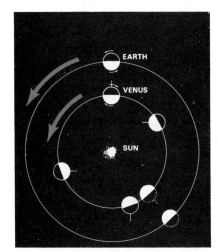

Figure 11-16. With respect to Earth, Venus rotates backwards about its axis. Thus, the sun rises in the west and sets in the east on Venus.

indicated they are much more translucent than the opaque clouds that surround the Earth.

Scientists were also surprised by the lack of sand or dust at the surface when none of the probes raised a dust cloud upon touching down on the rock-strewn landscape. Previously, many had pictured Venus as a desert suffocating in a thick greenhouse atmosphere. The rocky surface revealed a young, evolving planet in a cooling phase.

Since the vehicles landing on Venus were not able to move, the terrain information that scientists obtained was limited to a panoramic view of only one small location. Later radar images have revealed an abundance of information concerning Venus' topography. These include canyons larger than the Grand Canyon and plateaus roughly the size of the United States that rise nearly 11 miles above the planet's surface.

MARS

For decades, scientists and science fiction writers considered Mars the most likely planet to harbor life. Theories were built from Earth-based observations of the markings and changing colors on the planet's surface that seemed to correlate with "man-made" canals and growth of vegetation in the spring. But photographs from the first spacecraft to reach Mars, Mariner 4, led scientists to believe that Mars was a dead planet, resembling the moon with its cratered and scarred surface. Findings from later Mariner probes were also a disappointment to those expecting to see a multitude of Martian life forms. Mars appeared to be biologically and geologically dead.

When Mariner 9 began orbiting Mars in November 1971, scientific hopes for Martian life were once again raised. The spectacular photographs transmitted to Earth after a duststorm had obscured the planet for months revealed a diverse topography with an active geologic history. However, when the Viking missions reached the planet in 1976, biological experiments conducted aboard the landers could not detect life in the soil.

None of the samples taken from Martian soil have revealed signs of life.

Mars is about one-half the diameter of Earth. About half of its surface is very old and densely cratered. The other half looks more like Earth, and has younger terrain punctuated with what looks like fractured ocean basins with sedimentary and wind-borne deposits. The largest known volcano is located in this region. The base of the volcano is some 375 miles in diameter, and rises 17 miles above the surrounding plains, which is nearly three times the distance from sea level to the top of Mt. Everest. Another pronounced topographic feature of Mars is a huge canyon which follows the equator of the planet for 2,300 miles. It

Figure 11-17. Viking 1 sent photographs revealing rocks and finely granulated sand or dust on the Martian surface. The rocks in this region are consistent with terrain produced by volcanic activity.

plunges to 20,000 feet, or four times the depth of the Grand Canyon, and varies in width from 75 to 150 miles. [Figure 11-17]

Overall, the Martian atmosphere is very thin. Surface measurements revealed that the atmospheric pressure is about one-one hundredth as dense as the Earth's. Carbon dioxide is the major component of the atmosphere, with carbon monoxide, oxygen, and water vapor making up less than one percent of the total volume. On its descent to the surface, Viking 1 also measured traces of nitrogen and argon.

Infrared equipment aboard Mariner 9 recorded surface temperatures near 32°F in early afternoon, with some areas reaching 80°F. The temperature plunged to a frigid -190°F at night in the polar regions. Viking 1 recorded temperatures ranging from -24°F to -122°F. A wind sensor aboard the lander detected wind speeds averaging 19 m.p.h., with gusts up to 40 m.p.h.

JUPITER

Jupiter releases nearly twice as much heat as it receives from the sun.

Jupiter, the largest planet in our solar system, is nearly 2.5 times as massive as all of the other planets combined. If Jupiter were a hollow sphere, 1,400 balls the size of Earth could be placed inside it. The Pioneer and Voyager missions indicated that Jupiter is a blob of cold gases, composed almost entirely of liquid hydrogen, along with helium, methane, water, and ammonia. The atmospheric pressure of Jupiter is tremendous. At 16,000 miles below the cloud tops, the pressure reaches 3,000,000 times that found at sea level on Earth. Temperature variations are extreme on Jupiter. While the temperature is about -200°F at the cloud tops, findings from Pioneer showed that it's as hot as 34,000°F at the core. This value is nearly six times as hot as the sun's surface. Measurements also indicated that Jupiter radiates twice as much heat as it gets from the sun. [Figure 11-18]

Jupiter rotates quite rapidly in comparison to Earth, making one rotation on its axis in slightly less than ten hours. A drastic analogy is made by comparing the speed of rotation of a point on the Earth's equator with a similar point on Jupiter's equator. A point on the Earth's equator moves at 1,000 m.p.h. relative to the Earth's axis, while its counterpart on Jupiter moves at more than 31,000 m.p.h. This rapid rotation tends to make the planet bulge at the equator and produce a flattening at the poles.

Voyagers 1 and 2 provided thousands of images and a wealth of other information about the superplanet Jupiter and several of its moons. A scientific highlight was the discovery of live volcanoes on the moon Io — the first identification of volcanic activity anywhere except on Earth. Another startling discovery was a thin ring around the planet's equator. Jupiter may get a more extensive look when the Galileo spacecraft — an orbiter and an instrumented probe — investigates the Jovian atmosphere.

SATURN

The Pioneer and Voyager missions have revealed an abundance of new information about Saturn that was previously unavailable from Earth-based observations. Saturn is similar to Jupiter in many ways. The planet consists of a mixture of gases, mostly hydrogen and helium, and all we see are the cloud tops. Saturn radiates about twice as much energy as it receives from the sun. However, temperatures recorded near its cloud tops have been nearly -300°F. [Figure 11-19]

The most prominent feature of Saturn is its series of rings which extend to a distance equaling more than one-half that from the Earth to the moon. Although they appear as solid bands, they are actually hundreds of thin distinct rings composed primarily of ice particles that vary in size from minute crystals to huge boulders. Some dust also is found in the ring system.

Figure 11-18. The outer atmosphere of Jupiter is all that we see. The unique colorful patterns and bands that are visible are actually clouds formed by extremely high winds. Very little mixture occurs between these bands. The great Red Spot is a complex swirling hurricane that has raged for many years.

Figure 11-19. Photographs have revealed that the streams of clouds surrounding Saturn swirl at as much as 930 m.p.h.

THE OUTER PLANETS

After passing Jupiter, Voyager 1 was placed on a path that will take it out of the solar system. Voyager 2 continued toward a rendezvous with **Uranus** on January 25, 1986. Among the many new discoveries of the mission to Uranus were ten new satellites, ranging from 25 to 50 miles in diameter. The orbits of these new satellites all lie within the orbits of the five previously known moons.

Uranus is similar to Saturn in that it is a planet composed primarily of hydrogen and helium gases. Its rotation period is about 17 hours, but its axis of rotation is 98% from the vertical, which means Uranus revolves around the sun lying on its side. Another interesting property of Uranus is that its axis of rotation is offset nearly 60° from its magnetic axis. Although a series of rings somewhat similar to Saturn's was discovered in 1977, Voyager 2 uncovered a tenth major ring, and dozens of other lesser rings scattered among the major ones. The rings are made up mostly of boulder-sized particles.

Due to their tremendous distances from Earth, our knowledge of Neptune and Pluto is quite limited with respect to the other planets in the solar system. **Neptune** appears very similar to Uranus in size and structure. As Voyager 2 continues on its gravity-assisted mission, we hope to broaden our understanding of this planet, its rings and satellites. **Pluto** is the farthest known planet from the sun. Its unique elongated orbit actually carries it inside the orbit of Neptune for about 20 years of its nearly 248-year orbit of the sun. Pluto's orbit takes it out to such a great distance into the solar system that the sun would appear as a bright star when observed from the planet.

ASTEROIDS

During the night of January 1, 1801, an Italian priest, Father Giuseppe Piazzi was working in his observatory in Palermo, Sicily. He had surveyed the heavens systematically for months, but on this night, he came across a "star" that was not supposed to be there. He marked its position on his maps and searched for it again the following night. Much to his surprise, he found that it had moved. Night after night he watched this new body trace its path across the sky. He found that it moved faster than Jupiter and concluded that it must be a planet closer to the sun than Jupiter, yet he could only see it with his telescope. He deduced that the new planet must be small and, indeed, later observations revealed it to be an asteroid only 480 miles in diameter.

After Piazzi's time, a number of additional **asteroids**, which are small bodies believed to be the remains of one or more larger planets, were discovered, bringing the count to at least 2,000. Some experts believe that at least 44,000 and perhaps as many as 100,000 exist. Most asteroids are only a few miles in diameter; however, some are larger than 100 miles in diameter. All of these bodies revolve around the sun in the same direction as the planets. Although they generally orbit between Mars and Jupiter, they sometimes vary markedly. For example, one asteroid has an orbit which swings in as close as 18.5 million miles from the sun.

COMETS

A typical comet is composed of a nucleus, a coma or head, and sometimes a tail. Most of the comet's solid particles and, therefore, most of its mass is contained in the **nucleus**. According to one theory, the nucleus is like a "dirty snowball," basically a collection of rocky matter and dusty ice. The theory goes on to suggest that, as the comet nears the sun, heat causes the ice to vaporize, forming the coma.

The direction a comet appears to be heading is not necessarily the direction it actually is traveling because the tail always points away from the sun. The tail is formed when the solar wind carries dust and gas away from the comet's head. The length of the tail varies, becoming longer as the comet speeds toward the sun and shorter as it retreats. [Figure 11-20]

A comet's tail always points away from the sun because of the solar wind.

The continuing interest in Halley's comet is both historical and scientific. Halley's Comet is named after an eighteenth century British astronomer, Sir Edmond Halley. He was the first to believe that three previous comet sightings in 1531, 1607, and 1682, were the same celestial body. Halley plotted the comet's orbit and predicted it would return in 1758. Sir Edmond Halley became famous when the comet dramatically reappeared on Christmas Day in 1758.

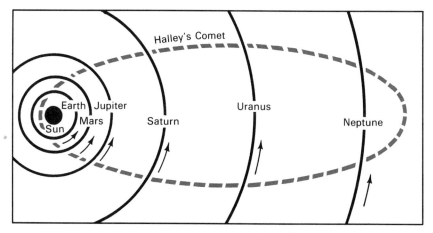

Figure 11-20. Some comets have orbits around the sun that are highly elliptical. Some orbital periods, or the time it takes for one complete circuit of the sun, exceeds 100 years. The most famous comet, Halley's Comet, has an orbital period of 76 years, and was last seen in 1986.

In 1986, five spacecraft from Europe, Japan, and the Soviet Union flew past Halley's Comet. The closest approach was by the European Space Agency's probe Giotto, which passed within 375 miles of the comet. Although it will take years to study the data, scientists found it is a black, peanut-shaped object about nine miles long and six miles across. The surface temperature is about 81°F on the sunlit side, much cooler than anticipated. As the comet rotates, it sheds its mass in jets of gas and dust that appear only on the sunlit side.

METEOROIDS

Meteoroids are pieces of matter ranging from microscopic size to rare massive chunks, smaller than asteroids. Explorer 16, the first NASA satellite designed exclusively for meteoroid study, proved that even the very small meteoroids, known as micrometeoroids, can puncture thin metal surfaces.

Meteoroids have three names that are applied to the same piece of matter. As long as it is in space, it is known as a **meteoroid**. When this same chunk of matter falls through the Earth's atmosphere and begins to glow, it is referred to as a **meteor** and is popularly called a "shooting star." If a meteor survives the fiery trip through the atmosphere and is found on the Earth's surface, it is then called a **meteorite**.

DISTANCES IN SPACE

Many people have difficulty comprehending distances here on the Earth's surface, and when it comes to distances such as those encountered in space, expressions of millions and billions of miles mean very little. This problem may be partly overcome by expressing distances in terms of travel time in more familiar vehicles such as automobiles. If you can imagine a highway from the Earth to the moon upon which an automobile could travel, the distance to the moon can be better comprehended. A person in an automobile traveling day and night at a steady speed of 60 miles per hour would arrive at the moon 166 days after departing from Earth. In contrast, the Apollo Lunar Landing Missions averaged 72 hours, or three days, on their journeys from the Earth to the moon. Light and radio waves, both of which travel at approximately 186,000 miles per second, require about 1.3 seconds to cover this distance.

Again using the automobile analogy, if you maintained a steady speed of 60 miles per hour, it would require 171 Earth-years for you to reach the sun, which is practically "next door" in terms of distances in space. Since this travel time spans several normal lifetimes, the automobile analogy must be abandoned in favor of some other standard, such as the speed of light. Light from the sun spans the distance to Earth in approximately 8.3 minutes. This same light, continuing to the outer reaches of the solar system, would require 5.5 hours to reach Pluto.

Another analogy may be helpful in understanding the distances and size scale of the solar system. Suppose the sun is scaled down to a sphere about 60 feet in diameter. If this scale is then extended to the planets, Mercury will be the size of a golf ball and about .46 of a mile from the sun. Venus can be represented by a cantaloupe at a little over .86 of a mile from the sun. Earth might be represented as another cantaloupe 2.3 miles from the sun, and Mars as a large baseball at a distance of 3.8 miles. At 6.3 miles, Jupiter might be represented as a sphere six feet five inches in diameter. At about 11.3 miles, Saturn could be shown by a sphere four feet eleven inches in diameter. The size decreases sharply to Uranus and Neptune, represented respectively by medicine balls two feet and one foot eleven inches in diameter, down to a baseball-sized Pluto. Pluto wanders at approximately 47 miles from the 60-foot wide sun.

Extending the scale and distance comparison to the nearest star beyond the solar system will again severely tax your imagination, for the star, Alpha Centauri, might be represented by a sphere smaller than the model sun at a distance of more than 262,000 miles. To continue with the relativity of the enormous distances in space, remember that our solar system is but a tiny island of matter in a vast sea of empty space.

Since conventional Earth measurements, in terms of miles, becomes relatively meaningless when discussing space, new units of distance measurement have been devised. One of these is called the **astronomical unit** (AU) and is based on the average distance from the sun to the Earth, or about 93,000,000 miles. The second unit of measurement, a much larger one, is called the **parsec**. This is a contraction of what scientists call a parallax second. Each parsec is equal to 19,150,000,000,000 miles.

The most familiar unit of space measurement is the **light-year**. This is the distance that light, traveling at the rate of 186,000 miles per second, would travel in one year. Each light-year is equal to 5,880,000,000,000 miles. One parsec is equal to about 3.26 light years.

Light travels at 186,000 miles per second.

CHECKLIST _____

After studying this section, you should have a basic understanding of:

✓ **The sun** — Why the planets orbit around it, what sunspots are, and how solar flares affect the Earth.

✓ **The moon** — How its atmosphere compares to the Earth's, and what scientists have discovered concerning rocks returned from the lunar surface.

✓ **Mercury** — What affect solar radiation has on this planet.

✓   **Venus** — How its rotation and atmosphere both differ from the Earth's.

✓   **Mars** — What scientists have discovered, and how it affects their view of the possibility of life existing on this planet.

✓   **Jupiter** — What the planet is composed of, and how its size compares to the other planets in the solar system.

✓   **Saturn** — What scientists have discovered about the planet's array of rings.

✓   **The outer planets** — What the unique features of Uranus, Neptune, and Pluto are and how they compare to the other planets.

✓   **Asteroids** — How they compare to other celestial bodies, and where their orbits are in relation to the closest planets.

✓   **Comets** — What the basic components of a comet are, and what we know about comets such as Halley's.

✓   **Meteoroids** — What the differences are between a meteoroid, meteor, and meteorite.

✓   **Distances in space** — Why new units of measurement have replaced conventional ones in measuring distances in space.

THE UNIVERSE

In previous sections, you studied the Earth's atmosphere and the characteristics of the space surrounding it. You also explored the solar system and became familiar with the tremendous distances between the various planets and the sun. In this section, you will find that the distances within the solar system actually are quite small when compared to the distances between galaxies and, particularly, when compared to the size of the observable universe. Distances on this scale are meaningful only when expressed in light years or parsecs.

COSMOGONY AND COSMOLOGY

When you study the universe, a logical place to start is by looking at how it originated, and how it has evolved to its current state. **Cosmogony** is the branch of astronomy that deals with the theories of the origin and evolution of individual stars, galaxies, and planetary systems making up the universe. The study of how our solar system originated falls within this field of research. **Cosmology** is the branch of study pertaining to the structure of the universe as a whole. It attempts to describe the universe as it now exists, and to trace changes from the beginning. These changes are described in terms of space, time, and matter.

THE BIG BANG THEORY

Although nobody knows exactly how the universe began, a highly supported theory suggests that it started about 15 to 20 billion years ago when most of the matter in the universe condensed into an infinitely hot primeval fireball that exploded. This explosion, referred to as the Big Bang, was so powerful that all the matter and energy and the space they occupied expanded at nearly the speed of light. According to the **Big Bang Theory,** the evolution of the universe began immediately following this tremendous explosion. Within microseconds, the temperature began to cool from billions of degrees. Minutes later, the temperature cooled enough to allow the formation of atomic nuclei.

The Big Bang is the most supported theory of cosmology.

The universe is still expanding as a result of the Big Bang, although its movement has slowed considerably due to the gravitational attraction of matter within it. Radiation resulting from the original explosion presently diffuses throughout space and is known as **background radiation**. Although this radiation was first released during the initial hot stages of the Big Bang, the average temperature of the universe has cooled to a few degrees above absolute zero, or approximately -455°F.

Within several minutes following the explosion, enormous amounts of helium and hydrogen had formed. In time, these atoms were attracted to one another by gravity, forming huge clouds that eventually resulted in galaxies. Within these enormous clouds, certain portions began to gather into small masses of helium and hydrogen gas. The gravitational attraction of these gaseous particles drew in more matter and resulted in a contraction which produced tremendous friction and subsequent heat. The temperature eventually became hot enough to produce a thermonuclear reaction that converted hydrogen into helium. The resulting pressure was high enough to stop the gases from contracting any more, and the energy produced radiated as a mass of heat and light known as a star.

THE OSCILLATING THEORY

Some difficult aspects of the Big Bang Theory pertain to the questions of exactly what existed before the Big Bang, and how the matter got packed into such a super-dense state prior to the explosion. These questions may be answered by the **Oscillating Theory** of cosmology.

The Oscillating Theory states that the universe expands and contracts in cycles.

The theory holds many of the same ideas as the Big Bang Theory. However, instead of the universe expanding indefinitely, it states that the expanding universe will gradually slow to a halt and begin contracting. The contraction is due to the gravitational attraction of the matter within the universe, just as a ball thrown into the sky will eventually fall due to the Earth's gravity.

According to the theory, as the universe begins to contract, it will build enormous momentum. The matter will eventually return to the original condensed point, where it will again explode, and the cycle will repeat itself over and over again. The question arises as to whether or not each new "bang" will produce changes in matter that will alter the laws of physics as they currently exist.

THE STEADY STATE THEORY

The Steady State Theory holds that new matter is created as the universe expands.

The **Steady State Theory** is an alternative premise which suggests that the universe is continuously expanding. It assumes that new matter is created at a rate which is, on the average, constant within space and throughout time. Instead of the universe thinning out as it expands, the theory suggests that new matter is spontaneously created, and replaces galaxies that are receding from one another. Since this new matter enables the universe to maintain a constant density, it maintains a "steady state."

The theory holds that the rate of creation of new matter is extremely small. However, this continuous creation of matter is the most controversial assumption of the theory because it seems to violate the **Law of Conservation of Mass-Energy**. This law states that mass (matter) and energy are equivalent and cannot be created or destroyed, only inter-changed. Some supporters of the theory explain that matter is created from negative energy.

THE MILKY WAY GALAXY

If you look overhead on a clear night, you can observe a faint diffused band of light running across the sky. What you are actually seeing is an inside view of the **Milky Way Galaxy**, which is a group of stars to which the sun and our solar system belongs. Although you might perceive the size of our solar system as very large, it is tiny with respect to the size of the entire galaxy, for our sun is only a single star in this huge collection of billions of stars. While our solar system is only about one-eight hundredth of a light-year across, the Milky Way is 100,000 light-years across. In addition, the Milky Way is only one of an estimated 100,000,000,000 galaxies. [Figure 11-21]

The Milky Way Galaxy is millions of times larger than the solar system.

The sun is located approximately 30,000 light-years from the center of the Milky Way. The galaxy makes a complete revolution on its imaginary axis in 200,000,000 years. Because of the galaxy's enormous radius, the speeds of the stars far from the center are very great. The sun has a speed of about 140 miles per second (about 826 times faster than a rifle bullet) relative to the center of the galaxy.

Although the Milky Way contains gas and dust, most of the mass of the galaxy appears to be concentrated in the form of stars. Their sizes range from those which are approximately that of the Earth to others

Figure 11-21. If you could view the entire Milky Way Galaxy from Earth, it would look somewhat like a flattened disc with spiral arms and a bulge near the center. The whole galaxy is thought to be rotating about an axis through its center at right angles to the disc.

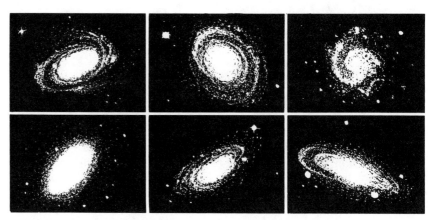

Figure 11-22. The galaxies within the universe vary considerably in their shape with globular, elliptical, irregular, and many variations of spiral-shaped galaxies scattered throughout the heavens. The galaxies themselves appear grouped into clusters of up to 1,000 or more.

that are so large that, if they were placed in the position of the sun, the orbits of Mercury, Venus, and Earth would fall within the star's body. [Figure 11-22]

STARS

As stars go, the sun is very ordinary in terms of size, color, and temperature. Other stars show great variations in these factors. For instance, the temperature at their surface may vary from 5,500°F to 145,000°F. A star's color is a general indication of its temperature. Red stars tend to be cooler; yellow stars, like the sun, somewhat hotter; and the hottest stars are blue-white in color. [Figure 11-23]

A star eventually consumes all of the hydrogen and nuclear fuels needed to sustain its life, then it gradually begins a cooling phase. As the core cools, the star begins to contract, causing the temperature and pressure within it to rise dramatically. This process ignites the remaining hydrogen, and the star swells and becomes a **red giant**. As the star continues to expand, its gravity is unable to hold it together, and the outer layers are expelled into space. This displaced matter forms a smoke-like shell around the star that is known as a **planetary nebula**. The remaining star is so hot that it turns white and is called a **white dwarf**. As the star slowly cools, it radiates its heat and energy into space. After billions of years of cooling, all that remains is a hunk of black matter called a **black dwarf**.

SUPERNOVA

A supernova is a dying star.

The death of some stars is very dramatic. As the star begins to run out of fuel and starts its cooling process, the drastic contraction and subsequent

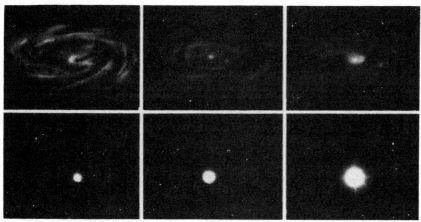

Figure 11-23. Stars seem to go through definite life cycles. The period of formation, as described earlier, occurs when gravitational attraction causes gaseous particles to contract. The resulting friction caused by the colliding atoms produces
enormous heat which eventually fuses hydrogen into helium. The resulting thermonuclear reaction releases tremendous amounts of heat and radiant energy. This
energy halts the contraction and a radiant star is born.

pressure may be too much for its core to support, and it suddenly col-
lapses. The result is a tremendous explosion, or **supernova**, that releases
so much energy that the dying star may shine millions of times brighter
than it did during any of its lifetime.

In February 1987, a supernova was observed that originated 170,000
light-years away in the Large Magellanic Cloud, which is the galaxy
nearest our own. Although dozens of supernova are witnessed each year,
this was the first one since 1604 that was close enough to be viewed by
the naked eye.

QUASARS

Some of the most mysterious and distant objects in the universe were
originally thought to be stars in the Milky Way. However, scientists discovered that they emit extremely strong radio waves which are more
characteristic of galaxies than stars. These celestial sources of radiation
were dubbed quasi-steller radio sources, or **quasars**. The light from a
quasar undergoes an increase in its wavelength as it moves away from
the Earth. This **red shift** indicates that quasars are receding from our
galaxy at tremendous velocities. Some of the most distant ones are estimated to be traveling at over 90% the speed of light.

Several ideas have been proposed to explain the characteristics of these
objects; one being that they are the most distant thing visible in the universe, existing billions of light-years from Earth. If this is correct, they
must be radiating enormous amounts of energy to appear as bright as

they do. Some estimates indicate that a quasar discharges hundreds of times more light than even the brightest galaxy. A puzzling aspect of a quasar is that the emitted light varies irregularly and rapidly enough that the source is thought to be relatively small. Perhaps they are the nucleus of distant galaxies which we are now observing as they existed during the early stages of the universe.

CHECKLIST ─────────────

After studying this section, you should have a basic understanding of:

✓   **The Big Bang Theory** — How this theory of cosmology attempts to explain the origin and evolution of the universe.

✓   **The Oscillating Theory** — How this theory differs from the Big Bang Theory, and what it states concerning the expansion of the universe.

✓   **The Steady State Theory** — What this theory suggests about the expansion of the universe, and how it explains the creation of new matter as the universe enlarges.

✓   **The Milky Way Galaxy** — What it consists of, and how the size of the solar system compares to that of the Milky Way and to the other galaxies in the universe.

✓   **Stars** — How the sun compares to other stars, and what happens during the life cycle of a star.

✓   **Supernova** — How they occur, and why the death of some stars produces such a tremendous explosion.

✓   **Quasars** — How they compare in brightness to other celestial objects, even though they are the most distant objects in the observable universe.

CHAPTER 12

ROCKETS AND SPACE FLIGHT

INTRODUCTION

This chapter includes a historical review of the significant events and hardware that helped us expand our knowledge of the solar system and beyond. You'll learn how rocketry has allowed us to gather information about ourselves, as well as other worlds, that is impossible to gather from earthbound observations. We'll also explore the principles of rocket propulsion and how spacecraft are placed into orbit.

HISTORY OF ROCKETRY

Rocketry has a long and colorful history. The vision of studying the heavens and visiting other worlds played an important role in getting us from the myths and legends of ancient China to the powerful boosters of today. However, these lofty goals were not always the reason for advances in rocket technology. The search for power, prestige, and riches lead to many important discoveries in rocketry.

THE FIRST ROCKETS

Many experts believe the discovery of **gunpowder** by the Chinese in about 900 A.D. is linked with the invention of the first rockets. Gunpowder was packed into a hollow tube that had one end open. When ignited, the burning powder would rush out the open end and propel the rocket forward. By 1100, simple rockets were being used to celebrate special occasions, as well as festive events. One legend even tells of the first manned rocket ascent. A Chinese official named Wan-Hoo fastened 47 rockets to a large wicker chair in an attempt to fly to the moon. According to the legend, Wan-Hoo disappeared in a large ball of smoke and fire when the rockets were ignited, never to be seen again.

Historians agree that powder-propelled fire arrows, as these early rockets were called, were used extensively during the Chinese-Mongolian War of 1232. At Peking, the Mongol cavalry was repeatedly pushed back by the many rockets fired by the Chinese.

PIONEERS OF ROCKETRY

As rocket technology spread into Europe, there were more reports of rocket use and experimentation. In 1242, Roger Bacon, an English scientist, described the chemical components of the gunpowder-type rocket fuel in common use at the time. By the early 1700's, rockets were assuming an increasingly greater role in military planning. The ability to launch large quantities of rockets at one time made up for the lack of accuracy.

Sir William Congreve (1772-1828) developed a series of rockets with improved accuracy and range.

The first big improvement in rocketry was made by Sir William Congreve, a British rocket pioneer, in the early 19th century. He added long wooden sticks to increase the stability and improve the range and accuracy of the rocket. [Figure 12-1]

Congreve's rockets were employed in the War of 1812 between Britain and the United States. A historical moment came during a bombing of Baltimore's Fort McHenry in 1814, when a young lawyer named Francis

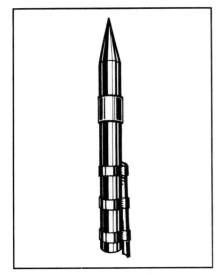

Figure 12-1. The early Congreve rockets were metallic cylinders with pointed nosecones. The propellant was a solid fuel packed within the cylinder. Guidance was improved when a long wooden stick was attached to the rocket.

Figure 12-2. On March 16, 1926, Dr. Goddard became the first person to successfully launch a liquid-fueled rocket. The flight lasted 2.5 seconds, reached a modest altitude of 41 feet, and traveled 184 feet from the launch site.

Scott Key wrote about "the rockets' red glare" in a verse that later became the national anthem of the United States. By the late 1800's, the Congreve rockets were replaced with a design introduced by an inventor named William Hale. He developed a rocket that would spin during flight, much like a bullet. This greatly improved the accuracy of the rocket.

The major developments in the late 1800's and early 1900's were the move toward **liquid fuels** and **multistaged vehicles**. The writings of the Russian theorist Konstantin Tsiolkovsky were instrumental in creating these changes. By 1898, he had worked out the mathematical formulas governing rocket operations. He then defined the need for liquid fuel and multistage designs that would allow rockets to achieve the velocities required to escape the earth's gravity.

Konstantin Tsiolkovsky (1857-1935) theoretically proved the use of liquid fuel and multistage rockets to achieve escape velocity.

A vision of the rocket as a space vehicle came from a Clark University professor, Dr. Robert H. Goddard. Although Dr. Goddard's early experiments centered around solid-fueled rockets, he concluded that they were inadequate for reaching the altitudes his studies had indicated were possible. Therefore, he turned to liquid fuel, particularly liquid oxygen and gasoline. Through research, Dr. Goddard concluded that it was possible to achieve escape velocity, that multistaged rockets were the way to achieve high altitudes, and that rockets could operate efficiently in the vacuum of space. Due to his pioneering work, Dr. Goddard is widely recognized as the father of modern rocketry. [Figure 12-2]

Dr. Robert H. Goddard (1882-1945) is considered the father of modern rocketry, due to his work with liquid fuels and multistage designs.

Dr. Goddard followed his historic flight with an instrument-carrying rocket in July of 1929. The rocket was equipped with a barometer, a thermometer, and a small camera designed to record the instrument readings at the maximum altitude. It is interesting to note that almost from the beginning of Dr. Goddard's experiments, he believed that a rocket would be the vehicle with which space travel might be achieved. [Figure 12-3]

The work of Hermann Oberth helped develop the German rocketry programs during the 1920's and 1930's.

At the time Dr. Goddard was beginning his pioneering work, another great developer of rocketry and space travel, Hermann Oberth, was working in Germany. Oberth's interest in space flight resulted in a number of studies that helped develop the rocket programs in Germany through the 1920's and 1930's. Prior to World War I, Oberth became interested in rockets designed for battle. He made proposals to the German War Department concerning the development of liquid fuels and long-range bombing missiles. After the war, he speculated on the feasibility of space flight.

Oberth's first book presented a discussion of almost every phase of rocket travel, including the effects of pressure on the human body. He

Figure 12-3. Dr. Goddard continued to improve his rocket designs by adding gyroscopes for inflight stability, fins for better control, and developing more reliable fuel pumps. These devices led to higher altitudes and also to larger vehicles, as shown in this photo of Dr. Goddard and his assistants working on a 1940 liquid-fueled rocket.

also gave a detailed description of a rocket which he called Model B. Describing the design of that rocket, he discussed the merits of alcohol and liquid hydrogen as rocket fuels and also described how the techniques might be applied. This book and an expanded second edition were important for the many new thoughts they presented about the problems of space travel; perhaps more important, they were an inspiration for other scientists to work on rockets. Oberth's work was largely independent of Dr. Goddard's, although many of the pioneering concepts of space flight were developed at the same time by these men.

Oberth's inspiration helped to develop the liquid-fueled rocket as an instrument of warfare, which led to the development and design of the German V-2 rocket. The first flight of a liquid-fueled rocket in Germany took place in March, 1931, when an 11-pound rocket rose to an altitude of about 1,000 feet.

At almost the same time, an Austrian rocketeer fired solid-propellant rockets which carried mail. The rockets delivered mail over a period of several years. In fact, regular rocket mail service was envisioned across the English Channel. These events were symbolic of German leadership in rocket flight between the two wars; however, important work was also performed in the United States, Russia, Britain, France, and Italy.

Most of the early experimenters were eager to pass along their information to others engaged in rocketry. This led to the founding of a number of rocket and space societies. It was through these societies that much of the theoretical and experimental work conducted in Europe and the United States was reported to members and certain other selected subscribers. Characteristic of the developments during this time was a successful rocket car and a rocket-powered glider built by German experimenters.

In 1933, the German government took control of the country's rocket development and began building a test facility at Peenemuende, on the Baltic coast. Between 1936 and 1945, the scientists at this facility, led by Dr. Wernher Von Braun, developed and produced a series of large rockets that were primarily designed as weapon delivery systems. The best known of these was the V-2, which was the most sophisticated weapon system known at the time. It was capable of delivering a one-ton payload 200 miles from the launch site. The first successful launch of a V-2 occurred in October, 1942. The first operational use of a V-2 was against England on September 6, 1944.

Following Germany's surrender, Dr. Von Braun and other German scientists, along with a number of captured V-2 rockets, were relocated to the White Sands Proving Grounds in New Mexico. Dr. Von Braun and these rocket scientists and technicians were the heart and backbone of the postwar rocket development in the United States. In fact, the technology we gained from this group and the captured V-2's must be recognized as one of the most fortunate events in our space history.

Dr. Von Braun (1912-1977) was a major contributor to the U.S. rocket and space programs following the war.

Figure 12-4. The original V-2, shown on the left, was a single-stage rocket that was 46 feet long, 65 inches in diameter, weighed about 28,000 pounds, and created 56,000 pounds of thrust. The middle photograph is a V-2 with a WAC Corporal rocket attached to the top as a second stage. The Jupiter-C, shown on the right, was a true multistage rocket that reached a record altitude of 682 miles and soared 3,400 miles downrange from Cape Canaveral in 1957.

A great number of V-2 rockets were fired between 1946 and 1951. Historical accounts show that almost every improvement in guidance, vehicle configuration, powerplant modification, and payload redesign involved the basic V-2 vehicle itself or many of its component parts.

As the supply of V-2's began to run out, development efforts resulted in the creation of the Redstone rocket. It was constructed at the U.S. Army Redstone Arsenal in Huntsville, Alabama, under the direction of Dr. Von Braun. The Redstone became operational in the early 1950's and was first used as a short-range ballistic missile, which is one that travels a high curving arc. The Redstone later served as the core of several early U.S. space boosters, which were designed to carry a payload, such as a satellite or spacecraft, into space. Modifications eventually resulted in the Jupiter series, which was first launched in 1957. [Figure 12-4]

CHECKLIST

After studying this section, you should have a basic understanding of:

✓   **The first rockets** — What powered them and how they were used.

✓   **Rocket pioneers** — Who the early rocket pioneers were and what they contributed to the development of rocketry.

✓   **Rocket developments** — How changes in stability, fuel, and staging improved rocket design and performance.

THE SPACE AGE

This section traces the history of the space age from the first orbiting satellite up through the space shuttle. This era and its technological achievements has given us the opportunity to study our world and others that would have been impossible had we stayed on Earth. It is human nature to explore the unknown and expand our understanding of our environment. Much has been accomplished and much remains to be explored.

THE SPACE AGE BEGINS

Many authorities consider October 4, 1957, as the dawn of the space age. On that day, the Soviet Union placed the world's first artificial satellite into orbit. **Sputnik 1** transmitted a series of beeps as it circled the Earth every 96 minutes. History will no doubt record this "electrifying" event as having a profound effect on education, communication, defense concepts, and politics.

The first artificial satellite, Sputnik 1, was launched by the USSR on October 4, 1957.

The Russians scored another space triumph less than a month later by orbiting Sputnik 2. The payload of this larger vehicle was a dog, Laika. Although Laika died after 10 days in space due to a lack of food, the flight proved that mammals could endure weightlessness and survive in space. [Figure 12-5]

Ten Sputnik series spacecraft were launched between October 1957 and March 1961. Most were sent into orbit by a Vostok launcher that was

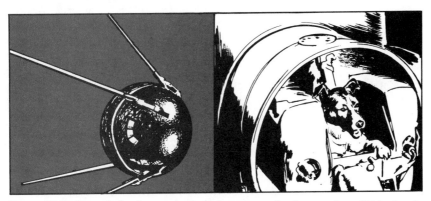

Figure 12-5. Sputnik 1, shown on the left, was an aluminum sphere 23 inches in diameter that weighed about 184 pounds. It remained in orbit for 92 days. Sputnik 2, shown on the right, was cone-shaped with a pressurized cylinder for Laika, the first mammal to orbit the Earth. The craft weighed about 1,120 pounds and remained in orbit for 163 days.

capable of producing a total first-stage thrust of over one million pounds. The Russians developed enormous boosters to carry their payloads, which gave them a significant edge in early space exploration. A number of experiments were conducted during the Sputnik series in preparation for the first manned flight. In the early 1960's, this series of satellites was renamed Cosmos. To date, the Russians have launched over 1,900 Cosmos satellites.

The U.S. effort to launch a satellite began in 1955 with the **Vanguard Project**, which was under the direction of the Navy. The original schedule called for the first launch to take place in October 1957 during the **International Geophysical Year** (IGY). The IGY was a concentrated effort by scientists throughout the world to study the Earth, its atmosphere, and the sun.

The first Vanguard launch attempt did not occur, however, until December 1957, and it used an untested second stage. The vehicle lost thrust after two seconds and was destroyed by flames. United States planners, somewhat humiliated by this failure, redirected efforts toward Dr. Von Braun and the Army Ballistic Missile Agency in Huntsville, Alabama. The Secretary of Defense authorized the preparation of a satellite, and the launch date was set for January 30, 1958.

The first U.S. satellite, Explorer 1, was launched on January 31, 1958.

With knowledge of the earlier success of Jupiter-C, Von Braun's group had no doubt that the rocket could be quickly adapted for a satellite launch. This modification, known as Juno 1, partially redeemed America's image by orbiting the first United States satellite, **Explorer 1**, on January 31, 1958, one day behind schedule. [Figure 12-6]

Many Explorer satellites were launched following this historic space shot. By the end of the program in 1975, 53 Explorer satellites were placed in orbit. It should be noted that the Vanguard program eventually succeeded on March 17, 1958, in placing the second U.S. satellite into orbit. **Vanguard 1** did not precisely follow the path predicted for it. This led scientist Ann Eckels to suggest that perhaps the Earth is not a smooth sphere. After she and her fellow scientists calculated the satellite's true orbit, she determined that the Earth is indeed somewhat pear-shaped. All orbit predictions and tracking are now based on that knowledge.

NASA

NASA was formed on October 1, 1958.

The passage of the National Aeronautics and Space Act of 1958 helped to organize the efforts of a variety of federal, industrial, and scientific groups into one national space program. This act created the **National**

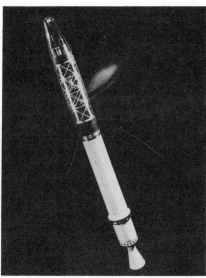

Figure 12-6. The left photograph is a Vanguard launch vehicle. It was developed using the basic systems and engine of a V-2, which was redesigned into a Viking rocket. A solid fuel third stage was added to make the Vanguard. On the right is Explorer 1, the first U.S. satellite to orbit the Earth. It weighed 30.8 pounds, was 80 inches long, and discovered the Van Allen Belts.

Aeronautics and Space Administration (NASA) on October 1, 1958, to oversee all nonmilitary aeronautical research and space programs. One nonmilitary Jupiter flight sounded a note for the future. During May 1959, two monkeys named Able and Baker were launched 300 miles high and 1,600 miles downrange in a Jupiter missile and were recovered alive. They were the forerunners of other living space payloads for the United States.

Even though the history of aviation and the history of rocketry and space have been treated separately, there has been a logical progression of aviation technology being refined and later applied to rocketry and space exploration. This was true of the effort to place a person in orbit around the Earth.

The United States program to explore the fringes of space produced the **X-15** rocket aircraft, which somewhat resembles a winged spacecraft. The first powered flight occurred in September 1959. The X-15, a product of an "X," or experimental, series of research aircraft provided unique experience in controlling a high-speed vehicle under flight conditions which closely resembled those of space. At high altitudes, aerodynamic controls do not produce the desired effect because the air is too thin. Therefore,

Figure 12-7. The X-15 was a joint military and NASA project. It collected data on high speed aerodynamics, heating, stability, and control. By the end of the program in the late 1960's, the X-15 had reached a speed of 4,534 m.p.h. (Mach 6.72) and an altitude of 354,000 feet (67 miles).

small stationary rockets in the nose and wings must be activated to control the aircraft's attitude and flight path. [Figure 12-7]

MANNED SPACE FLIGHTS

Yuri Gagarin, a Soviet cosmonaut, was the first person to fly in space.

The Russians scored another first on April 12, 1961, when cosmonaut Yuri Gagarin became the first person to fly in space. His flight lasted 108 minutes from liftoff to touchdown and orbited the Earth one time. The spacecraft, **Vostok 1**, reached a maximum distance, or apogee, of 203 miles and a minimum distance, or perigee, of 112 miles. During the flight, Gagarin ate, drank, and practiced writing under weightless conditions. This historic flight proved that people could function normally in space.

There were six Vostok flights between 1961 and 1963. The spacecraft was shaped like a ball 7.5 feet in diameter, and it weighed about 5,300 pounds. On June 16, 1963, Vostok 6 carried the first woman, Valentina Tereshkova, into space.

The United States' effort to place a person into Earth orbit began with **Project Mercury**. Through a highly selective screening process, seven astronauts were chosen for the project. Using the experience gained in ballistic missile tests and the X-15 program, a single-occupant capsule was designed. [Figure 12-8]

Alan Sheppard was the first U.S. astronaut to fly in space.

Initial success was scored on May 5, 1961, when a modified Redstone missile lifted a Mercury capsule from Cape Canaveral. Alan Sheppard was the astronaut for this suborbital mission which reached an altitude of 116 miles and which traveled 302 miles downrange.

Figure 12-8. On the left are the seven astronauts selected for the Mercury program. They were: (from left to right, front row) "Wally" Schirra, "Deke" Slayton, John Glenn, and Scott Carpenter; (back row) Alan Sheppard, "Gus" Grissom, and Gordon Cooper. The photograph on the right is a Mercury spacecraft being launched by a Redstone booster. The escape tower can be seen above the Mercury capsule. It could pull the capsule free in case of a booster malfunction.

Later that month, President Kennedy made his historic speech that unified the nation's spirit and efforts to reach the moon. ". . . I believe that this nation should commit itself to achieving the goal, before this decade is out, of landing a man on the moon and returning him safely to Earth . . . ." Much work remained to achieve this goal.

Two months later, Gus Grissom made another suborbital flight. The spacecraft and its systems performed well, although a malfunction after landing caused the hatch to eject and the spacecraft sank. The favorable data gained from the two missions enabled Project Mercury officials to move on toward orbital flights.

After several unmanned orbital flights testing the combination of the Atlas booster and Mercury spacecraft, the nation awaited the first attempt by the United States to place a human in orbital flight. Astronaut John Glenn was selected for the mission. At 9:47 a.m. on February 20, 1962, the powerful Atlas booster accelerated toward space. Five minutes later, the spaceship, dubbed Friendship 7, went into orbit.

On February 20, 1962, John Glenn became the first American to orbit the Earth.

During his three orbits, Glenn reported that weightlessness was not at all unpleasant and, in fact, it actually helped him perform his tasks. Some four hours after launch, there was concern that the capsule's heat shield might be loose; however, Glenn successfully fired his retrorockets and began his descent. Apparently, the loose heat shield indication was caused by a faulty sensor. Splashdown in the Atlantic Ocean was successful, and the world breathed a sigh of relief.

This first flight proved to the U.S. that human beings could perform well during almost five hours of weightlessness and successfully react to problems. Three additional orbital flights in the Mercury capsule perfected the technique of putting a human being into space and increased the time in orbit to slightly over 34 hours during the final Mercury flight on May 15, 1963.

The Mercury program enabled the United States to lay a foundation for space technology, prove the reliability of spacecraft control, and test the advanced tracking and communications network. It also demonstrated the ability of an astronaut to take charge in an emergency and that weightlessness resulted in few adverse effects upon the human body. Much valuable data and many photographs added to the fund of knowledge. At the end of the Mercury program, the United States had a group of highly trained astronauts for further explorations.

VOSKHOD

The first person to walk in space was Alexi Leonov on March 18, 1965.

On October 12, 1964, the Soviet Union launched the world's first multiman spacecraft, **Voskhod 1**. Aboard the craft were three cosmonauts. Due to the limited space inside the capsule and weight restrictions, they did not wear spacesuits. Voskhod 2 was modified for two crewmen. On March 18, 1965, Alexi Leonov became the first person to step outside a spacecraft and "walk" in space. There were only two Voskhod flights in this series of spacecraft.

GEMINI

The successor of the U.S. Mercury program was called **Gemini**, the Latin word for twins. As the name suggests, this was a dual-occupant spacecraft. This program was designed to be a bridge between the Mercury and Apollo program that would eventually land a person on the moon. The major objectives of the Gemini program were to gain experience in longer flights, to practice rendezvous and docking, and to conduct space walks or extra vehicular activities (EVAs).

Ed White was the first U.S. astronaut to walk in space.

Two unmanned orbital flights were launched before Gus Grissom and John Young made a three-orbit flight on March 23, 1965. During this flight, they became the first astronauts to change the orbit of a spacecraft. In the second manned flight, Gemini 4, astronauts James McDivitt and Ed White extended orbital flight to 62 orbits. One of the objectives of the program was realized when astronaut White left the capsule and conducted a space walk. [Figure 12-9]

During Gemini 7, astronauts Frank Borman and James Lovell set a record for time in space with 206 orbits. During that same mission, another spacecraft, Gemini 6, was launched and caught up with its sister craft. In a demonstration of precise and complex maneuvering, Wally Schirra and Tom Stafford came within one foot of the other capsule. The two spacecraft demonstrated for the first time that two vehicles could rendezvous in space. Further Gemini flights refined the rendezvous technique and achieved the first successful docking in space when Gemini 8 docked with an Agena target vehicle. [Figure 12-10]

The first U.S. spacecraft to rendezvous and dock with another vehicle was Gemini 8.

While the space walk, rendezvous, and docking are perhaps the most dramatic features of the Gemini program, each flight accomplished many other lesser objectives. For example, the Gemini astronauts took many color photographs, participated in medical experiments and measurements, and helped to determine whether mental ability changes in the prolonged stress of space flight. As far as could be determined, flights up to two weeks long did not damage the body or hinder the ability to make evaluations and observations. Gemini 12, launched on November 11, 1966, was the final flight in the Gemini series.

APOLLO

Another step in space was realized with the spectacular success of the **Apollo** lunar landing program. The command module was similar in

Figure 12-9. On June 3, 1965, astronaut Ed White used a hand-held propulsion unit to maneuver while outside Gemini 4. White was tethered to the spacecraft during this first U.S. EVA.

Figure 12-10. This is a photograph of Gemini 7 taken through the hatch window of Gemini 6. The two spacecraft flew in close formation for nearly eight hours.

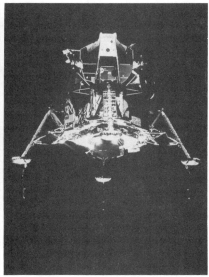

Figure 12-11. On the left is the Apollo command module that housed the three Apollo astronauts. The photograph on the right is the lunar excursion module. It was used to transport two astronauts to the surface of the moon.

shape to the earlier Mercury and Gemini spacecraft; however, it was considerably larger and designed for a crew of three. The service module that supplied the oxygen, water, and electrical power to the spacecraft was located directly behind the command module. The lunar excursion module (LEM) was stored in the Saturn V's third stage. It was extracted by docking once the mission was underway. [Figure 12-11]

The first six launches of the Apollo program were unmanned test flights of the spacecraft and booster rocket. The first manned flight was scheduled for February 1967, but a fire in the capsule during a simulated countdown took the lives of Gus Grissom, Ed White, and Roger Chaffee. The program was delayed 18 months while the Apollo craft was redesigned. On October 11, 1968, Apollo 7 was launched with complete success. Manned spaceflight was once again on course.

The first person to set foot on the moon was Neil Armstrong on July 20, 1969.

The first lunar landing was accomplished during Apollo 11. In a sense, a new age dawned when astronaut Neil Armstrong descended the ladder from the LEM on July 20, 1969, and became the first man to set foot on the moon. Armstrong was soon joined by Buzz Aldrin. Together they explored the surface of the moon, set up several experiments, and frolicked about in the one-sixth gravity of the moon while literally millions of people watched their activities on television. [Figure 12-12]

Apollo 13 ended in near tragedy when a malfunction in the fuel cells reduced the electrical generating capacity of the spacecraft and caused

Figure 12-12. Neil Armstrong's first step on the lunar surface and the safe return of Apollo 11 fulfilled President Kennedy's dream. The world heard Armstrong announce, "One small step for man, one giant leap for mankind."

Figure 12-13. This spectacular view of Earth was taken during Apollo 17, the last mission to the moon. The photograph extends from the Mediterranean Sea area to the Antarctic polar ice cap.

the moon mission to be aborted. The world joined in tense concern while the astronauts improvised and nursed their damaged spacecraft back to Earth to a successful splashdown.

Further Apollo missions studied the complex geology of the moon and permitted extended exploration away from the lunar module. Lunar rovers, or moon buggies, were first used on Apollo 15; they allowed astronauts far-ranging trips across the moon's surface. When the Apollo 17 command module splashed down in the Pacific Ocean on December 19, 1972, on board were the eleventh and twelfth men to have successfully landed on the moon. In the continuing adventure of manned space flight, the Apollo program will be remembered as the beginning of lunar exploration. [Figure 12-13]

Apollo 15 was the first mission to use the lunar rover to explore the moon.

SOYUZ

In 1967, the Soviet Union began launching the **Soyuz** series of spacecraft that were designed to carry up to three cosmonauts on long duration flights, as well as on rendezvous and docking missions. Soyuz 1 ended in tragedy on April 24, 1967, when Vladimir Komarov was killed during reentry. He was the first human to die in space during an actual mission. The Soyuz series is still being used by the Russians. In 1979, they began launching a modified Soyuz, called Soyuz T; in 1987, they introduced the Soyuz TM.

SPACE STATIONS

The world's first space station, **Salyut 1**, was placed into orbit on April 19, 1971, by the Soviet Union. The crew of Soyuz 11 were the first people

Salyut 1 was the first space station to orbit the Earth.

to live in the space station. The three cosmonauts spent 23 days aboard the craft in June 1971, but died during reentry due to a capsule pressure loss. Salyut was about 40 feet long and 13.5 feet in diameter at its largest point. It provided roughly 3,500 cubic feet of work area inside the craft. Seven Salyuts were launched between 1971 and 1982; they remained in orbit anywhere from a few months to several years. In 1986, the Soviets launched their next generation space station, called **Mir**. Since Salyut 7 was still aloft, this gave the Russians two functional space stations. Mir is a modular design that allows new sections to increase its size as needed. In December 1987, cosmonaut Yuri Ramanenko returned to Earth after living aboard the Mir space station for a record 326 days. This record was broken the following year by two more Soviets. To help resupply the space stations, the unmanned Progress tanker spacecraft was developed.

Skylab was the first U.S. space station. America's first manned space station, **Skylab**, was launched by a Saturn V vehicle on May 14, 1973. The station was a 100-ton cluster of units consisting of an orbital workshop and crew quarters. The entire cluster provided roughly 12,000 cubic feet of space. Three crews of astronauts lived aboard Skylab. Each crew used an Apollo command/service module to rendezvous and dock with Skylab. [Figure 12-14]

Most of the major research programs conducted by the three crews were aimed at improving life on Earth. These programs included:

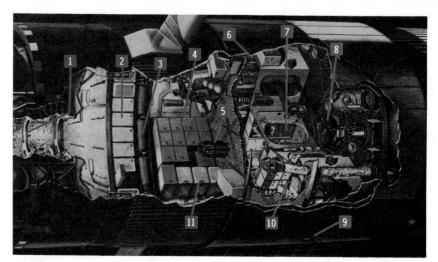

Figure 12-14. This illustration shows the various areas of the Skylab space station. They are the airlock (item 1), storage containers (item 2), water storage (item 3), food storage containers (item 4), waste management compartment ventilation system (item 5), sleep compartment (item 6), waste management compartment (item 7), trash disposal airlock (item 8), Earth observation window (item 9), wardroom (item 10), and food freezers (item 11).

1. Systems and techniques for gathering data on the Earth's resources and environmental programs

2. Solar telescopes to increase the knowledge of the sun and its influences on Earth's environment

3. Medical experiments to increase the knowledge of the human body and its relationship to the environment and adaptability to space flight

Skylab remained in orbit until 1979, when the drag of the Earth's atmosphere finally decayed the orbit. The greater portion of Skylab burned during reentry, but some large fragments fell on Western Australia.

The **Apollo-Soyuz Test Program** in 1975, was a major step in agreements between the United States and the Soviet Union to cooperate in space exploration. The main goals of the joint flight were to test and evaluate the compatibility of systems for rendezvous, docking, and the transfer of astronauts and cosmonauts between future manned spacecraft and stations. A standardized docking system, such as the one demonstrated by the program, was an essential first step for any future Earth-orbiting space stations employing the talents of citizens from different nations. [Figure 12-15]

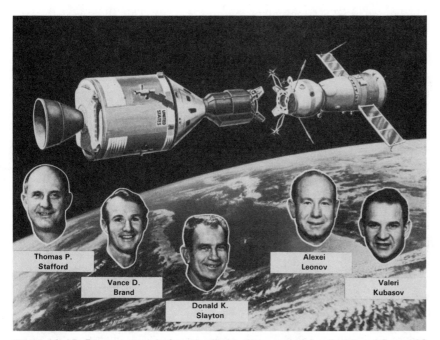

Thomas P. Stafford

Vance D. Brand

Donald K. Slayton

Alexei Leonov

Valeri Kubasov

Figure 12-15. For two years before the flight, the crews of Apollo 18 and Soyuz 19 exchanged visits and studied each other's language and equipment. During the nine-day flight, both crews experimented with processing materials in space.

THE SPACE SHUTTLE

The shuttle was the first reusable spacecraft.

The **space shuttle** was the first U.S. manned space mission after the Apollo-Soyuz Test Project. It is the principal element of a space transportation system (STS), and is the world's first reusable spacecraft. [Figure 12-16]

The orbiter was designed with a large cargo bay area to accommodate a variety of civilian and military payloads. The shuttle has distinct advantages over expendable booster systems for placing payloads in orbit, repairing or retrieving satellites, reusing components, and conducting scientific experiments.

The first orbital flight of the space shuttle occurred on April 12, 1981.

On April 12, 1981, 20 years to the day after Yuri Gagarin first orbited the Earth, the Space Shuttle Columbia lifted off on its first orbital flight. When it returned, Columbia made history by becoming the first spacecraft to end an orbital mission by making a conventional airplane-like landing at an Earth base. Crewmen for this historic flight were John Young and Robert Crippen. The near-flawless, first trip into space took slightly more than 54 hours. Another historical first occurred on November 12-14, when Columbia became the first spacecraft to complete a second flight. The first four flights of the shuttle were designed to test the systems and capabilities of the STS.

The launch of STS-4 took place on June 27, 1982. This flight was the last in the test segment phase of the program and the first to carry a classified military cargo. It also was the first with a paid **get away special** in which researchers put small, self-contained payloads of their own design

Figure 12-16. The space shuttle has three elements. The two recoverable solid rocket boosters (A), shown on the left, team with the orbiter's main engines to produce launch thrust. The huge, expendable external fuel tank (B) feeds the orbiter's main engines during the ascent phase. The recoverable shuttle orbiter, shown on the right, is the manned segment of the system.

aboard the orbiter. This flight was the first to carry a joint NASA/industrial payload which was an electrophoresis experiment for separating materials in low gravity. It also showed that the Canadian-built remote manipulator arm was easier to work than was previously expected. When the fourth flight concluded on July 7, Ken Mattingly and Henry Hartsfield piloted the Columbia to a perfect touchdown at Edwards Air Force Base, California.

STS-5 was considered the first operational spaceflight because two customers, Telesat of Canada and Satellite Business Systems, paid to have their respective communications satellites launched into geostationary orbit. This mission was launched on November 11, 1982, with Vance Brand, Robert Overmyer, William Lenoir, and Joe Allen aboard. Since the shuttle operates in a relatively low Earth orbit, the two satellites required the use of upper-stage propulsion units to put them into a higher orbit. This also was the first time four astronauts were launched in one spacecraft. The mission was completed on schedule when Columbia landed at Edwards Air Force Base. Later, it was transported back to the Kennedy Space Center. [Figure 12-17]

Two significant firsts in the U.S. space program occurred in 1983 with STS-7 and STS-8. On June 18, Sally Ride became America's first woman to go into space. Then, in August, Guion Bluford became the world's first black astronaut to orbit the Earth.

Sally Ride was the first U.S. woman to fly in space.

Figure 12-17. After some flights, it was necessary to transport the orbiter from its landing points in California or New Mexico to the Kennedy Space Center for the next launch. A specially modified Boeing 747 was used for this purpose.

In February 1984, astronauts Bruce McCandless and Robert Steward became the first to fly untethered away from a spacecraft. That same year, the crew aboard the Challenger Mission 41C fulfilled one of the STS goals by retrieving and repairing a satellite while in space. Solar Max was repaired by astronauts James van Hoften and George Nelson, then returned to orbit. In November, Dale Gardner and Joseph Allen retrieved the Westar 6 and Palapa B2 satellites that had been sent into improper orbits earlier in the year. An historical first occurred when both satellites were returned to Earth for refurbishing and future use. Through early 1986, 24 shuttle missions were successfully flown. Astronauts from West Germany, Canada, France, Saudi Arabia, the Netherlands, and Mexico participated. The European space agency's Spacelab, first flown aboard the shuttle in 1983, continued to provide valuable scientific information. Spacelab is a complete scientific laboratory that fits into the cargo bay of the shuttle orbiter.

On January 28, 1986, the Challenger exploded 73 seconds after liftoff.

Unfortunately, the shuttle program suffered a major setback on January 28, 1986, with the worst accident in the history of U.S. space activities. This particular mission was widely covered by news media because of the public's interest in one of the crewmembers, teacher Christa McAuliffe. She was to have been the first true civilian in space. A failure in the O-ring joint seal on the right solid rocket booster (SRB) caused a catastrophic explosion 73 seconds after liftoff from the Kennedy Space Center. The Challenger was destroyed and all seven astronauts were killed. Although this was the first time U.S. astronauts died in flight, the consequences have had far-reaching effects on U.S. space programs.

On September 29, 1988, the U.S. manned space program resumed with the successful launch of Discovery on Mission 26. The launch was the culmination of many shuttle hardware and NASA management changes following the Challenger accident. Highlights of Mission 26 included deployment of the Tracking and Data Rely Satellite (TDRS), photography of numerous Earth targets, and various experiments (such as protein crystal growth). By late 1988, the Soviets also demonstrated their capabilities with shuttle technology. The unmanned shuttle spacecraft **Buran**, which closely resembles the U.S. shuttle design, was successfully launched and recovered.

LIVING AND WORKING IN SPACE

Space is a hostile environment. To survive, a person must be protected from extreme temperatures, solar radiation, and micrometeoroids. Life support systems must surround the astronaut with an earth-like environment and provide air, water, food, and waste disposal for extended missions. To work in the weightless environment of space, special tools are required and maneuvering units are needed to move around or to remain stationary while working.

EXTRAVEHICULAR ACTIVITIES

Spacesuits and maneuvering units allow astronauts to leave the spacecraft and perform a variety of functions, such as deploying payloads, repairing and servicing satellites, assembling large structures, and performing experiments. The suit used on the shuttle is called the **extravehicular mobility unit** (EMU). It has a liquid cooling and venting garment, a flexible pressure vessel, and a primary life support system. These components are supplemented by a drinking bag, communications set, helmet, and visor assembly. The **manned maneuvering unit** (MMU) improves EVA mobility by allowing an astronaut to fly to any part of the shuttle or to a nearby satellite or payload. The MMU is used during satellite recovery and repair operations. [Figure 12-18]

The EMU and MMU allows astronauts to survive and work in space.

SPACE TOOLS

The tools used in space require a different design than those used on Earth. The problem arises because of weightlessness. Newton's Third Law of Motion states that for every action there is an equal and opposite reaction. When you tighten a nut or screw on Earth, the reaction force of the effort is not noticed because you are firmly held in place by gravity. In the weightlessness of space, however, an astronaut would start spinning in a direction opposite to the one in which the force was applied. To

The tools used in space are designed to overcome Newton's Third Law of Motion.

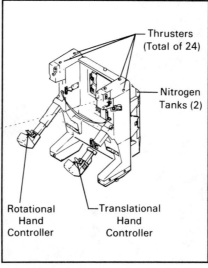

Thrusters
(Total of 24)

Nitrogen
Tanks (2)

Rotational
Hand
Controller

Translational
Hand
Controller

Figure 12-18. On the left is astronaut Robert Stewart as he hovers above the cargo bay of the Space Shuttle Challenger. The spacesuit he is wearing protects him from the hazards of space. He is attached to an MMU, shown on the right, that allows him to fly forward, back, up, and down, as well as rotate in the pitch, roll, and yaw axes.

cope with this problem, an astronaut must be anchored to the spacecraft or have tools that absorb or neutralize the reaction forces. [Figure 12-19]

SPACE FOOD

Mealtime in space has improved significantly from the semi-liquid toothpaste tubes used on the first Mercury missions to the real steak and strawberries on board the shuttle. On early manned flights, some experts were worried that food would be hard to swallow in a weightless environment; however, this did not prove to be a problem.

Figure 12-19. In this photograph, astronaut Allen is secured to the shuttle's remote manipulator arm by mobile foot restraints to enable him to stabilize the Westar satellite.

Day 1	Day 2	Day 3	Day 4
Peaches (T)	Applesauce (T)	Dried peaches (IM)	Dried apricots (IM)
Beef patty (R)	Beef jerky (NF)	Sausage (R)	Breakfast roll (I) (NF)
Scrambled eggs (R)	Granola (R)	Scrambled eggs (R)	Granola w/blueberries (R)
Bran flakes (R)	Breakfast roll (I) (NF)	Cornflakes (R)	Vanilla instant
Cocoa (B)	Chocolate instant	Cocoa (B)	breakfast (B)
Orange drink (B)	breakfast (B)	Orange-pineapple	Grapefruit drink (B)
	Orange-grapefruit	drink (B)	
Frankfurters (T)	drink (B)		Ground beef w/
Turkey tetrazzini (R)		Ham (T) (I)	pickle sauce (T)
Bread (I) (NF)	Corned beef (T) (I)	Cheese spread (T)	Noodles and chicken (R)
Bananas (FD)	Asparagus (R)	Bread (I) (NF)	Stewed tomatoes (T)
Almond crunch bar (NF)	Bread (I) (NF)	Green beans and	Pears (FD)
Apple drink (B)	Pears (T)	broccoli (R)	Almonds (NF)
	Peanuts (NF)	Crushed pineapple (T)	Strawberry drink (B)
Shrimp cocktail (R)	Lemonade (B)	Shortbread cookies (NF)	
Beef steak (T) (I)		Cashews (NF)	Tuna (T)
Rice pilaf (R)	Beef w/barbeque	Tea w/lemon and	Macaroni and cheese (R)
Broccoli au gratin (R)	sauce (T)	sugar (B)	Peas w/butter sauce (R)
Fruit cocktail (T)	Cauliflower w/cheese (R)		Peach ambrosia (R)
Butterscotch pudding (T)	Green beans w/	Cream of mushroom	Chocolate pudding (T) (R)
Grape drink (B)	mushrooms (R)	soup (R)	Lemonade (B)
	Lemon pudding (T)	Smoked turkey (T) (I)	
	Pecan cookies (NF)	Mixed Italian	
	Cocoa (B)	vegetables (R)	
		Vanilla pudding (T) (R)	
		Strawberries (R)	
		Tropical punch (B)	

Abbreviations in parentheses indicate type of food: T = thermostabilized, I = irradiated, IM = intermediate moisture, FD = freeze dried, R = rehydratable, NF = natural form, and B = beverage.

Figure 12-20. This is a typical four-day menu for a shuttle flight.

The primary objective of a food system is to provide food that is safe, nutritious, lightweight, compact, and easy to prepare and consume. The system on board the shuttle centers around a galley that is installed on the mid-deck of the orbiter. It features hot and cold water dispensers, a pantry, a forced air convection oven, food serving trays, and a personal hygiene station. Astronauts have a varied menu that features over 70 food items and 20 beverages. [Figure 12-20]

UNMANNED SPACE PROBES

This brief history should not neglect the important contributions of unmanned space vehicles to the present knowledge of space. For example, when the first astronauts landed on the moon, part of their success was due to programs such as Ranger, Surveyor, and the Lunar Orbiter series of unmanned spacecraft.

The **Ranger** series of probes was initially designed to hard-land on the moon and return data on moonquake activity. However, these early attempts were unsuccessful and the craft was redesigned as a purely photographic probe. The final three missions returned over 17,000 photographs that showed extremely fine detail of the lunar surface.

The **Surveyor** series of unmanned probes further explored the moon's surface. The Surveyor was a much more sophisticated vehicle that had the capability of soft-landing on the moon, a "mechanical hand" to scoop

The success of manned flights were, in part, due to unmanned probes.

up soil samples and chemically analyze them, and a television camera to photograph the moon's surface characteristics. The five Surveyors that soft-landed on the moon took over 87,000 pictures and gathered data for soil analysis. Detailed study of the photos and data indicated that the moon could be explored. Many of Surveyor's findings proved to be accurate when Apollo astronauts landed on the moon. [Figure 12-21]

The **lunar orbiter's** mission was to examine landing sites for the Apollo lunar landings. After the completion of five lunar orbiter flights, NASA was able to select five potential landing sites. In addition, the entire lunar surface was photographed to provide new maps containing many times the information that previously was available.

Figure 12-21. Apollo 12 landed close enough to Surveyor 3 to examine the spacecraft. When they returned its camera to Earth, they found that bacteria accidently carried with it had survived the hostile lunar environment.

Many probes were launched in the 1960's, 1970's, and 1980's in a continuing effort to explore the planets in our solar system. The information obtained from spacecraft such as Pioneer, Mariner, Viking, and Voyager has expanded our knowledge of interplanetary space.

SPACE STATION FREEDOM

In 1984, President Reagan committed NASA to the goal of building and launching a permanent, orbiting space station. The space station, which is now called **Freedom**, is scheduled to be completed in the late 1990's. Cooperation with Europe, Japan, and Canada is planned for this project. According to NASA, Freedom is the next logical step in manned space exploration. The space station can be used as the launch pad for further flight — a return to the moon and interplanetary travel to Mars and beyond.

CHECKLIST _____

After studying this section, you should have a basic understanding of:

✓ **The space age** — The event that began the space age.

✓ **Satellites** — Which sgnificant achievements of Russia and the United States were.

✓ **NASA** — When it was formed and its function.

✓ **Manned space flight** — What the significant achievements of Russia and the United States were.

✓ **Unmanned space flight** — What their contributions to manned flight were.

✓ **Space station Freedom** — What the basic plans for it are.

SECTION
C

ROCKET PROPULSION

For a rocket, satellite, or spacecraft to leave the ground, it must have some form of propulsion. In this section, you will learn the principles behind rocket propulsion. In addition, you will be introduced to the various methods which are currently being used and what might be expected for future interstellar flights.

PRINCIPLES OF ROCKET PROPULSION

In the seventeenth century, Sir Isaac Newton expressed three laws of physical motion. They are:

1. A body remains at rest, or in a state of motion in a straight line, unless acted upon by an external force.
2. A force acting upon a body causes it to accelerate in the direction of the force. The acceleration is directly proportional to the force and inversely proportional to the mass of the body being accelerated.
3. For every action, there is an equal and opposite reaction.

The third law contains the fundamental principle upon which jet and rocket engines operate. This principle can be demonstrated by releasing a highly inflated balloon. The **action**, in this example, is the sudden rush of air escaping from the balloon. The **reaction** is the rapidly accelerating movement of the balloon itself. In effect, this is exactly what takes place in a jet or rocket engine. The burning of fuel causes a continuous stream of tiny particles of gas to rush out of the exhaust nozzle at a high velocity. Simultaneously, a reaction of equal force, called thrust, is created in the opposite direction. [Figure 12-22]

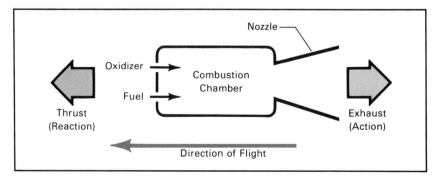

Figure 12-22. The thrust which results from the burning of fuel propels the jet or rocket forward.

In a jet engine, such as those powering many of today's airplanes, the escaping gas is created when fuel is burned. The surrounding air provides the oxygen for burning the jet fuel.

A rocket engine can operate in space, where there is no air, because its propellant tanks carry a supply of oxygen. As the fuel and oxygen are mixed and expelled as hot gases, they produce an accelerating force. The rocket accelerates as long as this force persists in accordance with Newton's Second Law of Motion.

Rocket engines can operate in space because they carry their own oxygen supply.

This law generally states that the greater the accelerating force, the greater the acceleration. It also implies that, with the same amount of force, a larger body experiences less acceleration than a smaller body, and vice versa. One common misconception is that a rocket or jet produces thrust by "pushing against the surrounding air." Contrary to this, a rocket operates with greater efficiency in the vacuum of space where the drag of air friction is not a factor.

ENERGY CONVERSION

The propulsive force provided by rocket engines may also be viewed in terms of energy conversion. **Potential energy** means stored energy. The basic potential energy forms which are relevant to rocketry are chemical energy and nuclear energy. These may also be changed to several intermediate forms; specifically, heat and electrical energy. The heat or electrical energy is further converted to **kinetic energy**, which is the energy a body has when it is in motion. In this discussion, it specifically applies to exhaust particles. [Figure 12-23]

Propulsion is created when potential energy is converted to kinetic energy.

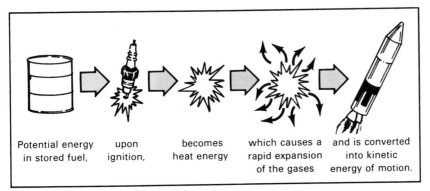

Potential energy in stored fuel,   upon ignition,   becomes heat energy   which causes a rapid expansion of the gases   and is converted into kinetic energy of motion.

Figure 12-23. Potential energy is contained in the chemical fuels of a rocket. When these fuels are ignited, potential energy is turned into heat energy. Because of the tremendous heat generated, there is a violent expansion of the gases. As the particles of gas rush from the rocket exhaust, heat energy is converted to kinetic energy.

CLASSIFICATION OF ROCKET ENGINES

Rocket engines are classified by the type of propellant used.

Rocket engines may be classified according to the type of propellant used to produce the high kinetic energy exhaust particles. These are:

1. Chemically fueled liquid propellant rockets
2. Chemically fueled solid propellant rockets
3. Nuclear rockets
4. Electric rockets
5. Photon rockets

CHEMICALLY FUELED LIQUID PROPELLANT ENGINES

In a liquid-propellant rocket, the propellants are stored in separate tanks and are forced into the combustion chamber the driving force of a high-pressure gas or by means of high-speed centrifugal pumps. Design of the pumps is one of the most critical aspects of the liquid-propellant system, since variations in pressure can result in wide variations in performance. In fact, pumps provide a means of controlling the amount of thrust produced by the rocket. [Figure 12-24]

Most larger liquid propellant rocket engines require the cooling of the combustion chamber. One of the most widely used methods is called **regenerative cooling** in which part of the liquid propellant is used as a coolant. It is piped around the outside of the combustion chamber before it is injected into the chamber.

Liquid propellant rockets can be bipropellant, using two different liquids, or monopropellant, where only one type of liquid is used.

Ordinarily, liquid propellant rockets are **bipropellant**. This means they use two different liquids — one liquid, such as refined kerosene (RP-1) as a fuel; the other, such as nitric acid or liquid oxygen (LOX) as the oxidizer. [Figure 12-25]

One of the objectives of propellant technology is to achieve a very high energy level. A number of exotic fuels and oxidizers, in various combinations, have been used in an attempt to attain this goal. As sophistication in ground support equipment has developed in the missile and space programs, some of the more exotic fuels have been tried, particularly for upper stage rockets.

One of the lightest fuels used is liquid hydrogen. Its density is about one-fifteenth that of more conventional fuels and its performance characteristics more than offset the additional tank volume required to handle such a low temperature fuel. Liquid hydrogen must be kept at a temperature lower than -423.1°F (-252.8°C) to prevent it from vaporizing.

An advanced type of liquid-fuel technology employs **hypergolic fuels** which ignite on contact with each other. This eliminates the need for

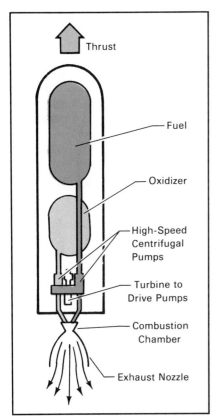

Figure 12-24. Rocket propellants consist of the fuel and the oxidizer. The oxidizer is the agent that supports the combustion of the fuel. When liquid propellants are mixed, they burn violently. The resulting mass of hot gases is then ejected from the combustion chamber through the exhaust nozzle.

Figure 12-25. One of the largest liquid-fueled engines was the Saturn V launch vehicle which was used to send the Apollo spacecraft and lunar module to the moon.

igniters and related ignition equipment. Use of hypergolic fuels also reduces or eliminates the necessity for keeping the fuel or oxidizer at very low temperatures.

There are also liquid **monopropellants**, such as hydrogen peroxide, which release their energy by decomposing under certain conditions, rather than by combining. A **catalyst** (substance which initiates a chemical reaction) may be necessary to start the process. Such monopropellants are not considered prime propellants, but are used in auxiliary applications, such as running small turbines or in the small attitude control jets which help to stabilize and maneuver a spacecraft in orbit.

CHEMICALLY FUELED SOLID PROPELLANT ROCKET ENGINES

A solid-propellant rocket is one in which the fuel and oxidizer are mixed in solid form, usually as a powdery or rubbery mixture known as the **grain**, or **charge**. The grain is packed in the rocket casing which serves as both a storage and combustion chamber. The shape and design of the grain control the thrust and burning time of the rocket. A large burning area means higher thrust and shorter burning time as compared to a smaller burning area. When the grain is cast, a hole or cavity in the form of a circle, star, gear, or other design is made through the center. The charge burns outward toward the case and along the entire length of the cavity.

Solid propellants may be those which have no separate fuel and oxidizer, as in double-base propellants like nitroglycerin and nitrocellulose. This type of propellant is somewhat like smokeless gun powder; that is, the unstable molecules break apart upon ignition and then rearrange themselves, releasing great quantities of heat energy in the process. The most commonly used propellants for solid-fuel rocket motors, however, are **composites** in which separate fuel and oxidizer chemicals are mixed and cast together to form the grain. [Figure 12-26]

Figure 12-26. The technique of casting propellants for large solid-fuel engines was one of the breakthroughs of modern rocket propulsion technology. It has resulted in large solid rocket boosters such as the ones used with the space shuttle.

In general, solid-propellant rockets are considered less complex than liquid-fueled rockets. At present, the burning rate of a solid mass, as in a solid-fuel rocket, cannot be controlled or throttled. However, it is possible to control combustion in a liquid-propellant rocket by regulating the fuel and oxidizer flow rates to the combustion chamber. On the other hand, a solid-fuel rocket simplifies propellant storage and eliminates the need for a complicated series of tanks, valves, and pumps to mix the propellants.

The burn rate of a solid-propellant rocket engine cannot be controlled like a liquid-propellant engine.

The performance available from rockets using solid or liquid chemicals as fuels is clearly limited. In order to obtain vehicles with performance great enough to carry out long-term and extreme-distance space missions, new propulsion systems with performance capabilities superior to those of the chemical rocket must be developed. With a look toward the exploration of the solar system, research is being conducted on a number of different propulsion systems.

NUCLEAR ROCKETS

A nuclear rocket is a powerplant which uses the enormous heat of **nuclear fission** in a reactor to heat a "working fluid" which might be hydrogen, helium, or ammonia in liquid form. This heated fluid changes to a gas, and the resulting rapidly expanding gases are channeled through a nozzle in conventional rocket fashion.

The latest idea for a nuclear rocket is to use **nuclear fusion**. A tremendous amount of energy is released by bringing atoms together to form new elements. [Figure 12-27]

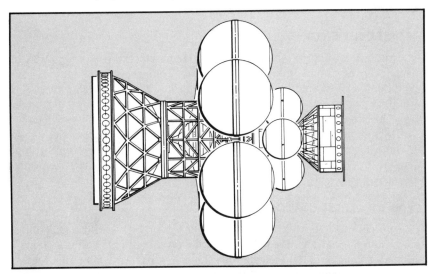

Figure 12-27. The British Interplanetary Society's Project Daedalus outlines a proposal to explore a nearby star with a robot spacecraft assembled in space and powered by a nuclear fusion reactor. Nuclear fusion powerplants will be safer and more efficient than nuclear fission reactors.

ELECTRIC PROPULSION

The first practical use of electric propulsion is in satellite station-keeping and attitude control. **Station-keeping** involves making slight changes in order to maintain a satellite's orbit. **Attitude control** refers to the turning, pitching, or rolling of the satellite to a desired orientation. Eventually, the electric rockets may be used for station-keeping and attitude control of large manned space stations and for midcourse maneuvers of unmanned interplanetary spacecraft. Studies are being conducted on the following kinds of electric propulsion engines.

ION ENGINES

The ion rocket engine produces thrust by electrically accelerating charged particles. One of the propellants used for ion engines is the rare metallic element called cesium, which readily ionizes when heated; that is, each atom of cesium gives up an electron. Removal of the electron which bears a negative electrical charge causes the remaining cesium atom (called an ion) to be positively charged. [Figure 12-28]

ARC JET ENGINES

The arc jet engine is similar to a chemical rocket except that it uses fuel and electrically created heat instead of fuel and an oxidizer. As an example, a propellant gas, such as liquid hydrogen, is passed through a high temperature electric arc where it is electrically heated to several thousand degrees Fahrenheit and expelled through the rocket nozzle. The exhaust velocity and thrust theoretically obtainable are far in excess of any known chemical or nuclear fission system.

RESISTOJET ENGINE

Like the arc jet engine, the resistojet system accelerates a propellant by electrically heating it to high temperatures. In the resistojet engine, however, heat is generated by passing an electric current through a tube with a high resistance to the current's passage. A phenomenon called **resistance heating** results. This is the principle on which electric toasters, waffle makers, irons, and other electrical heating appliances operate. As in the arc jet engine, a propellant gas is heated to an extremely high temperature, and as it expands through the exhaust nozzle, it generates thrust.

PLASMA ACCELERATOR

The plasma accelerator uses electric heat on a propellant gas whose atoms can be easily ionized. As a result, a stream of ions called plasma is created. A magnetic field accelerates the gas particles to very high velocities before ejecting them from the rocket nozzle.

Although the thrust of a plasma engine would be very low because the mass of the propellant is small, the thrust could be maintained over an

Figure 12-28. Ion rockets produce very little thrust. However, because the rate of fuel consumption is extremely low, they can sustain this thrust over long periods of time. Note the glow of ionized atoms as they rush from the engine.

Figure 12-29. Plasma-powered thrusters are presently used on satellites such as the one shown here. In order to keep the satellite in its proper position in orbit, each thruster will fire nearly two million times in a six-month period.

extended period of time, thereby obtaining extremely high velocities in a space environment. Because the velocity of the ionized particles ejected in the exhaust stream is extremely high, the plasma accelerator-type engine, used over an extended period of time, could attain the velocities required for deep space exploration. [Figure 12-29]

SOLAR ELECTRIC ENGINE

The solar electric propulsion unit combines an electric engine, such as an ion engine, with a system for converting sunlight. [Figure 12-30]

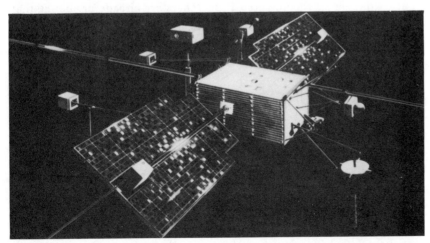

Figure 12-30. Solar panels made up of individual cells convert sunlight into electricity.

An advantage of the solar electric engine is that it can operate during an unmanned flight. For example, on a trip from Earth to Mars, controllers on Earth could match the speed of the spacecraft with that required for the mission. As a result, the spacecraft's velocity as it nears Mars would be lower than that of a chemically propelled rocket. Consequently, less **retropropulsion** (slowing down or braking power) would be required to place the spacecraft into an orbit around Mars or for a soft landing on the planet.

With chemical propulsion, a few rather large but short duration firings set a spacecraft on course. The velocity of a chemically propelled spacecraft as it approaches its planetary destination would tend to be much higher than that of an electrically propelled craft whose in-flight velocity could be adjusted frequently.

PHOTON ROCKET

Finally, one of the more advanced proposals for a rocket engine is the photon rocket, where **photons**, or light particles, would provide the thrust. Since this engine would approach the speed of light, it is thought to be the ultimate in rocket engines. In principle, however, it is not greatly different from the type of rocket propulsion used by the Chinese hundreds of years ago.

As one peers into the future, the world of rocket propulsion is broad and "open ended." Indeed, rocket propulsion will someday allow us to span not only the distances within our own solar system, but also to take giant strides across the universe. Researchers are already predicting that high energy density matter (HEDM) chemicals have the potential for dramatically increasing thrust when used to enrich existing rocket propellants.

ROCKET ENGINE PERFORMANCE

There are a number of measures of rocket engine performance. These factors are helpful in understanding the present chemically fueled rockets, the electric rockets, and the rockets envisioned for future interstellar flights.

The rate at which propellants burn and the velocity of the exhausted gases determine the amount of thrust.

Thrust is the reaction force exerted on the vehicle by the rocket exhaust. Two major factors determine the amount of thrust: the rate at which the propellant is burned, and the velocity at which the resulting gases are exhausted.

Thrust is measured in pounds. The thrust of a rocket vehicle launched vertically from the ground must be greater than the total loaded weight of the vehicle. This is because the rocket's engine must overcome the inertia of the entire launch vehicle. At liftoff, the total thrust of the engine is only slightly more than the total weight of the rocket. As fuel is consumed, however, the inertial resistance to acceleration lessens because there is less mass. Since the thrust remains constant, the rocket accelerates faster and faster until the propellant is used up.

For a rocket to lift off from the Earth's surface, thrust must be greater than the weight of the vehicle.

If large masses are to be lifted from the ground into an orbit about the Earth or sent further into space, correspondingly larger thrust ratings are required. However, when a specific job permits a small payload, a low thrust rating will suffice to accomplish the mission.

The comparison of the engine thrust with the vehicle's total weight is referred to as the **thrust-to-weight** ratio. It is particularly significant because thrust alone is not indicative of the vehicle's potential for velocity or range. Ten million pounds of rocket thrust will not lift a 10,000,000-pound vehicle from the ground. Yet, if the vehicle that weighs ten million pounds on the ground is already in orbit or is weightless, even a few pounds of thrust applied for an extended period can eventually accelerate it to tremendous velocities.

The Saturn V-Apollo combination can be used as an example of thrust-to-weight ratio. The entire assembly weighed about 6,000,000 pounds when ready for launch. The first-stage thrust was 7,500,000 pounds; thus, the thrust-to-weight ratio at launch was 7.5:6, or 5:4. This ratio changed as the vehicle gained altitude because thrust increased as atmospheric pressure dropped, and weight decreased as propellants were consumed and as the gravitational pull of the earth diminished.

The amount of thrust derived from each pound of propellant during one second of engine operation is its **specific impulse**. For example, a specific impulse of 200 seconds means the rocket engine produces 200 pounds of thrust for each pound of propellant burned in one second. To the rocket engineer, specific impulse means much the same as miles-per-gallon does to a motorist; it is a measure of the efficiency of the rocket propellants as they are being used to generate thrust.

Specific impulse is a measure of rocket engine efficiency.

It is important to remember that the greater the specific impulse number the more thrust is derived from each pound of propellant. This permits a reduction in the amount or weight of the propellant required for a given mission. A greater specific impulse enables a rocket to lift heavier payloads and send them farther into space. [Figure 12-31]

Eventually, nuclear rockets with a specific impulse of 800-1,000 seconds may become available. Beyond this, the ion rockets theoretically will have specific impulses of 10,000-15,000 seconds. These figures are clear evidence why rocket engineers look toward these more exotic rocket engines for propulsion of future spacecraft.

The speed at which the exhaust gases are expelled from the nozzle is called the **exhaust velocity**. This exit speed depends on the propellant's burning characteristics and the overall engine efficiency.

A rocket engine's mass ratio, exhaust velocity, and specific impulse are important factors in determining the velocity and range of a spacecraft.

The relationship between a rocket vehicle's total mass at takeoff and its total mass remaining after the propellants are consumed is its **mass ratio**. Excluding the effects of gravity and air resistance, a rocket vehicle with a mass ratio of 2.72:1 will achieve a speed equal to its exhaust velocity. A 7.4:1 mass ratio will produce speeds twice the exhaust velocity. The higher the ratio, the higher the velocity after the propellant is consumed. Since a higher mass ratio improves a rocket vehicle's total performance, any mass in the rocket assembly that can be eliminated after it is no longer needed should improve performance still further. This is the idea behind the **multistage** rocket.

In such a vehicle, a series of rockets is mounted on top of the other. The first rocket fires and carries the vehicle up to the maximum velocity of the first stage. At the end of the first-stage burn, it is jettisoned, thereby reducing the overall mass of the vehicle, and the second-stage rocket is ignited. When the second stage has finished its burn, it likewise is jettisoned and the third-stage rocket is ignited. This is continued for as many stages as are used in the combination. [Figure 12-32]

Using the principle of staging, the overall mass ratio of the combined system is improved far beyond that obtainable in single-stage vehicles. Roughly, the mass ratio for the combination is equal to the product of the mass ratios of the individual stages.

It should be obvious from the foregoing discussion that the design of a vehicle for space exploration is an extraordinarily complex task. The designer must take into consideration the weight, volume, and energy potential of the propellant; the weight, shape, and volume of the vehicle's structure; the weight and volume of the payload; and the weight and thrust of the engine or engines. Other factors include the effects of atmospheric resistance and gravity, both of which are constantly changing. It is only through the use of computers and the systems approach to engineering that all of these complex factors can be evaluated.

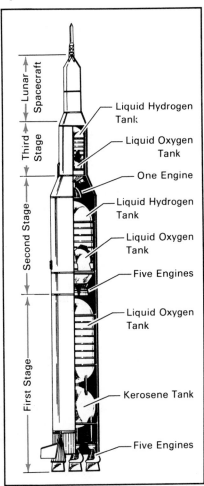

Figure 12-31. The Atlas-Centaur upper stages used liquid oxygen and liquid hydrogen for a specific impulse of 400 seconds.

Figure 12-32. The Saturn V used three stages which were dropped off in succession as their propellants were used up.

AIRFRAMES

The airframe of a space vehicle must be designed so it can contain or provide an attachment point for the engine, accessories, fuel, guidance system, and payload. The design also varies according to whether the vehicle is an aerodynamic spacecraft such as the space shuttle or a ballistic (free-falling) spacecraft such as the Mercury, Gemini, or Apollo command modules.

The aerodynamic spacecraft possesses some form of wing and tail assembly which can be used to control the vehicle in the Earth's atmosphere. In space, its directional control can be by auxiliary jets, or with a gimbaled engine (one that can change its direction of thrust). The ballistic spacecraft, on the other hand, has no wings and must use auxiliary jets or a gimbaled engine at all times.

The airframe of the aerodynamic and ballistic spacecraft must be structurally sound and able to withstand enormous amounts of heat and stress. The leading edges of some aerodynamic spacecraft are made of titanium, which has a very high melting point and retains its strength under extreme aerodynamic heating. The ballistic spacecraft may also be made of titanium with additional protection afforded by a heat shield, usually on the blunt end of the vehicle. In addition, other protective devices made from different materials might be used such as the coated silica tiles which are installed on the space shuttle. [Figure 12-33]

The spacecraft's airframe must be manufactured with great care and precision. Numerous techniques are used, such as welding, machining, forging, spinning, and extruding. The design and construction of airframes for spacecraft has created new techniques. Precision in every manufacturing technique from the blueprint to the launch pad is required in the construction of space vehicles.

Figure 12-33. A technician applies one of some 31,000 individual tiles to the Space Shuttle Orbiter Columbia. The tiles make up the thermal protection system that absorbs the intense heat of reentry following an orbital mission.

REENTRY

Reentry of a spacecraft into the earth's atmosphere probably imposes the most severe stress on the vehicle, both in terms of frictional heating and G-forces. Early intercontinental ballistic missiles made use of what is termed a **heat sink**. With this method, a large slab of metal was molded into a blunt nosecone shape. Upon reentry, the frictional heat was largely absorbed by the mass of the metal. The heat sink imposed a large weight penalty and, therefore, it was unsatisfactory for manned spacecraft.

The greatest stress on a spacecraft is during the reentry phase.

In the Mercury, Gemini, and Apollo spacecraft the blunt end had a heat shield made up with a thick layer of fiberglass coated with modified phenolic resins. This type of heat shield made use of a principle called **ablation**. In ablative cooling, the surface of the heat shield actually melted and streamed away, or it vaporized and carried a great amount of heat with it. These shields were very effective for that generation of spacecraft.

TYPES OF GUIDANCE

The types of guidance systems used to control missiles and spacecraft fall into several major categories. They are:

1. Homing
2. Command
3. Inertial
4. Celestial

With the exception of the homing system, each of the guidance systems must have the ability to measure the vehicle's velocity and position, compute the flight path corrections, and deliver corrective commands to the vehicle's control system so the required changes can be made.

HOMING GUIDANCE

Homing guidance systems have broad application in military operations. They are used on short-range missiles, and they require some type of detectable energy coming from the target. A common example is the heat-seeking missile which picks up infrared radiation that is emitted by any heat-generating object. Onboard sensors detect the direction the radiation is coming from and compare it with the missile's direction of movement. The guidance system then sends course corrections to the control system which result in target interception.

COMMAND GUIDANCE

With a command guidance system, such as the one installed in the Apollo spacecraft, the vehicle was controlled through its entire flight envelope by either manual or automatic controls. Data from ground stations or from the vehicle's sensors was constantly sent to on-board or ground-based computers. The computers swiftly compared the actual flight profile with the intended flight profile and commanded the necessary corrective action.

INERTIAL GUIDANCE

Fundamentally, an inertial guidance system is made up of three accelerometers (one in each plane of rotation) and an electronic computer. An accelerometer is a small mechanical device which senses any acceleration of the vehicle. Each accelerometer senses acceleration in a single direction and feeds this information into a computer, although the "weightlessness" encountered in space makes the accelerometer ineffective. Therefore, it can operate only during the powered flight phase. The forward, backward, and sideways motion of the vehicle is fed into the computer, analyzed, and appropriate corrections to the flight path are made through the vehicle's autopilot.

CELESTIAL GUIDANCE

Celestial guidance is performed by an automatic sextant which locks onto light radiation emanating from preselected natural celestial bodies (sun, stars, planets, moons). The automatic sextant then measures the angle between the actual path of the space vehicle and the path to a celestial reference; for example, a star. Information is fed into a computer where it is compared with the desired flight path. If any error exists, appropriate corrective signals are sent to the vehicle's control system.

If this type of guidance is used by itself, it is termed automatic celestial navigation (ACN). Celestial navigation usually is combined with some other type of guidance system such as the inertial guidance discussed previously.

A variation of celestial guidance is found in a system that senses the infrared radiation (heat) given off by a celestial body. The heat is picked up by a photoelectric device which changes it into tiny electrical currents. These currents, in turn, are fed into the computer and become a source of guidance information.

COMMUNICATIONS

As rocket propulsion and guidance technology has rapidly advanced, the science of communications has kept pace. To justify the rather large expense involved in a probe, a satellite, or a manned space flight, as much information as possible must be gained during the flight. To this end, the technology of **telemetry** has shown a rapid evolution. Telemetry means taking measurements at a remote location (probe, satellite, or spacecraft), and transmitting these measurements for dissemination at another location. The information obtained may be in a form suitable for display, recording, or use in computers.

In unmanned space exploration, telemetry has helped perfect the design of vehicles by monitoring their performance during flight. In manned flight, telemetered signals supplement the messages sent by the astronaut and permit the use of complex computing equipment on the ground which otherwise would be much too large to carry in the space vehicles. [Figure 12-34]

The power required to send telemetered signals from satellites and space probes is infinitely smaller than that required for commercial radio and television stations. For example, data was received from the Voyager 2 spacecraft as it passed by the planet Uranus some 1,700,000,000 miles away. One reason such ranges can be achieved with so little power is that the ground radio system used to communicate with the spacecraft has extremely sensitive receivers. [Figure 12-35]

Radio telescope studies have shown that, with sufficiently powerful transmitters and sensitive receivers, communications over interstellar (between stars) distances is possible. There are limiting factors, however. One is that, beyond the solar system, so many stars and other celestial bodies emit radio waves that they pose a threat to clear communications with a spacecraft.

Another limiting factor is distance itself. Radio waves travel at about the speed of light, or approximately 186,000 miles per second. It takes only

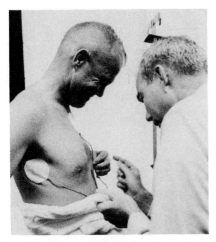

Figure 12-34. Biological sensors were taped to astronaut John Glenn's chest prior to the first U.S. Earth orbiting mission.

Figure 12-35. Large diameter antennas, such as this tracking and communications antenna near Goldstone, California, are about 50,000 times more sensitive than the average television antenna.

five minutes for a message sent from Earth to reach Venus when Venus is closest to Earth. However, a message from Earth to a spacecraft in the vicinity of Pluto would take more than five hours to reach its destination.

Present-day communications technology has permitted ground stations to communicate with, acquire data from, and track spacecraft with a high degree of accuracy. The crisp, clear communications and precise tracking exhibited during the Apollo lunar exploration missions was clear evidence of this advanced technology.

CHECKLIST

After studying this section, you should have a basic understanding of:

✓ **Principles of rocket propulsion** — How Newton's Three Laws of Motion relate to rocket movement and how energy conversion creates thrust.

✓ **Classification of rocket powerplants** — The different types of chemically fueled engines; and how nuclear, electrical, and photon engines produce thrust.

✓ **Rocket performance** — How thrust in a rocket engine is measured, and how thrust-to-weight ratio, specific impulse, exhaust velocity, and mass ratio affect performance.

✓ **Airframes** — What the difference is between aerodynamic and ballistic spacecraft and how a spacecraft can withstand the heat generated during reentry.

✓ **Guidance** — What the difference is between present, command, inertial, and celestial guidance and which ones can be used in space.

✓ **Communications** — What the meaning of telemetry is, how data is received from space probes, and some of the limitations of deep-space communications.

ORBITAL MECHANICS

Any man-made vehicle launched into space will move in accordance with the same laws that govern the motions of the planets about the sun and the motion of the moon about the Earth. As you study the following discussion on orbital mechanics, two terms will be helpful to you. An **orbit** can be defined as a closed or open path followed by a celestial body or a spacecraft. A **trajectory** is the path followed by a projectile such as an artillery shell, missile, or rocket after its propulsion is terminated.

NATURAL LAWS OF ORBIT

Prior to the time of Copernicus (the early 1500's), people generally accepted the belief that the Earth was the center of the solar system. However, efforts to explain the motions of planets on this assumption raised impossible contradictions. Copernicus pointed out that the difficulties in explaining the planetary movements disappeared if one assumed that the sun was the center of the solar system and that the planets revolved about it.

Copernicus, Galileo, and Kepler formulated and built upon the idea that the sun — not the Earth — was the center of the solar system.

Years later, Galileo took up the defense of Copernicus' theory with such experiments as the dropping of two different sized objects from the Leaning Tower of Pisa. Eventually, new ideas and experiments led to our current understanding of the laws of motion.

In the early seventeenth century, Johannes Kepler formulated three laws which describe the motions of the planets about the sun. They are:

1. Each planet revolves about the sun in an ellipse, which is an egg-shaped, closed orbit.

2. The **radius vector**, such as the line from the center of the sun to the center of a planet, sweeps out equal areas in equal periods of time. This means that a planet travels faster as it nears the sun and slower the farther away it is.

3. The square of a planet's period of revolution is proportional to the cube of its mean distance from the sun. In other words, the greater an

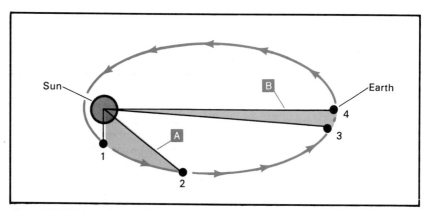

Figure 12-36. In a given period of time, the radius vector of Earth will sweep out the same area from the sun. (Area A is equal to Area B.) This means that Earth must travel faster between points 1 and 2 than it does between points 3 and 4.

object's mean orbital altitude, the longer it takes to go around the sun. For example, the Earth takes approximately 365 days to make one revolution around the sun. Pluto, on the other hand, takes approximately 248 years to make the same revolution. These laws apply not only to the sun and its family of planets, but also to satellites orbiting the Earth. [Figure 12-36]

Another law which governs orbits is Newton's Law of Gravity which may be described as follows: All bodies, from the largest star in the universe to the smallest particle of matter, attract each other with what is called **gravitational pull**. The strength of their gravitational pull is dependent upon two factors. First, the closer two bodies are to each other, the greater their mutual attraction. Secondly, the strength of their gravitational attraction is dependent upon their **masses** (a measure of how much material they contain).

The Earth and all other bodies in space have a gravitational pull. They pull anything within their sphere of influence toward them at an increasing velocity. This acceleration of gravity is used as a basic measurement. At the Earth's surface, it is known as one gravity, or one "G." The Earth's gravitational influence is believed to extend throughout the universe, although the force weakens with great distances until it becomes infinitely small and almost impossible to measure.

All bodies in space attract and are attracted by all other space bodies.

Any vehicle moving in space is subject to gravity. The vehicle has mass and is, itself, a space body. Therefore, it attracts and is attracted by all other space bodies. A vehicle moving between Earth and the moon would influence and be influenced by both bodies. Basic laws of motion take these concepts into consideration and explain how satellites can orbit the Earth and how it is possible for a vehicle to escape the Earth's gravitational attraction and travel to distant planets, or beyond.

TYPES OF ORBITS

An orbit actually describes the path of a body or spacecraft under the influence of gravity or some other force. There are two types of closed orbits — circular and elliptic — and two types of open orbits — parabolic and hyperbolic. [Figure 12-37]

A circular orbit is difficult to achieve because of the very precise aiming and velocities required. Most satellites and spacecraft follow elliptical orbits. These satellites and spacecraft, therefore, are constantly changing speeds. Such a body reaches maximum velocity at **perigee** — the low

The lowest point of an elliptical orbit around Earth is called the perigee. The apogee is the highest point.

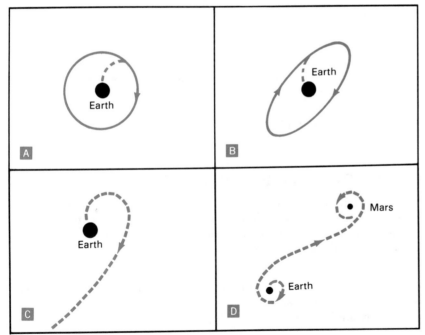

Figure 12-37. A body is in a circular orbit (A) when it is traveling around the Earth at a constant velocity and following a path which always maintains the same radius from the Earth's center of mass. A body is in an elliptical orbit (B) when it is traveling a path which resembles a closed loop. An elliptical orbit changes to a parabolic orbit (C) whenever a vehicle possesses the energy to break away from the gravitational field of a planet. A flight path is hyperbolic (D) whenever a space vehicle leaves the gravitational field of one planet and is transferred into the field of another planet.

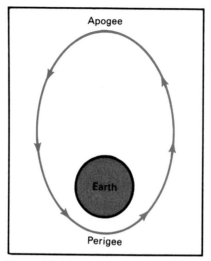

Figure 12-38. When an orbiting object reaches perigee, its centrifugal force is greater than the gravitational pull of Earth. Therefore, its momentum carries it upward or outward where excess speed is converted to distance. At its maximum distance (apogee), gravitational pull overcomes centrifugal force and the object "falls back" toward Earth.

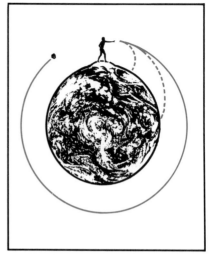

Figure 12-39. If a person throws a rock parallel to the Earth's surface, gravity will cause it to fall only a few feet away from the thrower. If the rock is thrown again at a velocity of several hundred miles per hour, it will go farther. When it is thrown a third time at several thousand miles per hour, its path will curve toward the surface at nearly the same rate as the Earth curves away.

point in its orbit, and minimum velocity at **apogee** — the highest point. [Figure 12-38]

HOW A SATELLITE IS ORBITED

Newton's First Law of Motion states that a body remains at rest or in a state of motion in a straight line unless acted upon by an external force. The external force which changes the straight path of a satellite to a curved path is the Earth's gravity.

Launching a satellite into orbit may be likened to a "super rock thrower" who can throw rocks at any velocity. The rocks, in this case, are not affected by air friction. [Figure 12-39]

For a satellite relatively close to the Earth (within 200 miles), the velocity required to achieve orbit is approximately 17,500 miles per hour. A vehicle placed in orbit around the moon (roughly 240,000 miles) needs an orbital velocity of only 2,000 miles per hour, but this does not mean that the attainment of the far-out orbit is easier. A considerable additional force still must be used to send a satellite out to that distance.

SUSTAINING ORBIT

In review, satellites are subject to the same physical laws which govern the motions of all bodies in space. These include Newton's Laws of Motion and Gravity, and Kepler's Laws of Planetary Motion. Newton's Second Law of Motion is useful in explaining how a satellite stays in orbit. A part of this law states that "a force acting upon a body causes it to accelerate in the direction of the force." This means that the force of Earth's gravity causes a satellite to fall toward Earth. What occurs in the case of a satellite is that gravity, to a degree, overcomes the kinetic energy (energy of motion) that tends to move the satellite in a straight line, and it veers toward the Earth. The satellite's kinetic energy, however, is pushing it forward every second that gravity is drawing it inward. The satellite has sufficient kinetic energy so that its downward curving path continually misses or overshoots the Earth. As a result, it traces an elliptical or circular orbit around Earth.

The number of degrees the orbit is inclined away from the equator is its **inclination**. This also indicates how far north and south a spacecraft or satellite travels in its orbit around Earth. An equatorial orbit has a zero inclination. [Figure 12-40]

Several satellites have been launched and maneuvered so they appear to stand still over one location on Earth. Among these are the Galaxy and Satcom communication satellites. [Figure 12-41]

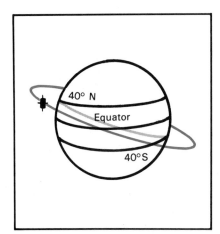

Figure 12-40. If a satellite is placed in an orbit with an inclination of 40° to the equator, it travels as far north as 40° north latitude and as far south as 40° south latitude. Because the Earth is rotating, it does not pass over the same areas of the Earth during each orbit.

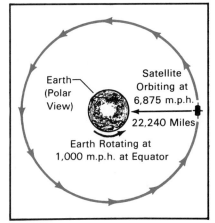

Figure 12-41. A geostationary satellite seems to remain over one spot on the Earth's surface.

Actually, these satellites are not stationary, but are moving at a speed of about 6,875 miles per hour. The Earth's equator, more than 22,000 miles below them, is moving at approximately 1,000 m.p.h. The relationships of the satellites to points on the Earth's surface may be likened to those of racers on a circular track. The competitor in the outside lane has to run faster to stay even with the one on the inside lane.

Satellites can remain stationary over a point on Earth because of the physical laws governing the motions of objects in space. Kepler's Third Law, which was discussed earlier, explains that a satellite's period of revolution (time to go around a planet) increases with its mean orbital altitude.

It follows logically that, at some altitude, a satellite's period of revolution is the same as Earth's period of rotation. This altitude is about 22,240 miles. A satellite orbiting at this altitude is termed a **synchronous** (same time) satellite.

To be geostationary, however, a satellite must have not only a synchronous orbit, but also a circular orbit lying in the plane of the equator. Kepler's Second Law says that a satellite in an elliptical orbit is always changing speeds, reaching maximum velocity at perigee and minimum velocity at apogee. Because of its speed variations, a synchronous satellite in an elliptical orbit would appear to oscillate east and west relative to an observation point on Earth.

An application of Kepler's Third Law involves rendezvous maneuvers in orbit. For example, when the space shuttle is trying to catch up with an unmanned satellite which is in the same orbit, it first slows down. The deceleration causes the shuttle to descend to a lower orbit where its speed increases. When it achieves proper position, the shuttle accelerates to raise its orbit and achieve rendezvous. This is all precisely controlled by the shuttle's on board computer system which is programmed with equations derived from the laws of Kepler, Newton, and others.

ESCAPE VELOCITY

A space vehicle must achieve escape velocity to achieve a parabolic orbit.

A spacecraft sent to the moon or to another planet must achieve what is termed **escape velocity**, which is the initial velocity required to escape the Earth's gravitational pull. For example, assume the rock thrower is able to cast the rock at approximately 25,000 miles per hour. In this case, the rock follows a parabolic path because it has enough momentum to leave the gravitational pull of Earth. As it races into space, it is slowed down because of gravity, but it continues outward until it becomes primarily influenced by the sun's gravity and never returns to Earth. Each planet or moon has a different escape velocity depending on the strength of its gravitational field. For example, when the astronauts returned from the moon, they had to reach an escape velocity of about 5,000 miles per hour.

Launching a spacecraft into an escape trajectory is somewhat analogous to rolling a ball up a smooth, frictionless hill whose slope is continuously decreasing. The diminishing slope of the hill may be compared to the decreasing force of gravity. If the ball is not rolled fast enough, it will gradually slow until its momentum is exhausted. At this point, it will momentarily pause before rolling back down the hill, arriving at the bottom with the same velocity with which it left. This part of the analogy is similar to an elliptical orbit. If the ball is rolled with sufficient force, however, it will slow as it rolls up the hill, but it will continue on over the top and never return to the starting point. This corresponds to the achievement of escape velocity.

GRAVITATIONAL ATTRACTION

During the Apollo Lunar Landing Missions, the spacecraft achieved escape velocity from Earth and then began a gradual slowdown as it hurtled toward a so-called gravitational "twilight zone" where the gravitational pull of Earth and that of the moon are about equal. Then, increasingly in the grip of the moon's gravity, the Apollo spacecraft accelerated from about 2,000 to 5,700 miles per hour as it began its sweep toward the backside of the moon. This gravitational "twilight zone" is closest to the moon because the mass of the moon is much smaller than Earth's mass.

On the return mission, the spacecraft again passed through the zone of equal gravitational attraction and then accelerated increasingly toward the narrow reentry corridor which is a forty-mile-wide "keyhole" in the Earth's atmosphere. The example from the Apollo missions illustrates some of the considerations that must be made for gravitational forces when journeys are planned between Earth and other planets. [Figure 12-42]

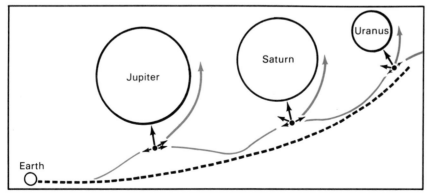

Figure 12-42. The parabolic flight path of a spacecraft is shown by the dashed line. The course the spacecraft would follow, if it were not corrected by bursts of power, is indicated by the large arrows. The smaller arrows depict the direction and relative magnitude of the gravitational forces exerted on the vehicle. The solid line represents the actual corrected course.

By using the gravitational pull of planets, scientists are able to accelerate a spacecraft like the Voyager 2 Space Probe. Then, by using the "sling-shot effect" which requires the application of breakaway power at just the right moment, they are able to send it hurtling toward its encounter with the next planet or into deep space.

CHECKLIST

After studying this section, you should have a basic understanding of:

✓ **Laws of orbital mechanics** — How the contributions of Copernicus, Galileo, Kepler, and Newton led to our current understanding of the laws governing orbital mechanics.

✓ **Types of orbit** — What the four types of orbits are, what each one means to an orbiting space vehicle, and how each is achieved.

✓ **Launching a satellite** — What speeds are needed to place a satellite into orbit and how the orbit is sustained.

✓ **Geostationary orbit** — How a synchronous orbit in the same plane as the equator makes a satellite appear to remain stationary.

✓ **Gravitational attraction** — How it affects bodies in space and how it is used for interplanetary or interstellar flights.

✓ **Escape velocity** — What it is for the Earth and why it is different for each planet or moon.

CHAPTER 13

CAREERS IN AVIATION AND AEROSPACE

INTRODUCTION

Aviation and aerospace are exciting and dynamic industries that employ a large part of the nation's work force. Efforts to improve air transportation and conquer space rely on the newest technologies and present a challenge to all who are involved. Although you are probably more familiar with the role of the pilot, you should keep in mind that most of the jobs in aviation and aerospace are ground-based activities that support flight operations, either directly or indirectly. The first section of this chapter briefly introduces some of the jobs available to pilots and other flight crewmembers. The next section looks at ground-based careers, and the last section contains some suggestions you can follow to prepare for an aviation/aerospace career.

FLIGHT CREW

Flight crewmembers include pilots, copilots (or first officers), and a variety of others who are essential to a particular flight. For example, flight engineers (or second officers) are required on some airplanes, and flight attendants are necessary for certain types of commercial operations.

PILOT CAREERS

In the early days of aviation, one of the main requirements for a pilot was the willingness to take risks. In fact, many of them were exploring the unknown. They were predecessors of modern-day test pilots. Most of today's pilots, however, are not required to perform test flights on a regular basis. Instead, they are concerned with reducing risks. Professional pilots very often have years of experience, as well as specialized training that emphasizes safe, efficient practices.

A pilot's duties include determining weather and flight conditions, making and filing flight plans, checking the airworthiness of the aircraft, and preparing it for flight. The pilot is then responsible for safely operating the aircraft; using its complex electronic, mechanical, and communications systems; and in the case of the captain, managing the crew.

If you decide to become a pilot, you may become involved in one of four general areas: general aviation, airline, military, and aerospace. Let's take a closer look at each of these.

GENERAL AVIATION PILOTS

General aviation is a broad category of flight operations that includes almost all civil flying except airline-type operations. The most common examples of general aviation activities are commercial, instructional, corporate, and private flying.

COMMERCIAL PILOTS

Commercial flying includes a wide variety of tasks that provide many different types of opportunities. Besides transporting passengers and cargo, commercial pilots may work in research, environmental, or service programs. Helicopter pilots are increasingly involved in fields such as construction, powerline and pipeline patrol, fire fighting and police work, news reporting, air ambulance, and agriculture. These are only some of the specialized types of flying in general aviation. [Figure 13-1]

1. Air taxi or charter operations may fly passengers or cargo on either a scheduled or on-call basis. Many air taxi companies have expanded their operations as larger air carriers have discontinued the less traveled routes.

2. Powerline and pipeline patrol consists of checking powerlines, towers, and pipelines for damage, and sometimes flying in repair crews.

3. Aircraft sales include demonstrating and selling aircraft, as well as transporting aircraft from factory to dealer or from dealer to customer.

4. Land survey and photography provide businesses and government agencies with information about commercial property, highway rights-of-way, and mining and drilling sites.

5. Sightseeing services fly tourists over scenic areas which may be hard to reach by other means. They also provide a different view of metropolitan areas and natural wonders.

Figure 13-1. Paramedics prepare to airlift a patient for emergency treatment.

6. Ambulance services are used by many hospitals. Helicopter pilots with trained paramedics lift critically ill or injured persons over ground traffic and get them to hospitals in a fraction of the time an ambulance would take. Specially equipped airplanes fly patients to other hospitals where more advanced treatment is available.

7. Construction site operations ferry workers, machines, and materials. When valuable machinery breaks down, it is more efficient to airlift parts and mechanics than to use ground transportation.

8. Agriculture and environmental services include spraying and crop dusting, seeding, herding livestock, fire fighting, and wildlife surveying.

9. Test flying involves checking aircraft and systems at various stages of design and production to make sure they meet safety and performance specifications.

10. Specialized agencies fly food, supplies, and medical workers to areas hit by disasters. When roads are destroyed by floods or earthquakes, victims often cannot be reached by any other means.

11. Law enforcement agencies use aircraft for traffic surveys, search and rescue missions, and border and coastline patrol.

12. News agencies often use helicopters to report on traffic congestion or special events, and to fly reporters to sites of accidents or crimes.

FLIGHT INSTRUCTORS

Another important area of commercial flying involves instruction and training. Many commercial pilots begin their careers as flight instructors. This requires training that goes beyond the commercial certificate. Flight instructor privileges depend on the particular aircraft category and class ratings that an applicant obtains. Some prefer to concentrate on primary training for beginning students, while others specialize in advanced training necessary for instrument, commercial, multiengine, and airline transport pilots. [Figure 13-2]

After acquiring considerable experience, it is quite common for instructors to move into air taxi, corporate, or airline flying. Others may work for professional flight schools or other training organizations that offer specialized or type-specific instruction in multiengine turboprops and jets. These schools usually provide comprehensive ground training and may also include flight simulator training.

Ground instruction is another career area that has its own certificate and ratings. It offers a wide variety of opportunities throughout the training industry. Flight and ground schools require chief instructors and assistants. Many also have designated examiners on staff who test students to see if they are ready to become certificated pilots.

Figure 13-2. Many flight instructors begin their careers by training student pilots in light airplanes.

CORPORATE PILOTS

Corporate pilots fly the aircraft owned by a particular business or industrial firm. They often have additional responsibilities such as supervision of aircraft maintenance. These pilots transport company executives and clients to meetings; carry products, materials, and machinery; and inspect company property or construction projects. They need to know as much as possible about the maintenance of their aircraft, since they sometimes fly into remote areas with few service facilities. In fact, pilots who also are certified maintenance technicians are typically in high demand. Large corporations often have fleets of aircraft and employ several pilots and maintenance technicians, as well as other flight crewmembers.

Many pilots work for small companies where they may have primary responsibilities in nonaviation areas such as advertising, research, or sales management and secondary duties as pilots. Others are employed by salespeople, lecturers, musicians, free-lance writers and photographers, and people in similar jobs who have unique transportation requirements. Corporate flying offers a wide range of opportunity and many pilot positions compete favorably with airline or military flying careers.

PRIVATE PILOTS

Thus far, we have discussed flying as an occupation; however, the largest segment of pilots consists of those who have taken up flying for recreation or personal business. An airplane allows you to take a vacation wherever there is a small airport, avoid crowds, and be independent of public transportation. Many people enjoy flying as a hobby because they appreciate the beauty of the world from the air; others find that flying relaxes them and takes their minds off everyday problems. Business people who make frequent trips often find they save considerable time and energy by flying themselves.

AIRLINE PILOTS

Flying for an established airline has traditionally been one of the most popular jobs in civil aviation. These pilots usually have good working conditions, the possibility of good pay and fringe benefits, and the use of some of the most sophisticated aircraft available. Because of the competition for jobs, airlines are able to choose the most experienced pilots with the highest skill levels. Most airlines prefer college graduates with considerable flying experience.

Usually, the cockpit crew consists of the captain, the first officer, and in some aircraft types, a flight engineer or second officer. The flight engineer is primarily responsible for monitoring the operation of the aircraft's systems. In the past, this person often was not a rated pilot. Today, however, the airlines prefer flight engineers who are pilots. After a period of training and experience, the engineer may advance to first officer and, eventually, to captain.

Although airline pilots normally fly preplanned routes, they coordinate each trip with the flight dispatcher. They also check such items as the aircraft weight and fuel supply, as well as enroute, destination, and alternate airport weather. Before takeoff, the captain is responsible for ensuring the aircraft is airworthy, briefing the flight crew and attendants, and completing all pretakeoff checklist procedures.

Cockpit management and crew coordination are important tasks associated with airline flight operations.

During flight, the captain, as pilot in command, is responsible for the safety of the airplane, its passengers, crew, and cargo. To fulfill this responsibility, the captain must be an effective manager of the flight crew. As indicated in Chapter 9, cockpit management is an important responsibility. A related task in operations with more than one cockpit crewmember is the ability to coordinate activities. **Crew coordination** involves the assignment of specific tasks to each crewmember and the use of prescribed checklists to accomplish these tasks.

FLIGHT ATTENDANT

In addition to the pilots, the crew may include one or more flight attendants. The flight attendants brief passengers, see that the cabin is in order, that food and supplies are available, and that emergency equipment is in working condition. They help passengers find their seats, store their luggage, and instruct them in emergency procedures. [Figure 13-3]

Flight attendants serve meals and beverages; answer questions; and give special attention to small children, the elderly, and the handicapped. They know first aid and are trained to deal with all kinds of situations. One of their most important functions is instructing and assisting passengers during emergency situations.

One of the most important functions of attendants is helping passengers during any kind of emergency that may occur.

Most airlines prefer flight attendant applicants who have some college background and have experience in dealing with the public. People with positive attitudes who can deal with strangers are most likely to be chosen for training. For overseas flights, attendants usually must speak at least one foreign language fluently.

MILITARY PILOTS

Military pilots are generally specialists who fly aircraft designed for specific missions. In many cases, they receive years of valuable training in some of the most advanced aircraft and weapons systems. Types of aircraft range from small trainers to the largest cargo and transport airplanes, as well as single-seat fighters, helicopters, and research and

Figure 13-3. A flight attendant's main responsibility is the safety and comfort of passengers.

experimental aircraft. Because of the quality of their training and experience, many former military pilots are able to obtain jobs in the aviation industry after they leave the armed forces.

The first duty of the military pilot is national defense, whether as a fighter pilot, a test pilot, or one engaged in support activities such as transporting troops, supplies, and equipment. Other military pilots are engaged in activities such as patrol, test flying new aircraft, and long-range military reconnaissance. In addition to pilots, flight crews on military aircraft may include navigators, specialists in electronic warfare or weapons systems, boom operators for in-flight refueling, flight engineers, and medical personnel.

ASTRONAUTS

Mankind's interest in space is probably as old as the interest in flying. Astronauts are the select few who have the chance to learn about space firsthand. The crew selected for a space flight depends on the nature of the mission. A space shuttle crew, for example, is normally made up of the commander, the pilot, and two or more mission specialists. Both the commander and the pilot are pilot astronauts who usually have had extensive military test pilot backgrounds. They also must have earned at least a bachelor's degree in either engineering, mathematics, or science, and be in excellent physical condition. Mission specialists have one or more advanced degrees in the sciences, engineering, or mathematics; for them, an aviation background is not as critical.

Although the nature of the work varies, their jobs most often consist of research and experimental work for governments and private businesses. They also work extensively with satellites, deploying new ones or testing and repairing those already in orbit. Using devices such as the **manned maneuvering unit** (MMU), astronauts are able to work outside an orbiting spacecraft. [Figure 13-4]

Working as a team with ground control facilities, astronauts perform many types of research not possible on earth. For example, they test living organisms, crystal formation, high-purity metals, and medical products. In addition, they gather data of interest to environmentalists, using the most sophisticated instruments available. In future projects, astronauts and mission specialists will be involved in setting up a manned space station.

Even though the training is long and difficult, there will be no shortage of candidates for this unique occupation. Those interested should begin early, and gain as much relevant experience as possible. In the future, mission specialists very likely will be selected on the basis of demonstrated expertise in the newest fields of science and engineering.

Figure 13-4. Astronaut Bruce McCandless II became the first man to fly freely in space, using an MMU, on February 7, 1984.

EMPLOYMENT OUTLOOK

Opportunities for a career as a professional pilot depend on many things. It has been forecast that U.S. passenger airlines may be carrying as many as 500 million passengers annually during the 1990's. Cargo traffic through these years is expected to grow annually at the rate of approximately eight percent. There will be increases in charter and air taxi service, as well as in aircraft owned and operated by businesses for their own uses. Deregulation has brought about many changes in the industry and has opened up new jobs. In addition, many people now choose early retirement, while others prefer to have two or three careers in their lifetimes. These factors tend to make room in the industry for newcomers. If the expected growth occurs, there will be an additional need for pilots, flight instructors, and flight attendants. Even though there will be many new jobs in the next few years, competition will be sharp for the best positions. As in most other jobs, factors such as the condition of related industries and the general state of the economy will always affect the aviation industry.

CHECKLIST

After studying this section, you should have a basic understanding of:

✓ **Commercial pilots** — What some of the specialized types of jobs are.

✓ **Corporate pilots** — Who employs them and what their responsibilities are.

✓ **Airline pilots** — What their responsibilities on a typical flight are.

✓ **Flight attendants** — What they do and what their most important functions are.

✓ **Military pilots** — What types of flying they do.

✓ **Astronauts** — What types of experiments and research they perform.

NONFLYING CAREERS

Each aircraft that flies depends on the work of hundreds of people in many different fields. These include aircraft designers and builders, maintenance technicians, airport operators, and a wide range of aircraft support operations. There are also many other opportunities within the aerospace industry which are not directly related to aircraft. These include working for military defense contractors, simulator designers and builders, construction firms, and various governmental agencies.

CIVILIAN CAREER OPPORTUNITIES

The manufacturing of an aircraft involves all of the research and development effort, the construction of the aircraft itself, and the installation of various systems and subsystems. Aircraft manufacturers seldom build every component in their aircraft. Instead, they usually contract out various components, such as the engines or navigation equipment, to other manufacturers with greater expertise on that system. This parting out, or **subcontracting**, of jobs increases the need for diverse aviation industries which all create additional jobs.

Most aerospace products are not designed and built by a single manufacturer.

Once the finished aircraft has been delivered, it must be maintained by properly certificated mechanics and technicians. If the airplane is used to help produce revenue, many others are involved in the day-to-day affairs of managing these operations. Beyond building, maintaining, and managing operations is the requirement for airport facilities. The airport can be thought of as an entire community where jobs and services are oriented to support aviation.

GOVERNMENT OPPORTUNITIES

Another major source of aviation jobs is with federal, state, and local governments. Some of the careers within the federal government include positions within the military, Federal Aviation Administration, National Transportation Safety Board, and the National Aeronautics and Space Administration. In addition, there are many career opportunities with state and local agencies.

FEDERAL AVIATION ADMINISTRATION

The Federal Aviation Administration (FAA) is responsible for the safe and efficient use of the nation's airspace by military as well as civil aviation. Additional tasks are fostering civil aeronautics and air commerce in the United States and abroad, and supporting the requirements of national defense.

Activities necessary to carry out these responsibilities include safety regulation, airspace management, the establishment and operation of a system for air traffic control service and navigation facilities, research and development in support of a national system of airports, setting standards and specifications for civil airports, administration of federal grants for developing public airports, and cooperative activities with the Department of Defense. Two of the many career opportunities within the FAA include air traffic services and aviation safety inspectors.

AIR TRAFFIC SERVICES

ATC is a service operated by the FAA to promote the safe, orderly, and expeditious flow of air traffic.

Air traffic control (ATC) specialists work at control towers and air route traffic control centers (ARTCCs) across the country. Air traffic control is a service operated by an appropriate authority to promote the safe, orderly, and expeditious flow of air traffic. At large airports, **ground controllers** monitor the safe flow of traffic on the surface. **Local controllers (towers)** issue takeoff and landing clearances. Once an airplane is in the air, **departure controllers** provide service to guide it out of the airport's airspace. **Approach controllers** perform the opposite function; they coordinate the flow of arriving aircraft.

Other air traffic control specialists are assigned to ARTCCs, where they work primarily with aircraft flying under instrument flight rules (IFR) and operating within the airspace of that center. When an airplane operating under IFR is about to leave the departure control area, the controller transfers it to the first **enroute controller**. As the airplane moves along its route, its flight is monitored by successive centers until it enters the airspace of the destination airport. Enroute controllers maintain contact with numerous agencies and give pilots the most current information about weather and flight conditions. If a pilot needs to change altitude to find better flying conditions, the radar controller checks to make sure the change will not interfere with any other airplanes along the route. [Figure 13-5]

Another group in the air traffic system is the **flight service specialists**. Unlike ATC specialists, flight service specialists do not work in tower facilities or ARTCCs. Instead they are located in flight service stations (FSSs) throughout the United States. The FSSs provide pilot briefings, enroute communications, and visual flight rule (VFR) search and rescue service. They also assist pilots of lost aircraft or aircraft in emergency situations, relay ATC clearances, originate Notices to Airmen, broadcast aviation weather and airspace information, receive and process flight plans, and monitor navigation aids. In addition, selected FSSs provide enroute flight advisory service (Flight Watch), take weather observations, issue airport advisories, and advise Customs and Immigration of transborder flights.

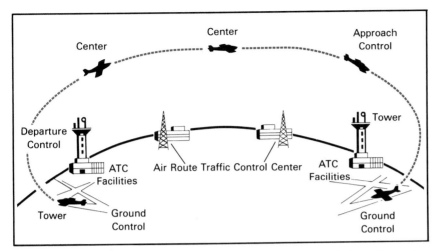

Figure 13-5. For flights under instrument flight rules, a team of air traffic control specialists provides flight following service for pilots from takeoff to landing.

Some flight service specialists may become controllers; however, controller applicants must enter the training program prior to their thirty-first birthday. In addition, applicants must be healthy, have good vision, and an aptitude for abstract reasoning and spatial relationships. Three years of work experience, or a college degree (or a combination of work experience and college courses) is required. Although not essential, a background as a military air traffic controller or as a pilot is beneficial. Competition for controller jobs is usually intense.

AVIATION SAFETY INSPECTORS

The FAA employs aviation safety inspectors to inspect aircraft and equipment manufacturing, maintenance and repair, and flight operations procedures. They usually specialize in either commercial or general aviation aircraft. These inspectors also test and certify pilots, pilot examiners, flight instructors, flight schools, and instructional materials.

Manufacturing inspectors check the design, materials, and methods of producing civil aircraft, engines, systems, and equipment to ensure that they meet FAA safety standards. They also work with aircraft manufacturing engineers from the blueprint stage through the entire production process to make sure that the finished product is airworthy.

Avionics inspectors check electronic communications and navigation equipment on the aircraft to ensure that established operational standards are met. **Maintenance inspectors** check maintenance procedures, methods, spare parts stock, employee training programs, instructional materials, and maintenance manuals. They also check repairs, alterations, general maintenance, and the airworthiness of airframes, engines, propellers, and aircraft components.

NATIONAL TRANSPORTATION SAFETY BOARD

The National Transportation Safety Board (NTSB) has the dual responsibility of safety and investigation of various types of transportation accidents. NTSB personnel with expertise in aviation may be assigned to aircraft-related accident investigation duties. These **aircraft accident investigators** conduct interviews and examine aircraft parts, instruments, engines, maintenance records, and flight records to determine the probable causes of accidents. They must be prepared to be dispatched, with short notice, to the scene of accidents, sometimes to very remote areas of the country. In some cases, this requires the use of helicopters or rough terrain vehicles to reach the accident site.

The findings of the NTSB investigator may result in recommendations for change. This can affect FARs, flight training procedures, airplane operating limitations, maintenance and inspection procedures, or even result in airplane modifications.

NATIONAL AERONAUTICS AND SPACE ADMINISTRATION (NASA)

The National Aeronautics and Space Administration (NASA) is a civilian agency of the federal government whose purpose is to conduct research in all aspects of space and aeronautics. It is an integral part of the aerospace industry, contracting out projects through various private companies. The work force at NASA is comprised mainly of scientists, engineers, and administrators. However, the agency also has jobs that are common in all businesses; for example, managers, accountants, lawyers, human resource personnel, and secretaries.

RESEARCH, DESIGN, AND PRODUCTION

Whether for civilian or governmental purposes, the aerospace industry designs and produces a wide variety of equipment. The products include completed aircraft, engines, aircraft and engine subsystems, sophisticated electronics, missiles, and defense hardware. The development of each of these products requires numerous individuals with a variety of educational and technical backgrounds. [Figure 13-6]

Technicians are specialists who work closely with engineers.

In addition to highly trained engineers, technicians are also required. **Technicians** are specialists in designing, repairing, testing, and maintaining complex equipment. Most receive their training in trade schools or

Figure 13-6. A list of engineers required for a particular contract might include aerodynamic, material, electrical, laser, robotics, propulsion, computer simulation, and ergonomic engineers.

community college programs that take two years or less; many receive equivalent training in the military. Those technicians who specialize in maintaining aviation equipment will be discussed later in this section. Because they are a part of every step of the designing and manufacturing process, and because their specialized skills also are needed to install, maintain, test, and repair equipment and systems, technicians have great opportunities in the aerospace industry. In addition to jobs in electronics, hydraulics, instrument and guidance systems, communications, and data systems, there are opportunities in many new fields.

Commercial artists also are an integral part of the design and production phase of a project. They must take the designer's ideas and convert them into visual concepts. Another important occupation combines the jobs of the artist, engineer, and computer operator into a function called **computer aided design/computer aided manufacturing** (CAD/CAM). CAD/CAM technology is becoming more and more important both for the accuracy of perspective it provides and for the time and money it saves.

CAD/CAM integrates the jobs of artist, engineer, and computer operator into a single function.

Some CAD/CAM technicians are robotics experts. They use information about manufacturing specifications stored in computer files to design and construct robots. These robots then become part of the manufacturing process, doing work that may be too strenuous, tedious, or dangerous for humans to do. CAD/CAM technicians may control or modify the

Figure 13-7. CAD/CAM preliminary drawings can be viewed from different angles or tested for estimates of strength, flexibility, and endurance. Construction materials can be changed, costs can be estimated, and the manufacturing process can be altered. When the design has been completed, tested, and approved, blueprints and schematics are drawn by computer-operated plotters.

robot's operation. They keep records of test results and production data and may use these to produce reports or charts. [Figure 13-7]

A growth area that has developed rapidly in recent years is simulation. **Simulators** are widely used for training, in engineering design, and for computer-aided education. Some simulators are so realistic that they are better than full-scale models.

Simulation engineers and technicians are in high demand.

The main advantage of simulators is that, once a system is developed, training costs and risks are decreased. Traditionally, simulators have been used to train aircrews in the operation of an aircraft and its systems. They are particularly well-suited to aircraft instrument and emergency procedures training. As simulators become more sophisticated, they are increasingly being used to train railroad, ship, and tank personnel, as well as heavy equipment operators. Increased demands for simulator engineers and technicians are forecast for the 1990's.

ASSOCIATIONS AND TRAINING

The aerospace industry also has a need for **technical writers**, **editors**, **photographers**, and **artists**. People with these skills help to convert high-technology data into a format that less technically oriented people can

Figure 13-8. Normally, technical writers, editors, artists, and photographers work together as a team to create printed and audiovisual materials. An aviation background is helpful for writers and editors, but it may not be essential.

understand. Large aerospace corporations often use technical publications to describe all phases of equipment operation and maintenance procedures. Some manufacturers also require technical data for logistical support, description of parts, and assembly. [Figure 13-8]

Technical communications specialists are also employed by trade journals, aviation magazines, training manual publishers, flight safety research organizations, insurance companies, and trade and industrial organizations. Some of these associations are: the Air Transport Association (ATA), American Institute of Aeronautics and Astronautics (AIAA), the Aerospace Industries Association (AIA), National Business Aircraft Association (NBAA), Aircraft Owners and Pilots Association (AOPA), General Aircraft Manufacturers Association (GAMA), National Association of State Aviation Officials (NASAO), Professional Aviation Maintenance Association, National Air Transportation Society (NATA), American Electronics Association (AEA), Society of Women Engineers (SWE), Aviation Space Writers Association, Society for Technical Communication (STC), the Ninety-Nines, Inc., and Future Aviation Professionals of America (FAPA). Many of these associations sponsor internships and on-the-job training opportunities. In addition, their publications may contain valuable articles about the specific area of the aerospace industry you are interested in, as well as job listings and free literature you can request.

MAINTENANCE TECHNICIANS

Aircraft maintenance is an important and highly specialized job in the aviation industry. The safety of air travel is partly due to the quality of work of aviation technicians, avionics technicians, and others such as machinists, sheet metal workers, drill press operators, and electricians. They service, repair, overhaul, and test airframes, engines, propellers, aircraft systems, electronic equipment, and instruments. In addition to the airlines and the armed forces, who together employ the majority of aircraft mechanics, thousands more work for air taxi operators, aerial applicators, fixed-base operators, aircraft manufacturers, and the FAA.

Most mechanics learn their jobs in trade schools certified by the FAA or in the military. Civilian technicians are licensed as powerplant mechanics, airframe mechanics, airframe and powerplant mechanics (A&P), or aircraft inspectors. **Powerplant mechanics** work only on the engines and propellers of aircraft, **airframe mechanics** work on all other parts of the aircraft, and **A&P mechanics** are qualified to work on all parts of the aircraft. **Aircraft inspectors** certify work done by other mechanics.

An aircraft inspector must have held an A&P license for at least three years.

Apprentice mechanics may work on various parts of the airplane under the supervision of a licensed mechanic, who must approve the finished work. The FAA requires at least 18 months of work experience as an apprentice for an airframe or powerplant license, and 30 months as an apprentice for the combined A&P license. An inspector applicant must have held an A&P license for at least three years. All applicants must pass written, oral, and practical tests.

The armed forces employ thousands of aviation technicians and mechanics to work on aircraft at military installations all over the world. For military personnel, these positions do not normally require FAA certification. Many civilians also work, either directly or indirectly, for the Department of Defense. The military is considered a good way to gain practical experience; with additional study, an applicant may pass the FAA licensing exam. Military experience is usually an advantage for a licensed applicant applying for a civilian job.

AVIONICS

Avionics technicians inspect, test, adjust, and repair communications, navigation, flight control radar, electrical, and autopilot systems on aircraft, spacecraft, and missiles. **Avionics** is a term formed by combining "aviation" and "electronics." Although many avionics technicians work with avionics engineers to develop new systems and components, most of them maintain and repair equipment already in use on aircraft and spacecraft.

To function properly, avionics equipment must meet exacting specifications. Once in use, it must be tested, calibrated, and repaired, if necessary, on a regular basis. An avionics technician completes testing and maintenance and verifies records to indicate the operational status of equipment.

The range of equipment in this field is so broad that these technicians often specialize in one type. FAA Repairman Certificates are issued on the basis of specific work experience and allow a technician to work only on those parts of the aircraft listed on the certificate. Since new equipment is constantly being introduced, avionics technicians must frequently attend classes and seminars to keep up with the most current developments. This type of training is usually provided by employers or manufacturers.

SUPPORT

Air transportation has become a highly competitive, 24-hour-a-day operation. Ground-based support services encompass hundreds of job classifications requiring diverse levels of education and training. The following is only a partial list of the jobs available: air traffic controller, meteorologist, airport manager, reservation ticket agent, travel agent, baggage handler, equipment operator, air cargo agent, passenger service agent, food service employee, clerical worker, car rental agent, security guard, and flight dispatcher.

Flight dispatchers work in airline facilities that have extensive communications equipment, as well as the most current weather, airways, and airport facility information. They prepare flight plans, choose the best route and altitude, compute fuel required, and calculate weight and balance data. Before a flight, the dispatcher and pilot in command discuss these details to ensure the flight is planned efficiently and safely. If weather changes during a flight, they must decide on alternate altitudes, routes, or landing sites. After the flight, the dispatcher may debrief with the captain, so the most current information can be used in planning subsequent flights. Dispatchers keep records of flight time for individual airplanes, engines, and crew members. They also keep records of flights, cancellations, and delays. Most dispatchers have worked for their employer either as an assistant dispatcher or as a pilot. Military service is another way to gain experience in this field.

Flight dispatchers work with pilots to increase the level of safety and efficiency of commercial flights.

The airport businesses that provide aviation services for pilots and aircraft are usually referred to as **fixed-base operators** (FBOs). They offer services such as aircraft repair, aviation fuel sales, flight school operations, the sale of new and used aircraft, and air taxi or charter flights. An FBO is a typical small business in the aviation industry and, depending on its size, may employ mechanics, flight instructors, and salespeople. [Figure 13-9]

Figure 13-9. The FBO also employs line service personnel who greet and service arriving aircraft. They may fill tanks with fuel, check oil, vacuum interiors, wash windshields, and report to the pilot any signs of trouble. Line service personnel are usually young people who are interested in aviation. While working on the flight line, they can gain experience in aircraft operations under the guidance of the fixed-base operator.

BUSINESS OPERATIONS

Every part of the aerospace industry from aircraft and system design to aircraft operation, or maintenance and support functions, requires expertise in the traditional business functions. These range from management of the various aspects of a project to accounting, marketing, and personnel administration.

The job of a manager in the aerospace industry is similar in many ways to that of managers in other industries. Since many facets of aviation and space exploration are new, managers in these areas should have knowledge and skills that are useful in the associated technology. Aerospace management fields include such areas as aerospace manufacturing, airline management, airport management, and fixed-base operations.

In manufacturing, managers must determine what contracts to bid on and how to fulfill the contracts. Managers also deal with personnel matters, governmental regulations, safety and environmental issues, production schedules, facilities planning, and profit objectives. They are responsible for meeting the needs of each customer by making new technology available in a timely and cost-effective manner.

Others are employed as **airport managers**. Airports may be privately owned by a single operator or owned and operated by a city, county, regional, or interstate government agency. Airports are usually directed by a manager who is responsible to either the owners of the airport or the appropriate government agency. An airport may cover hundreds of acres, have dozens of buildings, and employ thousands of people; or it may consist of a single runway, with a few buildings, and be owned and operated by one or two people. Whatever the size, the airport manager is concerned with safety, maintenance, operations, and service. They must be knowledgeable of federal, state, and local laws, work with the representatives of all these levels of government, do business with companies in many areas of the industry, manage employees in a variety of occupations, and deal with the public.

CHECKLIST _____

After studying this section, you should have a basic understanding of:

✓   **Civilian career opportunities** — What some of the different opportunities are which exist for civilians in the aerospace industry.

✓   **Government opportunities** — What the various governmental agencies are in the aerospace industry and the types of positions available.

✓ **Technicians** — What they do and what some of the newest fields of technology are.

✓ **Avionics** — What the term "avionics" means and what equipment avionics technicians maintain.

✓ **CAD/CAM** — What CAD/CAM is and how it is used in the aerospace industry.

✓ **Associations and training** — What some of the positions are within associations and training organizations.

✓ **Maintenance technicians** — What the various specializations are for maintenance technicians and what training is required.

✓ **FBOs** — What their purpose and function are and the types of people they employ.

✓ **Airport managers** — What the scope of their duties and responsibilities are.

SECTION C

GETTING STARTED IN AVIATION

This chapter has outlined various opportunities for employment throughout the aerospace industry. The next logical question is: "How do you get started?" Ideally, you should choose an occupational area that appeals to you from the start; however, you may not know exactly what career you want to pursue. If you haven't made a definite choice by your second or third year of college, you still can prepare for a career in the aerospace industry. Even though you haven't selected a specific objective, you may be attracted to aerospace employment in general. Of course, you must weigh this "general" approach against a specific objective so you can take full advantage of your educational opportunities. The more technical your career choice, the sooner you need to begin. This section is designed to give you some practical ideas for pursuing an aerospace career.

GENERAL EDUCATION

Good math and science skills are beneficial for any career in the aerospace industry.

Generally speaking, those who are most successful in this industry have good skills in math and science. Good written and verbal communication abilities also are important. This is not to say that people who have not developed these skills and abilities cannot find work in the industry; it only means that the better prepared you are, the better your opportunities will be. Another advantage of taking courses such as calculus, physics, and chemistry early in your education is that they help you determine your aptitudes and interests.

SPECIAL EDUCATION AND TRAINING

Most of the jobs in the aerospace industry require specialized education and training beyond the high school or even college level. Although the expense of acquiring the additional education is another hurdle to overcome, the enhancement of your qualifications and job opportunities usually is well worth it. To acquire additional education, you can attend schools or universities, or gain experience through an apprenticeship program. In many cases, scholarships, grants, or low interest loans are available to help you complete your education. These additional qualifications will greatly benefit your career objectives and broaden your employment opportunities in either private business or government.

FLIGHT TRAINING

You must be at least 16 years old to obtain a student pilot certificate.

If you are considering a career as a pilot, you may wish to begin your flight training early. The minimum age is only 16 to obtain a student pilot certificate, 17 for a private pilot certificate, and 18 for a commercial pilot certificate. However, before you begin your training, consider any general health or physical limitations you may have. All pilots are required to pass a physical examination. An aviation medical examiner (AME) can advise you in this area.

If you decide in favor of a career as a pilot, you can obtain flight and ground instruction from an individual instructor, at a flight school at your local airport, or at a professional pilot training establishment. Due to projections of a pilot shortage in the 1990's, airlines are also involved in unique pilot training programs. **Ab initio**, or training that takes the pilot from the beginning of flight training through airline qualification, has received a lot of attention in recent years. In addition, some colleges and universities offer academic and flight training as part of a professional pilot or aerospace career program. You receive an associate or bachelors degree and a pilot certificate. Your ground instruction will include subjects such as aerodynamics, meteorology, navigation, radio communications, aircraft systems, and FAA regulations. [Figure 13-10]

Before you can earn money as a pilot, you must hold a commercial pilot certificate, which usually means you also have an instrument rating. Depending on the training program you follow, you will be required to accumulate 190 to 250 hours of flight experience and successfully complete several written examinations and flight tests. Most newly certificated commercial pilots go on to obtain their flight instructor certificate and ratings. This allows them to earn an income while gaining additional flight experience. Flight instructors are permitted to log the time they are giving flight instruction as pilot-in-command time.

You must hold a commercial pilot certificate to earn money as a pilot.

Figure 13-10. During flight training, you learn to apply the knowledge acquired in ground school to the various required flight maneuvers.

Figure 13-11. The airlines usually are considered the pinnacle of aviation employment by younger pilots because they offer better pay and working conditions than many other flying positions. If you choose to pursue a career with an airline, you will probably have to work for a smaller airline or regional carrier for a period of time to gain experience in large aircraft. Competition for airline employment has always been very strong.

Many look for a position as a charter pilot, air freight pilot, corporate pilot, or pilot for one of the smaller airlines that operate only in a given region of the country (regional carrier). Your exact choice will vary with your objectives and the availability of jobs at the time. The larger airlines usually hire pilots with substantial flight experience or those with military flight experience. Generally, a four-year college degree also is required. [Figure 13-11]

TECHNICAL AND VOCATIONAL SCHOOLS

Technical and vocational schools provide formal training in specialized areas. In the aerospace industry, these include training in the repair and maintenance of avionics, robots, and computers among others. The length of training varies with the specialty.

A person may not become fully qualified at a particular trade through a technical or vocational school. Some practical experience and/or additional training often is required. For example, to be certified as an aircraft inspector, an applicant must hold a mechanic certificate with airframe and powerplant ratings for at least three years.

PRACTICAL EXPERIENCE

Often, it is possible to qualify for a particular position through on-the-job training and practical experience. Using the position of an aircraft maintenance technician as an example, it is possible to become a certified technician without attending school. This is done through an apprenticeship program. Apprentice technicians work on various parts of the airplane under the supervision of a licensed technician, who must sign an approval of the finished work. The FAA requires at least 18 months of work experience as an apprentice for an airframe or power-plant rating, and 30 months for the combined license.

You can become qualified for some aerospace positions through on-the-job training and practical experience.

COLLEGE

A college degree is highly recommended for many positions in the aerospace industry. Junior colleges, community colleges, and some other institutions offer two-year associate degrees. These institutions are usually more accessible to students and less costly. Typically, you can take the same courses during your first two years as at a four-year college, although you can usually specialize as well. This permits you to transfer the credit for the courses to a four-year degree college if you decide to obtain a four-year degree at a later date.

Overall, the four-year college or university offers a much broader curriculum. In addition, since it takes four years, you are more likely to obtain a higher level of knowledge than is possible in two-year institutions. Many four-year colleges also offer graduate degree programs.

Naturally, you must weigh the cost of attending a two- or four-year institution against your career goals and financial resources. Also consider the quality of the school you will attend and your abilities as a student. To enroll in many colleges and universities, you need to do well in high school and score high on the American College Test (ACT) or the Scholastic Aptitude Test (SAT). These tests are administered several times a year on a nationwide basis.

GOVERNMENT

Most positions in the private sector are also available within the government. In addition, the government offers several positions which are not found in the private sector. A good example of such a position is air traffic controller.

AIR TRAFFIC CONTROL

The responsibility for the training of air traffic control specialists lies with the Federal Aviation Administration (FAA). The training is technical and sophisticated. It requires students to take instruction at the FAA Academy in Oklahoma City and on-the-job training at the various air traffic control facilities. Generally, a minimum of three and a half years

Air traffic controllers are initially trained by the FAA in Oklahoma City.

of training and/or experience are required to become a fully qualified, professional controller.

At the FAA Academy, trainees become specialized for the type of facility they will work in such as an air route traffic control center (ARTCC), control tower, or flight service station. ARTCC and control tower trainees learn about radar, traffic separation, and instrument flight rules. Flight service specialists learn how to access, interpret, and communicate weather reports and forecasts and how to provide other flight planning information. Both FSS specialists and controllers learn how to provide assistance to aircraft in distress and how to help in search and rescue activities. Before they complete their training, both must pass a written exam which covers flight rules, air traffic control procedures, communications, operating procedures, air navigation procedures, aids to air navigation, and meteorology. Air traffic controllers also receive instruction in the rules that pilots must use, as well as courses specifically related to their specialty.

Generally, applicants applying for an air traffic controller position need a minimum of two years of college, with preferential consideration given to those applicants who hold an instrument rating. Air traffic controllers are civil service employees, so they must pass the appropriate civil service exam prior to consideration of their application.

ARMED FORCES

The armed forces train a large number of people each year in a variety of different occupations. By joining the armed forces, you can be trained as a technician, engineer, or even as a pilot at the government's expense. In fact, the armed forces may pay for you to attend a civilian college or university while you are completing your service obligation. The various services also have a number of technical programs of their own for specialized military training.

Some positions in the armed forces require a four-year college degree.

There are several ways you can enter the armed forces. One way is to enlist in the Army, Air Force, Navy, or Coast Guard after high school. If you have a college degree, you can apply for an officer training program. To qualify for certain positions within the armed forces, such as pilot, you must be an officer. Keep in mind that, if you do not have a college degree, you can enlist and attend college while you are serving. Then you can apply to become commissioned as an officer after you receive your degree.

Another way to join the armed services is through the Reserve Officer Training Corps (ROTC). These programs prepare you to be an officer at the same time you are completing school. Scholarship and financial assistance also may be available. ROTC classes are taken along with your other academic classes. In college, some ROTC credits can be applied toward your degree. You will normally be required to attend summer field training before your senior year as part of your officer training.

If you are planning a career as an officer in the armed forces, you should seriously consider attending one of the military academies. These institutions are fully accredited universities which, in addition to offering the full range of college courses, provide specialized courses for those seeking careers as military officers. The training in these academies is very rigorous and goes far beyond the classroom. Although a military academy can be much more demanding than most universities, the education and training can be of enormous value in your future career.

If you seek a career as an officer in the armed forces, you should consider applying at one of the military academies.

FUTURE EMPLOYMENT

The United States is a world leader in aerospace. Throughout the 1990's, government and industry will be spending huge amounts of money in research, development, and production of new aircraft and space vehicles. Forecasts indicate continued growth in commercial aviation as the primary public means of transportation between cities in the U.S. A large part of the fleet of commercial aircraft will have to be replaced. New space programs challenge the imagination. Spin-offs from these programs will promote technological advances in other areas and create new jobs. By the end of this century the demand for scientific and technical skills will be even greater than today. The best time to start preparing for a career in aerospace is now.

In the future, there will be an even greater demand for scientific and technical skills.

CHECKLIST ─────────────

After studying this section, you should have a basic understanding of:

✓ **General education** — What types of courses can be of general benefit in preparing for a career in the aerospace industry.

✓ **Flight training** — What the various sources are for obtaining pilot training and what you can expect as a career commercial pilot.

✓ **Technical training** — How to obtain technical training and how practical experience may be applied in lieu of formal training.

✓ **College** — What the differences are in the qualifications you can obtain from two- or four-year programs.

✓ **Air traffic control** — Who trains air traffic controllers and what the basic requirements are to become one.

✓ **Armed forces** — What the opportunities are in the armed forces and how to choose the best course of action.

PLOTTER AND WIND TRIANGLES

As indicated in Chapter 6, the plotter is a simple device that you can use to draw a straight line on a chart or measure direction and distance. Normally, you plan your flight with a plotter and a flight computer using the computer for basic calculations and for determining the effect of the wind on your airplane during the flight. While a flight computer is very useful, basic knowledge of wind triangles will help you visualize and understand the effects of wind.

WIND

Wind is the movement of an airmass over the earth. Its motion is made apparent through blowing trees, choppy water, or the tugging of clothing. A balloon simply moves with the wind and drifts above the terrain. An airplane, however, moves under its own power. Its speed and direction over the surface are the result of the combined effects of wind speed and direction and aircraft speed and direction.

Wind speed is the rate of progress of an airmass over the earth. You can obtain winds aloft information from flight service stations. Winds aloft are given in the true direction from which they are blowing, and wind speeds are given in knots. The term **knots** means nautical miles per hour. Remember that a nautical mile, which is 6,076 feet, is equal to one minute of latitude. The term **miles per hour** means statute miles per hour. A statute mile is 5,280 feet.

Wind above the surface level is normally reported in knots and in the true direction.

AIRCRAFT SPEED AND HEADING

To understand wind triangles, you need to be familiar with several types of speeds that relate to your aircraft. **Indicated airspeed** (IAS) is the uncorrected reading shown on the airspeed indicator. The actual speed of your airplane through the air is affected by nonstandard temperature and pressure. You can use a flight computer to correct indicated airspeed for these factors. The resulting value is called **true airspeed** (TAS). Indicated airspeed and true airspeed are equal only at sea level on a standard day. **Groundspeed** (GS) is the actual speed of your aircraft over the

Indicated airspeed and true airspeed are the same only at sea level on a standard day.

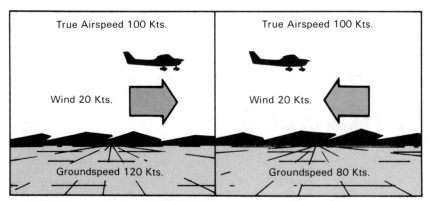

Figure A-1. If your airplane has a true airspeed of 100 knots and there is a 20-knot tailwind, your groundspeed is 120 knots. A 20-knot headwind produces the opposite effect; your groundspeed decreases to 80 knots. Your true airspeed, in either case, is not affected by wind.

ground. If there is no wind, it is the same as true airspeed. If there is a tailwind or headwind, however, groundspeed is affected. [Figure A-1]

In addition to speeds, you also need to remember the terminology that applies to aircraft headings. When plotting wind triangles, you normally use true north as the basic reference. **True heading** (TH) is the direction your aircraft is flying, and it is measured in degrees from true north. The path it makes over the ground is generally called **track. True course** (TC) is your intended path over the ground.

During most flights, the wind will be blowing at an angle to your true course. This **crosswind** will cause your airplane to drift in the same direction the wind is blowing. To maintain your ground track directly along your planned true course, you must fly a specific heading which corrects for wind. [Figure A-2]

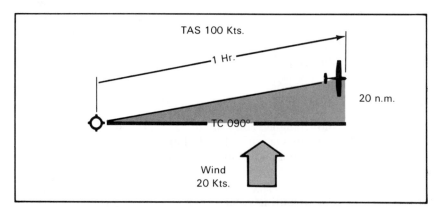

Figure A-2. Assume you want to fly a true course of 090° with a true airspeed of 100 knots, and you have a 20-knot crosswind from the right. If you maintain this heading for one hour, you will drift 20 n.m. north of the true course.

You counteract the effects of the wind by adjusting your heading into the wind. The number of degrees you use for this adjustment is the **wind correction angle** (WCA). You should also monitor your groundspeed to make certain that unexpected winds don't increase your time enroute and cause you to run short on fuel. Careful preflight planning will help you determine necessary wind corrections and fuel requirements.

WIND TRIANGLES

During preflight planning, especially for a cross-country flight, you should compute the effect of wind on your airplane. You can do this by constructing a **wind triangle**, which is a simplified vector diagram. As you learned in Chapter 1, a vector diagram consists of two or more vectors and a resultant. Each vector includes direction and speed (magnitude). The sum of the vectors is the resultant, and the resultant forms a third side, or the third vector, of a wind triangle.

With a plotter, you can draw a wind triangle which represents known values of direction and speed. Then, by using the plotter's protractor and mileage scales, you can find the unknown values. The 1:1,000,000 scale (WAC side) of the plotter is best for drawing a wind triangle, because its scale is easier to use on standard-sized paper. Make sure you use the same scale throughout. [Figure A-3]

If you know the relationships of the elements of a wind triangle, you can plot the known values and solve for the unknowns.

Perhaps the most effective way to understand wind triangles is to use one to work a problem. Let's assume that during your preflight planning you determine that your true course is 043°, your airplane's true airspeed is 114 knots, and the wind is 090° at 20 knots. Normally, this is the type of information you have before a flight. For a successful flight away from the local flying area, you need good estimates of your true heading

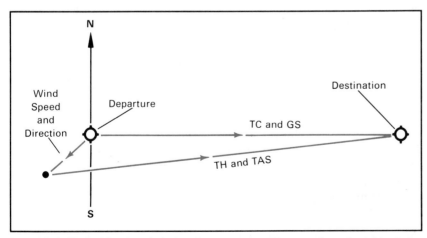

Figure A-3. Each side of a wind triangle represents different values. One side shows the wind speed and direction, another represents true course and groundspeed, and the third indicates true heading and true airspeed.

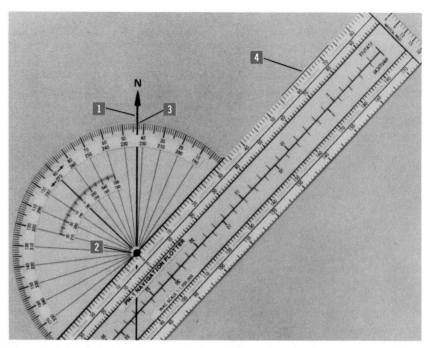

Figure A-4. Begin by drawing a vertical, north-south line that represents a meridian, or a true north line (item 1). Place a dot along this line to indicate your point of departure (item 2). Position the plotter so the center hole is over the departure dot and your TC of 043° on the protractor disc is over the north-south line (item 3). Then, draw a short reference line near the top of the plotter to show the position of the 043° true course line (item 4).

and groundspeed, so you can correct for the wind and compute your time enroute. True heading and groundspeed are the unknown values that you must compute. [Figure A-4]

The departure dot is the starting point for plotting vectors in the wind triangle. In a basic wind triangle problem, the length of the vector represents the distance traveled in one hour. [Figure A-5]

Your next step is to plot the wind vector. This vector also begins at the departure dot and extends in the direction the wind is blowing. With the protractor hole centered over the departure dot, rotate the plotter until 90° is aligned with the north-south line. Then, make a mark for a 090° reference line. [Figure A-6]

Now you have two sides of the wind triangle — the wind vector and the true course line. The missing information to complete the true course vector is the groundspeed. The resultant, or the third side of the wind

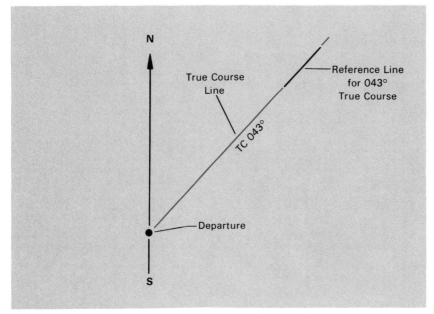

Figure A-5. Use the straightedge of the plotter to complete the true course line. It should extend from the departure dot through the short 043° true course reference line. Label the true course "TC 043°."

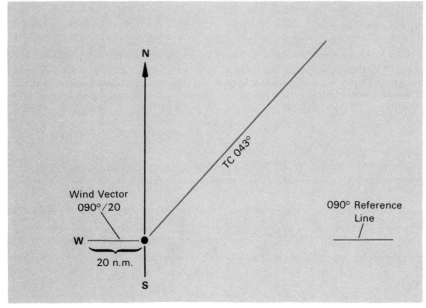

Figure A-6. Use the 090° reference line and the plotter's straightedge with the nautical miles scale to complete the wind vector. Since the wind is from 090° at 20 knots, the wind vector extends 20 n.m. in the opposite direction. Place an arrow at the end of the wind vector and label it "W" for wind.

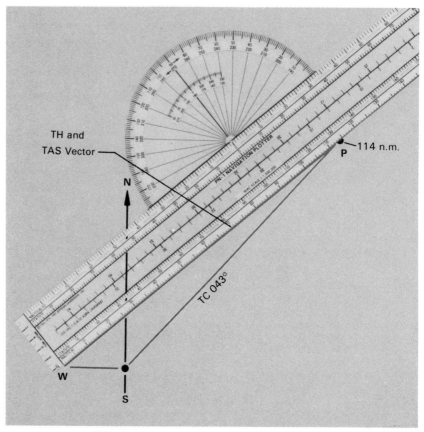

Figure A-7. To plot your true heading and true airspeed vector, align your plotter so the zero mark on the nautical scale is on the arrow end of the wind vector and the 114-mile mark intersects the true course line. Use your straightedge to draw a line connecting the two points; label the point formed by these two lines "P" for position.

triangle, contains the true heading, which you do not know at this point, and the true airspeed, which is 114 knots. [Figure A-7]

The point where the true airspeed and true course lines intersect represents the position of your aircraft at the end of one hour. To determine groundspeed, simply measure the true course line from the point of departure to the symbol "P." [Figure A-8]

True heading and true airspeed are also on a single line. The direction of the line is the true heading, while the length of the line is the true airspeed. [Figure A-9]

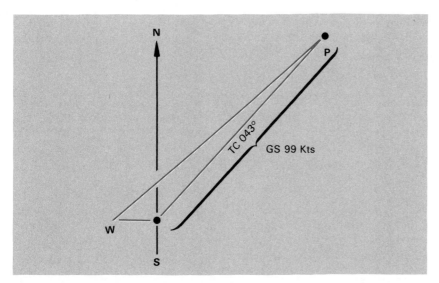

Figure A-8. The distance between the two points is 99 n.m. This means your groundspeed is 99 knots. Groundspeed and true course are always on one line in a wind triangle.

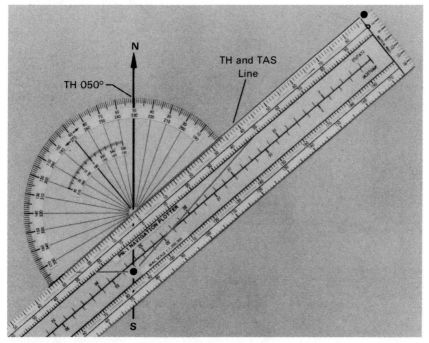

Figure A-9. To measure true heading, place the plotter with the protractor hole centered over the intersection of the true airspeed and north-south lines. Then, align the straightedge with the true airspeed line. The point at which the north-south line crosses the curved edge of the protractor is the true heading. In this case, it is 050°.

You can also determine true heading by first finding the wind correction angle. Remember the WCA is the angle between the true course and the true heading. [Figure A-10]

Apply the WCA mathematically to the true course to find your true heading.

In other words, you apply the wind correction angle to true course to find true heading. If the wind is from the right, add the WCA to true course. Conversely, if the wind is from the left, subtract the WCA. In this case, the wind is from the right, so you add the 7° wind correction angle to the true course of 043° to obtain a true heading of 050°.

Wind triangles clearly demonstrate the overall relationships between wind, true heading, TAS, true course, and groundspeed. Although you can derive these values through different methods, wind triangles help you to visualize their relationships.

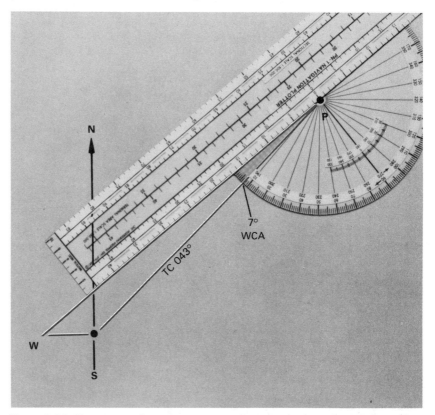

Figure A-10. First, center the protractor hole over the point labeled "P." Then, align the straightedge with the true airspeed line. The WCA is the angle formed by the two lines extending from point "P," and it represents the number of degrees you must add or subtract from your true course to maintain a planned track over the ground.

APPENDIX B

GLOSSARY

ABSOLUTE ALTITUDE — Actual height above the surface of the earth, either land or water.

ABSOLUTE CEILING — The altitude where a particular airplane's climb rate reaches zero.

ADVECTION FOG — Fog resulting from the movement of warm, humid air over a cold surface.

AGL — Above ground level.

AGONIC LINE — Line along which no magnetic variation occurs.

AIR DENSITY — The density of the air in terms of mass per unit volume. Dense air has more molecules per unit volume than less dense air. The density of air decreases with altitude above the surface of the earth and with increasing temperature.

AIR ROUTE TRAFFIC CONTROL CENTER (ARTCC) — A facility established to provide air traffic control service to aircraft operating on IFR flight plans within controlled airspace, principally during the enroute phase of flight. When equipment capabilities and controller workload permit, certain advisory/assistance services may be provided to VFR aircraft.

AIR TRAFFIC CONTROL (ATC) — A service provided by the FAA to promote the safe, orderly, and expeditious flow of air traffic.

AIRMASS — An extensive body of air having fairly uniform properties of temperature and moisture within a horizontal plane.

AIRMET — In-flight weather advisory concerning moderate icing, moderate turbulence, sustained winds of 30 knots or more at the surface, and widespread areas of ceilings less than 1,000 feet and/or visibilities less than three miles.

AIRPORT ADVISORY AREA — The area within 10 statute miles of an airport where a flight service station is located, but where there is no control tower in operation.

AIRPORT ADVISORY SERVICE — A service provided by flight service stations located at airports not serviced by a control tower. This service consists of providing pertinent information to arriving and departing aircraft.

AIRPORT RADAR SERVICE AREA (ARSA) — Regulatory airspace surrounding designated airports where ATC provides radar vectoring and sequencing on a full-time basis for all IFR and VFR aircraft. Participation is mandatory, and all aircraft must establish and maintain radio contact with ATC.

AIRPORT SURVEILLANCE RADAR (ASR) — Approach and departure control radar used to detect and display an aircraft's position in the terminal area and to provide aircraft with range and azimuth information.

AIRPORT TRAFFIC AREA — The airspace within a horizontal radius of five statute miles from the geo-graphical center of the airport and extending from the surface up to, but not including, 3,000 feet above the airport elevation. The airport must have an operating control tower for this area to be in effect.

ALERT AREA — Special use airspace which may contain a high volume of pilot training activities or an unusual type of aerial activity.

ALTIMETER — The instrument that indicates flight altitude by sensing pressure changes and displaying altitude in feet.

ALTIMETER SETTING — The barometric pressure setting used to adjust a pressure altimeter for variations in existing atmospheric pressure and temperature.

ALTITUDE — Height expressed in units of distance above a reference plane, usually above mean sea level or above ground level.

ANGLE OF ATTACK — The angle between the airfoil's chord line and the relative wind.

ANGLE OF INCIDENCE — The angle between the chord line of the wing and the longitudinal axis of the airplane.

APPROACH CONTROL — A terminal air traffic control facility providing approach control service.

AUTOMATIC DIRECTION FINDER (ADF) — An aircraft radio navigation system which senses and indicates the direction to an L/MF non-directional radio beacon (NDB) or commercial broadcast station.

AUTOMATIC TERMINAL INFORMATION SERVICE (ATIS) — The continuous broadcast of recorded noncontrol information in selected terminal areas. Its purpose is to improve controller effectiveness and to relieve frequency congestion by automating the repetitive transmission of essential but routine information.

B

BEARING — The horizontal direction to or from any point, usually measured clockwise from true north (true bearing), magnetic north (magnetic bearing), or some other reference point, through 360°.

BEST ANGLE-OF-CLIMB AIRSPEED — The best angle-of-climb airspeed (V_X) will produce the greatest gain in altitude for horizontal distance traveled.

BEST RATE-OF-CLIMB AIRSPEED — The best rate-of-climb airspeed (V_Y) produces the maximum gain in altitude per unit of time.

C

CALIBRATED AIRSPEED (CAS) — Indicated airspeed of an aircraft, corrected for installation and instrument errors.

CAMBER — The curve of an airfoil section from the leading edge to the trailing edge.

CATEGORY — (1) As used with respect to the certification, ratings, privileges, and limitations of airmen means a broad classification of aircraft (airplane, rotorcraft, glider, and lighter-than-air) and (2) as used with respect to the certification of aircraft means a grouping of aircraft by intended use or operating limitations (transport, normal, utility, acrobatic, limited, restricted, and provisional).

CEILING — The height above the earth's surface of the lowest layer of clouds or obscuring phenomena that is reported as broken, overcast, or obscuration and not classified as thin or partial.

CENTER OF GRAVITY (CG) — The theoretical point where the entire weight of the airplane is considered to be concentrated.

CHORD — An imaginary straight line between the leading and trailing edges of an airfoil section.

CLASS — (1) As used with respect to the certification, ratings, privileges, and limitations of airmen means a classification of aircraft within a category having similar operating characteristics (single engine, multi-engine, land, water, gyroplane, helicopter, airship, and free balloon) and (2) as used with respect to certification of aircraft means a broad grouping of aircraft having similar characteristics of propulsion, flight, or landing (airplane, rotorcraft, glider, balloon, landplane, and seaplane).

CLEAR AIR TURBULENCE — Turbulence that occurs in clear air, and is commonly applied to high-level turbulence associated with wind shear. It is often encountered near the jet stream, and it is not the same as turbulence associated with cumuliform clouds or thunderstorms.

COLD FRONT — The boundary between two airmasses where cold air is replacing warm air.

COMMON TRAFFIC ADVISORY FREQUENCY (CTAF) — A frequency designed for the purpose of carrying out airport advisory practices while operating to or from an uncontrolled airport. The CTAF may be a UNICOM, MULTICOM, FSS, or tower frequency and it is identified in appropriate aeronautical publications.

COMPASS HEADING — A compass reading that will make good the desired course. It is the desired course (true course) corrected for variation, deviation, and wind.

CONDENSATION — A change of state of water from a gas (water vapor) to a liquid.

CONTINENTAL CONTROL AREA — The airspace over the 48 contiguous states and extending 12 nautical miles out from the U.S. coast. It includes the District of Columbia, and portions of Alaska at and above 14,500 feet MSL, but not including the airspace less than 1,500 feet above the surface, or prohibited and restricted areas.

CONTROL ZONE — Controlled airspace from surface to base of continental control area. A control zone may include one or more airports, and it is normally a circular area with a radius of five statute miles and any extensions necessary to include instrument approach and departure paths.

CONTROLLED AIRSPACE — Airspace designated as control zone, airport radar service area, terminal control area, transition area, control area, continental control area, or positive control area within which some or all aircraft may be subject to air traffic control.

CONVECTION — The circular motion of air that results when warm air rises and is replaced by cooler air. These motions are predominantly vertical, resulting in vertical transport and mixing of atmospheric properties; distinguished from advection.

CONVECTIVE SIGMET — In-flight weather advisory concerning tornadoes, lines of thunderstorms, embedded thunderstorms, areas of thunderstorms, and/or hail greater than or equal to 3/4 inch in diameter.

CORIOLIS FORCE — A deflective force that is created by the difference in rotational velocity between the equator and the poles of the earth. It deflects air to the right in the northern hemisphere and to the left in the southern hemisphere.

COURSE — The intended or desired direction of flight in the horizontal plane measured in degrees from true or magnetic north.

CROSSWIND — A wind which is not parallel to a runway or the path of an aircraft.

CROSSWIND COMPONENT — A wind component which is at a right angle to the runway or the flight path of an aircraft.

D

DENSITY ALTITUDE — Pressure altitude corrected for nonstandard temperature variations. Performance charts for many older airplanes are based on this value.

DEVIATION — A compass error caused by magnetic disturbances from electrical and metal components in the airplane. The correction for this error is displayed on a compass correction card placed near the magnetic compass in the airplane.

DEWPOINT — The temperature to which air must be cooled to become saturated.

DISPLACED THRESHOLD — When the landing area begins at a point on the runway other than the designated beginning of the runway.

DISTANCE MEASURING EQUIPMENT (DME) — Equipment (airborne and ground) to measure, in nautical miles, the slant range distance of an aircraft from the DME navigation aid.

DOWNBURST — A strong downdraft which induces an outburst of damaging winds on or near the ground. Damaging winds, either straight or curved, are highly divergent. The sizes of downbursts vary from 1/2 mile or less to more than 10 miles. An intense downburst often causes widespread damage. Damaging winds, lasting 5 to 30 minutes, could reach speeds as high as 120 knots.

E

EMERGENCY LOCATOR TRANSMITTER (ELT) — A radio transmitter attached to the aircraft structure which operates from its own power source on 121.5 mHz and 243.0 mHz. It aids in locating downed aircraft by radiating a downward-sweeping audio tone.

EVAPORATION — The transformation of a liquid to the gaseous state, such as the change of water to water vapor.

F

FINAL APPROACH — A flight path of a landing aircraft in the direction of landing along the extended runway centerline from the base leg or straight in to the runway.

FLIGHT PLAN AREA — The geographical area assigned by regional air traffic divisions to a flight service station for the purpose of search and rescue for VFR aircraft, issuance of notams, pilot briefings, in-flight services, broadcast, emergency services, flight data processing, international operations, and aviation weather services. Three letter identifiers are assigned to every flight service station and are annotated in the A/FD.

FLIGHT SERVICE STATION — Air traffic service facilities that provide a variety of services to pilots, including weather briefings, opening and closing flight plans, and search and rescue operations.

FREEZING LEVEL — A level in the atmosphere at which the temperature is 32°F (0°C).

FRONT — The boundary between two different airmasses.

G

GROUND EFFECT — A usually beneficial influence on aircraft performance which occurs while you are flying close to the ground. It results from a reduction in upwash, downwash, and wingtip vortices which provide a corresponding decrease in induced drag.

GROUNDSPEED — Speed of the aircraft in relation to the ground.

H

HEADING — The direction in which the longitudinal axis of the airplane points with respect to true or magnetic north. Heading is equal to course plus or minus any wind correction angle.

HIGH — An area of high barometric pressure; also, a high pressure system.

HUMIDITY — Water vapor content in the air.

HYPERVENTILATION — The excessive ventilation of the lungs caused by very rapid and deep breathing which results in an excessive loss of carbon dioxide from the body.

HYPOXIA — The effects on the human body of an insufficient supply of oxygen.

I

INDICATED AIRSPEED — The speed of an aircraft as shown on the airspeed indicator.

INDICATED ALTITUDE — The altitude shown by an altimeter set to the current altimeter setting.

INDUCED DRAG — That part of total drag which is created by the production of lift.

INSTRUMENT FLIGHT RULES (IFR) — Rules that govern the procedure for conducting flight in instrument weather conditions. When weather conditions are below the minimums prescribed for VFR, only instrument-rated pilots may fly in accordance with IFR.

INVERSION — An increase in temperature with altitude — a reversal of the normal decrease of temperature with altitude in the troposphere.

ISOBAR — A line of equal or constant barometric pressure.

ISOGONIC LINES — Lines on charts that connect points of equal magnetic variation.

ISOTACH — A line of equal or constant wind speed.

ISOTHERM — A line of equal or constant temperature.

J

JET STREAM — A narrow band of winds with speeds of 50 knots and greater embedded in the westerlies in the high troposphere.

L

LAND BREEZE — A coastal breeze blowing from land to sea caused by temperature difference when the sea surface is warmer than the adjacent land; usually blows at night and alternates with a sea breeze which blows in the opposite direction by day.

LAPSE RATE — The rate of decrease of an atmospheric variable with altitude; commonly refers to a decrease of temperature or pressure with altitude.

LATITUDE — Measurement north or south of the equator in degrees, minutes, and seconds.

LOAD FACTOR — The ratio of the load supported by the airplane's wings to the actual weight of the aircraft and its contents.

LONGITUDE — Measurement east or west of the Prime Meridian in degrees, minutes, and seconds.

LOW — An area of low barometric pressure, also called a low pressure system.

M

MAGNETIC COURSE — True course corrected for magnetic variation.

MANEUVERING SPEED (V_A) — The maximum speed at which full and abrupt control movements will not overstress the airplane.

MEAN SEA LEVEL (MSL) — The average height of the surface of the sea for all stages of tide; used as a reference for elevations throughout the U.S.

MICROBURST — A small downburst with outbursts of damaging winds extending 2.5 miles or less. In spite of its small horizontal scale, an intense microburst could induce wind speeds as high as 150 knots.

MILITARY OPERATIONS AREA (MOA) — Special use airspace of defined vertical and lateral limits established to help VFR traffic identify locations where military activities are conducted.

MILITARY TRAINING ROUTE (MTR) — Routes depicted on aeronautical charts for the conduct of military flight training at speeds above 250 knots.

MILLIBAR — A unit of atmospheric pressure equal to a force of 1,000 dynes per square centimeter.

O

OBSTRUCTION LIGHT — A light, or one of a group of lights, usually red or white, mounted on a surface structure or natural terrain to warn pilots of the presence of a flight hazard.

OROGRAPHIC — Associated with or induced by the presence of mountains, such as orographic lift or orographic clouds.

P

PARASITE DRAG — That part of total drag created by the form or shape of airplane parts.

PILOT IN COMMAND — The pilot responsible for the operation and safety of an aircraft.

PILOT WEATHER REPORT — A PIREP is a report of meteorological phenomena encountered by aircraft in flight.

POSITIVE CONTROL AREA (PCA) — Designated airspace wherein aircraft are required to be operated under instrument flight rules (IFR). The PCA covers most of the conterminous United States and Alaska and extends from 18,000 feet MSL up to and including FL 600 out to 12 nautical miles from the U.S. coast.

PRECIPITATION — Any or all forms of water particles, whether liquid or solid, that fall from the atmosphere and reach the surface.

PRESSURE ALTITUDE — Height above the standard pressure level of 29.92 in. Hg. Obtained by setting 29.92 in the barometric pressure window and reading the altimeter.

PREVAILING WIND — The wind direction most frequently observed during a given period.

PROHIBITED AREA — Special use airspace of defined dimensions within which flight of aircraft is prohibited.

R

RADAR SERVICE — A term which encompasses a variety of services that a radar controller can provide to the pilot of an aircraft.

RADAR VECTOR — A heading issued by a radar controller to the pilot of an aircraft to provide navigational guidance.

RADIAL — A navigational signal generated by a VOR or VORTAC, measured as a magnetic bearing from the station.

RECIPROCAL — A reverse bearing, opposite in direction by 180°.

RESTRICTED AREA — Special use airspace of defined dimensions within which the flight of aircraft, while not wholly prohibited, is subject to restrictions.

RUNWAY HEADING — The magnetic direction that corresponds with the runway centerline extended, not the painted runway number. When cleared to "fly or maintain runway heading," pilots are expected to fly or maintain the heading that corresponds with the extended centerline of the departure runway. Drift correction shall not be applied; e.g., Runway 4, actual magnetic heading of the runway centerline 044, fly 044.

RUNWAY THRESHOLD — The beginning of the landing area of the runway.

RUNWAY VISIBILITY VALUE — Visibility determined by a transmissometer for a particular runway.

RUNWAY VISUAL RANGE — An instrumentally derived value representing the horizontal distance a pilot will see down the runway from the approach end, based on either the sighting of high intensity runway lights or on the visual contrast of other targets, whichever yields the greatest visual range.

S

SATURATED AIR — Air that contains the maximum amount of water vapor it can hold at a given temperature (relative humidity of 100%).

SEA BREEZE — A coastal breeze blowing from sea to land, caused by the temperature difference when the land surface is warmer than the sea surface.

SERVICE CEILING — The maximum height above mean sea level, under normal conditions, at which a given airplane is able to maintain a rate of climb of 100 feet per minute.

SIGMET — An in-flight advisory concerning severe icing, severe and extreme turbulence, widespread duststorms, sandstorms, or volcanic ash lowering visibility to less than three miles.

SPECIAL VFR CONDITIONS — Weather conditions which are less than basic VFR weather conditions, but permit flight under VFR in a control zone when authorization is received from ATC.

SQUALL LINE — Any nonfrontal or narrow band of active thunderstorms.

STANDARD ALTIMETER SETTING — An altimeter set to the standard pressure of 29.92 in. Hg, or 1013.2 Mb.

STANDARD ATMOSPHERE — A hypothetical atmosphere based on averages in which the surface temperature is 59°F (15°C), the surface pressure is 29.92 in. Hg (1013.2 Mb) at sea level, and the temperature lapse rate is approximately 2°C per 1,000 feet.

STRAIGHT-IN APPROACH-VFR — Entry into the traffic pattern by interception of the extended runway centerline (final approach course) without executing any other portion of the traffic pattern. (See Traffic Pattern)

SUBLIMATION — Process by which a gas is changed to a solid or a solid to a gas without going through the liquid state.

SUPERCOOLED WATER — Water that has been cooled below the freezing point, but is still in a liquid state.

T

TAXI INTO POSITION AND HOLD — Used by ATC to inform a pilot to taxi onto the departure runway in takeoff position and hold. It is not authorization for takeoff. It is used when takeoff clearance cannot immediately be issued because of traffic or other reasons.

TERMINAL CONTROL AREA (TCA) — Controlled airspace extending upward from the surface or higher to specified altitudes, within which all aircraft are subject to the operating rules and pilot/equipment requirements as specified in FAR Part 91.

TRACK — The actual flight path of an aircraft over the ground.

TRAFFIC ADVISORIES — Advisories issued to alert a pilot to other known or observed air traffic which may be in such proximity to their position or intended route of flight as to warrant their attention.

TRAFFIC PATTERN — The traffic flow that is prescribed for aircraft landing and taking off from an airport. The usual components are the upwind, crosswind, downwind, and base legs; and the final approach.

TRANSITION AREA — Controlled airspace designed to contain IFR operations for aircraft traveling between the terminal and enroute environment. Beginning at 700 or 1,200 feet AGL, transition areas terminate at the base of the overlying controlled airspace.

TRANSPONDER — An electronic device aboard the airplane that enhances an aircraft's identity on an ATC radar screen.

TRUE AIRSPEED (TAS) — The speed at which an aircraft is moving relative to the surrounding air.

TRUE ALTITUDE — The actual height of an object above mean sea level.

TRUE COURSE (TC) — The intended or desired direction of flight as measured on a chart clockwise from true north.

TRUE HEADING — The direction the longitudinal axis of the airplane points with respect to true north. True heading is equal to true course plus or minus any wind correction angle.

U

UNICOM — A nongovernment communications facility which may provide airport information at certain airports.

V

VARIATION — The angular difference between true north and magnetic north; indicated on charts by isogonic lines.

VICTOR AIRWAY — An airway system based on the use of VOR facilities. The north-south airways have odd numbers (Victor 11), and the east-west airways have even numbers (Victor 14).

VISIBILITY — The distance one can see and identify prominent unlighted objects by day and prominent lighted objects by night.

VISUAL FLIGHT RULES (VFR) — Rules that govern the procedures for conducting flight in visual conditions. The term "VFR" is also used to indicate weather conditions that comply with specified VFR requirements.

W

WARM FRONT — The boundary between two airmasses where warm air is replacing cold air.

WARNING AREA — Special use airspace which may contain hazards to nonparticipating aircraft over international and coastal waters.

WIND CORRECTION ANGLE (WCA) — The angular difference between the heading of the airplane and the course.

WIND SHEAR — A sudden, drastic shift in wind speed, direction, or both that may occur in the vertical or horizontal plane.

WINGTIP VORTICES — Circular patterns of air created by an airfoil when generating lift. Vortices from medium to heavy aircraft may be extremely hazardous to small aircraft.

ABBREVIATIONS

APPENDIX C

A

A/FD — Airport/Facility Directory
AAS — Airport Advisory Service
AC — Advisory Circular
ADF — automatic direction finder
ADIZ — air defense identification zone
ADM — aeronautical decision making
AFSS — automated flight service station
AGL — above ground level
AIM — Airman's Information Manual
AIP — Aeronautical Information Publication
AIRMET — Airman's Meteorological Information
ALS — approach light system
ARSA — airport radar service area
ARSR — air route surveillance radar
ARTCC — air route traffic control center
ARTS — automated radar terminal system
ASR — airport surveillance radar
ATA — actual time of arrival
ATC — Air Traffic Control
ATCRBS — ATC radar beacon system
ATD — actual time of departure
ATE — actual time enroute
ATIS — automatic terminal information service
AWOS — automated weather observing system
AWW — severe weather forecast alert

B

BFO — beat frequency oscillator mode of ADF
BHP — brake horsepower

C

CAP — Civil Air Patrol
CAS — calibrated airspeed
CAT — clear air turbulence
CDI — course deviation indicator
CFI — certified flight instructor
CG — center of gravity
CIG — ceiling
CL — coefficient of lift
CLC — courseline computer
CO — carbon monoxide
CO_2 — carbon dioxide
CRT — cathode ray tube
CSG — slide graphic computer
CTAF — common traffic advisory frequency
CW — continuous wave NDB signals
CWA — center weather advisory

D

DA — density altitude
DC — direct current
DEWIZ — distant early warning identification zone
DF — direction finder
DG — directional gyro
DME — distance measuring equipment
DR — dead reckoning
DUAT — direct user access terminal

E

EAS — equivalent airspeed
EFAS — enroute flight advisory service
ELT — emergency locator transmitter
ETA — estimated time of arrival
ETD — estimated time of departure
ETE — estimated time enroute

F

f.p.m. — feet per minute
f.p.s. — feet per second
FA — area forecast
FAA — Federal Aviation
    Administration
FARs — Federal Aviation
    Regulations
FBO — fixed base operator
FCC — Federal Communications
    Commission
FDC — Flight Data Center
FDs — winds and temperatures
    aloft forecast
FL — flight level
FM — frequency modulation
FREQ — frequency
FSDO — Flight Standards District
    Office
FSS — flight service station
FT — terminal forecast

G

g.p.h. — gallons per hour
GADO — General Aviation
    District Office
GAMA — General Aviation
    Manufacturers' Association
GPS — Global Positioning System
GS — groundspeed

H

HF — high frequency
HIRLs — high intensity runway
    lights
HIWAS — hazardous inflight
    weather advisory service
HSI — horizontal situation
    indicator
HVOR — high altitude VOR
Hz — Hertz

I

IAS — indicated airspeed
ICAO — International Civil
    Aviation Organization
IFR — instrument flight rules
ILS — instrument landing system
IMC — instrument meteorological
    conditions
in. HG — inches of mercury
IOAT — indicated outside air
    temperature
IR — IFR military training route
ISA — International Standard
    Atmosphere

J

J—AID — Jeppesen Airport and
    Information Directory

K

kHz — kiloHertz
KIAS — knots indicated airspeed
KTAS — knots true airspeed

L

L/MF — low/medium frequency
LAT — latitude
LF — low frequency
LIFR — low IFR
LIRLs — low intensity runway
    lights
LLWAS — low level wind shear
    alert system
LONG — longitude

LOP — line of position
LORAN — long range navigation
LVOR — low altitude VOR

M

mb — millibars
MB — magnetic bearing
MEF — maximum elevation figure
MH — magnetic heading
MHz — MegaHertz
MIRLs — medium intensity
    runway lights
MOA — military operations area
MSAW — minimum safe altitude
    warning
MSL — mean sea level
MTR — military training route
MULTICOM — frequency used at
    airports without a tower, FSS,
    or UNICOM NAS
MVFR — marginal VFR

N

n.m. — nautical miles
NAS — National Airspace System
navaids — navigation aids
NDB — nondirectional radio
    beacon
NFCT — non-federal control
    tower
NOAA — National Oceanic and
    Atmospheric Administration
NORDO — no radio, in reference
    to lost communications
NOS — National Ocean Service
NOTAM — notice to airmen
NTSB — National Transportation
    Safety Board
NWS — National Weather Service

O

OAT — outside air temperature
OBS — omnibearing selector
OTS — out-of-service

P

p.s.i. — pounds per square inch
P-factor — an element of asymmetrical thrust
PA — pressure altitude
PAPI — precision approach path indicator
PATWAS — pilots automatic telephone weather answering service
PCA — positive control area
PCL — pilot controlled lighting
PIREP — pilot report
POH — Pilot's Operating Handbook

R

r.p.m. — revolutions per minute
RAIL — runway alignment indicator lights
RAREP — radar weather report
RB — relative bearing
RCO — remote communications outlet
REIL — runway end identifier lights
RMI — radio magnetic indicator
RMK — remark
RNAV — area navigation

RRWDS — radar remote weather display system
RS — record special
RSC — runway surface condition
RVR — runway visual range
RVV — runway visibility value
rwy — runway

S

s.m. — statute mile
SA — surface aviation weather report
SAR — search and rescue
SCATANA — Security Control of Air Traffic and Air Navigation Aids
SDF — simplified directional facility
sfc — surface
SFL — sequenced flashing lights
SHF — super high frequency
SIGMET — significant meteorological information
SP — special report
SR—SS — sunrise — sunset
STC — sensitivity time control
STOL — Short Takeoff and Landing
SVFR — special VFR

T

TACAN — tactical air navigation
TAS — true airspeed
TC — true course
TCA — terminal control area
TEL—TWEB — telephone access to TWEB
TIBS — telephone information briefing service
TRSA — terminal radar service area
TVOR — terminal VOR
TWEB — transcribed weather broadcast

U

UFN — until further notice
UHF — ultra high frequency
UNICOM — aeronautical advisory station
UTC — Coordinated Universal Time (Zulu time)
UWS — urgent weather SIGMET

V

VASI — visual approach slope indicator
VFR — visual flight rules
VHF — very high frequency
VHF/DF — VHF direction finder
VMC — visual meteorological conditions
VOR — VHF omnidirectional receiver
VOR/DME — collocated VOR and DME navaids
VORTAC — VOR and TACAN collocated
VOT — VOR test facility
VR — VFR military training route
VSI — vertical speed indicator

W

WA — AIRMET
WAC — World Aeronautical Chart
WCA — wind correction angle
WILCO — understand and will comply
WP — waypoint
WS — SIGMET
WSO — Weather Service Office
WST — convective SIGMET
WW — severe weather watch bulletin

INDEX

C

D

NOTAMs

The NOTAMs Section is designed to inform you of recent developments that could affect your training.

AERONAUTICAL KNOWLEDGE AREAS

The following information pertains to areas of increased or new emphasis in aeronautical knowledge requirements for private pilot applicants.

AIRCRAFT MAINTENANCE

Rules pertaining to aircraft maintenance are covered in the Federal Aviation Regulations. Specific maintenance-related regulations include FAR Part 43 and FAR Part 91, Subpart E. Definitions which apply to maintenance, preventive maintenance, and alterations or repairs are listed in FAR Part 1.

PART 1

Maintenance means inspection, overhaul, repair, preservation, and the replacement of parts, but excludes preventive maintenance. Overhauling an engine or replacing a propeller are examples of maintenance.

Preventive maintenance means simple or minor preservation operations and the replacement of small standard parts not involving complex assembly operations. Servicing landing gear wheel bearings or replenishing hydraulic fluid are examples of preventive maintenance.

Alterations are classified as major or minor. A **major alteration** means an alteration not listed in the aircraft, aircraft engine, or propeller specifications that might appreciably affect weight, balance, flight characteristics, or other qualities of airworthiness; or that is not done according to accepted practices or cannot be done by elementary operations. **Minor alteration** means an alteration other than a major alteration. Major and minor repairs have definitions similar to major and minor alterations.

PART 43

Detailed maintenance procedures are prescribed in FAR Part 43. These rules govern the maintenance, preventive maintenance, rebuilding and alteration of civil aircraft. Generally, Part 43 applies to maintenance personnel; however, owners, operators, and pilots should be familiar with the basic requirements. As an example, anytime preventive maintenance has been performed on an aircraft, specific procedures must be followed. The signature, certificate number, kind of certificate held by the person approving the work, and a description of the work done must be entered in the aircraft maintenance records.

PART 91, SUBPART E

According to FAR Part 91, Subpart E, the owner or operator of an aircraft is primarily responsible for maintaining that aircraft in an airworthy condition. No person may perform maintenance, preventive maintenance, or alterations on an aircraft other than as prescribed in this Subpart and other regulations, including FAR Part 43. Each owner or operator of an aircraft shall have that aircraft inspected as required. When maintenance is completed, the owner/operator responsibilities include ensuring that maintenance personnel make appropriate entries in aircraft maintenance records indicating the aircraft has been approved for return to service. If alteration or repair substantially affects the aircraft's operation in flight, that aircraft must be test flown by an appropriately rated pilot with at least a private pilot certificate and approved for return to service before being operated with passengers aboard.

AIRSPACE RECLASSIFICATION FINAL RULE

The Airspace Reclassification final rule was published in the Federal Register on December 17, 1991. However, almost all of the provisions of this new rule will not become mandatory for pilot operations until the effective date of <u>September 16, 1993</u>. Among other provisions, this rule reclassifies U.S. airspace according to alphabetical designations from Class A through Class G, although Class F will not be used in the United States. The following table shows a simplified comparison of the current designations to the corresponding new designations.

Current Designation	Proposed Designation
Positive Control Area	Class A Airspace
TCA	Class B Airspace
ARSA	Class C Airspace
Airport Traffic Area	Class D Airspace
Other Controlled Airspace	Class E Airspace
Uncontrolled Airspace	Class G Airspace

The intent of airspace reclassification is to: (1) Simplify airspace designations; (2) achieve international commonality; (3) increase standardization of equipment requirements; (4) describe appropriate pilot certificate requirements, visual flight rules (VFR) visibility and distance from cloud rules, and air traffic services offered in each class of airspace; and (5) satisfy U.S. responsibilities as a member of the International Civil Aviation Organization (ICAO).

TRANSITION

A lengthy transition period has been established to ensure that the aviation community has time to become knowledgeable about the new airspace classifications. In addition, aeronautical charts must be updated. The FAA has begun to coordinate with a task group of the Interagency Air Cartographic Committee (IACC) and the National Ocean Service (NOS), which will begin to update aeronautical charts. During the transition, the FAA will update advisory circulars, handbooks, manuals, internal orders, and provide pilot/controller education. Significant dates in the transition process are described in the following table.

Tentative Date	Event
October 15, 1992	First sectional aeronautical charts (SAC), world aeronautical charts (WAC), and terminal aeronautical charts (TAC) will be published with legends that indicate both existing and future airspace classifications.
March 4, 1993	Initial charting changes will be completed for the SAC and TAC.
June 24, 1993	North Pacific, Gulf of Mexico, an Caribbean planning charts will be published with legends that indicate both existing and future airspace classifications.
September 16, 1993	New airspace classifications become effective. All charts begin publication with legends that indicate both the new airspace classification and the former airspace classification. All related publications will be updated.
March 3, 1994	First charts will be published with legends that only indicate the new airspace classifications.
August 17, 1994	All charts will be published with legends that only indicate the new airspace classifications.

CHART LEGENDS AND PILOT EDUCATION

The legends in aeronautical charts will include both the existing airspace classifications and the airspace classifications to be effective September 16, 1993. For example, the solid blue line that symbolizes a TCA will be annotated "TCA (Class B)." The first charts with a dual legend will be published October 15, 1992. Starting September 16, 1993, the legends on these charts will be reversed (e.g., a solid blue line will be annotated "Class B (TCA)"). Between March 3 and August 17, 1994, the use of dual indication legends will be phased out.

Between October 1992 and March 1993, educational materials such as pocket guides, a video, and posters will be issued to instruct the aviation public on airspace reclassification. The FAA will begin to update the AIM and other publications, as well as FAA orders, manuals, handbooks, and advisory circulars that must be revised to include the new airspace classifications and an explanation of the transition and implementation procedures.

FAR AMENDMENT

Currently, an amendment to Section 91.215(b)(2) of the Federal Aviation Regulations suspends, until December 30, 1993, the Mode C transponder equipment requirement for certain aircraft operations at specified general aviation airports within 30 miles of a terminal control area (TCA) primary airport (Mode C veil). This rule identifies approximately 300 airports at which operations by aircraft not equipped with Mode C transponders can be conducted at and below a specified altitude: (1) within a 2-nautical mile radius of a listed airport; and (2) along a direct route between that airport and the outer boundary of the Mode C veil. A list of the airports and the specified altitudes at which the Mode C transponder equipment requirements of Section 91.215(b)(2) do not apply is included in the *Airman's Information Manual* and in an appendix to FAR Part 91.